Sustainable Healthcare Architecture

Sustainable Healthcare Architecture

Robin Guenther, FAIA, LEED AP
Gail Vittori, LEED AP

WILEY

John Wiley & Sons, Inc.

Library of Congress Cataloging-in-Publication Data:

Guenther, Robin.
  Sustainable healthcare architecture / Robin Guenther, Gail Vittori.
     p. ; cm.
  Includes bibliographical references and index.
  ISBN 978-0-471-78404-3 (cloth : alk. paper)
  1. Hospital architecture—Environmental aspects. 2. Health facilities—Design and construction—Environmental aspects. 3. Sustainable architecture. I. Vittori, Gail. II. Title.
  [DNLM: 1. Facility Design and Construction. 2. Conservation of Natural Resources. 3. Health Facility Environment. 4. Hospital Design and Construction. WX 140 G937s 2008]
  RA967.G827 2008
  725'.51—dc22   2007030388

Printed in the United States of America

10 9 8 7 6 5 4 3

For our mothers, who instilled in us our sense of purpose and possibility:

Eleanor Guenther Wells and Doreen Dorothy Vittori

"Our lives are touched by those who lived centuries ago, and we hope that our lives will mean something to those who will live centuries from now. It's a great 'chain of being,' someone once told me, and I think our job is to hope, to dream and to do the best we can to hold up our small segment of that chain."

Dorothy Day

Contents

Foreword

THE GREEN BUILDING MOVEMENT is guided by a simple, yet revolutionary, idea: that the buildings in which we live our lives can nurture instead of harm, can restore instead of consume, and can inspire instead of constrain. The business case for green building is highly compelling, and it is a large part of the reason that we have made such great strides in the last 10 years. But it is important for us to remember that at its core, green building is about making the world a better place for people to live. As Robin Guenther and Gail Vittori show us in this important new book, nowhere is that fact more apparent than in the healthcare industry, where the sterile, imposing facilities of the past are being replaced by buildings that are filled with daylight, connected to nature, and, above all, designed to promote health and well-being.

The Opportunity

Buildings are human habitat. The way we design, construct, and operate these buildings has a profound impact on our health and the health of our environment. For too many years, the impact has been negative, from carbon dioxide emissions and construction waste to the wanton use of energy, water, and natural resources. Often, indoor air is more polluted than the air outside and has been linked to illnesses ranging from asthma to cancer.

That's the bad news. But the positive corollary is that changing the way we build offers unprecedented opportunities to have a positive impact on human and environmental health. Green buildings consume fewer resources, generate less waste, and dramatically curb CO_2 emissions. The people who live, work, learn, and heal in green buildings are healthier, happier, and more productive. And the communities we build with green homes, offices, schools, and hospitals are the foundation of a healthy, prosperous future for generations to come.

The convergence of these opportunities in the healthcare sector has brought us to a watershed moment for both the green building movement and the healthcare industry. Healthcare has a huge influence on our nation's economy and politics, and in no other sector are the human health impacts of buildings more explicit or more important. With the healthcare industry's leadership, we can dramatically advance green building throughout the marketplace, while increasing our focus on critical public and human health issues.

The Impact

Compared to other building types, healthcare facilities have an especially large impact on the environment. Healthcare construction is a $41 billion industry and is expected to grow 11 percent this year.[1] Operating those buildings to meet patient needs consumes tremendous energy and resources; hospitals use twice as much energy per square foot as office buildings and spend nearly $3 billion each year on electricity alone.[2]

Meeting patient needs is a hospital's top priority. But protecting the environment is a natural and necessary extension of this mission — as this book makes clear, you can't have healthy people on a sick planet. In the last decade, health care has made remarkable changes in its operations, such as creating safer, "no-burn" waste management practices and eliminating the use of mercury-based products. But the fact is that the healthcare sector can — and must — do more. Climate change is a ticking clock, a threat to the very systems on which we depend for life. Transforming the design, construction, and operations of our buildings is our best chance to stop time.

---

[1] Health Technology Center, Trends in Master Facilities Planning: The Intersection of Infection Control, Green and Evidence-Based Design, http://www.healthtechcenter.org/Common_Site/news/releases.asp

[2] Benjamin Lund, "Energy Star Label now Open to Hospitals," *Building Operating Management* (February 2002). http://www.facilitiesnet.com/bom /Feb02/feb02active.shtml.

The LEED Green Building Rating System

The US Green Building Council (USGBC) was founded in 1993 with a mission that was at once wildly ambitious and terribly urgent: to transform the building industry to sustainable practices. The origins of this mission can be traced to the energy crisis of the early 1970s, which prompted the architectural community to focus on energy efficiency in buildings. But recognizing that sustainability is about more than energy, architect Bob Berkebile asked a question that would fundamentally change the way we think about our built environment: "Are our designs improving quality of life, health, and well-being, and the quality of the neighborhood, community, and planet?"

USGBC was conceived as a coalition comprising every sector of the building industry, working together to transform the marketplace. Guided by the passion, vision, and commitment of early leaders like Berkebile, Bill Browning, and countless others (many of whose names you will find in this book's table of contents), we developed the LEED Green Building Rating System, a holistic framework for sustainable building design, construction, and operations.

Since its launch in 2000, LEED has been the catalyst for the explosive growth of the green building movement. Currently, more than one billion square feet of building space is being built to LEED standards, and organizations ranging from rural school districts to Fortune 100 companies have embraced LEED and green building as an immediate, measurable solution to the critical challenges ahead of us. It has also been used as a foundation for related green building tools, including the *Green Guide for Health Care.*

To better support the healthcare sector's transformation to sustainability, USGBC is developing LEED for Health Care. Recognizing the unique challenges of hospital buildings, LEED for Health Care affirms that a hospital's fundamental mission is to heal — placing emphasis on issues such as increased sensitivity to chemicals and pollutants; acoustical design; and access to daylight, nature, and the outdoors. Drawing upon the work of the environmental health advocates and healthcare industry leaders chronicled in these pages, LEED for Health Care demonstrates that meeting patient and staff needs does not preclude meeting environmental needs. Instead, the goals are complementary, so interwoven as to be inseparable.

A New Kind of Transformation

The current interest in green building results from the coincidence of our growing awareness about climate change with an ever-more-impressive business case. But there is another, equally important reason for building green: the direct impact building design has on human health and well-being. It doesn't make the *Wall Street Journal* as often as statistics about ROI and lease rates, but the way buildings make people feel is an essential part of the story. In the case of hospitals, we have ample evidence that design, construction, and operations are key determinants of patient health and staff well-being and productivity. Embracing green building is not just an opportunity to do what's right for the environment; it is also an opportunity for the healthcare industry to help us broaden and refine the definitions of green building to include human health and vitality.

In fact, the opportunities are endless. Sustainable design is bridging the traditional boundaries of building type, linking our homes and our schools and our hospitals with the common language of green building. By articulating green building in the context of health, the healthcare industry can help us to define the architecture of the twenty-first century. Together, the green building movement and the healthcare industry can enter a new era, one that is connected to the global imperatives of climate change, global toxification, fresh water shortages, and resource depletion — and one that recognizes how these imperatives are interconnected.

So how do we get there? In the end, green building comes down to people. Every green building, every LEED rating system, every new technology, happens because a passionate, committed person makes it happen. We see it in the projects and people described in this book, and we see it in the leadership of Robin Guenther and Gail Vittori. It has been my great privilege to know and work with both Robin and Gail for many years and to be part of a movement that has benefited so greatly from their vision. With this book, Robin and Gail show us how critical our green building mission is to the future of human health and secure a lasting legacy that will continue to challenge and focus the green building movement, the healthcare industry, and the world for years to come.

RICK FEDRIZZI
President, CEO, and founding chairman,
U.S. Green Building Council

Acknowledgments

WHEN WE BEGAN THIS BOOK IN EARLY 2005, sustainable healthcare design was still embryonic; we believed we would be limited to a few scattered case studies of completed buildings and isolated individual strategy examples. How quickly the work has evolved and matured! We are indebted to John Czarnecki and Wiley & Sons for recognizing the importance of this transformation and bringing this book to market.

This book would never have come together without the amazing skills of our team—Cynthia Atwood, Maya Sheppard, Justin Short, and Dylan Siegler—who worked with the project teams, tracked the essays and case studies, and offered us sage counsel and advice throughout the development of the text (thank you, Michael Green, for introducing us to Maya). Our Brazilian colleagues—Rodolpho Ramina and Lula Marcondes—enabled us to include the amazing Sarah Network of hospitals.

A special thanks to the Kaiser Permanente team, including Christine Malcolm, John Kouletsis, Tom Cooper, Scott Slotterback, Carol Antle, Kathy Gerwig, and Bob Eisenman, who make amazing changes happen in the industry. We also had the opportunity to conduct a groundbreaking set of interviews with sixteen executive teams engaged in sustainable healthcare building on behalf of Health Care Without Harm and the Center for Health Design, with funding from the Robert Wood Johnson Foundation. They collectively shaped this book far beyond their direct quotes, in particular: Kai Abelkis, Boulder Community Hospital; Patrick H. Dollard, CEO, the Center for Discovery; Richard Beam and Geoffrey Glass, Providence Health Systems; Mary McNeil, CEO, BC Cancer Research Agency; Roger Oxendale, CEO, University of Pittsburgh Medical Center/Children's Hospital of Pittsburgh; and Leo Gehring, FASHE, University of Arkansas for Medical Sciences.

There are many dedicated people whose own work has shaped this book, including Andrew Jameton, PhD, and Howard Frumkin, MD, MPH. Our essayists—many of them authors in their own right who have influenced our professional development—inspired us through their collective contributions. (They are listed individually in the contributor list.) In some instances they produced entirely different essays from their initial assignments; we thank each of them for sharing their insights and hope these relatively brief introductions inspire many of our readers to seek out their work. We are grateful to the people who worked with them: Aquene Freechild, David Macauley, John Gilmore, and Jessie Sackett.

The project teams who are collectively actualizing innovative healthcare projects—going into new territory and breaking barriers every day in the service of an ecologically informed vision of healthcare—tolerated our multiple requests for information, enthusiastically participated in the telephone interviews, and did it all while continuing to create these buildings. We are especially grateful to the designers who have been inspirational to us: Kristie Ennis of Boulder Associates, Tom Snearey of Karlsberger, and Andy Frichtl of Interface Engineering.

We owe special thanks to Jenny Russell of the Merck Family Fund for believing in and supporting the *Green Guide for Health Care*, which has served as a focal point for learning, exploring, and inspiring our work on high-performance healing environments. Tom Lent, our fearless co-coordinator and friend on the *Green Guide* development, offered extraordinary support that made this book possible. Throughout the process, the Green Guide Steering Committee members have offered wisdom and humor—in particular Kim Shinn, Walt Vernon, Jerry Smith, Ray Pradinuk, Craig Kneeland, and project coordinator Adele Houghton. We owe a debt of gratitude to Al Sunseri and Dale Woodin, ASHE, for their early understanding of the importance of sustainable design in healthcare. We have also relied on Gary Cohen, Bill Ravanesi, Jamie Harvie, Anna Gilmore Hall, and the other exceptional people within Health Care Without Harm for strategic advice and counsel.

For supporting us throughout this remarkable journey, tolerating our absences, and continuing to deliver work on time, we owe thanks to the staff of the Center for Maximum Potential Building Systems and Guenther 5 Architects, in particular codirector Pliny Fisk III and principals Jason Harper, AIA, and Peter Syrett, AIA, respectively.

Our friends and relatives both encouraged us to do this book and inspired us throughout its long and complex birth: Barbara Glickstein, RN; Steven Shelov, MD; Tracey Easthope; Robin Diane Orr; Kirk Hamilton; Bob Berkebile; Sarah Mecklem; Sharon Barnes, Lynn Monahan, Wendy Vittori, and Loeb Fellowship colleagues. Bill Walsh, we will never forget that you introduced us to each other.

And most importantly, thank you to Perry Gunther and Pliny Fisk III, who had never before experienced what it means to have life partners buried in books; thank you for your love, support and encouragement through seemingly endless late nights and weekends; and thank you to our children, Jyllian, Nicole, Ariel, Carson, Adam, and Noah, whom we know understand that this crazy life we lead is, after all, dedicated to their future. Imagine if we just tended the garden!

Introduction

IN THEIR EARLY YEARS OF ELEMENTARY SCHOOL, children are often guided through the intricacies of how the human body functions—what are the organs, the bones, the network of nerves; what are their individual functions and how do they work together as a system. This pedagogy offers the inquiring young mind a view into the invisible world of essential function and performance, of which it is astonishingly easy to remain unaware—except if you have the misfortune of needing to know because of illness, dysfunction, disease, or injury. This intentional exercise to make visible the invisible—not just the parts themselves, but how they are connected and work together—is a remarkable gift for these young children and provides an entrée into a world in which thinking trumps learning, a platform for informed engagement for the years ahead.

Those involved in creating and managing the built environment, whether as planners, designers, constructors, or operators, are often kept from entering this world of wonder as they pursue their life's work. Instead, they rush through the reality of the fast track—no longer the exception but the norm—responsible for delivering a project on time and on budget. In the process, it is easy, and common, to lose sight of how all the pieces fit together and whether the resulting building meets the intended quality standards, let alone whether it is a healthy building.

Considering buildings within a life cycle context and viewing them as part of an ecosystem or ecological metabolism, at least metaphorically, signals that buildings have much in common with the human body. Knowing that buildings are a principal determinant of human and global health means that a building that is healthy through the life cycle is key to creating a healthy planet.

Sustainability, though subject to many definitions, is universally regarded as coalescing the idea that a building is a system unto itself, a part of other nested systems at multiple scales. In a sense, sustainable buildings affirm their intrinsic interconnectedness. Neither islands nor isolated monuments, buildings define social, environmental, and economic realities, and they are the places where people in many parts of the world spend most of their time.

In healthcare, buildings are the physical manifestation of values and a means to communicate just what those values are—they are the clothing we put on our institutions. This extends from decisions about where the building is sited to the building's scale, from the materials and systems that are specified and installed to how the building is maintained and operated over its years of service. At the end of its life, is it indiscriminately hauled off to a landfill, with its constituent parts valued no more than the lowest common denominator's? Are there residual parts deemed persistently toxic that require special handling as hazardous waste? Does that option carry longer-term and perhaps even irreversible human health and ecological consequences? Or, does the building and its components become part of a continuous, vital supply chain, working like an organ donor program, so that one building's parts today become the "heart, lungs, and bones" for a building tomorrow.

It is a stunning commentary that in the first decade of the twenty-first century we continue to live in an era of sick building syndrome—one consequence of the chemical soup that has resulted from materials and technologies that emit a toxic potion that renders some buildings uninhabitable (or puts the people who live, learn, work, and heal in them at risk). Alarmingly, despite successes in ridding paint of lead and pipes, roofing, siding, and floor tile of asbestos, we are faced with an increasingly chemically complex and risky palette of materials that are sought after because they are inexpensive, look good enough, and meet minimum requirements for performance and safety. For many years, we have accepted this reality as a condition of our quest for building materials that can remain in place for decades without evidence of wear.

Now shift the frame of reference from the microscale to the macroscale: we live in cities with declining air quality (both indoor and outdoor), where the toxic emissions spewing out of factories located in one hemisphere influence the air quality in the other, on a planet beginning to bear the devastation of shifting climate patterns, in a biosphere in which the upper stratosphere that protects us from cancer-causing ultraviolet radiation is punctured, layering another cautionary note about the long-term sustainability of life on earth.

Schoolchildren are asked to peel back the skin on their anatomical models to reveal the inner workings of the human body. But what do we find when we peel back the skin of our buildings? Is it a healthy, vibrant system, in balance with its site, regional and global ecologies, and functioning with minimal maintenance and intervention during its expected life span? Or do we find a system that is dead on arrival, with pieces that fail the healthy litmus test on multiple fronts; that exact unnervingly high maintenance, repair, and replacement costs; that are destined for a premature death?

Indeed, an assessment of healthcare buildings in the US finds that the average age of a healthcare building is a mere twenty-eight years and, in the course of those years, hospitals are subject to extraordinary churn, as many buildings cope clumsily with the onslaught of new technologies and modes of caregiving that require radical renovations to respond. But the emerging generation of hospitals and other healthcare facilities replacing those built during the massive post–World War II construction boom funded by the Hill-Burton Act and responding to shifting population patterns is beginning to tell another story.

We can and must do better. Today's hospitals are informed by a new set of questions and challenges. Healthcare leaders are intentionally connecting buildings to mission and community benefit. They view these buildings as part of a life cycle continuum in which the invisible consequences of building decisions on human and ecosystem health — on the local, regional, and global scale — are as important as those that are visible inside the building's walls every day. They pay attention to details; consider long-term, loose-fit, and passive survivability; take seriously cautionary signals that begin to alert what may be the source of future concern; and, most of all, honor the fundamental precepts of prevention and precaution — the best choice of all is to avoid conditions that create potential problems in the future.

Hospitals and other healthcare buildings are a textbook opportunity to define what a healthy building is. As the civic institutions that not only treat illness but also restore health, they are the exemplars for reframing conventional assumptions that determine not what buildings are, but what buildings could — and should — be.

The global health challenges of the twenty-first century, and of this millennium, will not be solved or resolved by switching to a new kind of lightbulb, though that is a worthy initiative and something everyone should consider. The magnitude of the threats to global health require a unified call to arms to immediately and aggressively pull the plug from the dependencies responsible for the global calamity. We will not solve these issues using the same thinking that got us to this point in time. This transformation will not be easy, and will require new ways of thinking, new leadership, and a new vision of twenty-first century medicine, healthcare, and healing environments. This book is a first attempt to define this vision.

PART 1

CONTEXT

CHAPTER 1

Design and Stewardship

The standard for ecological design is neither efficiency nor productivity but health, beginning with that of the soil and extending upward through plants, animals, and people. It is impossible to impair health at any level without affecting it at other levels. The etymology of the word "health" reveals its connection to other words such as healing, wholeness, and holy. Ecological design is an art by which we aim to restore and maintain the wholeness of the entire fabric of life increasingly fragmented by specialization, scientific reductionism, and bureaucratic division.

—DAVID ORR

INTRODUCTION

What does *stewardship* mean, and what is the role of the design disciplines in furthering and developing this idea? The stewardship model of responsibility has its foundation in theological writings on the relationship between humans and the natural world—hence its prominent position in many of the mission statements of religious healthcare organizations. At many such organizations, stewardship of God-given natural resources has been reinterpreted in the modern era to include promotion of human health. Such an expanded view leaves the design industries a correspondingly broad role in terms of stewardship.

The concept of resource stewardship is pivotal in sustainable, or "green," design as it is currently defined and practiced throughout the design disciplines. The design of hospital buildings (as cultural artifacts) can be viewed as an important component of the larger practice of the design of habitats for humans—in this case, healing habitats. For the last half century, however, the design of hospital buildings has been remarkably independent of the broader trends in architectural design. As a particular typology, healthcare architecture has evolved in a world apart, responding, for the most part, to industry trends in technology and ever-more complex life-safety regulations. Until recently, healthcare owners, architects, and engineers have been unaware of the impact that sustainable design concerns have had on the larger design industry.

Stewardship of the environment is here taken as a defining principle of sustainable architecture. Architect Bill Valentine, FAIA, postulates below that "less is better" and challenges design professionals to reconsider scale and deliver better, healthier buildings using less. Designer and educator Pliny Fisk III presents an expanded definition of life cycle design, one that postulates a "new ecology of mind" and links to architect John Eberhard's work, which joins together architecture and neuroscience. Finally, architect Bob Berkebile, FAIA, challenges design to redefine itself as no less than "restorative" for our buildings, our health, and the planet.

The sustainable design movement, through such leaders as Paul Hawken, Amory Lovins, and Hunter Lovins, has given us new lenses for viewing the economy: *Natural Capitalism: Creating the Next Industrial Revolution* (2000) and *The Ecology of Commerce* (1993). The parallel ideologies of "clean production" and William McDonough and Michael Braungart's "cradle to cradle" are beginning to have a significant impact on building materials science, from revolutions in the petrochemical components of our material economy to end-of-life ideas such as "waste equals food." Science writer Janine Benyus, in *Biomimicry: Innovation Inspired by Nature* (1997), points to a future when science will look to nature for inspiration and technology. Just outside the silo that defines the current practice of healthcare architecture, notions of planetary stewardship linked to health are fundamentally redefining the design and production of the built environment.

LIVING PLANET INDEX, 1970–2003

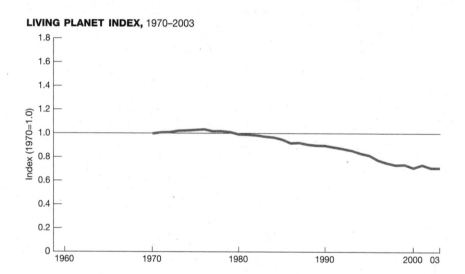

Figure 1-1: The Living Planet Index shows a rapid and continuing loss of biodiversity. It tracks the populations of 1,313 vertebrate species worldwide. Between 1970 and 2003, the index fell by approximately 30 percent (World Wildlife Fund International 2006).

HUMANITY'S ECOLOGICAL FOOTPRINT, 1961–2003

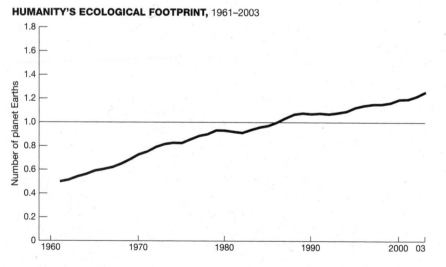

Figure 1-2:
Humanity's Ecological Footprint
Since the late 1980s, the ecological footprint has exceeded the earth's biocapacity—as of 2003, by approximately 25 percent (World Wildlife Fund International 2006).

THE CASE FOR STEWARDSHIP

The scientific community is in general agreement that human activity now exceeds the global carrying capacity of the earth's ecosystems, and that those ecosystems are degrading rapidly. *The Ecological Footprints of Nations* study (Wackernagel et al. 1997) estimates the world's economies are overshooting their capacity for natural resource regeneration by as much as 37 percent; the World Wildlife Fund's *Living Planet Report* (2006) more conservatively estimates 25 percent as of 2003. Environmentalist and writer Bill McKibben (1989) contends that there are no longer any ecosystems on earth uninfluenced by humans. From 10 to 15 percent of the earth's land surface is dominated by agriculture and urban development. Over 40 percent of the earth's land mass has been transformed by humans. Twenty years ago, *Science* magazine reported that humans consumed more than 50 percent of all available fresh water and almost 50 percent of the total terrestrial biological production (Vitousek et al. 1985).

The United Nations' *Millennium Ecosystem Assessment*, released in 2005, chronicles the continued degradation of the natural environment, amplifying the growing awareness that healthy people cannot live on a sick planet. Contributing to this global discord is that most financial ledgers do not monetize ecosystem "services"—fertile soil, the water we drink, the air we breathe—conservatively worth approximately $33 trillion (see Table 1-1).

In 1992, the Union of Concerned Scientists, on behalf of 1,600 scientists (including the majority of living Nobel laureates) issued the World Scientists' Warning to Humanity. It outlined the case for stewardship as essential to survival:

> We, the undersigned senior members of the world's scientific community, hereby warn humanity of what lies ahead. A great change in our *stewardship of the earth* [emphasis added] and the life of it is required, if vast human misery is to be avoided and our global home on this planet is not to be irretrievably mutilated (Union of Concerned Scientists 1992).

Table 1-1 Value of Various Ecosystem Services

Ecosystem Service	Value (in trillions of $)
Soil formation	$17.1
Recreation	3.0
Nutrient cycling	2.3
Water regulation and supply	2.3
Climate regulation	2.3
Habitat	1.4
Flood and storm protection	1.1
Genetic resources	0.8
Atmosphere gas balance	0.7
Pollination	0.4
All other services	1.6
TOTAL VALUE	$33.3

Source: Costanza et al. 1997

The principle of stewardship is intrinsic to the idea of sustainable development. This movement, global in scope while locally implemented, has broad implications for both medicine and the environments that support it.

> *The resilience of the community of life and the well-being of humanity depend upon preserving a healthy biosphere with all its ecological systems, a rich variety of plants and animals, fertile soils, pure waters, and clean air. The global environment with its finite resources is a common concern of all peoples. The protection of the Earth's vitality, diversity, and beauty is a sacred trust.*
> —EARTH CHARTER 2000

SUSTAINABLE DEVELOPMENT

Sustainable development was defined for the first time in the United Nations' 1987 *Brundtland Commission Report* as "development that meets the needs of the present without compromising the ability of future generations to meet their own needs." It quickly gained stature in the public lexicon. This definition both inserted an explicit value proposition into the international development domain and gave "green building" a broad conceptual foundation on which to grow.

In 1992, the first United Nations' Conference on Environment and Development (commonly referred to as the Earth Summit), convened in Rio de Janeiro, and resulted in Agenda 21, a blueprint for achieving global sustainability, and the Rio Declaration on Environment and Development. The Earth Summit produced some of the earliest statements on climate change and biodiversity. Adopted by more than 178 participating governments (including the United States) (UN 2004), its visionary declarations and action plans recognized the interconnections among all living systems on earth.

Two of these declarations would prove to be pivotal for sustainable building in healthcare. Principle 1 of the Rio Declaration states: "Human beings are at the centre of concerns for sustainable development. They are entitled to a healthy and productive life in harmony with nature." Principle 15 advances the principle of precaution, an important construct in medicine:

> In order to protect the environment, the precautionary approach shall be widely applied by States according to their capabilities. Where there are threats of serious or irreversible damage, lack of full scientific certainty shall not be used as a reason for postponing cost-effective measures to prevent environmental degradation.

THE PROFESSION OF ARCHITECTURE

Early environmental design initiatives were disparate, focusing primarily on the reduction of energy demands. In response to the energy crisis of the early 1970s, the American Institute of Architects (AIA) established the Committee on Energy to develop tools and policies to address mounting public concern about the building industry's reliance on fossil fuels. Parallel federal initiatives included the creation of the Solar Energy Research Institute (now the National Renewable Energy Laboratory) and the cabinet-level Department of Energy. Absent a larger framework for sustainable design, these departments focused on energy technologies and conservation.

In 1989, the AIA Committee on Energy transformed itself into the Committee on the Environment (AIA/COTE), reflecting a broader view of sustainability. In 1998, AIA/COTE announced the Top Ten Green Projects annual award program to recognize design excellence in sustainable architecture.

Inspired by the Earth Summit, the UIA/AIA World Congress of Architects (*UIA* stands for "International Union of Architects" in French) issued its *Declaration of Interdependence for a Sustainable Future* in 1993. Signed by more than three thousand participants, it states: "Buildings and the built environment play a major role in the human impact on the natural environment and on the quality of life" — a bold challenge to the profession at large to put a broader sustainability agenda into practice.

In 2000, the AIA unanimously approved Sustainable Design Resolution 00-3, a clear directive to incorporate sustainable design strategies as basic and fundamental to standard practice. Five years later, the AIA issued a more aggressive position statement on the responsibility of design professionals (AIA 2005):

> The AIA recognizes a growing body of evidence that demonstrates current planning, design, construction and real estate practices contribute to patterns of resource consumption that seriously jeopardize the future of the Earth's population. Architects need to accept responsibility for their role in creating the built environment and, consequently, believe we must alter our profession's actions and join our clients and the entire design and construction industry to change the course of the planet's future.

The statement continues with a commitment to achieve a 50 percent reduction in fossil fuel consumption for new and renovated buildings by 2010 and target continuing reduction thereafter, a commitment to integrate sustainable design education into the curricula of architecture schools (and ultimately into the licensing process), and a commitment to promote research into life cycle assessment methodologies. In 2006, architect Edward Mazria issued the 2030° Challenge, calling on architects to transform the design of buildings in order to achieve "carbon neutrality" by 2030 (see Chapter 12).

THE ETHICAL CHALLENGE FOR DESIGNERS

Ultimately, the built environment is the product of intentional design decisions, and waste signifies failure. *Metropolis* magazine editor Susan Szenasy (2004) sums up the challenge this way: "Designers today stand on the brink of being seen by society as essential contributors to its health, safety, and welfare. If you — together with the other design professions — decide to examine the materials and processes endemic to your work, as well as demand that these materials and processes become environmentally safe, you will be the heroes of the twenty-first century." Or, as David Orr (2004) sees it, "The larger challenge is to transform a wasteful society into one that meets human needs with elegant simplicity." As this change occurs, labels like *biomimicry* or *sustainable design* attempt to describe the efforts. The ethical challenge is, however, broad in scope. It is not simply about designing environmentally benign hospital buildings for an ever-expanding industrial-medical complex, but about formulating a system of healthcare that supports vital communities that nurture health and whole people "who do not confuse what they have with who they are" (Orr 2004). This broader vision of design can best be termed *ecological design.*

ECOLOGICAL DESIGN

Ecological design, Orr continues, "requires a revolution in our thinking." He suggests changing the kinds of questions we ask about a design, from, "How can we do the same old things more efficiently?" to ones such as:

- Do we need it?
- Is it ethical?
- What impact does it have on the economy?
- Is it safe to make and use?
- Is it fair?
- Can it be repaired or reused?
- What is the full cost over its expected lifetime?
- Is there a better way to do it?

By formulating the axiom "less is better" for the essay included here, Bill Valentine challenges all of us to consider these deeper questions. Orr conceives of ecological design not so much as an individual art practiced by individual designers as an ongoing negotiation between a community and the ecology of particular places. Ecologically designed buildings "grow" from the long-term knowledge that derives from intimate experience of a place over time; they "live" within a biotic framework established by an understanding of natural principles and man-made policies standing together.

University of Wisconsin Cancer Center

Johnson Creek,
Wisconsin

Figure 1-3: University of Wisconsin Cancer Center. *Credit: James Steinkamp*

Owner: Joint venture: UW Health, Watertown Memorial Hospital, and Fort HealthCare

Design team:

ARCHITECTS: OWP/P

MECHANICAL, ELECTRICAL, AND PLUMBING ENGINEERS: Affiliated Engineers, Inc.

CIVIL AND STRUCTURAL ENGINEERS: Graef, Anhalt, Schloemer & Associates

GENERAL CONTRACTORS: CG Schmidt, Inc.

SURVEY/SOILS/ENVIRONMENTAL CONSULTANTS: River Valley Testing Corp.

Building type: New construction

Size: 14,300 sq ft (1,330 sq m)

Program description: Medical and radiation oncology services, chemotherapy treatments, and clinical trials

Completion date: 2005

"By acknowledging the landscape, the building becomes a part of it. It's an inside-out kind of building. People actually take their treatments outside—the building allows for that," says Randy Guillot, OWP/P project manager. The building is located to disturb as little as possible of the surrounding site, and designed to follow the natural embankment of the land. Water runoff follows its natural patterns, draining around the building. "By pulling the building's components apart to allow light in, the sky and landscape become as much a part of the palette as the carpet or brick," Guillot adds.

The design goals included the development of a relationship with the surrounding community: "The nearby rural environment—older buildings, rustic architecture, and open spaces—inspired the design," Guillot continues. The project focuses on el-

Figure 1-4: Simple materials, honestly and elegantly expressed, reinforce the interdependence of the built environment and nature. *Credit: James Steinkamp*

Figure 1-5: Natural daylight serves as the primary light source during the day. Throughout the building, cancer patients continually experience the intersection between the clinical care environment and the natural world. *Credit: James Steinkamp*

egant exposure of natural materials and building structure. Remarking on the views from the interior, a staff member at the Cancer Center said, "We don't need to hang art in the building. Just look out the window. The changing of the seasons is the artwork."

Source: OWP/P

▨ *Less Is Better*

Bill Valentine, FAIA

*A*mericans consume too much of everything, including energy, land and natural resources, and consumer products. This mega-consumption is threatening to ruin our planet.

Consumer entitlement is close to being a national religion. Even Americans with modest incomes are able to buy more stuff than they ever dreamed about. Everywhere we turn we're barraged by messages telling us we don't have enough, we don't have what we need to live "the good life." So we work more, purchase more, and go further into debt. Yet the oh-so-elusive good life remains just out of reach.

Though we are fortunate to live in such an affluent society, we must be aware of the effect our material-

ism has on the rest of the world: our conspicuous consumption and quest for the good life, emulated by people in many other countries, is actually degrading everyone's quality of life.

The earth's resources are being consumed 20 percent faster than its ability to support renewal, and the average North American is by far the worst offender. We're facing a global crisis in terms of food, water, energy, climate change, biodiversity, and pollution.

OPPORTUNITIES IN THE CRISIS
In this crisis I see opportunities. The Chinese word for crisis, wei ji, is divided into two characters. One character represents danger, and the other signifies opportunity.

Architects have wonderful opportunities to make things better by enthusiastically promoting "less" in the buildings we design. This doesn't mean stripping away the elements that make our buildings beautiful. But we can design structures in simpler, more thoughtful ways that work with, instead of against, nature. And by doing so we can prove to people that less can be better in many aspects of their lives.

I believe in America. Efficient use of our resources helped us become a world power. Until World War II, our waste-not-want-not culture used resources intelligently and efficiently. Today, necessity is creating an environment in which we must reembrace that philosophy.

Built into the basic American consciousness are fantastic values such as innovation, freedom, opportunity, self-reliance, hard work, and competition. These values have profoundly impacted the world in the past —and they can continue to do so.

AT THE TIPPING POINT?

Though we can't legislate less in our culture, we're at a potential tipping point—that dramatic time popularized by Malcolm Gladwell's Tipping Point (2000) when something that had once been unique becomes common. Using less can become the norm.

US budget and trade deficits are growing. An energy crisis is mounting. In 2005 President George W. Bush signed the first national energy plan in more than a decade. The term peak oil has entered the lexicon of the average American. People are wary of rising gas prices and questioning our reliance on Middle Eastern energy sources.

To keep gasoline in their cars and heat their homes, people are cutting back on consumption. They're moving back downtown from the suburbs. More and more Americans believe that natural disasters such as Hurricane Katrina result from global warming, that human activity is the cause of global warming, and that global warming threatens our entire civilization. Hollywood celebrities are talking about their hybrid cars. Leading companies like General Electric and Wal-Mart are implementing policies related to sustainability. Green thinking is hitting the mainstream.

This is a perfect time for the "power of less" message to not only penetrate the psyche of our people, but even to garner a certain cachet. We need to build on the momentum.

ARCHITECTS FOR THE REAL WORLD

As architects for the real world, isn't it our job to ask clients if they really have to build new? Instead of adding to the clutter by making bigger buildings, let's be stewards and improve lives by using fewer resources to make better, healthier buildings.

The idea of building less resonates with all the large sustainable design ideas: less space, materials, waste, toxicity, energy, water—and less cost. Construction costs are rising. Tight budgets can go hand-in-glove with sustainability. Budget consciousness is a catalyst that forces us to think carefully about using less.

Do hospitals need loftlike atria? Do airports need gigantic ticketing halls? Do corporate office facilities need to be monuments? Developing smaller buildings without all the unnecessary "statement" spaces is the first step toward saving land. Only what is truly needed should be built.

Less encompasses smaller and simpler, but it's more than that. It means achieving clarity in design, flexibility over time, and reduced reliance on mechanical systems. Less is the elegance of simple, clear solutions that also happen to be smaller.

MORE EFFICIENT HOSPITALS

Designers should always be thinking about how to leverage technology to do more with less infrastructure. Many conventional architectural solutions provide opportunities for designers of all building types to use resources more efficiently. But perhaps our biggest current opportunity to use less in healthcare design involves using emerging technologies and breakthroughs in medical treatment to create more efficient hospitals.

The US arguably has the world's best healthcare system. Yet millions of people can't afford access to quality care or even to pursue healthy lifestyles.

A developing field carries the amazing potential to save more lives with fewer resources. Genetic (or personalized) medicine will allow physicians to treat patients for a specific disease subtype at a molecular level. Coupled with molecular imaging, which shows live images of the molecules of a disease instead of just the gross anatomical characterization, physicians will be able to create more effective courses of treatment.

Currently being led by our academic medical centers, this revolution in genetic medicine and molecular imaging on our doorstep will transform how hospitals are programmed and configured. Because the potential is for fewer surgeries, faster procedures, and fewer inpatient stays, hospitals should be able to deliver care in less intensive settings. The number of hospital beds per capita in the US (unadjusted for population growth or aging) should go down as treatments become less invasive and more effective. As populations grow and age, and as new treatments become possible for more disease types, the overall numbers of beds may still rise. Yet the increase will be smaller than what we would have experienced without these new technologies.

At broad societal levels, giving more people access to this type of pioneering treatment could have a profoundly positive impact on the overall health of our population. It would represent an incredible sea change that gives us double-pronged benefits: the environmental positives of using less along with healthier people.

This idea of using new technologies and reassessing our approaches to problem solving applies to all building types. Healthcare architects wanting to do more with less should use new technologies to reduce the size of buildings, their environmental impact, and their energy consumption. But technology always should inform, not drive, truly elegant design solutions.

HELP ME BE AN EVANGELIST
Can we work together to design smaller, more efficient buildings? If so, I believe we'll all be happier and healthier.

My message actually goes far beyond buildings and, I hope, straight to the heart of our culture. I'd like to trigger a move toward less in the building industry that also spreads across our society and catalyzes a profound cultural shift toward simplicity. Let's show people that all this stuff isn't required to live "the good life." Let's change our habits and reclaim our culture by making less a virtue. If we can make the idea of using less fashionable and chic in the US, our success could send ripples all over the world.

CLEANER PRODUCTION

The concept of stewardship requires a reexamination of materials, the units of production from which the built environment is created. Materials extraction and production processes as they evolved during the Industrial Revolution have come to be categorized as "beat, heat, and treat" methodologies. Industry thrived in an era of inexpensive energy, using industrial process to replace human labor in an ever-expanding era of raw material usage. Waste was seen as an inconvenience rather than a measure of inefficient production. In the early 1990s, in response to growing recognition of environmental degradation and resource depletion, the United Nations Environment Programme (UNEP 1989) defined "cleaner production":

> Cleaner Production is the continuous application of an integrated preventive environmental strategy to processes, products and services to increase overall efficiency, and reduce risks to humans and the environment....
>
> For production processes, Cleaner Production results from . . . conserving raw materials, water and energy; eliminating toxic and dangerous raw materials; and reducing the quantity and toxicity of all emissions and wastes at source during the production process.
>
> For products, Cleaner Production aims to reduce environmental, health and safety impacts over their entire life cycles, from raw materials extraction, through manufacturing and use, to the "ultimate" disposal of the product.

Advocates of cleaner production have developed "tool kits" for reducing pollution by substituting safer, more benign materials for hazardous materials; by optimizing production technologies; and by closing loops in manufacturing processes to recycle and reuse what had been waste materials. Pollution prevention programs, as defined by the healthcare industry, are examples of cleaner production initiatives in action. In some states, "toxic use reduction plans" are manifestations of cleaner production initiatives. Cleaner production demonstration programs have been launched all over the world and are now common not only in industrialized nations, but

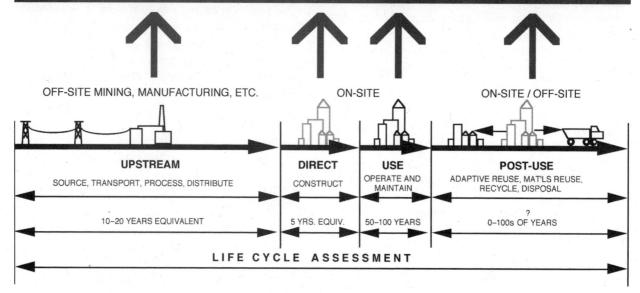

RESOURCE DEPLETION / RECYCLED CONTENT
BIODIVERSITY
CLIMATE CHANGE:
Greenhouse Gases
Ozone-Depleting Compounds
PUBLIC HEALTH:
Persistent Organic Pollutants
Criteria Air Pollutants
Toxic Releases Inventory
OCCUPATIONAL HEALTH & SAFETY

INDOOR ENVIRONMENTAL QUALITY:
Indoor Air Quality
Daylighting
Building Ventilation
ENERGY EFFICIENCY
DURABILITY
OCCUPANT HEALTH & PRODUCTIVITY
OCCUPATIONAL HEALTH & SAFETY
AMBIENT AIR QUALITY

BUILDING ADAPTIVE REUSE
MAT'LS REUSABILITY
MAT'LS RECYCLABILITY
MAT'LS SAFE DISPOSAL

OFF-SITE MINING, MANUFACTURING, ETC.   ON-SITE   ON-SITE / OFF-SITE

UPSTREAM
SOURCE, TRANSPORT, PROCESS, DISTRIBUTE

DIRECT
CONSTRUCT

USE
OPERATE AND
MAINTAIN

POST-USE
ADAPTIVE REUSE, MAT'LS REUSE,
RECYCLE, DISPOSAL

10–20 YEARS EQUIVALENT   5 YRS. EQUIV.   50–100 YEARS   ?
0–100s OF YEARS

LIFE CYCLE ASSESSMENT

Figure 1-6: Each building life cycle phase results in a range of environmental and health consequences—some of these are constants and some more variable based on building type, location, and programmatic focus. Using these indicators as evaluative criteria to compare material choices and design features leads to robust material specification and design decisions. *Credit: Center for Maximum Potential Building Systems*

also in developing nations. Generally speaking, cleaner production "design" activities achieve both environmental benefits and economic returns—and demonstrate improved stewardship of both resources through the life cycle.

LIFE CYCLE THINKING

Healthcare building design and construction processes have usually been cradle to grave, with ever-shorter use life spans. While many late-nineteenth-century healthcare buildings remain in use, they have often

been downgraded from acute care to ancillary facilities as the technology and the associated space requirements of acute-care buildings have escalated. After sixty years in service, the post–World War II Hill-Burton buildings throughout the US are presently the target of replacement. At the same time, mid- to late-1970s facilities are being downgraded after barely thirty years in service. Because the vast resource base that supported the expansion of the built environment in the nineteenth and twentieth centuries is diminished, the processes associated with buildings at every stage of their life cycle is being fundamentally reconsidered.

Broadly termed *life cycle thinking*, the production cycle for building design and construction will now be examined, beginning with the multiple processes from which building materials are derived — the extraction, production, and transportation consequences to ecosystems and human health that often, collectively, exceed the use-phase impacts of a building material.

Life Cycle Design: Toward an Ecology of Mind

Pliny Fisk III, MArch, MLArch

LIFE CYCLE DESIGN FUNDAMENTALS

Life cycle design (LCD) encourages design professionals to consider the use phase of a building (the energy expenditures and material interactions that occur while a building is occupied and operated) as a basis for design, specification, and procurement decisions — as well as any upstream and downstream human health and ecological ramifications. These might include processes related to supporting a region's resource base; tracking emissions, energy uses, and waste streams — both regionally and globally — caused by material sources, manufacturing, transportation, installation, and the function of building systems; and the consequences of a building's final deconstruction and disposal. LCD also addresses how a building responds to its site's and climate's specific cycles at a micro scale. LCD relies on the related frameworks of life cycle analysis and life cycle costing to compare options with the goal of designing a building with a long view toward economic, social, and environmental sustainability.

The aim of LCD is to reduce the harm caused by a building by expanding its system boundaries from the building outward, accounting for other natural and man-made life cycles that border and intersect it. Like the concepts of regenerative architecture or living buildings put forward elsewhere in this chapter, LCD can go beyond reducing the harm caused by the built environment and make buildings an active force for the common good. This essay provides a brief introduction to concepts that extend the reach of LCD into a behavioral realm and suggests that LCD has the po-

tential to engage our perceptions and alter our behaviors related to the resources we use, reconnecting humans to nature and its processes. (Life cycle design principles are outlined below.)

Life Cycle Design Principles

- Recognize the resource flows on which a building depends, and identify them and their multiple boundaries, from the building scale through to neighborhood, city, regional, and global scales.
- Evaluate and apply the source, transport, process, use, and re-source life cycle sequence in all resource-flow areas when considering the scales above, including energy, materials, water, and air. (In healthcare projects, food and medical waste are examples of operational resource flows that might be considered as well.)
- Increase resource-flow efficiency by basing decisions first on the scale of the building and site, progressing upward to tap into larger life cycle scales only as necessary.
- Support regionalized economic loops by respecting tight-knit regional integration. Each stage of the building life cycle supply chain should become a part of a regional economy.
- Plan for the extended use of a building through the separation of utilities, structure, and shell. Designing for flexibility extends the use phase of the building's life cycle.
- Create regionally relevant benchmarks throughout the world through comparisons with similar industrial bases, climates, and material conditions, as well as similar flora and fauna, using patterns supplied by the internationally accepted biome system.
- Reduce the size and complexity of the life cycle to enable it to relate more directly to people, involving the user with the resources associated with their everyday activities.
- If possible, incorporate both an input-output life cycle assessment and a process life cycle assessment, one supplying the perspective using national data, the other homing in on the low-hanging fruit identified.

Within the discipline of sustainable design, the advantages of LCD have thus far been evaluated on an easily recognizable, tangible level. For example, reducing the distance a material must be transported to a building site creates quantifiable reductions in fuel, emissions, and economic cost. Incrementally more sophisticated effects of LCD might include the development of regionalized economic loops incorporating virgin and by-product materials, local producers, and locally appropriate resources, or the advancement of a building vernacular based on such a regional network.

Drawing on neuropsychological research, this thinking may be extended to suggest that LCD could have even deeper and more remarkable ramifications. The hypothesis is based on an understanding of how humans engage with their environments through life cycle events—when we directly encounter the life cycles of water, energy, food, air, and materials often remote from our everyday experience. This reflects our lack of knowingly playing a role with life cycle "events," such as how oxygen is produced or carbon is absorbed by a certain quantity of vegetation and soil systems. The fact is that approximately 5000 sq ft (465 sq m) of temperate forest is needed to support an individual's oxygen needed for breathing, and 7500 sq ft (697 sq m) is needed for carbon sequestering—these essential life-giving threads have not been part of our 'event' vocabulary, but should be. In the model outlined here, buildings are designed to mimic and illuminate the life cycle events around us, causing humans to experience resource flows and cycles, understand resource dependencies, and adapt their behavior accordingly.

This is a new LCD framework not driven solely by the physical and engineering manipulation of resources and analyses of building phases, but instead by the idea that our relationship with life cycle events might be related to behaviors based on the evolution of the brain itself. In this new conception of LCD, miniaturizing the life cycle—for example, bringing the cycle of water (from capture to use to waste treatment) within the site boundary so that the processes are no longer removed and abstracted—is recognized to trigger brain functions that may better connect us to these significant environmental sequences. Buildings, then, extend our perceptions and connect us to the resources we use on a deeper level than previously imagined.

A NEUROLOGICAL BASIS FOR LIFE CYCLE DESIGN

Early humans, like other animals, organized around what might be referred to as resource events, existing in relation to what was directly visible around them in time and space: they saw food, sourced and transported it, then discarded the remains. Their ability to predict conditions of change from the patterns around them was limited. As resource events eventually became connected to conceptions of time past and time future—evidenced in prehistoric paintings—human brains evolved to perceive sequence, seasons, and mistakes engendering an increasingly sophisticated trial-and-error adaptive strategy. These perceptions evolved into the uniquely human trait of critical thinking, located in the neocortex, which makes up the majority of the human brain.

The neocortex is responsible for our senses, parts of our motor function, spatial reasoning, and conscious thought and language. According to neuroscientists, the neocortex is also responsible for interval pattern recognition (Wright 2002). This part of the brain responds to activity sequences and controls our ability to adapt when confronted with new patterns, in contrast to the part associated with the circadian clock—those daily and seasonal rhythms focused on in biophilic design. The neocortex can quickly develop feedback loops that reinforce or discard past conditions, but also propose entirely new ones. There is also evidence that this part of the brain tends to seek new stimuli to feed itself: its food for evolutionary growth is the new, the different, the challenge of solving, of patternizing in rapid-response sequences (Biederman and Vessel 2006). Recent discoveries have shown that when properly and sufficiently stimulated, this part of the brain actually grows new neurons (Gould et al. 1998).

Currently, our neocortex's information hunger is satiated at least partially by the creation of and interaction in a resource-unconscious world of electronic information technology that takes us into make-believe realms disconnected from much of the actual physical world around us. Some analysts who have studied global population in conjunction with the trend of interhuman communication propose the possibility of a point at which arises a truly omnipresent awareness of each other and each other's actions—the point at which we function as an entire adaptive organism, or a truly compassionate society (Teilhard de Chardin 1955;

von Foerster 2003). That population appears to be between 16 to 18 billion (Kursweil 2005), disturbingly far above what resource analysts refer to as the earth's holding capacity: optimistically between 10 to 12 billion people (Durning 1989; Durham 1992).

Today we face not the simplistic resource events of prehistory, but life cycle events of mammoth proportions and grave concern due to their transformative effects on humans and planetary life in general — climate change, for instance, or the long-term toxic effects of industrial and technological processes. Thanks to our advanced neocortex's ability to record and propose alternative action strategies, science is able to project potential ecological catastrophes. But in many cases, what our brains are willing to see and predict surpasses nature's ability to respond to. Even if we take action, success or failure may not be evident for decades or centuries. This discrepancy between nature's time and the human neocortex's time may indeed be at the core of our increasing disconnect from nature and its processes.

Understanding these relationships may provide a platform for designers of all building types (healthcare facilities among them) to begin to redirect the neocortex to conceptualize the resource problems of the everyday world before the advent of planetary devastation. Life cycle design has the potential to serve as a link between human brain capacity and the key life-support capabilities of the natural processes around us. But to properly address the future through design, humans must first become engaged with life cycle events in the built environment in a time frame close to what the neocortex craves — so that the gap between natural processes and human consciousness begins to close.

Another step toward closing the gap between nature time and neocortex time might be a massive human response on the order of what evolutionary biologists refer to as "connected behavior," based on their studies of swarming animal populations. Further evidence of whether such behavior occurs in significant ways in human populations is needed. Recent work shows evidence of this type of mass-population response as convincing as that pointing to individual neocortical responses; text messaging using cellular telephones is one recent example of this, demonstrating the redirection of public opinion resulting in mass action (Rheingold 2003).

Environmental psychologists De Long and Lubar (1979) have identified conditions (not yet attributed to a specific physical area of the brain) that suggest humans perceive a strong relationship between space, size, and time, with larger spaces slowing down perceived time and smaller spaces speeding up perceived time. The relationship between time perception and space has been shown to reduce proportionally: humans dealing with one-sixth scale models perceive time at one-sixth its regular rate. We exhibit an increasing tendency to accelerate time when faced with two-dimensional images — when information is viewed on a smaller screen, time perception during the period of engagement decreases, and information retention increases (Brickey 1994). Following this theory, designers would focus on scale and size — of, for instance, an event sequence in relation to the place where it occurs — in seeking to alter our ability and speed in perceiving and responding to patterns.

A space and the events within that space, then, can be designed so that occupants witness more thoroughly their interaction with a resource and the life cycle that creates it; turning on a faucet, for example, triggers a recognition of the rainwater cistern the water comes from and, further, an understanding of the life cycle of water we rely on. Synchronizing with the brain on this level, then, may become a primary design goal, increasing designers' abilities to alter perception and ultimately, behavior. Such an idea might be used in tandem with biophilic design, which utilizes the more primitive brain function of circadian rhythm to influence our synchronization with natural processes in the world around us.

Further, this space-time correlation may form a critical link to the time-interval element of the neocortex, accelerating or decelerating how we perceive sequenced events (De Long et al. 1994) and potentially satisfying our evolutionary need to stimulate brain growth. The design principles outlined below represent a distillation of the above hypothesis, the launch of an "ecology of mind" (Bateson 1972) that introduces a dimension to enrich life cycle design not addressed by biophilia.

Elements of an Ecology of Mind

- Consider life cycle events in a building—direct interactions with the natural life cycles of water, air, energy, and materials—as microcosms of the life cycle events around us, and treat them with the same awe and respect as natural life cycle events, eliciting engagement with and response to these cycles through design.

- Identify the full range of ecosystem life cycles and life cycle events in and around our buildings, and consciously cover all environmental life cycle phases (or in behavioral terms, "events") from source (e.g., rain) to re-source (e.g., drinking water).

- Conceive of the life cycle as successions of resource events that can be balanced and the user part of the balancing act, so that people understand both the parts (i.e., the individual events) and the whole.

- When designing, differentiate between building elements that stimulate human brain activity at the circadian and interval scales, so that life cycle involvement can occur at both levels.

- Go beyond circadian brain rhythms by engaging the interval time function of the brain's neocortex through the miniaturization of the life cycle.

- Synchronize the scale of everyday life cycle events with the interval time of the neocortex through two- and three-dimensional means and miniaturization.

- Project from past to future and from locus to region the effects of our actions, not just at the individual scale but also at the community, regional, and global scales. Consider simulation and gaming environments so the neocortex is enticed to participate with the life cycles that support us.

Sustainable design, in this eventuality, bridges the widening gap between human brain capacity and key life-support capabilities of the natural processes around us. The neocortex fulfills its evolutionary potential as an advanced, internal consequence-mapping tool, its drive for information sated by engagement with life cycle events made explicit in the design that surrounds us, its dominance directed to resource-related reasoning that contributes to continuing life on earth.

CRADLE-TO-CRADLE DESIGN

- *Waste equals food.* In nature, one organism's waste is food for another.

- *Use current solar income.* Plants use sunlight to manufacture food. In fact, fossil fuels are "ancient sunlight" —past solar income. Both energy and material inputs are renewable rather than depleting.

- *Celebrate diversity.* Nature's diversity provides many models to imitate in the design of systems and processes: biomimicry.

Informed by ecological design approaches, industrial designers are beginning to use an alternative framework for reengineering both products and processes as a response to the limits of "cradle-to-grave" ideology. Architect Bill McDonough and chemist Michael Braungart (2002) developed the "cradle-to-cradle" (C2C) design paradigm based on three key principles (see sidebar).

Benyus (1997) suggests nine principles that define natural systems (see below). These design axioms provide a roadmap for how we might further broaden and re-vision an approach to life cycle design, an idea that is explored in Fisk's essay. As industry redesigns material production in accordance with C2C and biomimicry principles, it remains the task of designers to reimagine buildings based on similar tenets.

NATURAL SYSTEMS

Nature runs on sunlight.
Nature uses only the energy it needs.
Nature fits form to function.
Nature recycles everything.
Nature rewards cooperation.
Nature banks on diversity.
Nature demands local expertise.
Nature curbs excesses from within.
Nature taps the power of limits.

LIVING BUILDINGS

What would ecological design mean for the typology of healthcare buildings? "In the century ahead we must chart a course that leads to restoration, healing, and wholeness" (Orr 2004). Bob Berkebile's essay introduces the concept of living buildings—buildings that actually restore the ecosystems within which they are situated.

Architect Bob Berkebile and designer Jason McLennan (1999) define the future of architecture as a future of living buildings, operating on these six principles. Living buildings will:

1. Harvest water and energy needs on site
2. Be adapted specifically to site and climate and evolve as conditions change
3. Operate pollution free and generate no wastes that aren't useful for some other process in the building or immediate environment
4. Promote the health and well-being of all the inhabitants, as a healthy ecosystem does
5. Comprise integrated systems that maximize efficiency and comfort
6. Be beautiful and inspire us to dream

This is not a future predicated on less, but rather one inspired by doing more—and doing better—with less. To move building design toward this vision, McLennan and the Cascadia Region Green Building Council (2006) developed the Living Building Challenge. Initiatives such as this will have a dramatic impact on the design of the built environment in the next decade.

Restoring Our Buildings, Restoring Our Health, Restoring the Earth

Bob Berkebile, FAIA

"The future belongs to those who give the next generation reason to hope."
— PIERRE TEILHARD DE CHARDIN

The vital connection between human health and the built environment, between our human behavior and the health of the planet, has been studied and documented for decades. While still an architecture student more than forty years ago, I took on a research project at the famous Menninger Clinic, then located in Topeka, Kansas. During that semester, I studied how varying a patient's physical environment can affect his or her mental, emotional, and physical well-being. The variables we used were simple—color, temperature, daylight, humidity, and acoustic levels. Nor were our measurements particularly sophisticated. Yet we were able to observe how patients responded to changes in color (red made them more agitated and "eye-ease" green, more calm) as well as the effects of light and temperature on their appetites. It was obvious to me even then that the environment we create for people can dramatically affect their health, heart rate—even their ability to feel good about themselves.

Thirty years later, I began to understand this connection differently and on a much broader scale. I was privileged to visit the South Pole in 1993 as part of a National Science Foundation team there to explore ways to make US facilities in Antarctica more sustainable. Scientists understand that our individual actions, our community patterns, what we design, build, and operate—all dramatically affect the planet's well-being, which in turn affects our own well-being. In that amazing place, where scientists collect data on the ocean's thermohaline circulation and other global phenomena, I gained a new awareness of hard science: it was no longer general, no longer merely theory.

WHAT'S THE ISSUE—AND THE OPPORTUNITY—
BEFORE US?
In the last few decades, we've acquired a tremendous body of knowledge concerning the direct links between buildings and human health and productivity. In schools, better environments result in greater learning potential, a fact documented in studies from Alberta to Massachusetts to North Carolina to Brazil.

The Rocky Mountain Institute (RMI) reported on the power of daylighting to improve standardized test scores in California, Colorado, and Washington (Burns and Eubank 2002). In two school districts studied, students in classrooms with the most daylighting showed scores 7 to 18 percent higher than those with the least. Strategic consulting firm Capital E has also cited benefits based on data compiled from thirty green schools nationwide (Kats 2005). Not only are these schools saving energy and water while reducing costs associated with waste and emissions, but studies demonstrate positive health or productivity impacts from improvements in air quality and related building-comfort conditions as well.

This connection between human health and the built environment goes even deeper. The Academy of Neuroscience for Architecture (ANFA) is now mapping the brain; recent research has identified a cortical region containing voxels, described by John Eberhard, former director of research for AIA, as collections of neurons that have the function of recognizing buildings. This part of the brain doesn't appear to exist for any other reason: researchers never find it active unless the body is reacting to its environment. Over time, we will be able to use this information to inform our designs and their impact on many variables of well-being that up until now have been deemed anecdotal or difficult to measure.

Similarly, the macroscopic view of earth from space and humanity's ongoing imprint on the planet is revealing our interdependence. Through sophisticated satellite imaging, infrared photography, and computer modeling, scientists are discerning changes on a global scale never previously imagined. This "large-pattern science" is showing us pollution levels, temperature swings, the fragility of the ozone layer, even the toxicity of the soil in extreme detail—all from miles and miles overhead. As a result, we are now receiving alarming reports about climate change and global warming as scientists precisely measure the amount of ice melt on the polar caps, the decline of thermohaline circulation, and the further degradation of our life-support systems.

RESTORING THE EARTH: WHAT'S POSSIBLE?

"The significant problems we face today cannot be solved by the same level of consciousness that created them."
—ALBERT EINSTEIN

We have come to a place where there is no longer any doubt that our actions as a society or as a collection of societies influence global economics, culture, and climate. A seemingly endless list of journal articles, television broadcasts, news stories, books, reports, environmental initiatives, and foundation programs bear witness to this obvious and inevitable trajectory. It appears that our ability to measure and track our own environmental demise has far outpaced our ability or will to understand it, let alone do anything about it. Despite this, we should remain encouraged by recent signs of increased interest among institutions, business, and government in understanding our impact on the health of the environment.

If we are to trust Einstein's maxim, our solutions must involve an opposing doctrine of connectivity, integration, and interdependence. It is a matter of changing not just the way we live, but the way we think and the way we work. It is not sufficient to use fewer raw materials and minimize emissions. A culture of change and a spirit of teamwork and interconnectedness that is far different from our current state of isolation and adversarial tendencies is required. This enlivened consciousness and understanding accelerates the potential for change.

Compelling new ideas, new technologies, and new models of integration are emerging that provide a glimpse into a more hopeful future. We know enough today; there is no reason to wait for the rest of the evidence, to wait until it's all absolutely scientifically proven. The pattern is strong enough to allow us to take these next steps and employ these new capabilities. Significant advances are already under way, with the rise of the US Green Building Council, AIA's Committee on the Environment, and the Healthy Building Network, as well as evolving benchmark tools such as Leadership in Energy and Environmental Design (LEED) and the Green Guide for Health Care.

In her revolutionary book Biomimicry, Janine Benyus explores the seemingly infinite realm of natural systems—evolving, adaptive, and sustainable—and how a growing number of innovators are capitalizing on this wisdom. The movement toward biomimetic architecture and high-performance design holds tremendous promise for new products and methods of construction that emulate life's genius. Incredible new tools that offer better design efficiency, resourcing, and integration are also emerging. Building information modeling (BIM), for example, has the potential to reveal relationships between complex systems and accelerate toward a language and practice of sustainability. It's now a matter of using these tools to create integrated design options and evaluate material selection, system selection, and building performance, including environmental and health impacts.

WHAT'S NEXT, AND HOW CAN WE PROCEED?

> "The best way to predict the future is to design it."
>
> BUCKMINSTER FULLER

The promise of BIM and our willingness to learn from nature will help us move more quickly to healthy buildings. These are, in fact, integrated issues: on one level, it is about human health and our local environment, which includes buildings, neighborhoods, and communities; beyond that, it is about the larger environment: the planet. And each element can and should be part of the design definition.

For me, Fuller's early lessons resonate today more than ever—particularly his advice to young architecture students to practice "anticipatory design" for the future: "Architects, if they are really to be comprehensive, must assume the enormous task of thinking in terms always disciplined to the scale of the total world pattern of needs, its resource flows, its recirculatory and regenerative processes" (Fuller and Marks 1963). This moment in time represents the largest window of opportunity for a major shift in thinking in my lifetime. The immensity of these issues, of these needed changes, is manifest to most people.

But what will it take to make that shift? In part, it requires a convincing—and consistent—sense of urgency. In addition, we must offer up approaches that are clear, comprehensible, and attractive, so people will want to reach out for them.

It is critical that we begin to move beyond green buildings, even beyond the current generation of green building tools, and embrace the concept of living buildings or even restorative buildings. In BNIM's work for the David and Lucille Packard Foundation (Packard 2002), we defined the living building as having no net impact on people or the environment: it harvests all its own water and energy needs, is adapted specifically to site and climate, is built primarily of local materials, and generates zero wastes. The restorative building goes even further: it produces more energy than it consumes, purifies more water and air than it pollutes, and can actually restore a degraded environment through its very existence. We have the ability to design and build restorative buildings now—to create environments that are inspiring and uplifting and where people can gain, or regain, their health just by virtue of being in them.

We also have much more to learn. But we do know enough about sustainable architecture to move toward a regenerative future in our communities. Addressing this ultimate design challenge will require us to successfully realign human nature with Mother Nature, the built environment with natural environments. More than that, it will require of us a new way of thinking, of imagining something unimaginable not so long ago, of looking through new eyes to a world of buildings that restore.

THE NEXT GENERATION

Physical manifestations of this expanded vision of design are already being realized. While we have not yet seen the first generation of climate-neutral healthcare buildings, the projects in this book suggest new approaches to bioregionalism and specific adaptations to location and site context. They embrace the goals of promoting the health and well-being of all inhabitants. They are integrating systems in innovative ways. Many, in fact, are beautiful and inspire us to dream.

BC Cancer Agency Research Center

Vancouver,
British Columbia

Figure 1-7: BC Cancer Agency Research Center. *Credit: Nic Lehoux, Nic Lehoux Photography*

Owner: BC Cancer Foundation
Design team:
  ARCHITECTS: IBI Group/Henriquez Partners Architects in joint venture
  STRUCTURAL ENGINEERS: Glotman Simpson
  MECHANICAL ENGINEERS: Stantec Consulting Ltd.
  ELECTRICAL ENGINEERS: R. A. Duff and Associates Inc.
  LAB CONSULTANTS: Earl Walls Associates
  PROGRAM AND PROJECT MANAGERS: Stantec Consulting Ltd.
  GENERAL CONTRACTORS: Ledcor Construction Ltd.
  LANDSCAPE CONSULTANTS: Durante Kreuk Ltd.
Building type: New medical research laboratory facility
Size: 233,000 sq ft (21,650 sq m)
Program description: Cancer research center, genomics facility, laboratories, offices, interstitial service floors
Completion date: 2004
Awards/recognition: Canada Green Building Council LEED: gold certified

This fully integrated cancer research center includes facilities for advanced therapeutics, cancer control research, cancer endocrinology, cancer genetics and developmental biology, cancer imaging, molecular oncology and breast cancer program, and medical biophysics; a genome sciences center; and the Terry Fox Laboratory, a multidisciplinary research unit dedicated to improve cancer diagnosis and treatment.

The site, in a transitional neighborhood in downtown Vancouver between commercial and residential areas, was zoned for less floor area and more parking than was required for the program. The decision to build a sustainable building accelerated the review process. The city agreed to double the allowable floor area and modify height and setback regulations once it became clear that the massing of the building, which separated the labs and offices into distinct, smaller-scale units to achieve daylight and ventilation objectives, would not overwhelm adjacent properties.

The building is broken up into 35 percent office and 65 percent laboratory blocks, each with its own architectural expression. In cross-section, two floors of offices correspond to one floor of laboratories and its interstitial service floor. A total of 68 large, round "petri dish" windows (one for each principal investigator), each 15 feet in diameter, reduce the apparent height of the laboratory block.

Based on the calculation of staff use of public transportation and bicycles, the agency successfully reduced the on-site parking in favor of research space. The commitment to environmental stewardship eased the process of removing the land (previously occupied by a for-profit parking concession) from the property tax rolls.

When asked what researchers appreciate most about the building, Mary McNeil answers that it is the operable windows and dual-flush toilets: "Both are moments when people interact with the building to elicit control over resource use—a way to live their values." Twelve floors of office space look out on ocean and mountain views through multicolored glass strips. The office block's vertical, striplike window pattern is an

Figure 1-8: Organic forms are expressed in the rooftop terrace, a welcome outdoor place of respite for building occupants.
Credit: Nic Lehoux, Nic Lehoux Photography

Figure 1-9: The open double helix stair—recalling the structure of DNA—is a central organizing element and visual symbol. Clustering conference rooms at each floor landing promotes walking and interaction among researchers. *Credit: Nic Lehoux, Nic Lehoux Photography*

abstraction of a sequence of chromosome six, a subject of study in cancer research. These windows open to allow for natural airflow.

Another important element is the open stair—a double helix that recalls human DNA. "We wanted to encourage the researchers to use the staircase and not the elevators," recalls McNeil, "but that won't work if you put a dark staircase in the middle of a building. All of the meeting rooms abut this staircase, which is located with the best views in the building. Again, the city loved it; it's a visible extension of activity on the street."

KEY BUILDING PERFORMANCE STRATEGIES

Water
- Reduction of 43 percent in potable water demand
- Dual-flush toilets, waterless urinals, and low-flow faucets

Energy
- Energy savings of 42 percent below code using HCFC-free air conditioning equipment
- Heat recovery system for exhaust air and condensing units
- Variable air-volume supply and exhaust boxes in the perimeter zone to reduce air volumes during nonpeak load times
- Radiant heating and cooling in office areas
- Natural ventilation in all laboratories and offices
- Highly reflective roofing membrane
- Operable windows reduce reliance on mechanical cooling.

Materials
- 24 percent of materials contain recycled content
- 98 percent of construction waste recycled
- Formaldehyde-free composite wood

Environmental quality
- Low-emitting carpets, paints, and sealants
- Large, round windows daylight the laboratory space
- 90 percent of occupied spaces (including laboratories) have access to daylight, views, and operable windows

Source: Henriquez Partners Architects

Figure 1-10: Deventer Ziekenhuis. *Credit: Courtesy of Deventer Ziekenhuis*

Deventer Ziekenhuis

Deventer,
Netherlands

Owner: Dutch Care Federation (Nederlandse Zorgfederatie)
Design team:
  ARCHITECTS, ENGINEERS, AND CONTRACTORS: de Jong Gortemaker Algra
  LANDSCAPE ARCHITECTS: Buro Poelmans Reesink Landschapsarchitectuur
Building type: New replacement hospital
Size: Main hospital: 592,015 sq ft (55,000 sq m); psychiatric center: 61,354 sq ft (5,700 sq m); radiation therapy clinic: 55,972 sq ft (5,200 sq m); site: 27 acres (11 ha)
Program description: 380-bed acute teaching hospital with specialty clinics for psychiatry and radiation therapy
Completion date: 2007
Awards/recognition: European Union Hospitals Project demonstration facility

Formed in 1985 in a merger of two smaller facilities, Deventer Hospital is a large teaching hospital with a staff of 2,000. The hospital's new facility, under construction on a greenfield site east of the city of Deventer, will serve a population area of 170,000.

The project's design focuses on energy efficiency, driven primarily by the Dutch Care Federation's pledge to reduce facility energy consumption by 30 percent below 1988 levels. Designers anticipate that the energy efficiency measures will result in annual emissions reductions of 1.943 tons of carbon dioxide (CO_2), 8.71 tons of sulfur oxide (SOx), and 3.35 tons nitrogen oxide (NOx). This is a reduction of 69 percent from the average Dutch hospital.

As a European Union Hospitals Project demonstration facility, the hospital design has benefited from consultations with outside engineers and energy modelers. Designers were concerned with patient comfort; locating single-, double-, and triple-patient rooms away from public waiting rooms and high-traffic circulation areas; and improving patient access to daylight and views.

KEY PERFORMANCE STRATEGIES

Site

- About half of the 950 parking spaces located in underground decks
- Space for 200 bicycles

Water

- High proportion of pervious cover reduces storm water runoff
- System of wadis (originally an Arabic word describing a dry riverbed), swales, and small ditches funnels rainwater and functions as landscaping when dry in summer
- During ten-year storm events, ditch system overflows into a large canal nearby
- Green roof filters rainwater and reduces storm water runoff

Energy

- Annual energy cost savings estimated at €154,545 from a baseline case, with a simple payback time for the owner of 13.4 years, or 8.7 years after European Union incentives
- Heating system energy use reduced an estimated 73 percent (to 44 kWh/sq m) and cooling by half compared with a conventional system through the use of geothermal heat and cooling storage, a heat pump, ventilation heat recovery, and combined heat and power (CHP) plant
- Electricity consumption reduced an estimated 16 percent compared with a standard Dutch hospital's
- Increased building envelope insulation
- Low-E glazing
- Floors and areas with similar use periods grouped to reduce space-conditioning and lighting energy demands

Environmental quality

- Built using Dutch government DuBo (*duurzaam bouwen,* or "sustainable building") principles, which consider project life cycle costs from design to disposal
- Planted sedum roof of 139,930 sq ft (13,300 sq m) over outpatient area filters rainwater and provides views of living vegetation for upper levels
- Building wings designed as "fingers" to maximize daylighting
- Operable windows in patient rooms

Sources: Deventer Ziekenhuis and EU Hospitals Project

CHAPTER 2

The Built Environment and Human Health

Can we move nations and people in the direction of sustainability? Such a move would be a modification of society comparable in scale to only two other changes: the Agricultural Revolution of the late Neolithic and the Industrial Revolution of the past two centuries. These revolutions were gradual, spontaneous, and largely unconscious. This one will have to be a fully conscious operation, guided by the best foresight that science can provide.... If we actually do it, the undertaking will be absolutely unique in humanity's stay on Earth.

— WILLIAM RUCKELSHAUS

INTRODUCTION

The built environment influences health. As a species, humans need structures for physical shelter, as manifestations of social and cultural values, and as embodiments of spiritual and emotional needs. As population growth accelerates, the production of the built environment becomes more resource intensive, stressing indigenous building materials and methodologies beyond their sustainable capacities. Resource depletion, in turn, negatively impacts human health.

Clinical medicine and public health do not always define health as the mere absence of disease. The World Health Organization, for example, defines health as a state of physical, mental, and social well-being. Architecture and planning can promote this broader conception of human health and well-being.

In the nineteenth century, infectious diseases such as smallpox, tuberculosis, typhoid, pneumonia, and rubella were responsible for the majority of deaths. To a large degree, these could be, and eventually were, controlled through environmental and clinical public health interventions — sanitation and innoculation (Turner 1995). Many of these health improvements were achieved through urban planning and zoning mechanisms, reflecting a close partnership among urban planning, public health, and allopathic medicine.

Moving into the twenty-first century, long-term chronic illnesses such as cancer, heart disease, and strokes began claiming the most lives. In the last twenty years, chronic respiratory afflictions such as asthma and sick building syndrome have emerged as widespread threats to public health. While we have created a large allopathic medical structure to deal with these issues, growing evidence indicates that a renewed partnership among urban planning, architecture, public health, and medicine will be necessary to prevent these illnesses before they occur.

There are important differences between the public health concerns of the late nineteenth century and those of the twenty-first century. The public health challenges of today — asthma, developmental disabilities, diabetes, obesity, reduced fertility, cancer — have significant linkages to the technological and environmental changes of the twentieth century. At the same time, the built environment is and has been a significant contributor to these technological and environmental changes through its prodigious resource use.

What does all this mean for the healthcare industry? As long as human health continues to be impacted negatively by environmental stress, the healthcare industry will build larger, resource-intensive structures to deal with the downstream health consequences of environmental degradation. In so doing, it will unwittingly contribute to the very problem it is trying to solve. Beyond the production and operation of its own buildings, the culture of automobile dependence and suburban sprawl is further challenging the medical-care infrastructure.

This chapter examines the global-, community-, and occupant-level health impacts associated with the built environment. Insofar as healthcare construction is both a major player in the construction economy and a resource consumer, the contributions of the industry to environmental stress are significant.

THE GLOBAL IMPACTS OF THE BUILT ENVIRONMENT

As the condition of the natural environment deteriorates, we face an increasingly complex and difficult global public health crisis. Today, up to one-third of the global disease burden, measured in disability-adjusted life years (DALYs), is related to environmental factors such as poor nutrition, contaminated water, indoor smoke, vector-borne disease, and unhygienic living conditions (UNEP 1999). The World Health Organization (WHO) estimates that environmental hazards kill three million children under the age of five each year (WHO, UNICEF, and UNEP 2002). As the environment declines, environmental heath issues such as nutrition, clean water, and hygiene become more complex.

A host of contemporary environmental problems — climate change, ozone depletion, acid rain, toxic pollution, decreased biodiversity — can be linked to the production and maintenance of the built environment. Buildings are resource intensive in both their construction and ongoing operation. On a provocative 2003 cover, *Metropolis* magazine proclaimed "Architects Pollute"; a story by architect Edward Mazria chronicled the sector's significant offenses (Mazria 2003). According to Roodman and Lenssen (1995), building-related activities are responsible for 35 to 45 percent of atmospheric carbon dioxide (CO_2) releases, a precursor to global warming. Even more startling, while industrial CO_2 emissions are leveling off, they are rising significantly in the building and transportation sectors, where they have more than doubled, from 300 million metric tons (mmt) in 1960 to 700 mmt in 2000 (Mazria 2003). Worldwatch estimates that buildings use 40 percent of energy resources; Mazria increases that estimate to 48 percent when the transportation of building materials is included. Building construction activities account for 40 percent of the raw stone, gravel, sand, and steel generated; and consume 25 percent of the world's virgin lumber (Roodman and Lenssen 1995). Building construction and demolition generates about 51 percent of nonindustrial municipal solid waste (EPA 1998). Buildings further deplete the stratospheric ozone layer by using refrigerants and products manufactured with ozone-depleting compounds, including insulation materials. Buildings use over 75 percent of the polyvinyl chloride (PVC or vinyl) produced; chlorine production, one of the world's most energy intensive industrial processes, consumes approximately 1 percent of the world's total electricity output — 47 billion KwH per year — equivalent to the annual output of eight medium-sized nuclear power plants (Thornton 2003).

Material production also has public health consequences. "A focus on improving public health or protecting ecological systems without addressing the production, use, and disposal of industrial materials will prove inadequate and ineffective," writes Dr. Kenneth Geiser, director of the Massachusetts-based Toxics Use Reduction Institute. "Depletion of the resources of the environment and impairment of human health are the symptoms of a poorly designed and functionally flawed industrial production and consumption economy, not of an unprotected environment" (Geiser 2001). As resources are depleted, materials must be shipped longer distances in response to growing worldwide demand. Because built environments are now produced in a global materials marketplace, cleaner production and life cycle–assessment methodologies have an impact on that marketplace.

CLIMATE CHANGE AND PUBLIC HEALTH

Climate change is projected to continue to impose unique health threats on populations worldwide. In 2000, the US Global Change Research Program released an assessment of the potential consequences of global warming on the United States that included an analysis of its health impacts (Figure 2-1). Certain health outcomes

are known to be associated with weather, including illnesses associated with extreme temperature and precipitation events, air pollution, water contamination, and diseases carried by ticks, mosquitoes, and rodents. While the causes of climate change are global, the health impacts manifest at the community level.

While the precise health impacts associated with global climate change are unknown, there is increasing political pressure to reduce CO_2 emissions (see Chapter 12). The Kyoto Protocol (1997) called for the reduction of greenhouse gas emissions 7 percent below 1990 levels by 2012. Although the United States is not a signatory, as of May 2007 the mayors of 496 American cities —from the Northwest to the Deep South and everywhere in between, representing 64 million citizens— have signed on through the 2005 US Mayors Climate Protection Agreement (US Conference of Mayors 2005). This agreement is precautionary in nature; by taking steps now, its signatories hope to avoid or reduce future impacts. Ultimately, greenhouse gas reductions can only be achieved through strategies targeting both the transportation and building sectors—as well as the development and urban planning philosophies that underlie twentieth-century suburban development patterns.

Figure 2-1: Potential Health Effects of Climate Variability and Change
Moderating influences include nonclimate factors that affect climate-related health outcomes, such as population growth and demographic change, standards of living, access to healthcare, improvements in healthcare, and public health infrastructure.

Adaptation measures include actions to reduce the risks of adverse health outcomes, such as vaccination programs, disease surveillance, monitoring, use of protective technologies (e.g., air-conditioning, pesticides, water filtration/treatment), use of climate forecasts and development of weather warning systems, emergency management and disaster preparedness programs, and public education. Source: United States Global Change Research Program *Credit: USGCRP 2000.*

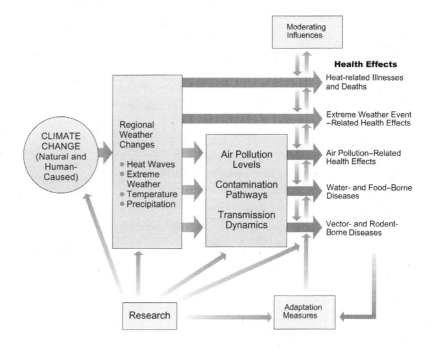

URBAN PLANNING AND PUBLIC HEALTH

By the middle of the nineteenth century, business leaders, physicians, planners, and architects throughout the industrialized world saw daily the effects of unhealthy urban environments. Most evident were communicable diseases—cholera and tuberculosis, for example—associated with poor housing conditions, overcrowding, limited access to light and air, unfit drinking water, mosquitoes, and uncarted waste. Virtually every family had lost a loved one to an infectious disease of environmental origin. Controlling these diseases required improved sanitation, urban planning, and building regulations.

In the United States, more than just engineers and doctors pressed for the funding for large urban improvements and public sanitation efforts. Jacob Riis, a newspaperman, published his book *How the Other Half Lives* in 1890; in it he described the appalling conditions in which immigrants in New York lived. The book strengthened the anti-tuberculosis movement's arguments for improved housing and led to the enactment of zoning and building regulations that provided for increased ventilation and access to light and air (Crisci 1990).

Such infrastructure improvements could not have occurred if each of the professions had remained isolated within its specialty. According to physician and public health advocate Richard Jackson, MD, MPH, "Doctors had to care about sewers, architects about sunlight, and politicians about public health accountability." The success of these efforts has been magnificent. Average American life spans have doubled since that time—from forty to eighty years—and only a small part of those added years have come from medical care. Most of the decreased mortality can be attributed to better housing, nutrition, water, workplaces, and immunizations (Preston 1996).

This public health approach to design extended to hospital environments as well. In the nineteenth century, the view that the circulation of fresh air was the primary requirement for institutional health was unchallenged. Medical historian Charles Rosenberg (1987) observes:

> Hospital planners, including Florence Nightingale, were quick to invoke arbitrary but seductively precise formulae for the numbers of cubic feet each hospital patient (or schoolchild or tenement dweller) required to avoid infection. The maintenance of health reduced itself to the placement of beds and windows, the arrangement of flues and ventilators, and the proper design of heating systems.

Sociologist Paul Starr (1949) observed that ideas about dirt have serious political implications, as is evidenced by today's environmental struggles. "A broad conception of dirt," he noted, "may imply a need for a correspondingly large investment in cleaning things up. A more narrow conception may be much cheaper." Despite the major health advances, the turn of the century brought forward the idea that dirt, per se, did not cause infectious disease. By 1910, a reconsideration of public health advocacy initiated a "new public health," with two defining characteristics: an emphasis on education in personal hygiene, and the role of the physician to examine and diagnose.

The separation of diagnosis from treatment, of public health from allopathic medicine (and more generally preventive medicine from curative medicine), was the beginning of the fragmentation of the medical system — a fragmentation that remains with us today. Likewise, the separation of public health from urban planning — resulting in the rise of the suburb and automobile-oriented land-use and development patterns in the United States — has engendered a set of emergent chronic health issues. Ranging from the increase in asthma among children in urban populations to obesity and diabetes in the general population, they are challenging the delivery of healthcare in terms of both cost and scale of services.

In response to this awareness, public health practitioners are reinvigorating the relationship between urban planning and public health. In their essay "Good Places — Good Health," physicians and public health advocates Richard Jackson, MD, MPH, and Marlon Maus, MD, MPH, challenge the previously linked fields to join together once again to support more livable communities that promote healthier lifestyles. Arguing that the US healthcare system, already the largest and most resource-intensive in the world, will be unable to provide the clinical services required to "clinically solve" the twenty-first century's chronic disease challenges of obesity, diabetes, depression, and asthma, Jackson and Maus offer a vision of prevention through design that designers and healthcare executives alike should heed.

Good Places — Good Health

Richard Jackson, MD, MPH, and Marlon Maus, MD, MPH

Urban planning and public health were partners in the historic effort to prevent epidemics of infectious diseases a century ago. Over the course of the twentieth century, however, the major causes of death in developed countries shifted from infectious to chronic diseases, and the two disciplines neglected their shared heritage. Health professionals became increasingly concerned with biomedical and behavioral factors and forgot how much the built environment shapes well-being; urban planning and architecture lost sight of design's important contributions to the population's health (Corburn 2004). This essay explores the effects of the built environment on health and how the worlds of design and public health could partner to build in ways that enhance well-being and prevent or delay disease.

At the close of the twentieth century it became increasingly evident that planning, design, and health needed to revitalize their common roots. In 2001 the US Institute of Medicine of the National Academies published the report Rebuilding the Unity of Health and the Environment, which defines the environment as the multifactorial interplay of the built and natural physical environments, as well as the ecological, social, aesthetic, and economic environments (Hanna and Coussens 2001). Further work suggests ways in which a healthy built environment can be created by recognizing the connection between land-use decisions and public health, particularly with regard to obesity, asthma, and mental health (Dannenberg et al. 2003).

AN ERA OF CHRONIC DISEASE

Today America must confront a different set of serious epidemics: epidemics of chronic, long-lasting diseases like diabetes, obesity, depression, osteoporosis, and cancer. They are devastating to quality of life — and costly. In 1960 the United States spent 5.1 percent of its gross domestic product on healthcare; in 2003, the portion was 15.3 percent, or $1.7 trillion, a tripling in the ratio in just forty-three years (2003). The one-year increase in dollars spent over 2002 was 7.7 percent.

The epidemic of obesity will only increase these staggering costs. One in seven youths is now classified as obese. The most rapidly increasing surgery in adults — and in children — is bariatric surgery, or stomach stapling. There were approximately 130,000 bariatric procedures in the United States in 2005; as many as 218,000 are expected in 2010 (Santry, Gillen, and Lauderdale 2005; Davis et al. 2006). The direct cost of obesity and physical inactivity has been estimated at 9.4 percent of US healthcare expenditures (Colditz 1999). Obesity increases the risk of becoming diabetic

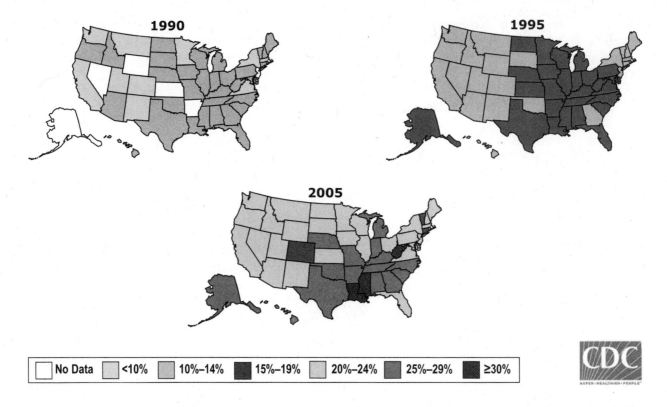

| | No Data | | <10% | | 10%–14% | | 15%–19% | | 20%–24% | | 25%–29% | | ≥30% |

Figure 2-2: Obesity among Adults by State
Obesity is defined as a body mass index of greater than 30, corresponding to a weight of about 185 pounds for a height of 5'6", 210 pounds for a height of 5'10", and 230 pounds for a height of 6'1". The states in white (in the 1991 map) are missing data. The shades of gray correspond to the obesity prevalence percentage shown in the legend. *Source: CDC 2006*

in adulthood nearly forty times (Stein and Colditz 2004). In the past it was unusual to see a child with Type 2, or adult-onset, diabetes; now it accounts for as much as one-third of pediatric diabetes cases. Developing diabetes before age forty shortens life by fourteen years on average, and diminishes the quality of life by twenty years (Flegal et al. 2004). Today's children may be the first generation in American history with a shorter life span than their parents' because of overweight and lack of fitness.

To prevent chronic diseases in the twenty-first century, their root causes must be confronted. Many of these root causes must be approached through what the World Health Organization (WHO) calls "healthy urban planning" —by reconnecting public health and planning (Duhl and Sanchez 1999). Doctors urging their patients to eat and drive less and to exercise more have had only limited success.

Although much of the obesity epidemic is due to a "toxic" nutritional environment (an abundance of cheap, high-calorie food and drinks, even at school, and a saturation of junk food advertising), it is exacerbated by a change in walking behaviors: we no longer walk to where we need to do our life's work: schools, sports fields, friends' homes, libraries, shops, or churches (Martin and Carlson 2005).

SPRAWL AND PUBLIC HEALTH
While technology has eliminated a lot of backbreaking labor from our lives, we have also designed most walking out of our lives. In 1969, an average of 48 percent of all students—and 90 percent of those living within a one-mile radius of their school—walked or bicycled to school. In 1999, only 19 percent of children walked to or from school, and 6 percent rode bicycles (Koplan, Liverman, and Kraak 2005). Overall, Americans walk or

bike a trivial amount—for only about 6 percent of our trips—compared with close to 50 percent of all trips for the people of chilly Scandinavia (Pucher and Dijkstra 2003). Among primary school–aged children, walking to school is associated with higher levels of overall physical activity compared with those who travel to school by motorized transport (Cooper et al. 2005). People in the US are simply less likely to walk or bike for transportation (French, Story, and Jeffrey 2001). From 1960 to 2000, per person driving more than doubled—from four thousand to close to ten thousand miles per year. An American mother spends more than one hour per day in her car, and half of that time is spent chauffeuring children or doing errands—again, up from a generation ago.

But this lifestyle, enabled by increased affluence compared with previous generations, is not making us healthier and happier. Beyond basic shelter and necessities, increased wealth does not translate into contentment. In 1957, 35 percent of Americans reported being "very happy"; in 1993, 32 percent said the same thing—in spite of a doubling in the affluence of Americans overall (Myers and Diener 1995). Just in the last ten years the number of days that the average American reports as feeling unwell or outright sick has increased by twelve (Duhl and Sanchez 1999). Expenditures for antidepressants have skyrocketed; for many health plans, they are the second-largest prescription expense—after cholesterol-lowering medications (Olfson et al. 2002). The effects of depression—missed days of work and limited social activity among them—are also enormous (Kouzis and Eaton 1994). WHO has declared that depression is rapidly becoming one of the most burdensome diseases in the world (Mutangadura 2004).

The direct costs of lack of physical activity, defined conservatively as absence of leisure-time physical activity, are approximately $24 billion, or 2.4 percent of US healthcare expenditures (Colditz 1999). Our children—many of whom have little chance for home- or school-based exercise—are increasingly

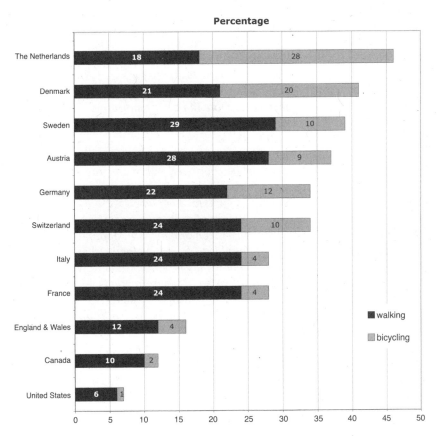

Percentage

Figure 2-3: Proportion of Trips in Urban Areas Made by Walking and Bicycling (1995)
A combination of more walkable built environments and different social attitudes results in a dramatic increase in walking in other countries. *Source: Frumkin, Frank, and Jackson 2004*

medicated for inattentiveness or hyperactivity (Zito et al. 2000; Zuvekas, Vitiello, and Norquist 2006). The effects on learning and resultant behavior problems, including youth violence, have been devastating, particularly in low-income populations (Simpson et al. 2005).

This information may feel overwhelming, but it does not surprise the average American. For many of us, things don't feel right. We can afford homes, but they are far from work and we spend more time working and commuting than our parents did. The average American works 1,815 hours per year, more than in any other developed country (Germans, for example, work 1,444 hours per year) (Miller, Bashford, and Strem 2003). What is the best nonmedicated way to treat depression? Exercise and social connectedness. What is the best nonmedicated way to treat type 2 diabetes? Exercise and weight loss. And what is the safest form of exercise? Walking. What are the most fuel-efficient, least-polluting ways to commute? Walking and biking. For people with diabetes, walking for exercise just two hours per week reduces their death rate by nearly 40 percent (Gregg et al. 2003).

Population changes in the twenty-first century will astonish us. Our nation will have 392 million people by 2050, a more than 50 percent increase from its 1990 population. California's population in 2000 was thirty-four million; the estimate for 2050 is 54.8 million. Yet we continue to build subdivisions as if land were limitless (California Department of Finance 2004). In 1945, Los Angeles County was one of the most productive agricultural lands in the nation; today it is covered with sprawling development.

Reducing opportunities for walking as exercise is a national health threat. Through changes to the design of the built environment, it is possible to encourage people to make healthy choices. Prescribing a minimum of physical activity is useless if there is nowhere to exercise. How a neighborhood is designed is associated with whether people choose to walk or bicycle — or drive. Transit-oriented neighborhoods are designed with gridded street patterns that have four-way intersections as compared to automobile-oriented neighborhoods, which have random street patterns (Cervero and Gorham 1995). Transit-oriented neighborhoods generate 120 percent more pedestrian and bicycle trips

than automobile-oriented neighborhoods. For every one thousand households, nineteen more trips took place in public transit than in automobiles.

A VISION OF THE FUTURE

For public health and urban planning professionals to work together it will be necessary for them to learn each others' language, to understand each others' goals, and to produce a common working framework. To address these challenges, Active Living Research (www.activelivingresearch.org) is taking a transdisciplinary approach to prioritize a research agenda, build the capacity of investigators from multiple disciplines to conduct research, and communicate findings to policy makers and advocates. It anticipates influencing four domains of active living: recreation, transport, occupation, and household (Sallis, Cervero, and Ascher 2006).

There is an "overarching goal of equality and democracy" that underlies projects, programs, and policies in this area (Northridge and Sclar 2003). The link between public health and urban planning must be based on sound science and an understanding of the two disciplines' connections to the social and economic problems that are at the root of many of today's health problems. Widening disparities in health by race, ethnicity, socioeconomic class, gender, and sexuality are in many cases more important indicators than any biomedical explanations and cures (Northridge and Sclar 2003).

For prevention to be effective, the confluence of threats must be countered with a congruence of benefits: what is good for us as individuals is good for community and is good for the planet. As individuals, we need to eat plenty of fruits and vegetables and use meats and oils as condiments. This approach would save agricultural land from development and increase consumption of locally produced food; it would also engender gardens and farmers' markets near our homes, schools, and neighborhoods. The reorientation of our food sources would mean that as individuals, we would walk as a major form of exercise — the recommended ten thousand steps a day.

If we lived closer to work we could get those steps in, and if we did not need so much car time, we might have more time with the people we love and who care about us. We should take the stairs instead of the elevator; climbing stairs is a good weight-bearing exercise, and climbing one flight of stairs burns approximately eight to ten calories per minute. Five minutes of stair climbing over the course of a day can result in a weight loss of five pounds in one year!

We need to belong to a community — one that is the hub and support for the important tasks of life: working, playing, learning, shopping, socializing, rejoicing, and mourning. Well-designed communities make this much easier. To accommodate the growing population and at the same time increase social capital we must re-create denser communities that have privacy, safety, beauty, tranquility, and culture. Such communities need to cluster near mass transit; people who use mass transit walk more and pollute less. Well-designed communities can also be safe havens during the weather disasters that climate change will bring us. Green and sustainable building and community design must advance past sustainability and become restorative.

The biggest challenge is not knowledge (though plenty more research is needed) and it is not good will (we all want to give our children a planet as healthful, diverse, and beautiful as the one we were given). The biggest challenge is one of leadership. We need to articulate and take ownership of a vision of healthy communities that provide optimal support for families, children, old people, workers, and parents, as well as the natural world around us. The importance of the healthcare industry's leadership in advocating for this vision cannot be underestimated. Much more can be accomplished to improve health when communities are well designed — when they are a place of the heart, as well as the wallet.

SPRAWL AND AIR QUALITY

The Vermont Forum on Sprawl (2007) defines sprawl as "dispersed, auto-dependent development outside of compact urban and village centers, along highways, and in rural countryside." Sprawl is associated with increased vehicle miles of travel. In spread out cities like Atlanta and Houston, there is as much as 50 percent more vehicle miles of travel per capita than more compact cities with similar populations. This assessment comes from T. Keith

Lawton (2001), transportation planner in Portland, Oregon, who comments, "When looking at the amount of travel in US cities, it is clear that those cities with lower densities and a larger road supply consume significantly more vehicle miles of travel." Likewise, Australian transportation scholars Peter Newman and Jeff Kenworthy (1998, 1993) have revealed the same relationship on a global scale — comparing decreased urban density with increased vehicle miles traveled. More vehicle miles generate more vehicle exhaust, which in turn results in reduced air quality. Exposure to air pollution has public health consequences. Ground-level ozone can exacerbate respiratory illness and reduce lung function. Exposure to carbon monoxide, sulfur dioxide, and nitrogen dioxide can cause respiratory illnesses and alter the lung's defense systems (USGCRP 2001).

Numerous studies link increases in emergency department visits with increases in community ozone levels. One study links these increases to motor vehicles. During the Atlanta Olympic Games in 1996, morning peak traffic flow decreased by 22 percent, one-hour peak ozone levels decreased by 28 percent, and various measures of acute asthma decreased between 11 percent (for emergency hospital admissions) and 44 percent (for urgent care through health maintenance organizations) (Frumkin, Frank, and Jackson 2004).

Increasing temperatures in urban areas are another manifestation of global warming. In heat-sensitive regions, populations in urban areas are most vulnerable to adverse heat-related health outcomes. Heat indices and heat-related mortality rates are higher in the urban core than in surrounding areas, a situation that is exacerbated by air conditioners, which transfer heat from building interiors to the outdoors.

The absence of nighttime relief from heat for urban residents is a factor in heat-related deaths.

In 1995 during a five-day heat wave in Chicago, maximum temperatures ranged up to 104°F. The number of deaths increased 85 percent over the number recorded during the same time period the preceding year. At least seven hundred excess deaths were recorded, most directly attributable to the heat. The elderly, young children, the poor, and people who had underlying medical conditions were at particular risk (USGCRP 2001).

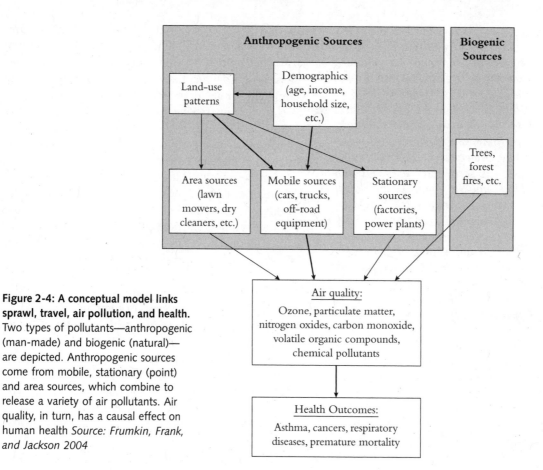

Figure 2-4: A conceptual model links sprawl, travel, air pollution, and health. Two types of pollutants—anthropogenic (man-made) and biogenic (natural)—are depicted. Anthropogenic sources come from mobile, stationary (point) and area sources, which combine to release a variety of air pollutants. Air quality, in turn, has a causal effect on human health *Source: Frumkin, Frank, and Jackson 2004*

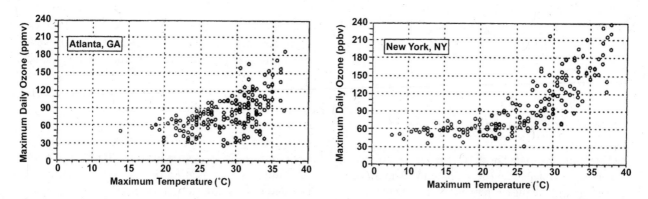

Figure 2-5: Ground-Level Ozone Concentration and Temperature
These graphs illustrate the observed association between ground-level ozone concentrations and temperature in Atlanta and New York City (May to October 1988–1990). Projected higher temperatures across the US in the twenty-first century are likely to increase the occurrence of high ozone concentrations. Ground-level ozone can exacerbate respiratory diseases and cause short-term reductions in lung function. *Source: USGCRP 2001*

SMART GROWTH AND HEALTHY CITIES

It is a cruel irony that the development of low-density suburban neighborhoods that Jackson and Maus so vividly critique from a public health perspective was in some respects a public health response to the overcrowded urban experience. Just as the public health infrastructure advanced through zoning and building regulations, improving urban health, the invention of the automobile fed the growing belief that suburban living was healthier. As the results of this belief contribute to a new age of chronic health problems, organizations dedicated to reinvigorating a healthy, higher-density development model have emerged.

In 1987, the World Health Organization initiated its Healthy Cities Project (www.healthycities.org). With more than eighteen national networks in Europe, North America, and Australia, its members are "conscious of health and striving to improve it" through a portfolio of activities. The program's major focus is health promotion; more than one thousand cities have undertaken many of its missions. In the United States, corresponding state initiatives include California Healthy Cities and Communities and the Indiana Healthy Cities and Communities Network. Canadian physician Trevor Hancock has assisted North American communities to envision and create a healthier urban future.

In 1996, the US Environmental Protection Agency (EPA) and several nonprofit organizations formed the Smart Growth Network (www.smartgrowth.org) to assist communities in boosting their economies, protecting their environment, and enhancing their vitality. Smart Growth Network strategies include mixed land use, decreased automobile dependence balanced by transportation alternatives, and increased density balanced by the preservation of undeveloped green space. Related initiatives include the Congress for the New Urbanism (www.cnu.org), a planning and architecture movement with similar goals. New Urbanism argues for a return to traditional neighborhood development — the compact, higher-density, mixed-use, transit-oriented, walkable developments that were the norm prior to the 1950s. All of these initiatives aim to mitigate the health and social consequences of sprawl outlined by Jackson and Maus.

SMART GROWTH PRINCIPLES

- Mix land uses.
- Take advantage of compact building design.
- Create a range of housing opportunities and choices.
- Create walkable neighborhoods.
- Foster distinctive, attractive communities with a strong sense of place.
- Preserve open space, farmland, natural beauty, and critical environmental areas.
- Strengthen and direct development toward existing communities.
- Provide a range of transportation choices.
- Make development decisions predictable, fair, and cost-effective.
- Encourage community and stakeholder collaboration in development decisions.

Source: Smart Growth Network 2006

A final related initiative is the Community Indicators Movement. More than two hundred communities in the United States — from Missoula, Montana, to Jacksonville, Florida — have developed alternative ways to measure progress and engage community members in a dialogue about health, the future, and changing community outcomes (Redefining Progress 2007). Some use a healthy communities framework, while others focus on sustainability. The common goal is to bring diverse community sectors together, foster new alliances and relationships, provide citizens with the tools to understand problems and opportunities, and foster healthy change. This will give the healthcare sector, a major employer and service provider within local economies, increasing opportunities to advocate for healthy planning and design innovation.

AIR POLLUTION

In addition to the health issues that arise from community planning, there are a range of community health issues associated with local point sources of chemical contamination, most of which affect either air or water. Many of these stressors are related to commonly manufactured materials and products. In fact, most of what we have learned about the impacts of exposures to industrial pollutants—silica, asbestos, tobacco, and other materials—has been through studies of industrial workers since the Industrial Revolution (Christiani 1993).

Since the advent of the twentieth century, whole communities have been engulfed by air pollution, resulting in serious illness and death from cardiopulmonary disease. In her book *When Smoke Ran Like Water* (2002), Devra Davis recounts the story of Donora, Pennsylvania, in 1948. In the worst of such episodes, in London in 1952, the death toll exceeded four thousand. Based on these incidents, individual governments moved to enact laws aimed at improving air quality. But pollution knows no boundaries or national borders. With continued population growth

and worldwide industrial expansion, worldwide air quality, including indoor air quality, continues to decline. In fact, air pollution remains a leading factor in the high mortality rates for acute respiratory disease in children under five in developing countries (four million annually). In the United States, it is among the leading causes of increased asthma rates in children.

POTABLE WATER POLLUTION AND SCARCITY

John Snow's 1854 discovery that cholera was being spread from a water pump in London energized the efforts to improve the infrastructure of cities worldwide. It was not until the 1970s, however, that the hazards associated with industrial and agricultural activity were deemed a major threat to potable water supplies. De-

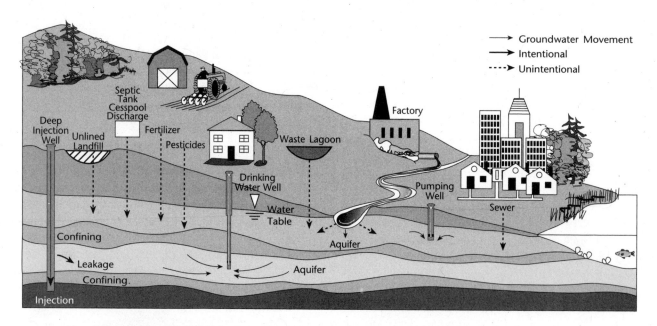

Figure 2-6: Sources of Groundwater Contamination
Groundwater contamination can occur from point sources such as leaking underground storage tanks, spills, landfills, waste lagoons, and industrial facilities. Groundwater quality degradation can also occur over a wide area due to diffuse nonpoint sources such as agricultural fertilizer and pesticide application. In some cases, contaminants introduced into the subsurface decades ago are only now being discovered. *Source: EPA 2000*

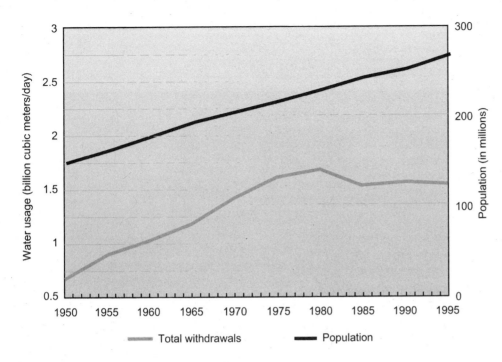

Figure 2-7: Water Withdrawals and Population Trends in the US
Although US population has continued to increase, water withdrawals have declined on a per capita basis. Reductions are due to increased efficiency and recycling in some sectors, and a reduction in acreage of irrigated agriculture. While this trend is encouraging, availability of fresh water in the US is subject to regional climatic variability and usage patterns.
Source: USGCRP 2001

spite the major improvements, the threat to health posed by both potable water contamination and scarcity remain high. As of 1996, the World Health Organization estimated nearly 25 percent of the global population lacked access to safe water for drinking (World Bank Group 2001). Water contamination is often difficult to detect, and many chemicals that were once thought safe are now believed to be hazardous (Hu and Kim 1993).

According to the EPA (2000), the contamination of groundwater with relatively new contaminants (e.g., methyl tertiary butyl ether, or MTBE) is increasing. Groundwater remains the source of drinking water for almost half the nation's population. The built environment is directly responsible for ten of the top twenty sources of its contamination. The most important contaminants are heavy metals (lead, arsenic, cadmium, and mercury) and volatile organic chemicals (gasoline and the halogenated solvent trichloroethylene). In addition, water contamination impacts the food chain, hence the widespread health advisories against consuming fish or shellfish products.

Overall US trends in water withdrawal are encouraging. While the population continues to increase, total water withdrawals appear to have leveled off. Industries that consume large amounts of water have been actively engaged in curbing their water usage, while improvements in irrigation methods have also contributed to this leveling trend.

Overall trends can, however, be misleading. Water availability is not uniform across the US. Arid regions of the Southwest, for example, struggle with chronic potable water shortages. The Midwestern areas dependent on the Ogallala Aquifer are withdrawing potable water far faster than the natural recharge rate. Municipalities in drought-prone areas are installing recycled water infrastructure (Austin, Texas, calls its reclaimed water system the "purple pipe" because of its distinctive color to differentiate it from potable water supply). These systems reduce the use of potable water for irrigation and process uses. Likewise, many cities also require storm water management design strategies to maximize groundwater recharge in an effort to sustain potable water sources.

GAVIOTAS HOSPITAL

Figure 2-8: The Gaviotas Hospital. *Credit: © ZERI Foundation; Luis Camargo*

Gaviotas, a village founded in 1971 in the remote savannas of eastern Colombia by Professor Paolo Lugari, is a self-sufficient community of about two hundred. The sixteen-bed, 7,266-square-foot (674-square-meter) solar-powered hospital was designed and built by community members and visiting friends between 1982 and 1986. Without a hospital within a day's drive, the hospital served Gaviotas residents as well as the indigenous Guahibo population and fighters on both sides of the Colombian political conflict. Heralded by a Japanese architectural journal in 1995 as "one of the thirty most important buildings in the world," the hospital—elegant in its pragmatic functionality—manifests a humanistic core value that underscores Gaviotas's self-declared identity as "an oasis of imagination and sustainability" (Friends of Gaviotas 2007).

When the Gaviotas community began, many people were suffering from gastrointestinal disorders attributable to unclean drinking water, and occupational accidents related to new forestry initiatives had increased; medical assistance with childbirth was also needed. But doctors were increasingly scarce due to travel dangers. Adhering to the Gaviotas way of life, villagers filled the need for a hospital in a participatory, experimental, socially conscious, and environmentally sound manner. The hospital's provision of purified water—for example, using simple solar energy distillation technology—immediately reduced deaths and illnesses previously plaguing the villagers.

Figure 2-9: The Gaviotas clinic's water purification plant relies on simple, appropriate technology and addresses an urgent public health need for clean water. *Credit: © ZERI Foundation; Luis Camargo*

INDOOR AIR QUALITY

No discussion of the impacts of the built environment on human health can be complete without acknowledging the health impacts of indoor air quality. The EPA estimates that people spend 89 percent of their time indoors, with the balance split between automobiles (6 percent) and outdoors (5 percent). Further estimates suggest that the level of pollutants indoors is up to five times greater than outdoor levels. Extensive driving not only impacts pollution levels within the air shed, but also creates particular problems for those people who spend much of their time in cars (Frumkin, Frank, and Jackson 2004).

Asthma affects 20 million people in the US, including 6.3 million children. Since 1980, the largest increase in asthma cases has been in children under five. In 2000, there were nearly 2 million emergency room visits and nearly 1.5 million hospitalizations due to asthma, at a

As with all Gaviotas's buildings, the hospital functioned as an off-the-grid structure, relying on solar and wind power for the building's modest energy demands. This was made possible, in part, by passive design strategies for cooling. A series of underground ducts enabled the building's interior to maintain cool temperatures by creating a convective loop: cool underground air entered the building, and warmer air escaped through honeycombed-shaped air channels in the double-layered corrugated roof. Despite frequent 100 percent humidity, a passive dehumidification system inspired by the workings of a termite mound contributed to comfortable indoor conditions

Figure 2-10: Gaviotas's off-the-grid passive solar hospital building augments its modest energy needs with solar and wind power. Thatched roof malocas, built by the Guahibo Indians, provide hammocks for patients and families and are connected to the hospital by a vine-covered walkway. *Credit: © ZERI Foundation; Luis Camargo*

—the surgical room maintained 17 percent humidity year-round. The lush landscape was replete with organic produce and medicinal herbs. People were kept connected to the outdoors through operable skylights, daylit spaces, and a retractable galvanized metal roof over patient areas, which provided a view of the stars at night. A separate wing, Las Malocas, was built by the Guahibo Indians and connected to the hospital by a vine-covered walkway. Rather than providing rooms with beds, this open air porch was outfitted with hammocks for patients and families under a thatched roof.

With the Colombian government's prohibition of hospital operations lacking a minimum level of equipment, staff, and insured patients, the Gaviotas hospital closed between 1997 and 1998 and now operates as a purified water-bottling plant. Gaviotas's founder, Gunter Pauli, maintains that the conversion expresses the community's allegiance to public health more than a reaction to new legislation. By redirecting the service of healthcare from within the walls of a single building to the entire village, the hospital building—reborn as water purification plant—now services the community through prevention rather than treatment. Indeed, the continuing need for clean drinking water outstripped the need for acute medical care as clean water, health and occupational safety education, and midwifery became public health realities.

Sources: Friends of Gaviotas 2007

cost of almost $2 billion and 14 million missed school days (EPA 2006). In addition to concerns about outdoor air pollution, increasing scrutiny of indoor pollutant sources, ranging from dust to formaldehyde, from phthalate plasticizers to pesticides to cleaning products, is yielding new data about the importance of source control as in the example of the Atlanta Olympics.

According to the National Institute for Occupational Safety and Health (NIOSH), occupational lung disease, including occupational asthma, is the leading work-related disease (NIOSH 1988). As a group, healthcare workers account for more than 40 percent of occupationally related adult-onset asthma with exposures tied to cleaning products (Rosenman et al. 2003). Because of concerns for worker safety, a new generation of "greener cleaners" is being introduced in healthcare settings. The following essay chronicles emerging ideas about quantifying the indoor air impacts of building materials.

Good Air, Good Health

Anthony Bernheim, FAIA

Clean water and clean air are critical for good health. We can choose to drink bottled water, which is labeled at the bottling plant, so that we know, for the most part, what it contains. But the air we breathe is not labeled, nor can we choose what air we inhale. This is particularly true of patients in healthcare facilities, confined in a building because of a health condition and subsequent treatment.

HEALTH AND SUSTAINABILITY

Genuine long-term environmental sustainability entails an integrated approach to energy conservation and efficiency, indoor environmental and air quality, and the efficient use of site, water, and material resources resulting in deep green, restorative buildings (McLennan 2004). These buildings enhance the environment by producing more energy than they consume, and they provide comfortable indoor environments with healthy indoor air quality (IAQ).

BUILDING OCCUPANT HEALTH

The EPA estimates that Americans spend about 89 percent of their time indoors (at home and at work), 6 percent in vehicles, and about 5 percent outdoors, and that indoor air is about two to five times more concentrated with chemical pollutants than outdoor air. Our bodies, which are not designed for the high levels of chemical concentrations to which we are exposed for the vast majority of our lives, are responding with new health afflictions: Sick Building Syndrome symptoms (short-term health effects with coldlike symptoms that cannot be traced to specific pollutant sources), Building-Related Illnesses (diagnosable illnesses whose symptoms can be identified and whose causes can be directly attributed to airborne building pollutants), and Multiple Chemical Sensitivity (a condition in which a person reports sensitivity or intolerance to a number of chemicals and other irritants at very low concentrations).

IAQ is dependent on a number of factors. They include the quality of the outside air used for building ventilation; the chemical emissions from the building's materials, furnishings, and equipment; the efficacy of the ventilation systems used to purge the indoor air; the activities of the building occupants; and long-term building maintenance and cleaning. These factors contribute volatile organic compounds (VOCs); microbial organisms and microbial volatile organic compounds (MVOCs) from mold; semivolatile organic compounds (SVOCs) from fire retardants, pesticides, and plasticizers (Bornehag et al. 2004); inorganic chemicals such as carbon monoxide, nitrogen dioxide, and ozone; and particulate matter generated outdoors by fuel combustion and manufacturing practices and indoors by occupant activities and equipment. These factors take on particular significance in complex multifunctional healthcare facilities, especially considering these additional issues:

- *Patients, staff, and visitors may be exposed to numerous airborne chemicals — sensitizing and allergenic agents, direct toxins, mutagens[1] and teratogens[2], and infectious aerosols — emitted from the chemicals, pharmaceuticals, and medical therapies used in patient treatments. Additional contributors to poor air quality may include exposure to latex allergens (e.g., airborne latex dust), surgical smoke produced during laser surgery, anesthetic gases, and aerosolized medications (McCarthy and Spengler 2001).*
- *Some patients may be very infectious themselves, or may have compromised immune systems that make them more susceptible to the health impacts of VOCs.*
- *Patients, staff, and visitors may be exposed to the VOC emissions from the numerous disinfectants and sterilizing agents used for cleaning medical equipment and room surfaces.*
- *Hospitals operate twenty-four hours per day, seven days per week, which requires special care for ongoing maintenance, repair work, and regular cleaning while patients, staff, and visitors are occupying the building.*

---

[1]A mutagen is an agent that tends to increase the frequency or extent of mutation.

[2] A teratogen is a chemical that can cause birth defects by adversely altering the development of an embryo or fetus without necessarily altering the organism's genetic structure.

- New medical procedures and technologies require building upgrading and remodeling, which necessitates construction while the building is occupied and functional.
- Medical facilities are, in effect, small villages with many different functions housed in one building. Functions requiring different indoor environments and climates include patient rooms, operating rooms, intensive care units, food preparation areas, cafeterias and restaurants, staff work rooms and offices, and visitor areas.

While achieving healthy indoor air quality might appear to be a complex and almost insurmountable challenge for healthcare facilities, it is possible to overcome that challenge. Recent research, developments in the building material manufacturing and construction industries, and practical building experience have aided the development of basic indoor air quality principles and best practices that are moving us toward healthier indoor environments.

Building owners, architects, interior designers, engineers, contractors, and the building engineers who operate facilities can have a major impact on a building's IAQ. Experience with completed projects has confirmed that healthier buildings result from the adherence to four basic principles (see sidebar).

INDOOR POLLUTANT SOURCE REDUCTION

There have been many developments in the science and practical application of improved indoor air quality. Most recently, these developments have been in the area of source control for which the industry has developed effective guidelines and best practices. Efforts began in the 1980s with the indoor air quality guidelines of the American Society of Heating, Refrigerating and Air-Conditioning Engineers (ASHRAE), and advanced through the 1990s with Lars Mølhave's research on the human-health effects of total VOC concentrations (Levin 1998). More recently, IAQ guidelines and building material specifications were developed for the State of California (Alevantis et al. 2002).

Used appropriately, these guidelines and practices can inform building owners and operators about the quality of the air in their facilities. Indoor air samples, taken in a building pre- and post-occupancy and during its functional life as part of an ongoing commis-

FOUR DESIGN PRINCIPLES FOR HEALTHY INDOOR AIR QUALITY

1. *Source control:* Minimize the indoor chemical concentrations by reducing or eliminating pollutant sources. For healthcare facilities, this involves two separate strategies:
   - *The building:* Select and install building materials and finishes that minimize or eliminate indoor pollutant sources.
   - *The building's contents:* Substitute low-emitting furnishings, medical products, materials, and cleaning agents for the previously used, more toxic materials. Examples of this include the use of PVC-free furniture and window shades and the use of nonlatex gloves (McCarthy and Spengler 2001).

2. *Ventilation control:* Provide adequate ventilation to dissipate and purge indoor air pollutants. (Refer to Chapter 10 for additional information.)

3. *Building and IAQ commissioning:* This is a process used during design and construction to verify that a building is constructed as designed and operates as intended. Recommissioning should occur regularly to ensure that the building continues to perform as intended. (Refer to Chapter 6 for additional information.)

4. *Operations and maintenance:* Perform regular inspection, maintenance, and cleaning (adhere to a green housekeeping regimen) of the building and its contents. (Refer to Chapter 7 for additional information.)

sioning program, can be analyzed for chemical concentrations. The goal is to design, construct, and operate healthcare facilities so that the indoor concentrations of chemicals of concern—carcinogens, reproductive toxicants, and chemicals with chronic or long-term health effects—are low enough to minimize their harmful effects or not adversely impact occupant health.

In 2000, California's Office of Environmental Health Hazard Assessment (OEHHA) developed a list of chemical compounds commonly found in buildings and determined the impact of long-term exposure to these chemicals on the human body. It also created a chronic reference exposure level (CREL) for each chemical: the concentration or dose "at or below which adverse health effects are not likely to occur from an acute and chronic exposure to hazardous airborne substances. [The data] are intended to protect individuals from chemical injury, including sensitive sub-populations" (OEHHA 2005).

To address indoor building materials and finishes and their associated health impacts, this author and a team of green building experts developed the Special Environmental Requirements Specifications, Section 01350, which requires emissions testing for interior materials and sets maximum modeled indoor volatile organic compound and formaldehyde concentrations

for the materials and finishes, based on the CRELs. This specification also establishes minimum material recycled content and procedures to deal with mold on construction sites (Bernheim, Levin, and Alevantis 2002).

Armed with the OEHHA's chronic reference exposure levels and Section 01350, building owners and managers can take two important steps to ensure good indoor air quality when renovating existing healthcare facilities or building new ones. They can require building designers to select materials that comply with Section 01350 requirements. They can also implement an indoor air–testing program to identify chemicals of concern and to verify that the indoor chemical concentrations in the completed facilities do not exceed the OEHHA-recommended CREL for each chemical.

There is still significant work proceeding in this area. One current development intended to protect

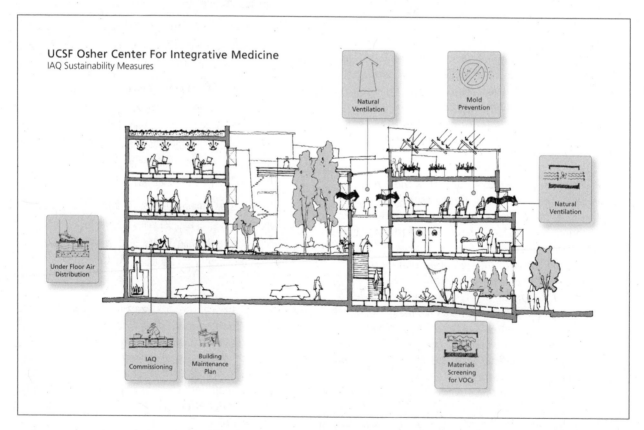

Figure 2-11: This diagram of the Osher Center for Integrative Medicine, University of California–San Francisco illustrates both projected sources of indoor pollutants and the system responses to improved source control. *Credit: SMWM*

patients, staff, and visitors from short-term health effects in healthcare facilities where building repair work is in progress close to occupied areas is the refinement of Section 01350 into Section 01351, which will incorporate material-testing requirements for wet applied products such as paints and adhesives. The chemicals of concern to be identified include those listed with both acute reference exposure level (AREL) (OEHHA 2000) and minimum risk levels (MRL) based on chemical inhalation as developed by the Agency for Toxic Substance Disease Registry (ATSDR), a unit of the US Centers for Disease Control (CDC) (ATSDR 2005).

The design of a ventilation system can also reduce indoor pollutant sources. Providing high-performance filtration media will reduce the induction of particulate matter (e.g., diesel particulates and related diesel gases), formaldehyde, and ozone into interior spaces from outdoor air. Ozone causes the oxidation of indoor VOCs, adding new compounds to the indoor air (see Chapter 10).

THE BUILDING INDUSTRY'S CONTRIBUTION
Many building product manufacturers are reformulating their products (e.g., carpets, ceiling materials, resilient flooring, and paint) to reduce VOC emissions in compliance with Section 01350, and reduce SVOC emissions by eliminating PVC from products such as carpets, resilient flooring, and bumper guards. Industry trade groups have developed or are in the process of developing certifications to indicate a level of compliance. Examples include the Carpet and Rug Institute's Green Label Plus program and the Resilient Floor Covering Institute's FloorScore Seal. Additionally, Scientific Certification Systems has developed indoor air quality certifications for building products, called Indoor Advantage and Indoor Advantage Gold. Recently, the GreenGuard Environmental Institute (2007) introduced its Product Emission Standard for Children and Schools, a certification program for low-emitting products and materials commonly used in school buildings, classrooms, and day-care facilities to make it easier for building designers to select and specify materials that meet Section 01350 low–VOC emission standards.

While the US Green Building Council's LEED and Green Guide for Health Care rating systems reference Section 01350, actual building material emissions and postoccupancy indoor air quality measurement and verification is a better way to ensure, with test data, that good indoor air quality has been achieved.

BREATHING EASIER
Over the last twenty-five years, much attention has been paid to improving indoor air quality as a result of the practical application of scientific research. With a new consciousness about occupant health, architects and engineers are producing new building designs, systems, and specifications. The manufacturing industry is responding with both reformulated and brand new green products. Some independent, third-party material certifications are now available, giving building material specifiers more confidence in selecting healthy materials, and the construction industry is responding by incorporating green construction methods. Scientific testing proves and qualitative feedback from occupants of these enhanced IAQ buildings confirms: improved indoor air quality improves every breath staff, visitors, and especially patients take and how they feel throughout the day and night—factors of particular importance in healthcare facilities.

Bernheim's essay examines the complex issue of measuring and assessing the impacts of the built environment itself on the resultant indoor air quality in healthcare settings, recognizing that ultimately it is the product of the quality of the outdoor air, contaminant sources from the building materials within the space, the ventilation systems servicing the space, and the materials used to maintain the systems and finishes. Achieving superior indoor air quality was a project priority in the Fachkrankenhaus Nordfriesland, a psychiatric hospital, a discussion of which follows. The designers' emphasis on healthy, low-emitting materials was a response to the hospital administration's belief that indoor air quality improvements would markedly improve the treatment of patients with environmentally related illnesses.

Fachkrankenhaus Nordfriesland

Bredstedt,
Germany

Figure 2-12: A green roof mitigates storm water runoff and provides sound attenuation while enhancing outdoor air quality. *Credit: Olaf Bruun Jorgensen, European Union Hospitals Project*

Owner: Fachkrankenhaus Nordfriesland Gruppe, a private foundation
Design team:
    ARCHITECTS: Detlefsen + Lundelius
    ENERGY CONSULTANTS: Esbensen Consulting Engineers A/S
Building type: Addition
Program description: Inpatient and outpatient psychiatric facility with 120 beds. Existing campus included buildings dating from the late nineteenth century through the 1970s.
Completion date: 2007
Awards and recognition: European Union Hospitals Demonstration Project

This small-town psychiatric hospital near the North Sea specializes in psychiatry, psychosomatic disorders (e.g., chronic fatigue syndrome), environmental medicine (e.g., multiple chemical sensitivity, electromagnetic sensitivity), and substance abuse, and it handles general medicine as it relates to those specialties. Aligned with its specialization areas is an environmental consciousness in management; administrators pay close attention to indoor air quality in particular. Environmentally sensitive patients receive 100 percent organic foods, with other patients' meals comprised of organic foods where cost-efficient.

As a European Union Hospitals Demonstration Project, the hospital's renovation was inspired primarily by energy conservation concerns, but the nature of some of the disorders the hospital treats—10 percent of patients are treated for multiple chemical or electromagnetic sensitivities—prompted innovation in materials selection and careful attention to ventilation. Close cooperation by designers and hospital officials was necessary to align the design scrupulously with patient needs, and some budget reallocation was necessary to fulfill both objectives.

KEY BUILDING PERFORMANCE STRATEGIES

Site
- Mold-free environment safeguards sensitive patients
- Previously diverted creek now flows to a 300-sq-ft (27.9 sq m), patient-accessible duck pond
- Green roof

Water
- Rainwater captured and used in atrium water features
- Coastal wetland site restored, including formerly diverted streams and pond

Energy
- Energy demand for heating (space conditioning and water) reduced by 41 percent compared with German standard
- Energy demand for electricity (e.g., lighting, fans) reduced by 57 percent compared with German standard
- Double skin facades
- Solar mass walls with transparent insulation
- Combined heat and power (CHP) plant
- Transparent photovoltaics, considered for roof, were eliminated due to cost

Materials
- Metal elements avoided in rooms for electromagnetically sensitive patients: electronic equipment housed elsewhere, and metal-free furniture used where possible
- Wood floors instead of carpet in all areas
- Hard materials preferred to soft ones to eliminate off-gassing

Environmental Quality
- Single-patient rooms average 215 sq ft (20 sq m), with high ceilings to increase air volume per person and to dilute interior airborne contaminants
- Energy savings projected to result in annual emissions reduction of 262 t of carbon dioxide (CO_2), 0.23 t of sulfur oxide (SOx), and 0.0002 t of nitrogen oxide (NOx), accounting for an overall emissions reduction of 46 percent

As a European Union (EU) Hospitals Demonstration Project, the facility's design and some of its performance results will be monitored and disseminated. The hospital is also a voluntary participant in the EU's Eco-Management and Audit Scheme (EMAS) program, which provides ongoing third-party verification of an organization's environmental goals and claims.

Sources: Olaf Bruun Jørgensen, Esbensen Consulting Engineers; Fachkrankenhaus Nordfriesland and European Union Hospitals Demonstration Project

EDUCATING A NEW GENERATION OF PUBLIC HEALTH PRACTITIONERS

This expanded vision of a public health partnership with medicine and ecology is being realized at graduate programs in public health, which are embedding these values in the buildings they construct. At Harvard University, for example, the School of Public Health delivered the first LEED-certified university project: the Landmark Center. The University of Arkansas for Medical Sciences (UAMS) in Little Rock established its College of Public Health adjacent to its medical and nursing schools, financed with an allocation of tobacco settlement proceeds. The following case study focuses on the use of sustainable building strategies in a project with a stated mission to "promote and support the health of Arkansans."

Figure 2-13: The renovated office space in Harvard's Landmark Center introduces transparent dividing walls and natural, low-emitting materials to create a work environment conducive to staff productivity and well-being. *Credit: © Greg Premru*

CASE STUDY

University of Arkansas for Medical Sciences College of Public Health

Little Rock, Arkansas

Figure 2-14: University of Arkansas for Medical Sciences College of Public Health. *Credit: ©Tim Hursley*

Owner: University of Arkansas for Medical Sciences

Design team:

ARCHITECTS: Wilcox Group Architects

LANDSCAPE ARCHITECTS: Roberts & Williams Associates

MECHANICAL, ELECTRICAL, AND PLUMBING ENGINEERS: TME, Inc. Consulting Engineers

STRUCTURAL ENGINEERS: Crafton, Tull, Sparks & Associates

GENERAL CONTRACTORS: Nabholz Construction

Building type: New building addition

Size: 126,000 sq ft (11,706 sq m)

Program description: Faculty, research, and teaching facility; six-story vertical addition to an existing two-story classroom building

Completion date: 2003

To support the newly established College of Public Health, the building contains faculty, research, and educational spaces for the new program. The solution, a vertical addition to an existing two-story building, interfaces directly with an existing nine-story building to the south. As such, the basic building footprint, structural grid, and lateral bracing were fixed, and the project began with a building reuse baseline.

Arkansas voters stipulated that the tobacco settlement proceeds that provided the majority of the project's funding be used to promote and support the health of Arkansans; the project team championed sustainable building for a facility built to promote public health. By establishing the College of Public Health and ensuring that the physical structure embodied principles of healthy building, the university met the public's stipulation. "We started this project based on the idea that we needed the building to express an enlightened view of public health," Leo Gehring explains.

The principal goal for the new building was a sense of openness, transparency, and accessibility that would welcome the public—a departure from the traditional "institutional" aesthetic. The second goal was to showcase the benefits of health and well-being that come through sustainable building methods and through the integration of interior features that promote a healthy lifestyle. Central to both these goals is a monumental, six-story open stair that promotes physical exercise and improved communication among program components.

Figure 2-15: The monumental stairway provides an opportunity for social interaction and engagement among staffers while also encouraging exercise. *Credit: ©Tim Hursley*

We asked ourselves: "How can we use this project to demonstrate what's good for the community, the nation—the environment?" By pushing the boundaries of building forward, students learn to see this as what they should continue to do. But it teaches everyone across the board, from our students all the way through to the mechanical equipment vendors.

—LEO GEHRING, CHSM, SASHE, VICE CHANCELLOR FOR CAMPUS OPERATIONS, UAMS

Energy
- Energy wheel recovers 80 percent of the sensible and latent (moisture) energy in the exhaust air stream
- Building pressure control
- High-performance roof and glazing systems
- High-performance mechanical systems

Materials
- Low-emitting materials
- Recycled content materials

According to Gehring, this building catalyzed a transformation in thinking at UAMS. "With this building, the university acquired a new lens for looking at its building program and saw how it related to being responsible community citizens. Through that change in mindset, we can better advocate for the health of all Arkansans."

Source: Wilcox Group Architects

THE FUTURE

According to the US Census Bureau, the population is projected to increase to 570 million—nearly double today's population—by 2100. Metropolitan areas will continue to grow at rates faster than other areas. The challenge is not to find the resources to construct ever-larger emergency departments to service ever-expanding populations with asthma related to air pollution or intestinal disorders from contaminated water, but to make compelling arguments within communities that these problems are increasingly overburdening our healthcare system and consuming an ever-greater percentage of our paychecks and gross domestic product.

A larger healthcare infrastructure will mean more energy, more materials, and more development. The challenge before us, and the healthcare industry, is how to support and advocate community growth that is healthy, socially just, and environmentally sustainable. Without the transformation of the building sector in healthcare, continued system expansion will increase the ecological resource burdens within communities. The

healthcare sector should not be the victim of this vicious cycle, but use its prominence and scale to transform it. As Jackson and Maus make clear, there is no basis for the belief that we can achieve improved health without a public health approach to chronic disease issues: we never have.

The transformation of the materials marketplace in the service of indoor air quality will be challenging, but as Bernheim's essay recounts, the journey is underway. The enormous purchasing power of the healthcare industry, advocating for standards such as California's *Section 01350*, greener cleaning products, and improved indoor air quality can have a major impact on moving toward cleaner production.

For those who believe that this upstream, precautionary approach is outside the realm of the healthcare industry, the projects in this book demonstrate that it is not. Many healthcare leaders understand that such advocacy fits within their mission. Their stories of leadership inspire us to recognize and act on the good work that the myriad of research studies cited here give us the background to understand.

CHAPTER 3

Environment and Medicine

> The mirage of modern medicine (to use René Dubos's image) is one facet of the dream of progress as increasing material comfort and mastery over nature, a dream that is drifting into nightmare. The expansionist mindset strives for the gradual and eventually perfect victory over disease, disability, and perhaps even over aging and death. While in this dream state, medicine remains oddly oblivious to the large-scale constraints of ecosystems.
>
> —JESSICA PIERCE AND ANDREW JAMETON

INTRODUCTION

The twentieth-century divergence between public health and medicine signaled the shift in medicine's focus from prevention to cure and, with it, the centralization of medicine and medical education on the acute-care medical center campus. For the last sixty years, the US has invested in an ever-expanding system of acute-care hospitals to "cure" sickness. However, the late-twentieth-century emergence of chronic disease, with its complex mix of environmental, social, and medical factors, has resisted purely medical cures. Cancer, heart disease, and obesity are seen as the emergent disease burdens of wealthy, industrialized economies; the United States currently leads the world in obesity rates. Medical professionals and the general public alike increasingly view these chronic conditions as linked to lifestyle and environmental and industrial causes.

The study of the relationship between ecological and human health encompasses the disciplines of environmental health and ecological medicine. Through these emerging disciplines and the treatment of chronic diseases, public health and medicine are once again finding common ground—linked through prevention and lifestyle.

Can the healthcare industry become a model for the larger world in developing an ecological approach to these environmental and health challenges? Central to these approaches to medicine is the axiom, "First, do no harm." This seminal principle forms the basis of a medicine that embraces a broad definition of health and recognizes the primacy of prevention and restoration as preferable to treatment on a planet with a finite carrying capacity.

What is health in a world dominated by degraded ecosystems? What will a healthcare system that values restoration look like? The work of Jessica Pierce and Andrew Jameton (2004), excerpted here, represents the beginning of an answer. Inevitably, a discussion of medicine and ecology raises the question of scale—scale of the industry, resource use, and the buildings that support medical care. Commonweal Institute founder Michael Lerner, PhD, in his persuasive, personal essay, proposes that medicine and healthcare will increasingly engage in the struggle to preserve environmental health in an "ecological renaissance." Environmental activist Gary Cohen discusses the healthcare industry's recognition that healthy people cannot exist on a sick planet. Finally, physician and public health advocate Ted Schettler responds to the question, what is health? and posits a new challenge for medical care providers and designers alike.

THE STATE OF HEALTH IN THE WORLD

In the fourth century BCE, Hippocrates, the father of Western medicine, prophetically wrote: "Human health cannot be treated separately from the natural environment." As outlined in Chapter 2, through the end of the nineteenth century, medicine and public health were linked; urban planning, architecture, and healthcare improved the health of increasing urban populations through such seemingly unrelated initiatives as zoning, sanitation systems, and the construction of hospitals.

By the end of the nineteenth century, however, scientific and technical advances created a divergence in these previously linked fields. Medical practice evolved toward education and training based on the recognition and treatment of disease. Medicine became increasingly specialized toward the goal of individual patient outcomes, leading to the emergence of a wide range of medical specialties. Despite tremendous advances in the field of public health, including the eradication of numerous infectious diseases, the attention focused on clinical medicine has increasingly dissociated our health from environmental issues.

The World Bank (1993) reports that global health conditions improved more in the past half century than in all of the years before. Life expectancy has increased to an average of 65 years, and death rates have declined. In wealthy countries, life expectancy climbed from 67 years in 1950 to 77 years in 1995. In developing countries, life expectancy jumped more significantly—from 40 to 64 years—due to the public health measures (improved sanitation, water, and food supplies) associated with development and access to expanding healthcare services. Yet alongside this progress is the reality that huge disparities still exist between the richest and poorest countries. At the close of the twentieth century, nearly 20 percent of all people in developing nations were not expected to survive to age 40 (UNDP 1997). Add to this the background of unsustainable resource extraction and continued population growth, and the picture becomes even more disturbing.

With life-expectancy increases come epidemiological transitions: changes in the types of diseases and illnesses a society experiences. In *The Nature and Etiology of Disease*, Gaydos and Veney (2002) describe three such transitions. The first was associated with the development of urban centers and resulted in communicable diseases (such as cholera) due to contaminated water and viral diseases (like measles and smallpox) associated with density. Tuberculosis and respiratory diseases were even more serious problems, with social and cultural

> *Nature's goods and services are the ultimate foundations of life and health, even though in modern societies this fundamental dependency may be indirect, displaced in space and time, and therefore poorly recognized. This [is] a call to the health sector, not only to cure the diseases that result from environmental degradation, but also to ensure that the benefits that the natural environment provides to human health and well-being are preserved for future generations.*
>
> —LEE JONG-WOOK, MD, FORMER DIRECTOR GENERAL, WORLD HEALTH ORGANIZATION
>
> Source: Corvalan, Hales, and McMichael 2005

overlays related to harsh working conditions and overcrowding. The second transition, experienced by industrialized nations in the second half of the twentieth century, was the shift from acute infectious disease to chronic, noninfectious, degenerative diseases, their prevalence related to increases in longevity. Finally, Gaydos and Veney identify a third epidemiological transition —the reemergence of infectious diseases with antibiotic resistance. The result of the interaction of social and environmental changes resulting in the adaptation of the microbe, it has the potential to be global in scope.

Ironically, they point out, "the technological advances that have allowed for increased longevity can also cause an increase in environmental degradation, and these advances arguably lead to new chronic diagnoses.... Many of the diseases of the second transition share common factors related to human adaptation, including diet, activity level, mental stress, behavioral practice, and environmental pollution." Global warming, ozone depletion, habitat destruction, and toxic chemicals are major global environmental concerns with defined human and ecosystem health impacts. Over the last twenty years, the study of these issues and their complex impacts on ecosystem health has evolved into the fields of environmental health and ecological medicine. In the following essay, Michael Lerner, the president and cofounder of Commonweal, examines the intersection between environment and human health and its opportunities for medicine through a new lens.

The Recovery of the Sacred in Healthcare in the Ecological Renaissance: The Age of Extinctions

Michael Lerner, PhD

We indubitably live in an Age of Extinctions. Conservation science has demonstrated this beyond reasonable doubt. This is the sixth great spasm of extinction in the history of the earth. The last comparable spasm of extinctions took place at the end of the Age of Dinosaurs, 65 million years ago. What is distinctive about this Age of Extinctions is that it is the first to be caused by the activity of a single species: man.

The great challenge of our time is to move from this Age of Extinctions to what David Orr has called an ecological renaissance. To do so, we must understand the great outlines of the diseases and disorders of our time, both personal and planetary.

Scientists tell us there are five major drivers of this Age of Extinctions. Climate change, ozone depletion, toxic chemicals, habitat destruction, and invasive species are the five drivers of this great cutting back of the tree of life. Three of these five—climate change, ozone depletion, and toxic chemicals—are directly the result of the past Hydrocarbon Century and the misuse of the carbon resources once safely stored under the earth's mantle.

But these are not the only drivers of this Age of Extinctions. Bill Joy has eloquently written of our present shift from an era of weapons of mass destruction to an era of technologies of mass destruction in his prescient essay "Why the Future Doesn't Need Us" in Wired magazine. The information technologies, biotechnology, nanotechnology, and robotics are flooding the world with genetically modified organisms and nanoparticles—robotic entities will soon follow.

There is much more threatening both human and planetary life. In response to the threat of climate change, nuclear power is resurgent. Nuclear weapons are proliferating everywhere. Disparities of wealth and poverty are growing and with them the inevitable disparities in health. Wireless technologies have created an awesome transformation of electromagnetic fields with health consequences that are only beginning to be understood.

Another way to look at the drivers of extinction is to use the simple formula that states that our impact on the biosphere equals production x consumption x technology, or $I = P \times C \times T$. We can reduce our impact on the biosphere by altering any or all of these three factors. We can reduce the population, reduce or transform what we consume, and move from more toxic to less toxic, or even biologically regenerative, technologies.

Yet another useful formula suggests that the way to a sustainable world is described in three principal terms: green energy, green materials, and green chemistry. Fortunately, the three are closely linked and interrelated. We can to an amazing degree develop far less toxic chemicals from living plants than from dead carbon; we can then use these chemicals to create green materials and to support the production of green energy.

These facts are, individually, well-known. What we rarely look at is the whole behind the facts, the pattern language of comprehensive human and ecological disaster that contemplation of the whole reveals.

THE EMERGING ENVIRONMENTAL HEALTH MOVEMENT

A decade ago I wrote an essay called "The Age of Extinctions and the Emerging Environmental Health Movement" in which I proposed that in the face of this Age of Extinctions we were witnessing an emerging environmental health movement that linked people and organizations around the world in an unprecedented effort to protect human and ecosystem health. I also proposed that the emerging environmental health movement would be led to a remarkable degree by women, who are more readily disposed than most men to recognize holistic patterns that threaten personal, familial, community, and planetary health.

We have, over the past decade, seen dramatic growth in the environmental health movement. It has driven the issue of climate change to the top of the global agenda. Awareness of the threat of destruction of the ozone layer resulted in the Montreal Protocol on Substances That Deplete the Ozone Layer in the hopes of reducing the use of the chemicals destroying this fragile layer protecting life on earth. More recently, the Stockholm Convention on Persistent Organic Pollutants became the first global treaty to ban the use of a dozen of the most toxic chemicals. Likewise, efforts to protect and restore the habitats of endangered species have gathered strength around the world, preserving imperiled lands and oceans on an unprecedented scale.

The efforts to address the threats of biotechnology, nanotechnology, and electromagnetic field disruption are newer and far smaller, but they are gathering strength. And networks working on global poverty have succeeded in making poverty almost as potent a global issue as climate change. But in the midst of all this heroic work to preserve human and ecosphere health, the global forces that are causing this Age of Extinctions continue to gather strength.

THE ENVIRONMENTAL HEALTH SCIENCE REVOLUTION

This is the context in which serious men and women around the world have tackled the critical issue of green healthcare design. Green healthcare design gained prominence through a global initiative called Health Care Without Harm: The Campaign for Environmentally Responsible Health Care, in whose inception I played a small part, and which I have followed closely ever since.

Health Care Without Harm (HCWH) was the first of a new generation of grassroots, market-focused, industrial-sector environmental health campaigns. Its leadership recognized that in the United States the traditional approaches to reform—passing new laws, improving enforcement of existing laws, improving administrative regulation, and seeking redress through the courts—were largely unavailable because the country was in a period of governance hostile to public health and environmental values.

The environmental health science revolution is demonstrating with growing certainty that the old paradigms regarding the health effects of these toxic chemicals is entirely outdated. The old paradigm focused on high doses of chemicals and their direct impact on health. The new paradigm focuses on much lower doses of endocrine-disrupting chemicals and their widespread effects on both fetal development and young children. It also focuses on the extraordinarily complex interactions between genes, gene expression, chemicals, nutrition, infectious agents, poverty, stress, and much more. Other campaigns modeled in part on HCWH have followed, addressing the greening of other industrial sectors by replacing egregious chemical technologies, products, and processes with more health-friendly practices.

THE COLLABORATIVE ON HEALTH AND THE ENVIRONMENT

For the past five years my own efforts in environmental health have focused on the Collaborative on Health and the Environment, an international partnership of individuals and organizations seeking to raise the level of public and professional dialogue on the impact of the environment on health. The principal focus of the Collaborative on Health and the Environment (like that of HCWH) has been the impact of chemicals on human health. Its principal goal has been to alert patients, health professionals, and health-affected community groups across the country and around the world to the implications of the environmental health science revolution. It is not a coalition, like HCWH, but a network that focuses on delivering science to a concerned global partnership and fostering constructive dialogue about how chemicals and other environmental factors affect human health.

In its first five years, the Collaborative on Health and the Environment has had a powerful impact, developing high-level communities of concern among scientists, health professionals, and patient groups in the disease sectors of learning and developmental disabilities, infertility and pregnancy compromise, and breast cancer. It is having a rapidly developing impact among patients and health professionals concerned more broadly with cancer, Parkinson's disease, and other neurodegenerative diseases. (Asthma, heart disease, diabetes, endometriosis, autoimmune diseases, allergies, and chemical sensitivities are among other conditions for which there is strong evidence of an etiological role of chemicals.)

The Collaborative on Health and the Environment developed a widely used online database that catalogs the impact of chemical contaminants on almost two hundred diseases, disorders, and conditions. Its partner teleconference calls attract top scientists, government officials, health professionals, and patient and community representatives for discussions committed to "science and civility."

FROM NEUTRALITY TO THE PATIENT-HEALER PERSPECTIVE

Up to this point I have used the neutral language of science and policy. Now I will write as both a patient and a health educator who has focused his work on the interface between personal and planetary healing. For over thirty years, we at Commonweal have worked to help children with learning and behavior disorders. For over twenty years, a large part of my own work at Commonweal has focused on week-long retreats for people with cancer—mostly women, many young mothers with metastatic breast cancer whose greatest concerns are dying while their children are young and whether their daughters will develop cancer them-

selves. Having been close to well over one thousand people living with cancer in the Cancer Help Program, I have seen far too many people killed and maimed by senseless and preventable destruction of life to maintain a neutral distance.

Nor is my experience only with the Cancer Help Program. I am myself a DES son. My mother took diethylstilbestrol while she was pregnant with me, her first child, because her previous six pregnancies had ended in miscarriage. DES was eventually the first endocrine-disrupting chemical to be recognized. If I had been a girl, chances are I would have had some form of reproductive cancer.

Both my parents had cancer. My half sister Pamela died of cancer as a young mother, leaving two young children. And there are four children on the autistic spectrum in my immediate family. I have two brothers. All the children we fathered required intensive medical interventions before or at birth. I had a learning disability as a child. I have also had benign prostatitis—associated in rats with DES—since I was a young man, and live with a gradually neurodegenerative essential tremor that makes many daily tasks of living a challenge. And, despite a very healthy lifestyle, I had a heart attack before age sixty. Asthma, endometriosis, chemical sensitivities, and allergies are some of the other environmentally related diseases in my immediate family.

The central purpose of the Collaborative on Health and the Environment is to help people realize that many (if not most) of the common, and even epidemic, diseases, disorders, and conditions of our time would be far less prevalent if we were not all carrying many hundreds of toxic chemicals in our bodies that were not present in the bodies of our relatives just a century ago.

But the science, the policy work, and the advocacy are not enough. The deeply felt experience of the truth of chemical contamination of the sacred body of life comes to us most profoundly when we realize that we and the people we love are suffering unnecessarily because of the profligate carelessness with which we have let greed design our use of toxic chemicals. And so it is most fitting that green healthcare should lead the way into an ecological renaissance of green building design. For those who believe that protecting life is sacred work, green healthcare design becomes a deep dimension of that work.

We may, if we are fortunate, become, when we are wounded, the carriers of an inner light that Carl Jung called the awakening of the wounded healer in us. This is the essence of the ancient shamanic tradition. The shamans, wounded themselves by an initiatory illness, discovered that their own personal recovery was less important than recovering to help others who had been wounded. They also were the guardians of the balance of the forces around the community that could preserve the health of all.

As far back in history as the healing temple of Asclepius, where patients in search of healing entered dark chambers and awaited powerful dreams of healing, places of healing have been associated with the sacred. The Hippocratic tradition is a sacred lineage. Green healthcare, and green healthcare design, is at the heart of that lineage.

I have a personal dream of green healthcare. I dream of living to see a time when the world comes to realize that the whole body of life on earth—not just human life—is sacred. I dream that we recognize that since the body of life is essentially one, we cannot allow toxic materials, toxic energy sources, or toxic chemicals to continue to destroy this infinitely complex and beautiful natural design.

I dream that healthcare continues to pioneer what a deeply green design for healing work can be. I dream of a healthcare system accessible to all, rich and poor alike, where every dimension of healing work has been reexamined so that it strengthens and reinforces health wherever possible.

I dream of a time when all the patient groups, large and small, and the health professionals who support them, have become one of the strongest forces on earth for the ecological renaissance. For they understand better than anyone else that an ounce of prevention is worth a pound of cure, and that prevention of disease by the green design of our homes, work places, communities, and nations is at the heart of the healer's task.

That is the vision to which this book is dedicated. I am proud to be associated with that great vision.

ENVIRONMENTAL HEALTH

The natural, social, and built environments, and their complex interrelationships, affect human health. Together, they comprise environmental health. According to the World Health Organization (WHO), environmental health is "the study of the direct pathological effects on health of chemical, physical and biological agents . . . and the effects of the broad physical and social environment on human health." The direct health impacts of degraded ecosystems—air and water—have historically been documented in the public health literature. The asthma epidemic (annual self-reported asthma prevalence increased 73 percent between 1980 and 1996) (Mannino et al. 2002) may be attributable to increased exposure to indoor allergens and poor indoor air quality (the built environment), combined with more time spent indoors (90 percent on average), and decreased physical activity (behavior). As chronic diseases like asthma are linked to this complex set of factors, studying these interrelationships propels environmental medicine from the fringes of medical discourse into the mainstream.

BIOETHICS

In the late 1960s, Van Rensselaer Potter coined the term *bioethics* to join environmental and medical concerns with the goal of the "long-term acceptable survival of the human species" (Potter 1971). However, just as medicine and public health diverged in an era of major technological advances, a similar bifurcation in bioethics has suppressed global environmental concerns in favor of debate over clinical technologies and patient care. Environmental medicine is just beginning the integrative work of defining environmental bioethics, drawing on the work of philosopher Herschel Elliot (1997): "An acceptable system of ethics is contingent on its ability to preserve the ecosystems which sustain it."

In formulating environmental health ethics, Andrew Jameton (2005), who sits on the faculty of preventive

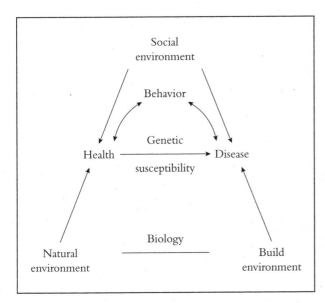

Figure 3-1: Environmental health is the study of the complex interrelationship between the natural, built, and social environments and how they create the conditions for health and disease. *Credit: Samuel H. Wilson, MD, 2004*

and societal medicine at the University of Nebraska Medical Center, outlines three compelling implications:

1. Methods of accounting that discount future health risks must be reconsidered. The notion that diminished human and ecosystem health is "the price we pay" for technological or economic progress is unacceptable.
2. The full life cycle cost of environmental health measures must be considered in development decisions. Whether a sewage treatment plant, a nuclear power plant, or a new hospital campus, the local health benefits must be weighed against the life cycle impacts of the construction and operation of the facility.
3. While there is an observed correspondence between the wealth of a nation and the average health of its citizens (World Bank 1993), if a nation overburdens its environment in pursuit of wealth, that nation will undermine everyone's health in the long run.

ECOLOGICAL MEDICINE

More recently, a global movement of concerned scientists, doctors, and environmentalists began "a field of inquiry and action to reconcile the care and health of ecosystems, populations, communities and individuals" (Myers et al. 2002). Ecological medicine draws on public health, ecology, conventional medicine, complementary and alternative medicine, conservation medicine, and conservation biology in framing the following basic tenets (Ausubel 2004):

- The first goal of medicine is to establish the conditions for health and wholeness, thus preventing disease and illness. The second goal is to cure.
- The earth is also the physician's client. The patient under the physician's care is one part of the earth.
- Humans are part of a local ecosystem. Following the ecopsychological insight that a disturbed ecosystem can make people mentally ill, a disturbed ecosystem can surely make people physically ill.
- Medicine should not add to the illnesses of humans or the planet. Medical practices themselves should not damage other species or the ecosystem.

Humans cannot have a moral duty to deliver the impossible, or to supply something if the act of supplying it harms the ecosystem to the point where life on earth becomes unsustainable. Moral codes, no matter how logical and well reasoned, and human rights, no matter how compassionate, must make sense within the limitations of the ecosystem; we cannot disregard the factual consequences of our ethics. If acting morally compromises the ecosystem, then moral behavior must be rethought. Ethics cannot demand a level of resource use that the ecosystem cannot tolerate.

—HERSCHEL ELLIOTT AND RICHARD LAMM (2002)

Principles of Responsibility

The architecture, organizational design, strategic planning, management, and budget of the GHC embody principles of responsibility to nature and future generations.

Interdependence

Each of us is deeply connected with Earth's ecosystems; each of our lives is only a moment in the grand scale of time. Ultimately, we all depend on the health of the global community and of Earth's biosphere for our own health and happiness. Individuals cannot live healthy or happy lives in poisoned ecosystems and unhealthy communities. By the same token, healthy communities and biological systems depend on human restraint and responsibility in technologies, population, production, and consumption.

Model Behaviors

The GHC encourages staff and patients to live in environmentally sound ways that express a modest level of consumption.

Conceptions of Health

The GHC employs ecologically sound conceptions of health, recovery, and rehabilitation.

Resilience

Health in humans and ecosystems is not a steady state but a dynamic one marked by resilience. Both medicine and ecosystem science and management should focus on promoting and restoring the innate ability of biological systems to protect themselves, to recover, and to heal. Systems that draw upon or mimic the elegance, economies, and resilience of nature offer promising paths for health care research and development.

Occupational Safety

The GHC monitors, minimizes, and equalizes environmental risks to GHC employees.

Minimize Harm

The GHC provides health care in ways that minimize harm to human and ecosystem health.

"First, do no harm."

Health care should not undermine public health or the environment. This precautionary principle should be applied to decisions affecting the ecosystem, populations, communities, and individuals.

Therapies and Products

The GHC provides ecologically sustainable therapies and products.

Treatment Options

The GHC provides services to patients with any health condition but may limit the range of therapies offered in order to reduce ecological impacts and increase efficiency.

Appropriateness

"Medicine," in its Greek origins, means "appropriate measures." The goal is to achieve maximal health with minimal intervention, promoting good health that is appropriate to an individual's stage of life without overburdening Earth's life-sustaining processes.

Research-based Assessment

The GHC engages in a continuous process of assessment and evaluation of its services, in light of both patient satisfaction and research into environmentally preferable technologies.

Diversity

Health is served by diverse approaches, including many traditional healing systems, local adaptations, and indigenous science around the world. Ecological Medicine encourages freedom of medical choice, guided by informed consent and compassionate practice.

Responsibility

The GHC pays its share of the environmental and social costs of providing health care.

Market Transformation

The GHC encourages institutions with which it has business relations to operate in environmentally responsible ways.

Cooperation

In order to gain knowledge and improve practices, patients should be partners with practitioners, and medical professionals should cooperate with ecologists and other students of the natural world. Health care organizations should be managed with the active participation of the communities they serve, while communities must learn to integrate their welfare with that of their regional ecosystems.

Community Educator

The GHC acts as a community educator, advocating principles of sustainability in every aspect of life.

Equitable Access

The GHC provides high quality services at a level inexpensive enough that they can be made equally available to all.

Reconciliation

Individual health care services should be economically sustainable, equitable, modest in scale of high quality, noncommercial, and readily available to all. Societies should build and maintain infrastructures that assure all citizens the capability to meet basic needs such as health, nutrition, family planning, shelter, and meaningful work while minimizing harm to the Earth. Societies should increasingly devote their material and creative resources to policies and projects that restore and maintain the health of biological and human neighborhoods. All efforts to improve human welfare must be conducted within a cooperative framework established by the health of the Earth.

Responsible Citizen

The GHC pays its share of the environmental and social costs of providing health care.

Figure 3-2: The concepts and values of ecological medicine inform the development of core principles of a green health center (GHC) as articulated by Jessica Pierce and Andrew Jameton (2004). *(Ecological medicine principles reprinted with permission from the Science and Environmental Health Network.)*

In a call to reconcile the care and health of ecosystems, populations, communities, and individuals, ecological medicine integrates the concepts and values enumerated in Figure 3-2.

How might these concepts and values manifest in the healthcare delivery system and the buildings that define it? It is not so simple to make the conceptual leap from these visionary statements to the reality of healthcare delivery in the industrialized world. Pierce and Jameton (2004) led a group of inspired medical professionals and students in strategizing a set of principles they bundled into the definition of a "green health center." These thirteen core principles, viewed in Figure 3-2 alongside the precepts of ecological medicine, are an initial attempt at mapping the edges of this brave new world.

Built examples of this ecological view of medicine are difficult to pinpoint today. The case studies that follow, the Sambhavna Trust Clinic in Bhopal, India, and the Joseph F. Sullivan Center — a graduate architecture student project from Clemson University's Architecture + Health program — represent primary-care facilities both in the developing world and in the US that demonstrate this ecological vision of medicine. Many of the case studies in other chapters of this book also embody aspects of these principles; hopefully, this dialogue will inform the transformation ahead.

Figure 3-3: Sambhavna Trust Clinic. *Credit: Maude Dorr*

CASE STUDY

Sambhavna Trust Clinic

Bhopal,
India

Owner: Sambhavna Trust
Design team: House of Consultants, Delhi
   ARCHITECTS: Shri Kishore Charavarti and Shri Yatin Choudhary
   CIVIL ENGINEERS: Vishnu Chilotre
Building type: Replacement ambulatory care building
Size: 22,000 sq ft (2,044 sq m)
Design energy intensity: 10–20 kWh/sq m (.93–1.86 kWh/sq ft) depending on season and intensity of occasional medical procedures (such as surgery)
Program description: A freestanding clinical services building catering to victims of the 1984 Union Carbide chemical leak, including a medicinal garden and an associated traditional medicine manufacturing facility.
Completion date: 2005
Awards/recognition: 2002 Margaret Mead Centennial Award

On December 3, 1984, a methyl isocyanate leak from a tank at a Union Carbide pesticide production plant in Bhopal, India, exposed an estimated 200,000 local residents to the lethal gas. While estimates vary, the toll on human life was staggering. About

3,800 of the city's 1.7 million residents died instantly. Perhaps more than 20,000 are said to have died in total. The clinic maintains that 120,000 to 150,000 of the area's people are chronically ill, many from allegedly contaminated water. Located in a neighborhood where many were affected by the incident, the Sambhavna Trust Clinic serves 5 to 10 new patients per day, and about 10,000 patients total per year, using both traditional ayurvedic and Western allopathic techniques.

The clinic, funded through individual donations, was founded in 1996, by the Sambhavna Trust, to fill a need for medical services that volunteer trustees believed were not being adequately provided by the government following the disaster. *Sambhavna*, defined as both "possibility" and "compassion" in Sanskrit and Hindi, focuses on personal, participatory patient care delivered in a holistic, sustainable setting. The clinic's design works within the local vernacular to provide a tranquil, verdant, non-threatening place for treatment of a sometimes medicine-wary clientele. Primary goals for the clinic include:

- Making survivors from surrounding communities coming for care feel welcome by offering space, tranquility, and natural vegetation.
- Training the community to grow medicinal plants and produce medicines from them.
- Providing health education and training to the community.
- Demonstrating environmentally sustainable techniques and their relationship to health through the use of energy, construction and daily-use materials, and waste disposal.

The facility's sustainable design strategies inform every aspect of the building, from the rainwater harvesting systems to the microshade offered by the textured exterior surfaces.

Figure 3-4: Patients gather in the exterior waiting room constructed of handcrafted natural materials and shaded by roof overhangs. *Credit: Maude Dorr*

KEY BUILDING PERFORMANCE STRATEGIES

Site

■ Landscaping and tropical gardens designed to enhance microclimate

■ "Environment management design" integrates landscape, trees, gray water, rainwater, storm water, solid-waste management, and energy

Water

■ Extensive rainwater harvesting: roof rainwater captured during the monsoon season and stored in 150,000 liter (39,626 gal) underground tanks; water filtered for domestic use during the dry summer months

■ Gray water used for landscape irrigation

Energy

■ 10-kW photovoltaic system supplements grid energy

■ Rooftop solar collectors heat water

■ Passive ventilation: stack effect in central courtyard exhausts heat from building

■ Bioclimatic design, surface shading

■ Building designed for hot local climate: inward looking, northern orientation, Venturi effect, gable wind catcher for prevailing breezes, verandas, roof overhangs, small-opening windows, double (cavity) walls on west side, textured surfaces, double-insulated roof, solar orientation (short walls face east and west), minimized surface-to-volume ratio

Materials

■ Local materials used in natural form and color (i.e., not painted or stained) wherever possible

Environmental Quality

■ Designed to be welcoming and familiar to patients and to promote tranquility

■ Human-scale building

■ More than 50 percent of occupied spaces require no electrical lighting during the day

The Sambhavna Trust envisioned the new facility as "a model setting for holistic healthcare with community involvement." More specifically, the building was specified to be low-cost and durable, to combine beauty with function while blending in with the local landscape, to be passively cooled, daylit, and well ventilated, and to harvest its own rainwater. Trust spokesman Satinath Sarangi affirms that in practice, all these goals have been achieved.

Sources: Sambhavna Trust and House of Consultants

Figure 3-5: The lush gardens, irrigated with gray water, temper the intense heat and provide a source of medicinal herbs used in the clinic. *Credit: Maude Dorr*

Joseph F. Sullivan Center at Clemson University

Figure 3-6: A flexible building system comprised of modular components is designed to adapt to changing programmatic needs over time, minimizing waste and reliance on resources. *Credit: David Allison, AIA, ACHA; Dina Battisto, PhD; Allen Buie; and Megan Gerend: Clemson University Architecture & Health Studio*

Figure 3-7: The proposed 20,000 sq ft (1,850 sq m) Sullivan Center takes advantage of the site's sun, wind, and water resources, creating a human-scale, daylit space constructed with nontoxic materials. *Credit: David Allison, AIA, ACHA; Dina Battisto, PhD; Allen Buie; and Megan Gerend: Clemson University Architecture & Health Studio*

Partnership and collaboration between designers and medical practitioners is fundamental to instilling a public health–inspired ethic in twenty-first-century healthcare facilities. In the years ahead, today's students will be the stewards of this ethic. Clemson University's Architecture + Health program is one of a few graduate-level programs in the US that bridges the disciplines of architecture and public health. An example of Clemson's pioneering work is its partnership with the campus-based Joseph F. Sullivan Center, established in 1978, now one of the oldest continuously operating nurse-managed health centers in the United States.

Recognizing that the Sullivan Center's facilities were impeding the effective delivery of its broad array of services, an interdisciplinary studio in both architecture and landscape architecture was offered in the spring of 2005, coordinated by professors Dina Battisto and David Allison. The resulting design—a winner in the 2005 Healthcare Environment Awards Competition student category—provides a blueprint for integrating green design, healthcare, and community development.

The project's central organizing principles evolved from four primary tenets, with associated benefits:

1. **Principle:** A setting designed to use natural capital—sun, wind, and water
   Benefits: Reduces operating costs and maintenance; uses renewable resources
2. **Principle:** A setting that harms the environment as little as possible; one that pollutes less, consumes less, and uses fewer nonrenewable resources
   Benefits: Fosters a healthy environment and protects natural ecosystems
3. **Principle:** A setting that provides a healthy interior environment—daylit, free of toxic materials, and connecting its occupants to nature
   Benefits: Improves workplace productivity, reduces stress, increases job satisfaction, and improves comfort
4. **Principle:** Uses an integrated building approach and life-cycle assessment

Source: Clemson University 2004

Pending a successful fundraising campaign, the new center will be built on the edge of the Clemson campus on a reclaimed brownfield site, and will emphasize health promotion as a core service, in addition to treating illness and disability. Consistent with this public health commitment are plans for a weekend farmers' market and community garden plots. There is a flexible building plan, abundant daylight, shaded courtyards, therapeutic gardens, and tucked-under parking for staff (Battisto 2006).

Source: Battisto, Allison, and Crew 2006

HEALTHCARE AND THE ENVIRONMENT

In stark contrast to the preceding goals and case study examples, the existing healthcare industry is increasingly environmentally paradoxical. Pierce and Jameton (2004) summarize the dilemma:

> The materials and methods of healthcare contribute to pollution, add to global warming and ozone depletion, and rely on an extensive natural resource base — the extraction, manufacturing, and use of which incurs a significant environmental burden both locally and globally. This is partly a problem of scale. The United States maintains the world's largest healthcare system, spending close to half of all the money spent in the world on healthcare. Maintaining such a large healthcare system requires a large economy. That economy, however, is making a substantial contribution to the decline in the state of the world's environment. And environmental decline is in turn harming human health and creating more illnesses in need of treatment. As the need for healthcare increases, this already oversized healthcare system, caught in the vicious positive feedback cycle, is likely to respond by growing and thereby continuing to further compound health problems. As such, healthcare frustrates its own practical and moral commitment to promote and maintain human health.

As this book goes to print, the US expenditure on healthcare has surpassed 17 percent of the gross domestic product, while the average health status of its citizens has begun to decline. Despite having the highest per capita expenditure on healthcare per year ($5,700), the US global ranking based on a spectrum of health indicators has been in decline for the past twenty years.

The irony of healthcare's role in environmental degradation provides compelling insight into what is wrong with the delivery of healthcare and foreshadows a path to the future that recognizes the ethical, economic, and environmental dimensions of service delivery and the construction and operation of buildings. The work of Health Care Without Harm is transforming the industry on both policy and operational levels. Environmental health issues are increasingly appearing in mainstream medical literature. The next essayist, Gary Cohen, founder and coexecutive director of Health Care Without Harm, provides a blueprint for medical service delivery in the twenty-first century that recognizes that healthy people cannot exist on a sick planet.

PROBLEMS OF SCALE IN US HEALTHCARE

- Access to healthcare is narrowing.
- International competitiveness of US healthcare is declining.
- Medical error rates are rising: between 50.000 and 100,000 deaths annually are attributed to medical error.
- The ecological footprint of healthcare services is large and continues to increase.
- Many physicians believe that over 50 percent of healthcare is ineffective, wasteful, or both.

Source: Jameton 2005

Transforming Healthcare

Gary Cohen

What is the role of medicine in a world where new diseases are emerging due to global warming and where toxic chemicals have trespassed not only into our food and buildings but also into the womb? What does the Hippocratic oath mean in a healthcare sector addicted to petrochemicals in its products and operations? What does "the environment of care" signify in a society in which close to 40 percent of adult work-related asthma is triggered in hospital environments?

OUR RISING DISEASE BURDEN
Chronic diseases and disabilities now affect more than ninety million men, women, and children — more than one-third of our population (CDC 2005a). Despite medical advancements, the best available data shows an increase in the incidence of asthma, autism, birth defects, childhood brain cancer, acute lymphocytic

leukemia, endometriosis, Parkinson's disease, and infertility (Trasande and Landrigan 2004, Jahnke et al. 2005).

The picture is profoundly troubling. The human toll on families and communities is immense, particularly on those already disadvantaged by persistent economic disparities. By 2020, healthcare and lost productivity costs for these diseases will exceed $1 trillion yearly (Goldman 2001).

The new field of environmental health is linking each of these diseases and disorders to exposure to toxic chemicals (CHE 2006, Heindel 2003). In the past five years, the Centers for Disease Control and Prevention (CDC) has released three biomonitoring studies detailing toxic chemical loads among the American population. The CDC's Third National Report on Human Exposure to Environmental Chemicals looked at 148 environmental chemicals—including lead, mercury, cadmium; dioxin, furans, and polychlorinated biphenyls or PCBs; and 42 pesticides—in the bodies of thousands of participants (CDC 2005c). The conclusions are startling.

Without our knowledge or informed consent, all of us carry the products and by-products of the chemical industry—carcinogens, reproductive toxins, neurotoxicants, mutagens, and chemicals that impact a broad set of bodily systems. Our exposures come from food, building materials, cleaning and disinfection products, personal-care products, pesticide and herbicide applications, emissions from chemical manufacturing and disposal sites, pharmaceuticals, and a multitude of other sources, some known and some unknown. In the last twenty-seven years, only five chemicals or chemical classes have been restricted due to their impact on public health via the Toxic Substances Control Act of 1976, yet thousands of new chemicals have entered the marketplace without comprehensive toxicity testing (Wilson 2006). Essentially, the chemical industry is conducting an uncontrolled experiment on us and our children. The overall social, public health, and environmental costs of toxic chemical poisoning are borne by society instead of the companies that are trespassing into our bodies.

HIGHLIGHTS OF AMERICANS' DISEASE BURDEN

- The lifetime risk of getting cancer is 1 in 2 for men, and 1 in 3 for women; 1 in 12 men and 1 in 11 women will develop invasive cancer before the age of sixty (ACS 2005).

- The risk of breast cancer has almost tripled from more than 1 in 20 to 1 in 8 in the last forty years (ACS 2005b).

- Annual self-reported asthma prevalence increased 73 percent between 1980 and 1996 (Mannino et al. 2002).

- The incidence rate of non-Hodgkin's lymphoma has nearly doubled since the late 1970s (NCI 2006).

- In America, 127 million people are overweight; 60 million are obese (AOA 2006).

- Between 1997 and 2004, the incidence of diabetes increased 45 percent among eighteen to forty-four-year-olds (CDC 2005b).

- Endometriosis, which has been linked to dioxin exposure, now affects 10 percent to 15 percent of American women (Holloway 1994; Suchy and Stepan 2004).

HEALTHCARE'S CONTRIBUTION TO CHEMICAL CONTAMINATION

Dioxin is one of many chemicals that new environmental health science considers unsafe at levels previously thought to be benign (Mahaffey 2000; Keitt, Fagan, and Marts 2004). Processes such as combustion, the chlorine bleaching of pulp and paper, certain types of chemical manufacturing, and other industrial procedures that include the combustion of chlorine produce dioxin as a by-product.

Dioxin is one of the most infamous of the persistent bioaccumulative toxicants (PBTs), one of the most potent carcinogens known to science, and one of the few targeted by international treaty for elimination. Health effects linked to dioxin exposure in humans and/or animals include cancer, endometriosis, testicular atrophy, immune and neurological system damage, increased miscarriages and birth defects, and alterations in hormone function. Intimately linked to dioxin is polyvinyl chloride (PVC), used widely in the production of IV and blood bags, plastic tubing, and an array of other hospital products. Because of its high chlorine content, PVC contributes to dioxin formation when it is manufactured and incinerated.

The US Environmental Protection Agency (EPA) estimates that humans receive more than 95 percent of their dioxin intake through food (FDA 2006); the dioxin in dairy products, meat, and fish is ingested and stored in fatty tissue for years, building up over time. Dioxin's global distribution means that every member of the human population is exposed. This is especially problematic for childbearing women, who pass dioxin to an embryo or fetus in utero, and to a child through breast-feeding. In its reassessment of dioxin-related science, the EPA (2001) also estimated that the average amount of dioxin in all Americans' bodies is "at or approaching levels" that will begin to cause a variety of adverse health effects.

Another chemical, di(2-ethylhexyl) phthalate, or DEHP, is a plasticizer used to make flexible PVC-based products such as IV tubes and blood bags. DEHP can leach out of these products and enter patients' bodies. In 2000, new environmental health science led the National Toxicology Program to conclude that DEHP is a reproductive toxicant and that infants in hospitals are at risk from exposure to it (NTP 2000). The Food and Drug Administration (FDA) followed with a health advisory to hospitals, urging healthcare facilities to seek safer alternatives, especially for vulnerable patient populations (FDA 2002).

Pharmaceuticals are also emerging as a major environmental and public health threat that until recently was virtually unknown. Many pharmaceuticals contain hormone-disrupting chemicals that migrate from hospitals and homes to bodies of water, where they negatively impact aquatic life. They also wind up in our drinking water (Fox 2005; Heinzmann 2005). Many drugs also contain compounds that persist in the environment and/or bioaccumulate in the food chain. As Americans consume more drugs, these biologically active agents build up. More than one hundred pharmaceuticals or their metabolites have been found in bodies of water in Europe and the United States, some of them in drinking water supplies (Hemminger 2005; Heberer et al. 1997).

EVOLVING THE HIPPOCRATIC OATH

Physicians and other healthcare professionals are taught to "first, do no harm," so healthcare institutions and the industries that support them have a special responsibility to ensure that their operations are not major sources of environmental harm. Until recently, healthcare professionals and administrators were unaware of their contribution to chemical contamination and broader societal disease burdens. The curricula for physicians, nurses, and hospital administrators do not provide the latest scientific information on the environmental consequences of healthcare delivery.

Over the last ten years, the information gap has begun to close. With the emergence of Health Care Without Harm, healthcare's leaders have learned about their industry's contribution to chemical exposure issues and made steady progress toward solving some of their environmental problems. For example, due to the rising costs of complying with dioxin emission regulations and the educational work of HCWH, more than five thousand medical-waste incinerators have closed since the mid-1990s. In response to the changing regulatory climate, hospital administrators chose to reduce waste and adopt safer waste-disposal and treatment technologies.

Mercury elimination in the American healthcare sector, although not yet complete, is a powerful success story about how hospitals can collectively use their enormous purchasing power to reduce their environmental and public health footprint and also drive markets for safer alternatives to problematic chemicals and technologies (H2E 2005). In 1998, the American Hospital Association and the EPA entered into a memorandum of understanding to eliminate products containing mercury from the healthcare sector by 2005. As hospitals and major healthcare systems adopted mercury phase-out procurement policies, virtually all the major pharmacy chains in the country stopped selling mercury thermometers. The largest healthcare-related group purchasing organizations (GPOs) — Premier, Novation, Consorta, Amerinet, Broadlane, and MedAssets — have committed to eliminate mercury-based products from their catalogs.

There is more to this success story. Healthcare leaders are seen as trustworthy and occupy a highly respected place in American society. As hospitals eliminate mercury from their operations, political momentum to eliminate mercury from other sectors — and other products in our economy — is generated. Since hospitals began eliminating mercury, more than twenty-nine states have passed laws restricting mercury-based products (EIA 2005). Moreover, as leaders within the American Nurses Association and affiliated organizations learn about environmental threats linked to hospital operations, they have become active in more than eight states to support policies to phase out chemicals linked to cancer, birth defects, and genetic damage. In 2005, HCWH launched a Web site called the Luminary Project (www.theluminaryproject.org) to honor those leaders in the nursing profession who are guided by the precautionary principle and engaging in preventive medicine through environmental activities in their institutions and in society at large.

HEALTHCARE'S PATH TO ECOLOGICAL MEDICINE
Once the link between healthy people and a healthy environment is made, opportunities emerge for hospitals wanting to model environmental responsibility.

DESIGN FOR HEALTH
The healthcare sector's eager acceptance of the Green Guide for Health Care is encouraging. If hospitals redefine green building by including environmental health as a key component, the healthcare sector could become a leader in going beyond first-cost capital accounting. If the health and environmental services of a building are accounted for over its entire life, the life cycle costs and benefits can be defined during its design.

As hospitals evaluate buildings using environmental health criteria, an entirely new chapter in evidence-based design research in healthcare begins. The healthcare sector can lead a far-reaching and significant research agenda that documents how healthy buildings contribute to healthier people and greater productivity both within the hospital and beyond.

HEALTHY FOOD IN HEALTHCARE
The United States' dominant industrial food system contributes significantly to a host of preventable health and environmental problems. Poor nutrition, for example, is a risk factor for four of the six leading causes of death — heart disease, stroke, diabetes, and cancer. Pesticide drift, field runoff, waste burning, and diesel exhaust

from transporting food long distances are all factors of food production that contribute to air and water pollution. Ever-expanding large-scale animal feedlot operations have led to the demise of independent family farms and contaminated groundwater with nitrates, hormones, and other products of untreated animal waste, creating the conditions for the spread of virulent pathogens.

Rather than fresh fruits and vegetables, whole grains, and other high-fiber foods important for health, our current food system favors the production of feedlot-raised animal products and highly refined, calorie-dense foods. This is not only a food system misaligned with governmental dietary guidelines, it is also a food system largely reliant on production and distribution methods that undermine public health and the environment in which we live (Koc and Dahlberg 2004).

This puts hospitals in a richly ironic position. How can we expect the larger society to understand the links between good food and human health if our healing spaces are filled with products that are part of the problem? Hospital leaders are beginning to rise to this challenge. Several large healthcare systems are promoting better health and responsible farming practices by purchasing fresher, better tasting, and nutritious food for their patients and staff and for the broader community. Both Kaiser Permanente and Catholic Healthcare West (CHW) have passed overarching food policies that clearly align their institutions with both healthy food choices for their patients and staff and sustainable agriculture practices.

CHW recognizes that food production and distribution systems have wide ranging impacts on the quality of ecosystems and their communities, and so; CHW recognizes that healthy food is defined not only by nutritional quality, but equally by a food system which is economically viable, environmentally sustainable and which supports human dignity and justice, and so; CHW aspires to develop a healthy food system.

— CATHOLIC HEALTHCARE WEST 2006

Beginning in 2004, Kaiser Permanente (2006) established farmers' markets at the majority of its hospital campuses. In some locations, the Kaiser Permanente lobby is the only place to get fresh and organic produce in the community. Large GPOs, which purchase 72 percent of the healthcare sector's supplies, are developing specifications to buy meat produced without the use of nontherapeutic antibiotics (KnowledgeSource 2006). This change alone could help ensure that essential antibiotic drugs are not rendered ineffective by agricultural overuse (Huffling 2006; Shea 2004). From sponsoring farmers' markets to adopting better procurement guidelines, hospitals can make a difference. And by supporting food production that is local, humane, and protective of the environment, healthcare providers can lead the way to more sustainable agricultural practices in their communities. These sweeping changes help redefine the term community benefit and allow the hospital to expand its health-promotion mission beyond the four walls of its facility.

SAFER CHEMICAL POLICIES
Clearly, if our society could eliminate these chemical exposures linked to cancer, immune-related diseases, learning disabilities, and asthma, the rates of these preventable diseases could be reduced, thus avoiding the enormous burden on the healthcare system and society as a whole. Healthcare systems are developing their own chemical policies to purchase safer chemicals. This far-reaching framework is a powerful signal to the marketplace that the healthcare industry plans to use its purchasing power to drive markets for safer products.

> Kaiser Permanente aspires to create an environment for its workers, members, and visitors that is free from the hazards posed by chemicals that are harmful to humans, animals, and the environment. Kaiser Permanente's mission is to provide affordable, high-quality healthcare services to improve the health of our members and the communities we serve. Our concern for the health of our communities extends to the air we breathe and the water we drink.
>
> —KAISER PERMANENTE 2005

As healthcare systems and GPOs adopt chemical policies to guide their overall procurement, the healthcare sector demonstrates to other business sectors that replacing dangerous chemicals with safer ones is not only good for the American economy, but good for the health of the American people. In fact, healthcare leaders are beginning to advocate for broader chemical policy changes. Leaders from Kaiser Permanente, Consorta, the American Nurses Association, and Catholic Healthcare West have testified before state legislatures about the need for chemical policy reform. This expanded role reflects the growing awareness that healthcare leaders can transform not only their own institutions, but also the society at large.

CONCLUSION
As the full dimensions of the planet's environmental crisis become apparent, healthcare is in a unique position to provide leadership at many levels, to firmly embrace the essential link between healthy people and a healthy environment, and to build a new vision of ecological medicine. Healthcare leaders must understand that it is difficult to have healthy people on a sick planet. The twenty-first-century hospital can promote the health of its patients, staff, the general public, and the environment in its design and operations; it can support the local economy through purchasing an array of safe products and technologies; it can model the kind of environmentally responsible institutions every community should have. The hospital, in essence, can situate itself within the broader ecology of its community and region and act as a healing force.

THE PRECAUTIONARY PRINCIPLE

Of paramount importance to this dialogue is the acknowledgment of prevention and precaution as bases for decision making. As articulated by Ted Schettler, Carolyn Raffensperger, and others, science and industry must first assess the health and environmental impacts of their activities before they act, and in the face of uncertainty, precautionary action is an appropriate basis for preventing harm (Schettler 2001; Tickner and Raffensperger 1999). Author and social entrepreneur Kenny Ausubel (2004) sums it up as follows: for generations, the "risk paradigm" has allowed us to accept the inevitability that a "certain amount of pollution and disease is the price we have to pay for modern life." This presumes there are acceptable levels of contamination that our bodies, and the earth, can tolerate, and leaves the burden of proof of harm to society at large. "The risk paradigm is at best a high-stakes game of biological roulette with all the chambers loaded." In contrast, the precautionary principle:

- Recommends the study of industrial innovations' risks *before* they are accepted
- Shifts the burden of proof so that proponents must demonstrate that a practice is sustainable
- Assumes it is preferable to avoid harm than to incur benefits
- Takes a long-term view

The precautionary principle is emerging globally, fostered by the recognition that science cannot reliably predict consequences and possible harm, and our rapidly acquired "fast knowledge" is often repudiated over time. The precautionary approach is not a new idea in medicine — the pharmaceutical industry, for example, has operated according to a form of precaution for a generation or more. Ecological medicine and environmental health practitioners, joined by organizations such as the American Nurses Association, the American Public Health Association, and Physicians for Social Responsibility, are actively promoting the expansion of precaution in the choices surrounding matters of health and the environment.

MEDICINE'S ROLE IN ENVIRONMENTAL IMPROVEMENT

Increasingly, major academic medical centers and universities are recognizing environmental medicine and reinvigorating the dialogue between allopathic medicine and public health. This book includes numerous case study examples of how nursing and public health schools are embracing sustainable construction as an outward expression of their environmental values. Curricula in medical schools are responding not only to "mind-body" medicine, but also to the growing awareness of environmental issues that impact health.

The Paris Appeal (2004), an International Declaration on diseases due to chemical pollution, has been signed by scientists, Nobel laureates, approximately one thousand nonprofit organizations in the European Union, and two million European physicians (represented by the Standing Committee of European Doctors). Highlights of the problem statement include:

The development of numerous current diseases is a result of the deterioration of the environment.

Chemical pollution represents a serious threat to children and to humanity's survival. As our own health and that of our children and future generations is under threat, the Human race itself is in serious danger.

Among the measures the Appeal supports are the use of the Precautionary Principle, promoting the adoption of toxicological standards, and an appeal to States to act forcefully enacting measures to curb greenhouse gas emissions.

Source: The Paris Appeal

In his essay earlier in this chapter, Michael Lerner predicts that advocates for children and medical and public health communities have a pivotal role to play in the emerging environmental health arena. The fact that so many of these chronic diseases and environmental threats affect children first is a key motivator for both pediatricians and educators. The rise of chronic health conditions that require a public health solution, like obesity, is signaling "a new era of cooperation" between medicine and public health, one that is likely to impact the physical structure of healthcare delivery.

In the following essay, physician Ted Schettler presents a new vision of public health and medicine predicated on an ecological view of human health, one nested within both ecological and public health in the missions and goals of healthcare institutions. He recognizes that the ethical challenges raised by this definition represent new territory — the territory that sustainable design is beginning to open for debate.

From Medicine to Ecological Health

Ted Schettler, MD, MPH

During much of the twentieth century, the sciences and practices of medicine, public health, and ecology developed on largely separate trajectories, with only occasional and sometimes uncomfortable, competitive interactions. While this approach accomplished much, it required that many relationships among these disciplines be ignored or remain invisible. When they are viewed as nested spheres of inquiry and practice, however, vivid patterns and interrelationships become apparent. In the fundamentally new world of the twenty-first century, inevitable and incontestable relationships among human disease patterns, community health, and the health of ecological systems demand attention.

Essayist, farmer, and ecologist Wendell Berry (1983) suggests "solving problems for pattern." By that he means finding solutions that solve multiple problems, while minimizing the creation of new ones. This is an idea worth exploring. What are the implications for medicine, public health, and ecology? Solving problems for pattern will require healthcare and public health institutions to revise their missions, goals, strategies, and technologies with the guidance of the ecological sciences and evolutionary biology. Practitioners and policy makers will confront fundamental questions about the meaning of health itself and the scope of medical and public health ethics. An integrated analysis and approach to problem solving is likely to conclude that medical and public health practitioners must also become planetary healers in their daily work.

WHAT IS HEALTH?

Some people prefer to think of health as the absence of disease, while others insist that health is a state of physical, mental, and social well-being. An ecologist might define health differently. Wendell Berry (1995) says that health is membership. The word health, *he wrote, comes from the same Indo-European root as the words* heal, whole, *and* holy. *To be healthy, then, is to be whole, and to heal is to make whole.*

> *Can our present medical industry produce an adequate definition of health? My own guess is that it cannot do so. Like industrial agriculture, industrial medicine has depended increasingly on specialist methodology, mechanical technology, and chemicals; thus, its point of reference has become more and more its own technical prowess and less and less the health of creatures and habitats. I don't expect this problem to be solved in the universities, which have never addressed, much less solved, the problem of health in agriculture. And I don't expect it to be solved by the government.*
>
> —WENDELL BERRY (1995)

Years earlier, ecologist Aldo Leopold had concluded from his field work that "a thing is right when it tends to preserve the integrity, stability and beauty of the biotic community. It is wrong when it tends otherwise." Leopold thought that health was the capacity for self-renewal and insisted that aesthetics and ethics must combine with the sciences of ecology and evolutionary biology if we are to understand how best to live on the land as "plain members of the biotic community" (Leopold 1949).

Clinical medicine largely ignores health as a community attribute and focuses primarily on individuals, emphasizing the diagnosis, treatment, and cure of diseases rather than their prevention. Hospitals and offices are designed, built, and remodeled to house the people and services associated with a vast and growing medical-industrial complex. The ecological footprint of capital equipment expenditures, buildings, material throughput, transportation, water and electricity use, and pharmaceuticals is large. Much of clinical medicine in the US is based on technologies that are unsustainable over time and cannot be transferred to other parts of the world because of economic and resource constraints (Pierce and Jameton 2003).

Public health practice is what we as a society do collectively to ensure conditions in which people can be healthy. Public health emphasizes primary prevention and explicitly acknowledges the social, cultural, political, and economic determinants of health as well as the influential roles of the natural and built environments. Historically, public health focused on sanitation, housing conditions, and infectious diseases. Although this portfolio has expanded considerably, differences between individualist and communitarian ideologies, as well as competition for resources, create a tension between clinical medicine and public health, keeping them from truly integrating and comfortably coexisting. Public health efforts benefit from only a small fraction of the monetary resources devoted to clinical medicine and research. Consequently, the public health infrastructure in the US—and in most countries—is in desperate need of overhaul.

THE FUNDAMENTALLY NEW WORLD OF THE TWENTY-FIRST CENTURY

Unique and dramatic changes in populations, geopolitics, and planetary ecosystems during the twentieth century brought us onto a new and unfamiliar stage. Empirical data is forcing medical and public health professionals to consider their disciplines in the context of planetary health. Reporting on the state of the world's ecosystems, the United Nation's 2005 Millennium Assessment described an unprecedented "newness" in planetary systems, most of which are degraded and used unsustainably by humans. The report warns of the likelihood of nonlinear, accelerating, abrupt, and potentially irreversible changes with important consequences for human well-being (MEA 2005). Change, of course, has and will always be the norm in evolutionary systems throughout human history, but in scope and scale, today's patterns are unique.

Nested within those larger ecosystems, and significantly influenced by them, are changes in patterns of human disease. Throughout the world, obesity, diabetes, cardiovascular disorders, asthma, some malignancies, birth defects, and mental health problems are increasing. Mega-cities and mega-slums facilitate the emergence and transmission of infectious diseases, which are then spread around the world. These trends have resulted from the complex interaction of many factors, including population growth, diet and agricultural systems, industrialization, land use, war, and political and economic policies.

ECOLOGICAL HEALTH: A NEW NECESSITY FOR MEDICINE AND PUBLIC HEALTH

Disciplinary isolation and specialization, along with sociopolitical and economic choices, encourage the sprawling medical-industrial complex to focus on the most proximate causes of disease and disability, reducing resources for preventive efforts that could address the complex interrelationships across and within levels of ecological organization. Neither medicine nor public health gives much coherent attention to the status of, or its impact on, the larger ecological systems on which people's health depends.

This approach no longer serves the public as well as it once might have. It is true that if I were sick or injured, I would deeply appreciate skillful medical care. But we need to ask if that care is delivered with respect for living things, realistic understanding of interconnectedness, acknowledgement of the limits of the earth to assimilate human activity without becoming inhospitable to human existence, and a sense of moral responsibility for current and future generations (Jameton 2005; Jonas 1984). These ideas belong to the realm of bioethics.

INCORPORATING MEDICAL AND PUBLIC HEALTH ETHICS INTO BIOETHICS

Medical ethics emphasizes autonomy, beneficence, nonmalfeasance, justice, dignity, and truthfulness. Public health ethics adds a communitarian dimension that is sometimes discordant with individual autonomy but, like medical ethics, largely avoids recognizing the deep and fundamental interrelationships among communities of humans, other species, and ecological systems.

Van Rensselaer Potter, an oncologist, coined the term bioethics in 1970 (Potter 1971, 1988). It was originally based on the notion of biological wisdom and the idea that any practical ethic must address the real problems of its time. Potter thought that any ethic for the human species had to be based on the possibility of a severely degraded quality of life—even extinction. He believed that each of us has the capacity—and the responsibility—to figure out how we ought to live, and that we could therefore avoid the fate of most other species. By incorporating environmental concerns, bioethics includes, but extends its reach beyond, medical and public health ethics. Bioethics addresses values, duties, obligations, and responsibilities with an ecological awareness of the coexistence, codependence, and coevolution of individuals, communities, and ecosystems.

THE ROLE OF HEALTHCARE INSTITUTIONS
Interconnections within and across boundaries of consideration in complex systems make it untenable to continue to define health exclusively in terms of individuals or communities of people. People are members of entire ecological systems that are also within the wholeness of health and on which our lives depend. Making the healthcare system bigger by steadily increasing healthcare expenditures is not going to change the trajectory documented by the Millennium Assessment or the changing patterns of disease, though surely some people will profit from that approach.

If medicine and public health incorporate a view of human health as nested within a broader concept of ecological health and adopt an expanded scope of bioethics that incorporates medical and public health ethics, what is likely to follow?

- Among their basic responsibilities, medical and public health institutions will commit to appropriately promoting, restoring, and fostering the health of individuals, communities, and ecological systems of which we are members and that the institutions serve and/or impact. Appropriateness implies wisdom in knowing why, where, how, and on what scale to intervene.
- Medical and public health institutions will explicitly commit to promoting the health and restoration of the natural, social, and built environments. These commitments will extend to the soil, water, landscapes, and other features that contribute to the integrity, beauty, and resilience of the entire biotic community. They will extend to the social determinants of health and disease. Institutions will demonstrate their commitments through community actions, advocacy, and education.

- Medical and public health institutions will also translate these commitments into a variety of operational initiatives—reduced resource consumption, green building, environmentally preferable purchasing, recycling, disposing of waste materials in ways that substantively reduce their ecological footprint, and purchasing and serving nutritious food produced in respectful, just, and sustainable ways, among many others.

And there is more. Currently, the US medical community and the general public remain enamored with the treadmill of ever-improving technological achievements that hold out promises of rescue from both old and new diseases, many of which are preventable and some of which are the consequences of profound ecological change. Unmodified, this love affair keeps us on an unsustainable trajectory featuring increasing consumption of medical services, ecological degradation, discrimination, and injustice. Emergent ecologically framed missions will initiate careful reexamination of health-related services with a larger view in mind. What might more radical efforts at primary prevention look like? What is ecologically appropriate care? How might pharmaceutical prescribing practices, surgery, end-of-life care, and a range of diagnostic procedures, among many others, be modified in order to help ameliorate the decline of ecosystems? How will resources, education, and practice meaningfully shift to disease prevention from treatment and cure?

This is new territory. It will not be explored without controversy. It is, however, an opportunity for essential and wise leadership to emerge from the medical and public health communities. Medicine and public health are mixtures of art, science, ethics, sociology, economics, and politics. Each routinely confronts uncertainty and complexity. Single causes and single outcomes are uncommon. The concept of prevention is deeply embedded in public health practice. Preventive, precautionary action—action with foresight—aimed at increasing the resilience and well-being of the whole biotic community and having salutary effects on individual community members *necessitates an expanded ethical framework. As a practical undertaking in institutions with ecologically framed missions, bioethics will embrace its original intent as a guide toward a science for survival and an aid in securing lives of quality. Instead of focusing solely on individual rights and responsibilities, bioethics adds individual membership in larger ecological communities and their health to its frame of reference. Anything less perpetuates a worldview belonging to a story that should no longer be told as the way things are.*

Pierce and Jameton (2004) issue this summary challenge:

> As a significant element of culture, ethics has an important role to play in making this change, and thus in helping mitigate and remedy the global ecological crisis. Among other things, we can change our modes of production and how we practice healthcare. It may even be possible…to improve the sense of meaningfulness of our lives, increase happiness, build community, and begin to maintain an adequate, sustainable global level of human healthiness.

University of Texas Health Science Center School of Nursing and Student Community Center

Houston, Texas

Figure 3-9: University of Texas Health Science Center at Houston/ School of Nursing and Student Community Center. *Credit: ©Paul Hester*

Owner: University of Texas Health Science Center
Design team:
    ARCHITECTS: LakelFlato Architects and BNIM Architects
    LANDSCAPE ARCHITECTS: Coleman & Associates, Inc.
    MECHANICAL, ELECTRICAL, AND PLUMBING ENGINEERS:
      Carter & Burgess, Inc.
    CONSTRUCTION MANAGERS: Jacobs/Vaughn, Inc.
Sustainable strategies: Elements, Center for Maximum
    Potential Building Systems, and Rocky Mountain
    Institute
Building type: New Academic
Size: 194,000 sq ft (18,023 sq m)
Program description: Nursing school and student center
    with classrooms, labs, and multifunctional lecture fa-
    cilities
Completion date: 2004
Awards/recognition: LEED gold certification, 2006 AIA
    COTE Top Ten Green Award

Figure 3-10: Shading devices along the building's east facade control glare while providing abundant daylight for classrooms and offices. *Credit: © Assassi*

The project began by defining a series of goals to create a building and landscape that would integrate building purpose, program, and academics. Designed for one hundred years, the landmark building was inspired by a commitment to "building as pedagogy," promoting health, wellness, and community through the teaching/learning environment, and reinforced through the building's flexible design and resource efficiency. "A building that houses programs about health ought to be as healthy as possible," says Greg Papay, a partner at LakelFlato Architects. The building, adjacent to Houston's Grant Fay Park, includes an auditorium, restaurant, and library for students and visitors at ground level, welcoming interaction with the broader community.

The project focused on energy performance and indoor environmental quality (through abundant daylighting and the use of nontoxic materials). Given the orientation of the restricted site, optimizing energy performance required the careful integration of exterior shading devices. Attention was also paid to material life cycle, leading to reliance on reclaimed, recycled, and regional materials.

KEY BUILDING PERFORMANCE FEATURES

Site
- Previously developed site on the Texas Medical Center campus
- Green roof for improved storm water retention

Energy
- Usage 41 percent below ASHRAE 90.1-1999
- High-performance facade elements, including insulation, glazing, and solar-shading devices
- Roof structure in place for future photovoltaic installation

Materials
- Exterior aluminum window mullions 100 percent recycled content; exterior aluminum panels 92 percent recycled content
- Portland cement replaced with 51 percent fly ash
- Rebar 65 percent recycled content
- Exterior wood walls and soffit panels 100 percent reclaimed cypress
- Brick on exterior 100 percent reclaimed

Environmental Quality
- Aluminum light shelves increase daylight penetration
- Interior atria on top three stories of building increase daylight penetration
- Operable windows throughout
- Low-emitting materials

Source: BNIM Architects

Figure 3-11: The building's interior atrium, located below rooftop monitors, ensures daylit spaces for the building's central open offices and circulation areas. Exposed structure and low-emitting finish materials contribute to enhanced indoor air quality. *Credit: ©Assassi*

Figure 3-12: Generous glazing in meeting rooms afford expansive views of adjacent Grant Fay Park and medical center buildings while also offsetting reliance on electrical lighting. *Credit: ©Assassi*

David R. Obey Health Sciences Center, Northcentral Technical College

Wausau, Wisconsin

Figure 3-13: David R. Obey Health Sciences Center at Northcentral Technical College. *Credit: Steven Hall @ Hedrich Blessing*

Owner: Northcentral Technical College
Design team:
    ARCHITECTS AND INTERIOR DESIGNERS: Kahler Slater Architects, Inc.
    LANDSCAPE ARCHITECTS: Rettler Corporation
    MECHANICAL/PLUMBING ENGINEERS: Arnold & O'Sheridan, Inc.
    ELECTRICAL ENGINEERS: Lang & Associates, Inc.
    STRUCTURAL ENGINEERS: Graef, Anhalt, Schloemer & Associates, Inc.
    CONTRACTORS: Miron Construction
Building type: New medical education facility
Size: 126,000 sq ft (11,700 sq m)
Program description: Education and training facilities for nurses as well as dental, laboratory, surgery, radiography, and emergency medical technologists, including both classrooms and clinical teaching spaces
Completion date: 2005
Awards: LEED silver certification

To advance the way future healthcare professionals approach patient care, Northcentral Technical College's new Health Sciences Center's curriculum and building were designed to promote enhanced collaboration and communication among students and faculty and in turn, enhance overall patient safety, efficiency, and effectiveness. The building has a forty-chair public clinic; hands-on teaching spaces for the dental hygiene, radiology, and nursing programs; medical technician and surgical technician laboratories; a computerized health learning resource lab; lecture halls; high-tech classrooms; a variety of administrative offices and support services; and chemistry, biology, anatomy, physiology, physics, and computer labs equipped with distance-learning capabilities.

The greenfield site had major outcroppings of granite, an important and abundant local resource. In order to excavate for foundations, the project team first had to dynamite the outcroppings and remove the stone to below footing elevation. The recovered, blasted-out stone was then reused in the new sidewalks, landscaping, and retaining walls, and was carved and polished to make bollards and tiles at the front entrance and upper terrace area. The fairly steep slope facilitated the insertion of one floor level with the hill; natural water drainage patterns were enhanced by a water feature at the front of the site that both retains rainwater and slowly dissipates it into the soil.

Figure 3-14: The laboratories feature low-flow fume hoods and indirect lighting. *Credit: Steven Hall @ Hedrich Blessing*

KEY BUILDING PERFORMANCE FEATURES

Site
- High-reflectance roofing
- Open stair encourages walking behavior in building

Energy
- HVAC system that includes energy-recovery wheels, low-flow fume hoods in laboratories, and nighttime shutdown of unused areas
- Building orientation minimizes summer heat gain

Materials
- Local materials used throughout building, including Wausau red granite at the interior waterfall and massive boulders for retaining walls around the exterior green spaces and terraced planting areas

Environmental Quality
- Narrow floor plate maximizes daylight penetration in offices, classrooms, and clinical environments

Wausau is known for its waterfalls and lumbering, and is home to a world-class whitewater kayak and canoe course. To connect the new Health Sciences Center with the natural surroundings of the Wausau community, the project team designed the building using metaphors specific to the area: a historical reference to the Wisconsin River can be found in the water feature; wood, granite, and other natural materials used in and around the building are native to Wausau; and the integration of the building within the existing landscape is characteristic of the land found throughout the region.

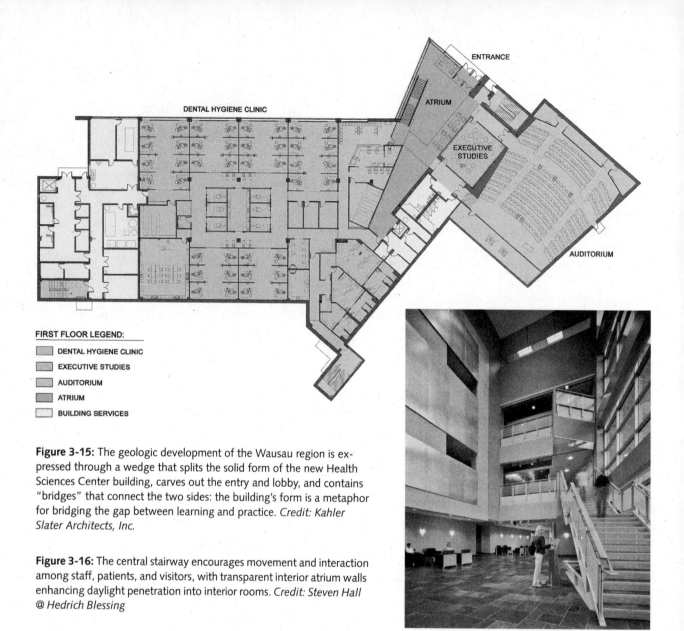

FIRST FLOOR LEGEND:

- ☐ DENTAL HYGIENE CLINIC
- ☐ EXECUTIVE STUDIES
- ☐ AUDITORIUM
- ☐ ATRIUM
- ☐ BUILDING SERVICES

Figure 3-15: The geologic development of the Wausau region is expressed through a wedge that splits the solid form of the new Health Sciences Center building, carves out the entry and lobby, and contains "bridges" that connect the two sides: the building's form is a metaphor for bridging the gap between learning and practice. *Credit: Kahler Slater Architects, Inc.*

Figure 3-16: The central stairway encourages movement and interaction among staff, patients, and visitors, with transparent interior atrium walls enhancing daylight penetration into interior rooms. *Credit: Steven Hall @ Hedrich Blessing*

Project success measures were developed early on and used to inform decisions made throughout the project. At the beginning, every staff member expected an enclosed office. Through many meetings, however, staff members came to understand that open offices would improve communication, increase energy and spatial efficiency, and still allow for privacy when needed through enclosed shared spaces at the center core. Today, the Health Sciences Center's space is filled with natural light and fantastic views of nearby Rib Mountain, tree-lined hillsides, and views of the existing campus.

Source: Kahler Slater Architects

CHAPTER 4

Nature and Healing

Our ability to perceive quality in nature begins, as in art, with the pretty. It expands through successive stages of the beautiful to values as yet uncaptured by language. The quality of cranes lies, I think, in this higher gamut, as yet beyond the reach of words . . . .
When we hear his call, we hear no mere bird. We hear the trumpet in the orchestra of evolution. He is the symbol of our untamable past, of that incredible sweep of millennia which underlies and conditions the daily affairs of birds and men.

—ALDO LEOPOLD

Through its infinite complexity, nature is an instructive and inspirational influence that can expand the aesthetic horizons of the building arts and confirm the inalienable right of humanity to try to salvage a place on this planet before it's too late. The mission now in architecture, as in all human endeavor, is to recover those fragile threads of connectedness with nature that have been lost for most of this century.

—JAMES WINES

The "control of nature" is a phrase conceived in arrogance, born of the Neanderthal age of biology and the convenience of Man.

—RACHEL CARSON

INTRODUCTION

Medicine has long-standing ties with the natural world. Whether through the harvesting of willow bark in the early formulation of salicylate (aspirin), the public health work of Florence Nightingale, or Thomas Mann's description of nineteenth-century tuberculosis sanatoriums in *The Magic Mountain*, where people huddled under blankets to "take the cure," the interrelationships between nature and healing have been a part of the slow knowledge universally acquired and understood across diverse cultures and traditions. As the Industrial Revolution progressed, the medical profession moved away from acknowledging this partnership. The pharmaceutical industry, as it increased in scale, converted from natural to synthetic petrochemical derivatives, and North American healthcare buildings became sealed, totally artificial environments with severely limited access to natural light and ventilation. Today, allopathic medicine rarely acknowledges that healing is, fundamentally, a natural process.

Just as twentieth-century industrial processes are out of sync with biological systems, medical technology has become ever more aggressive in battling disease. The common refrain, "If the disease doesn't kill you, the treatment will," accompanies many of our more advanced medical interventions, and we describe our medical research as "wars" on disease. Since the early twentieth century, metaphors of nature have given way to machine metaphors in our approach to medicine and medical buildings. Designer Jason McLennan (2000) observed that the machine metaphor "implies a relationship with nature that is exploitative and relies on brute force combined with great amounts of energy to solve problems."

When was it determined that nature is somehow in opposition to healing, a precept that is clearly reflected in hospital architecture today? As the twenty-first century emerges, can medicine, and the buildings that clothe it, be reimagined in partnership with natural processes and flows? Can medicine and hospital architecture be regenerative? What form might such a partnership take? How might this relate to the bioethical constructs in medicine outlined in Chapter 3?

Chapter 4 explores new ways to integrate nature and healing in the service of ecological design. First, biophilic design elements serve to reconnect building occupants to nature. Then, an ethic of conservation as a component of an expanded view of bioethics leads to a fundamental reexamination of the hospital's place in the landscape — an intervention of restorative land planning. Finally, the idea of landscapes that heal is introduced through an exploration of therapeutic or restorative garden design.

THE TRADITION OF NATURE AND HEALING

Nature has been recognized as a source for healing throughout history. In ancient times, healing rituals were conducted in sacred spaces defined by the presence of awe-inspiring nature. Among the earliest surviving Western manifestations of architecture for health are the open halls of Asclepieia in ancient Greece, where in the fourth century BCE priests converted patients' dreams into therapeutic regimens. Such early places of healing

THE STORY OF TAXOL

The drug Taxol is one of the success stories of the National Cancer Institute's 1960s screening program to identify plants, animals, and microbes with anticancer properties. Taxol was discovered in 1963, and preclinical work began in 1977 when it was shown to inhibit the replication of human tumor cells. The first clinical trials began in 1983, and in 1992 it was approved for use in treating ovarian cancer.

Taxol is found in the bark and needles of the Pacific yew, a slow-growing, understory evergreen tree from the family *Taxaceae,* which grows in the virgin rainforests of the Pacific Northwest. To obtain the bark, the tree must be killed. The five pounds of bark harvested from a two-hundred-year-old tree yields a tiny amount of Taxol: to treat one woman with cancer throughout her illness requires approximately six to eight yew trees.

Spurred by the destruction of old-growth forests and the expanded harvest of yews, the Environmental Protection Agency (EPA) issued a warning in 1993 and, as a result, significant resources were allocated to finding alternatives to Taxol. A semisynthetic form of the drug has been processed from the needles of the European yew, a more abundant species that contains a compound more efficient than Taxol. While approved by the Food and Drug Administration (FDA), more noticeable negative side effects have reduced its popularity. Another alternative is derived from the needles of the English yew, but the extraction procedure leaves impurities in the drug.

The majority of Taxol today is a semisynthetic compound, produced through synthetic alternatives based on fossil fuel production. The Pacific yew is now an endangered species, and the pharmaceutical industry is allied with environmentalists in attempts to preserve the tree from extinction. Taxol's manufacturer agreed to cease harvesting Pacific yew trees from public lands in 1993. At the same time, Taxol appears to have life-saving benefits for cancer patients, making exclusion of the treatment ethically problematic.

Sources: National Cancer Institute Cancer Facts 2002; Stephenson 2002

included patient beds, treatments, medication, and diet and exercise regimens, taking their architectural placement from nature: the sun and prevailing winds.

Since that early vision, advancements in medical education, care, and technology have defined the hospital as the primary typology of healing architecture. Until the late nineteenth century, courtyards, daylight, and natural ventilation produced hospital buildings that focused on convalescence, as interventional treatment modalities were limited. Clean air and water were seen as essential in hospital settings. Florence Nightingale, in *Notes on Hospitals* (1859), reinforced prescriptive design measures, including ward dimensions and window sizes, for providing abundant daylight and fresh air. "To deprive the sick of pure air," she wrote, "is nothing but manslaughter under the garb of benevolence."

The nineteenth-century pavilion hospitals were often situated remote from the dense urban environment, where access to light and air was still achievable. As cities expanded, hospitals eagerly sought sites at their edge, alongside rivers or at high elevations, to ensure access to water, fresh air, and light. Continued urbanization throughout the nineteenth and twentieth centuries eventually engulfed many of them in the cities they had initially hoped to stay clear of.

The development of anesthesia, surgical techniques, and medical treatment modalities further separated the late-nineteenth-century hospital from its beginnings in convalescence. Resort spas, tuberculosis sanatoriums, residential psychiatric facilities, and other specialty-care settings maintained a focus on the restorative aspects of landscape, while the twentieth-century hospital followed the broader pursuit of mastery over nature.

The case studies that follow, on the Laguna Honda Replacement Hospital and the Southeast Regional Treatment Center at the Madison State Hospital in Indiana, are examples of late-nineteenth century residential facilities located on promontory sites. Laguna Honda Hospital is situated on a hillside site overlooking San Francisco; Madison State Hospital is on a bluff overlooking the Ohio River. At both, recent major expansion and rehabilitation projects pursued sustainable building strategies that recognized the value of these historic nature-based healthcare buildings and sites.

Laguna Honda Replacement Hospital

San Francisco, California

Figure 4-1: Laguna Honda Replacement Hospital. *Credit: Anshen + Allen/Chong Architecture, a joint venture*

Owner: City and County of San Francisco

Design team:

ARCHITECTS: Anshen + Allen/Chong Partners in Joint Venture

LANDSCAPE ARCHITECTS: The Office of Cheryl Barton

MECHANICAL, ELECTRICAL, AND PLUMBING ENGINEERS: ARUP, SJ Engineers, FW Associates

CIVIL ENGINEERS: Olivia Chen Consultants

STRUCTURAL ENGINEERS: Rutherford & Chekene, Forell/Elsesser Engineers, Inc.

CONSTRUCTION MANAGERS: Turner Construction Co.

Type: New long-term care and rehabilitation hospital

Size: New construction: 700,000 sq ft (65,000 sq m); renovation: 150,000 sq ft (13,900 sq m); Site: 62 acres (25.1 ha)

Program description: Acute medical, acute rehab, and 1,170 skilled nursing beds in a combination of new and renovated buildings

Completion date: 2011

Recognition: *The Green Guide*'s 2006 top ten green hospitals; *Green Guide for Health Care* pilot

---

Dating back to 1866, when it was known as the Almshouse, this convalescent and rehabilitation hospital is the largest provider of long-term care services in San Francisco. Laguna Honda houses chronically ill, disabled, and elderly city residents, 50 percent of whom are wheelchair bound. Tobacco settlement funds and a special bond issue funded the replacement hospital project on the existing site. While the community initially requested a low-rise, garden-style building to minimize viewshed impact, the design team successfully demonstrated that a taller solution preserved more forest and open site. The overall goal is to create a building that is innovative, technologically advanced, and flexible, yet humane and less institutional than most hospitals.

The project is designated as a city of San Francisco green-building pilot project, but has no additional funding to meet its LEED certification goal. In a conversation about the project, Larry Funk, Executive Administrator, described the decision to proceed with

Figure 4-2: The steeply sloping wooded site integrates the new link building to the existing historic residential structures.
Credit: Anshen + Allen/Chong Architecture, a joint venture

green building as "an opportunity for the city to demonstrate environmental stewardship for the occupants, for the community, and for global environmental issues."

The new hospital program highlights the residential aspect of the design. Each of four wings on each floor houses fifteen residents in a "household" with its own living and dining areas. In turn, each floor of sixty residents comprises a "neighborhood" where group projects and activities are shared. The new link building contains all the community service aspects of the hospital—beauty salon, barber shop, library, convenience store, swimming pool —which are equally accessible from the historic hospital and new building.

Figure 4-3: The Laguna Honda Replacement Hospital, under construction, will be completed in 2011. *Credit: Perretti & Park Pictures*

KEY BUILDING PERFORMANCE STRATEGIES

Site
- Improved access to existing public transportation for staff
- Removal of existing ancillary structures created open space, restored natural water flow and site drainage, and offset impact of new structures
- Site design incorporates outdoor places of respite

Energy
- Energy demand reduced 30 percent below ASHRAE 90.1 (20 percent below California Title 24 requirements) using evaporative-cooling and heat-recovery systems
- New Link building roof designed to accommodate future installation of 360 megawatt photovoltaic array

Materials
- Targeting 75 percent of construction waste recycled
- PVC-free as per city of San Francisco ordinance

Environmental Quality
- Operable windows in resident rooms
- 75 percent of occupied spaces receive ample daylight

Operations (currently under development by the City and County of San Francisco)
- Green housekeeping program
- Integrated pest management program
- Composting program for kitchen waste
- Education and outreach program highlighting sustainable features

Source: Anshen + Allen

Southeast Regional Treatment Center at Madison State Hospital

Madison,
Indiana

Figure 4-4: Southeast Regional Treatment Center at Madison State Hospital. *Credit: © Jeff Millies @ Hedrich Blessing*

Owner: Madison State Hospital/Indiana State Office Building Commission
Design team:
> ARCHITECTS: RATIO Architects, Inc.
> ASSOCIATE ARCHITECTS: Hellmuth, Obata + Kassabaum (HOK)
> CIVIL ENGINEERS: Jacobi, Toombs, and Lanz, Inc.
> STRUCTURAL ENGINEERS: Fink Roberts & Petrie, Inc.
> MECHANICAL/ELECTRICAL ENGINEERS: Biagi, Chance, Cummins, London, Titzer, Inc.
> CONSTRUCTION MANAGERS: Shiel Sexton Construction
> ENERGY ANALYSIS AND COMMISSIONING: William Tao & Associates, Inc.

Building type: Renovation and restoration of four historic buildings; two new buildings
Program description: 160-bed specialty hospital for patients with mental illness and/or developmental disabilities.
Completion date: 2006
Recognition: US Green Building Council LEED certified

The hospital, which serves eighteen counties in southeast Indiana, was built in 1910 to consolidate four overcrowded state hospitals. The site, selected over seven other possible locations throughout the state, is 650 acres (263 hectares) located on a 600-

foot (183 meter) bluff overlooking the city of Madison and the Ohio River. The new hospital will use only the 40-acre (16.1 ha) riverfront portion of the original campus. The balance will be put under the auspices of a reuse authority whose goals include the preservation of the historic buildings.

The treatment center includes the renovation of four of the six early-twentieth-century bluff buildings, with modifications to ensure program fit and regulatory compliance while meeting historic preservation requirements. Two small buildings were demolished and replaced with new connector buildings to maximize efficiency and provide effective patient care.

While the state of Indiana requires LEED certification for its facilities, the project team realized the historic buildings and heavily wooded site embodied special opportunities to simultaneously promote a healing environment and sustainability. In addition to implementing sustainable building strategies, the treatment center incorporates sustainable operation as a component of day rehabilitation programs: patients' daily activities include staffing the recycling program.

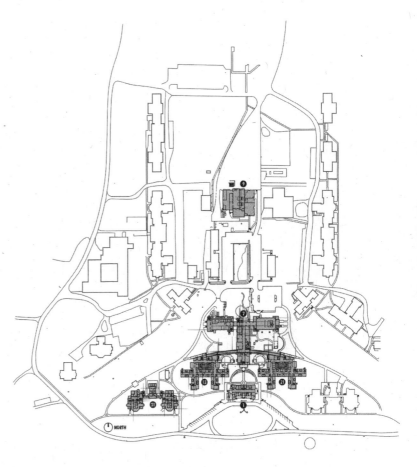

Figure 4-5: The original buildings are clustered in a 40-acre portion of this wooded, 650-acre campus, on a bluff overlooking the Ohio River. *Credit: HOK*

Figure 4-6: The project includes both new construction to link the individual historic residential structures and significant rehabilitation of the historic buildings, while preserving the mature landscape. *Credit: HOK, courtesy of Laura Linn*

Figure 4-7: The new structure features extensive glazing that increases daylight penetration and contrasts with the existing historic masonry buildings. *Credit: HOK, courtesy of Laura Linn*

KEY BUILDING PERFORMANCE STRATEGIES

Site

- Preservation of open space and landscape
- Bike racks and showers to encourage alternative transportation

Energy

- Envelope improvements, including high-performance windows
- New building management system

Materials

- 80 percent of construction waste recycled, including brick from demolished structures for future site buildings

Environmental Quality

- Large existing windows optimize daylight

Source: Hellmuth, Obata +Kassabaum

THE THERAPEUTIC SPA MOVEMENT

As hospitals focused on medical education and technology, the resort spa movement in Europe and the United States continued to focus on nature as a therapeutic modality. Dedicated to the notion of reconnecting highly stressed individuals in the industrial economy to their bodies and health, these typologies emerged in the private sector as the most powerful and potent connection to disease prevention. During urban epidemics, the wealthy routinely retreated to the refuge of the resort spa.

As the Industrial Revolution progressed, an antiurban commune movement endured, offering an alternative view of man's inherent humanism and need to connect with authentic nature. Initially, these buildings included tuberculosis sanatoriums. Alvar Aalto's sanatorium in Paimio, Finland (1929–1933), a surviving example of the early-twentieth-century hospital building, retains a strong connection between nature and healing that postwar twentieth-century North American hospitals, with their focus on technology, left behind.

NATURE RECONSIDERED

By the 1980s, a body of research emerged indicating that a connection to nature positively influences medical outcomes and staff performance. The studies on the therapeutic importance of views supported reconnecting nature with the healthcare environment (Ulrich 1984). In 1993, the nonprofit Center for Health Design (www.healthdesign.org) began advocating for a critical reexamination of the hospital building. Recognizing that the built environment impacts both the patient experience and medical outcomes, the center gathered a coalition of environmental design researchers to define evidence-based design in support of life-enhancing environments that promote health and healing.

The influence of this work in the healthcare industry is compelling. New hospitals routinely emphasize improved access to nature, interpreted to mean windows at the ends of corridors, "healing gardens," and a new focus on patient and staff amenity areas. In *The Business Case for Better Buildings*, Leonard Berry (2004), Derek Parker, and others define a better building as one that reduces stress, improves safety, and contributes to ecological health. Nature, they contend, has an important role in defining this "better building."

At the same time, there is no pattern language or tool kit to assist in the reintegration of nature in hospitals. Outdoor places of respite, therapeutic landscaping, and views of nature are all increasingly appearing in hospitals. Sustainable design considerations extend the vocabulary further, by introducing another set of prescriptive design strategies — restorative habitat, for example, or green roofs. What are the emergent ideas that can catalyze a new approach to healthcare's integration of nature?

BIOPHILIA

Increasing evidence suggests that contact with nature can foster human health, productivity, and well-being, and that humans possess a basic need for contact with natural systems and processes (Kellert 2005). The entomologist E. O. Wilson (1984) coined the term *biophilia* to describe humans' inherent inclination to affiliate with nature, most particularly with life and ecosystem features of the natural environment. More recently, Wilson collaborator and social ecologist Stephen Kellert has extended the definition of *biophilic design* to include buildings and constructed landscapes that foster a positive connection between people and nature in places of cultural and ecological significance. In the essay that follows, he and environmental psychologist Judith Heerwagen offer a glimpse into the extensive research on the role of nature in therapeutic settings, as well as a comprehensive approach to integrating nature references at all levels of building design — from organization to materials.

Nature and Healing: The Science, Theory, and Promise of Biophilic Design

Stephen R. Kellert, PhD, and Judith H. Heerwagen, PhD

*N*ature nurtures. There is no longer any doubt about the therapeutic value of contact with the natural environment, whether it is through window views, gardening, walking through the woods, or watching the sun set over the ocean. Positive benefits occur even through simulations of nature — in posters and photographs, for example.

As envisioned here, biophilic design is more than the inclusion of nature and natural elements in buildings. It incorporates both organic/naturalistic design and vernacular/place-based design that can be conveyed symbolically as well as through the actual use of nature and natural systems.

THE BENEFITS OF NATURE CONTACT
Over the past several decades, research in a variety of fields has shown that contact with nature generates emotional, physiological, social, and cognitive benefits in a wide array of contexts. Specific benefits at the individual level include improved emotional functioning, improved attention capacity and feelings of self-worth, and reduced mental and physical stress. Social benefits are also evident from studies of recreational activities and gardening. Being in a natural setting strengthens group ties and promotes prosocial behaviors. Many of these benefits have been found in both laboratory and field studies, and through active as well as passive contact with natural settings. However, not all nature is equally beneficial. Spaces with large trees, water features, birds, and a variety of shrubs and flowers are perceived more positively than spaces with only grass (Heerwagen and Orians 1993).

FINDINGS FROM FIELD AND LABORATORY SETTINGS
The most consistent findings across studies, regardless of whether they are controlled laboratory experiments or field applications, are mood improvement and

stress reduction related to contact with nature. The contact can be multisensory active engagement (e.g., walking, running, gardening), or purely visual and passive (i.e., viewing only). Although it has long been intuited that being in a natural setting is therapeutic, the first well-controlled empirical test of this hypothesis was conducted in a hospital setting (Ulrich 1984). Using data from hospital records, Ulrich tested the effect of window views on patient outcomes. Half of the patients had a room with a window that looked out on a brick wall; the others had a view of a landscape with trees. The two view groups were matched for age, gender, and general health conditions; all patients had the same kind of surgery. Ulrich found that patients with the view of the trees used fewer narcotics and milder analgesics, indicating that they experienced less pain. They also stayed in the hospital for a shorter time and had more a positive postsurgical recovery overall than did the patients who had the view of the brick wall.

In Ulrich's laboratory and field experiments he has consistently found that subjects exposed to a stressor recover faster and more positively if they are shown nature scenes or urban scenes with nature rather than urban scenes devoid of natural elements (Ulrich et al. 1991; Ulrich 1993). Subjects viewing the completely natural scenes do the best overall, with the greatest and most rapid reduction in physiological stress and more rapid mood enhancement. And Ulrich's work has shown that contact with nature can be beneficial whether it is real or simulated. In fact, in many environments, such as windowless spaces, simulations may be the only way to create a beneficial experience. A study of windowed and windowless offices by Heerwagen and Orians (1986) supports this conclusion. They found that people in windowless spaces used twice as many nature elements (posters and photos especially) to decorate their office walls than those who had views to natural areas outdoors.

Other researchers have also found improvements in emotional functioning and reductions in stress. For instance, a laboratory study of "green exercise" tested the effects of projected scenes on physiological and psychological outcomes of subjects on a treadmill (Pretty et al. 2005). They found that all subjects benefited similarly in physiological outcomes, but the subjects who viewed pleasant nature scenes (both rural and urban) scored higher in measures of self-esteem than those viewing totally urban scenes or "unpleasant" rural scenes with destroyed landscapes.

In a study of office workers doing similar kinds of tasks, Kaplan (1992) found that those who had views of a natural landscape scored lower on a measure of psychological stress and frustration, and higher on a measure of patience and overall life satisfaction, than similar workers who had a window lacking a view of nature. Other benefits of nature views include improved ability to concentrate (Tennessen and Cimprich 1995) and higher scores on memory tasks (Heschong Mahone Group 2003).

Access to outdoor urban nature also has benefits. A study of public housing projects found that large trees had a significant impact on residents' social behavior (Kweon, Sullivan, and Wiley 1998; Sullivan, Kuo, and Depooter 2004). In contrast to barren, treeless spaces, those with large trees lured people outdoors, and, once there, they talked to their neighbors and developed social bonds and a stronger sense of community than people in similar housing projects without green space and trees.

NATURE AND HEALTHCARE SETTINGS

Given the evidence of the health and well-being benefits that accrue from contact with nature, it is somewhat surprising that healthcare institutions have been slow to incorporate nature into building and site design. However, a recent spate of studies in hospital settings support Ulrich's early findings and demonstrate that natural features — including gardens, sunlight, and landscape views — have positive effects on both patient and financial outcomes.

Sunlight in patient rooms is also associated with a reduction in pain, stress, and depression, more positive moods, and/or shorter hospital stays. In a study of patients hospitalized for severe depression, Beauchemin and Hays (1996) found that patients in sunny rooms remained in the hospital fewer days than those in dimly lit rooms. Similar results were found for heart patients in another study (Beauchemin and Hays 1998). Patients assigned to a sunny critical-care room had lower mortality rates than those in north-facing rooms lacking sunlight.

A more recent study in Pittsburgh assessed patient outcomes in bright hospital rooms compared with those in which sunlight exposure was blocked by a building wing (Walch et al. 2005). The researchers found that patients in the bright rooms, who were exposed to 46 percent higher light levels, experienced less perceived stress, took less analgesic medication per hour, and accrued 21 percent less pain medication costs than patients who underwent the same type of surgery but were housed in the more dimly lit rooms. A recent review of the health effects of sunlight (Kiraly et al., 2006) found that its physiological benefits also extend to the central nervous system through a wide range of hormonal effects. (The effect of the sun on bone health through the production of vitamin D has, of course, been long understood.)

SUMMARY OF FINDINGS

A wide array of methods and contexts shows that a connection to nature in everyday life settings yields a consistent set of benefits, including stress reduction, an improved sense of well-being, and enhanced emotional and social functioning. These benefits also occur in hospital settings. Connection to nature, however, embodies more than the incorporation of views of nature or sunlight into hospital design.

EXPLAINING THE HUMAN-NATURE-HEALTH DEPENDENCY

Humans evolved in a natural rather than artificial or human-constructed world. Biophilia developed as a genetic tendency because of our species' long dependence on functionally adapting to the natural environment for fitness and survival. The evolutionary context for human development has been a diverse environment that challenges the senses, dominated by such natural stimuli as light, sound, odor, wind, vegetation, landscape, water, animals—and more. The development during the past five thousand years of small- and large-scale agriculture, technology, industry, and cities is but a small fraction of the much longer period of human biological evolution. It is, thus, unreasonable to assume human physical and mental well-being could have escaped the requirements of adapting to a largely natural heritage. Yet many people today assume human distinctiveness, progress, and civilization is marked by

our species' capacity to separate from and transcend our genetic roots. This assumption is an illusion. Ongoing contact with natural systems and processes functions as an anvil on which human health and fitness continues to be forged, even in an increasingly built and urbanizing world.

Yet biophilia is not a hard-wired instinct like breathing and eating; it is a "weak" genetic tendency that must depend on experience, learning, and social support to become functionally manifest. Biophilia is a series of genetically programmed tendencies to value the natural world, but it relies on adequate stimulation and cultural reinforcement to actuate, although as a "genetically prepared learning rule," it can be triggered easily and learned relatively fast. Biophilia reflects the unusual human capacity for choice and free will in responding to much of our biology and genetics. People may be born with inclinations to affiliate with nature, but this tendency remains nascent and atrophied absent adequate stimulation and robust expression. The genius of humanity is its extraordinary capacity for learning, creative innovation, progress, culture, and designing the built environment. Yet, this seeming release from the dictates of a rigid biology is a two-edged sword carrying with it the equivalent potential for creative construction and unrivaled self-destruction.

Biophilia is a biocultural phenomenon through which biological tendencies are shaped and molded into distinctive forms by human ingenuity and culture. This volitional ability produces extraordinary variability, yet the functionality of these diverse constructions remains ultimately subject to the test of biological fitness and survival: not all constructions are equally functional, and some inevitably prove maladaptive. The design and development of the modern urban built environment reflects this positive or negative potential for fostering or threatening human health and well-being.

Unfortunately, the prevailing paradigm of design and development of the modern built (especially the modern urban built) environment has largely encouraged widespread environmental degradation, as well as increasing the separation of people from beneficial contact with natural systems and processes (Kellert 2005). Reflecting this tendency, the built environment today consumes huge and unsustainable quantities of natural and energy resources, generates excessive wastes and chemical contaminants, and increasingly alienates people from necessary contact with nature. This lamentable condition is viewed as a design failure rather than an intrinsic flaw of modern urban life.

Efforts at remedying this design failure have been laudable but inadequate and narrow. Most so-called sustainable or green design has emphasized using energy and resources more efficiently, avoiding toxic products and materials, reducing and recycling wastes, and maintaining a healthy indoor environment (Mendler, Odell, and Lazarus 2006). These low-environmental-impact strategies are necessary but insufficient. For the most part, they fail to heal the breach between people and natural systems characteristic of much of the modern urban built environment. The way most sustainable constructions and places positively connect people with nature—directly, indirectly, or metaphorically—has been neglected. A broader strategy, which seeks not only to minimize and avoid adverse environmental effects, but also to foster beneficial biophilic ties between people and nature in places of ecological and cultural significance and security, is therefore required. This broader approach has been referred to as restorative environmental design; its goal is both low and positive environmental impact, or what we like to call biophilic design.

In other words, biophilia is a missing link in current attempts at sustainable design. Our challenge is to restore in the built environment all of our inherent biophilic values of nature. Only by harmonizing the natural and built environments in an increasingly urban world can we arrest the ominous trends of environmental destruction and alienation from nature so pervasive in modern life. Restorative environmental design affirms how even in the modern city, ongoing contact with nature remains endowed with an abiding sense and spirit of place and is an indispensable basis for physical health and emotional and intellectual soundness.

ELEMENTS OF BIOPHILIC DESIGN
We define biophilic design as buildings and constructed landscapes that foster a positive connection between people and nature in places of cultural and ecological significance and security. This definition encompasses two broad goals: an organic or naturalistic design strategy that encourages shapes and forms in the built environment that directly, indirectly, or symbolically elicit a human affinity for nature; and a vernacular or place-based approach that emphasizes buildings and landscapes that connect well with the culture, history, and ecology of a locality. In turn, this leads to a series of biophilic building design and construction elements and attributes that promote human health and well-being.

Biophilic design elements are encountered in buildings and landscapes in direct, indirect, and symbolic ways. Direct expressions involve relatively unstructured contact with self-sustaining elements of nature; indirect expressions include typically structured contact with real environmental features that require nearly continuous human input and management to survive; while symbolic expressions involve no contact with real or living nature but rather the representation or image of natural features and processes. These biophilic design elements can be grouped into six (often overlapping) categories: environmental features, natural shapes and forms, natural patterns and processes, light and space, place-based relationships, and evolved human relations to nature. A simple list of the most frequent expressions of these six biophilic design elements follows.

CONCLUSION
Effectively incorporating these biophilic design elements in constructed buildings and landscapes to varying degrees and in various combinations can enhance human health and well-being. This list of biophilic design elements can guide healthcare designers and hospital developers in addressing the inherent human affinity for nature. Yet the effectiveness of the design always depends on the creativity and integrative talent of the development more than on following a prescribed list. A checklist can never assure that even a well-intentioned project will produce a harmonious and beneficial design. Like all great constructions, the whole always remains more than the simple sum of its parts.

1. Environmental features:
   - Natural materials
   - Natural colors
   - Sunlight
   - Water
   - Natural ventilation
   - Plants and animals
   - Natural views and vistas
   - Facade greening
   - Geological and landscape forms
   - Habitats and ecosystems
   - Fire

2. Natural shapes and forms:
   - Botanical motifs
   - Animal motifs
   - Shell and spiral forms
   - Egg, ovular, and tubular forms
   - Arches, vaults, domes
   - Columns and treelike supports
   - Shapes that resist right angles
   - Simulation of natural features
   - Biomorphism (resemblance to organic forms)
   - Natural morphology (e.g., stratified surfaces and rooted relationships)
   - Biomimicry (mimicry of organic structures and functions)

3. Natural patterns and processes:
   - Sensory variability
   - Information richness
   - Time, aging, and change
   - Growth and efflorescence
   - Central focal point
   - Patterned whole
   - Bounded spaces (e.g., borders, territories)
   - Transitional spaces (e.g., gateways, thresholds)
   - Complementary contrasts (e.g., light/dark, high/low)
   - Dynamic balance and tension
   - Similar forms at different scales (e.g., fractals)
   - Hierarchically organized scales
   - Ordered complexity
   - Relation and integration of parts to whole
   - Linked series and chains

4. Light and space:
   - Natural light
   - Filtered and diffused light
   - Light and shadow
   - Reflected light
   - Light pools
   - Warm light
   - Light as shape and form
   - Spatial variability
   - Spaciousness
   - Space as shape and form
   - Spatial harmony (the integration of light, mass, and scale)
   - Inside/outside spaces (e.g., atria, colonnades)

5. Place-based relationships:
   - Historical connection to place
   - Cultural connection to place
   - Geographical connection to place
   - Ecological connection to place
   - Use of indigenous materials
   - Compatible orientation to landscape
   - Landscape features that define building form
   - Landscape ecology (connections, corridors, biodiversity)
   - Integrating culture and ecology
   - Sense or spirit of place
   - Avoiding placelessness

6. Evolved human relations to nature:
   - Prospect and refuge
   - Exploration and discovery
   - Mystery and enticement
   - Order and complexity
   - Change and metamorphosis
   - Information and cognition
   - Attraction and beauty
   - Mastery and control
   - Security and protection
   - Affection and attachment
   - Fear and awe
   - Reverence and spirituality

Two basic dimensions distinguish biophilic design: the human experience of nature—organic or naturalistic design—and the context where this experience occurs—vernacular or place-based design. Both low-environmental and biophilic design must work in complementary relation to achieve a true and lasting sustainability. This broader approach to sustainability seeks to avoid and minimize harmful impacts on the natural environment and human health as well as provide and restore beneficial contact between people and nature in the built environment.

LANDSCAPE PERCEPTION

Related to environmental psychology, the field of environmental aesthetics encompasses the question: what is the nature of nature? How do we perceive landscape and nature settings, and what does this mean for reconnecting nature and healing? Landscape, as a concept, derives from the seventeenth-century Dutch *landschap,* referring to the background of a painting. Geographer J. Douglas Porteous (1996) notes that the British expanded the concept to include "a visually pleasing prospect whether on the ground or on canvas." It delighted all the senses and was best appreciated kinesthetically, by moving through it, rather than simply gazing upon it. Porteous observes that in the United States, landscape has always been seen as reflecting the dominant value system that lauds freedom, individualism, power, and progress. In fact, the United States has long defined landscape as a commodity, or a means of wealth-production—the waterfront view, the mountain vista property.

As long ago as the eighteenth century, we developed our sense of the beautiful in landscape design. Aristocrats reshaped the countryside to fit contemporary theories of how landscapes should look. The pastoral/beautiful was seen as the antidote to the Industrial Revolution's urban landscape—a manifestation of the tranquility of nature. In the nineteenth century, the writers Ralph Waldo Emerson and Henry David Thoreau argued for a return to an authentic, emotional contact with wilderness and nature—the development of the system of the country's national parks was partially inspired by this challenge. Porteous (1996) observed that rapid population growth and urban development won out: "As Western societies developed the tools for making over the earth, the 'feel' for harmony between humankind and nature was lost in the frantic exploitation of 'resources.'"

"THE SAVANNA GESTALT"

"When people are confined to crowded cities or featureless land, they go to considerable lengths to recreate an intermediate terrain, something that can tentatively be called the savanna gestalt" (Wilson 1984). Presumably,

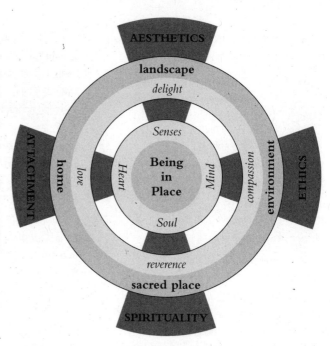

Figure 4-8: Humanity's intangible relationships with the environment directly informs the consideration of therapeutic or healing landscape in healthcare settings by recognizing the complex attributes of well-being—thought (mind), feeling (heart), intuition (soul), and sensation (senses). *Source: Porteous (1996). Redrawn with permission from Routledge Taylor.*

this has its roots in human evolution, supposedly to have taken place in the savannas of tropical Africa, where natural selection favored individuals in lower-risk environments: the savanna afforded long views and was therefore relatively safe (Orians and Heerwagen 1992). Related to this are the notions of prospect (the long view) and refuge (the safe place), concepts that form part of Kellert and Heerwagen's evolved human affinities for nature.

According to Wilson (1984), given free choice, people will move to open, tree-studded land on prominences overlooking water. The compelling healing garden atop the Yawkey Center for Outpatient Care illustrates Wilson's principles in action. A candid journal entry by a twelve-year-old child, reproduced at the garden entrance, reads: "Coming here is the best medicine" (Ravanesi 2006).

The Howard Ulfelder, MD, Healing Garden at the Yawkey Center for Outpatient Care, Massachusetts General Hospital

Boston, Massachusetts

Figure 4-9: The Howard Ulfelder Healing Garden at the Yawkey Center is a place of respite, a meditation space with wood furniture and extensive plantings. It is quiet and tranquil; when people leave the oncology department with serious thoughts—radiation, chemotherapy, death—they have a place to be with families and friends in relative solitude. *Credit: © Halvorson Design Partnership, Ben Watkins*

After attending the Design for Health Summit in 2004 (described in Chapter 8), Partners HealthCare System determined to incorporate additional green features in the Yawkey Center, a major building 60 percent through construction at the time. One of the resultant initiatives is a magnificent outdoor healing garden adjacent to the oncology department that provides expansive views of the urban and natural worlds and transforms the experience of the tight, complex urban site.

The healing garden looks out to the west over the Charles River, with a stunning panoramic view of both the Boston and Cambridge skylines and the Longfellow Bridge in the foreground. This westerly view allows patients, visitors, and staff to take in the sunsets. The beautifully landscaped garden also has a small reflecting pool with trees, grassy areas, granite benches, and wood furnishings. Cambridge Seven Associates, Inc., was the building architect, with Halvorson Design Partnership, Inc., providing the landscape architecture.

Figure 4-10: Visitors to the Howard Ulfelder Healing Garden look west over the Charles River, with a view of the Boston and Cambridge skylines. *Credit: © Halvorson Design Partnership, Ben Watkins*

HEALING LANDSCAPE

Healing, for the purposes of this discussion, embodies the three ideas articulated by landscape architect Clare Cooper Marcus (1999): relief from symptoms of illness, stress reduction, and improvement in the sense of overall well-being. In fact, she maintains, the healing garden is emerging as a supplement to drug- or technology-based treatments. Marcus has led a lifelong exploration of the principles that inform healing landscapes in healthcare settings and underlie the worldwide therapeutic landscape movement. This extensive body of work informs the essay "Design with Rhythm" that follows.

As landscape architects Jody Rosenblatt-Naderi and Jerry Smith note, the challenge is to situate healing and therapeutic landscape design in the broader context of sustainable site planning. They argue for a land-planning ethic in partnership with natural cycles, rather than the planning process rooted in mastery over nature that prioritizes linear time — the travel distance from points A to B — that characterizes much healthcare site planning today.

Design with Rhythm

Jody Rosenblatt-Naderi, ASLA, and Jerry Smith, ASLA

> Yesterday, I sat in a field of violets
> for a long time perfectly still,
> until I really sank into it —
> into the rhythm of the place.
> Then, when I got up to go home
> I couldn't walk quickly or evenly
> because I was still in time with the field.
>
> —ANNE MORROW LINDBERGH

Healing gardens, or therapeutic landscapes, are by definition places of renewal. Therapeutic benefits derive from contact with nature because the spatial experience encourages people to connect with a deeper part of themselves and with their natural surroundings. These deep connections, in turn, renew the spirit and help people find a strength that is a crucial part of healing.

Gardens designed to heal should themselves be in a healthy relationship with their biophysical and cultural contexts. Successful gardens tend to transport people away from the intensity of healthcare through contrasts and distractions. But, in doing so, they may, ironically, inadvertently displace nature with generic healing gardens. Tucked into the harsh landscapes of courtyards and hospital rooftops, these gardens can be an oasis, but are at risk of failing by being out of step with the ecology of the ambient landscape.

Taking cues from the history of ecological and sustainable design literature, evidence favors survival based on the diversity of the indigenous palette (Ndubisi 2002). However, behavioral and landscape-preference research suggests that most people prefer a more controlled, familiar, or even domestic landscape (Marcus 1997). How can a Disneyesque, domesticated landscape impart the healing force of nature honestly and sustainably? Given the constraints and environmental boundaries that are often imposed on outdoor places of respite within today's built environments of care, is the designed landscape able to impart that same sense of healing that nature provides?

To find our footing in sustainable healthcare garden design, we need to understand how to grasp the deeper nature of a landscape. In doing so, we must look beyond the footprint of the built environment to better understand the context of the site itself. Every site has a voice that can be heard within the broader context of the landscape. An empty site tells a lot of stories that can show us where to place buildings, roads, and utilities so that the natural character of the site is preserved or restored. Working with the natural contours of the site, the flow of the water, the sun angles, and the shade benefits the therapeutic value of the landscape as a whole and embeds placemaking in the cyclical rhythms of nature. By taking our cues from the basic cycles of nature — solar and lunar cycles, annual seasonal cycles, circadian rhythms, and the tempo of the heartbeat of life as we know it — we may find a sense of security in knowing that some things are familiar and can be relied on, even in an ever-changing world.

If we recognize how embedded these cycles are in our understanding of health and well-being, we may be more able to form landscape design principles for gardens that yield positive health outcomes. The emerging principles that surround the design of contemporary healing gardens suggest that we achieve this deeper understanding by working more closely with the cyclical dimension of nature.

THERAPEUTIC LANDSCAPES: EMERGING DESIGN PRINCIPLES

The principles below are not comprehensive; they are derived from literature published over the last fifty years as well as from the authors' experiments, professional experience, and field observations with the healing dimensions of the built environment (Naderi 2004).

Preference for nature: Since Hippocrates in the fourth century BCE, physicians have known that nature heals. Nature promotes reflections on the continuity of life and offers positive distraction from the anxiety and stress of the hospital (Marcus and Francis 1997; Kaplan and Kaplan 1990). Views of trees strengthen patient recovery, shorten hospital stays, and reduce pain and stress (Horsburgh 1995; Stigsdotter and Grahn 2003; Ulrich 1999). A view, textures, familiar smells, fresh air, and sunlight all provide respite from the stressors of hospital interiors. Preferences for different types of nature (forest, trees, meadows—even mowed lawns) necessitate inquiry prior to design (Kaplan and Austin 2004). Providing a variety of phenomenological experiences of nature in landscape of healing gardens maximizes their potential healing outcomes. This is the therapeutic dimension of the garden design. Greening the therapeutic garden is about organizing natural features and welcoming contextual nature into the environment of care experience.

Contrast: Gardens have historically included features in contrast with the surrounding environment: water channels in desert gardens, dry stone arrangements in cypress forests, deep shade and pools under blistering sunlight. The contrast enhances the spatial experience of contemplation and restoration. The healing garden stands in contrast to the hospital context, providing patients, visitors, and staff with an escape from the intensity of hospital activities. The healing garden draws from the palette of the surrounding landscape while remaining unique within it. It is an inner sanctuary.

Choice: Loss of control and lack of autonomy characterize a hospital visit. Providing choice increases patients' and visitors' sense of control, and has been found to improve overall health (Zeisel and Eberhard 1981). The garden layout provides choice through celebrating both spatial and natural diversity. A path with multiple connections to each node gives walkers multiple routes to choose from. The microclimatic variations of sunlight/shade and coolness/warmth can be manipulated with tree canopy and sun pockets, providing both multiple seating choices throughout the day and richer plant diversity. Supporting social groupings with small tables and chairs as well as larger picnic grounds gives people the choice of being alone or in a place where larger groups can congregate.

Archetypes, favorite places, and metaphors: People can reduce their stress by returning to favorite places where they feel nurtured, secure, and protected (Myss 2005; Barrie 1996; Tuan 1977; Abram 1996). Favorite places as archetypes might be a swing, a front porch with a chaise lounge, under a tree, around the kitchen table at a grandmother's house, or next to a sparkling stream in the woods (Marcus 1997). Sacred places as archetypes, such as paths, caves, bluffs, glades, mountaintops, and waterfalls, have echoed through the ages as places for personal renewal and transformation (Downing 2000; Messervy and Abell 1995). Metaphors of favorite places and features, both sacred and domestic, can trigger patients' and visitors' memories, shifting their focus to the energy of nature in the garden and providing a respite from the health troubles at hand.

Chance encounters and places of repose: Gardens and connecting spaces can be designed with attractive transitional spaces along the way to encourage chance encounters during the ebb and flow of daily activities. In ecology, edge conditions exhibit the highest concentration of biological activity; this is also the case in the garden. Transitional spaces and paths can be arranged to provide enough space to support a casual conversation while still allowing passage (10 to 14 feet, 3 to 42 meters). Including a variety of spaces furnished with a range of seating groupings provides flexible gathering spots for anything from an impromptu encounter between two people to a yoga class for thirty. Microclimatic placement of ergonomic benches that are easy to sit in and rise from can allow for visually stimulating views and create diverse people-watching opportunities (Yancey 1972; Gehls 1987; Hall 1969; Alexander, Ishikawa, and Silverstein 1977).

Kinesthetics and connectivity: Walking and physical activity are a part of nearly every health regimen because of their multiple benefits on the physical, psychological, and spiritual levels (Naderi 2003). The spatial experience of walking along paths and transitional, transformative experiences such as crossing thresholds or gateways, sitting to contemplate, seeing a glimpse of infinity, being surrounded by green edges for shade and microclimatic protection, and being oriented to the celestial movement of the sun, moon, and stars all provide time and space for personal transformation.

Spiritual renewal: *Employing the language of sacred architecture and creating traditional places of contemplation or prayer can enhance spiritual renewal (Lane 1988). Material transformations in the garden can act as a metaphor for internal transformation and promote a sense of renewal as well (Barrie 1996; Geva 2002; Tabb 2003). Both traditional and contemporary places of renewal are characterized by juxtaposition: deep greenery and stone, water and earth, light and darkness, inside and outside, path and verticality. Spiritual experience can be enhanced by mystery, revelation, and repetition (Kaplan, Kaplan, and Brown 1989). The kinetic considerations of design have a significant influence on spiritual experience. The duration of the approach to a sacred object or place of transformation has a pace of its own that must be respected. The path-and-pause sequence can be designed to maximize opportunities for transformative experience by considering the slower pace of a contemplative walk and the need for simple edge treatment and focal point with natural materials.*

When these principles are applied in landscape design, they can weave together to address physical, psychological, and spiritual health outcomes. Alignment with the contextual natural systems of water, earth, plants, light, and breezes will continue to affect the designed landscape and distinguish the sustainable therapeutic environment.

THE CYCLICAL DIMENSION OF NATURE AND RENEWAL

Making nature's cyclical dimension primary to the design process (and potential health outcomes) will ensure harmony between a garden and its contextual environment—natural or built. These cycles present a design framework that builds on and reveals the harmony of the site's intrinsic natural rhythms. Design outcomes that create opportunities for a spontaneous

awareness of nature's cycles establish a context for healing. The familiarity of acknowledging and remembering such basic rhythms of life through nature helps reduce the imposed stress factors of the unknown and uncertain. As a complement, conservation, efficiency, and recycling ensure outcomes that go with, rather than against, the flow of the cycle.

The temporal dimension of a site is measured at multiple scales. Like spatial dimension, time units are also defined by edge conditions. "Events" are the edges that bound and define the temporal scales of a site. Events enclose time, as walls enclose space: sunrise-to-sunrise, solstice-to-solstice, season-to-season, hurricane-to-hurricane. Together, these cycles shape and renew the site. Layers of time are part of the rhythms of life that sustainable design utilizes in the new garden, acknowledging the site's intentions.

SUMMARY OF LANDSCAPE DESIGN PRINCIPLES FOR HEALING

- Celebrate the rhythm and cycles of nature through design by acknowledging seasonal change, natural patterns, and the movement of sun, water, terrain, and natural materials.
- Connect to the sacred dimensions of the subculture and biophysical setting unique to each hospital community.
- Present seasonal experiences with views of infinity aligned with contextual celestial movements of the sun, moon, and stars.
- Engage all the senses with plants, wind, water, earth, movement, and music.
- Utilize horizontal and vertical dynamics that draw the visitor into the garden and provide visual focus beyond it.
- Evoke memory and familiarity.
- Contrast with the intensity of the healthcare experience through changing scale, materials (nature over man-made), microclimate (e.g., fresh air, dew, breeze, and sunlight), sound levels (in contrast with the public address system) and views (e.g., infinity at the micro and macro scale, reflections, from windows). Employ ergonometric and spatially comfortable details for patients, visitors, and staff.

These unique features tell the story of interdependence and constant change that are fundamental to human nature and ecosystems (Wilhelm and Baynes 1987). This empowering axiom is realized by designing with the complexities and choices embedded in designing with time. Recycling water and allowing fields to go fallow—all contribute to the spatial experience of renewal. The garden is an opportunity to celebrate these cycles and achieve a sustainable relationship with these refreshing flows through time. Provided with those concepts and guiding principles that reinforce the natural progression of transformation and renewal, therapeutic garden design can support our own need to be one with ourselves, in tune and accepting of our own personal cycle of life, whatever that may be.

CONCLUSION

Healing and healthy landscape outcomes are enabled through opportunities to restore or regenerate natural systems as well as to develop therapeutic landscape experience location(s) around which the buildings are often sited. Following this framework, the ideal environment of care could be said to inhabit a particular location because that's where the site "tells us" the building belongs, based on landscape features such as solar orientation, prevailing winds, views, and vistas. Historically, environments of care were strategically located on hilltops or higher planes for those very benefits of the site. Bringing that traditional site-design concept back into today's complex urban environment through outdoor places of respite may enable those known health outcomes in today's environments of care.

With the acceptance of that premise, the site and the designed landscape alike (defined as places of natural cycles) have powerful identities that need to be considered in the earliest phases of the design process and carried through implementation and stewardship. The physical potential of a garden to meet the most basic personal needs is best realized when life's natural rhythm is considered in the organizing principles of the design process. When what is viewed and experienced and translated in its simplest form can bring the viewer back to that basic appreciation of life and living, then that place has been renewed and revived and empowered through design with rhythm and the tempo of nature.

SUGGESTED DESIGN METHODS FOR ENABLING HEALING

- Provide places for pause along paths that are comfortable, semiprivate, sited in response to microclimate, and present natural elements through interesting views, smells, textures, and sounds.
- Provide paths connecting transitional spaces to facilitate chance encounters.
- Maximize the number of paths and intersections to facilitate informal walking circuits, path choice, and contemplative walking.
- Plant trees along paths, around seating, and within view of windows.
- Increase the variety of social spaces and seating groups.
- Engage the site's natural preconstruction condition to celebrate the genius loci of the hospital location.
- Provide signage and accessibility to the garden for all mobility types.

Hospital siting is no longer determined based on affinity for view or natural and cyclical properties of sites, but rather by commercial real estate interests. The hospital landscape, for the most part, has been obliterated by surface parking requirements, helipads, and service and emergency vehicle access. While a patient room window may frame a natural vista of distant views, the view across the intermediate landscape is rarely satisfactory. Often, the middle ground is dominated by vehicle access or urban structures. In rare cases, like at the Yawkey Center, an urban hospital creates a solution that instantly and profoundly connects occupants to the landscape. In so doing, it demonstrates both the challenges inherent in reconsidering the fundamental relationship of the building to its site, and the power of doing so.

In developing new hospital campuses on urban sites, ideas of therapeutic landscape merge with sustainable site-planning principles in developing healing gardens, green roofs, and native plantings. The work of Walker Macy at Legacy Salmon Creek Hospital illustrates how developing structured parking and orienting patient room vistas toward adjacent wooded areas achieved a profound healthcare experience.

Legacy Salmon Creek Hospital Landscape

Vancouver,
Washington

Figure 4-11: Legacy Salmon Creek Hospital Landscape. *Credit:* © *Eckert & Eckert*

For the landscape design of Legacy Salmon Creek Hospital, Walker Macy developed a series of gardens using native and adapted planting strategies, permeable paving, water features in the campus forecourt, and an intimate healing garden on a rooftop nestled between inpatient wings. Mauricio Villarreal, project landscape architect with Walker Macy Landscape Architects and Planners of Portland, Oregon, stated: "Plantings and water features are designed to be comforting and to put people at ease by providing outdoor green spaces which are accessible through visits to the gardens and views from the surrounding facilities" (Simpson 2004). The building case study is presented in Chapter 9.

Figure 4-12: The forecourt garden plan develops the space between the parking garage, hospital, and ambulatory care building into a series of stepped terraces featuring native and adapted planting and permeable pavers linked by a continuous water feature. *Credit: Walker Macy*

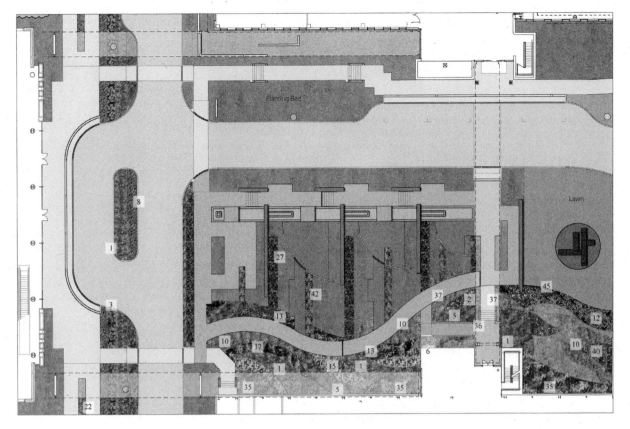

Plant names:

1. Fragrant sarcococca *Sarcococca ruscifolia*
2. White rockrose *Cistus x hybridus*
3. Girard's Pleasant White azalea *'Girard's Pleasant White'*
4. Yellow Queen columbine *Aquilegia chrysantha 'Yellow Queen'*
5. Oceanlake rhododendron *Rhododendron 'Oceanlake'*
6. Dwarf fothergilla *Fothergilla gardenii*
7. Sungold butterfly bush *Buddleia x weyeriana 'Sungold'*
8. Variegated Japanese sedge *Carex morrowii 'Aureo-Variegata'*
9. Fire Power nandina *Nandina domestica 'Fire Power'*
10. Swordfern *Polystichum munitum*
11. Blue Mist fothergilla *Fothergilla 'Blue Mist'*
12. David viburnum *Viburnum davidii*
13. Deutschland astilbe *Astilbe x arendsii 'Deutschland'*
14. Lemon Drop Cape fuschia *Phygelius 'Lemon Drop'*
15. Chionoides rhododendron *'Chionoides'*
16. Compact Korean Spice viburnum *Viburnum carlesii 'Compactum'*
17. Bear's Breech *Acanthus mollis*
18. Convex Leaf Japanese holly *Ilex crenata 'Convexa'*
19. Carol Mackie daphne *Daphne x burkwoodii 'Carol Mackie'*
20. Kobold Spiked gayfeather *Liatris spicata 'Kobold'*
21. Red spurge *Euphorbia amygdaloides 'Rubra'*
22. Lady's-mantle *Alchemilla mollis*
23. Bressingham Comet Red-Hot poker *Kniphofia uvaria 'Bressingham Comet'*
24. Bourgatii sea holly *Eryngium Alpinum 'Bourgatii'*
25. Snowcap Shasta daisy *Leucanthemum x superbum 'Snowcap'*
26. Silver Light bergenia *Bergenia 'Silberlicht'*
27. Box-leaf euonymus *Euonymus japonicus 'Microphyllus'*
28. Silver Dragon liriope *Liriope 'Silver Dragon'*
29. Midnight Blue lily of the Nile *Agapanthus 'Midnight Blue'*
30. SeaFoam rose *Rosa 'Sea Foam'*
31. Gemander *Teucrium fruticans*
32. White Swan echinacea *Echinacea 'White Swan'*
33. Minnesota Snowflake mock orange *Philadelphus 'Minnesota Snowflake'*
34. Catlin's Giant carpet bugle *Ajuga reptans 'Catlin's Giant'*
35. Variegated Mariseii big-leaf hydrangea *Hydrangea macrophylla 'Mariesii Variegata'*
36. Dwarf lily of the nile *Agapanthus africanus 'Peter Pan'*
37. Fringe cup *Tellima grandiflora*
38. Foamflower *Thalictrum rochebrunianum*
39. Cunningham's Blush rhododendron *Rhododendron x 'Cunningham's Blush'*
40. Mount Airy fothergilla *Fothergilla Major 'Mount Airy'*
41. Privet honeysuckle *Lonicera pileata*
42. Big Blue liriope *Liriope muscari 'Big Blue'*
43. Rusty foxglove *Digitalis ferruginea*
44. Fairy bells *Dierama pulcherrimum*
45. Palace Purple alumroot *Heuchera micrantha 'Palace Purple'*
46. Dwarf germander *Teucrium chamaedrys 'Prostratum'*
47. Sky Pencil Japanese holly *Ilex crenata 'Sky Pencil'*
48. Purple Gem rhododendron *Rhododendron 'Purple Gem'*
49. Whirling Butterflies gaura *Gaura lindheimeri 'Whirling Butterflies'*
50. Dropmore catmint *Nepeta x faassenii 'Dropmore'*
51. Plum Passion nandina *Nandina domestica 'Plum Passion'*
52. Purple sage *Salvia officinalis 'Purpurascens'*
53. Dora Amateis rhododendron *Rhododendron 'Dora Amateis'*

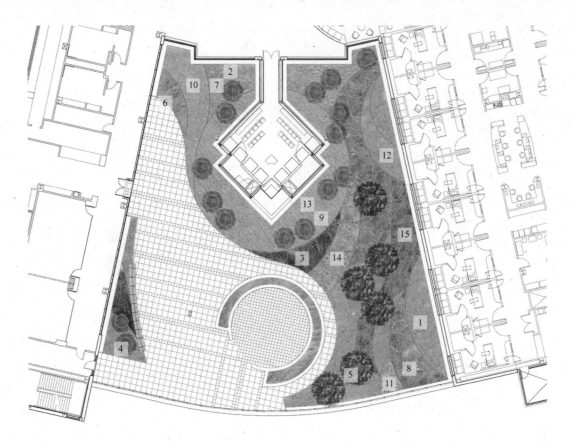

Figure 4-13: Native and adapted perennials and grasses provide both visual stimulation and scent in the therapeutic healing garden. A key to the plant species is available for visitors. *Credit: Walker Macy*

Plant names:
1. Golden Glory euphorbia *Euphorbia amygdaloides 'Golden Glory'*
2. Jerusalem sage *Phlomis russelliana*
3. Feather reed grass *Calamagrostis x acutiflora 'Karl Forester'*
4. Golden bamboo *Phyllostachys aurea*
5. Purple smoke bush *Cotinus coggygria 'Royal Robe'*
6. Black Flower fountain grass *Pennisetum alopecuroides 'Moudry'*
7. Sweet variegated iris *Iris pallida 'Variegata'*
8. Camas *Camassia quamash*
9. Purple silver grass *Miscanthus 'purpurascens'*
10. Dark Horse weigelia *Weigelia florida 'Dark Horse'*
11. Adjective Hybrid Daylily *Hemerocallis x 'Adjective'*
12. Otto Quast Spanish lavender *Lavandula stoechas 'Otto Quast'*
13. Ice Dance Japanese sedge *Carex morrowii 'Ice Dance'*
14. Superbum sea holly *Eryngium alpinum 'Superbum'*
15. Russian sage *Perovskia atriplicifolia*

Figure 4-14: The meditation room floats in the healing garden, a landscaped roof space between the two inpatient tower wings. See plan, Fig. 4-13. The garden was designed as an integral component of a horticulture therapy program. *Credit: © Eckert & Eckert*

SUSTAINABLE LANDSCAPE

Landscape architect and professor Ian McHarg, the pioneer of ecological land planning, devoted his life to revealing the complexity of contemporary site planning hubris — the widespread belief that nothing in nature should constrain what humans do to the land they own. Most importantly, McHarg advocated for three important principles of sustainable site planning (Sorvig 2006):

1. Sustainable site planning depends on proactive advocacy for the land itself.
2. Landscape architecture is equal in importance to architecture and civil engineering.
3. It is both possible and essential to recognize and map sites for their inherent natural, cyclical patterns and flows.

> *Our eyes do not divide us from the world, but unite us with it. . . . Let us abandon the self-mutilation which has been our way and give expression to the potential harmony of man-nature. The world is abundant; we require only a deference born of understanding to fulfill man's promise. Man is that uniquely conscious creature who can perceive and express. He must become the steward of the biosphere. To do this he must design with nature.*
>
> —IAN MCHARG (1969)

As research on the therapeutic benefits of a connection with nature and sustainable healthcare emerges, the critical significance of McHarg's work becomes more evident. As hospital patients reconnect with the outdoors, situating hospital buildings in seas of parking, devoid of any direct connection to the landscape, will become unacceptable.

THE ETHICS OF CONSERVATION

E. O. Wilson (1984) suggests that the future of the conservation movement relies on linkages to bioethics. Like other visionary thinkers, including Ted Schettler, an essayist in Chapter 3, Wilson returns to the original meaning of bioethics — the relationship between human beings and other species, and the impact of mass extinction and environmental degradation on humanity. Likewise, part of the answer to developing a deep conservation ethic stems from the notion of biophilia — the development of a deep affinity for the natural world. Or, as evolutionary biologist Stephen Jay Gould (1991) so eloquently expressed: "We cannot win this battle to save species and environments without forging an emotional bond between ourselves and nature as well — for we will not fight to save what we do not love."

Dell Children's Medical Center of Central Texas Therapeutic Gardens

Austin,
Texas

The planning approach places the inpatient units opposite parking areas, and develops a therapeutic garden between and around the twenty-four-bed units. Patient rooms provide views of the gardens and more distant vistas of the downtown Austin skyline. In addition, the two-story diagnostic and treatment block is pierced with four plan-enclosed courtyards. Each of these has a distinctive garden response based on native plants from the seven eco-regions (forty-two counties) served by the children's hospital. The diverse palette results in unique, bioregionally focused experiences connecting children to the familiar while educating them about broader regional differences.

Within the parking areas, trees are positioned to reduce heat island impacts. The perimeter site landscaping is based on native, drought-tolerant plants. Where required, drip landscape irrigation is provided by the municipal reclaimed water system (described in Chapter 2).

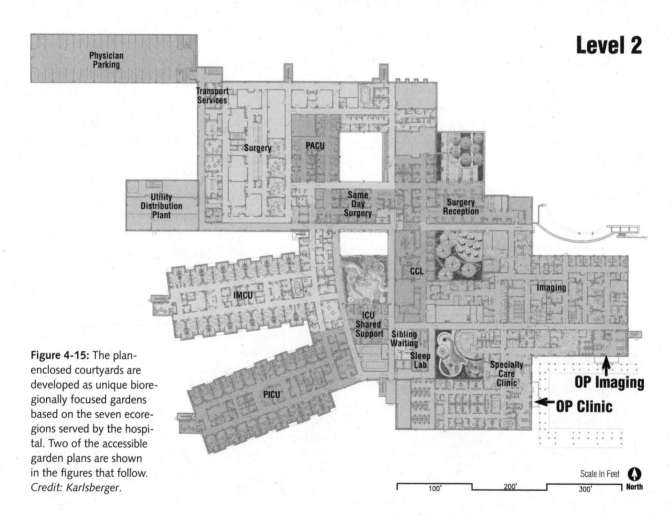

Figure 4-15: The plan-enclosed courtyards are developed as unique bioregionally focused gardens based on the seven ecoregions served by the hospital. Two of the accessible garden plans are shown in the figures that follow. *Credit: Karlsberger.*

Figure 4-16: The Therapy Garden features four distinct seating areas of varying scale, shade trellis, and organic paving and pathways. *Credit: TBG Partners*

Figure 4-17: The Lost Pines Garden focuses on a stand of seven pine trees flanked by benches and paved pathways. In this garden, the trees provide the only source of shade. *Credit: TBG Partners*

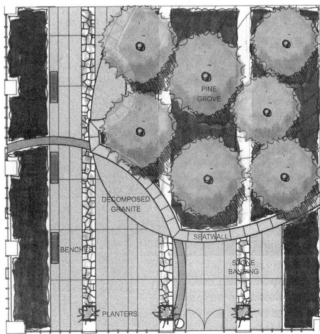

CONCLUSION

More than one hundred years of the systematic decoupling of nature and healthcare buildings will not be overcome easily. No longer are sacred natural sites reserved for buildings for healing, thanks to the simultaneous commoditization of health and the landscape. Healthcare buildings are no longer intentionally sited alongside hot springs, nor on promontories with water views that resonate with humans in times of stress—places of strong biophilic content for humans in their greatest hour of need.

The dictates of technology and fear of contamination and infection have eliminated most traces of nature from hospital buildings: the lack of natural ventilation or operable windows, the dependence on artificial lighting over natural daylight, the deep floor plate building, the rejection of courtyards and other nature-inclusive spaces for patient use. Sustainable building challenges this typology; the projects in this book, at this moment of transformation, demonstrate a renewed partnership between buildings and nature. The creative introduction of healing landscapes can assist in developing and strengthening the biophilic connections to nature, and further reconnection to the therapeutic powers of nature.

Sustainable building calls the question of whether buildings that purport to heal and restore people can restore the natural surroundings they are sited within. As the projects in this book demonstrate, the disciplines of land planning and landscape design bring coherence to the relationship between healing people and healing the earth. While engaged on a healthcare campus, people can and should experience a positive, restorative natural setting.

PART 2

ACTUALIZING
THE VISION

CHAPTER 5

The Business Case

> When one tugs at a single thing in nature, one finds it
> attached to the rest of the world.
>
> —JOHN MUIR

Ever since sustainability became foreshortened as a
quantifiable term in public consciousness, i.e., reduced
purely to measurements of energy use, it has become
fashionable, achieving wide recognition as a discipline.
The many facts and more subtle aspects of
sustainability, for example the unity of nature and the
human being, or the long overdue redefinition of
"comfort," are essentially lost in the shuffle. Here too,
the prevalent orientation is apparently exclusively to
the quantifiable. It is important to counter
this development.

> —BEHNISCH, BEHNISCH & PARTNER

INTRODUCTION

In *Redefining Health Care: Creating Value-Based Competition on Results,* their analysis of the US health system, business strategist Michael Porter and innovation expert Elizabeth Olmsted Teisberg (2006) begin with a sweeping critique: "The U.S. health care system is on a dangerous path, with a toxic combination of high costs, uneven quality, frequent errors, and limited access to care." Their central thesis—that hospitals are failing to deliver value to patients—corresponds with trends linking value to mission and differentiates the assessment of healthcare's definition of bottom line from other businesses'. Their aim is to convert this dysfunctional healthcare system into one in which value-based competition produces better health and greater efficiency.

> Healthy competition is competition to improve value for customers, or the quality of products or services relative to their price. It leads to relentless improvements in efficiency. Product quality and customer service improve. Innovation propels advances in the state of the art. Quality adjusted prices fall, and the market expands and more customer needs are met. Choice expands. It is a far cry from what we see today in health care.
>
> —PORTER AND TEISBERG (2006)

Indeed, healthcare is held to higher moral and ethical standards than virtually any other business sector. One demonstration of this is a blurring of distinction between for-profit and nonprofit hospitals. While nonprofit hospitals have a legal obligation to deliver community benefit, it is common for for-profit systems to also make visible investments in this realm. Healthcare providers recognize the value of community health as creating a visible connection with mission — and as a means to gain advantage in a competitive marketplace (Schlessinger and Gray 1998).

Increasingly, as the causal links between public health, environmental quality, and buildings are better understood, the reasons for extending the definition of community benefit beyond public health to include environmental stewardship become axiomatic. Joined with the necessity to be economically sustainable, this broader construct is underpinning how the hospitals of tomorrow are being defined. The three concepts of economy, community, and environment define a "triple bottom line" for sustainable business ventures.

This chapter explores the complex, multidimensional business case for sustainable building in the healthcare sector. Beginning with a review of basic sustainable-building economics, it builds upon an essay included in *Improving Healthcare with Better Building Design* (Roberts and Guenther 2006), the 2004 Massachusetts Design for Health Summit, and a series of lectures by the authors to healthcare audiences beginning in 2004. The business case remains a work-in-progress, informed by each sustainable healthcare project team experience.

THE TRIPLE BOTTOM LINE

The idea of a triple bottom line dates back to the mid-1990s (SustainAbility and UNEP 2002) and gained popularity with the publication of the British edition of *Cannibals with Forks: The Triple Bottom Line of 21st Century Business* by John Elkington (1998). The triple bottom-line concept describes a framework for measuring and reporting business performance against economic, social, and environmental parameters, rather than simply maximizing profits or growth. Figure 5-1 demon-

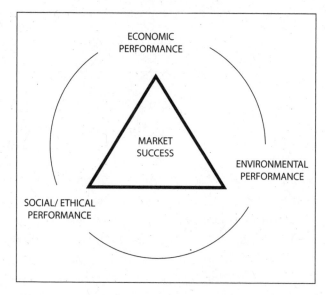

Figure 5-1: Triple bottom-line frameworks balance economic, ethical (social), and environmental issues to determine optimal intersections.

strates the triple bottom line of socially responsible businesses, which seek to integrate environmental, social, and economic values in their products and services.

Corporations have realized that businesses lacking social and ecological integrity are not economically viable over the long term; their costs eventually increase and their customer loyalty declines. Conserving nonrenewable resources, protecting the environment, and focusing on good corporate citizenship has become integral to maintaining long-term profitability. Product innovations that transform wastes into economic assets for increased production while using fewer costly, nonrenewable resources are increasingly viewed as essential to long-term economic profitability. Developing and maintaining better relationships with their workers, customers, and others in the communities in which companies operate can lead to reduced labor costs and create new markets (Hawken, Lovins, and Lovins 1999).

This concept has taken on a number of different labels — green economics, full-cost accounting, natural capital, social capital — but can also simply be thought of as good business. Increasingly, CEOs believe that sustainability is vital to the profitability of any company, as evidenced by a PricewaterhouseCoopers (2002) survey of one thousand CEOs from forty-three countries. *Building Design and Construction* (2006) pronounced that green building had entered a new reality, having graduated "from environmental cause to financial opportunity." Showcase green building projects for influential corporate owners — Bank of America, Swiss Re, Starbucks, Toyota — have completed at close to, and sometimes even below, their budget and cost projections.

HEALTHCARE AND THE TRIPLE BOTTOM LINE

That the healthcare industry has a responsibility beyond the economic bottom line is undeniable. David Lawrence (2000), former CEO of Kaiser Permanente, said, "Just as we have responsibility for providing quality patient care [and]...keeping our facilities and technology up to date, we have a responsibility for providing leadership in the environment." Lloyd Dean (2000) of Catholic Healthcare West, agreed: "We will not have healthy individuals, healthy families, and healthy communities if we do not have clean air, clean water, and healthy soil."

As a largely nonprofit sector, the healthcare industry is always engaged in triple bottom-line accounting. Often, healthcare service lines are developed and continued despite poor economic performance for the sake of social goals. Healthcare executives often use the concept of "margin into mission" to describe this reality. If healthcare organizations based their service decisions solely on economic criteria, the US healthcare system would be very different indeed!

Private, for-profit business has traditionally emphasized economic performance; socially responsible models seek a more balanced framework. Socially responsible business models demand a multifaceted business case — one that responds to each aspect of triple bottom-line thinking. In developing such a business case, solutions emerge that reflect the triple-bottom-line's multiple aspects — delivering benefits across all categories.

A useful construct for examining this complexity begins with defining three distinct business perspectives that accompany triple bottom-line approaches in healthcare. Environmental business writer Carl Frankel (2004) developed an insightful and useful characterization of these perspectives — the seeker, the citizen, and the strategist. The seeker governs environmental and overall organizational performance, the citizen governs social and community values, and the strategist governs economic outcome. Figure 5-2 illustrates the interplay among the seeker's, citizen's, and strategist's perspectives.

In healthcare organizations, each of these viewpoints combines to provide a complex decision-making structure that attempts to balance multiple priorities and perspectives. Governing principles for the healthcare sector and its margin-to-mission reality are more

Figure 5-2: The business case for sustainable healthcare must be multifaceted and respond to each of the stakeholders in the decision-making process. Ultimately, sustainable building strategies that deliver benefits to multiple stakeholders will define excellence. *Credit: Guenther 5 Architects*

complex and multidimensional than simple economic accounting might suggest, as the various administrative roles come together to define business success. A unique business case is delineated for each: an economic business case for the strategist, a social business case for the citizen, and a visionary leadership business case for the seeker. Ultimately, the task for healthcare leaders is to weave together to form a unified case for change.

THE STRATEGIST: THE ECONOMICS OF SUSTAINABLE HEALTHCARE

A prevalent notion in today's market is that green buildings cost more. "More than what?" is the first question that should be carefully framed. Does a green hospital cost more than the exact same building without the green features (also termed a "brown building")? More than the available capital budget? Or more than a neighboring comparable building of the same size and complexity? A related question is, of course, just how much does a hospital cost to construct? And, finally, what is the cost of *not* constructing a green hospital? Already, it is clear that this is a complex question requiring careful analysis.

In the absence of a sufficient database of green buildings to analyze, early financial models predicted that sustainable buildings would carry cost premiums related to their level of sustainability. For example, a basic LEED-certified building would have a lower initial cost premium than an exemplary LEED platinum building, which might encounter capital costs related to strategies such as on-site renewable energy. While initial data seemed to support this notion (Kats 2003), Amory Lovins and Rocky Mountain Institute (RMI) proposed a powerful countervailing cost model. RMI postulated that while capital costs would initially increase as sustainable building features were added on to conventional buildings, an integrated design process would ultimately lead to synergies between building systems that would "tunnel through the cost barrier" and drive initial construction costs lower than conventional construction. In fact, a number of case studies have realized exactly this outcome.

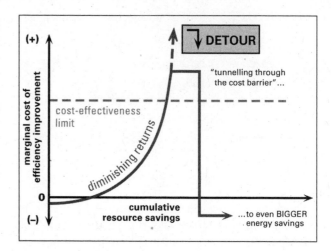

Figure 5-3: This cost model proposes that as strategies are added to produce increased cumulative resource savings, a cost-effectiveness limit is reached, after which strategies no longer produce resource savings. However, stretching design beyond this boundary condition will ultimately "tunnel through the cost barrier," with system synergies that realize more resource savings with lower costs. *Credit: Rocky Mountain Institute*

Studies based on completed buildings have shown that the anticipated cost premiums have been largely overstated, especially as green building practices and expertise mature. As early as 2003, *Building Design and Construction* magazine concluded that many green build-

In late 2003, Greg Kats and others released a study showing that the average construction premium for a sample of 33 LEED-registered buildings across the country was 1.84 percent, as seen in the accompanying table.

LEED certification level	Number of buildings	Construction cost premium
LEED certified	8	0.66 percent
LEED silver	18	2.11 percent
LEED gold	6	1.82 percent
LEED platinum	1	6.50 percent

Source: BDC 2006.

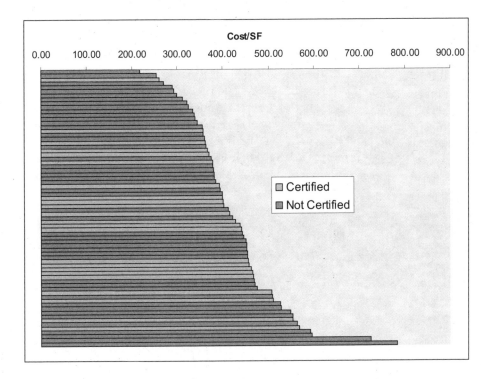

Cost/SF

| 0.00 | 100.00 | 200.00 | 300.00 | 400.00 | 500.00 | 600.00 | 700.00 | 800.00 | 900.00 |

□ Certified
■ Not Certified

Figure 5-4: This comparison of unit costs for new laboratory buildings (2006 data) demonstrates that the green buildings continue to be randomly distributed throughout the total pool of projects—there are both high-cost green lab buildings and low-cost green lab buildings. Factors that influence construction cost more significantly than sustainable measures include program components, regional construction market variation, and the experience of the design team in the building type. *Credit: Matthiessen 2007*

ings cost no more than their brown equivalents (Cassidy 2003). Greg Kats (2003) reviewed more than thirty-three completed LEED-registered office and school buildings and concluded that the average first-cost premium was slightly less than 2 percent. More importantly, these studies point to a consistent set of key factors that affect building costs:

- The earlier the green features are incorporated into the design, the lower the cost.
- Costs decline with increasing experience and as market transformation occurs.
- Green buildings provide financial benefits that brown buildings do not.

Kats (2003) outlined these advantages for green buildings: "The financial benefits are in lower operating costs, lower environmental costs, and increased productivity and health. Over twenty years, the benefits are over ten times the additional costs." Matthiessen and Morris (2004) concluded, "Sustainability is a program issue rather than an added requirement; perhaps the most important thing to remember is that . . . [it] is not a below

the line item." That 2003 study, which compared completed green and brown laboratory buildings, found no correlation between construction cost and level of sustainable design features. Instead, it concluded:

- Great variation exists in costs of buildings, even within the same building program type.
- There are low- and high-cost green buildings; there are low- and high-cost brown buildings.

In 2004, Lisa Fay Matthiessen and Peter Morris of real estate consultant Davis Langdon used their firm's proprietary construction cost database to compare the cost of forty-five buildings seeking LEED certification against ninety-three conventional buildings. They concluded, "Many projects achieve sustainable design within their initial budget, or with very small supplemental funding." Further, "the costs per square foot for buildings seeking LEED certification fall into the existing range of costs for buildings of similar program type" (BDC 2006).

CAPITAL TRADING COST FOR OPERATIONAL SAVINGS

There are no conclusive data that prove in the aggregate that green buildings cost more than their brown equivalents. However, as design teams begin to consider sustainable design features, there is a tendency to evaluate the first-cost implications of individual strategies against conventional solutions. In fact, Mathiessen and Morris (2006) prepared a first-cost analysis of *Green Guide for*

Health Care construction credits, using data derived from the Davis Langdon construction-cost database and interviews with *Green Guide* pilot teams. They concluded that many *Green Guide* credits can be implemented with minimal or no additional first cost, while some can reduce first cost "through improved design, or reduced complexity of design" (Mathiessen and Morris 2006).

In considering green strategies in isolation that cost more than their brown equivalents but deliver operational savings, the operational savings must find their

---

ENERGY EFFICIENCY MEASURES AT OREGON HEALTH & SCIENCES UNIVERSITY CENTER FOR HEALTH AND HEALING

(See also the case study in Chapter 10.)

Often, the cumulative results of energy-efficiency measures (EEMs) stem from a large number of small changes. For this project, the many ideas that were implemented are presented in terms of their relative payback at today's energy prices compared to base-case building design (adapted from Yudelson 2005).

EEMs That Pay Back Immediately (after incentives)

- Garage fan use based on carbon monoxide levels
- Premium efficiency motors
- Variable-flow water-heating system
- Lab exhaust heat-recovery system
- Lab occupancy sensors
- Reduced garage lighting levels
- Emergency light sweep
- On/off switches for daylighting controls (versus dimmable ballasts)
- Double fan variable air volume (VAV)
- Fan wall with low-pressure air filters
- Natural ventilation for stairwells
- Radiant heating and cooling for first-floor lobby

EEMs That Pay Back in One to Five Years

- High-efficiency chilled water plant
- High-efficiency glazing
- Water-heating demand reduction from water conservation measures
- High-efficiency boiler for domestic water heating
- Carbon dioxide sensors on ventilation systems
- Chiller heat recovery
- Dual-bank exam lighting

EEMs That Pay Back in Six to Ten Years

- 300-kW microturbine plant
- Extra floor insulation (from 5 to 12 in.) (12.7 cm to 30.5 cm)
- Occupancy sensors to control lighting and HVAC systems
- Optimized lighting fixture selection

EEMs That Pay Back in More Than Ten Years

- Extra wall insulation
- 60-kW photovoltaic array (with federal tax rebate)
- Solar air collector

---

way into the equation. Examples of such operational savings include energy and water efficiency or material selections that reduce maintenance costs. The Environmental Protection Agency (EPA) estimates that every dollar saved in operation is equivalent to $20 in new healthcare revenue (Reed 2000). At the Boston Design for Health Summit (see Chapter 8), hospital CFOs agreed that economic models must be developed to recognize this tradeoff, and healthcare organizations need to be creative in finding incremental capital to invest in

strategies that deliver long-term operational savings. The case studies presented in this book have taken many different approaches to this challenge, whether by defining simple acceptable payback periods or minimum acceptable returns on investment (ROIs), or by using public incentive programs to offset capital expenditures. Whatever the technique, project teams are finding their way through the complexity to deliver resource reduction strategies (primarily related to energy and water) that have measurable operational paybacks.

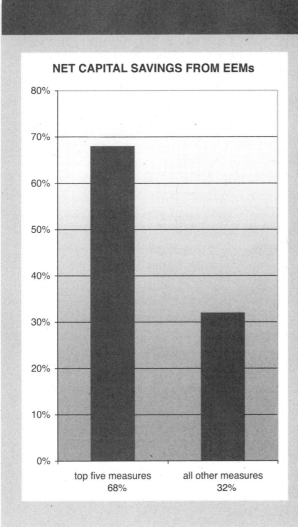

NET CAPITAL SAVINGS FROM EEMs

top five measures 68%

all other measures 32%

While some energy-efficiency measures do have higher costs, project savings associated with other measures were used to offset the first-cost premium of the most cost-effective EEMs, using life cycle cost analysis.

Cost of Energy-Efficiency Measures (EEMs)

Summary of Individual EEMs	+ Cost
Double fan VAV	$161,500
Chiller heat recovery	140,000
Hot water use reduction	89,165
Chilled beams	86,250
Fan-powered VAV	85,125
Occupancy sensors	79,100
High-efficiency boiler	70,000
Subtotal	**711,140**
All other measures	264,159
Total: All EEMs	**$975,299**

Figure 5-5: In this project, five energy-efficiency measures provided more than 68 percent of the net capital cost savings for the project. For example, naturally ventilating the stairwells generates initial capital savings. *Credit: Interface Engineering.*

Kaiser Permanente Modesto Medical Center

Modesto, California

Figure 5-6: Kaiser Permanente Modesto Medical Center. *Credit: Lionakis Beaumont Design Group*

Owner: Kaiser Permanente
Design team:
    ARCHITECTS: Lionakis Beaumont Design Group
    ASSOCIATE ARCHITECTS: Smith Group
    LANDSCAPE ARCHITECTS: Pollock & Partners, Inc.
    MECHANICAL ENGINEERS: Capital Engineering Consultants, Inc.
    ELECTRICAL ENGINEERS: Harry Yee & Associates
    GENERAL CONTRACTORS: Harbison-Mahony-Higgins Builders, Inc.
Building type: New acute-care medical center campus
Size: 683,000 sq ft (63,453 sq m)
Program description: 400,000 sq ft (37,161 sq m), five-story hospital with two nursing towers; 29,000 sq ft (2,694 sq m) central utility plant; 254,000 sq ft (23,597 sq m), four-story hospital support building with ambulatory surgery center
Completion date: 2007
Recognition: *Green Guide for Health Care* pilot

The medical center is one of four Kaiser Permanente templated hospitals implementing the *Green Guide for Health Care*'s principles of high-performance healing design. The economic assessment of the sustainable site strategies began with a discussion of permeable paving. While the constructor initially indicated that such a paving system would be more expensive than conventional concrete, negotiations with the city of Modesto resulted in its approval for substituting required underground storm water retention

Figure 5-7: The photovoltaic array screens rooftop mechanical equipment. By substituting the installation of a conventional screen and capturing utility incentives, the difference in the capital cost of the photovoltaics fell within Kaiser's three-year payback criteria. *Credit: Lionakis Beaumont Design Group*

systems with the paving. Once these savings were calculated, the porous paving actually reduced the overall budget. Only after the paving was installed were the other benefits understood —during periods of intense rain, there are no puddles in the parking lot, and virtually no water is ever tracked into the building. Kaiser predicts that slip-and-fall accidents, as well as day-to-day maintenance, will be reduced as a result.

Solar lighting in the parking lot delivered a similar economic return. By offsetting the increased cost of the solar fixtures through the elimination of the installation of conduits and wiring associated with conventional lighting, the solar system became cost neutral while providing operational cost savings.

KEY PERFORMANCE STRATEGIES

Site
- Porous paving throughout parking lot areas mitigates storm water runoff on-site

Energy
- Solar photovoltaic lighting in parking lot
- On-site photovoltaic array screens roof-mounted mechanical equipment

Materials
- Wall-protection systems polyvinyl chloride (PVC) free
- Carpet with polyvinyl butyral (PVB) backing system

Figure 5-8: The porous paving installation reduced the construction cost of the parking areas by eliminating the underground storm water management system. An added, though more difficult to quantify benefit, was the reduction of the slip-and-fall risk associated with wet paving and puddles. *Credit: Lionakis Beaumont Design Group*

POROUS PAVING AT KAISER PERMANENTE MEDICAL CENTER MODESTO

First-cost premium to install porous paving:
- Eliminated the fees associated with connecting to the municipal storm water system
- Avoided the cost of installing an on-site storm water piping system
- Simplified environmental review of project
- Yielded significant cost savings overall

Figure 5-9: The building's interior features a range of low-emitting and high performance materials, including rubber and ecopolymeric flooring and PVC-free wall-protection systems. *Credit: Lionakis Beaumont Design Group*

THE CITIZEN: THE SOCIAL VALUE OF SUSTAINABLE HEALTHCARE

At the same time the strategist deals with the financial implications, the citizen reviews the social implications of sustainable building practices and prioritizes the relationship between buildings and health. It is in this realm that the intersection with evidence-based design is most clearly revealed. In the Fable Hospital study, outlined in *The Business Case for Better Buildings* (Berry et al. 2004), the authors used data from the Center for Health Design Pebble Project to define a range of financial returns associated with constructing buildings that reduce stress, improve safety, and contribute to ecological health. This groundbreaking study monetizes a range of organizational benefits ranging from improved staff recruitment, performance, and retention to reduced medical errors and nosocomial infections. While it is possible to assign financial value to these benefits, such avoided or indirect costs are more difficult to quantify and measure.

The Fable Hospital study defined a series of evidence-based best practices in design that increased the capital cost of an average 350-bed community hospital by approximately 12 percent. Through improved performance, however, payback was achieved in just over one year. Some of the innovative design strategies considered in the study resonate with sustainable building, including increased access to daylighting and an increased program emphasis on places of respite. (For an example of the complexity of applying such an analysis to sustainable design strategies, see the sidebar.)

In Chapter 10, a series of studies that correlate improved health with increased indoor air quality are presented to support the idea that sustainable building practices can result in documented and, in some cases, quantifiable health improvements for building occupants (see Figure 10-35). The table below presents estimates of productivity gains that might be realized from improved indoor environmental quality (IEQ) — a combination of daylight, views, and access to improved ventilation and outdoor air.

Estimated Health and Productivity Gains from Improved IEQ for the US

Health effect	Low	Medium	High
Reduced respiratory disease*	6	10	14
Reduced allergies and asthma	2	3	4
Reduced Sick Building Syndrome symptoms	10	20	30
Health-related total	**18**	**33**	**48**
Improvements in productivity/performance unrelated to health	20	90	160
Combined health and productivity total	**38**	**123**	**208**

*All figures in $ billions.
This chart aggregates the financial savings attributable to health and productivity gains that arise from improved building IEQ.
Source: Adapted from Fisk 2000

THE COSTS AND BENEFITS OF AN EMERGING BEST PRACTICES HOSPITAL

This study identifies building fabric and infrastructure capital innovations that could be implemented in the design and construction of a five-hundred-bed tertiary-care replacement hospital in Vancouver, British Columbia, in order to realize a set of specific, quantifiable building operations and care-delivery benefits during the first thirty years of operation. A resonant guiding principle established for the St. Paul's Hospital renewal component of the Providence Legacy Project was to "develop the building to maximize the efficiency of clinical and nonclinical service delivery over the long term."

The study posed two fundamental questions:

1. What specific innovations could be made to improve care delivery—and at what cost?

2. Translated into dollars, how much more productive, and how much less dangerous to patients, would healthcare delivery be?

This study identifies design innovations representing improvements on Canadian hospital construction practices in the mid-1990s. Operational benefits considered are highly dependent upon or facilitated by the built environment. These include reduced nosocomial infection, medical error, patient falls, and medication use by inpatients; increased caregiver productivity; reduced horizontal and vertical travel time and patient transfers; reduced energy consumption; and reduced costs for future layout modifications.

The study places conservative estimates on both costs and benefits. Benefits anticipated to accrue include shorter stays, fewer patient deaths from nosocomial infection or other adverse events, or from reduced litigation costs are not quantified. The significant supportive role of policy and management in implementing and maintaining productivity gains and improved patient safety is also not addressed within the scope of the study.

While many of the recommended design innovations have been implemented individually and their costs and benefits quantified by North American hospitals, there are no built hospitals in Canada or the United States that incorporate all of them. The study aggregates nineteen specific design innovations in order to define an emerging best practices standard.

The design innovations and their costs were organized into four categories:

1. Energy and environment
2. Indoor environmental quality (IEQ)
3. Operational efficiency
4. Infection control

Several design innovations bridged multiple categories, though were categorized in only one. For example, single-acuity adaptable rooms, while primarily intended to reduce nosocomial infections, also substantially reduce patient transfers, improve staff-patient communication, reduce medical errors and in-hospital medication costs, increase privacy for patients, and allow patients to get more rest and better sleep.

Seventeen operational cost savings and/or productivity gains resulting from the recommended design innovations are identified in four cost areas:

1. Building operations
2. Patient care staff labor
3. Human resources
4. Patient care physician labor

There are few instances of a one-to-one correspondence between capital improvements and operational benefits resulting in an overall spider web pattern of interdependent design innovations and operational benefits (see Figures 5-10A and B). A reduction in medical error and other adverse events, for example, is linked to eight design innovations:

(continued)

1. Better air quality and distribution
2. Daylighting
3. Artificial lighting
4. A quiet work environment

5. Work path planning
6. An upgraded communications system
7. Same-handed standardized rooms
8. Single-acuity-adaptable inpatient rooms

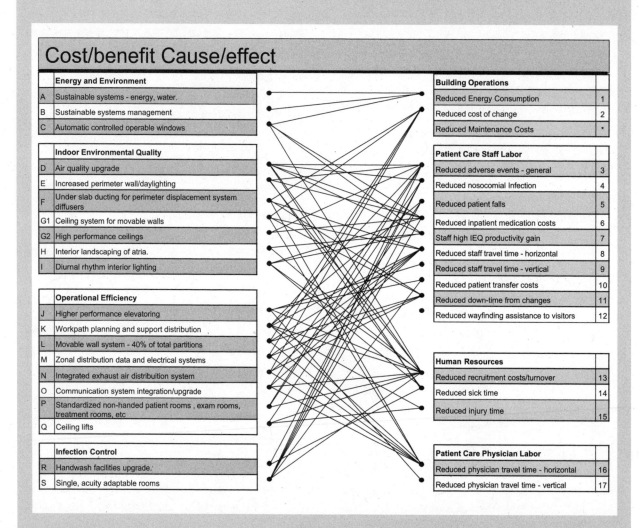

Cost/benefit Cause/effect

	Energy and Environment
A	Sustainable systems - energy, water.
B	Sustainable systems management
C	Automatic controlled operable windows

	Indoor Environmental Quality
D	Air quality upgrade
E	Increased perimeter wall/daylighting
F	Under slab ducting for perimeter displacement system diffusers
G1	Ceiling system for movable walls
G2	High performance ceilings
H	Interior landscaping of atria.
I	Diurnal rhythm interior lighting

	Operational Efficiency
J	Higher performance elevatoring
K	Workpath planning and support distribution
L	Movable wall system - 40% of total partitions
M	Zonal distribution data and electrical systems
N	Integrated exhaust air distribution system
O	Communication system integration/upgrade
P	Standardized non-handed patient rooms , exam rooms, treatment rooms, etc
Q	Ceiling lifts

	Infection Control
R	Handwash facilities upgrade.
S	Single, acuity adaptable rooms

Building Operations	
Reduced Energy Consumption	1
Reduced cost of change	2
Reduced Maintenance Costs	*

Patient Care Staff Labor	
Reduced adverse events - general	3
Reduced nosocomial Infection	4
Reduced patient falls	5
Reduced inpatient medication costs	6
Staff high IEQ productivity gain	7
Reduced staff travel time - horizontal	8
Reduced staff travel time - vertical	9
Reduced patient transfer costs	10
Reduced down-time from changes	11
Reduced wayfinding assistance to visitors	12

Human Resources	
Reduced recruitment costs/turnover	13
Reduced sick time	14
Reduced injury time	15

Patient Care Physician Labor	
Reduced physician travel time - horizontal	16
Reduced physician travel time - vertical	17

Figure 5-10 A and B: There is a complex web of interdependent relationships between design innovations and operational benefits. Figure 5-10A identifies twenty sustainable and evidence-based design innovations and seventeen potential benefits across operations, staff performance, and patient and workplace safety; the interconnected lines demonstrate the web of relationships. Figure 5-10B highlights the evidence-based and sustainable-design innovations linked to reduced medical error. *Credit: Stantec Architecture, Pradinuk 2005, and N. MacConnel*

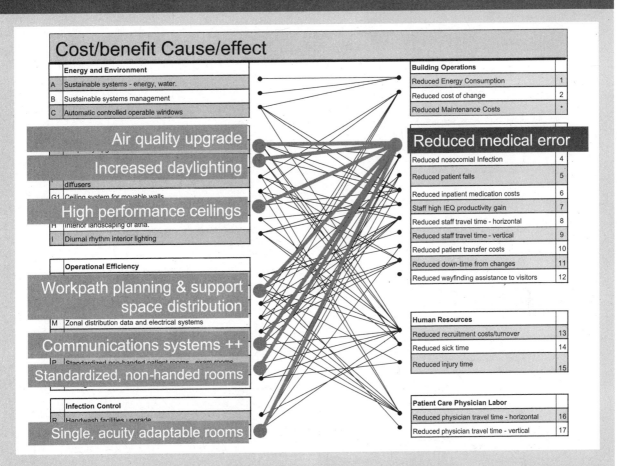

Cost/benefit Cause/effect

	Energy and Environment
A	Sustainable systems - energy, water.
B	Sustainable systems management
C	Automatic controlled operable windows

Air quality upgrade

Increased daylighting

diffusers

| G1 | Ceiling system for movable walls |

High performance ceilings

| | interior landscaping or atria. |
| I | Diurnal rhythm interior lighting |

	Operational Efficiency

Workpath planning & support space distribution

| M | Zonal distribution data and electrical systems |

Communications systems ++

| P | Standardized non-handed patient rooms, exam rooms |

Standardized, non-handed rooms

	Infection Control
R	Handwash facilities upgrade

Single, acuity adaptable rooms

Building Operations	
Reduced Energy Consumption	1
Reduced cost of change	2
Reduced Maintenance Costs	*

Reduced medical error	
Reduced nosocomial Infection	4
Reduced patient falls	5
Reduced inpatient medication costs	6
Staff high IEQ productivity gain	7
Reduced staff travel time - horizontal	8
Reduced staff travel time - vertical	9
Reduced patient transfer costs	10
Reduced down-time from changes	11
Reduced wayfinding assistance to visitors	12

Human Resources	
Reduced recruitment costs/turnover	13
Reduced sick time	14
Reduced injury time	15

Patient Care Physician Labor	
Reduced physician travel time - horizontal	16
Reduced physician travel time - vertical	17

The beneficial effects of the innovations are cumulative: they are greater than the sum of their parts. More emphasis was placed on design innovations that would save caregiver travel time, including high-performance elevatoring, remote charting and finer grained support-space distribution, and extensive use of movable walls and associated systems to allow an incremental adaptation of spatial configuration to program. Time savings were calculated at hourly rates and valued as time freed for improved care rather than as time that could be pooled to reduce full-time equivalent (FTE) staff. Some financial savings were supported by the research data presented in the "Business Case for Better Buildings" (Berry et al. 2004).

The benefits as a package were calculated to have a payback period of just over three years (see Figure 5-11), highly favorable considering the British Columbia government is now entertaining paybacks as high as fifteen years for measures to reduce hard costs such as energy use on publicly funded projects. The existing hospital, together with other comanaged facilities in the region, has already implemented service consolidation and process redesign strategies that have saved approximately 15 percent on operating costs. The business case for the new building will include operating savings equivalent to an additional 12 percent of the in-scope operating budget, of which 7.5 percent is directly building related.

Source: Ray Pradinuk, Stantec Architecture and N. MacConnel

Figure 8: Cost / benefit sub-groupings and yearly benefit as a % of capital cost

	Costs		Benefits		Yearly benefit as % of cost
	Building Operations - Energy		**Energy Cost Savings**		%
A	Sustainable systems - energy, water.	$ 5,000,000	1 Reduced Energy Consumption	$ 1,730,500	
B	Sustainable systems management	$ 5,000,000			
	sub - total	$ 10,000,000	sub - total	$ 1,730,500	17%
	Indoor Environmental Quality		**Operational Impacts - Improved IEQ**		
C	Automatic controlled operable windows	$ 4,000,000	4 Reduced adverse events - general	$ 550,000	
D	Air quality upgrade	$ 10,000,000	6 Reduced inpatient medication costs	$ 3,375,000	
E	Increased perimeter wall/daylighting	$ 9,000,000	7 Staff high IEQ productivity gain	$ 4,500,000	
G2	High performance ceilings	$ 100,000	14 Reduced recruitment costs/turnover	$ 450,000	
H	Interior landscaping of atria.	$ 750,000	15 Reduced sick time	$ 1,125,000	
I	Diurnal rhythm interior lighting	$ 1,200,000			
	sub - total	$ 25,050,000	sub - total	$ 10,000,000	40%
	Operational Efficiency - flexibility & workpath planning		**Operational Impacts - flexibility & workpath planning**		
F	Under slab ducting for perimeter displacement system diffusers	$ 1,850,000	2 Reduced cost of change	$ 2,250,000	
G1	Ceiling system for movable walls	$ 4,000,000	9 Reduced StaffTravel time - horizontal	$ 6,750,000	
L	Movable wall system - 40% of total partitions	$ 7,200,000			
M	Zonal distribution data and electrical systems	$ 1,600,000	12 Reduced down-time from changes	$ 657,000	
N	Integrated exhaust air distribution system	$ 3,180,000			
K	Workpath planning and support distribution	$ 2,500,000	17 Reduced Physician Travel time - horizontal	$ 1,250,000	
O	Communication system integration/upgrade	$ 7,000,000			
	sub - total	$ 27,330,000	sub - total	$ 10,907,000	40%
	Operational Efficiency - high performance elevators		**Operational Impacts - high performance elevators**		
J	Higher performance elevatoring	$ 5,000,000	10 Reduced Staff Travel time - vertical	$ 1,125,000	
			18 Reduced Physician Travel time - vertical	$ 1,250,000	
	sub - total	$ 5,000,000	sub - total	$ 2,375,000	48%
	Operational Efficiency - improved wayfinding		**Operational Impacts - improved wayfinding**		
P	Standardized non-handed patient rooms,		Reduced patient falls	$ 3,795,000	
	Staff Safety		**Staff Safety Impacts**		
Q	Ceiling lifts	$ 4,500,000	16 Reduced injury time	$ 825,000	
	sub - total	$ 4,500,000	sub - total	$ 825,000	18%
	total	$ 96,280,000	total	$ 37,600,000	39%

33% annual rate of return

3.5 year payback period

Costs $96,280,000 | **Yearly Benefit $37,600,000** | **39%**

Figure 5-11: The total cost of all evidence-based and sustainable design innovations totaled $96.28 million while delivering annual benefits estimated at $37.6 million, for a 33 percent rate of return and a 3.5 year payback. Measures related to improved indoor environmental quality—perimeter for daylighting, operable windows, improved ventilation—added $25 million in initial cost while yielding approximately $10 million in operational savings annually, for a 2.5 year payback. The largest contributing factor to savings came from reduced medication costs. All figures in Canadian dollars. *Source: Stantec Architecture, Pradinuk 2005, and N. MacConnel*

Often, additional organizational social benefit is achieved through an integrated design process that engages a wide group of stakeholders, where the building design is viewed as only one component of an institution-wide environmental improvement initiative that involves everyone. As Lance Secretan (2005) put it: "There is no actual nursing shortage. There is a shortage of places that nurses want to work."

Defining organizational and community benefits that arise from sustainable building strategies is the current challenge in healthcare. These benefits need to be defined, quantified, and communicated through industry, much the way the Fable Hospital and examples of best-practices hospitals here provide important initial data to use in quantifying benefits such as staff illness and absenteeism, improved staff performance (through reduced medical errors), reduced hospital-acquired infections, and improved staff recruitment and retention. Yet despite these studies and examples, health and productivity benefits continue to elude quantification. *Building Design and Construction* (2006) offers this conclusion:

> Perhaps the bottom line on the health and human performance benefits of green buildings comes to this: a) if we know from personal and anecdotal experience that having a thermally comfortable, well-lit, properly ventilated work space, preferably with daylight and a view of nature, is likely to have a positive effect on our well-being and morale, and therefore would inspire greater work performance; and b) if sustainable physical elements, such as adequate air exchange, produce any positive benefits in employee health and well-being; and c) if we can build green offices to a high standard at little or no extra cost, then d) why wouldn't we do so?

Interestingly, this search for best practices continues globally. The UK architecture and engineering firm Building Design Partnership (BDP) undertook a comparison of French and British approaches to hospital construction in an effort to determine the factors that contribute to improved building efficiency and health status of French citizens. (See below for a summary of the findings.)

At the same time, hospitals have realized that enormous social benefits accrue from implementing improved environmental performance strategies through operations. Whether organizations receive recognition for recycling programs, reductions in medical waste incineration, or implementation of farmers' markets on-site, environmental improvement programs resonate with communities. To date, many sustainable healthcare projects have engaged in sustainable design to reduce both real and perceived community impacts from their development footprint. Some municipalities have instituted expedited approval processes for LEED projects, particularly for sites with drainage and water-quality challenges.

A REPORT ON FRENCH HOSPITALS

What distinguishes cost and performance between hospitals in the UK and in France? To answer this question, the UK-based architecture and engineering firm BDP undertook a study to "improve the way design and construction is procured, taking the best of both UK and French thinking" and to highlight "areas where design makes a difference to healthcare outcomes and where design and build practice determines the cost of construction and operation" (BDP 2004).

Among the key findings:

- *Construction costs:* At 2002 rates, French hospitals cost between one-half and two-thirds of the British hospitals per square meter; the costs per bed are similar. In France, single-bed wards are standard, hence the area per bed is much higher in France. Arguably, each French bed space outperforms its British counterpart.

- *Utility costs:* Utility costs in France are less than half those in the UK. Ambitious automation and information and communications technology (ICT) are used in France.

- *Building costs:* Building-envelope costs dominate French examples, reflecting the French plan for natural daylighting and ventilation that generate more gross plan area per building perimeter than British examples.

(continued)

- **Construction efficiencies:** Contractor-led detail design seems to contribute to the economy of means in French hospitals.

- **Benefits to patients and staff:** The French approach contributes to better health outcomes. Single-bed wards hasten recovery. Daylit plans and good amenities aid staff well-being. Better architecture fosters community pride and user morale.

- **Decentralized services:** Other published research suggests that future healthcare-related building needs to put more emphasis on local and home-based care, aided by ICT. There will still be a need for hospitals to cater to the more seriously ill, but they will need to be built more quickly, economically, flexibly, sustainably—and based on life cycle economics. Supportive design features will speed patient recovery.

- **Research agenda:** Further design research is suggested on single-room economics, servicing and sustainability, the supportive environment, design-quality indicators, labor-saving systems, and lifetime costing. Existing links to research teams should be expanded.

- **French hospitals as a model of best practices:** Healthcare architecture is in a period of rapid change, with rising aspirations meeting new thinking about needs and construction. French practice could form a valuable model for the UK, combining the best thinking from both countries.

Source: BDP 2004

Key to the French success is their universal use of single-patient rooms and abundant daylight and views throughout their buildings, supported by decades of practice and by legal requirements. Since the 1980s, single-patient rooms have been standard in all new French hospitals, while French law requires daylight in all regularly occupied spaces: windows in operating theaters, for example, are standard. The study notes that health outcomes in French hospitals are generally superior to those in the UK, and that public trust in the French system exceeds that in the UK. The BDP's comparative data are compelling, particularly as the value of design features is understood within the context of outcomes and construction costs.

RISK AVOIDANCE

Another factor in the business case is the perception that green building provides a reduction in obsolescence and reduces risks such as employee errors, slip-and-fall accidents (due to improved materials), and mold occurrence. A range of "future-proofing" discussions accompany sustainable building benefits. The Fireman's Fund became the first US insurance company to offer discounted premiums on green buildings. Globally, more than 190 green-based insurance products and services have been documented by Ceres, a Boston-based environmental research organization (Mills and Lecomte 2006). Another important benefit, passive survivability, describes the ability of the hospital to remain in operation during prolonged disruption to utility supplies or service deliveries. Sustainable design measures provide an added level of resilience to buildings that may be required to remain in service through prolonged service disruption—whether from extreme weather events or utility infrastructure disruption.

THE SEEKER: ENVIRONMENTAL LEADERSHIP

Until there are enough green healthcare buildings to study and the business case is proven, sustainable healthcare construction will be accomplished by a select group of industry leaders. Why do healthcare organizations strive to be leaders in this area? They do it to enhance patient outcomes, their community and medical reputations, improve staff recruitment and retention, and increase market share, philanthropic support, and research grants. Each of these considerations is directly affected by sustainable building practices.

For many leaders undertaking green buildings, there are sustainable building strategies that have no quantifiable direct or indirect financial benefits. Yet organizations are undertaking them anyway. For example, Boulder Community Hospital restored degraded wetlands and returned 32 of its 49-acre (16-hectare) site to the city as permanent open space. How is that benefit captured?

Many healthcare organizations look to private philanthropy to assist in funding those initiatives that have no direct or indirect financial return, but have demonstrated social or environmental benefit. Examples of these initiatives might include features such as therapeutic gardens or habitat restoration. Some early adopters have directly attributed their green building initiatives to private gifts. Lacks Cancer Center at St. Mary's Health Care describes its LEED project as a testimony to three things: the commitment of Richard Lacks to fund a consolidated cancer care facility in honor of his father and grandfather; Peter Wege's gift directed specifically toward sustainability; and the willingness of St. Mary's to take on a new challenge. It began when Peter Wege invited the hospital to an opening of a LEED-certified office building in Grand Rapids, Michigan.

In 2003 the Kresge Foundation launched a green building initiative, becoming the first major philanthropic organization to commit to fund green building. Since then, Kresge has funded a number of the *Green Guide*'s pilot and LEED-certified case study projects presented in this book, either through planning grants or its capital challenge grant program. Between 2003 and 2006, Kresge distributed $7.2 million to forty-two nonprofits as LEED bonus grants, rewarding capital challenge grant recipients with significant bonuses for achieving certification. With a stated mission to "ad-

> *With Peter Wege's involvement, the momentum and the spirit captured us all. He was giving us a tour of Steelcase's new facility, and we began to think that we could incorporate similar strategies in our new building. Peter Wege, the retired vice-chairman of the board of Steelcase, had not yet decided at that point in his gift giving that his financial contributions had to be used toward LEED (or sustainable) buildings. We said, "We think it's important to do because we can see the benefits." The more we talked, the more excited we all became and realized it was possible and doable. We loved the challenge. That was in 2001.*
>
> —PHILIP H. MCCORKLE, JR., PRESIDENT AND CEO, ST. MARY'S HEALTH CARE, GRAND RAPIDS, MICHIGAN

vance the well-being of humanity," it is not surprising that the Kresge Foundation would make a link between sustainable building and health (Kresge 2007).

The public and private business sectors are accelerating green building initiatives with programs ranging from tax credits to utility-based demand-reduction incentives. In some regions, substantial programs are in place for subsidizing on-site renewable energy installations. In the nonprofit healthcare sector, utility incentives are a strong motivator. The Oregon Health & Science University (OHSU) Center for Health & Healing (see the case study in Chapter 10) received more than $1.6 million in incentives

> *The Kresge gift was a major boost because it validated to our board of trustees that this was a good thing to do. Kresge stayed with us, and ultimately we received a challenge grant and a LEED bonus grant. It's been a rewarding partnership. The building is a remarkable care asset that has people in the agency saying, "To focus on improved indoor air quality when your predominant population has upper-respiratory concerns is a good idea."*
>
> —PATRICK DOLLARD, CEO, THE CENTER FOR DISCOVERY

(as a partnership with a private developer, approximately half of the incentives were achieved through tax-credit programs). The Center for Discovery in Harris, New York (see the case study in Chapter 11), received approximately $200,000 in utility incentives through the New York State Energy Research and Development Authority (NYSERDA). The Providence Newberg Medical Center in Providence, Oregon (see the case study in Chapter 10), received approximately $200,000 from the Energy Trust of Oregon for energy-efficiency measures. The Heinz Endowments, located in Pittsburgh, has been a major supporter of the University of Pittsburgh Medical Center's (UPMC) green building initiative, presented in the case study below.

Children's Hospital of Pittsburgh/ University of Pittsburgh Medical Center (UPMC)

Pittsburgh, Pennsylvania

Figure 5-12: Children's Hospital of Pittsburgh/University of Pittsburgh Medical Center. *Credit: © 2006 Astorino*

Owner: Children's Hospital of Pittsburgh of UPMC
Design team:
ARCHITECTS, INTERIOR DESIGNERS, COMMISSIONING, LEED CONSULTANTS, LANDSCAPE ARCHITECTS, AND STRUCTURAL ENGINEERS: Astorino
ELEVATOR, MATERIALS, AND WASTE MANAGEMENT CONSULTANTS: Lerch, Bates & Associates, Inc.
SITE/CIVIL ENGINEERS: KAG Engineering, Inc.
MEDICAL EQUIPMENT CONSULTANTS: Gene Burton & Associates, Inc.
Building type: New and renovation
Size: 1,450,000 sq ft (134, 709 sq m)
Program description: Clinical services with 9 floors of inpatient and outpatient care areas; 41-bed emergency room and trauma center; 13 operating suites; 36-bed pediatric intensive care unit; 12-bed cardiac intensive care unit; 31-bed neonatal intensive care unit; 10-story research facility; 2 office buildings, 3 parking garages; library, healing garden, day care and fitness center, conference center, and atrium
Completion date: 2009
Awards/recognition: *Green Guide for Health Care* pilot

The new UPMC Children's Hospital of Pittsburgh is under construction on the urban campus of a former hospital in the Lawrenceville neighborhood of the city. In his article "Environmental Sensitivity in Children's Healthcare" (2006), architect Timothy Powers of Astorino writes: "By opting to locate the new hospital on this existing campus, the hospital will benefit from many of the assets already in place while the increased economic activity it will generate will help revitalize the immediate urban neighborhood."

KEY PERFORMANCE STRATEGIES

Site
- Easy access to public transportation
- Available bike racks and showers
- Preferred parking for car pools

Water
- Water-efficient landscaping
- Recycling of water where appropriate
- Installation of water fixtures that reduce water use

Energy
- Campuswide central plant to improve efficiency at the source level

Figure 5-13: This experiential rooftop healing garden is an exterior extension of an adjoining four-story inpatient atrium, providing patients and their families the opportunity to experience nature without leaving the safety of the inpatient unit. *Credit: © 2006 Astorino*

Materials

- 30 percent of the existing building area will be reused
- Local and regional construction materials
- Low volatile organic compound (VOC)–content sealants, adhesives, paints, and carpets
- Low mercury content and polyvinyl chloride (PVC) reduction

Environmental Quality

- Maximum daylight and views
- Installation of air filtration systems that increase indoor air quality
- Quiet building emphasizes acoustic environment

Source: Astorino

UPMC has established a green team to initiate a range of green operation initiatives in anticipation of the building's completion. It is now working with its Community Development Corporation on incentive programs that will allow staff to purchase housing in the immediate Lawrenceville area. "Doing things differently is really challenging," says Roger Oxendale, president and CEO of Children's Hospital of Pittsburgh. "What do we do in terms of pest control and environmental services? How will recycling impact our purchasing policies?"

> *Another major theme that emerged in our design process was that of transformation, whether it was a patient coming in ill and leaving well or an employee saying, "This day I want to be able to have a significant impact on the care of this organization and on people's lives."*
>
> —ROGER OXENDALE, PRESIDENT AND CEO, UPMC CHILDREN'S HOSPITAL OF PITTSBURGH

There is no shortage of public relations and marketing benefits from green building initiatives. Many healthcare organizations' spokespeople remark that it is difficult to get positive local press —until they undertake green building. Such are among the most powerful benefits that early adopters have realized; most have been surprised by the consistent level of interest locally and regionally. In some markets, public relations saturation may already be approaching, but for healthcare, the groundswell is only beginning. As healthcare organizations develop and sell their improved building and operational performance, the market will continue to respond.

In the summer of 2006, Gail Vittori, Robin Guenther, FAIA, and Jean Hansen, IIDA, Chong Partners, interviewed Kaiser Permanente's John Kouletsis, AIA, national director, planning and design services; and Tom Cooper, manager, strategic sourcing and technology, on the topic of how Kaiser Permanente builds a business case for sustainable building initiatives. The interview is excerpted here:

JEAN HANSEN: *How does Kaiser Permanente define its sphere of influence for green building? Your mission is to take care of your members—and the communities they live in. How does sustainable building reinforce that broader vision?*

JOHN KOULETSIS: Kaiser's leadership gets it. Our current CEO, George Halvorson, and previous CEO, David Lawrence, have been consistent in their commitment to environmental stewardship. Because of the way this issue is interwoven with our core values, it's been supported very vigorously at the highest levels of management for at least twenty years.

Having said that, one could ask, "Why is healthcare so far behind many other industries in terms of sustainable design?" I don't think anyone could argue that healthcare has a sterling silver record around sustainability. It's an industry that has not made money for a long time. Sustainability has always been conflated with "more money." I constantly hear, "Healthcare just can't afford to do that." We counter that argument with two points: first, it doesn't need to cost more if you determine and focus on the right issues; second, we cannot afford not to be involved. This is absolutely a defining, seminal issue for the healthcare industry. It's unconscionable that healthcare should be behind the curve.

There are people out there developing solid frameworks for making decisions about sustainable buildings (rather than generalized notions like, "well, this seems like a good thing to do"). It's clear that we are degrading our environment at an alarming rate; we have to turn that around. So let's base our actions on some strong (though

> *Sustainability doesn't need to cost more if you determine and focus on the right issues. And we cannot afford not to be involved. This is absolutely a defining, seminal issue for the healthcare industry. It's unconscionable that healthcare should be behind the curve.*
>
> —JOHN KOULETSIS, AIA, NATIONAL DIRECTOR, PLANNING AND DESIGN SERVICES, KAISER PERMANENTE

not incontrovertible) causal evidence and find ways to do it that are economically achievable. What we discovered is that the information is out there. We are getting there—we might just be moving more slowly than we'd like.

We don't look at sustainability as the single banner under which all Kaiser Permanente gathers—but it's integral to Kaiser Permanente's three safety banners—workplace, patient, environment. None is separable from the other. As we look at sustainability's benefits and impacts beyond just being a good steward of the earth, there are safety improvements, labor-management improvements, and environmental health improvements. Environmental health is a huge piece of our promise to the labor-management partnership that we will not compromise about—we will not put our staff in harm's way.

TOM COOPER: There is a longstanding relationship between Kaiser Permanente and its employees around workplace safety issues and a longstanding alliance with the labor unions. We understand that the people who work for us are also members, that their health is important to our success and mission, and that they are in our buildings for extended time periods. If we can reduce sick days and reduce injuries, there's a business case around those issues that both benefits the bottom line and improves our relationship with our employees. The same thing is true with patient safety. A lot of these new materials appear to improve patient safety and connect to other environmental initiatives as well. This program fits well into the larger program at Kaiser Permanente: the Three Safeties. *(continued)*

Once different stakeholders within the company — members, labor unions, caregivers — are educated about what's going on, the demand increases internally to drive up that bar. Our office is doing that education — creating the customers for each building team. They bring up these issues and generate more demand internally. It's a long journey — it's a huge company. Our members — consumer demand — will also drive the change.

JOHN KOULETSIS: How do you communicate with 145,000 employees to tell them what you are doing to improve their workplace? Our national union rep, who is very interested in measures to protect our workers from exposure to potentially harmful chemicals in the indoor environment, sits on our executive committee. At our monthly leadership meetings, his excitement about communicating our work back to his membership is phenomenal. He's a key part of getting information to and support from this large workforce.

JEAN HANSEN: *How would you apportion the effort you put behind various sustainability issues? How do you make decisions about the level of attention you place on topics such as energy, water, materials, and environmental quality? A lot of architects think about energy as the top sustainability issue, and in California, water is certainly our next big issue. Why does market transformation rank highly in view of these other important and perhaps competing priorities?*

TOM COOPER: Energy is low-hanging fruit. Because we own and operate 64 million square feet of physical plant in over nine hundred buildings, we are very conscious about our operating budgets. For fifteen years we have looked at energy decisions on a total-cost-of-ownership basis — including operating and capital costs. We recognize that the lowest first-cost equipment is often less efficient, and the savings is dwarfed by the energy costs — you end up paying the savings twenty times over. We did things around energy before we ever did anything around materials because they impacted our economic bottom line and were so obvious.

But that also means that life cycle cost analysis is thoroughly embraced, because we understand that it's about the total cost of ownership, not the first cost. We are a healthcare company. That the benefits you get from best-practice, efficient operations accrue to the system permeates the way we do things. We benchmark against other systems — that's part of our culture.

On materials, it's not only that many new products are healthier and eliminate toxins — polyvinyl chloride or brominated flame retardants or other chemicals of concern — many of the new products outperform the generation of materials they are replacing. People forget that today's products have some performance disadvantages — they confuse convenience with performance. They've gotten so used to them that their performance disadvantages are no longer evident. These new materials have other performance attributes that move them out in front of the existing products in life cycle cost assessment — in the case of flooring, for example, it's reduced slips and falls, easier cleaning protocols, and that they're quieter and softer underfoot.

JOHN KOULETSIS: There's also a recognition that history has given us reason to think about material hazards — asbestos, for example. Once you know that there are toxic chemicals in products you are using in your buildings, you have an obligation to do something about it. Kaiser Permanente is beginning to use the precautionary principle to manage risk: in five or ten years, there may be the science to definitively prove that we should have avoided this material, so let's try to move away from it earlier. Individuals — and healthcare organizations — have to stand up and say that we will not wait for someone else to take action, that we will vote with our purchasing power and stand for safer alternatives.

TOM COOPER: We will continue to push the market to develop alternatives to those materials in the building process that contain chemicals of concern in order to improve patient, staff, and environmental safety. While the movement of health providers that share our concerns may seem small now, it's going to keep growing geometrically, and more and more products will be introduced in the US. The market for safer products is going to grow in huge waves, and we want to be positioned to collaborate with other like-minded companies pushing it forward, whether it's jacketing on wiring and cable or the technologies associated with HVAC-related renewable energy. Operationally, energy costs are huge, and as they increase, we are likely to see more interesting system development.

Our principle with regard to market transformation or new products has always been: it can't cost Kaiser Permanente more money. That's the first thing we look at. The challenges are associated with cost and product performance.

GAIL VITTORI: *One question: the statement, "It can't cost more money—are you determining that based on first cost or some form of life cycle cost that you talked about earlier relative to energy? How are you playing those two pots of money?*

TOM COOPER: We first look at first cost. Our goal, initially, is to not pay a first-cost premium for a preferred material. If that's not possible, we look at payback and life cycle cost. So there has to be something else about the product that reduces maintenance or impacts some other aspect of our operations like reducing injuries. We can use that savings to pay for the increased first cost. But when we approach manufacturers to partner with us on a new sustainable product—it doesn't matter what it is—we tell them that it can't cost more than what we currently pay for a comparable product. Generally, we look at achieving less than a three-year payback for increased first costs.

ROBIN GUENTHER: *Does that mission translate into "improving the health of the communities we serve"? How are you envisioning making the life cycle cost analysis more sophisticated in order to better understand what are now identified as " intangibles," particularly at the community scale, in terms of the benefit analysis.*

TOM COOPER: Part of this is about marketing. We have the Thrive Campaign, which is looking at health and lifestyle. Our marketing folks are very interested in the sustainable building program because it fits in perfectly with the broader campaign. By building smarter, better buildings that have fewer impacts on the communities we serve, we're promoting that same view that the campaign is projecting to potential members.

JOHN KOULETSIS: We have recent examples of how this resonates with our members and among the communities where we operate. The Modesto facility, one of the first templated hospitals, has a great sustainability champion in Mike Hrast, our project director, who has really advocated for green building—whether it's photovoltaic screens for rooftop mechanical equipment, biodiesel, porous paving—any number of innovative strategies. He's reported back to us that the marketing people are taking companies that might want to join Kaiser Permanente through the facility and talking about how the design speaks to the mission statement. We're curious to see what happens with Modesto—the greenest building we've built to date. Will it have an impact on membership?

JEAN HANSEN: *Just because a product meets environmental standards, it doesn't mean it meets your needs. How do you work with design teams to define and solve the right problem?*

JOHN KOULETSIS: When we go to new medical centers and talk about xeriscaping—we tell them it will use fewer chemicals and save hundreds of thousands of gallons of water—they say: "You mean I don't have to mow it and pick up dead leaves? That's great." They focus on their pinch points—in this case staffing. If they don't have the staff to maintain that turf grass lawn to the satisfaction of management and members, they are ready for a change that is easier for them to take care of. After that, they'll look at the environmental benefit. If we step into their world for a moment, the conversation changes.

(continued)

TOM COOPER: It's all about change. You're introducing something that's different from what people are used to. If they don't have a comfort level with a new product or system, it won't work if all you can tell them is that it's better for the environment. For example, I was in a facility last week that has been almost totally renovated with an alternative resilient floor product. There are a few places with problems—and that's all the staff wants to focus on and talk about. When I toured the facility, I was stunned by how beautiful it looked and how important the floor is to that transformation. But because of the few problems, they want it removed. At some point, they don't care about environmental performance or even the aesthetic—their issues are, who's going to complain about the problem spots next? and how am I going to deal with this today?

JEAN HANSEN: *Talk a bit about how you create champions and innovations projects. Can any organization develop champions deeply embedded in this work and within their organizations?*

TOM COOPER: We have a High Performance Buildings Committee, which is what we call our green buildings committee. It includes representation from different sectors of the organization—different stakeholders, regions, disciplines of the company that are all affected by this work. We also have representation from the design consultants and contractors we use as well as from nongovernmental organizations—Health Care Without Harm and the Healthy Building Network. We recently established two tiers—permanent and rotating members. Because the rotating members are often project team architects and contractors, they become members and champions of the committee work in the projects they do for us. They go out and spread that information to their peers.

We also have a series of innovations projects. Using the *Green Guide for Health Care,* we developed a checklist. Category 1 points are items incorporated in our Kaiser Permanente standards or required by code. These become the minimum requirements for our project teams. Category 2 are items that are not in our standards but are reasonably simple to implement with a modest amount of research by us or our project teams—we encourage them to research items in collaboration with us in the context of innovations projects. Items that teams are looking at include displacement ventilation, renewable energy, hybrid chiller plants, and innovative materials. We provide them with support and guidance, but the teams take ownership of the innovation—that's another way in which we spread credit for developing great ideas and implementing positive changes for Kaiser Permanente. Eventually, this will spread geometrically within the organization, forming a web of champions among us and our outside architects and contractors. We believe the process will produce a stronger base of better, smarter buildings for Kaiser Permanente, based on a standard while responsive to local community and individual team vision.

CONCLUSION

Ultimately, healthcare is making business cases using economic, social, and environmental benefit calculations. The innovators and fast followers have not waited for a proven business case, but have forged ahead and created it as they have designed their buildings. For most, they viewed the business case in terms of improved health coupled with a certain risk-reward equation. Whatever the risk, there was an inherent belief that the rewards would ultimately emerge—whether in reduced utility bills, improved staff retention and morale, occupant health, or perceived community leadership. Most did not choose to study or quantify those benefits through peer-reviewed research projects. None initially believed they would be seen as the leaders they have become through constructing these buildings. They chose, simply, to lead their organizations into the future. In so doing, they have defined a new path for healthcare.

CHAPTER 6

Design Process

> We need to cultivate and bring together both the inspiration which gives moral force to our ideas and the sense of listening to environment which makes those ideas appropriate.
> —CHRISTOPHER DAY, *Places of the Soul*

> When you build a thing, you cannot merely build that thing in isolation, but must also repair the world around it, and within it, so that the large world at that one place becomes more coherent, and more whole; and the thing which you make takes its place in the web of nature, as you make it.
> —CHRISTOPHER ALEXANDER, *A Pattern Language*

INTRODUCTION

Successful sustainable building requires reconsideration of the traditional project delivery process—a daunting undertaking in the healthcare sector. There's an axiom in healthcare parlance that the shortest projects take five years to complete and major projects often require ten. With the increasing scale of healthcare buildings, costs of major new projects commonly approach $1 billion. Program and regulatory complexity, site acquisition, and environmental impact reviews, followed by the complex sequencing of the design and construction process, make healthcare projects among the most challenging to actualize.

Green buildings outperform traditional brown buildings—a demonstrated benefit of design integration (Kats 2003, Matthiessen and Morris 2004). The siting, shell, materials, and systems are optimized in a systemic way throughout the whole building, rather than component by component. Finely calibrated design integration creates synergies, reducing initial cost and delivering sustained, improved performance. Optimizing the results, however, begins with reengineering the design and construction process.

Current project delivery processes are not necessarily delivering optimized value. Often, the design and construction processes are unable to keep up with the pace of technological innovation, resulting in buildings that are approaching obsolescence when they open their doors. Traditional forms of project delivery—design-bid-build and construction management—are being challenged to respond to the need for flexibility and

129

innovation in healthcare projects as cost and schedule considerations prevail. Increasingly complex regulations —most recently, infection control risk assessment (ICRA) guidelines— have emerged in response to issues around the health and safety of building occupants in the midst of construction.

This chapter examines how health-based sustainable design considerations influence the design and production process of healthcare buildings. The integrative design process frames the discussion of "whole building" design. Architect Bill Reed discusses the importance of mindset, who sits at the design table, and whole-systems and living-systems thinking as it informs the design process. Engineer and educator J. A. Vanegas applies a health mindset and articulates a proactive construction process informed by sustainable building considerations. The chapter also includes case studies of sustainable healthcare buildings whose design teams have pursued innovative design processes to achieve their sustainable building goals.

INTEGRATED DESIGN PROCESS

A key principle behind sustainable building practice is an integrated design process. This approach is distinguished from conventional design by establishing a highly collaborative, multidisciplinary team at a project's inception and empowering this team to understand and develop all the aspects of the building, its site design, and, in some cases, its operation. Many in the sustainable building movement trace this concept to the workshops, squatter sessions, and charrettes developed by architects in the 1960s, most notably the firm of Caudill Rowlett Scott in Houston and the Architects Collaborative in Boston.

A traditional, iterative design process respects professional silos. The site engineer may receive a base drawing and instructions for moving forward at a meeting that does not include plumbing engineers or landscape architects. Mechanical systems are sized using rule-of-thumb principles largely uninformed by the particulars of orientation or building envelope. The tendency is to believe that client and consultant services are optimized through strict definition and by monitoring traditional service boundaries. An integrated design process proposes that the best ideas emerge when participants cross the usual boundaries because their views are not as limited by familiarity with the way things are usually done (Malin 2005). In sustainable design, nonstandard strategies that increase costs in one discipline or trade often reduce costs in another. But without a highly integrated process for tracking design decision making, many of these benefits (or synergies) could not be realized.

Integrated design may carry many other names— often, consultants believe *integrative design* is more evocative of process. Others use the term *whole building design* to connote the goal of a team optimizing the design of the "whole building" rather than merely its members' particular department or system. Whatever the term, the process is fundamentally, radically different from the traditional design approach to major healthcare projects and requires a new definition of team, a new process, and specialized tools. It also demands a new mindset, new forms of communication, and strong leadership. Integrated design is not more expensive, nor does it require more time, though it may reallocate time and dollars to the early phases of design that later get recouped as the design process ensues. By definition, integrated design requires no outside expertise, nor does it demand a strong vision —vision is, in fact, one of the process's most important deliverables. Once defined, this vision defines and guides the project from inception to completion.

Because healthcare buildings are among the most complex, program-driven project types and often require a broad range of specialty subconsultants and large numbers of user-stakeholders, construction managers, and owner-representatives, it is tempting to believe that the industry is already practicing integrated design. After all, how many more people could one actually engage in a design process? In fact, the firms that developed squatter sessions and charrettes designed complex, program-driven buildings that needed highly interactive processes to resolve competing interests.

Are the right people on the team? Have the right questions been framed? Is the team challenged? Do the members value their participation, and are they creating a shared vision that optimizes the owner's resources toward the best project possible? How is the project defined? How are competing values, interests, and needs resolved?

MINDSET

Mindset is the foremost challenge to designing a successful sustainable building. Mindset describes the mental models that form our views of the world, green building, and healthcare design. "Mindset can be thought of as the implicit worldview that we carry without even realizing that we're carrying it" (Malin 2005). When a design team operates within the usual set of assumptions and relationships, green measures will be sacrificed to schedule and budget constraints:

some ideas will simply challenge conventional wisdom and be discarded. In an integrated design process, however, conventional solutions are viewed as unacceptable, and the team is committed to seeking new design solutions.

In her landmark essay "Leverage Points: Places to Intervene in a System," scientist and systems analyst Donella Meadows (1999) ranked numbers (cost, subsidies, rebates, etc.)—which we tend to focus on defining —as least effective at shifting systems. In her words, fixation with this is "diddling with details, arranging the deck chairs on the Titanic." Mindset, or paradigm shift, she contends, is considered the most important leverage point. She summed up the challenge as follows: "I don't think there are cheap tickets to system change. You have to work at it.... In the end, it seems that leverage has less to do with pushing levers than it does with disciplined thinking combined with strategically, profoundly, madly letting go."

In the following essay, architect Bill Reed explores the use of whole-systems health principles to reveal opportunities for a design team to link social, technical, and physical (i.e., earth) systems into a mutually supportive built environment. He terms this process "integrative design."

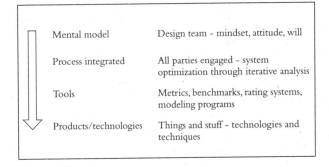

Mental model	Design team – mindset, attitude, will
Process integrated	All parties engaged – system optimization through iterative analysis
Tools	Metrics, benchmarks, rating systems, modeling programs
Products/technologies	Things and stuff – technologies and techniques

Figure 6-1: While much of the design team's attention is focused on product and technologies, the team requires effective design tools to optimize selection and specification. In turn, design tools must be utilized as part of an intentional process. The design process is often a product of the mental model. Sustainability requires a fundamental shift in the mental model. *Source: Diagram based on the work of Barbra Batshalom and Bill Reed (2005).*

Bill Reed, AIA

*T*he integrative design and delivery process is acknowledged by experienced green designers as the essential aspect of achieving a building project with high levels of cost-effective environmental performance. Yet shifting the nature and practice of design from a linear, simplistic cause-and-effect process to one that considers issues from multiple and interrelated systems perspectives is resisted more than any other aspect of green design. The process of change is certainly hard, but knowing something about the change required may help us work toward the purpose of this process.

SHIFTING MENTAL MODELS

Green building rating systems are important tools when effectively used in an integrative process. When rating-system checklists are relegated to a series of add-on strategies, cost and inefficiency complicate and negatively impact the design process.

Sustainable design requires a mindset or mental model that facilitates looking at systems in a more complete way. Instead of examining just the physical elements of the building, the invisible connections among the elements must also be understood. These invisible connections and patterns may manifest in the downstream impact of toxins in building materials, the multiple efficiency and cost relationships among the many variables in a heating, ventilating, and air-conditioning (HVAC) system and the building envelope, or the impact on social systems due to logging practices or any raw material extraction. Since no one has all of this knowledge individually, the role of the team takes on great importance in systems understanding.

Holding design charrettes puts us in a position to begin a systems approach but does not necessarily mean we have changed the way we think and how we understand and process the complexity of technical and living systems. While most of us feel we are systems designers because of the nature of our work—we deliver complex buildings—we usually are not. A whole-systems approach requires a different mental model.

In order to achieve different results, it is necessary to think differently.

WHOLE-SYSTEMS AND LIVING-SYSTEMS THINKING

The fundamental aspect of this new mental model is whole-systems thinking. Western culture generally lives in a conceptual world of either-or logic and simplistic cause-and-effect thinking. We fragment, isolate, bifurcate, and package complex issues—humans versus nature, science versus religion, tangible versus spiritual—into those that can be analyzed by reduction and others not easily quantified or impossible to measure. As a result, we separate understanding into realms of mind and heart, realism and idealism, logic and intuition, quantity and quality. But the world is not really an either-or phenomenon; it is a whole of both-and.

The result of conventional thinking is a reductionist and incomplete mental model. Scientists reduce the interactions of complex systems into a worthwhile but incomplete understanding of the elements that make the system healthy and functional. Medical doctors treat cancer but fail to address the health of the whole patient. Society permits the sources of cancer to continue to be manufactured while paying the price for ineffective and incomplete healing. Architects and engineers address the efficiency of buildings while failing to understand the earth systems that are the very ones we are trying to sustain. Urban planners use formal design guidelines to pattern communities that are "alive" without understanding or addressing the health of the ecosystems that sustain and inform life in the place they are creating.

One of the difficult issues our culture has in defining sustainability is that people are looking for a definition of what "it" is. Our culture and language are so dominantly object oriented that we have a difficult time moving into a worldview that requires both quantitative and qualitative understanding—a world of interrelationships and processes of life, not simply of things. The nature of this broken perception is reflected in a comparison of language between two worldviews. "An Algonquin Indian... when he has to speak English instead of his MicMaq language says, 'he feels he is being forced to interact with a world of objects, things, rigid boundaries and categories in place of a more familiar world of flows, processes, activities, transformations and energies'" (Peat 1995).

The essence of sustainability is sustaining life. Life is not a static thing; a static condition is dead. Life is an evolving process. Sustainability is not a thing, nor does the process of sustainability have an end point. Achieving a sustainable condition requires us to engage with life on its own terms—as a living, evolving, interconnected, and mutually supportive enterprise. Sustainability is a progression toward a functional awareness that all things are connected; that the systems of commerce, technology, building, society, geology, habitat, soil, and other earth systems are really one system of integrated relationships; and that these systems are coparticipants in the evolution of life.

An integrated design process, by definition, will address all these systems in a way that helps us understand and link the parts of the whole—the whole process of all the subsystems that make up the processes of life. There are no boundaries that limit the scope of integration other than the boundaries we assume.

MAKING AND SUSTAINING THE SHIFT

An integrated design process creates opportunities for the design team to link the many parts of social, technical, and earth systems into a coherent and mutually supportive whole system. To do this effectively we need to shift our worldview from making pieces of the system more efficient to understanding that every aspect of the planet is in a relationship with the others—a shift from doing things to the system to participating in the system.

As practitioners evolve in their capability to function in a more integral way, design teams will initially need to create some boundary around the scope of the integration effort (see sidebar).

If we continue to try to justify green design from a perspective of cost savings and a better way to build, at the end of the day, we will still be operating from the same incremental and fragmented perspective that put us in this situation in the first place. The process of transformative change is the leap we must make to move quickly toward achieving a truly sustainable condition. A deep integrative design approach built on a foundation of aligning the participants around a systems perspective and purpose for this work—sustain-

SCOPING THE INTEGRATIVE DESIGN EFFORT

1. Understand the process of linking the technical systems in a building—the typical example is the reduction of air-conditioning equipment size and cost by spending an equivalent amount on high-performance glazing and daylighting techniques. For the same cost, buildings use less energy and the occupants benefit through higher indoor environmental quality.

2. Link microclimate, site, and landscape aspects to further reduce energy use in the building, reduce the cost of infrastructure for storm water, and increase water quality and groundwater recharge. A further ring of issues relates to transportation and energy sources for the building: the efficiency of electricity production, sunlight for energy, and so on.

3. Develop a relationship between people and their place, growing an understanding of how the health of living systems (humans, streams, habitat, air quality, etc.) can be restored, how the process of engaging the stakeholders can breathe new consciousness in their care of that place, and how social systems can be seen to interrelate with the health of the ecosystem. A healthy community evolves from this conscious awareness of reciprocal benefit.

ing life as an integrated, healthily evolving whole—should ultimately be the objective of any sustainable design process. This may not seem to be practical at this stage in society's willingness to embrace ecologic thinking; however, there are practitioners and communities that have been designing and thinking at this level for decades—Curitiba, Brazil, for one.

There is no simple, cause-and-effect recipe for embracing a whole-systems design approach. A nonlinear, whole system requires multiple access points and different ways of seeing, or lenses, that reinforce each other until a whole picture emerges. The multiple access points come from the various participants in an integrative design process representing different subsystems and stakeholders (energy, water, habitat, social, economic, etc.). The different lenses may be healthy building materials, carbon dioxide balancing, the Natural Step, input/output analysis, life cycle assessment, LEED, or the Green Guide to Health Care (GGHC). The process of understanding a whole system is similar to how a blind man understands the whole of the elephant. The approach requires circling around all the issues multiple times, iterating and optimizing the relationships that will fulfill the purpose of this work: long-term health.

BASIC ASPECTS OF AN INTEGRATIVE DESIGN PROCESS

- All participants should be co-learners—those with a willingness to change.
  - Don't engage insecure "experts." Avoid egos.
  - The integrated design process should create time for true interactive dialogue to allow change to occur.
- Before the design process begins, understand the health-generating patterns of place.
  - What are the forces and relationships that made this place? What has degraded it? What keeps it healthy? There are typically only a few key systems that function as health-generating leverage points.
  - Address how human activities and aspirations can move into alignment with earth-system functions.
- Identify the deeper purpose for our activities and decisions.
  - Don't try to solve problems without understanding why they are being solved.
  - Avoid solving design problems by addressing how solutions are measured (e.g., LEED or GGHC requirements). Address the overall health of the system.
- Align the team around the essential, deepest, and core purpose of why the project is proposed. Develop a health mission statement for the project.
- Commit to measurable goals for the key systems in order to realize the core purpose.
- Map the design process in order to manage this new pattern of design.
  - This will allow for the time and cost of this work to be optimized.
  - If you don't, people will fall back into traditional, linear patterns of design.
  - This level of design is front-loaded. The payoff occurs in much quicker approvals and support from the community.

- Iterate ideas and optimize systems through the design process.
- Assemble a core team to hold the core aspirations of the project.
  - This team is meant to hold the vision and evolve it during—and long after—the project is complete and consultants gone.
- Set up a feedback process.
  - This process will inform the core team and stakeholders so adjustments can be made and the evolving relationships can be addressed and sustained.

Some aspects of a living-system worldview that must be embraced in order to make a shift:

- Natural systems have the ability to heal themselves—if we provide the opportunities.
- We are nature and an integral part of nature.
- A conscious relationship between humans and earth systems is essential to realize a sustainable condition.
  - Dialogue (i.e., humble co-learning) is necessary to achieve mutually beneficial understanding.
- Whole-systems design is most easily sustained in our places.
  - Sustainability issues are both planetary (energy, toxics) and local (habitat, soil health, water management, social health). Place-based engagement can frame and integrate the planetary issues in a manageable, meaningful, and, literally, grounded context (a word that comes from the Latin contexere, "to weave together").
- The building and development process must become a place-based healing process. An approach that merely limits the damage is just a slower way to degrade the planet.

A fundamental question in the integrative design process should be: where and when do we stop integrating? The answer is that we can't. Life doesn't stop interrelating. We are an integral part of the process of life, and the more focused our intention, the deeper our sustainable relationships. In a typical building project, it is not the design team's job to be engaged forever and continue the integration process. It is the design team's job to open the door to the potential of this thinking. It is the owner's job to continue this work and evolve the health of the project along with the place the project is built. If the community is not working toward an understanding of whole-systems health, it is unlikely the building project will be sustainable in the long run. Any time we build we are creating the potential for learning about these significant interrelationships — the integration process is a learning process. The design and client team should become, in effect, a learning organization.

Learning involves . . . a movement of mind. Real learning gets to the heart of what it means to be human. Through learning we re-create ourselves. Through learning we become able to something we never were able to do. Through learning we re-perceive the world and our relationship to it. Through learning we extend our capacity to create, to be part of the generative process of life (Senge 1990).

LEARNING ORGANIZATIONS

Many healthcare organizations are, in fact, teaching organizations. Can they become learning organizations to realize the potential suggested by engineer and author Peter Senge in the closing words of Reed's essay? According to Senge (1990), "A learning organization is human beings cooperating in dynamical systems that are in a state of continuous adaptation and improvement . . . . There is within each of us a deep hunger for this type of learning." Since the publication of his groundbreaking book, *The Fifth Discipline*, businesses worldwide have used the concept of learning organizations to transform longstanding static management practices into more agile, dynamic decision-making processes.

Integrated design plays a pivotal role in defining and realizing the goals of a learning organization. While an integrated design process, as defined in this chapter, relates to the design of the physical facility, it exists within a framework of culture and decision making whose transformational potential must be acknowledged by owner and design team consultants alike. In other words, integrative design will be understood and embraced by learning organizations as an important tool in their organizational evolution.

David Orr (2004) challenged academic organizations to reinvent themselves for an ecological era:

This requires rethinking principles and procedures at a higher level of generality. It would mean changing routines and old ways of doing things. It would require a willingness to accept the risks that accompany change. It would require a more honest accounting to include environmental costs. Instead of bureaucratic fragmentation, the transition would require boundary crossing and systems ways of thinking and doing. Instead of being reactive organizations, they would become proactive, with an eye on a distant future. Instead of defining themselves narrowly, they would redefine themselves and what they do in the world at a higher and more inclusive level.

While Orr may have intended this message for institutions of higher learning, it has resonance for the healthcare industry.

ORGANIZATIONAL CULTURE

What is the "mindset" of healthcare organizations? It is often characterized as organizational culture; organizational culture, in turn, is often cited as a major factor in the inability of the healthcare industry to respond appropriately to rising costs, staffing shortages, and the challenges of infection rates and errors. "The organization's culture is a powerful set of norms, habits, policies and procedures that guide behavior. The artifacts and outward signs of the culture, including its buildings, are based on the organization's 'values' — both expressed and observed — along with deep underlying assumptions" (Shein 1992). An organization acquires a distinctive competence (what it actually does better than any other) or sense of mission when it has not only answered the question, "what shall we do?" but also the question, "what shall we be?" (Wilson 1989).

Architect D. Kirk Hamilton and healthcare organizational consultant Robin Orr (2005) observe: "We desperately need to redesign our organizations to rekindle a commitment to healing, hope, optimism, innovation and creativity." Individuals who have created major innovations in healthcare delivery, like Orr with Planetree's patient- and consumer-centered approach, or Clarian Health's Ann Hendricks with acuity-adaptable "universal" rooms, have coupled a facility redesign with major organizational change. Hamilton and Orr recognize that "the symbols of culture appear from the moment one encounters the site and include signage, landscape or urban context, layout of the property, drives, parking, plantings and site amenities. The design of a campus and appearance of each building can be attractive and welcoming, ambiguous and confusing, or simply forbidding . . . . These nonverbal cues signal something about the organization." They are evident in the organization of a nursing station, the design of a patient room, and the food service. Ultimately, they conclude:

> Organizational theory supports the concept of simultaneous interventions to generate change. Sociotechnical theory suggests that joint optimization of the social aspects (including culture) and technical aspects (including architecture) of an organization will more often deliver the desired results. This strongly suggests that healthcare executives leading a change process should work

Visionary leaders must point the way to a better future, launch the change process, protect the champions, nourish their efforts, and celebrate the successes every day. Such a process demands an interdisciplinary team committed to synergistic collaboration and prepared to passionately devote long hours over several years to achieve the goal. Many champions are needed to play many important roles. Most of all, there must be a commitment to act.

—D. Kirk Hamilton, FAIA, and Robin Orr

simultaneously with both organizational consultants and architects who actively collaborate. It also suggests that architects and organizational consultants should more often *integrate their activities* [emphasis added].

The integrated design process provides a vehicle to integrate an organization's project vision and goals with its health mission.

San Juan Regional Medical Center in Farmington, New Mexico, engaged in a series of "visioning sessions" related to patient experience, safety, and sustainability. Early on, the team identified a need for deep overhangs on the building's south facade, but the energy demand reduction was insufficient to fund the incremental capital costs of the shading devices. At the same time, the visioning session experience revealed that families wanted the ability to stay alongside patients and valued the opportunity to sleep outdoors. In the integrated design process, the two ideas converged to create screened patient balconies directly accessed from each patient room.

Figure 6-2: San Juan Regional Medical Center. *Credit: Steven Hall @ Hedrich Blessing*

San Juan Regional Medical Center

Farmington, New Mexico

Owner: San Juan Regional Medical Center
Design team:
 ARCHITECTS AND INTERIOR DESIGNERS: Kahler Slater Architects, Inc.
 LANDSCAPE DESIGNERS: Laskin & Associates, Inc.
 MECHANICAL, ELECTRICAL, AND PLUMBING ENGINEERS: Ring & DuChateau, Inc.
 CIVIL ENGINEERS: Cheney-Walters-Echols, Inc.
 CONSTRUCTION MANAGERS: M. A. Mortenson Company
 GENERAL CONTRACTORS: Arviso/Okland Construction
Building type: Addition and renovation
Size: 155,946 sq ft (14,490 sq m)
Program description: 168 beds; acute-care, diagnostic, treatment, and support services
Completion date: 2006

San Juan Regional Medical Center in Farmington, New Mexico, lies within sight of the San Juan Mountains of Colorado and the desert highlands of Utah and Arizona, and is in the heart of the picturesque San Juan River Valley. The region is known as Four Corners, so named because it is the only place in the United States where the borders of four states—Arizona, Utah, Colorado, and New Mexico—touch. There

Figure 6-3: The curving concourse level features clerestory glazing, increasing the level of available daylight. *Credit: Steven Hall @ Hedrich Blessing*

The additional construction costs for the balconies were offset by reduced mechanical A/C equipment infrastructure sizing. The porches provide an important occupant amenity, while keeping the intense sun off the exterior walls and windows, decreasing the cooling load. The large doorways allow a patient bed to be wheeled outdoors in a private setting. This is a community that lives for the outdoors. They value their connection to nature.

—DOUG FRARY, VICE PRESIDENT OF SUPPORT SERVICES, SAN JUAN REGIONAL MEDICAL CENTER

are four outlying mountain ranges that provide a protective barrier for the community, in which diverse cultures and rich geographical context converge. A Navajo reservation borders Farmington at its west and southwest limits, contributing culturally and economically to the community.

"This is a great example of an independent community hospital with strong leadership and vision willing to partner with its design team for innovation," says Jim Rasche of Kahler Slater. "With awareness comes curiosity." San Juan's regional leadership saw the confluence of global environmental stewardship issues and indoor environmental quality issues. "This is a region with a fragile ecology, threatened by overdevelopment," notes Matt Tendler, AIA. "The local aging coal-burning power plant produces observable air pollution—the hospital treats the asthma. There are dire predictions about regional availability of water in the next twenty years." The design team's approach built on ongoing operational issues—like microfiber mops and digital imaging—designed to reduce water usage.

KEY BUILDING PERFORMANCE STRATEGIES

Water
- Closed-loop cooling tower
- Low-flow fixtures in public toilets (project specified prior to market availability of low-flow toilets)
- No potable water used for irrigation
- Native drought-tolerant landscaping

Figure 6-4: The screen porches on patient and staff break rooms manifest an effective integrated design process. Initially conceived solely as deep overhangs for solar shading, the team evolved the design to incorporate screened sleeping porches for patients and families. *Credit: Steven Hall @ Hedrich Blessing*

Energy

- Balconies serve as solar-shading devices for patient rooms
- Extensive shading devices for passive courtyard cooling
- Lumen adaptation compensation control: lighting controls in patient rooms and corridors allow for lower light levels at night when the human eye is accustomed to less light

Materials

- Locally sourced sandstone cladding used on 40 percent of building's exterior
- 75 percent recycled content ceiling tiles
- Supplementary cementitious materials (SCM) replace cement in the concrete mix design
- Concrete, a locally sourced material, used in lieu of steel as the primary structural material
- Stained concrete flooring combines structure and finish, making it resource efficient
- Rubber flooring used in lieu of vinyl products and maintained without wax or other chemicals
- Carpet-backing free of latex or polyvinyl chloride (PVC)
- 100 percent recycled content synthetic gypsum board

Environmental Quality

- Balconies allow patients and visitors to connect with the outdoors and control their thermal and luminous environment
- Integrated daylighting: view glass and clerestory windows increase daylight penetration with user daylighting control
- Construction-phase IAQ plan implemented
- Low-emitting materials used

Source: Kahler Slater Architects, Inc.

HEALTH MISSION

A pivotal component of the integrated design process is the initial development of a health mission statement. This statement is an early outcome of the project team and becomes the touchstone for the project mindset. A health mission statement is intended to embody the healthcare organization's commitment to promoting health through the building's design and operation at all levels: occupant, community, and global.

Creating a health mission statement demands the same questioning and examination that the design of the building requires. It calls on the healthcare organization to consider what makes a good corporate and community citizen and challenges design and construction professionals to reflect that commitment in the building's bricks and mortar.

This statement can demonstrate the team's understanding of the health-generating patterns of place and carry the deeper purpose for activities and decisions—both important aspects articulated by Reed. The mission statement might also include a series of health-based project goals articulated by the entire team—a desire to ensure healthy indoor air by minimizing materials' volatile emissions, for example.

St. Mary's/Duluth Clinic (SMDC) Health System compiled a health mission statement at the start of its First Street Building project, the case study that follows. According to the design team, this mission statement guided design decisions throughout the process. The statement is included in the sidebar.

CASE STUDY

St. Mary's/Duluth Clinic First Street Building

Duluth,
Minnesota

Figure 6-5: St. Mary's/Duluth Clinic First Street Building. *Credit: Blake Marvin*

Owner: St. Mary's/Duluth Clinic Health System
Design team:
    ARCHITECTS AND INTERIOR DESIGNERS: HKS, Inc.
    LANDSCAPE ARCHITECTS: SWA Group
    STRUCTURAL ENGINEERS: Meyer, Borgman and Johnson, Inc.
    MECHANICAL, ELECTRICAL, AND PLUMBING ENGINEERS: ccrd partners
    CIVIL ENGINEERS: LHB
    PROGRAM MANAGER/OWNER REPRESENTATIVE: Kirk Program Management Inc.
    GENERAL CONTRACTORS: Mortenson
    LEED CONSULTANTS: James Scott Brew FCSI AIA/ LHB Engineers & Architects
    ENERGY ANALYSIS: The Weidt Group
Building type: New
Size: 225,000 sq ft (20,900 sq m)
Design energy intensity: 132.6 kBTU/sq ft/year
Program description: Ambulatory care and cancer center building
Completion date: 2006
Awards and recognition: US Green Building Council LEED gold certified

Figure 6-6: An urban brownfield site with views of Lake Superior was selected for this new LEED-Gold certified cancer center building. *Credit: Blake Marvin*

St. Mary's viewed sustainability as a core mission of its institution. In a project description of St. Mary's, HKS states, "Creation of a project-focused health mission statement was a key element in the success of the sustainable aspects of the project." Innovation was achieved by going above and beyond threshold levels in LEED in areas such as recycled content and green power purchasing. Green housekeeping protocols were implemented when the building opened.

Figure 6-7: "Warm wood tones and the blues, grays, and greens of the Lake Superior shoreline are captured in the hospital's interior design. The extensively glazed south elevation will reflect the changing nature of the sky and water—one of the most striking site features. Water serves as a healing and relaxing element for the patients and their families." David Urling, senior interior designer, HKS, Inc. *Credit: Ed LaCasse*

KEY BUILDING PERFORMANCE STRATEGIES

Site
- Brownfield remediation
- Places of respite: an outdoor healing garden near the cafeteria area

Water
- No potable water used for landscaping irrigation
- Water use reduced 52 percent through low-flow fixtures
- Chemical-free water treatment in cooling tower

Energy
- Energy demand reduced 22 percent
- 100 percent green power purchase

Materials
- PVC avoidance; linoleum and latex/wood pulp wall coverings
- Local and regional materials
- Recycled content materials exceeded LEED thresholds
- Certified wood

Environmental Quality
- Low-emissivity materials
- Occupied spaces, including waiting, exam, and treatment rooms, with views of Lake Superior

Source: HKS, Inc.

RECOGNIZING INTEGRATED DESIGN

What does a successful integrative process look like? How does a team recognize that it is engaging in integrative design? In the following excerpt, sustainable design advocate Barbra Batshalom offers salient observations about recognizing a successful process.

RESEARCH AND INNOVATION

Because design teams are realizing the importance of research in the early stages of design, and not just on clinical innovation and site visits of similar facilities, they are conducting building energy modeling, considering solar-shading options, and making daylighting studies. Zimmer Gunsul Frasca Architects LLP, for example, teamed with the Energy Studies in Buildings Laboratory at the University of Oregon to conduct a patient-room daylighting study to determine an optimum patient-room configuration (see case study, Chapter 11). At Mills-Peninsula Health Services Replacement Hospital, in Burlingame, California, Anshen + Allen, together with Arup, defined particular facade design goals as part of their integrated design process and performed a series of analyses to optimize orientation and solar-shading strategies.

You know you are participating in an integrative design process when:

- You are pushed out of your comfort zone. (You either find this exciting and invigorating, or terrifying and disturbing!)
- You are asked for your input on a wide range of issues—including those outside of your immediate area of expertise.
- The expectations of your work are clear and detailed—the results have targeted performance goals.
- Other people's work depends on yours. No one's efforts are completely independent—instead, they are interdependent. No one goes off and hides in a corner to push through deliverables. Stakeholders solve problems together.
- The interactions of the group inspire creativity—working sessions are more fun.
- You feel more respected and valued than in a traditional project, and you feel obligated to return the same attitude. Morale is higher among the group and there is greater pride in the outcome.
- The process is mapped clearly. Stakeholders spend time planning how they will solve problems together, and they make decisions in a transparent way.
- Innovative solutions are encouraged. (Innovation does not, however, mean high-tech or risky strategies.)
- Decision makers (i.e., owners and clients) are involved in a significant way.

Source: Barbra Batshalom, the Green Roundtable

Mills-Peninsula Health Services Hospital Replacement Project

Burlingame, California

Owner: Mills-Peninsula Health Services: A Sutter Health Affiliate

Design Team:

ARCHITECTS: Anshen + Allen

LANDSCAPE ARCHITECTS: Antonio Bava Landscape Architects

STRUCTURAL ENGINEERS: Rutherford & Chekene

MECHANICAL, ELECTRICAL, AND PLUMBING ENGINEERS: Ted Jacob Engineering Group, Inc.

ENERGY ANALYSIS: Architectural Energy Corporation

THERMAL COMFORT ANALYSIS: Arup

CIVIL ENGINEERS: KCA Engineers, Inc.

GEOTECHNICAL ENGINEERS: Treadwell & Rollo, Inc.

CONTRACTOR: Turner Construction Co.

Building type: New acute-care hospital

Size: Hospital: 440,000 sq ft (41,000 sq m); administrative/support: 150,000 sq ft (13,935 sq m)

Program description: A 313-bed hospital includes adult medical/surgical and critical-care beds, 30-bed family birthing center, 6-bassinet neonatal intensive care unit. A 5-story administrative/support building includes administration, a conference center, a cafeteria and dietary, a laboratory, medical-records storage, and a medical library. A 4-level parking structure contains 830 parking spaces that supplement the 632 surface spaces.

Completion date: 2010

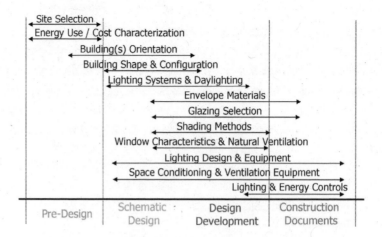

Figure 6-8: Energy and Daylighting Considerations during the Design Process
This diagram indicates the range of studies that design teams undertake, and when in the process each begins. This illustrates the front-loaded aspect of the integrated design process.
Credit: Anshen + Allen

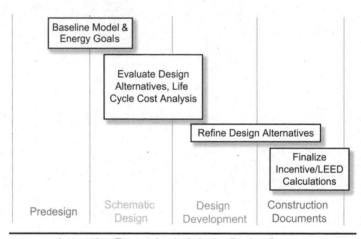

Figure 6-9: Integrating Energy Analysis in the Design Process
Energy analysis begins early. A baseline energy model can be constructed during concept or predesign; establishing energy goals early will drive initial system selections. *Credit: Anshen + Allen*

The design team engaged in a front-loaded design process, recognizing that early decisions on orientation, systems, and envelope solutions have the greatest impact on building performance. It performed analyses of energy conservation, thermal comfort, and life cycle costs for a range of envelope, glazing, and solar-shading solutions. The purpose of these analyses was to optimize a coordinated design solution—a key goal of integrated design processes. Such a process ensures that each individual system component is evaluated and optimized as part of a complete system and prevents inadvertent value engineering of critical system components later in the process. The outcome of these analyses included:

- The lowest life cycle cost–option also reduced the initial cost by $167,000.
- Over a twenty-five-year period, Mills-Peninsula is projected to save $13 million on the cost of HVAC energy: $50 million versus $63 million.

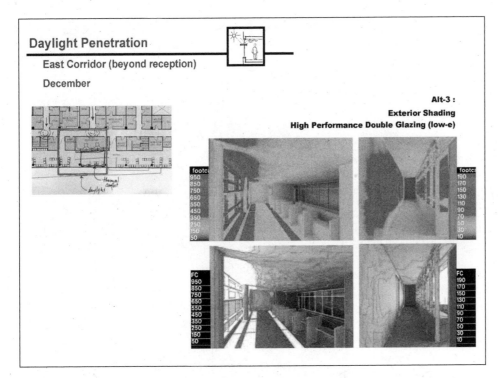

Daylight Penetration

East Corridor (beyond reception)

December

Alt-3 :
Exterior Shading
High Performance Double Glazing (low-e)

Figure 6-10: At Mills-Peninsula, the team carefully studied daylight penetration over daily and annual cycles. It also developed specific solar shading design strategies for each face of the freestanding buildings. *Credit: Anshen + Allen*

- Total energy costs were reduced from baseline $2.7 million to $1.8 million annually—a 33 percent energy savings or $900,000 cost reduction (using 2006 as baseline energy costs).
- The rightsizing of equipment eliminated two air-handling units (AHUs), two cooling towers, and one chiller, and reduces size of ductwork distribution system.

Source: Anshen + Allen

MUDA AND MINDSET

Taiichi Ohno, the creator of the Toyota Production System, coined the term *muda* (roughly translated from the Japanese as "waste" or "purposelessness") to describe any human activity that absorbs resources without creating value. In their landmark text *Lean Thinking*, industrial experts Dr. James Womack and Daniel Jones (1996) have translated the lessons learned by Toyota into a systems approach to eliminating waste from all aspects of industrial production. Lean thinking emphasizes simplification and scale: what's the right size for the task? Rightsizing is an example of a system attribute.

The construction process is rife with examples of *muda*—Womack and Jones include "mistakes which require rectification, production of items no one wants so that inventories pile up, processing steps which aren't actually needed, movement of employees and transport of goods from one place to another without any purpose, groups of people in a downstream activity standing around because an upstream activity has not delivered on time, and goods and services which don't meet the needs of the customer." Engineer and educator J. A. Vanegas often asks a workshop participant to produce a five dollar bill, which he promptly tears and discards half of in order to illustrate his research finding that nearly

50 percent of every US construction dollar disappears as *muda*—whether through drawing and document translation inconsistencies, incorrect product fabrication, mistakes in the supply chain, or problems of matching upstream and downstream activities on a construction site.

The application of lean principles in construction is just beginning, but the eradication of waste in the process of design and construction is a fundamental concept of sustainable thinking. According to Vanegas, recovering even 1 percent of the wasted half of every construction dollar would transfer enough value to fund notable sustainable design features. On a planet where resource use exceeds carrying capacity by almost 30 percent, identifying and reducing *muda* is a global imperative.

One initial outcome of applying lean approaches in manufacturing is the consideration of selling services rather than things. For example, the Schindler Group has moved to leasing vertical transportation services rather than selling elevators. The more reliable and efficient the product they install, the more money they make through operational savings. And Seton Healthcare Network negotiated a contract to purchase both electricity and thermal energy from Austin Energy through a combined cooling, heating, and power (CCHP) plant constructed by Austin Energy, off-loading the capital cost of a central plant and allowing Seton to invest its limited financial capital resources toward building strategies that reduce its heating and cooling load; this, in turn, freed excess CCHP capacity for Austin Energy to sell to other customers. Both producer and consumer are benefiting: the efficiency of the plant is so much greater than conventional energy production that the cost of the energy is well below what Seton would have paid for conventional natural gas boilers and chiller plants. These examples illustrate the power of innovative thinking facilitated by an integrated design process.

MINDSET AND CONSTRUCTION

In a traditional design-team approach, the constructor's role is often limited to providing input on constructability, cost, and scheduling. Sustainable design parameters

THE SUTTER PROTOTYPE HOSPITAL: LEAN PRINCIPLES IN ACTION

As this book goes to press, David Chambers is leading Sutter Health in a competition process to develop three community hospital prototypes using lean principles to achieve a series of measurable improvements in healthcare delivery processes. The adjusted patient discharge (APD) is the unit of production against which process efficiencies are measured. Integrated design process goals include the following benchmarks:

- 30 percent reduction from baseline building area per APD as modified for case mix index
- 40 percent reduction from baseline for required full-time employees per APD as modified for case mix index
- 50 percent decrease from baseline aggregated clinical procedure cycle times
- 50 percent decrease from baseline for time to build (including design, permitting, and construction)
- 25 percent reduction in natural resource use per APD

Ulrich and Zimring (2004) contend:

Many hospital settings have not been rethought as jobs have changed, and, as a result, the design of hospitals often increases staff stress and reduces their effectiveness in delivering care. While much research in the hospital setting has been aimed at patients, there is a growing and convincing body of evidence suggesting that improved designs can make the jobs of staff much easier.

Competition participants are rejecting standard medical planning solutions and fundamentally reengineering the delivery of care and the buildings in which the care is delivered, using lean tools such as value-stream mapping, time and motion analysis, and target-value design.

Competition results will be compiled in a forthcoming publication.

Source: David Chambers, director of planning, architecture, and design, Facility Planning and Development, Sutter Health

create expanded opportunities and responsibilities for construction professionals engaged in healthcare construction. An integrative design process supports the introduction of lean thinking in eliminating waste in both the design of the building and its construction process. Improved communication, building-system synergies, and the rightsizing of facilities, equipment, and systems are all facilitated through an expanded, albeit front-loaded, design process.

In the following essay, J. A. Vanegas expands the role of the construction professional further as he advocates for health and safety throughout the development of the project, beginning with building materials and processes in the preconstruction phases. This expanded role of construction professionals is illustrated by the case study on Skanska — the first construction firm to become certified through the International Standards Organization for environmental performance using the ISO 14001 program (see Chapter 7 for further discussion of the ISO program). As part of achieving its certification requirements, Skanska developed and implemented a high-hazard chemical screening process that is utilized on all its construction projects in the European Union.

Construction and Health

by J. A. Vanegas, PhD

Construction has been, is, and will always be, the provider and custodian of the built environment, which in turn is the foundation upon which any society exists, develops, and survives. Increasingly, evidence reveals construction activity to be a direct definer of human and ecosystem health. How can the construction industry be a more proactive, positive contributor to the health of people and ecosystems?

An initial response to this question is that it must formally and explicitly:

1. *Educate a project's construction team, increasing its awareness and understanding of construction-related health issues, concerns, and problems*
2. *Encourage the team to be more proactive in the identification, development, and implementation of solutions for any potential health concerns or prob-*

lems associated with the project during preconstruction, construction, or postconstruction activities

By achieving these two objectives, the construction team can transcend the current emphasis on meeting cost, time, quality, and safety criteria and include health as a fundamental decision-making criterion. Primarily applicable during the construction phase, which is under the construction team's direct responsibility, there are two other opportunities to contribute construction knowledge and experience: the preconstruction phase, in support of the planning and design processes; and the postconstruction phase, in support of the management, operations, and maintenance processes. In the same way that quality-, safety-, and more recently, sustainability-driven planning, design, and construction have become prevalent factors in the delivery of construction projects, health can and should be an essential driver.

In general, the construction phase is about the effective and efficient management of:

- *Procurement processes followed to their source and the acquisition of all necessary resources for a project, as dictated and specified by the plans and specifications*
- *Construction operations and work tasks that use labor, materials, equipment, and methods to transform the design solution into a constructed facility*
- *Commissioning, start-up, and turnover processes required to make the constructed facility fully operational from a building systems point of view*

Especially important for the construction team is to ensure that field-construction activities enhance health rather than contribute to health concerns or problems and, more specifically, avoid:

- *Poor craftsmanship, which can lead to construction defects that, over time, result in the development of moisture and allergenic molds and the release of mycotoxins by toxic molds such as penicillium, aspergillus and stachybotrys; can emit harmful chemicals and odors within sealed and poorly ventilated spaces; and can lead to exposure to carbon dioxide and carbon monoxide emissions as a result of the improper installation of furnaces, space heaters, or gas-fired central heating systems.*

- Poor procurement practices, *which can lead to inefficient use and significant consumption of building materials that:*
  - *Have a history of failure, such as hardboard or oriented strand board (OSB) exterior siding, exterior insulation and finish systems (EIFS), and asphalt roofing shingles*
  - *Perform significantly below their inflated claims, such as "lifelong" plastic plumbing systems, "impermeable" roofs, and "leak-proof" doors and windows*
  - *Have negative health and environmental impacts resulting from their manufacture and disposal, such as polyvinyl chloride (PVC), chromated copper arsenate (CCA)–treated wood and products made with ozone-depleting substances*
  - *Have the potential to cause respiratory problems and allergic reactions through off-gassing (i.e., the evaporation at normal atmospheric pressure of the volatile chemicals within a material for years after the product is initially installed), such as paints, stains, varnishes, carpets, insulation, flooring, plywood, particleboard, and paint strippers*
- Poor construction equipment and methods, *which can:*
  - *Cause excessive disturbance and other environmental burdens to the project site and to the surrounding environment*
  - *Generate excessive amounts of noxious emissions and effluents as well as demolition and waste debris*
  - *Compromise the health and safety of construction workers at the project site and of people in the surrounding areas*
  - *Consume excessive amounts of energy and water*
  - *Preclude the effective implementation of on-site recycling efforts*

Despite the importance of what can be done during a project's construction phase, involving construction team members trained in health issues during the preconstruction phase can impact the project even more positively. By providing both input and feedback in the development and review of the planning and integrated design solution in the preconstruction phase, enhancements and corrections can be made to the project execution plan, to the plans and specifications,

HEALTH-BASED PRECONSTRUCTION PRACTICES

- Evaluate the physical context, including the geographical location, surface and subsurface conditions, ecological and environmental conditions, existing infrastructure, and surrounding activities or assets.
- Assist in developing the functional solution, including the nature and type of interrelationships among people, activities, and processes.
- Actively participate in the formal/physical solution, including the site layout, the spatial solution, and the specification of the materials, products, equipment, and technologies.
- Determine the standards of quality and reliability, with an emphasis on the key parameters and levels of performance that must be achieved and the mechanisms for preventing partial or total failures.
- Develop and refine the cost model, transcending the anticipated total installed cost (TIC) estimate by including life cycle cost analyses.
- Develop and refine the time model, transcending the anticipated overall project schedule through to substantial completion by also including analyses of the cycle times of the project's commissioning, start-up, and turnover phases.

and to the construction production process plan before construction begins.

Especially important in the preconstruction phase is for the construction team to provide input on best practices to the planning and design teams to eliminate, prevent, or mitigate potential health concerns or problems stemming from the project, and to ensure that the project's quality, cost, and time models reflect the implementation of these best practices, as outlined in Figure 6-11.

These best practices contribute to:

- *Reducing the areas of developed land, paved surfaces, and contaminated sites*

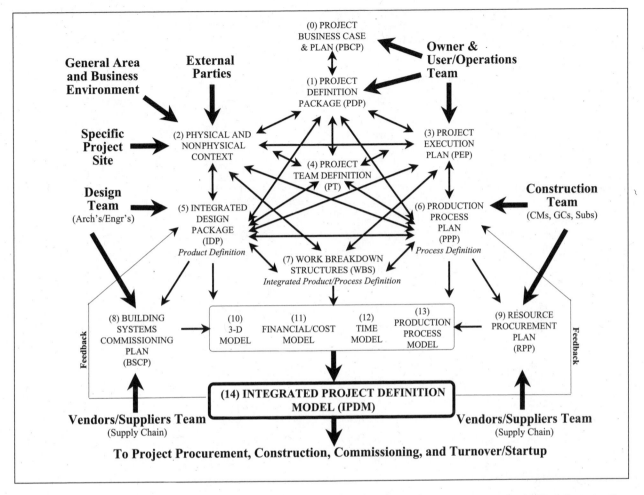

Figure 6-11: These are the entry points for health-based best practices during preconstruction services. This diagram illustrates the complex integrated process that informs the development of the integrated design package (IDP), which defines the products, and the production process plan (PPP), which defines the process. *Credit: Jorge Vanegas*

- Minimizing disruptive impacts to, and the reduction of areas of, wildlife habitats and wetlands within or close to the project site
- Minimizing water use, sewage and solid waste generation, and construction and demolition waste accumulation during construction
- Improving the facility's energy performance, reducing the energy consumed during construction activities, and identifying opportunities to use renewable energy sources during construction, operations, and maintenance phases

- Proper management and execution of indoor environmental quality measures during construction
- Implementing processes and procedures to enhance the physical, mental, and emotional quality of life and well-being for construction workers during the construction phase, and subsequently for the facility's users and operators during the operations and maintenance phases
- Selecting materials and methods that enable or facilitate the future reuse of the facility or of the facility's systems, equipment, products, and materials

Skanska is the first international construction company to have its environmental management systems (EMSs) certified to the ISO 14001 standard across all its business units. Skanska USA Building, Inc. is the first construction management firm in the United States to achieve ISO 14001 certification. Skanska project teams comply with a well laid-out corporate EMS and develop job-specific environmental management programs.

The company's leadership realized that even taking small steps toward environmental enhancement can make a significant impact if they affect thousands of projects. According to Staffan Soderberg, Skanska's sustainability manager, the company's triple bottom-line approach embodies both specialization in energy solutions and advocacy for safer, more environmentally sustainable building materials globally.

Its development of a materials filter, or high-hazard screening protocol, for example, was an early health-based initiative in Skanska's Swedish business unit. As early as 2001, Skanska in Sweden had reviewed five thousand material safety data sheets (MSDSs) for common building chemical products, and found as many as 30 percent of the reports inaccurate. As part of its decision to substitute known or suspected hazardous substances with safer alternatives, Skanska developed a restricted substances list banning materials such as arsenic, brominated flame retardants, mercury, and lead from all project sites. It also developed a phase-out list to move toward eliminating materials that contain known or potential carcinogenic, mutagenic, or reproductive toxicants—a list based on the precautionary principle. This effort has continued to expand during the last five years, as indicated in the table above.

The impact of materials-screening protocols is visible in the marketplace. New databases have emerged—including a Swedish Construction Federation R & D–initiative database known by a Swedish acronym, BASTA, (*byggsektorns avveckling av särskilt farliga ämnen,* or "phasing out very

Environmental Performance Measures at Skanska

Number of materials evaluated

	2005	2004	2003	2002	2001
Chemical products	10,909	10,299	8,693	7,588	4,749
Construction materials	2,938	1,543	1,783	1,402	—

Source: Skanska 2005 annual report

dangerous substances from the construction industry") manipulated by one letter to become the Italian word for "enough," which is referenced regularly by Skanska. Skanska has also developed a "spider"—an Internet search tool that automatically hunts for and uploads MSDSs. Clients tend to react positively to the leadership initiated by a construction management firm, and manufacturers are eager to understand the emerging protocols as they innovate product lines.

Skanska has embarked on a responsible wood-procurement initiative, as well as an examination of carbon footprints associated with projects in particular sectors and regions. It supported REACH (Reallocation, Evaluation and Authorisation of Chemicals), the European Union legislation to reallocate safety risks associated with chemicals from the consumer to the producer, passed in 2006. Skanska is beginning to transfer knowledge regarding energy solutions between business units worldwide in an effort to provide decentralized but integrated solutions aimed at reducing carbon footprint. Its 2005 annual report states that 115 projects in the UK, US, and Finland are either engaged with the Building Research Establishment Environmental Assessment Method (BREEAM) and its adjunct NHS Environmental Assessment Tool (NEAT), the UK green building rating system (see Chapter 8), or LEED (including National Health Service/Coventry, an early NEAT project, and Providence Newberg, the first US LEED gold-certified hospital), reflecting a commitment to environmental responsibility.

Source: Staffan Soderberg, Skanska sustainability manager

Finally, involving construction team members trained in health issues in the project's postconstruction phase facilitates follow-up and follow-through on earlier recommendations during the complete service life of the constructed facility. More specifically, construction knowledge and experience can play an important role in:

- *Preventing potential health concerns or problems associated with the facility's operability and maintainability, particularly regarding craftsmanship issues and the materials and methods used in the operations and maintenance processes*
- *Maintaining the highest standards of indoor environmental quality for the constructed facility to protect and enhance the safety, health, and well-being of users and operators*
- *Protecting and/or enhancing the ecosystems, resource base, and the well-being of people with whom the constructed facility coexists and interacts*
- *Maximizing the potential reuse of the facility, and/or of its systems, equipment, products, and materials at the end of their service life*

The construction industry's role in the delivery and use of healthcare buildings and related infrastructure is poised to shift from its current role — contributing to environmental and health decline — to a more intentional one that contributes to a built environment that fosters the health of both the people who inhabit it and of the ecosystems with which it coexists.

COMMISSIONING

Commissioning ensures that building systems are designed, installed, integrated, and tested to perform according to the design intent or the owner's project requirements, and optimized to the building owner's operational needs. It is an essential part of the integrated design process and a key to a project's ultimate success. Green building rating tools, including both the *Green Guide* and LEED, emphasize commissioning in both fundamental project requirements (i.e., prerequisites) and as optional points. (Both the *Green Guide*'s operations section and LEED for Existing Buildings deal with ongoing recommissioning.) Engineers and commissioning professionals Tia Heneghan and Rebecca T. Ellis describe the critical role of the building commissioning authority in an integrated design process in the following essay.

▒ Commissioning

Tia Heneghan, PE, and Rebecca T. Ellis, PE

*O*ver the past century, and particularly during the past twenty years, numerous innovations in healthcare facility design have been implemented to enhance the hospital experience for patients and healthcare professionals alike, and to reduce the risk of exacerbating patients' conditions from facility-related factors. The emphasis on an integrated design process and creating more sustainable facilities can add a level of complexity related to the collaboration this requires — and result in changing roles and responsibilities for the designers and construction professionals involved.

Often, standard design and construction processes do not result in a high level of confidence that building systems will operate as intended. How can that confidence level be increased? And beyond that, sustainable design and construction places a high value on systems optimization in the service of improved building performance — reduced energy demand, improved indoor air quality, and so on. The building systems commissioning process integrates into and fills this void in the traditional design and construction process through a systematic procedure.

To realize its full benefits, commissioning requires an extended project team effort, but ultimately it enhances a building project's quality assurance. For example, the commissioning process verifies that critical space-to-space pressure relationships in healthcare facilities are maintained under multiple normal and emergency operating modes. A typical end-of-construction air-balancing report will document that the pressure relationship was maintained under a specific set of design conditions. The commissioning process takes this further, physically creating or simulating nor-

mally expected operational scenarios (e.g., partial occupancy and equipment loads, seasonal variances) and emergency conditions (e.g., loss of power, equipment failure) to verify that the intended pressure relationships will be maintained at all times.

Commissioning begins with the development of a project-specific commissioning (Cx) plan that serves as the roadmap for the process, from predesign through design, construction, and occupancy. It lays out the roles and responsibilities for each team member during the various project phases and identifies the systems to be commissioned and the level of rigor for each system. It also establishes expectations early to minimize any surprises later on.

A TEAM SPORT

The Cx process is facilitated by a Cx specialist (also known as a Cx authority). However, commissioning is a team sport; the Cx specialist's primary role is that of coach. The commissioning team is comprehensive and includes the owner's project and operations staff, the design team, and the contractor team. If possible, engaging the Joint Commission on Accreditation of Healthcare Organizations' (JCAHO) compliance manager as a team member early in Cx planning and execution will allow the Cx process to dovetail with and support the certification process.

The Cx process helps the team understand the owner's building systems' performance goals; it is a step-by-step process meant to enhance the potential for successfully achieving those goals at the end of construction and prior to owner occupancy. The following are some of the fundamental elements of Cx (in chronological order):

1. Prepare Cx plan.
2. Define owner's systems performance acceptance criteria.
3. Review design documents for compliance with acceptance criteria.
4. Prepare Cx specification section for bidding documents.
5. Review shop drawings and equipment submittals for compliance with acceptance criteria.
6. Observe installation for future maintenance and operations accessibility issues.
7. Verify that equipment is installed and started per manufacturers' recommendations.
8. Provide appropriate time in the construction schedule for coordinating and executing system-level activities such as air and water testing and balancing, controls programming and quality control ("checkout"), and intersystem communications.
9. Verify functional performance of the systems and integrated systems to confirm final compliance with the acceptance criteria.
10. Train owner's staff in equipment maintenance and systems operation.
11. Provide system-level operations documentation for future reference and training of owner's staff.
12. Develop recommissioning and/or continuous commissioning plans for the owner's execution throughout the life of the facility.

One of the most important parts of the Cx process is documenting the owner's project requirements (OPR). The systems acceptance criteria need to be defined in quantifiable and measurable terms so success can be objectively determined at the project's end. Criteria to include in the OPR should go beyond the functional requirements of the building systems and include the facility's long-term operational and maintenance needs. A target energy budget may be part of the OPR, as well as the ability to monitor and meter system performance over the life of the system.

Any system whose performance can be defined in measurable terms can be included in the commissioning process. In healthcare facilities, this goes far beyond typical energy systems and includes normal and emergency electrical power, life safety systems, medical gas, medical information systems, security, lighting controls, and the building envelope.

Bringing the Cx specialist onto the project team early — ideally before the architects and engineers are selected and prior to the creation of the OPR — is critical to integrating Cx into a project. The Cx specialist can then review and critique the OPR and facilitate its inclusion into the request for proposal for design services. This will facilitate a communication process that results in a design that the owner really wants — rather than one that the design team believes the owner should have. Owners, on the other hand, must be willing to define and commit to verifiable operational objectives; owners won't sustain the operation of systems that are not viewed as beneficial, are not understandable, or which they have not helped to develop.

QUALITY CONTROL

During construction, the Cx process does not replace the quality control component of a project, but rather enhances the quality process itself. Quality control focuses on the static elements of the project (e.g., equipment, piping, conduit, and installation coordination). Commissioning goes a step further, to focus on how all of the static elements work together dynamically as systems. It is only through the interaction of system elements that the owner's project requirements can be met.

The Cx specialist is the eyes and ears of the operations staff during the design and construction process, while the Cx process brings the long-term view of the facility to the forefront of all decisions. When budget, schedule, and quality decisions are made, the Cx process gives the quality issues as much weight as the other critical project goals. Quality will not always take precedence, but the owner will be able to make informed decisions with an understanding of the true long-range cost of each decision.

TRAINING AND DOCUMENTATION

Commissioning offers a substantial benefit to a design and construction project by providing a framework within which the entire project team can successfully achieve their operational, schedule, and budget goals. However, the greatest value from Cx accrues to the facility owner through focused planning, documentation, and training for the ongoing operation and maintenance of the new systems. This is the truly "sustainable" contribution of commissioning to a project.

Although the traditional project close-out activities include the training of the owner's staff, that training is typically limited to the preventive maintenance and troubleshooting of individual pieces of equipment. Commissioning takes this further by focusing on systems operation training. If the facilities engineering staff responsible for operating the systems are inadequately prepared — because of a lack of training, documentation, and commissioning process involvement —

the systems are almost certain to perform less than efficaciously.

Systems training consists of an explanation of the system performance criteria and how the designers' systems achieve the stated criteria. The goal is to convey how all of the individual pieces of equipment are uniquely configured to operate as a system, emphasizing schematic diagrams and automatic and manual control sequences.

In the interest of proper sustained operation of the equipment and systems, Cx underscores the importance of complete, accurate, and easy-to-use systems documentation. This documentation should be designed with the new owner-employee in mind, as the building systems will outlast most of the staff working with them. Ideally, a new employee training program would be developed to transfer knowledge from the initial project staff to all future personnel. The traditional process of word-of-mouth training from exiting staff to entering staff will quickly result in an operational staff that doesn't understand the systems for which they are responsible.

RECOMMISSIONING

Also critically important to sustaining (and improving) the building systems' optimal performance throughout the life of the facility is the implementation of a recommissioning and/or continuous commissioning program. Such programs combine system monitoring with periodic functional performance testing similar to the tests conducted at the culmination of the new construction Cx process. By building these activities into the owner's regular maintenance program, the operations and maintenance staffs can do more than just respond to comfort complaints and repair equipment; they can proactively identify and prevent many problems before the building occupants become aware of them. This is especially important for healthcare facilities, in which patients may not be able to tolerate improperly operating systems.

Ongoing Cx makes sense from a healthcare service provider's perspective; it also makes economic sense. Continuous Cx has been shown to save up to 40 percent of a facility's energy consumption by identifying and correcting problems before they result in excess energy use (Lewis 2003).

Commissioning benefits three proponent groups associated with a healthcare facility:

1. Building occupants
2. Design and construction project teams
3. Facilities operations and maintenance teams

The project team benefits from improved communication and coordination, on-time successful completion and turnover of the building to the owner, and far fewer callbacks after project completion. The owner receives a building that works as intended at the time of occupancy, while the designers and contractors have a satisfied customer and a more profitable project. Additionally, the owner's facilities team operates a building it understands and in which it has confidence. It is also given the tools to successfully serve its customers, the building's occupants.

A well-commissioned facility will result in improvements in healthcare staff productivity and well-being. Most important to healthcare providers, however, is the knowledge and documentation that they have done their best to provide a safe and healing environment for their patients.

ENVIRONMENT OF CARE

Since JCAHO coined the term, the healthcare industry has manifested its organizational culture by defining the environment of care (EOC). With the publication of the 2006 edition of the American Institute of Architects' *Guidelines for Hospital and Healthcare Construction,* the clear definition and description of the environment of care is now a required component of the functional program for any facility. As architect Alberto Salvatore notes: "Every cultural and organizational model has a physical and operational consequence. In the development of service delivery models, they must be considered in a cohesive and integrated manner *simultaneously.*"

While it is beyond the scope of this book to examine all the components of the environment of care, it is crucial to understand that EOC considerations can all be components of an integrated building design process

formed around sustainable design values. The sustainable design process that begins with consideration of a health mission statement may well fulfill environment of care goals and requirements.

The adoption of an integrated design process is also strongly implied in the 2006 AIA guidelines, whether the ultimate objective is to achieve the environment of care goals or improved building performance. The integrated process, as described in Reed's essay, cultivates an understanding of sustainable design among team members and a process for tracking throughout design and construction. For Mills-Peninsula, the integrated design process included a new level of teamwork and research, and led to research-based recommendations for the design of a new acute-care building.

THE VALUE OF THE PROCESS

The true value of an integrated process is an improved building with less waste in its production and operation. These better building improvements include reduced operating costs, rightsizing, the improved health and productivity of the staff, and enhanced patient experience. By inserting a systems approach early, the design process maintains a focus on the whole, and long-term value and benefits become as much a part of the metrics of success as quality, schedule, and value.

As Albert Einstein exhorted in *The World As I See It* (1935), "We can't solve problems by using the same kind of thinking we used when we created them." The integrated design process breaks through silos that have concentrated on optimizing individual components rather than optimizing the building as a system. Understanding the interrelationships and synergies among systems —that improving glazing performance, for example, can have cascading benefits including reducing mechanical equipment sizing while also enhancing the indoor environment—leads to best-value solutions. Further, by recognizing that the building sits within a dynamic ecosystem, providing a context to become *part of* rather than *apart from,* injects an additional layer of integration that has lasting value.

CHAPTER 7

Integrating Operations

But really, this cannot go on indefinitely, can it? Does anyone rationally think it can? My companies' technologies and those of every other company I know of anywhere, in their present forms, are plundering the earth. This cannot go on and on and on...we breathe what we burn to make our products and our livings.

—RAY ANDERSON, Founder and Chairman, Interface, Inc.

INTRODUCTION

At many healthcare organizations, it is difficult for administrators to think about undertaking green building when the cafeteria still uses Styrofoam cups. Hospital leaders recognize that pursuing sustainable building requires operational initiatives to support it. At the same time, a major building program represents a chance to shift the organizational culture in support of sustainable design and operations objectives. Just as design is actualized during construction, both design and construction create operational realities. During operations, the building becomes a metabolic processor managing a dizzying array of inputs and outputs both front stage and backstage. These measurable, oftentimes visible operational patterns become the distinguishing features of our buildings for decades. How are these patterns aligned with

mission? How do they shape the experience of giving and receiving care? What are the best practices that, in the twenty-first century, are viewed as an intelligent response to global realities?

Within a single generation of healthcare operation, massive amounts of disposable products replaced reusable ones as the economy of cheap waste disposal was weighed against the labor associated with processing for reuse. From cafeteriaware to surgical supplies, hospitals are awash in throwaway supplies. Hospitals eliminated food preparation in favor of industrialized cook-chill systems, traded their dishwashing areas for plastic—and generated ever more garbage in the process. Throughout the late 1980s and into the 1990s, waste disposal costs crept higher as limitations to landfill capacities were recognized. As syringes washed up on beaches, regulations surrounding medical waste increased, and with them, the cost of compliant disposal. Hospitals viewed the escalating costs of waste disposal as a cost of doing business, but were rarely proactive about stemming the flow.

At the same time, the healthcare industry was in the ironic position of consuming and disposing of a myriad of toxic chemicals in the process of making people healthy. Mercury in thermometers, lead in radiation shielding, sterilants, pharmaceutical disposal, and caustic cleaning chemicals are among the major pollutants in hospitals. As hospitals moved from reusable glass to disposable plastic medical products, from landfill to incineration, dioxin emissions associated with polyvinyl chloride (PVC) incineration increased.

In 1998, a memorandum of understanding between the US Environmental Protection Agency (EPA) and the American Hospital Association (AHA) began to change that trajectory. This chapter traces the evolution of pollution prevention initiatives in healthcare, as it pertains to both waste management and persistent bioaccumulative toxicant (PBT) elimination. Interwoven are building case studies that demonstrate a high degree of green operation integration.

Healthcare design has traditionally focused on clinical process — mapping patient and staff flow. Materials flow is the territory of an array of specialized subconsultants — food service, materials management, security — the actual operation of the building is viewed as "backstage" and subordinate to care delivery. Programming for waste management, for example, rarely begins with a review of an overall waste management plan. Environmental managers' goals for recycling (and the space that may require), alternative waste treatment technologies, and the process for collection and/or site source separation are rarely discussed with the design team. Operations space is often viewed as non-revenue-generating space, which relegates strategic conversation to second or third tier. What lean thinking brings forward — and resource scarcity drives — is the concept that waste equals money. In the closing essay of this chapter, "Integrating Operations in the Design Process," Janet Brown, Laura Brannen, and Sarah O'Brien propose that operational

wayfinding become an important design component for high-performance healing environments — ensuring a sustained level of environmental stewardship in the ongoing operation of healthcare buildings.

POLLUTION PREVENTION

In 1996, the healthcare industry got the opportunity to affirm its commitment to environmental stewardship. That year, the EPA categorized medical waste incineration as the second leading quantified contributor to airborne dioxin releases. One year later, it was named the fourth largest contributor to anthropogenic mercury releases (EPA 1997). Dioxin and mercury are persistent bioaccumulative toxic chemicals: dioxin is a known carcinogen; mercury, a potent neurotoxin. Responding to this challenge, a coalition of hospitals, healthcare systems, and environmental organizations founded Health Care Without Harm. Its self-stated goal is "to transform the health care industry so it is no longer a source of harm to people and the environment."

The voluntary 1998 memorandum of understanding between the American Hospital Association and the

Figure 7-1: Health Care Without Harm is a global coalition of 443 organizations in 52 countries working to protect health by reducing pollution in the healthcare industry. Its Web site is www.noharm.org.

Figure 7-2: Hospitals for a Healthy Environment (H2E) was jointly founded in 1998 by the American Hospital Association, the US Environmental Protection Agency, Health Care Without Harm, and the American Nurses Association. Its Web site is www.h2e-online.org.

EPA launched a series of pollution prevention initiatives (EPA and AHA 1998). Building on healthcare's principle of "first, do no harm," this landmark agreement identified three action steps designed to reduce the environmental impacts associated with healthcare operations (see above). The same year, Hospitals for a Healthy Environment (H2E), a nonprofit membership organization, was formed to work on the ground with hospitals in order to transform the environmental footprint of healthcare operations.

The combined organizational effort to reduce solid waste and divert the incinerated waste stream has yielded impressive results. In 1996, more than 6,200 medical waste incinerators operated in North America; in 2005, fewer than one hundred remained (HCWH 2005). The reduction of incineration has been achieved through packaging reduction, recycling, segregating waste streams to reduce regulated medical waste, and diverting chlorinated plastic waste from incineration. According to EPA dioxin reassessment data, atmospheric dioxin levels have declined from their mid-1990s peak, and the estimated contribution from regulated medical waste incineration has fallen from 2,570g to 378g between 1995 and 2000 (EPA 2006). At the same time, many hospitals continue to utilize municipal waste incinerators for their nonregulated waste streams, representing an ongoing threat to environmental and human health.

In 2001, with assistance from Health Care Without Harm, H2E launched a campaign called Making Medicine Mercury Free that not only targeted incineration, but also attempted to shift healthcare markets from manufacturing and procuring mercury-containing medical devices (such as thermometers and blood-pressure devices) to safer digital alternatives. At the opposite end of the life cycle, H2E assisted the industry in establishing best-practice protocols for mercury capture and recycling. Today, formerly commonplace mercury-containing devices have all but disappeared from healthcare settings, and protocols for capture are widely understood. A 2005 AHA survey of hospitals revealed that 97.3 percent of hospital respondents are actively engaged in eliminating mercury (H2E 2005).

These initial waste-reduction strategies not only delivered environmental benefits; they also saved hospitals money. Diverting waste from the regulated waste stream reduced waste-handling charges. Dartmouth-Hitchcock Medical Center, for example, reported annual savings approaching $1 million in 2003 as a result. Before these initiatives, environmental performance was not a core business value for hospitals. There were few incentives to either monitor or improve performance beyond minimum regulatory requirements.

While the industry had some ability to track the aggregate value of these initiatives, individual hospitals lacked the tools necessary to measure their incremental improvements. In the absence of a comprehensive tool

Dartmouth-Hitchcock Medical Center in Lebanon, New Hampshire, has achieved a 40 percent recycling rate—among the highest in the nation. It closed an on-site medical waste incinerator and installed an autoclave to treat its regulated medical waste, after which it is safely landfilled. Dartmouth-Hitchcock also implemented a red-bag waste reduction program that saved $250,000 the first year and continues to pay for itself with sustained operational cost reductions.

Source: H2E

with which to measure and track performance, rewarding pollution-prevention achievement was only possible for individual measures.

Early attempts to classify or rank performance met with limited success. In a paper presented at CleanMed 2001, Ted Schettler, MD, MPH, the science director of the Science & Environmental Health Network, identified three tiers of environmental performance evolving in hospitals:

- **Tier 1:** Minimum local, state, and national environmental regulatory compliance
- **Tier 2:** Beyond compliance to measures that save money
- **Tier 3:** Informed by the inextricable link between environment and human health and moving beyond both compliance and monetary savings, with a long-term plan to reduce environmental footprint — a triple bottom-line approach (Schettler 2001).

Schettler contended that applying triple bottom-line approaches to pollution prevention initiatives — that is, measuring economic, social, and environmental benefits — would deliver significant benefits for healthcare organizations and the communities they serve. Early Tier 3 hospitals supported this notion. Named one of the state's top four recyclers, the University of Michigan Health System described its program's social benefit as "an institution-wide initiative that engages everyone" (UMHS 2001). A 25 percent reduction in solid waste yielded $30,000 in savings in 2000 and diverted more than 830 tons of waste from the community landfill.

POLLUTION PREVENTION AT UNIVERSITY OF MICHIGAN HEALTH SYSTEM

From the inception of its pollution prevention program, the safety management staff at the University of Michigan Health System set out to significantly reduce its medical and general waste flows. Initial achievements in recycling office paper and cardboard were achieved by aggressive signage and education campaigns. Once the obvious contributors were captured, the team moved on to recycling 109 tons of scrap metal and 25 tons of cooking grease. As part of the hospital's mercury-free pledge (an endeavor that as of September 2001 had reclaimed and recycled over 2,000 pounds of mercury and allowed the hospital to declare itself mercury free), the medical center sent 22,300 fluorescent lightbulbs and ballasts, each containing about 300 mg of mercury, to mercury recycling facilities in Michigan. Through this aggressive recycling and waste reduction campaign, the University of Michigan Medical Center saved approximately 19,000 trees, 4,000 cubic yards of landfill space, 7.8 million gallons of water, more than 2,780 barrels of oil, and 8,175,347 kilowatt hours of electricity.

The medical center currently recycles 30 percent of its total waste stream and has bold goals for the future. Its recycling and waste-reduction policies prove that a large hospital system can attain a viable and productive pollution prevention policy while improving its financial bottom line.

Source: H2E Awards

C. S. Mott Children's and Women's Hospitals

Ann Arbor,
Michigan

Figure 7-3: C. S. Mott Children's Hospital. *Credit: HKS, Inc.*

Owner: University of Michigan
Design team:
    ARCHITECTS AND STRUCTURAL ENGINEER: HKS Inc.
    LANDSCAPE DESIGNER: Talley Associates
    CONSULTING ENGINEER: ccrd partners
    CIVIL ENGINEER: Cummins & Barnard, Inc.
    CONSTRUCTION MANAGER: Barton Malow Co.
Building type: Replacement hospital
Size: 1,100,000 sq ft (102,190 sq m)
Program description: 855,000 sq ft (79,432 sq m) inpatient services, with 234 pediatric beds, including a 46-bed pediatric intensive care unit, 40-bed neonatal intensive care unit, 26-bed bone marrow transplant unit, and 30-bed birthing center; 245,000 sq ft (22,761 sq m) outpatient services; approximately 180,000 sq ft (16,723 sq m) will be constructed as shell space for future expansion
Completion date: 2011

The University of Michigan is constructing a replacement children's hospital on an open-surface parking lot adjacent to the Nichols Arboretum on the existing medical campus. The sustainability drivers include the mandate to remedy existing site water-flow erosion of the arboretum, a long history of operational environmental leadership in the community, and energized and engaged pediatric residents at the medical school.

Given that the existing site had been totally covered with impervious paving, overall site permeability will be significantly increased through the use of ground-level gardens and green roofs, which patients will be able to view from their rooms. Inspired by a tour of a similar major green roof installation at the nearby Ford Motor Company Rouge River plant, and with the support of the arboretum's management, the project team's commitment to a green roof solution was secured.

The sheer scale of the building preempts on-site parking; enhanced transportation systems, including a campus monorail system and extended bus and shuttle system, will transport staff to remote parking areas. Visitors will park in an existing adjacent garage.

The building's orientation prioritizes views of the arboretum and the Huron River, maximizing daylight and a direct connection to nature. The form incorporates both curves and insets to provide deep daylight penetration to the interior and reduce the scale.

During the design process, the university and the medical students advocated for a sustainable building approach. "Aside from being very, very bright, they're influential, and they're persuasive," said Dr. Robert Kelch. "They may not be fully informed about the economics of healthcare, but they are very well informed about the environment and sustainable building."

Source: HKS Inc.

UNIVERSITY OF MICHIGAN 2006 H2E SUSTAINED ENVIRONMENTAL LEADERSHIP AWARD WINNER

The University of Michigan Health System's longstanding commitment to environmental responsibility has been recognized through H2E Awards in 2002, 2004, and 2005, and now with this 2006 Sustained Environmental Leadership Award for their continued environmental initiatives. In 2005, the health system recycled 1669.8 tons (1696.6 tonnes) of waste, including 26,377 fluorescent lightbulbs, 16,050 pounds (7280 kg) of ballasts, and 10,286 pounds (4666 kg) of batteries. Recycling 700 pounds (317.5 kg) of compression sleeves saved the facility $60,821. The university follows the EPA Energy Star program for all lighting and mechanical retrofits and replacements; motion sensor lighting controls are installed in many restrooms, classrooms, and offices. Lead X-ray aprons are being phased out and responsibly recycled, and the pathology lab currently distills and recycles alcohol, formalin, and xylene. Foam peanuts are even returned to the shipping and receiving department for reuse, and unused food is donated to a local charitable organization for distribution.

Source: H2E

The challenge is clear: moving beyond Tier 1 performance requires education and tools to assist hospitals in setting and achieving measurable goals for pollution prevention. As hospitals increasingly view environmental performance improvements as good business, the demand for user-friendly tools that both measure performance and rank achievement grows.

As of June 2007, H2E has 1,358 partners representing 7,312 healthcare facilities—1,641 hospitals, 3,718 clinics, 918 nursing homes and 1,035 other types of healthcare facilities. Environmental programs aimed at reducing healthcare's operational footprint are approaching an industry tipping point. The H2E awards programs have experienced rapid growth—in 2006, they recognized close to two hundred hospital and health system members for pollution prevention through multiple award categories. The winners of the 2006 Partners for Change Award collectively accomplished the improvements chronicled here. The case studies that follow showcase both sustainable building and award-winning operation initiatives.

PARTNERS FOR CHANGE AWARD

The H2E Partners for Change Award honors H2E partner facilities that have made significant and sustainable progress toward reducing waste, preventing pollution, and eliminating mercury. Recipients of this annual award reduce, reuse, and/or recycle at least 10 percent of their total waste and have initiated comprehensive waste minimization and pollution prevention programs. The many achievements of individual 2006 Partners for Change Award winners include:

- Increasing a facility's recycling rate from 7 percent to 14 percent in one year
- Saving 2 to 5 million gallons of water each month by using recycled water for landscaping
- Piloting the *Green Guide for Health Care* to self-certify progress toward integrating green building and greener operations
- Working toward certification in the LEED Green Building Rating System
- Transitioning from the use of ethylene oxide to hydrogen peroxide for the on-site sterilization of reusable instruments
- Reducing regulated medical waste from 9 to 6 percent in one year
- Instituting an on-site incineration-free technology for the treatment of regulated medical waste, resulting in a cost reduction from $0.30 to $0.05 per pound

- Collecting 465 pounds (211 kg) of batteries for recycling
- Using building materials with minimum 25 percent recycled content, including carpeting, acoustical tiles, wallpaper, wall protection systems, structural steel, concrete, terrazzo, and aluminum
- Reprocessing single-use devices with a third-party processor
- Implementing a reusable pharmaceutical bin collection program, resulting in an annual reduction of 80,000 pounds (36,287 kg) of regulated medical waste
- Recycling 68,000 pounds (30,844 kg) of bricks, 48 cubic yards of wood, 633 tons (643 tonnes) of asphalt, 2,480 pounds (1125 kg) of corrugated cardboard, 121,000 pounds (54,885 kg) of scrap metal, 2,521 pounds (1144 kg) of aluminum, 783 pounds (355 kg) of copper, and 7 pounds (3 kg) of brass during a construction project
- Hiring an energy manager as part of the EPA's Energy Star partner program and initiating a conservation program, resulting in a 5.2 percent energy reduction and 1.5 percent water reduction
- Transitioning to digital imaging, reducing use of chemical fixer by 50 percent
- Switching to the use of di(2-ethylhexyl) phthalate (DEHP)–free IV bags and tubing
- Contracting for the purchase of antibiotic-free poultry and milk
- Using rapidly renewable materials like cork and agrifiber-based board for construction projects

Metro Health Hospital at Metropolitan Health Care Village

Wyoming, Michigan

Figure 7-4: Metro Health Hospital. *Credit: Kevin Ruff*

Owner: Metro Health Hospital
Design team:
    ARCHITECT; LANDSCAPE ARCHITECT; STRUCTURAL, MECHANICAL, ELECTRICAL, AND CIVIL ENGINEER; INTERIOR DESIGNER; AND SUSTAINABILITY CONSULTANT: HDR Architecture
    CONSTRUCTION MANAGER: Turner Construction Co. and the Christman Company (Turner-Christman)
Building type: Replacement hospital
Size: 480,000 sq ft (44,600 sq m)
Program description: Acute care hospital/outpatient services building
Completion date: 2007
Recognition: *Green Guide for Health Care* pilot

Since first achieving a Making Medicine Mercury Free Award in 2001, Metro Health has been engaged in improving environmental performance. The new Metro Health Village—which includes the new Metro Health Hospital, built on a greenfield campus—reaches past operational improvements to sustainable building. The design of the facility identified several key objectives, including sustainability, evidence-based design, and connection to the community. A major driver was the development of a building that directly benefits the patient experience and healing process.

The hospital building is the anchor facility on a large, multiuse campus. Site planning features native landscape, on-site storm water management, and integrated,

> *I started talking about green roofs, and our senior team didn't know what I meant. To reinforce my point, I tied it back to our core values. Then I had a simple picture drawn of a green roof on our hospital. We're planning to have a very large roof right below our patient room windows, so I thought, we'll have to address that problem. I wanted to replace those black roofs with flowering sedum. Now the senior team is thinking, We've got to get the $600,000 for the roof, because we can't afford not to.*
>
> —JEFF SMILEY, DIRECTOR OF ENGINEERING AND REAL ESTATE, METRO HEALTH VILLAGE, A PROJECT OF METRO HEALTH

Figure 7-5: The diagnostic and treatment program is placed alongside the public and inpatient tower. A green roof system is a key functional element in the storm water management system and improves the view from the patient rooms. *Credit: HDR Architects*

therapeutic gardens that are open year-round. A major green roof on the extended diagnostic and treatment block provides an important visual amenity for the patient rooms that overlook it and mitigates storm water runoff as well.

The interior design team created an environmentally preferable purchasing furniture, fixtures, and equipment (FF&E) initiative to assist Metro in evaluating how initial and ongoing FF&E purchasing would comply with LEED, *Green Guide for Health Care,* and other environmentally focused programs. In addition, waterless urinals and low-flow fixtures reduce potable water consumption, and a rainwater collection system is used for irrigation.

KEY OPERATIONAL STRATEGIES

Paper recycling (cost savings)
A paper-recycling program compliant with the Health Insurance Portability and Accountability Act (HIPAA) of 1996 captures white paper for recycling.

Cafeteria recycling (cost savings)
The Metro Café recycles glass, metals, and plastics.

Electronic equipment recycling (cost plus)
A hardware and peripherals recycling program was implemented.

Glutaraldehyde substitution (cost neutral)
The use of glutaraldehyde, a medical disinfectant, was eliminated.

Metro Health Hospital received both H2E's Partner for Change and Making Medicine Mercury Free awards for making strides in its environmental program through the development of a green team and its Clean Corporate Citizen Program. Metro implemented a mercury elimination policy and a DEHP-free policy and has begun phasing out both. All thermometers, sphygmomanometers, clinical devices, lightbulbs, and batteries are recycled, and the hospital is transitioning to a mercury-free laboratory fixative, rounding out its commitment to near-total elimination of mercury.

Source: H2E

Fiber-mop system (cost savings)

The traditional mop-and-bucket system was replaced with a fiber-mop system, resulting in fewer chemicals in the work environment, a decrease in employee injuries, and a significant reduction in water use.

Food waste composting (cost savings)

Food waste from patients and the cafeteria was captured and composted locally. The estimated annual waste reduction is 67 tons.

Reusable sharps containers (cost savings)

Single-use sharps containers that were previously incinerated are now replaced. The estimated annual reduction is 7.8 tons of regulated medical waste.

Instrument reprocessing (cost savings)

Single-use surgical instruments previously treated as disposable are now reprocessed.

Rigid containers (cost savings)

Disposable wraps and trays in central processing were replaced with reusable rigid containers, resulting in significant reductions of blue plastic wrap and labor costs for the operating room staff. Estimated annual waste reduction: 4 tons; annual savings: $30,000.

Electronics waste is contracted out for responsible removal and recycling. All new employees receive annual training in the facilities' recycling operations. Metro integrated its HIPAA (Health Insurance Portability and Accountability Act) and paper recycling programs into one controlled method of paper recycling (taking measures to ensure patient confidentiality), reducing costs in the process. A sustainability officer coordinates all of Metro's programs. Created during design and construction of Metro Health Hospital, the position was transitioned to address operational initiatives. The *Green Guide for Health Care* is used to track operational progress.

Source: HDR Architecture

Advocate Lutheran General Hospital and Lutheran General Children's Hospital Patient Care Tower

Park Ridge,
Illinois

Figure 7-6: Advocate Lutheran General Hospital. *Credit: OWP/P*

Owner: Advocate Health Care
Client: Advocate Lutheran General Hospital
Design team:
    ARCHITECTS AND STRUCTURAL ENGINEER: OWP/P
    LANDSCAPE ARCHITECT: Conservation Design Forum, Inc.
    MECHANICAL ENGINEER: Grumman/Butkus Associates
    ELECTRICAL ENGINEER: Dickerson Engineering, Inc.
    CIVIL ENGINEER: Gewalt Hamilton Associates, Inc.
    GENERAL CONTRACTOR: Power Construction
Building type: New construction and renovation
Size: New: 384,000 sq ft (35,675 sq m); renovation: 45,000 sq ft (4,180 sq m)
Program description: 192-bed replacement acute care tower, including 102 medical/surgical beds, 22-bed intensive care unit, 15-bed pediatric intensive care unit, and 28-bed mother-baby unit
Completion date: 2009
Recognition: H2E Partners for Change Award

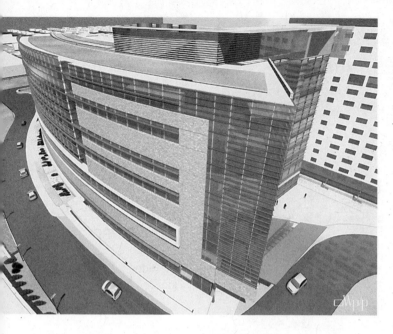

The vision for Advocate Lutheran Hospital's new inpatient building is to "create a facility that expands and enhances the hospital's leadership in providing quality healthcare," according to Dr. Bruce Campbell, the hospital's CEO and the project's sustainability champion. A primary driver for the replacement tower is to increase the number of single-occupancy patient rooms. Randy Guillot, AIA, Design Principal at OWP/P, says, "Dr. Campbell's commitment to the vision of the project truly focused and improved the design process as we worked toward a LEED project."

The design team emphasized sustainability in presentations to the local community. "We stressed that this is not just another big building that's going to create a lot of dust and noise while it goes up," Guillot continues. "Its real purpose is to take care of the community and be good stewards of the environment at the same time."

Figure 7-7: The Lutheran General Children's Hospital patient care tower will transform the image of the hospital. It features green roofs as a component of on-site storm water management. *Credit: OWP/P*

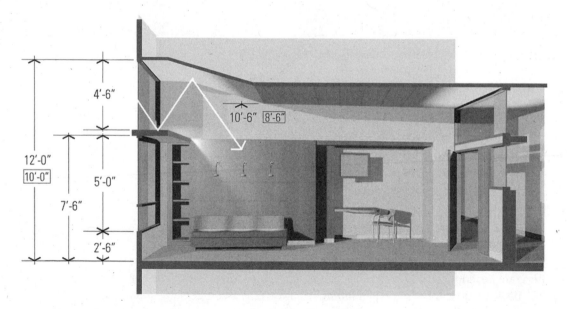

Figure 7-8: The patient room section has been carefully reconsidered to incorporate clerestory glazing at the exterior and at the corridor wall. The ceiling height increases at the perimeter to maximize daylight penetration to the interior corridor. *Credit: OWP/P*

The biggest challenges to sustainable design strategies came from local and state officials concerned about storm water management. The project features green roofs that reduce storm water runoff and permeable pavement that facilitates groundwater recharge. The patient tower's roofs and the connection corridor leading to the new hospital entrance will be blanketed with soil and sedum, a drought-tolerant, ground-cover plant that is easy to maintain.

KEY BUILDING PERFORMANCE STRATEGIES

Site
- On-site storm water management
- Green roofs mitigate heat island impacts

Energy
- Projected 20 percent reduction in energy below ASHRAE 90.1-2004

Water
- No potable water for landscape irrigation

Materials
- Recycled content and rapidly renewable materials
- Certified wood

Environmental Quality
- Low-emitting materials
- Indoor pollutant source control

Source: OWP/P

2005 H2E PARTNER FOR CHANGE AWARD

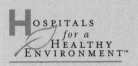

The Recycling Task Force coordinates Advocate Lutheran General Hospital's environmental improvement initiatives. The program's theme is "We can do better!" Recycling and switching to reusable dishware assisted in achieving a 13.6 percent diversion rate. Proper segregation of regulated medical waste has led to an impressive 7.4 percent generation rate. Current program efforts include increasing the recycling rates, reusable coffee mugs for employees, and the implementation of recycling for aluminum and steel cans and for plastic and glass—launched on America Recycles Day. Mercury elimination efforts include the development of a mercury elimination commitment statement, 100 percent elimination of thermometers and sphygmomanometers containing mercury, and recycling fluorescent lightbulbs and batteries.

Source: H2E

ISO 14001

In 2001, Cambridge Memorial Hospital, in Cambridge, Ontario, became the first hospital in North America to receive ISO 14001 certification for environmental performance. With no healthcare-specific tool in place to recognize or reward environmental leadership, Cambridge turned to the International Organization of Standardization (ISO) Environmental Management System (EMS), traditionally used by the manufacturing sector to certify overall environmental performance. In 2002, the Detroit Medical Center, a system of eight hospitals,

became the first healthcare system in the United States to achieve ISO certification. Trillium Health Centre, based in Mississauga, Ontario, certified its multisite system in 2004.

ISO 14001 standards were developed for environmental management—that is, "what the organization does to minimize harmful effects on the environment caused by its activities, and continually to improve its environmental performance" (ISO 2006). The voluntary standard includes twenty-one specific requirements in the areas of environmental performance. The six EMS components are (ISO 2006):

"Inspired by our hospital's vision of being 'an excellent community hospital that contributes to making our community as healthy as possible,' we were ready to take on a nontraditional area of healthcare: the environment," says Helen Wright, CEO at Cambridge Memorial Hospital. "The first steps in achieving our vision started directly inside the organization. We knew we had to get our own house in order."

Some of the results of a comprehensive environmental management program—and the less tangible benefits associated with an improved waste-minimization program—include (Wright, Hanley, and Quigley 2001):

- *Increased community goodwill:* A good system assures the community of the hospital's commitment to demonstrable environmental management.

- *Improved risk-management profile:* A proper EMS minimizes the possibility of environmental problems and is important in demonstrating due diligence.

- *Recognition as a leader in the healthcare sector:* Proactive measures on environmental issues fit the sustainable development strategy adopted by Cambridge Memorial.

- *Self-regulation:* An EMS minimizes the need for regulatory intervention and facilitates a cooperative approach by regulatory agencies. The assurance of compliance heads off any negative publicity or adverse effects on public confidence in Cambridge Memorial's services that could result from regulatory violations.

- *Control:* Examining practices associated with waste management, discharges, and resource consumption can identify inefficiencies that lead to cost reductions.

- *Decrease in airborne contaminants:* Neighbors' air quality is improved by negating the release of materials such as dioxins and nitrogen oxides from burning of plastic and other materials.

- *Employee awareness of the environment:* Employees have adopted both the policy and work wholeheartedly in order to maintain the EMS for the health of the environment.

1. *An environmental policy,* in which the organization states its intentions and commitment to environmental performance;

2. *Planning,* in which the organization analyses the environmental impact of its operations;

3. *Implementation and operation:* the development and putting into practice of processes that will bring about environmental goals and objectives;

4. *Checking and corrective action:* monitoring and measurement of environmental indicators to ensure that goals and objectives are being met;

5. *Management review:* review of the EMS by the organization's top management to ensure its continuing suitability, adequacy and effectiveness; and

6. *Continual improvement.*

ISO 14001 standards are generic—an environmental management system can be applied to any organization, large or small, whether its products are goods or services. To achieve certification, Cambridge Memorial diverted 60 tons of paper from landfill; recycled 60 percent of recyclables, reduced regulated medical waste (biohazards) by 41 percent, and implemented fluorescent lamp and battery recycling programs. Compliance can be self-declared, or the EMS can be registered, reviewed, and certified by a third party—at Cambridge, AQSR, a management system registrar, presented the certificate. In 2004, Cambridge's certification was renewed as it continued to improve environmental performance.

ISO 14001 promised a means for Tier 3 healthcare organizations to be recognized as leaders, certified by a third party for their progress in reducing the environmental burdens associated with their operations. According to Helen Wright, CEO of Cambridge Memorial Hospital, ISO 14001 certification generated resumés from nursing applicants across Canada energized by the idea of working at an environmentally responsible organization. At the same time, most guides to ISO 14001 certification are not customized to healthcare operations and require significant resources to adapt. Issues of fit, combined with the need to continuously monitor improvement, have greatly impeded healthcare organizations' abilities to attain ISO 14001 certification.

As of 2005, approximately thirty hospitals in North America had achieved either ISO 9001 or ISO 14001 certification. ISO 14001 certification is more common abroad. The UK's National Health Service (NHS) has developed a computerized EMS called Greencode that allows NHS hospitals to manage environmental systems with an option of seeking ISO certification. As of 2004, six NHS hospitals were ISO 14001 certified through Greencode.

Greencode is an innovative, comprehensive, computer-based environmental management tool. It enables organizations to implement coherent, structured management systems and achieve full ISO 14001 certification swiftly and cost-effectively. Designed by the NHS, it is now extensively used in the healthcare, retail, and manufacturing sectors throughout the UK.

Source: HFS 2007

In 1998, Changi General Hospital became the first ISO 14001 certified hospital in Singapore. Changi General demonstrates how operational initiatives can be integrated in the design of a building. At the same time, it demonstrates the challenges inherent in improving environmental performance while dramatically expanding the size and scope of buildings and medical services.

CASE STUDY

Changi General Hospital

Simei, Singapore

Figure 7-9: Changi General Hospital. *Credit: Changi General Hospital*

Owner: Singapore Ministry of Health

Design team: CPG Corporation Pte. Ltd.

Building type: Replacement regional hospital

Size: 1,152,000 sq ft (107,000 sq m); site: 12.8 acres (5.2 ha)

Program description: 776 inpatient beds and 30 adult intensive care beds on 25 units, 8 operating theaters, emergency department, and ambulatory care in 23 medical specialties.

Completion date: 1997

Recognition: ISO 14001 certified; Singapore National Environmental Agency Green Leaf Award, 2002

The building was designed around the ideal of improving interior traffic flows by segregating uses, and was the first hospital in Singapore to be ISO 14001 certified. An H-shaped ward tower stacked on a diagnostic and treatment base defines the building's organization. It is oriented to maximize daylight, minimize solar gain, and take advantage of prevailing winds for natural ventilation.

Many of the hospital's green initiatives extend beyond the built environment and support the goal of improved environmental performance. Building on the momentum of a volunteer gardening club popular at the hospital's former site, the Changi General prides itself on landscaped grounds that include six koi ponds (four of which are located in the hospital lobby), an accessible planted roof yielding cherry tomatoes and herbs for use in the kitchen (while cooling the roof), and an active composting program through which kitchen and landscaping waste is used as landscaping fertilizer on-site, helping remediate previously damaged soil.

Figure 7-10: Rooftop gardens provide shade to reduce solar heat gain and yield a variety of herbs and 440 lbs (200 kg) of cherry tomatoes annually for the hospital's food service. *Credit: Changi General Hospital*

Figure 7-11: Drip irrigation and container systems separate plants from the building's roof membrane. *Credit: Changi General Hospital*

KEY BUILDING PERFORMANCE STRATEGIES

Energy

- Chiller heat recovery for domestic hot water eliminated gas hot-water heaters
- Thermostats maintain room temperatures between 23° and 24°C (73° and 75°F), clearly marked for nursing staff
- Automatic doors separate air-conditioned and non-air-conditioned areas
- Motion sensor lights, electronic ballast lighting, and energy-saving bulbs
- User-accessible shade devices
- Variable air volume (VAV) system
- Efficient ceiling fans save 146,905 kWh annually compared with old ceiling fans
- Fourteen out of twenty-five wards are mechanically air-conditioned
- All patient rooms have operable windows
- New automatic condenser tube cleaning system has reduced energy consumption 15 to 25 percent

Water

- Low-flow fixtures
- Occupant education for awareness-based conservation

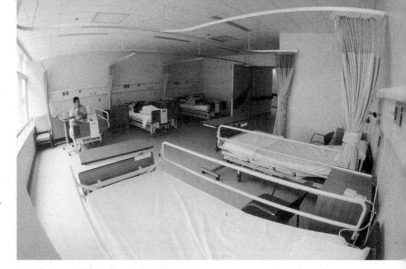

Figure 7-12: Patient rooms feature large, fully operable windows to facilitate daylighting and ventilation. *Credit: Changi General Hospital*

    To maintain its ISO certification, the hospital submits to ongoing, regular environmental monitoring systems, tests, and maintenance measures. While the hospital's architectural design incorporates passive techniques, in its first year of operation, it consumed more energy than anticipated, largely due to an increase in air-conditioned areas compared with the former facility; water use also increased drastically. A variety of postoccupancy strategies were then employed—from microscale and user-focused energy- and water-saving initiatives such as compact fluorescent bulbs, thermostat setbacks, low-flow fixtures, shade devices, and a chiller heat recovery system—yielding an electricity use reduction of more than 3.5 million kilowatt hours per year, or 12 percent of total energy use, by the end of the second year of operation. Water efficiency measures reduced use by 25 percent during the same time period. Total energy and water conservation are reported to save $800,000 annually. The ISO process assisted the hospital in identifying and measuring the savings achieved through each measure.

Source: Changi General Hospital

For the next generation of hospital buildings in Singapore, the Ministry of Health set ambitious goals for both building and operational performance. In the Alexandra Hospital, operational guidelines will accompany the building, but no specific initiatives have yet been drafted. The hospital will be rated under Green Mark for Buildings, a new green building assessment tool implemented by Singapore's Building and Construction Authority, and will be reviewed semiannually for ongoing compliance.

Alexandra Hospital at Yishun

Yishun, Singapore

Figure 7-13: Alexandra Hospital at Yishun. *Credit: Hillier Architecture*

Owner: Singapore Ministry of Health
Design team: Hillier Architecture and CPG Corporation Pte. Ltd.
Building type: Replacement hospital
Size: 1,100,556 sq ft (102,245 sq m); site area: 7.4 acres (3 ha)
Design energy intensity: 105 kWh/sq m (projected)
Program description: 550-bed replacement hospital with 107,600 sq ft (10,000 sq m) underground disaster-preparedness facility
Completion date: 2009

Singapore's 2003 experience with the SARS epidemic and the 2004 tsunami challenged the government to develop new high-tech facilities capable of handling increasingly complex scenarios. The hospital, known as AH @ Yishun, incorporates a large underground disaster-preparedness facility, and will aim to prevent the spread of disease using thermal scan technology to identify infected patients and visitors. Energy costs, meanwhile, have driven a focus on efficiency.

With humid temperatures that average 85°F (29°C), designers were challenged to reduce energy costs while addressing comfort, infection control, and security. The hospital will consume less than half the average Singapore hospital kilowatt hours per bed per month in grid electricity, according to Mitch Green, director of healthcare at Hillier Architecture. To accomplish this, only 30 percent of the hospital (including labs and operating areas) will be air-conditioned, with the remaining areas

Figure 7-14: Designed as a "hospital in a garden," the courtyard allows deep daylight penetration into the underground clinical areas. *Credit: Hillier Architecture*

cooled using passive strategies—shading devices, green roofs and walls, cross ventilation, building orientation, and a high-performance exterior envelope. Meanwhile, a gas-fired cogeneration plant will provide enough energy to power the hospital fifteen hours per day. Daylighting will reduce energy consumption and heat gain from electric lighting.

KEY BUILDING PERFORMANCE STRATEGIES

Site
- Landscaping aids in reducing heat-island impacts
- Inpatient units face on-site pond
- Extensive tree planting

Energy
- Gas-powered combined cooling, heating, and power plant will reduce energy demand 50 percent
- Extensive use of natural ventilation—only 30 percent is mechanically air-conditioned

Water
- Storm water detention pond to be landscaped and remediated
- Gray water system to be used for toilet flushing and irrigation

Materials
- Indoor air quality to be considered in interior specifications

Environmental Quality
- "Inside-out" design places corridors on exterior so they can be daylit
- Light shelves and shading devices direct and control daylight
- Accessible courtyard gardens at basement, ground, and terrace levels and roof

Sources: Hillier Architecture and Green, Gifford, and McCarter 2006.

Figure 7-15: At Alexandra Hospital continuous vegetated balconies act as solar-shading devices. *Credit: Hillier Architecture*

Geriatriezentrum Favoriten (Favoriten Geriatric Clinic)

Vienna, Austria

Figure 7-16: Geriatriezentrum Favoriten (Favoriten Geriatric Clinic). *Credit: Courtesy of Favoriten Geriatric Clinic and the KAV of Vienna*

Owner: Wiener Krankenanstaltenverbund (Viennese Hospital Group)
Design team: ARCHITECT: Anton Schweighofer
Building type: New Geriatric Residential
Size: 183,000 sq ft (17,000 sq m)

Program description: 192-bed residential geriatric clinic that also accommodates 50 day patients; sister facility to an adjacent 140-bed hospital, Kaiser-Franz-Josef-Spital; clinic is 100% occupied

Completion date: 2003

Awards/recognition: CleanMed Europe Best Practice Award 2004, architectural design category

Located in urban Vienna, Favoriten is a residential geriatric facility run by the city-funded eighteen-facility Viennese Hospital Group. The 192 full-time residents and fifty day patients are divided among eight classes of care, with a nearly one-to-one patient-to-caregiver ratio, including physicians and specialists.

Figure 7-17: Careful site design buffers the building entrance from traffic, providing a welcoming, human-scale approach for incoming patients and visitors. The wood-clad exterior and continuous outdoor balconies exude a warm, noninstitutional aesthetic, while bicycle racks near the entrance encourage healthy living practices. *Credit: Courtesy of Favoriten Geriatric Clinic and the KAV of Vienna*

The inclusion of the clinic's sustainable design features was motivated by a qualitative sense of patient well-being that includes reducing social isolation and promoting direct contact with nature. In addition, goals for energy reduction and air quality were achieved mostly through heating, ventilating, and air-conditioning (HVAC) and refrigeration technology. While local codes motivated the facility's polyvinyl chloride (PVC) avoidance and its carbon dioxide reduction strategies, no other formal performance benchmarks were set and no other management systems were applied. Simple climate-appropriate strategies were preferred (e.g., operable windows) to mechanical cooling systems. Patient health concerns drive the clinic's use of 45 percent organic foods, preference for seasonal produce, and avoidance of processed food products. The clinic participates in international Biofair organic purchasing initiatives. Affirming the clinic's success, it has been 100 percent occupied since it opened.

KEY BUILDING PERFORMANCE STRATEGIES

Site
- Minimized building footprint
- Pedestrian-only main entrance
- Patient access to greenery — even for those bedridden — maximized through on-site trees and planted facades and roofs visible from large, operable windows

Energy
- Passive solar design incorporates user-controlled natural ventilation in summer: no air conditioning in office spaces
- Motion detectors control corridor lighting
- Lavatory thermostats set back to 22°C from 24°C (72°F from 75°F)

- Heat recovery system uses waste heat to warm fresh air
- Heat transfer losses reduced by an estimated 90,000 kilowatt hours per year, compared with traditional building
- Interior architecture improves energy efficiency; balconies in patient room accessed through a buffer room that shields interiors from cold and may be opened in warm weather to form loggias
- Cabinetry on exterior walls provides insulation
- Energy-efficient kitchen equipment

Materials
- Resource-efficient construction practices
- Wood design elements preferred in patient spaces
- PVC (polyvinyl chloride) use minimized in accordance with 1992 Vienna City Council resolution; window frames are wood or aluminum; flooring is india rubber
- No synthetic surface finishes; no materials manufactured with ozone-depleting halogenated chemicals

Environmental Quality
- All office spaces have operable windows; none is air-conditioned
- Patient rooms have access to private balconies, providing daylight and views

Translation assistance provided by Michele Meditz.

Source: Favoriten Geriatric Clinic

FROM OPERATIONAL IMPROVEMENT TO BUILDING DESIGN

In North America, operational performance advocacy signaled the start of a more coordinated approach to design and operations. As predicted in an article on the pollution prevention initiatives of H2E and Health Care Without Harm in *Healthcare Design*, "While the issues surrounding sustainable building practices have not yet surfaced with these organizations, it is only a matter of time before their achievements in the arena of waste management allow a refocusing of their agenda to the built environment" (Guenther 2001).

At the same time, operational improvement initiatives often fell short of achieving their objectives; in many instances, building design appeared to limit success. As far back as the early 1990s, Janet Brown, Waste Manager at Beth Israel Medical Center, New York, identified three core issues — space, money, and time — preventing the widespread implementation of operational improvements, sentiments echoed in the AHA publication, *An Ounce of Prevention: Waste Reduction Strategies for Health Care Facilities* (McRae, Shaner and Bisson 1993). In fact, the 2001 *Guidelines for Construction of Hospital and Health Care Facilities* (FGI 2001), which define minimum space standards for healthcare buildings, included no language for either receiving areas or waste handling facilities. The 2006 edition of the document includes language mandating program consideration of these important operational issues (FGI 2006).

Through sponsorship of the *Green Guide for Health Care*, H2E has participated in the development of a more comprehensive tool that both measures operational performance and integrates operations with design considerations. This positioned the North American healthcare industry to move forward on a coordinated path.

Operations

				Integrated Operations	5 Points
Y				Prereq 1 Ongoing Self-Certification	Required
Y				Prereq 2 Integrated Operations & Maintenance Process	Required
Y				Prereq 3 Environmental Tobacco Smoke Control	Required
Y				Prereq 4 Outside Air Introduction & Exhaust Systems	Required
Y	?	N	NA	Credit 1.1 Building Operations & Maintenance: Staff Education	1
Y	?	N	NA	Credit 1.2 Building Operations & Maintenance: Building Systems Maintenance	1
Y	?	N	NA	Credit 1.3 Building Operations & Maintenance: Building Systems Monitoring	1
Y	?	N	NA	Credit 2.1 IAQ Management: Maintaining Indoor Air Quality	1
Y	?	N	NA	Credit 2.2 IAQ Management: Reduce Particulates in Air Distribution	1

				Transportation Operations	3 Points
Y	?	N	NA	Credit 1.1 Alternative Transportation: Public Transportation Access	1
Y	?	N	NA	Credit 1.2 Alternative Transportation: Low Emitting & Fuel Efficient Vehicles	1
Y	?	N	NA	Credit 1.3 Alternative Transportation: Carpool Programs	1

				Energy Efficiency	18 Points
Y				Prereq 1 Existing Building Commissioning	Required
Y				Prereq 2 Minimum Building Energy Performance	Required
Y				Prereq 3 Ozone Protection	Required
Y	?	N	NA	Credit 1.1 Optimize Energy Performance: Energy Star score of 63	1
Y	?	N	NA	Credit 1.2 Optimize Energy Performance: Energy Star score of 67	1
Y	?	N	NA	Credit 1.3 Optimize Energy Performance: Energy Star score of 71	1
Y	?	N	NA	Credit 1.4 Optimize Energy Performance: Energy Star score of 75	1
Y	?	N	NA	Credit 1.5 Optimize Energy Performance: Energy Star score of 79	1
Y	?	N	NA	Credit 1.6 Optimize Energy Performance: Energy Star score of 83	1
Y	?	N	NA	Credit 1.7 Optimize Energy Performance: Energy Star score of 87	1
Y	?	N	NA	Credit 1.8 Optimize Energy Performance: Energy Star score of 91	1
Y	?	N	NA	Credit 1.9 Optimize Energy Performance: Energy Star score of 95	1
Y	?	N	NA	Credit 1.10 Optimize Energy Performance: Energy Star score of 99	1
Y	?	N	NA	Credit 2.1 On-Site & Off-Site Renewable Energy: 1% on or 5% off	1
Y	?	N	NA	Credit 2.2 On-Site & Off-Site Renewable Energy: 2% on or 10% off	1
Y	?	N	NA	Credit 2.3 On-Site & Off-Site Renewable Energy: 5% on or 25% off	1
Y	?	N	NA	Credit 2.4 On-Site & Off-Site Renewable Energy: 10% on or 50% off	1
Y	?	N	NA	Credit 3 Energy Efficient Equipment	1
Y	?	N	NA	Credit 4 Refrigerant Selection	1
Y	?	N	NA	Credit 5.1 Performance Measurement: Enhanced Metering	1
Y	?	N	NA	Credit 5.2 Performance Measurement: Emission Reduction Reporting	1

Figure 7-18: The *Green Guide for Health Care* operations section, with ten prerequisites and seventy-two optional points, has eight categories incorporating much of Hospitals for a Healthy Environment's pollution prevention initiatives and those found in LEED for Existing Buildings, organized according to healthcare administrative definition. *Credit: GGHC 2007*

Water Conservation — 8 Points

Y						Required
Y				Prereq 1	Minimum Water Efficiency	Required

Y	?	N	NA	Credit 1.1	Water Efficient Landscaping: Reduce potable water use by 50%	1
Y	?	N	NA	Credit 1.2	Water Efficient Landscaping: Eliminate potable water use	1
Y	?	N	NA	Credit 2.1	Building Water Use Reduction: Reduce 10%	1
Y	?	N	NA	Credit 2.2	Building Water Use Reduction: Reduce 20%	1
Y	?	N	NA	Credit 2.3	Building Water Use Reduction: Reduce 30%	1
Y	?	N	NA	Credit 2.4	Building Water Use Reduction: Reduce 40%	1
Y	?	N	NA	Credit 2.5	Building Water Use Reduction: Reduce 50%	1
Y	?	N	NA	Credit 3	Performance Measurement: Enhanced Metering	1

Chemical Management — 5 Points

Y				Prereq 1	Polychlorinated Biphenyl (PCB) Removal	Required

Y	?	N	NA	Credit 1.1	Community Contaminant Prevention: Airborne Releases	1
Y	?	N	NA	Credit 1.2	Community Contaminant Prevention: Leaks & Spills	1
Y	?	N	NA	Credit 2.1	Indoor Pollutant Source Control & Other Occupational Exposures: Chemical Management & Minimization	1
Y	?	N	NA	Credit 2.2	Indoor Pollutant Source Control & Other Occupational Exposures: High Hazard Chemicals	1
Y	?	N	NA	Credit 3	Chemical Discharge: Pharmaceutical Management & Disposal	1

Waste Management — 6 Points

Y				Prereq 1	Waste Stream Audit	Required

Y	?	N	NA	Credit 1.1	Total Waste Reduction: 15%	1
Y	?	N	NA	Credit 1.2	Total Waste Reduction: 25%	1
Y	?	N	NA	Credit 1.3	Total Waste Reduction: 35%	1
Y	?	N	NA	Credit 2.1	Regulated Medical Waste Reduction: <10%	1
Y	?	N	NA	Credit 2.2	Regulated Medical Waste Reduction: Minimize incineration	1
Y	?	N	NA	Credit 3	Food Waste Reduction	1

Environmental Services — 9 Points

Y	?	N	NA	Credit 1.1	Outdoor Grounds & Building Exterior Management : Implement 4 strategies	1
Y	?	N	NA	Credit 1.2	Outdoor Grounds & Building Exterior Management : Implement 8 strategies	1
Y	?	N	NA	Credit 2	Indoor Integrated Pest Management	2
Y	?	N	NA	Credit 3	Environmentally Preferable Cleaning Policy	1
Y	?	N	NA	Credit 4.1	Sustainable Cleaning Products & Materials: 30% of annual purchases	1
Y	?	N	NA	Credit 4.2	Sustainable Cleaning Products & Materials: 60% of annual purchases	1
Y	?	N	NA	Credit 4.3	Sustainable Cleaning Products & Materials: 90% of annual purchases	1
Y	?	N	NA	Credit 5	Environmentally Preferable Janitorial Equipment	1

Environmentally Preferable Purchasing — 11 Points

Y	?	N	NA	Credit 1.1	Food: Organic or Sustainable	1
Y	?	N	NA	Credit 1.2	Food: Antibiotics	1
Y	?	N	NA	Credit 1.3	Food: Local Production / Food Security	1
Y	?	N	NA	Credit 2	Janitorial Paper & Other Disposable Products	1
Y	?	N	NA	Credit 3	Electronics Purchasing & End of Life Management	1
Y	?	N	NA	Credit 4.1	Toxic Reduction: Mercury	1
Y	?	N	NA	Credit 4.2	Toxic Reduction: DEHP	1
Y	?	N	NA	Credit 4.3	Toxic Reduction: Natural Rubber Latex	1
Y	?	N	NA	Credit 5	Furniture & Medical Furnishings	1
Y	?	N	NA	Credit 6.1	IAQ Compliant Products: 45% of annual purchases	1
Y	?	N	NA	Credit 6.2	IAQ Compliant Products: 90% of annual purchases	1

Innovation in Operation — 7 Points

Y	?	N	Credit 1.1	Innovation in Operations	1
Y	?	N	Credit 1.2	Innovation in Operations	1
Y	?	N	Credit 1.3	Innovation in Operations	1
Y	?	N	Credit 1.4	Innovation in Operations	1
Y	?	N	Credit 2	Documenting Sustainable Operations: Business Case Impacts	1
Y	?	N	Credit 3.1	Documenting Productivity Impacts: Absenteeism & Health Care Cost Impacts	1
Y	?	N	Credit 3.2	Documenting Productivity Impacts: Research Initiatives	1

Operations Project Total — 72 Points

Key

Y – (yes) you are moderately confident that you can attain the credit.

? – (maybe) it will be challenging for this project and you are uncertain of your ability to attain it but you will try.

N – (no) while technically possible, you currently don't expect to try to achieve this credit in this project due to the cost or other tradeoffs with project goals.

NA – (not applicable) it is inherently physically unattainable for this particular project regardless of effort due to physical conditions or project scope.

Examples would include: Sustainable Sites Credits 3.1-3.3 (Brownfield Redevelopment) for a project not on a brownfield site, Materials & Resources Credits 1.1-1.3 (Building Reuse) if no portions of an existing building are part of the project, Environmental Quality Credit 8.1d-8.1e (Daylight & Views, Inpatient) if there are no facilities for inpatients, and Sustainable Sites Credit 7.1-7.2 (Heat Island Effect) if the scope of the project is only interior renovation.

The case study projects presented in this chapter have a history of pollution prevention initiatives that predate their undertakings in sustainable building. For some, their success in pollution prevention community leadership made sustainable building a requirement for maintaining leadership positions. For others, establishing high-level environmental leadership councils or green teams created leadership capabilities that propelled green building initiatives forward.

Achievements in pollution prevention require a shift in mindset (as discussed in Chapter 6) and creative ways around the barriers of money, time, and space. Early adopters have demonstrated that monetary savings

We launched a group that we call Stewards for a Sustainable Environment, or S2E. It's an interdisciplinary team of four people. We meet monthly at 7 AM, and we are all early for the meeting. In the midst of all the rest of the work we have to do, we find time to move on these environmental initiatives because of our passion for them!

—GEOFFREY GLASS, PE, DIRECTOR, FACILITY AND TECHNOLOGY SERVICES, PROVIDENCE ST. PETER HOSPITAL, OLYMPIA, WASHINGTON

through waste reduction can fund positions for environmental managers and recycling coordinators. Green teams, in some instances led by these new personnel, emerge, energized, from within organizations. At the same time, as the following essay chronicles, facility design decisions can have a dramatic impact on the ultimate success of environmental management programs.

Integrating Operations in the Design Process

Janet Brown, Laura Brannen, and Sarah O'Brien

You've designed and built the healthcare environment of your dreams—with natural daylighting, meditative space for workers and staff, healthier materials, and visual inspiration. Now, fast forward to occupancy. The supplies arrive in corrugated boxes that are opened and piled up by the service elevator; disposable plastic ID cards are stamped for each patient; covered trash receptacles become table tops for the empty cafeteria trays holding disposable polystyrene dishware and the untouched slice of white bread, still in its clear plastic wrap; the pest control contractor walks through on his scheduled pesticide application rounds. You get the idea.

It would be wonderful if workers could just step into a new green building and through healthy materials-daylighting-meditative-space-osmosis and get with the program and have an environmental attitude adjustment. It would be nice if all the operations in the new environment could get an automatic environmental makeover, and if the high-performance healing environment would never transform into a green envelope holding the same old toxic habits (pouring lab chemicals down the drain), unhealthy processes (using toxic cleaning chemicals for general-purpose cleaning) and wasteful inefficiencies (upgrading and disposing of computers constantly). But in reality, less-than-healthy processes will continue unless they are addressed before creating and populating a space.

As with preventive medicine, it's easier and more effective to engage operational issues at the outset of the planning process than trying to cope with them after a space is built. It doesn't make sense to create a building and then wonder where the recycling baler or the housekeeping chemicals should be stored. To create a healing environment—an environment that minimizes stress for building occupants, reduces ecological impact, and improves safety—the flow of people, equipment, air, materials, and sounds connected with ordinary, everyday healthcare operations must be mapped out and clearly understood by the design team.

Simply reviewing current waste handling processes, for example, can lead to better flow control and storage options. Similarly, if a hospital is no longer going to use ethylene oxide for instrument sterilization, it may not need as much air-handling capacity and safety elements. By developing a shared understanding of the building's basic operations, we can successfully address the challenges as a group. If not, a mismatch between building and operations may result in disappointment on both sides, as well as unrealized opportunities and unnecessary costs. Some facilities have hired a sustainability coordinator during construction and kept this person on in a staff position following building completion to ensure the sustainability of continuing operations. Environmental management and improvement does not stop when the construction is complete. It just takes a different form.

WAYFINDING TO GREENER OPERATIONS

Walk into most facilities and you will find a hodgepodge of waste and recycling receptacles for a hodgepodge of materials. Good design should make it easier and more obvious how to handle waste materials. We are all accustomed to wayfinding in a facility, but wayfinding is usually focused on helping patients navigate to their destination. Incorporating environmental wayfinding—standardized methods and containers for material collection, storage, transport, and removal, with consistent color coding and snazzy signage throughout the facility—could help staff follow proper waste procedures without having to work so hard to do the right thing! Maintenance closets with straightforward, clearly designed signage (and good lighting with which to read it) can help reinforce staff training and improve compliance with best practices when using dispensing systems and new methods that employ green cleaning chemicals. In healthcare—where environmental management involves numerous full-time and contract staff, multiple languages, and, at teaching institutions, students who go in and out of rotations frequently—simplicity equals success.

WASTE MANAGEMENT

US healthcare generates more than two million tons of waste annually—an environmental and financial problem that we can do something about. Because it's garbage, there's a tendency to underestimate the complexity of waste-management operations in healthcare. Don't be fooled—it takes serious study and planning to build high-functioning waste and housekeeping systems that comply with regulations and meet staff and patient needs. If highly developed environmental and waste-reduction expertise is not available in-house, include healthcare environmental experts in the design process.

Three basic steps will go a long way to put waste-reduction programs into practice:

1. Design for waste management: *Spaces themselves can help staffers engage in environmentally sound waste-management practices, but this requires an understanding of how hospitals generate waste, what kind of waste is avoidable, and what space is needed for optimal operational efficiency. In considering a material's exit strategy, remember that*

THREE ELEMENTS OF A WASTE-REDUCTION PROGRAM

1. Buy less, and buy the right stuff. Integrate reusable, durable, less toxic products that use less packaging, are recyclable, and ultimately generate less waste into all aspects of operations.

2. Use less stuff. Choose efficient, effective products, and engage staff members about changes in their individual work practices.

3. At the end of a material's useful life, dispose of it in a way that minimizes its health and environmental impacts. Always consider reuse and recycling options before throwing any material in the trash.

waste materials require as much oversight as materials entering a facility: waste has to be segregated by type, weighed, scanned for radioactivity, and trafficked through the fewest pickups in order to reduce per pound hauling costs. If possible, create separate docks for incoming materials and outgoing wastes. A commitment to the environment is about control—if there is inadequate space or supervision over the flow of materials, control is lost; this can result in regulatory infractions, negative press, or even worse, an actual safety problem that causes illness or injury.

2. Review the facility's waste-management plan: Assess the efficacy of the existing operations and make enhancements before beginning a new design. There's no sense designing a new facility based on inefficient or environmentally unsound waste management. Such an assessment also ensures there is a documented system for controlling the various waste and recycling streams. If a facility is doing very little recycling, donating, or reprocessing, or is still using a lot of disposables, it may make sense to employ a waste-reduction consultant to discuss an overall plan to minimize the generation of all waste types.

3. Design for the real world: If you are sizing a treatment technology for regulated medical waste (RMW) (also referred to as infectious waste or red-bag waste), you don't need space for a system generating 40 percent RMW when the achievable target is 8 to 15 percent. A high generation rate means there is an opportunity for improved segregation and cost savings. (Red-bag waste usually costs five times more per pound to dispose of than regular waste.) Receiving dock space must accommodate a system that recycles cardboard: cardboard alone accounts for up to 15 percent of total waste and the vast majority of it enters the system through the receiving department. (Locate a baler or compactor at the receiving dock and capture the cardboard there.) With the next generation of best practices, facilities may be able to replace most cardboard by using reusable toters to transport materials from centralized warehouses; consider using reusable containers to deliver supplies to the floors.

WASTE MANAGEMENT AND SPACE

Environmental improvements don't necessarily reduce space needs, but they do affect the configuration of the space required. Environmentally preferable purchasing practices can reduce the need for both solid-waste and recyclable storage space. Alternatively, increased recycling may reduce waste storage needs but increase the need for recycling storage.

Regulatory requirements vary by region. Staffers' levels of training and awareness will also influence generation rates. Each facility is unique. Only with clear, data-driven knowledge of the generation rates of its various waste streams can waste-reduction opportunities and appropriate storage needs be identified.

ENVIRONMENTAL PURCHASING

Purchasing is inevitably linked to waste generation and management. Material is garbage and garbage is material—it's only a matter of time. Some supplies become garbage in minutes, others in weeks, months, or years. Making informed purchasing decisions through environmentally preferable purchasing (EPP)—the process of purchasing products and services that have a reduced impact on human health and the environment when compared with comparable alternatives—goes a long way to reduce waste and toxicity at its source and is gaining broad adoption in healthcare. EPP is being supported by the labeling protocols and expanded choices of group purchasing organizations.

If we take a close look at "back door" waste material, we can learn a lot from it. By introducing the front door (purchasing) to the back door (housekeeping) and having the two departments report waste- and toxicity-reduction successes to the same person, facilities can address the material-to-garbage connection directly. This presents opportunities to reduce toxicity and waste through purchasing—not only when designing a building, but throughout its many years of operation. All too often, housekeeping is in charge of the waste budget, so waste prevention, reduced toxic chemical spills, and other "waste"-related costs aren't appreciated in the purchasing department, which focuses only on upfront pricing. By establishing a reporting structure that links the upfront cost and quality with waste and worker protection costs, the value of reducing toxic baggage (e.g., disposal, air-quality testing, spill cleanup, and protective equipment) becomes much more obvious to both departments.

RESPECT FOR WORKERS

The physician lounge is a locked, "gated community," and the housekeeping lounge is next to the morgue! If this is a slight exaggeration, it is meant to illustrate the severe discrepancy in worker environments and speak to the critical importance of employee satisfaction for all workers and its connection to patient satisfaction, staff retention, and overall quality of care.

All employees have basic rights—first and foremost to a safe working environment, but also to a clean, aesthetically pleasing spot for a meal or a break or to change clothes; proper training on work practices; and recognition for a job well done. By taking the time to engage all workers—housekeepers, lab technicians, food servers, engineers, risk managers, administrators, and so on—designers can learn about the way a facility really operates and glean useful suggestions from those involved in its day-to-day work. Healthcare facilities at which designers consult early with the housekeeping staff won't end up with countertops that stain easily when washed with common cleaning products or rooms that are too small to allow staffers to change the linens easily. Consider mocking up a model space and allowing the housekeepers to try working in it—you'll likely get an earful of useful advice.

Employee and patient satisfaction is a primary goal in the creation of a healing environment. When transforming a healthcare facility's operations, employees are asked to do things a new way. For some, it may mean changing the way they have done something for the past twenty-five years, whether it's switching to a different cleanser, putting paper in a different bin, or putting sharps in a reusable container. Employees need to be actively educated and supported, and understand their critical role in the healing environment.

This involves a lot of listening—and learning. If you listen to the workers out on the floors, you'll learn about the way things are really done (and that way isn't always what you read about in the policies and procedures manual. Surprise!). There is deep wisdom on those floors, but it can remain an unopened gift. Often no one asks for that information, and it may take some time to establish enough trust for it to be offered up anyway. An environment of care has to be built collaboratively to endure and thrive. By demonstrating to frontline workers that their ideas will be heard and sometimes acted upon, healthy communication can grow.

Integrating greener operations has to be a continuous quality-improvement process—it's not something that will be finished upon the completion of construction. If introduced too quickly, changes in operations may fall flat. Maintaining programs takes work—a fact that is sometimes overlooked. We have to keep supporting existing initiatives as we introduce new ones; if too many changes are required at the same time, progress can become mired in confusion. Success does not happen by itself. It requires support, creativity, passion, and strong leadership from someone ready to guide the effort throughout the life of the facility.

Committing to healthier operations encompasses a broad range of initiatives, including environmentally preferable purchasing, material-flow control, reducing toxicity and the volume of materials and waste, engaging the staff and making environmental programs easy to participate in, and creating respectful, efficient workspaces. Working collaboratively with the building's facility management and housekeeping staff to develop such initiatives is critical to the creation of a truly healing environment—a place where the environmental and healing missions go beyond a plaque on the wall by the elevator and become something that you can feel by visiting, working in—or healing in—the space.

ADDRESSING THE CHALLENGES

The following analysis of two hypothetical 425-bed hospitals that each generate 2,400 tons of waste annually —Brown Medical Center and Green Memorial Hospital —illustrates the monetary savings achievable through implementing comprehensive and progressive waste-management programs. Green Memorial has an innovative recycling program through which 38 percent (900 tons) of its waste is diverted from landfill as well as a regulated medical waste (RMW) management program that maintains a consistent generation rate of 10 percent (an achievable benchmark value). In total, Green Memorial spends $245,000 annually on waste disposal. This performance, while exemplary, is achieved in most progressive H2E member hospitals — disposal costs are average. Brown Medical Center, on the other hand, doesn't have a waste segregation or recycling program, and splits the 900 tons of material that Green Memorial recycles between RMW and solid waste. Brown spends $596,000. The difference, annually, is a staggering $351,000 (see Figure 7-19).

Ultimately, the implementation of successful environmental programs requires leadership and commitment, much the same as sustainable building processes. Laura Brannen, executive director of H2E, summarized the power of linking building performance and operation:

> There is a clear vision of the health care facilities of the future: high-performance buildings that use less energy, less water, require fewer chemicals to maintain, that are designed for maximum operational waste management systems; where materials are purchased with health and environmental considerations; where materials are used efficiently, staff take responsibility for and participate in waste minimization programs; and end-of-life considerations are maximized and include reuse and recycling. Today . . . no facility has to start from scratch or go it alone to achieve that vision (Brannen 2006).

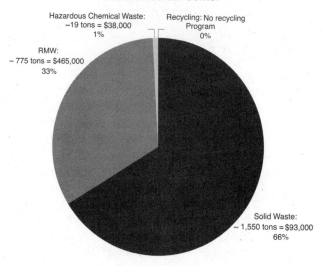

Brown Medical Center

Hazardous Chemical Waste: ~19 tons = $38,000 1%

Recycling: No recycling Program 0%

RMW: ~ 775 tons = $465,000 33%

Solid Waste: ~ 1,550 tons = $93,000 66%

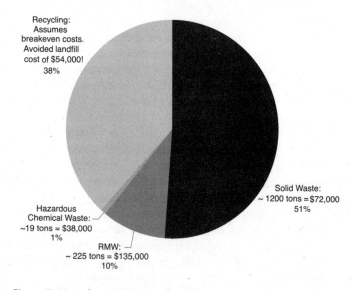

Green Memorial Hospital

Recycling: Assumes breakeven costs. Avoided landfill cost of $54,000! 38%

Solid Waste: ~ 1200 tons = $72,000 51%

Hazardous Chemical Waste: ~19 tons = $38,000 1%

RMW: ~ 225 tons = $135,000 10%

Figure 7-19: In this comparison of two hypothetical 425-bed hospitals, aggressive source segregation and recycling programs reduce annual waste disposal costs by $351,000. *Credit: Brannen 2006.*

CHAPTER 8

Tools

Never doubt that a small group of thoughtful, committed citizens can change the world. Indeed, it's the only thing that ever has.
—MARGARET MEAD

INTRODUCTION

The prospect of establishing green building protocols for the healthcare sector is daunting, given the technical sophistication of its buildings. The promise of quantifying performance benefits, however, makes such tools essential. What defines a high-performance healing environment? Attributes that make healthcare settings unique—from 24/7 operations, infection-control concerns, extensive construction amid ongoing occupancy, and hazardous chemical use to creating physical environments conducive to healing patients and optimizing work conditions for staff—are precisely those that make them challenging.

What if the healthcare industry, informed by ecological and human health considerations, recalibrated its standard approach to planning, design, and construction? What if healthcare organizations became community leaders by recognizing that decisions made within their walls have a profound effect on health outside their

walls? What if the healthcare industry motivated manufacturers of building products and materials to take responsibility for the environmental health consequences of their enterprises and catalyzed industry toward manufacturing practices aligned with a mission of "first, do no harm"?

Healthcare is, in fact, in the midst of this transformation—aided by an expanding network of customized tools, policies, programs, and projects—both in the US and abroad. A journey that began years ago, it has been undertaken by both individuals and organizations, influenced by international policy and modest individual hospital initiatives, informed by green building tools, and inspired by a vision of health and healing. With each successive policy and development tool, the journey moves the industry closer to actualizing this unique vision for healthcare in the twenty-first century.

IN THE BEGINNING: SUSTAINABLE DESIGN TOOLS, PRINCIPLES, AND POLICIES

The 1990s witnessed a proliferation of tools, best-practice procedures, and policy frameworks structured to promote and support sustainable planning, development, design, and construction. Ranging from international policies to local sustainability guidelines, building industry leaders recognized the importance of green buildings and began moving the agenda into practice. From these early efforts emerged a powerful definition of sustainability and the first comprehensive tools for rating buildings. While the healthcare industry was largely untouched by these early developments, they ultimately provided the framework for healthcare's green building tools.

In 1990, the US Environmental Protection Agency (EPA) funded the American Institute of Architects' Committee on the Environment (AIA/COTE) to develop the first US guide to building materials, systems, and processes based on a life cycle framework. *The Environmental Resource Guide* (AIA 1996), first published in 1992, is credited with initiating the transformation of the building sector toward sustainability.

Since then, a continuum of federal policies and programs supporting green building has ensued in earnest. In 1998, the first executive order, "Greening the Government through Waste Prevention, Recycling, and Federal Acquisition" (OFEE 1998), was issued, with many more to follow. Additionally, the *Whole Building Design Guide* (2007), initially released in 1998, continues to serve as an online information how-to resource; it is managed by the National Institute for Building Sciences (NIBS).

EARLY RATING TOOLS

The 1992 United Nations Earth Summit recognized the first comprehensive rating tool for building performance, a tool that guided much of the first generation of rating-tool development. The City of Austin Green Building Program, conceived in 1989 through a public-private partnership between the city of Austin and the Center for Maximum Potential Building Systems (CMPBS), was the first rating tool to extend the metrics associated with green building beyond energy performance to include materials, water, and waste in a life cycle context (Austin Energy 2007). The UN Earth Summit Award recognized the seminal framework developed by CMPBS that scores of future green building programs would follow.

Coincident with Austin's Green Building Program, the UK's Building Research Establishment (BRE) released its building assessment tool. The Building Research Establishment's Environmental Assessment Method (BREEAM 1990) was the first environmental assessment tool to be used internationally. According to BRE, the rating tool provides "the measure of best practice in environmental design and management" for both new and existing commercial office buildings, though its methodology has wide applications in other sectors and has expanded to include tools customized for the residential, school, industrial, and healthcare markets. BREEAM has been a model for other international tools, most notably the Green Building Council of Australia's Green Star scheme, and continues to command strong support and implementation in the UK. It is referenced specifically in the healthcare sector through the British National Health Service's Environmental Assessment Tool, or NEAT, which is discussed in later sections of this chapter. A companion reference document, "The Green Guide to Specification" (BRE 2002), provides in-depth life cycle assessment data on a range of building materials and assemblies.

Soon after the release of these early tools, the American Society for Testing and Materials Technical Committee E-50 on Environmental Assessment introduced Subcommittee E-50.06, chaired by developer and US Green Building Council cofounder David Gottfried. This subcommittee, charged with developing criteria to evaluate the environmental performance of commercial buildings, also viewed a voluntary rating system as a necessary

Figure 8-1: The Building Research Establishment's Environmental Assessment Method (BREEAM) logo. Its Web site is: www.breeam.org. *Credit: BREEAM is a registered trademark owned by the Building Research Establishment.*

part of putting green building into practice (EBN 1992). While this effort did not result in releasing a green building standard in the time frame anticipated, it nonetheless reflected the broad national interest and investment in creating a robust framework to advance green building.

Throughout the remainder of the decade, local and regional sustainable design tools proliferated, both nationally and internationally. The initial release of the US Green Building Council's Leadership in Energy and Environmental Design (LEED) Green Building Rating System in 1998 marked the culmination of a short but rich history of efforts to define and measure green building performance.

Figure 8-2: The US Green Building Council (USGBC) logo. Its Web site is: www.usgbc.org. *Credit: © US Green Building Council*

THE US GREEN BUILDING COUNCIL AND LEED

The US Green Building Council (USGBC), a nonprofit organization founded in 1993, held its first conference in Chicago, in conjunction with the International Union of Architects/American Institute of Architects (UIA/AIA) convention. Organized by a dedicated and diverse group of building-related professionals, the council undertook an assessment of national best-practice efforts that sup-

ported its mission to accelerate the adoption of green building practices, technologies, policies, and standards. Acknowledging the need for a design tool that quantified green building design and performance strategies as a basis to validate green building claims and to extend the earlier efforts of the American Society for Testing and Materials, the USGBC's initial goal was to create a whole-building sustainability rating system. Over the next five years, this independent rating system — LEED — was developed and launched. (For details on the development of LEED, see www.usgbc.org.)

Figure 8-3: The US Green Building Council's LEED family of products is structured to provide tailored green building rating tools that address specific construction phases and market segments. *Credit: © US Green Building Council*

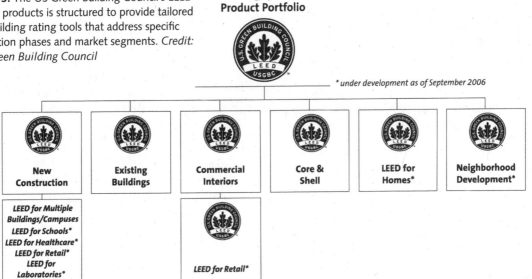

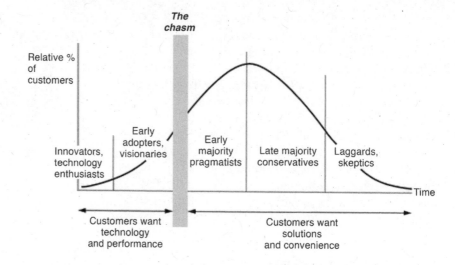

Figure 8-4: The technology adoption life cycle reflects successive stages of adopters: innovators are the pioneers who embrace new technologies; early adopters view new technologies as an opportunity to gain advantage; the early majority are pragmatists unwilling to take risks but ready to take advantage of proven technologies; the late majority prefer tradition to progress; and laggards resist and block new technologies. *Credit: © 1998 D. A. Norman. Used with permission of the author.*

In 1998, the USGBC's membership approved an initial commercial building rating system document—LEED for New Construction Version 1.0. The first major update, Version 2.0, followed less than two years later, addressing a myriad of content issues, emphasizing performance versus prescriptive practices, and rewarding an expanding set of recognized best practices. These products propelled USGBC growth—by 2003, it was the fastest growing nonprofit organization in the United States.

Developed by a multi-stakeholder consensus committee process including design, construction, engineering, manufacturer, government, real estate, finance, building owner, and environmental nonprofit representation, LEED targeted the top 25 percent of the commercial building marketplace with regard to sustainable best practices for third-party recognition and certification. In so doing, it catalyzed the building materials marketplace toward product innovation and transformation.

THE LEED RATING SYSTEM

LEED is both a point-based metric tool to define best practice in sustainable design and construction and a third-party certification system to verify achievement. Through a rigorous registration, documentation, submission, and certification process, buildings attain a rat-

ing at one of four levels: certified, silver, gold, or platinum. In 2001, the USGBC launched a professional accreditation program. Using a standardized testing methodology to gauge command of the use of LEED and sustainable design, the council began accrediting professionals to signal baseline sustainability knowledge. As of 2006, more than thirty thousand people had achieved LEED accredited professional (LEED-AP) status.

LEED's success in the marketplace reflects its distinguishing features:

- *Simplicity:* LEED's basic framework is easy to follow, comprised of prerequisites and credits structured around six categories. By maintaining consistency within product-development cycles, users can establish in-house protocols, standard specifications, and performance indicators aligned with the LEED structure.
- *Branding:* LEED is recognized as a mark of approval by manufacturers, building owners and operators, design firms, and increasingly by utilities, real estate developers, financial institutions, and the general public.
- *Competition:* LEED provides a basis of comparison, both among LEED- and non-LEED certified buildings, and among LEED-certified buildings—from the basic, certified level to platinum, the highest level.

LEED was almost immediately adopted within the regulatory arena, reflecting a demand on the part of federal, state, and local governments for a third-party certification tool tied to a regulatory performance standard. Before LEED, governments, such as the City of Austin, had been developing their own green building rating tools. While the initial intent of LEED was to reward the leading edge of marketplace best practices, it has been increasingly referenced as a minimum standard in green building legislation. As of May 2007, more than ninety LEED-related initiatives, including resolutions, legislation, ordinances, executive orders, policies, and incentives, had been promulgated by city, county, state, and federal regulatory bodies in the US and Canada, further embedding LEED as the de facto standard for green building (USGBC 2007).

Inevitably, the American market shifts toward green building have resonated globally, echoing the pattern of tool development that occurred in the United States. The Green Building Council of Australia, for example, launched its own green building tool, Green Star, and has gone on to modify it for several sector-specific applications, including healthcare.

MARKET TRANSFORMATION

By the onset of the new millennium, sustainable design had achieved broad recognition and acceptance — in the US and internationally — that distinguished it from earlier dispersed, more singularly focused efforts. By 2003, a decade after its founding, the USGBC had grown to more than two thousand organizational members, with thirty-one certified LEED projects and about five thousand LEED-registered projects representing over 4 percent of all new commercial construction in the US, based on square footage (USGBC 2003). By the end of 2006, membership had ballooned to more than seven thousand, with approximately seven hundred LEED-certified projects, and five thousand registered (Glaser 2006). Fueling this expansion is the growing suite of LEED tools, customized for specific sectors and building phases.

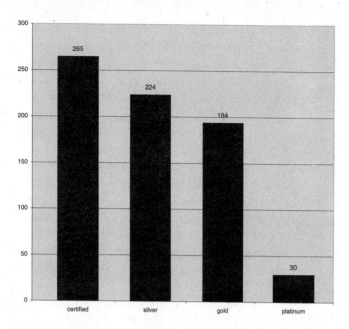

Figure 8-5A: This diagram indicates the achievement thresholds of the 713 LEED certified projects as of December, 2006.

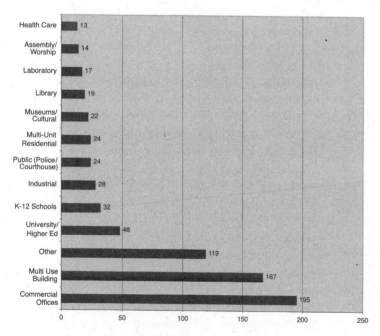

Figure 8-5B: The healthcare sector ranks twelfth out of all LEED certified project building types as of December, 2006, representing just under 2 percent of the total.

Viewing LEED as a "journey, not a destination" (Moore 2006), USGBC leadership has cultivated an entrepreneurial approach to LEED. The next generation of LEED products is anticipated to transform both the rating system's fundamental structure and marketplace delivery, with an initial release expected in late 2007. LEED continues to be the market leader in third-party certification tools for green building in North America: in July 2006, a report prepared for the US General Services Administration (GSA) concluded, "LEED is not only the US market leader, but is also the most widely used rating system by Federal and state agencies" (Fowler and Rauch 2006).

At the same time, the next generation of rating tools, such as the Cascadia Region Green Building Council's Living Building Challenge — a tool with no credits, only prerequisites — continues to raise the bar for building performance. Institutions and governmental bodies enact specialized green building standards, while industry-sector-sponsored self-certification tools, such as Green Globes, challenge the definition of sustainable buildings.

GREEN BUILDING IN HEALTHCARE: THE BEGINNING

Viewed through healthcare's lens, however, this momentum was virtually invisible. Described by *Building Design and Construction* in 2004 as "The Lost Sheep of Sustainable Design" (Cassidy 2004), healthcare's lagging engagement was characterized as ironic, especially as green buildings were increasingly defined as "environmentally responsible, profitable and healthy places to live and work" (USGBC 2006). As traced over a short history of gatherings, collaborations, and tool development, the coalescing of green building and healthcare interests is quickening; what were distanced spheres of interest are coming together as shared spheres of concern.

The Living Building Challenge, released in November 2006 by the Cascadia Region Green Building Council, is a prerequisite-only tool meant to "raise the bar and define a closer measure of true sustainability in the built environment. Projects that achieve this level of performance can claim to be the 'greenest' in North America and as close to true sustainability as currently possible." By structuring the Living Building Challenge around only performance-based prerequisites—and not credits—the authors' intention is to inspire a balanced state between the built and natural environments while encouraging diverse solutions reflecting building type and bioregion. The sixteen prerequisites are organized within a framework of six categories:

1. *Site:* responsible site selection, limits to growth, habitat exchange
2. *Energy:* net zero energy
3. *Materials:* materials red list, construction carbon footprint, responsible industry, appropriate materials/services radius, leadership in construction waste
4. *Water:* net zero water, sustainable water discharge
5. *Indoor environmental quality:* civilized work environment, healthy air/source control, healthy air/ventilation
6. *Beauty + inspiration:* beauty and spirit, inspiration and education

Source: Cascadia Region Green Building Council (2006)

SETTING HEALTHCARE'S ENVIRONMENTAL AGENDA

In October 2000, healthcare industry leaders representing healthcare systems, public and nonprofit policy advisors, and professional associations gathered in San Francisco to assess healthcare's unique environmental opportunities and challenges. The conference coincided with the eve of the nation's most ambitious hospital rebuilding program since the Hill-Burton period. Kaiser Permanente, for example, the nation's largest nonprofit healthcare provider, with a significant building portfolio in California, expects to spend upward of $13.1 billion before 2013 on twenty-five new hospitals (replacements or significant additions) and more than four hundred new medical office buildings due to changes in the state of California's seismic requirements. Convened by Health Care Without Harm, Kaiser Permanente, and Catholic Healthcare West, the landmark conference, Setting Healthcare's Environmental Agenda (SHEA), began with a challenge issued by environmental health advocate Michael Lerner: "The question is whether health care professionals can begin to recognize the environmental consequences of our operations and put our own house in order. This is no trivial question" (Lerner 2000).

Healthcare system executives in attendance echoed the recognition of leadership responsibility. David Lawrence, chairman and CEO of Kaiser Foundation Health Plan, Inc., declared, "Just as we have responsibility for providing quality patient care [and] . . . keeping our facilities and technology up to date, we have a responsibility for providing leadership in the environment" (Lawrence 2000). Lloyd Dean, president and CEO of Catholic Healthcare West, agreed, adding this challenge: "We will not have healthy individuals, healthy families, and healthy communities if we do not have clean air, clean water, and healthy soil" (Dean 2000).

Prior to the SHEA conference, the healthcare industry had not formed a position about green building, nor did it have familiarity with green building examples. An Internet literature search in 2000 yielded virtually no results for *green healthcare* or *sustainable healthcare* as specifically related to healthcare facilities, save for a few European examples. SHEA participants endorsed a health-based framework to guide the healthcare design and construction sector: "Guidelines and regulations overseeing hospital design and construction should be evaluated based on their impacts on environmental quality and human health and revised so that they reflect these as priority considerations" (Vittori 2001).

The concept of health as an explicit performance metric within the broader range of emerging green building metrics was acknowledged as both a necessary and defining component of a green building protocol for the healthcare sector. The conference achieved its objective: by its close, the participants had, in fact, set the agenda for the development of the healthcare sector's approach to environmental performance.

AMERICAN SOCIETY FOR HEALTHCARE ENGINEERING INITIATIVES

The American Society for Healthcare Engineering (ASHE) published healthcare's first green building guidance tool. Sensing that green building held great promise for the industry, executive director Al Sunseri, PhD, believed that establishing a sustainable design recognition program for healthcare would convey an important first signal. He convened a Green Building Task Force to draft a guidance statement for the ASHE Vista Awards Committee to use in assessing award applicants. Released in January 2002 as the ASHE *Green Healthcare Construction Guidance Statement*, the introductory statement of principles asserts the importance of protecting health at three scales (ASHE 2002):

1. Protecting the immediate health of building occupants
2. Protecting the health of the surrounding community
3. Protecting the health of the larger global community and natural resources

In addition, the guidance statement includes a specific reference to the precautionary principle, one of the basic tenets of the Agenda 21 agreement ratified at the 1992 UN Earth Summit:

> Prevention is a fundamental principle of health care and public health. Indeed, to prevent disease is preferable to treating disease after it has occurred. In the face of uncertainty, precautionary action is appropriate to prevent harm. This public health approach makes sense both in the clinical setting and in response to environmental and public health hazards. Similarly, a precautionary and preventive approach is an appropriate basis for decisions regarding material selection, design features, me-

chanical systems, infrastructure, and operations and maintenance practices (ASHE 2002).

Expanding upon the six recognized LEED categories — sustainable sites, water efficiency, energy and atmosphere, materials and resources, indoor environmental quality, and innovation in design — the guidance statement adds sections for integrated design, construction practices, commissioning, operations, and maintenance. These reflect an intrinsic health-based value system, as well as attributes unique to healthcare facilities. The specific approach to integrated design was inspired by healthcare's operational realities, from initial project planning through construction practices, building commissioning, and operations and maintenance. Each category includes a vision statement, goals, and suggested strategies.

Soon after its release, it became apparent that a key element in moving the healthcare industry toward green building — a performance metric — was missing. While the USGBC's LEED for New Construction was a standard to rate buildings based on a numerical achievement of LEED points, it posed challenges for healthcare buildings. And while development of a LEED tool customized for healthcare was slated for the future, its development wasn't yet underway.

The astonishing surge in healthcare construction activity throughout the United States added a sense of urgency for a customized green building tool for healthcare. In California, following the SHEA Conference, Kaiser Permanente produced its Eco-Toolkit, comparing LEED strategies to the ASHE guidance statement approach in an effort to define a systemwide green building tool. Knowing that the ASHE guidance statement had already spurred demand among healthcare providers and industry architects and engineers, the timing was right to launch the next phase of green building tools for the healthcare sector.

THE GREEN GUIDE FOR HEALTH CARE

With initial funding provided by the Merck Family Fund in early 2003, the development of the *Green Guide for Health Care* began. A steering committee of profession-

GREEN GUIDE for Health Care™ GGHC

Figure 8-6: "The *Green Guide for Health Care* is a joint project of Health Care Without Harm and the Center for Maximum Potential Building Systems; the Merck Family Fund provided initial funding. The *Green Guide* may be downloaded from www.gghc.org. *Credit:* Green Guide for Health Care *2007.*

ally and geographically diverse healthcare experts was convened by the Center for Maximum Potential Building Systems to create "the health care sector's first quantifiable sustainable design toolkit integrating enhanced environmental and health principles and practices into the planning, design, construction, operations and maintenance of their facilities" (GGHC 2004).

The *Green Guide for Health Care* sought to incorporate and build on existing industry momentum; the breadth of the undertaking proved enormous. The *Green Guide* adopted the ASHE *Green Healthcare Construction Guidance Statement of Principles.* It reaffirmed a principle of precaution, echoed in medicine and international sustainable design policy. From LEED, with permission, it gained credit structure, content, and organization. Building upon the work of Hospitals for a Healthy Environment (H2E), it reinforced the commitment to the 1998 Memorandum of Understanding by the Environmental Protection Agency and the American Hospital Association (see Chapter 7) and defined a comprehensive approach to healthcare operations. From the early green building adopters in healthcare, it evolved rigorous materials evaluation requirements, particularly with regard to emissions and persistent bioaccumulative toxic (PBT) chemical avoidance. It reinforced principles of evidence-based design through an emphasis on daylighting, acoustics, and places of respite.

Finally, the *Green Guide* recognized that the healthcare industry was in the early stages of sustainability development. Consequently, it did not establish minimum achievement thresholds. Instead, it developed as a self-certification tool, promoting best practices within the industry by instilling a culture of internal assessment, evaluation, and continuous improvement. Since its initial release in 2003, the *Green Guide's* goal of transforming the healthcare sector's building portfolio into healthy, high-performance healing environments is being realized through a measured approach grounded on best practices, industry partnerships, and implementation feedback. As an evolving document, it continues to be refined through periodic updates.

Scope and Structure

The first distinguishing feature of the *Green Guide* is its comprehensive approach to both construction and operations. Version 2.2's construction section includes twelve prerequisites and ninety-seven optional points in seven categories that generally correspond to LEED for New Construction. The operations section, with ten prerequisites and seventy-two optional points, has eight categories that incorporate much of Hospitals for a Healthy Environment's (H2E) pollution prevention initiatives and those of LEED for Existing Buildings, organized according to healthcare administrative definition (Figure 7-18 is the operations checklist; Figure 8-7 is the construction checklist). Together, these credits respond to the enormous breadth of the industry's ecological footprint and the wide range of strategies that may be implemented to reduce environmental and health burdens linked to building design and operations.

Construction

Construction
Project Checklist

Key
Y – (yes) you are moderately confident that you can attain the credit.
? – (maybe) it will be challenging for this project and you are uncertain of your ability to attain it but you will try.
N – (no) while technically possible, you currently don't expect to try to achieve this credit in this project due to the cost or other tradeoffs with project goals.
NA – (not applicable) it is inherently physically unattainable for this particular project regardless of effort due to physical conditions or project scope.

Note: an Excel spreadsheet of this checklist is available for download at www.gghc.org

Integrated Design

Y	Prereq 1	Integrated Design Process	Required
Y	Prereq 2	Health Mission Statement & Program	Required

Sustainable Sites — 21 Points

Y	Prereq 1	Construction Activity Pollution Prevention	Required

Y ? N NA	Credit 1	Site Selection	1
Y ? N NA	Credit 2	Development Density & Community Connectivity	1
Y ? N NA	Credit 3.1	Brownfield Redevelopment: Basic Remediation Level	1
Y ? N NA	Credit 3.2	Brownfield Redevelopment: Residential Remediation Level	1
Y ? N NA	Credit 3.3	Brownfield Redevelopment: Minimizing Future Hazards	1
Y ? N NA	Credit 4.1	Alternative Transportation: Public Transportation Access	1
Y ? N NA	Credit 4.2	Alternative Transportation: Bicycle Storage & Changing Rooms	1
Y ? N NA	Credit 4.3	Alternative Transportation: Low-Emitting & Fuel Efficient Vehicles	1
Y ? N NA	Credit 4.4	Alternative Transportation: Parking Capacity	1
Y ? N NA	Credit 5.1	Site Development: Protect or Restore Open Space or Habitat	1
Y ? N NA	Credit 5.2	Site Development: Reduce Development Footprint	1
Y ? N NA	Credit 5.3	Site Development: Structured Parking	1
Y ? N NA	Credit 6.1	Stormwater Design: Quantity Control	1
Y ? N NA	Credit 6.2	Stormwater Design: Quality Control	1
Y ? N NA	Credit 7.1	Heat Island Effect: Non-Roof	1
Y ? N NA	Credit 7.2	Heat Island Effect: Roof	1
Y ? N NA	Credit 8	Light Pollution Reduction	1
Y ? N NA	Credit 9.1	Connection to the Natural World: Outdoor Places of Respite	1
Y ? N NA	Credit 9.2	Connection to the Natural World: Exterior Access for Patients	1
Y ? N NA	Credit 10.1	Community Contaminant Prevention: Airborne Releases	1
Y ? N NA	Credit 10.2	Community Contaminant Prevention: Leaks & Spills	1

Water Efficiency — 6 Points

Y	Prereq 1	Potable Water Use for Medical Equipment Cooling	Required

Y ? N NA	Credit 1	Water Efficient Landscaping: No Potable Water Use or No Irrigation	1
Y ? N NA	Credit 2.1	Potable Water Use Reduction: Measurement & Verification	1
Y ? N NA	Credit 2.2	Potable Water Use Reduction: Domestic Water	1
Y ? N NA	Credit 2.3	Potable Water Use Reduction: Domestic Water	1
Y ? N NA	Credit 2.4	Potable Water Use Reduction: Process Water & Building System Equipment	1
Y ? N NA	Credit 2.5	Potable Water Use Reduction: Process Water & Building System Equipment	1

Figure 8-7: The *Green Guide for Health Care* Version 2.2 construction section includes twelve prerequisites and ninety-seven optional points in seven categories that generally correspond to the LEED for New Construction framework. *Credit: GGHC 2007*

Energy & Atmosphere — 21 Points

Y						
Y				Prereq 1	Fundamental Commissioning of the Building Energy Systems	Required
Y				Prereq 2	Minimum Energy Performance	Required
Y				Prereq 3	Fundamental Refrigerant Management	Required
Y	?	N	NA	Credit 1.1	Optimize Energy Performance: 3.5%/10.5%	1
Y	?	N	NA	Credit 1.2	Optimize Energy Performance: 7%/14%	1
Y	?	N	NA	Credit 1.3	Optimize Energy Performance: 10.5%/17.5%	1
Y	?	N	NA	Credit 1.4	Optimize Energy Performance: 14%/21%	1
Y	?	N	NA	Credit 1.5	Optimize Energy Performance: 17.5%/24.5%	1
Y	?	N	NA	Credit 1.6	Optimize Energy Performance: 21%/28%	1
Y	?	N	NA	Credit 1.7	Optimize Energy Performance: 24.5%/31.5%	1
Y	?	N	NA	Credit 1.8	Optimize Energy Performance: 28%/35%	1
Y	?	N	NA	Credit 1.9	Optimize Energy Performance: 31.5%/38.5%	1
Y	?	N	NA	Credit 1.10	Optimize Energy Performance: 35%/42%	1
Y	?	N	NA	Credit 2.1	On-Site Renewable Energy: 0.05 watts of renewable generating capacity / sf of building area	1
Y	?	N	NA	Credit 2.2	On-Site Renewable Energy: 0.10 watts of renewable generating capacity / sf of building area	1
Y	?	N	NA	Credit 2.3	On-Site Renewable Energy: 0.15 watts of renewable generating capacity / sf of building area	1
Y	?	N	NA	Credit 3	Enhanced Commissioning	1
Y	?	N	NA	Credit 4	Enhanced Refrigerant Management	1
Y	?	N	NA	Credit 5	Measurement & Verification	1
Y	?	N	NA	Credit 6.1	Green Power: 20%	1
Y	?	N	NA	Credit 6.2	Green Power: 50%	1
Y	?	N	NA	Credit 6.3	Green Power: 80%	1
Y	?	N	NA	Credit 6.4	Green Power: 100%	1
Y	?	N	NA	Credit 7	Equipment Efficiency	1

Materials & Resources — 21 Points

Y				Prereq 1	Storage & Collection of Recyclables	Required
Y				Prereq 2	Mercury Elimination	Required
Y	?	N	NA	Credit 1.1	Building Reuse: Maintain 40% of Existing Walls, Floors & Roof	1
Y	?	N	NA	Credit 1.2	Building Reuse: Maintain 80% of Existing Walls, Floors & Roof	1
Y	?	N	NA	Credit 1.3	Building Reuse: Maintain 50% of Interior Non-Structural Elements	1
Y	?	N	NA	Credit 2.1	Construction Waste Management: Divert 50% from Disposal	1
Y	?	N	NA	Credit 2.2	Construction Waste Management: Divert 75% from Disposal	1
Y	?	N	NA	Credit 2.3	Construction Practices: Site & Materials Management	1
Y	?	N	NA	Credit 2.4	Construction Practices: Utility & Emissions Control	1
Y	?	N	NA	Credit 3.1	Sustainably Sourced Materials: 10%	1
Y	?	N	NA	Credit 3.2	Sustainably Sourced Materials: 20%	1
Y	?	N	NA	Credit 3.3	Sustainably Sourced Materials: 30%	1
Y	?	N	NA	Credit 3.4	Sustainably Sourced Materials: 40%	1
Y	?	N	NA	Credit 3.5	Sustainably Sourced Materials: 50%	1
Y	?	N	NA	Credit 4.1	PBT Elimination: Dioxins	1
Y	?	N	NA	Credit 4.2	PBT Elimination: Mercury	1
Y	?	N	NA	Credit 4.3	PBT Elimination: Lead & Cadmium	1
Y	?	N	NA	Credit 5.1	Furniture & Medical Furnishings: Resource Reuse	1
Y	?	N	NA	Credit 5.2	Furniture & Medical Furnishings: Materials	1
Y	?	N	NA	Credit 5.3	Furniture & Medical Furnishings: Manufacturing, Transportation & Recycling	1
Y	?	N	NA	Credit 6	Copper Reduction	1
Y	?	N	NA	Credit 7.1	Resource Use: Design for Flexibility	1
Y	?	N	NA	Credit 7.2	Resource Use: Design for Durability	1

Environmental Quality — 24 Points

Y				Prereq 1	Minimum IAQ Performance	Required
Y				Prereq 2	Environmental Tobacco Smoke Control (ETS)	Required
Y				Prereq 3	Hazardous Material Removal or Encapsulation	Required

Y	?	N	NA	Credit 1	Outdoor Air Delivery Monitoring	1
Y	?	N	NA	Credit 2	Natural Ventilation	1
Y	?	N	NA	Credit 3.1	Construction EQ Management Plan: During Construction	1
Y	?	N	NA	Credit 3.2	Construction EQ Management Plan: Before Occupancy	1
Y	?	N	NA	Credit 4.1	Low-Emitting Materials: Interior Adhesives & Sealants	1
Y	?	N	NA	Credit 4.2	Low-Emitting Materials: Wall & Ceiling Finishes	1
Y	?	N	NA	Credit 4.3	Low-Emitting Materials: Flooring Systems	1
Y	?	N	NA	Credit 4.4	Low-Emitting Materials: Composite Wood & Insulation	1
Y	?	N	NA	Credit 4.5	Low-Emitting Materials: Furniture & Medical Furnishings	1
Y	?	N	NA	Credit 4.6	Low-Emitting Materials: Exterior Applied Products	1
Y	?	N	NA	Credit 5.1	Chemical & Pollutant Source Control: Outdoor	1
Y	?	N	NA	Credit 5.2	Chemical & Pollutant Source Control: Indoor	1
Y	?	N	NA	Credit 6.1	Controllability of Systems: Lighting	1
Y	?	N	NA	Credit 6.2	Controllability of Systems: Thermal Comfort	1
Y	?	N	NA	Credit 7	Thermal Comfort	1
Y	?	N	NA	Credit 8.1a	Daylight & Views: Daylight for Occupied Spaces: 6% above 'square-root base' daylit area	1
Y	?	N	NA	Credit 8.1b	Daylight & Views: Daylight for Occupied Spaces: 12% above 'square-root base' daylit area	1
Y	?	N	NA	Credit 8.1c	Daylight & Views: Daylight for Occupied Spaces: 18% above 'square-root base' daylit area	1
Y	?	N	NA	Credit 8.1d	Daylight & Views: Daylight for Occupied Spaces: 75% of regularly occupied spaces	1
Y	?	N	NA	Credit 8.1e	Daylight & Views: Daylight for Occupied Spaces: 90% of regularly occupied spaces	1
Y	?	N	NA	Credit 8.2	Daylight & Views: Connection to the Natural World: Indoor Places of Respite	1
Y	?	N	NA	Credit 8.3	Daylight & Views: Lighting & Circadian Rhythm	1
Y	?	N	NA	Credit 9.1	Acoustic Environment: Exterior Noise, Acoustical Finishes, & Room Noise Levels	1
Y	?	N	NA	Credit 9.2	Acoustic Environment: Sound Isolation, Paging & Call System, & Building Vibration	1

Innovation & Design Process — 4 Points

Y	?	N	Credit 1.1	Innovation in Design:	1
Y	?	N	Credit 1.2	Innovation in Design	1
Y	?	N	Credit 1.3	Innovation in Design	1
Y	?	N	Credit 2	Documenting Health, Quality of Care & Productivity Performance Impacts: Research Initiatives	1

Construction Project Total — 97 Points

Secondly, the *Green Guide*'s section on construction includes one category drawn from the ASHE *Green Healthcare Construction Guidance Statement:* integrated design. While it may seem obvious to many practitioners that an integrated design approach is fundamental to green building, a dedicated integrated design section supports the idea that the design process is such a clear determinant of project success that it warrants a stand-alone category. Given the critical relationship among operations, building program, and design, the *Green Guide* encourages design teams to collaborate with facility staff early in an integrated design process to establish shared commitments to the operations-related strategies.

A third major distinguishing feature is the health issues statement, which highlights specific health concerns associated with each credit. This unique feature of the *Green Guide* differentiates it from every other rating system or tool; it also emphasizes that every decision associated with the built environment brings with it direct or indirect health consequences. This focus positions the healthcare sector as the leader in raising health issues as a fundamental underpinning of green building. *Architectural Record* proclaimed, "Its health-based approach adds a rich layer of information to the original LEED structure" (Solomon 2004).

Redefining what constitutes green building performance metrics has far-reaching implications for education, consumer awareness, and market transformation. For example, reducing energy demand is typically viewed as having economic benefit (reduced energy costs) and environmental benefit (reduced global warming impacts), but its social benefit (improved air quality and community health) is less widely acknowledged, though the data are well documented. In healthcare, energy conservation has been associated with concerns for decreased occupant health and safety, while its strong potential for public health benefit has not been advanced. The *Green Guide*, through its health-issues statement and extensive resources list, narrows this gap significantly.

Lastly, the *Green Guide* modifies and extends the scope of LEED credits to address the distinctive realities and specific regulatory requirements of the acute care hospital sector. Many of the essays in this book examine and extend these unique healthcare credit strategies in detail, addressing topics such as process-water reduction, energy source and energy performance improvements, acoustical control, and daylighting.

GREEN GUIDE PILOT PROJECTS

The *Green Guide*, a largely Web-based, open-source document, has been continuously refined and edited since its initial release. An extensive public comment period accompanied its initial release; the subsequent release was followed by a pilot project registration program. As it evolves, it continues to incorporate emerging green building and pollution prevention knowledge to remain at the leading edge of industry best practices. In the two years following the release of *Pilot Version 2.0*, *Green Guide* registrants climbed to more than eleven thousand,

representing every state in the US; six hundred from Canada and nine hundred from eighty-three other countries. In addition, pilot participants represented over 30 million square feet and included projects in the US, Canada, China, Malaysia, Guatemala, and eastern Europe. In the US, these early adopter pilot projects constitute a significant percentage of the estimated annual 100 million square feet of healthcare-related construction. The pilot provided an opportunity to glean insight as to the *Green Guide*'s market relevance, appropriateness of credit thresholds, and effectiveness at adding value to design, construction, and operations (see page 199). Many case study projects in this book are *Green Guide* pilots.

Figure 8-8: The Dell Children's Medical Center of Central Texas is both LEED registered and a *Green Guide* pilot. The project has been instrumental in informing the *Green Guide* daylighting credits. *Credit: Karlsberger*

Figure 8-9: The open design of the Donald Dexter Dental Clinic in Eugene, Oregon, brings a bright natural light ambience to all work areas in the clinic. *Credit: Donald Dexter*

Figures 8-10 A and B: The critical access hospital prototype carefully articulates the building section to achieve daylighting in interior circulation zones. *Illustrator: Insight Animation, LLC; Credit: Department of Health and Human Services and Health Resources and Services Administration*

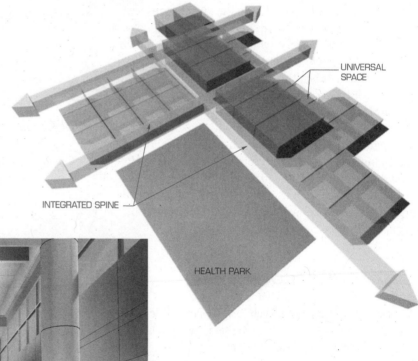

UNIVERSAL SPACE

INTEGRATED SPINE

HEALTH PARK

The Green Guide for Health Care Pilot Program

Adele Houghton, AIA, *Green Guide for Health Care* project manager

The Green Guide for Health Care *Pilot Program has en-abled a cross-section of leading healthcare institutions to collaborate in an active development process. Over two years, the* Green Guide *Pilot Program generated a wide-ranging set of comments and suggestions to im-prove and enhance the next version of the* Green Guide *toolkit,* Green Guide Version 2.2, *which was released in January 2007. Throughout 2006, the program grew to over 115 pilot projects representing more than 30 mil-lion square feet of construction in the US and abroad—an increase of 45 percent over the previous year. Pilot projects vary greatly in size, building type, building phase, and region, demonstrating the* Green Guide's *versatility.*

The majority of Green Guide *pilot projects are lo-cated in the United States. Five projects are in Canada, and four others are located overseas. In the US,* Green Guide *protocols have been implemented across the country—not merely concentrated on the two coasts. In regions with a critical mass of engagement,* Green Guide *pilot projects are creating a climate for innova-tion and exemplary performance. Boston is particularly notable for the large number of institutions that have pledged to achieve at least fifty credits in the* Green Guide's *construction section.*

The Green Guide's *flexible structure accommodates all sizes of pilot projects, from small renovations to major replacement facilities and operations, with the majority (41 percent) falling between 100,000 and 500,000 square feet. New construction projects domi-nate, representing 50 percent based on construction type, and 60 percent based on facility type.*

Although the Green Guide *is tailored to acute care facilities, medical office buildings, retirement facilities, and specialty hospitals, pilot participants reached equivalent levels of achievement using the construc-tion section. For the operations section, the best per-forming projects are renovations and specialty hospitals. In many cases, renovation projects have been registered with the* Green Guide *at the instigation*

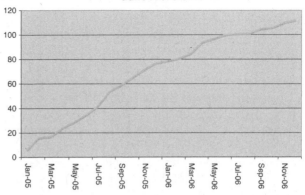

Figure 8-11: Over a one-and-a-half year period, *Green Guide* pilots grew to 115 projects, with about ten projects joining each month. *Credit: GGHC 2007*

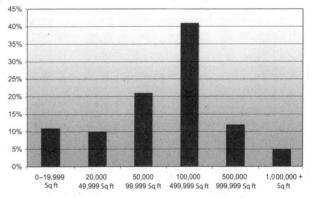

Figure 8-12: *Green Guide* pilot projects range from under 20,000 sq ft (1,858 sq m) to over 1 million sq ft (92,903 sq m), with over 40 percent between 100,000 sq ft (9,290 sq m) and 499,999 sq ft (46,451 sq m). *Credit: GGHC 2007*

of the healthcare institution rather than the design team, reflecting an established awareness of the facil-ity operations' ecological footprint and a desire to move toward green operations and maintenance pro-tocols. Hospitals familiar with Hospitals for a Healthy Environment's pollution prevention and waste reduc-tion programs will find many familiar criteria in the Green Guide's *operations section credits.*

The most striking characteristic of the Green Guide *pilots that break past the twenty-six-point threshold—*

the minimum number of points required for basic LEED certification—is their ability to reach into the upper levels of credit achievement. Over 30 percent of the pilots are projecting the equivalent of LEED gold or platinum point achievement levels using the Green Guide's self-certification system, illustrating the power of integrated design to capitalize on synergistic strategies across building systems.

Average credit achievement for each construction type (Figure 8-13) is consistent with the average Green Guide pilot credit achievement profile for the sustainable sites, energy and atmosphere, and environmental quality sections (Figure 8-14). The water efficiency

section has proved difficult for all of the pilots; however, with new construction projects, the opportunity to design the entire facility's mechanical system and purchase new equipment has contributed to improved achievement levels. Renovation projects, on the other hand, have demonstrated higher achievement in the materials and resources section. In many cases, their more limited scope compared to new construction projects has provided the opportunity to concentrate on healthy materials selection; other Green Guide credits, such as landscaping or upgrading mechanical systems to improve energy efficiency, often fall outside of a renovation project's scope of work.

The Green Guide for Health Care Pilot Program demonstrates the value of having a customized green building tool for healthcare in the marketplace. As a first step into green building for many healthcare projects, the Green Guide provides a knowledge and resource base, while catalyzing a process that inserts a broad spectrum of health outcomes as a measure of success, beginning with design through to a building's operation.

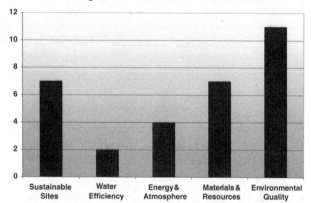

Figure 8-14: In addition to fulfilling Integrated Design prerequisites, Green Guide pilots pursued credits in all of the credit categories, with the greatest number of points pursued in environmental quality. Credit: GGHC 2007

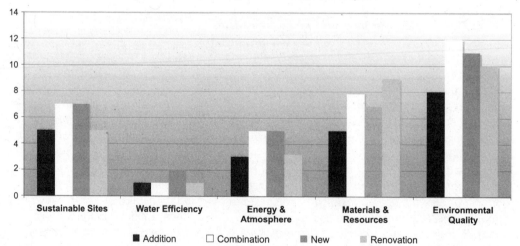

Figure 8-13: Green Guide credit distribution, based on pilot projects, varies by building type, indicating its flexibility to address many types of healthcare facilities. Credit: GGHC 2007

LEED FOR HEALTH CARE

The *Green Guide's* rapid market uptake demonstrates that despite regulatory and financial challenges, healthcare market leaders are gaining comfort with green building protocols, motivated in part by the emerging quantitative and qualitative data asserting the value of green buildings. The *Green Guide*, largely by aligning its structure with LEED, anticipated early on that LEED for Health Care would eventually emerge in the marketplace.

By January 2004, the development of LEED for New Construction Application Guide for Healthcare began in earnest; the core committee representatives included significant crossover with the *Green Guide for Health Care's* steering committee. The objective embraced by committee members and USGBC was to bring to market a third-party certifiable leadership tool for the healthcare sector. The close relationship between the *Green Guide* and LEED for Health Care served the committee well, as the members of the respective groups continued the collaborative nature of tool development.

LEED FOR HEALTH CARE MISSION STATEMENT

LEED for Health Care supports sustainable planning, design, and construction of healthcare facilities by adapting the U.S. Green Building Council's LEED to respond to the unique set of opportunities and challenges presented by the healthcare sector. By affirming healthcare's fundamental mission of '... first, do no harm,' LEED for Health Care recognizes the profound impact of the built environment on the health of occupants, local communities, and global ecology and encourages design strategies that enhance the healing environment for patients, healthy and productive work environments for staff, and responsible ecological stewardship.

Source: LEED for Health Care Core Committee 2004

The anticipated launch of LEED for Health Care in early 2008 is expected to introduce breakthrough credit enhancements into the LEED portfolio of products. While not yet subject to public comment and balloting, the drafted credits include increased emphasis on integrated design, life cycle exposures to PBTs, and explicit attention to human health consequences associated with building-related actions — all outgrowths of the pioneering work of the *Green Guide* — as such, they will extend the parameters of green building and enrich the mindsets of green building practitioners whether or not they are associated with healthcare.

In early 2007, a relatively small percentage of USGBC members represented healthcare organizations. Similarly, of a total registered project pool of about five thousand, the healthcare sector represented only one hundred projects, or about 2 percent (Glaser 2006). A scant thirteen out of over seven hundred LEED-certified buildings are healthcare projects, and only four are acute care hospitals (For the list of certified healthcare projects as of the end of 2006, see page 228. A sampling of the projects are shown in Figures 8-15 through 8-21.)

Eight years after the release of LEED, interest in green building within the healthcare sector is shifting from a small group of innovators test driving green building to early adopters — and even a group of fast followers. The number of healthcare facilities engaged in sustainable new construction, renovation, and operations is climbing steadily. This burgeoning commitment to evolve a values-oriented approach to healthcare design, construction, and operations is redefining the building experience as it relates to patients, staff, and the broader ecological context of the twenty-first century. Defining what constitutes a high-performance healing environment has grown from theory to practice.

These successes have benefited from the tools described in this chapter. In some cases, the accomplishments accrue from augmenting the tools with regional, real-world efforts that introduce concentrated expertise and resources to accelerate market adoption and momentum. One success story is the Design for Health summit, held in Massachusetts in 2004.

Figure 8-15: Boulder Community Hospital, Boulder, Colorado, is the first LEED-certified hospital, achieving LEED silver certification (case study, Chapter 9). *Credit: Courtesy of OZ Architecture*

Figure 8-16: Discovery Health Center, Harris, New York, is the first ambulatory care building to achieve LEED certified status (case study, Chapter 11). *Credit: David Allee, courtesy of Guenther 5 Architects*

Figure 8-17: The Winship Cancer Institute of Emory University, Atlanta, Georgia, achieved LEED certified status in 2005 (case study, Chapter 9). *Credit: Gary Knight + Associates, Inc.*

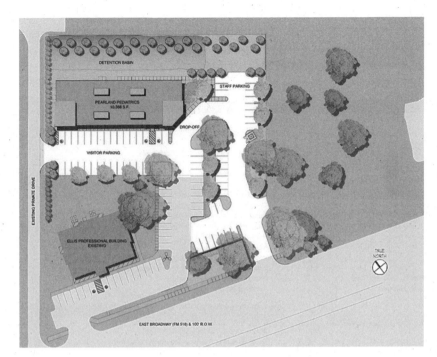

Figure 8-18: The 10,400-sq-ft (966-sq-m) Pearland Pediatrics in Pearland, Texas, achieved LEED certified status in 2006. *Credit: Browne Penland McGregor Stephens Architects*

Figure 8-20: Providence Newberg Medical Center, Newberg, Oregon, is the first hospital to achieve LEED gold certification (case study, Chapter 10). *Credit: Eckert & Eckert*

Figure 8-19: Pearland Pediatrics is the first healthcare project to achieve the daylight credit as defined by LEED for New Construction Version 2.1. *Credit: Browne Penland McGregor Stephens Architects*

LEED·NC

Providence Newberg Medical Center
LEED® Project # 1869
LEED Version 2 Certification Level: GOLD
4-August 2006

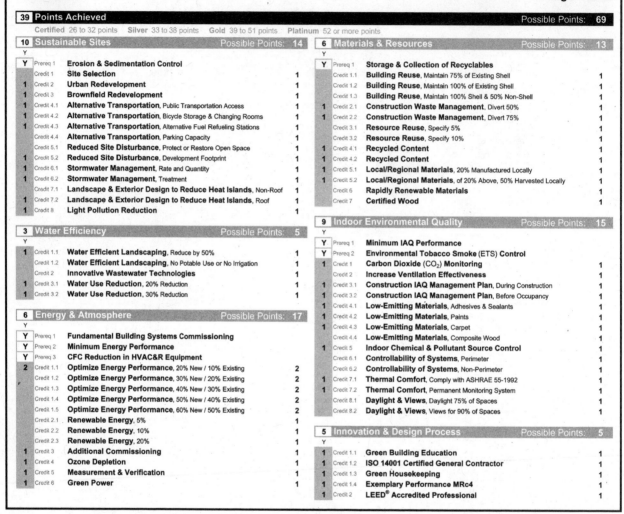

39 Points Achieved — Possible Points: **69**

Certified 26 to 32 points   Silver 33 to 38 points   Gold 39 to 51 points   Platinum 52 or more points

10 Sustainable Sites — Possible Points: 14

Y	Prereq 1	Erosion & Sedimentation Control	
	Credit 1	Site Selection	1
1	Credit 2	Urban Redevelopment	1
1	Credit 3	Brownfield Redevelopment	1
1	Credit 4.1	Alternative Transportation, Public Transportation Access	1
1	Credit 4.2	Alternative Transportation, Bicycle Storage & Changing Rooms	1
1	Credit 4.3	Alternative Transportation, Alternative Fuel Refueling Stations	1
	Credit 4.4	Alternative Transportation, Parking Capacity	1
	Credit 5.1	Reduced Site Disturbance, Protect or Restore Open Space	1
1	Credit 5.2	Reduced Site Disturbance, Development Footprint	1
1	Credit 6.1	Stormwater Management, Rate and Quantity	1
1	Credit 6.2	Stormwater Management, Treatment	1
	Credit 7.1	Landscape & Exterior Design to Reduce Heat Islands, Non-Roof	1
1	Credit 7.2	Landscape & Exterior Design to Reduce Heat Islands, Roof	1
1	Credit 8	Light Pollution Reduction	1

3 Water Efficiency — Possible Points: 5

1	Credit 1.1	Water Efficient Landscaping, Reduce by 50%	1
	Credit 1.2	Water Efficient Landscaping, No Potable Use or No Irrigation	1
	Credit 2	Innovative Wastewater Technologies	1
1	Credit 3.1	Water Use Reduction, 20% Reduction	1
1	Credit 3.2	Water Use Reduction, 30% Reduction	1

6 Energy & Atmosphere — Possible Points: 17

Y	Prereq 1	Fundamental Building Systems Commissioning	
Y	Prereq 2	Minimum Energy Performance	
Y	Prereq 3	CFC Reduction in HVAC&R Equipment	
2	Credit 1.1	Optimize Energy Performance, 20% New / 10% Existing	2
	Credit 1.2	Optimize Energy Performance, 30% New / 20% Existing	2
	Credit 1.3	Optimize Energy Performance, 40% New / 30% Existing	2
	Credit 1.4	Optimize Energy Performance, 50% New / 40% Existing	2
	Credit 1.5	Optimize Energy Performance, 60% New / 50% Existing	2
	Credit 2.1	Renewable Energy, 5%	1
	Credit 2.2	Renewable Energy, 10%	1
	Credit 2.3	Renewable Energy, 20%	1
1	Credit 3	Additional Commissioning	1
1	Credit 4	Ozone Depletion	1
1	Credit 5	Measurement & Verification	1
1	Credit 6	Green Power	1

6 Materials & Resources — Possible Points: 13

Y	Prereq 1	Storage & Collection of Recyclables	
	Credit 1.1	Building Reuse, Maintain 75% of Existing Shell	1
	Credit 1.2	Building Reuse, Maintain 100% of Existing Shell	1
	Credit 1.3	Building Reuse, Maintain 100% Shell & 50% Non-Shell	1
1	Credit 2.1	Construction Waste Management, Divert 50%	1
1	Credit 2.2	Construction Waste Management, Divert 75%	1
	Credit 3.1	Resource Reuse, Specify 5%	1
	Credit 3.2	Resource Reuse, Specify 10%	1
1	Credit 4.1	Recycled Content	1
1	Credit 4.2	Recycled Content	1
1	Credit 5.1	Local/Regional Materials, 20% Manufactured Locally	1
1	Credit 5.2	Local/Regional Materials, of 20% Above, 50% Harvested Locally	1
	Credit 6	Rapidly Renewable Materials	1
	Credit 7	Certified Wood	1

9 Indoor Environmental Quality — Possible Points: 15

Y	Prereq 1	Minimum IAQ Performance	
Y	Prereq 2	Environmental Tobacco Smoke (ETS) Control	
1	Credit 1	Carbon Dioxide (CO_2) Monitoring	1
	Credit 2	Increase Ventilation Effectiveness	1
1	Credit 3.1	Construction IAQ Management Plan, During Construction	1
1	Credit 3.2	Construction IAQ Management Plan, Before Occupancy	1
1	Credit 4.1	Low-Emitting Materials, Adhesives & Sealants	1
1	Credit 4.2	Low-Emitting Materials, Paints	1
1	Credit 4.3	Low-Emitting Materials, Carpet	1
	Credit 4.4	Low-Emitting Materials, Composite Wood	1
1	Credit 5	Indoor Chemical & Pollutant Source Control	1
	Credit 6.1	Controllability of Systems, Perimeter	1
	Credit 6.2	Controllability of Systems, Non-Perimeter	1
1	Credit 7.1	Thermal Comfort, Comply with ASHRAE 55-1992	1
1	Credit 7.2	Thermal Comfort, Permanent Monitoring System	1
	Credit 8.1	Daylight & Views, Daylight 75% of Spaces	1
	Credit 8.2	Daylight & Views, Views for 90% of Spaces	1

5 Innovation & Design Process — Possible Points: 5

1	Credit 1.1	Green Building Education	1
1	Credit 1.2	ISO 14001 Certified General Contractor	1
1	Credit 1.3	Green Housekeeping	1
1	Credit 1.4	Exemplary Performance MRc4	1
1	Credit 2	LEED® Accredited Professional	1

Figure 8-21: This sample checklist from Providence Newberg, a LEED gold-certified project, is an example of the LEED rating tool in action. *Credit: US Green Building Council*

DESIGN FOR HEALTH: SUMMIT FOR MASSACHUSETTS HEALTHCARE DECISION MAKERS

In September 2004, more than eighty healthcare executives and their facility management and design teams from throughout Massachusetts convened in a two-day summit to collectively assess the state of Massachusetts' healthcare building portfolio. Coordinated by Health Care Without Harm and the Rocky Mountain Institute, with principal funding from the Merck Family Fund, this inaugural Design for Health summit set the stage for a bold challenge to deliver healthy hospitals: healthy for patients, staff, community, the environment, and the hospitals' financial status. A roster of nationally recognized presenters sparked breakthrough thinking about sustainable facility design, construction, and operations; the dialogue was sharpened with the participation of policy and government regulators, including Boston Mayor Thomas Menino. As in most regions in the US, at the time of the summit the notion of a green healthcare facility was an unfocused aspiration. The follow-through actions during the subsequent two years have been remarkable.

CASE STUDY

Carl J. and Ruth Shapiro Cardiovascular Center at Brigham and Women's Hospital

Boston, Massachusetts

Figure 8-22: The Carl J. and Ruth Shapiro Cardiovascular Center at Brigham and Women's Hospital. *Credit: Cannon Design*

Owner: Brigham and Women's Hospital

Design team:

ARCHITECT: Cannon Design

LANDSCAPE ARCHITECT: Halvorson Design Partnership

INTERIOR DESIGNER: Cannon Design/Chan Krieger & Associates

STRUCTURAL ENGINEER: McNamara/Salvia, Inc.

MECHANICAL/ELECTRICAL ENGINEER: BR+A Consulting Engineers, LLC

PLUMBING ENGINEER: R. W. Sullivan Engineering

CIVIL ENGINEER: Vanasse Hangen Brustlin, Inc.

CONSTRUCTION MANAGER: W. A. Berry & Son, Inc.

COMMISSIONING: Sebesta Blomberg & Associates

LEED CONSULTANTS: Environmental Health & Engineering, Inc./The Green Roundtable

Building type: New Acute Care

Size: 420,000 sq ft (39,019 sq m)

Program description: Ten-story hospital with cardiac and vascular surgery operating rooms, 136 beds for cardiovascular patients, outpatient cardiovascular clinics, café, conference space, and family support spaces

Completion date: 2008

Awards/recognition: *Green Guide for Health Care* pilot

Brigham and Women's Hospital (BWH), a teaching affiliate of Harvard Medical School, embraced sustainability and integrated design as cornerstones for its Shapiro Cardiovascular Center. From the onset, the design team emphasized indoor air quality and energy efficiency, reflecting the hospital's commitment to environmental stewardship. "The center is a study in connectivity, transparency, and urban design," writes Gina Kish, AIA, of Cannon Design, maintaining an immediate, intimate connection "with the BWH community, the neighborhood, and the general public through a transparent glass facade, publicly oriented facilities on the bottom floors, and a second-floor bridge extending the hospital's main pedestrian thoroughfare." The design team's objective to achieve an exceptional healing environment was pursued in concert with enriching the urban fabric and environmental quality.

"Connective features are a direct manifestation of BWH's deeply held institutional commitment to do the right thing," Kish continues, "a commitment that, combined with the hospital's deep-seated energy consciousness, bottom-line orientation, and identification with leadership in innovation, has yielded numerous sustainability initiatives over the years. The unwavering support, from day one, of BWH administration for the sustainable design of the center lies at the root of the effort's success."

KEY BUILDING PERFORMANCE STRATEGIES

Site

- Development density
- Access to public transportation, bicycle-friendly showers, alternative fuel refueling stations, parking capacity

Figure 8-23: The building places circulation and public space at the perimeter and features large expanses of glass to maximize daylight penetration. *Credit: Cannon Design*

Figure 8-24: Despite the deep floor plate and constrained urban setting, the building incorporates multiple-height spaces linked by an open stair adjacent to an exterior garden. *Credit: Cannon Design*

- High-reflectance roofing to reduce heat-island effects
- Light pollution reduction

Energy
- Hydrochlorofluorocarbon reduction in heating, ventilating, air-conditioning (HVAC) and refrigerating equipment
- Energy performance optimized
- Enhanced building systems commissioning
- Measurement and verification protocols

Water
- No potable water for landscape irrigation
- Cooling tower water reuse

Materials
- Recyclables stored and collected
- 75 percent of construction waste diverted from landfills through construction waste management
- 20 percent of materials manufactured regionally; 10 percent contain recycled content
- FSC-certified wood

Environmental Quality
- Environmental tobacco smoke control
- Carbon dioxide monitoring
- Indoor chemical and pollutant source control
- Daylighting of 90 percent of indoor spaces
- Indoor air quality management plan during construction and before occupancy
- Low-emitting materials, adhesives, sealants, paints, carpets, composite wood

Source: Cannon Design

Figure 8-25: Brigham and Women's Hospital opted to relocate existing triple-decker houses on the site of its proposed new tower rather than demolish the historic, moderate-income multifamily residences, strengthening community relationships and reducing the waste associated with demolition. *Credit: Arthur Mombourquette*

Spaulding Rehabilitation Hospital

Boston, Massachusetts

Figure 8-26: Spaulding Rehabilitation Hospital. *Credit: Perkins + Will*

Owner: Spaulding Rehabilitation Hospital
Design team: Perkins + Will
Building type: Replacement rehabilitation hospital
Size: Building: 240,000 sq ft (22,300 sq m); site: 2.6 acres (1.05 ha)
Program description: 150 beds with rehabilitation program support; 300 underground parking spaces
Completion date: 2010
Awards/recognition: *Green Guide for Health Care* pilot

The project is located on a Charlestown Navy Yard brownfield property—a vacant former industrial land parcel that directly influenced the design and sustainable building philosophy. The site emphasizes the direct relationship between the rehabilitation of the earth and the rehabilitation that will take place inside the hospital. "We're committed to cleaning up the site," says Judith Waterston, president of Spaulding Rehabilitation Hospital "and a building that reflects what we want to do for the environment from that point forward."

To emphasize this connection to nature, the building features two types of green roofs: one engineered to manage storm water, and the other a therapeutic garden. The team is working closely with the Northeast Sustainable Energy Association to develop sustainable energy strategies.

The inpatient and outpatient gymnasiums are situated in a low-rise waterfront structure that creates opportunities to segregate building energy systems. The team is

Figure 8-27: The site is in the former Charlestown Navy Yard, at the convergence of Little Mystic Channel and Boston Harbor. *Credit: Perkins + Will*

Figure 8-29: Prior to beginning construction, Spaulding will remediate the contaminated brownfield site. *Credit: Deborah Rivers*

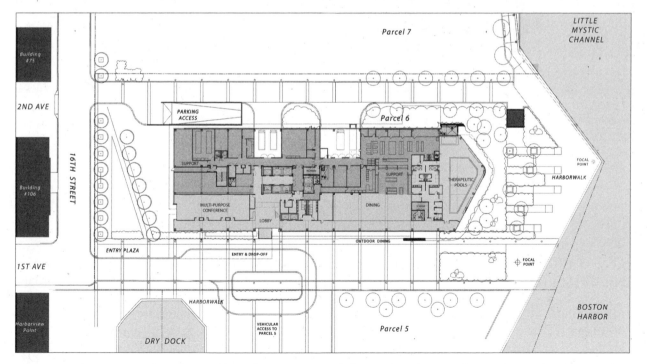

Figure 8-28: The narrow site dimensions and limited area necessitates below-grade parking. A public riverfront esplanade is included; an accessible walkway continues the pedestrian access from the adjacent residential street grid to the water. *Credit: Perkins + Will*

actively investigating operable windows and natural ventilation strategies for the gyms that will allow the building to open itself to the activity, sounds, and smells of Boston Harbor. Spaulding, which is currently located on a river site, will continue its active water therapy program.

As might be expected given its present urban location, more than 60 percent of its staffers use public transportation. As there is capacity for only three hundred parking spaces on-site, Spaulding has been advocating for improved public transportation access throughout the Navy Yard redevelopment zone.

Figure 8-30: From the Boston Harbor, the building reduces in scale and articulates the gymnasium volumes. Individual terraces on each floor allow residents to easily experience the sights and sounds of the water. *Credit: Perkins + Will*

KEY BUILDING PERFORMANCE STRATEGIES

Site

- Brownfield redevelopment
- Green roofs and outdoor places of respite, including a central therapeutic garden and terraces on inpatient units
- Alternative transportation available through shuttle bus service to existing public transportation infrastructure

Water

- Storm water collection for landscape irrigation

Energy

- 30 percent reduction in energy below ASHRAE 90.1-2004

Environmental Quality

- Narrow floor plate and articulated massing achieves daylight for occupied spaces—approximately 42 percent of occupied space is within 15 feet of a window
- Potential for natural ventilation of gymnasiums

Source: Perkins + Will

GREAT BRITAIN'S NATIONAL HEALTH SERVICE

Great Britain's National Health Service (NHS) is aligning its core principles of "improving health and preventing disease" to its approach to health delivery, and to the scale, location and environmental performance of its buildings. While it is a work in progress, the NHS's initia- tives provide insights into how such a unified vision can yield cascading benefits on many levels. While applying many of these tools and policy initiatives in the vast, diverse, and complex US system would not be achievable, these efforts are having significant impacts on the form and future of the NHS building and service portfolio, and are useful tools in the continued development of sustainable healthcare best practices.

Established in 1948, the NHS is trailblazing organizational transformation, exploring sustainable design and operational improvements and creating unique benchmarking tools relevant to the global healthcare sector. Its enlightened view of healthcare is deeply rooted in organizational culture, captured in one of its founding principles: "[to] improve health and prevent disease, not just provide treatment for those who are ill" (NHS Department of Health 2004). Sustainable design and operations are emerging as keystone components of a broad commitment to achieve effective quality healthcare for all citizens of the United Kingdom.

The NHS is the largest employer in Europe (NHS 2007a). With an annual budget of more than £80 billion (approximately $155.5 billion), the tax-funded NHS employs more than 1.3 million people and represents 7.7 percent of the UK's gross domestic product (WHO 2004). In this decade, the NHS expects to spend £11 billion ($21.7 billion) on new hospital buildings accompanied by an estimated £17 billion ($33.5 billion) on goods and services annually. This magnitude of capital investment, coupled with enormous sustained purchasing volume, renders the NHS a formidable economic power capable of catalyzing market transformation both in design methods and materials. Already, its specific responses to climate change illustrate its organizational values and ability to act (these are further elaborated in Chapter 12). Having effective tools in place to guide this trajectory is key to the NHS's ability to measure and manage its organization's massive environmental impacts.

Reflecting a commitment to change "the way it works to make sure patients always come first" (NHS 2007b), the NHS is pursuing an aggressive path to transform how it manages its vast portfolio of properties and infrastructure, using triple bottom-line assessment methods (see Figure 8-31). As described in "Sustainable Development in the NHS":

> The environment in which people live and work has a key influence on their health. Environmental considerations must therefore be taken into account when building or adapting facilities in which NHS services are delivered. In addition, NHS facilities can have an impact on the surrounding environment. Job opportunities can bring social benefits to a community; traffic congestion and noise pollution can have a detrimental impact. Environmental impact assessments should therefore be undertaken by all new and existing facilities (NHS Department of Health 2006b).

This snapshot of the NHS's myriad tools, programs, and partnerships provides a window into its organizational commitment to values-driven, health-focused ecological transformation.

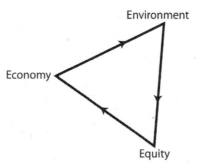

Figure 8-31: National Health Service triple bottom line. Triple-bottom-line accounting, developed in the late 1990s, reflects the interrelationships between social, environmental, and economic dimensions of sustainability and the vulnerability of decisions that fail to valuate each of these three performance indicators. *Source: NHS Department of Health 2006b*

NEAT: A GREEN BUILDING TOOL

Developed in 2002 by the Building Research Establishment with funding from the NHS and the Department of Trade and Industry, the NHS Environmental Assessment Tool (NEAT) is a self-assessing software tool designed to evaluate negative environmental impacts associated with NHS facilities. NEAT assesses day-to-day activities and ranks facilities—existing sites, new builds, and refurbishments—as either "excellent" or "very good." NEAT is an outgrowth of the *Sustainable Construction Action Plan*, which requires all new construction to achieve an excellent rating, and all refurbished buildings to achieve a rating of very good. At the beginning of 2007, about one-quarter of operational NHS facilities had voluntarily undergone the NEAT self-assessment; since 2002, when it became a requirement, all new NHS facilities have used the tool. While data on the actual number of assessments are not currently collected, the UK's Department of Health is working to fold NEAT into the BREEAM family of assessment tools as *BREEAM for Healthcare*—its expected launch is in early 2008. In this new context, external assessors will evaluate new and renovated healthcare facilities' environmental performance, similar to the way LEED certification is conducted. The following case study, on University Hospital in Coventry, is an example of a large British replacement hospital project that has used the NEAT tool.

NEAT is a green building and operations rating tool that has the potential to reduce the environmental impact of the building site and associated services. It is structured around ten distinct issue areas:

1. *Management:* commissioning, environmental management systems, education and training, purchasing policy
2. *Energy:* carbon emissions (including a carbon calculator), heating and lighting control, energy monitoring, daylighting, alternative electricity tariffs
3. *Transport:* car parking provision, cyclists' facilities, public transport nodes, distance to local amenities, green transport plan
4. *Water:* leak detection, water meters, low-flush toilets, gray-water reuse
5. *Materials:* new-build building material specifications, hazardous substances prohibitions, existing-build asbestos survey, asbestos removal
6. *Land use and ecology:* new-build use of contaminated land, change in ecological value, existing build-protection of ecological features, introduction of natural habitat
7. *Pollution:* monitoring, ozone-depleting substances, nitrogen oxide emissions rates, noise pollution, incineration practices
8. *Internal environment:* new-build budget for plants, views out, existing-build high-frequency ballasts, signage, decor and art
9. *Social:* links with community and local agenda, sharing of facilities, staff and patient empowerment
10. *Operational waste:* recycling facilities, waste-stream analysis, staff waste interviews, recycling storage

Source: NHS Department of Health 2006b

Owners: University Hospitals Coventry & Warwickshire NHS Trust

Design team:

ARCHITECT: Nightingale Associates

STRUCTURAL ENGINEER: Arup

CONTRACTOR: Skanska UK

Building type: Replacement hospital, new construction

Size: Buildings: 1,663,024 sq ft (154,500 sq m); site: 75 acres (30 ha)

Design energy intensity: 55 GJ/building

Program description:

1,212 bed acute care university hospital, including medical-surgical; Caludon Center (geriatrics); 132-bed, 118,404-sq-ft (11,000-sq-m) mental health building; and 102,258-sq-ft (9,500-sq-m) university clinical sciences building

Completion date: 2006

Awards/Recognition: Public Private Finance Awards, 2003; each of the three buildings achieved an excellent rating using NEAT as a preconstruction self-assessment tool

University Hospital

Coventry, UK

Figure 8-32:
Universtiy Hospital Coventry.
Credit: Courtesy of Nightingale Associates

The largest NHS-commissioned hospital in recent history, the Coventry New Hospitals complex replaces a number of outmoded regional facilities with a "superhospital" incorporating a cancer center; a women's hospital; twenty-seven operating theaters; major trauma, cardiac, and cancer specialty centers; and a children's hospital with a dedicated emergency department. The hospital is located on the suburban former site of Walsgrave Hospital, which opened in 1970.

KEY BUILDING PERFORMANCE STRATEGIES

Site

▪ Preservation of ancient hedgerows provides habitat and prevents erosion

▪ Creeks rehabilitated as site amenity

Water

▪ Green roof filters rainwater and mitigates storm water runoff

▪ Custom-designed construction wash-out station instituted on job site to divert potentially hazardous waste streams

Figure 8-33: Daylight illuminates the University Hospital Coventry entrance. Transparent facade materials create a transition between the interior and exterior lobby areas. *Credit: Courtesy of Nightingale Associates*

Energy
- Energy modeling–tested shading, natural ventilation, and insulation strategies before implementation
- HVAC efficiency measures such as heat recovery yielded impressive life cycle cost savings

Materials
- Low-volatile organic compound (VOC) paints
- Construction waste recycling program exceeded benchmark of 65 percent diversion rate
- First British project to institute large-scale recycling of waste wallboard
- Reuse of existing concrete on-site saved estimated eight thousand haul-off truck trips

Environmental Quality
- Daylighting maximized in patient and public areas, including lobbies and entries
- Sheltered courtyards accessible from mental health unit
- Wards have views of Warwickshire countryside

Sources: Skanska UK; Nightingale Associates; Nightingale 2006

Defining Corporate Citizenship

Developed by the UK's Sustainable Development Commission for the NHS, *Good Corporate Citizenship* is one publication in a four-part series that assesses how the NHS can contribute to sustainable development. It includes a good corporate citizenship web-based self-assessment checklist model designed to help healthcare organizations "promote social cohesion, strong local economies and a healthy environment" (SDC 2006). The self-assessment tool is structured to instill an understanding of what good corporate citizenship means, to appreciate its importance, and to evaluate project-specific performance and encourage continuous improvement. The Norfolk and Norwich University Hospital, a 987-bed acute care general hospital with more than 5,390 employees, was the first trust facility to test the good corporate citizenship self-assessment model. Its findings prompted the creation of new facility waste-management and car-sharing programs. While not entirely appropriate to US healthcare organizations, it is nonetheless a powerful framework for challenging prevailing notions of community benefit and corporate citizenship for all hospitals engaged in shifting traditional measures.

CABE: Promoting Architectural Excellence

Founded in 1999, the Commission for Architecture and the Built Environment (CABE) serves as the British government's advisor on architecture, urban design, and public space, and is dedicated to "inspiring the nation to understand and demand better design, [i]nfluencing decision makers to insist on and choose good design; and [i]mproving the quality of what gets built" (CABE 2006a). CABE has had a particular focus on healthcare and the NHS. Its Web site offers these key elements of good healthcare buildings:

- Good integrated design
- Public open space
- A clear plan
- Materials, finishes, and furnishings
- Natural light and ventilation
- Adapting to future changes
- Out-of-hours community use

Using the metaphor of a virtuous circle, CABE advocates for a multipronged alignment with its essential operational components, including employment, food, and buildings (CABE 2006c). In describing its advocacy, CABE lays out an impressive agenda (see sidebar).

In *Designed with Care: Design and Neighbourhood Healthcare Buildings*, CABE (2006d) articulates its concern with building scale and emphasizes the built environment's pivotal role in the debate on health and well-being. The publication challenges the country's portfolio of healthcare buildings to "provide a high-quality facility for both patients and staff . . . in particular recognizing the importance of integrating the planning and development of neighbourhoods with the design of individual healthcare buildings." Included in the report are fifteen case studies of exemplary neighborhood-scale healthcare buildings in the UK, including the Kaleidoscope Children and Young People's Centre, included in this chapter. In *The Cost of Bad Design*, CABE researchers

call for mandatory and regularly scheduled postoccupancy analysis of every healthcare building following occupancy (CABE 2006b), a forceful acknowledgment of the value of continuous commissioning and postoccupancy evaluation.

Also intended to address design excellence, the NHS's *Achieving Excellence Design Evaluation Toolkit* (NHS 2007c) assists individual trusts (hospitals) and the NHS in determining and managing design requirements. AEDET is a benchmarking tool focused on three impact areas:

1. *Functionality:* uses, access, and spaces
2. *Impact:* character and innovation, form and materials, staff and patient environment, urban and social integration
3. *Build standards:* performance, engineering, and construction

THE CABE ADVOCACY AGENDA

- *Job training as an antidote to poverty:* "[People will] start coming into the hospitals as workers rather than as patients. Getting jobs makes them less vulnerable to illness; ...it can create a virtuous circle helping to improve health in the community, reducing preventable disease, lessening the burden on the NHS and freeing it up to provide better care for those with unavoidable illness."

- *Nutritious food:* "If the NHS uses its resources more carefully—arranging its purchasing and catering policies so that it provides nutritious food in ways that encourage patients to eat and enjoy—it could do marvels not only for patients' health, but for staff and visitors, too. It could also use its power as one of the largest food purchasers in the country, to encourage local and sustainable food production, strengthening local economies, to reduce the environmental damage caused by shipping foods across vast distances, and to promote organic and other environmentally sound agricultural practices."

- *Appropriate buildings:* "[T]here could be a much smaller number of high-quality specialist centres, combined with a larger number of small (possibly mobile) community-based clinics and care centres. This would be a lot more

effective and give far better value for money. And every building that does go ahead could meet high standards of sustainable development. And here, again, is the chance to create a virtuous circle. A sustainable building can provide a healthy environment to work in, reducing absenteeism and improving staff performance. It can provide a good environment to receive treatment and care in—improving patient recovery rates. Building design can affect the ease with which infections such as MRSA can be isolated, or spread. A building can be constructed using sustainable materials and local labour. It can make maximum use of natural heating and ventilation, reducing the amount of energy it consumes. It can be located and designed to facilitate water conservation, minimize waste and encourage walking, cycling and public transport rather than private car use. It can be situated on a brownfield site, helping to preserve green spaces. It can be part of the local community. By managing energy, waste and water sustainably, by creating environments that reduce staff sickness and hasten patient recovery, this approach can make very substantial financial savings over time."

Source: Coote 2006

Project teams are invited to establish project-specific weighting valuations. The NHS contends that the convergence of these three areas, akin to the historical architectural notions of commodity, firmness, and delight, creates added value and, ultimately, design excellence. Example evaluative criteria under the form and materials and staff and patient environment categories are:

- The building has a human scale and feels welcoming.
- The design takes advantage of available sunlight and provides shelter from prevailing winds.
- There are good views inside and out of the building.
- Patients and staff have good access to the outdoors.
- There are high levels of both comfort and control of comfort.
- There are good facilities for staff, including convenient places to work and relax without being on demand.

Figure 8-34: This diagram illustrates the NHS-AEDET concept that added value and excellence reside at the intersection of function, impact of the building design, and building quality. *Credit: Extracted with permission from the Department of Health Web site*

Evelina Children's Hospital

London, England

Figure 8-35: Evelina Children's Hospital. *Credit: © Paul Tyagi/VIEW*

Owner: Guy's and St. Thomas' NHS Foundation Trust
Design team:
    ARCHITECT: Hopkins Architects
    MECHANICAL AND ELECTRICAL ENGINEER: Hoare Lea
    STRUCTURAL ENGINEER: Buro Happold
    QUANTITY SURVEYOR: Davis Langdon
    CONTRACTOR: M. J. Gleeson Group PLC
Building type: New construction on existing St. Thomas' Hospital campus
Size: 177,605 sq ft (16,500 sq m)
Program description: Seven-story, 140-bed acute care children's hospital
    (including a twenty-bed intensive care unit) specializing in neonatal
    care
Completion date: 2005
Recognition: NHS Building Better Health Care Award for Hospital Design,
    November 2006; design team won initial Royal Institute of British Archi-
    tects design competition

Wedged into the crowded Guy's and St. Thomas's hospital complex on the banks of the River Thames, Evelina Children's Hospital is the first new children's hospital in London in more than one hundred years, replacing children's hospital services offered throughout Guy's and St. Thomas'. The seven-story building uses a four-story conservatory to distribute daylight from a 325-feet-long (100-meter-long) curved greenhouse facade.

Prompted by formal consultations with the young patients during the design process, designers aimed to create a hospital without an institutional feel, with fresh air, access to daylight, views, and opportunities for socializing—and without long, frightening corridors. Indoor air-quality goals directed designers toward greener materials (such as rubber flooring) and patient-controlled natural ventilation. Because it was Hopkins Architects' first hospital project, the team felt free to ask basic questions about hospital space efficiencies and to challenge embedded notions about how hospitals should be designed and function. Through this exploration, the firm discovered overlaps between green features and patient comfort. A children's board comprised of local schoolchildren and patients was consulted on furnishings, menu, and wayfinding. One result was foldout beds for parents in each patient room.

Since the building's opening, anecdotal information from Evelina's pediatric management team suggests improved staff retention and recruitment. For instance, of approximately fifty new staffers in housekeeping and patient services, forty-seven remained after the first year and applications for clinical posts have increased. The average patient length of stay has been reduced, although the hospital notes that no formal study points to the new building as a factor for this change.

KEY BUILDING PERFORMANCE STRATEGIES

Site
- Patient rooms overlook the Archbishop of Canterbury's Lambeth Palace Gardens and/or the conservatory
- Flexible floor plan allows for additional patient rooms to be added in the future

Energy
- Stack ventilation in the conservatory provides passive cooling
- Building orientation to maximize solar performance characteristics

Materials
- Rubber flooring
- Terra-cotta exterior cladding
- Interior materials used without finishes wherever possible

Environmental Quality
- Operable louvers in all patient rooms (including intensive care units) control the flow of fresh air
- Displacement ventilation throughout patient rooms
- Patient rooms communicate with larger hospital community through connection to public conservatory space
- Daylight available throughout hospital, including some operating theaters

Sources: Andrew Barnett, Hopkins Architects; Guy's and St. Thomas's NHS Foundation Trust

---

NHS ASPECT includes eight sections:

1. *Privacy, company, and dignity:* control of privacy and interaction with others (e.g., patients can choose to have visual privacy or be alone)

2. *Views:* patient and staff ability to see out of and around the building (e.g., spaces where staffers and patients spend time have windows, patients and staff can easily see the sky and ground, the view outside is calming)

3. *Nature and outdoors:* patient and staff contact with the natural world (e.g., patients can go outside, have access to usable landscaped areas, and/or can easily see plants, vegetation, and other forms of nature)

4. *Comfort and control:* comfort level of staff and patients and their ability to control those levels (e.g., variety of artificial lighting patterns appropriate for day, night, summer, and winter)

5. *Legibility of place:* staffers', patients', and visitors' ability to understand healthcare buildings (e.g., the entrance is obvious)

6. *Interior appearance:* what the interior of healthcare buildings looks like (e.g., interiors feel light and airy, ceilings look interesting)

7. *Facilities:* buildings meet patients' needs (e.g., patients' relatives and friends are able to stay overnight)

8. *Staff:* ability to lead personal lives and perform professional duties (e.g., staffers can rest and relax in places segregated from patient and visitor areas)

ASPECT: An NHS Evidence-Based Design Tool

Drawing on a database of more than six hundred research studies, ASPECT (A Staff and Patient Environment Calibration Tool) was developed to support the use of AEDET (described above) or to be used as a stand-alone tool. This research-rich tool enables a detailed evaluation of the design of healthcare environments and demonstrates the intersection of sustainable design with features that contribute to an expanded definition of design excellence. Using an Excel-based scoresheet that allows individuals or teams to score based upon agreement with a series of statements about the design, ASPECT provides a simple format for arriving at a shared evaluation of the performance of a building design based upon eight major performance areas (see sidebar). While ASPECT is not directly concerned with sustainable building measures, its focus on daylight, views, connection to nature, occupant control, and staff performance intersects with green building initiatives.

Food Procurement

Each year the NHS prepares and serves more than 300 million meals for patients and staff, representing an annual expenditure of about £500 million ($986 million) (NHS Purchasing 2006). The NHS *Purchasing and Supply Agency's Food Procurement Action Plan* "promotes public procurement of food that supports delivery of the Government's Sustainable Farming and Food Strategy for England" (NHS PASA 2006a). The plan includes fourteen key objectives, including purchasing organic food and buying from British and local food suppliers, complying with fair trade practices and healthier eating strategies, minimizing waste, and reducing vehicle emissions in food delivery.

In the plan's June 2006 update, the NHS stated its full commitment "to the principles of sustainable food procurement both to provide improved services to customers (including but not limited to NHS patients, staff and visitors) and to enrich the communities served by the NHS" (NHS PASA 2006b).

Figure 8-36: ASPECT Logo. *Credit: Extracted with permission from the Department of Health Web site*

The NHS serves over 300 million meals a year to staff, patients, and visitors. The opportunity to impact on health and to give the right messages about sustainable food is enormous.

— DR. FIONA ADSHEAD, DEPUTY CHIEF MEDICAL OFFICER, DEPARTMENT OF HEALTH

Having burger chains and junk food vending machines on hospital grounds is not an acceptable way forward. The NHS should be leading by example.

—JONATHON PORRITT, CHAIRMAN, SUSTAINABLE DEVELOPMENT COMMISSION

Sustainability and improving the health of the nation must be integral to public procurement. Sustainable food procurement offers the opportunity to deliver benefits across the board, from working with UK suppliers to improving environmental and health outcomes.

—DUNCAN EATON, CHIEF EXECUTIVE, NHS PURCHASING AND SUPPLY AGENCY

Source: SDC 2004

As an example of the plan's influence, the London Hospital Food Project, led by the London Food Link and the Soil Association, initiated a four-hospital pilot program with an initial goal of ensuring that 10 percent of the food served in these pilot hospitals is locally produced, seasonal, and organic (Hockridge & Longfield 2005).

Sustainable Procurement

Initiated in December 2005 and designed to reinforce the NHS's stated commitment to "make a significant contribution to the health and sustainability of the communities it serves" (HM Government 2005), the NHS *Sustainable Procurement Action Plan*'s objective is to embed sustainability considerations — including environmental and social impacts — in purchasing decisions. According to the NHS Purchasing and Supply Agency (PASA), the program's key strategies are to:

- Deliver training and development activity that helps embed sustainable procurement objectives within the agency and wider NHS procurement activity

- Develop policies to facilitate and promote sustainable procurement and communicate progress to achieve sustainable procurement objectives to stakeholders

- Develop and embed tools that enable sustainability objectives to be addressed in the procurement process

- Work with suppliers to improve sustainability performance through the supply chain and stimulate innovation

- Develop and utilize indicators of sustainable procurement performance (NHS PASA 2006c)

Included in the plan is the Supplier Sustainability Assessment Framework. This tool characterizes suppliers based on their adherence to sustainable values, with relative weightings reflecting their corporate policies, accountability, stakeholder and supply chain management, operational procedures, future proofing, and continuous improvement/assessment. For example, in the policy category, a supplier's ranking could range from *embedded* at the high end — reflecting "clear and assertive targets, fully integrated into corporate culture and values with continuous reviews and communication cycle in place" — to *detractor* at the low end — reflecting "no written policy" (NHS PASA 2005).

Where to find NHS Resources:
- NHS general information: www.dh.gov.uk
- NEAT (NHS Environmental Assessment Tool): www.dh.gov.uk/PolicyAndGuidance/
- Good Corporate Citizenship Assessment Model: www.corporatecitizen.nhs.uk
- CABE (Commission for Architecture and the Built Environment): www.cabe.org.uk
- AEDET (Achieving Excellence Design Evaluation Toolkit): www.design.dh.gov.uk/content/connections/aedet_evolution.asp
- ASPECT (A Staff and Patient Environment Calibration Tool): www.design.dh.gov.uk/content/connections/aspect.asp
- Sustainable Purchasing Action Plan: www.pasa.doh.gov.uk/sustainabledevelopment
- Purchasing and Supply Agency Food Procurement Action Plan: www.pasa.doh.gov.uk/sustainabledevelopment/food/actionplan.stm

Figure 8-37: Gravesham Community Hospital. *Credit: James Brittain Photography*

Owners: Grosvenor House Group PLC; Dartford, Gravesham & Swanley PCT NHS; and Kent County Council
Design team: Steffian Bradley Architects
Building type: New construction, replacement geriatric hospital
Size: 64,500 sq ft (5,992 sq m)
Program description: 102-bed acute and social services facility incorporating an ambulatory care center, intermediate care beds, and a day center in a neighborhood setting
Completion date: 2006

This three-story urban hospital, developed through the NHS's private finance initiative, addresses the region's need for neighborhood-level care while replacing an outdated facility. Acute health services are provided alongside the elderly residential and day center Gravesham Place, which is considered part of the hospital. The hospital was designed to provide intermediate care for the elderly at the community level as part of the UK's 2001 National Service Framework Programme for Older People, a ten-year initiative to improve the quality of healthcare for the aged.

Located on a brownfield site in downtown Kent, the hospital is integrated into a strip of row houses bridging the city's residential and commercial districts and was designed to promote accessibility, especially for elderly patients. Views from ward areas take in the River Thames, and the hospital makes use of natural ventilation and extensive daylighting to promote high indoor air quality and patient comfort. Future growth flexibility, energy efficiency, and patient comfort inspired sustainable design features.

Figure 8-38: The entry lobby is designed with carefully placed light wells and exterior glazing, providing daylight and views to enhance the interior environmental quality while protecting the building from solar heat gain.
Credit: James Brittain Photography

KEY BUILDING PERFORMANCE STRATEGIES

Site
- ▣ Brownfield site
- ▣ Urban location with minimal parking availability curbs automobile dependence and mitigates suburban sprawl

Energy
- ▣ Double-glazed low-E windows
- ▣ Solar-tinted glazing prevents heat gain

Materials
- ▣ Timber used for exterior cladding certified through Canadian Standards Association sustainable forestry management standard
- ▣ Steel framing in clinic allows for future space flexibility
- ▣ Masonry-bearing wall functions as thermal mass and dampens noise

Environmental Quality
- ▣ Operable windows in patient rooms admit fresh air
- ▣ Courtyard assists in daylighting and provides views
- ▣ Light wells in lobby areas provide daylight
- ▣ Building oriented to take advantage of views of the River Thames
- ▣ Wood cladding and other wood design elements contribute to noninstitutional aesthetic

Source: Steffian Bradley Architects

Figure 8-39: Gravesham Community Hospital features operable windows in patient rooms that provide fresh air and balconies for convenient access to the outdoors. The wooded courtyard provides a tranquil setting for reflection; the light-color facade maximizes daylight in the courtyard.
Credit: James Brittain Photography

Owner: NHS Lewisham Primary Care Trust

Design team:

ARCHITECT: van Heyningen and Haward Architects

LANDSCAPE ARCHITECT: Edward Hutchison

STRUCTURAL ENGINEER: Price & Myers LLP

BUILDING SERVICES ENGINEER: Max Fordham LLP

CONTRACTOR: Verry Construction

QUANTITY SURVEYOR: Davis Langdon

Building type: New construction

Size: 43,056 sq ft (4,000 sq m)

Program description: One-stop pediatric and adolescent ambulatory care center offering specialist acute health as well as mental health, social care, and educational services

Completion date: 2006

Recognition: Firm won initial CABE design competition

Kaleidoscope, Lewisham Children and Young People's Centre

Borough of Lewisham, London, England

Figure 8-40: Kaleidoscope, Lewisham Children and Young People's Centre. *Credit: © Tim Crocker 2007*

This five-story outpatient clinic combines services previously spread throughout Lewisham, in South London, through a partnership between the Lewisham Primary Care Trust, the South London and Maudsley NHS Foundation Trust, the London Borough of Lewisham's Directorate for Children and Young People, and a number of nonprofit organizations serving children and adolescents. The NHS's goals for this low-income area, which has a high proportion of single-parent families who rely exclusively on public transportation, include consolidating children's healthcare services under one roof. The facility houses 250 staffers and includes a gymnasium, café, and accessible outdoor space, as well as community meeting and event rooms. The architects, chosen through a 2003 competition held by the Commission for Architecture and the Built Environment, consulted extensively with patients, families, and healthcare staff members from local facilities on the facility's design. The impact, build quality, and functionality of finalists' designs were evaluated using the AEDET (discussed on page 215).

Design goals to enhance operational efficiency are being realized: locating secondary referral doctors on the premises has reduced appointment volume; patient feedback surveys indicate reduced waits and travel time—and more cohesive appointments in-

Figure 8-41: The plan is organized around a central garden space, which recesses the operable windows from the active urban street to reduce noise and create a respite from the city. *Credit: © Nick Kane*

volving less duplication of services; and staff members report improved interagency coordination and information sharing, as well as reduced workload pressure due to greater efficiency.

KEY BUILDING PERFORMANCE STRATEGIES

Water
- Landscaped roof filters rainwater

Energy
- Thermally active radiant-slab system provides energy-efficient heating and cooling
- Natural ventilation and operable windows
- Lighting controls include occupancy sensors
- User-controlled shade devices for courtyard glazing
- Building responds to solar orientation; exterior shading devices reduce solar heat gain

Materials
- Materials chosen for durability

Environmental Quality
- U-shaped plan arranged around courtyard garden
- Daylighting available to most interior spaces; glazing makes up 30 percent of total exterior wall space
- Internal circulation space overlooks courtyard, eliminating enclosed corridors (per user requests)
- Ground floor has larger footprint than upper stories to reduce scale from perspective of children's courtyard
- Landscaped roof and courtyard visible from upper stories
- Unified color scheme for each floor aids wayfinding

Sources: van Heyningen and Haward Architects; Kaleidoscope, Lewisham Children and Young People's Centre

---

CONCLUSION

The expanding portfolio of green building tools—both in the US and abroad—catalyze, reinforce, and extend the breadth and rigor of sustainable healthcare design, construction, and operations. It represents, in a sense, a process of discovery, as the ecologic, economic, and health-related dimensions of this endeavor become better understood. Rather than

an individual, isolated journey to determine what works best, this promises to be a pilgrimage shared by the collective whole whom healthcare design represents: design practitioners, facility owners and operators, medical professionals, policy makers—and the general public. It can only benefit from sharing the richness and diversity of that collective experience, wisdom, and hope as the process continues to evolve ever-more effective tools.

PART 3

VISIONING
THE FUTURE

CHAPTER 9

Pioneers and Benchmarks

Boldness has genius, power, and magic in it.
Begin it now.
—JOHANN WOLFGANG VON GOETHE

The future can't be predicted, but it can be envisioned
and brought lovingly into being. Systems can't be
controlled, but they can be designed and redesigned.
We can't surge forward with certainty into a world of
no surprises, but we can expect surprises and learn
from them and even profit from them.
—DONELLA MEADOWS, from "Dancing with Systems," 2001

INTRODUCTION

Pioneers were the early adopters, the innovators, the project teams far enough ahead of the curve to actualize a vision of sustainable healthcare building. In some instances, these projects were registered as *Green Guide for Health Care* pilots or with LEED; in other instances, they were not. Collectively, however, these completed projects now define a new baseline of healthcare building performance. Their early accomplishments demonstrate that sustainable healthcare is not only possible but achievable, even within the constraints and challenges of the healthcare and construction industries today.

Late in the year 2000, a Web search generated virtually no results for green healthcare buildings. Despite this lack of interest, most, if not all, of these healthcare innovators, were already well on the path toward sustainabil-

ity: the vocabularies and knowledge bases of green building and visionary healthcare design had not yet found each other. Some projects were already under construction. Only a small number had registered with the US Green Building Council (USGBC). The Center for Discovery, for example, was LEED project number 077. Architect Peter Syrett, project manager for Guenther 5 Architects, recalls that no drop-down menu choice even existed for a healthcare project on the LEED Web registration page in 2001. After registering healthcare as "other," a USGBC staff person called to congratulate him for being the first registered healthcare project in the program.

By 2002, many had seen the American Society for Healthcare Engineering's *Green Healthcare Construction Guidance Statement* (ASHE 2002). With the arrival of the

Green Guide for Health Care Version 1.0 in late 2002, even more cited the use of this tool in refining their design. By 2004, this group of initial sustainable projects was largely operational.

The 2005 American Society for Healthcare Engineering (ASHE) Vista Award winners, while not formally engaged in sustainable building initiatives, collectively demonstrated the extent to which sustainable ideology had penetrated the marketplace. Vista Award criteria emphasized team performance, and award-winning teams described the influence of sustainable-design thinking and tools in their design process on projects that completed in 2003 and 2004.

What were the drivers for the innovators and early adopters to take on green building in healthcare? How did these projects measure their success before rating tools were available? These project teams moved forward with innovation in the absence of a proven business case and often without readily available market alternatives for sustainable products and systems. This makes their accomplishments all the more noteworthy. The market uptake of sustainable building in healthcare is accelerating rapidly, and the bar for exceptional performance continues to rise. This chapter examines the initial group of projects that established new benchmarks for sustainable performance.

INTRODUCING THE PIONEERS

Benchmark projects are listed below, and include North American LEED-certified projects as of the end of 2006, selected *Green Guide for Health Care* (GGHC) pilots, and other early adopters. It includes the 2005 ASHE Vista Award winners. These projects were completed and began operation between 2003 and 2006.

North American Sustainable Healthcare Pioneers

Project Name	State or Province	Completed	Achievement
Boulder Community Hospital	CO	2003	LEED silver
Discovery Health Center	NY	2003	LEED certified
University of Arkansas for Medical Sciences College of Public Health	AR	2003	2005 ASHE Vista
Providence St. Peter Hospital	WA	2003–2004	2005 ASHE Vista
BC Cancer Agency's Research Centre	BC	2004	Canada Green Building Council (CaGBC) LEED gold
D'Amour Center for Cancer Care	MA	2004	2005 ASHE Vista
McGowan Institute for Regenerative Medicine	PA	2004	LEED gold
Winship Cancer Institute	GA	2004	LEED certified
Angel Harvey Infant Welfare Society	IL	2005	LEED certified
Gabrellian Women's and Children's Pavilion at Hackensack University Medical Center	NJ	2005	GGHC pilot
Jewish Hospital Medical Center South	KY	2005	LEED silver
Kaiser Modesto Medical Center	CA	2005	GGHC pilot
Lacks Cancer Center	MI	2005	LEED silver
Legacy Salmon Creek Hospital	WA	2005	
Washington Veterans Home	WA	2005	LEED gold
Isaac Ray Treatment Center	IN	2006	LEED silver
Metro Health Hospital	MI	2006	GGHC pilot
Pearland Pediatrics	TX	2006	LEED certified
Providence Newberg Medical Center	OR	2006	LEED gold

COMMUNITY CITIZENSHIP

Many of the innovators credit surrounding environmentally progressive communities with triggering their decision to move forward with sustainable design initiatives. "They view their buildings as manifesting the values embedded in the communities they serve; within environmentally progressive communities, the health care sector's environmental leadership is essential. The converse is also true: community health providers recognize that standing with or being ahead of the community awareness level is key to maintaining market leadership" (Guenther, Vittori, and Atwood 2006). Reflecting a long-standing heritage of environmental awareness, the Pacific Northwest, Colorado Rockies, and Michigan are regions with innovators and early adopters.

In the Grand Rapids, Michigan, case studies that begin this chapter, three very different organizations demonstrate sustainable building across differing healthcare typologies—acute care, assisted living, and cancer care (Metro Health Hospital, the acute care project, is profiled in Chapter 7). Why Grand Rapids, Michigan? According to Micki Benz, vice president for development at St. Mary's Health Care, "This part of the state is very interested in sustainable design. It's part of our heritage. It stems from the forest industry and from living with the land. It's tied to the psyche of the local population." In addition, progressive furniture manufacturers, including Herman Miller and Steelcase, constructed early examples of sustainable manufacturing and commercial office buildings here—and used those buildings to research the positive impact of sustainable building on staff performance.

CASE STUDY

The Lacks Cancer Center at St. Mary's Health Care

Grand Rapids, Michigan

Figure 9-1: The Lacks Cancer Center. *Credit: HKS Architects*

Owner: Saint Mary's Health Care

Design team:

ARCHITECT: Trinity Design (now HKS Architects, Inc.)

LANDSCAPE ARCHITECT: Grissim Metz Andriese Associates

CIVIL ENGINEER: Fleis & Vandenbrink Engineering, Inc.

ELECTRICAL/MECHANICAL ENGINEER: Wolf Wineman

STRUCTURAL ENGINEER: Ehlert/Bryan Consulting Structural Engineers

GENERAL CONTRACTOR: Triangle Associates, Inc.

Building type: New construction

Size: 172,000 sq ft (15,978 sq m)

Program description: Forty-two private inpatient oncology beds; treatment spaces consisting of medical oncology, radiation oncology, and breast center; surgical suites; outpatient services; healing garden

Completion date: 2005

Recognition: US Green Building Council LEED certified silver

The Lacks Cancer Center at Saint Mary's Health Care is situated in a high-density historic urban setting. Because the site is bordered by a road and other buildings, there were limited opportunities for sustainable site strategies. Instead, the project team focused on material selection, such as locally manufactured products and formaldehyde-free products and those low in volatile organic compounds (VOCs). "Selecting and reviewing materials requires a lot of diligence," notes Bob Miller of HKS, "and you need to have a lot of staying power."

Peter Wege, a Grand Rapids philanthropist and environmentalist, challenged the center to create a LEED-certified building in 2001, two years after project initiation but prior to the completion of design. The Lacks family supported the creation of a consolidated cancer center in order to reduce the transportation and patient stress associated with the dispersed cancer care in the region. The design team recognized that many of the design features that contribute to a green building are also recommended for improving patient health and reducing stress levels.

KEY BUILDING PERFORMANCE STRATEGIES

Site

■ Thermal and storm water benefits from gardens that cover 65 percent of roof

Water

■ High-efficiency irrigation technology reduced potable water irrigation consumption by 50 percent

■ No turf grass; drought-tolerant xeriscaping includes bed plantings that require minimal irrigation

Energy

■ Building oriented for optimal sun exposure

We wanted to take this challenge because we believed it would be better for our patients, the environment, and the community.

—PHILIP J. MCCORKLE JR., CEO, ST. MARY'S HEALTH CARE

- Light sensor and dimming ballasts; light tailored to individual departments and rooms; light shielding on exterior to prevent light pollution
- Waste steam condensate from Kent County municipal incinerators heats domestic water and snow-melting systems in the driveway

Materials

- More than 20 percent of materials manufactured within a 500-mile radius of Grand Rapids
- 98 percent of previous building recycled
- Reduced floor-to-floor heights minimize mass and material usage

David Hathaway, manager of construction projects at St. Mary's Health Care, describes the team's journey as early adopters: "Back in 2001, which seems a generation ago, none of us even knew what LEED meant. The process of realizing this building became a testimony to three ideas: first, Peter Wege's devotion to saving the environment; second, our design and construction team's willingness to learn a major new skill; and third, St. Mary's ability to take on new challenges."

Source: HKS Architects, Inc.

Figure 9-2: The design optimizes floor-to-floor heights; providing a gracious lobby space with abundant daylight. *Credit: HKS Architects*

Dominican Sisters Marywood Center

Grand Rapids, Michigan

Figure 9-3: Dominican Sisters Marywood Center. *Credit: Chris Barrett © Hedrich Blessing*

Owner: Grand Rapids Dominicans

Design team:

ARCHITECT: Perkins Eastman

STRUCTURAL ENGINEER: Graef, Anhalt, Schloemer & Associates, Inc.

MECHANICAL, ELECTRICAL, AND PLUMBING ENGINEER: OWP/P

CIVIL ENGINEER: Moore & Bruggink, Inc.

GENERAL CONTRACTOR: Erhardt Construction

Building type: New construction

Size: 80,000 sq ft (7,435 sq m)

Program description: Fifty-one-bed senior residence with assisted living, skilled nursing, and dementia care

Completion date: 2005

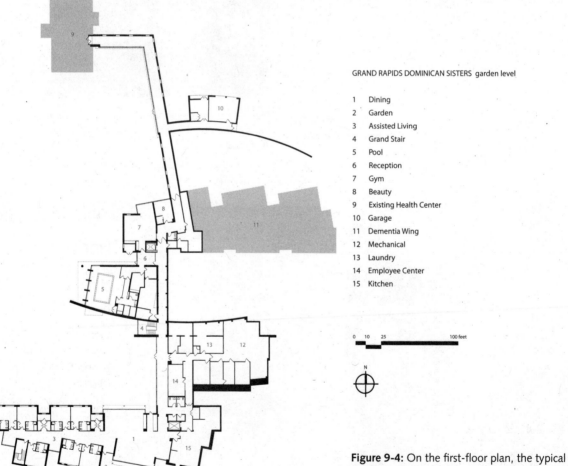

GRAND RAPIDS DOMINICAN SISTERS garden level

1   Dining
2   Garden
3   Assisted Living
4   Grand Stair
5   Pool
6   Reception
7   Gym
8   Beauty
9   Existing Health Center
10 Garage
11 Dementia Wing
12 Mechanical
13 Laundry
14 Employee Center
15 Kitchen

0   10   25   100 feet

N

Figure 9-4: On the first-floor plan, the typical double-loaded corridor is deconstructed to allow deep penetration of daylight and views to the exterior. *Credit: Perkins Eastman*

From the start of the design process, the Grand Rapids Dominican sisters emphasized their commitment to sustainability and during the integrated design process, conducted research on sustainable strategies alongside the project architects. "We reviewed everything system by system, material by material," said architect Ramu Ramachandran of the Perkins Eastman project team. "We would say, 'if you want to be standard, you can do this. If you want to be sustainable, here are the options you have.'"

The campus employs a natural storm water management system; storm water moves directly through bioswales and grading into retention areas on-site. From those retention areas, the water irrigates indigenous prairie-style plantings. This system enabled the removal of piping, sewer lines, and concrete curbs and gutters, allowing the buildings to blend more gracefully into the site.

The building design is inherently flexible and will accommodate future conversion of the property, either floor-by-floor or in its entirety, with limited modifications. The typical double-loaded corridor plan is deconstructed to allow deep penetration of daylight and views to the exterior.

KEY BUILDING PERFORMANCE STRATEGIES

Site
- Natural storm water management system linked to prairie-style native plantings
- High-reflectance metal roofing and ethylene propylene diene monomer (EPDM) rubber membrane

Energy
- Hydronic heating and cooling system
- Energy management system and occupant lighting controls

Materials
- Natural cork and cork/rubber flooring
- Focus on local and regional materials

Source: Perkins Eastman; Hassel, Walleck, Ramachandran 2006.

Figure 9-5: The entrance hall interior focuses on views to the courtyard between the building's wings and to the broader site beyond. *Credit: Chris Barrett © Hedrich Blessing*

ENVIRONMENTAL STEWARDSHIP

In these initial case studies, environmental stewardship was also framed as a core value of the religious organizations involved. As Philip McCorkle notes, "The mission statement of Trinity Health System includes the phrase, 'We will steward the resources entrusted to us.'" In discussing the Providence Health System's early leadership in sustainable building, Geoffrey Glass, PE, director of facility and technology services, notes, "One of Providence Health System's core values as a Catholic organization is stewardship. I was able to stand up in front of leadership and say, 'Our organization needs to commit to an environmental initiative because this allows us to connect to our very mission as a Catholic organization.'"

Environmental stewardship manifests in the acquisition or maintenance of sites that are ecologically valuable or cherished by communities. Laguna Honda Hospital in San Francisco and Southeast Regional Treatment Center at Madison State Hospital in Madison, Indiana, (see Chapter 4) are examples of sustainable design approaches embedded in modernization programs on the campuses of sprawling, hundred-year-old psychiatric hospitals now revered as large, undeveloped parcels of historic and environmental significance. Boulder Community Hospital in Boulder, Colorado, (below), demonstrates how sustainable design considerations emerged in an environmentally progressive community increasingly concerned about the negative impact of real estate development on ecosystem health. Harris, New York's Discovery Health Center, another early innovator, restored a damaged agricultural site to accommodate its building and mitigate previous runoff negatively impacting the adjacent organic farm (see page 347).

CASE STUDY

Boulder Community Hospital

Boulder, Colorado

Figure 9-6: Boulder Community Hospital. *Credit: OZ Architecture*

Owner: Boulder Community Hospital

Design team:

ARCHITECTS: OZ Architecture/Boulder Associates, Inc.

LANDSCAPE ARCHITECT/SITE PLANNER: Civitas

INTERIOR DESIGNERS: OZ Architecture/Boulder Associates, Inc./SO Design

STRUCTURAL ENGINEER: Monroe & Newell Engineers, Inc.

MECHANICAL ENGINEER: Shaffer Baucom Engineering & Consulting

ELECTRICAL ENGINEER: BCER Engineering, Inc.

CIVIL ENGINEER: Drexel, Barrell & Co.

CONTRACTOR: Gerald H. Phipps, Inc.

LEED CONSULTANT: Architectural Energy Corporation

COMMISSIONING: Farnsworth Group

Building type: New campus

Size: Acute care: 154,000 sq ft (14,306 sq m); outpatient: 67,000 sq ft (6,224 sq m); 49 acre (19.8 ha) site

Program description: Sixty-bed women's and children's hospital, including outpatient services building, imaging, surgery, labs, and emergency care

Completion date: 2003

Recognition: First US Green Building Council LEED-certified hospital in the United States (LEED silver); 2006 Hospitals for a Healthy Environment (H2E) Environmental Leadership Award

The project site was an unincorporated parcel that the city of Boulder had identified for development. Surrounding development had severely deteriorated the health of the site, which included both a large wetland zone and a sizable resident prairie dog colony. The colony was safely relocated away from the development zone; the wetland area was increased sixfold. The particulars of the site, along with Boulder Community Hospital's commitment to pollution prevention, set the project on a sustainable development path.

The project is located along several bus routes, and two new bus stops were provided for employees, patients, and visitors. Signed carpool spaces encourage employees to share a ride, and bike racks, showers, and changing facilities encourage employees to bike or walk to work. The site is linked to an existing city of Boulder bike path located along Boulder Creek.

Encouraging the use of alternative transportation and reducing storm water runoff worked hand in hand: accessibility to bus service, carpooling spaces, and bike racks enabled a reduction in the number of parking spaces to 25 percent below the city requirement. This, in turn, reduced the amount of impermeable surface on the site, which reduced storm water runoff by 25 percent in the parking areas. Additionally, grass pavers were used to construct the fire lane. In one area, the fire lane is incorporated with the pedestrian walks in the courtyard, eliminating duplication of surfaces.

Figure 9-7: Phase One Site Plan. *Credit: CIVITAS, Inc.*

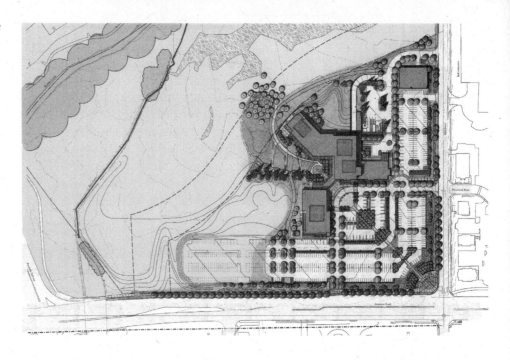

Figure 9-8: When fully developed, the site disturbance will only be marginally greater than it is presently (Fig. 9-7), while the total built area will increase to 400,000 sq ft (37,161 sq m). Thirty-two acres of the 49-acre site have been returned to the city of Boulder as permanent open space. *Credit: CIVITAS, Inc.*

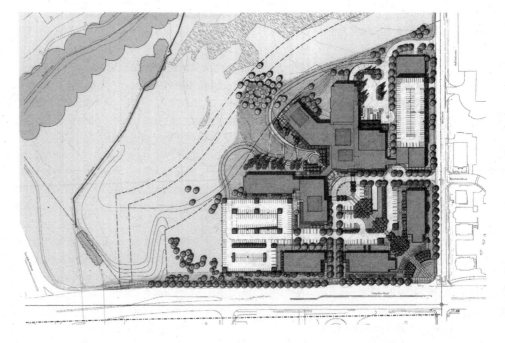

KEY BUILDING PERFORMANCE STRATEGIES

Site

- Reduced site disturbance
- Habitat restoration
- Grass paver system at fire lanes
- Alternative transportation encouraged, resulting in reduced parking requirements
- High-reflectance, Energy Star roofing

Water

- Xeriscaping with native vegetation saved an estimated 40 percent in water consumption over a more typical project of the same size
- Low-flow fixtures; waterless urinals

Energy

- High-performance building envelope
- Building form incorporates solar shading
- On-site central utility plant with high-efficiency, partial-load, low–nitrogen oxide emitting boilers (nitrogen oxide emission level is 70 percent lower than that of standard equipment)
- 35 percent reduction in energy demand below ASHRAE 90.1-1999 baseline
- Air-side economizer cycle to maximize free cooling

Materials

- Local and regional materials used
- 64 percent construction-waste recycling
- Recycled-content materials employed
- Polyvinyl chloride (PVC) avoidance
- Use of linoleum and rubber flooring

Environmental Quality

- Operable patient room windows interlocked to variable air volume (VAV) system, which shuts down when windows open
- Control system notifies plant manager if open windows cause system to run inefficiently

Sources: Boulder Associates, Inc.; OZ Architecture; Civitas

We encourage people to reflect their community values by recycling, riding their bike to work, and taking the bus. People tell me this is what they believe in and how they want to live and work. I keep adding more bike racks — more people are biking to the hospital. The singular belief system that drives the work that I do is the direct link between the quality of the environment and the quality of health.

—KAI ABELKIS, ENVIRONMENTAL COORDINATOR, BOULDER COMMUNITY HOSPITAL

2006 H2E ENVIRONMENTAL LEADERSHIP AWARD

HOSPITALS *for a* HEALTHY ENVIRONMENT™

With an impressive 31 percent recycling rate, this LEED silver–certified facility boasts comprehensive recycling programs. Boulder Community Hospital demonstrated its deep commitment to the environment throughout the construction of its new facility. The purchasing department is permitted to spend an additional 15 percent for green products, and the hospital works closely with its group purchasing organization to provide environmental guidance, impacting product selection for the group purchasing organization's entire membership. In 2005 the facility invested in reusable containers for sterilizing operating room instruments, reducing costs by over $100,000 per year.

Source: H2E

SUSTAINABLE OPERATIONS

Overlaying community engagement is an underlying commitment to pollution prevention and other operational environmental improvements. Boulder Community Hospital, for example, engages in an expanding range of pollution prevention initiatives. For many large health system innovators and early adopters serving environmentally progressive Pacific Northwest and California markets (e.g., Providence Health System, Legacy Health System, and Kaiser Permanente), achievements in operations directly impacted sustainable building pursuits. Legacy Health System, for example, won an H2E award for its leadership in recycling in 2006. Its first sustainable building project, Legacy Salmon Creek Hospital, blends a focus on the patient experience with sustainable building.

Trash	46
Regulated medical waste (RMW)	7
Recycling	46
Hazardous waste	1

hazardous waste
1%

recycling
46%

trash
46%

regulated medical
waste (RMW)
7%

Figure 9-9: Legacy Health System sets a new industry standard as it recycles 46 percent of its operational solid waste; it has a combined total of only 8 percent in regulated medical and hazardous waste. *Credit: H2E*

LEGACY HEALTH SYSTEM 2006 H2E ENVIRONMENTAL LEADERSHIP AWARD

Legacy Health System is setting the standard for waste minimization in the healthcare sector with an outstanding 46 percent recycling rate. The system has spearheaded an innovative sterile blue wrap recycling program: materials are brought to Legacy Health System for responsible disposal from other hospitals across the state. In 2005, Legacy recycled more than 105 tons of blue wrap, resulting in savings of more than $25,000. Legacy also has a centralized recycling center where staffers sort a variety of materials. By launching a brand new "healthy hospitals" sustainability campaign in the upcoming year, Legacy Health System will continue to set a high bar for environmental excellence.

Source: H2E

Legacy Salmon Creek Hospital

Vancouver,
Washington

Figure 9-10: Legacy Salmon Creek. *Credit: Eckert & Eckert*

Owner: Legacy Health System
Design team:
    ARCHITECT: Zimmer Gunsul Frasca Architects LLP
    LANDSCAPE ARCHITECT: Walker Macy
    MECHANICAL, ELECTRICAL, AND PLUMBING ENGINEER: AEI Affiliated
      Engineers Inc.
    STRUCTURAL ENGINEER: KPFF Consulting Engineers
    CIVIL ENGINEER: Olson Engineering, Inc.
    GENERAL CONTRACTOR: Skanska USA
    CONSTRUCTION MANAGER: Hammes Co.
Building Type: New hospital campus
Size: Hospital: 469,000 sq ft (43,600 sq m), 220 beds; outpatient: 189,000
    sq ft (17,600 sq m); garage: 460,000 sq ft (42,700 sq m), 1,400 cars; site
    area: 24 acres (9.7 ha)
Program description: Acute care hospital and physician medical center; two
    four-story medical office buildings; seven-story parking garage
Completion date: 2005

This freestanding medical center complex is located in Salmon Creek, the most rapidly growing area of Clark County, Washington. The campus aggregates to just over 1.1 million square feet (102,193 sq m) of development on the compact 24-acre (9.7 ha) site adjacent to a wooded forest area. The site, as developed, is approximately 46,000 square feet per acre (10,560 sq m per ha).

Indigenous drought-tolerant landscaping, pervious surface treatments, natural storm water retention design, and sensitive site lighting are incorporated as sustainable design features in consideration of this protected area. Daylighting studies were

Figure 9-11: The building's primary facade of travertine stone extends into the main public spaces as interior finishes. Other exterior materials include brick, glass, and metal. *Credit: Robert Canfield*

performed by the University of Oregon's daylighting lab in Portland to determine the amount of sunlight and glazing necessary to achieve the facility's daylighting performance goals throughout the building, including patient rooms. Legacy Health System prioritized indoor air quality for patients and staff, recycling, and waste reduction.

A central courtyard with a water feature, sculpture, plazas, and seating connects the complex on the ground level, providing opportunities for visitors and staff to interact outdoors. The design also creates south-facing outdoor terraces off the cafeteria, chapel, and conference rooms. (For the case study on the hospital's garden, see page 96.)

KEY BUILDING PERFORMANCE STRATEGIES

Site
- Rooftop healing garden
- Central courtyard with water feature, sculpture, plazas, and seating connects the complex to the ground level and provides a community amenity
- Sand-set pavers increase permeable surfaces

Water
- Site landscaping with drought-tolerant plants and storm water detention system

Energy
- Daylighting maximized using low-E-coated glazing and clerestory glazing in patient rooms

Materials
- Recycled content materials used, including cabinet substrate
- Persistent bioaccumulative toxic (PBT) chemicals avoided
- 75 percent construction-waste recycled
- Local and regional materials employed—including exterior brick, curtain wall assemblies, ceiling panels, gypsum board, and steel trusses

Environmental Quality
- Patient towers angled to maximize views of adjacent natural habitat and Mount Hood; balconies on inpatient units give patient and staff access to outdoors

In addition to first costs, Legacy Health Systems conducted an analysis of life cycle and long-term operating costs as design decisions were made. Some sustainable design features, such as the green roof healing garden, increased first costs but added important program amenities for patients, visitors, and staff.

Source: Zimmer Gunsul Frasca Architects LLP

Figure 9-12: The 24-acre Legacy Salmon Creek site includes more than 1.1 million sq ft (102,193 sq m) of building—a 220-bed acute care hospital, a 189,000-sq-ft (17,559-sq-m) outpatient facility, and structured parking for 1,400 cars. The patient care towers are oriented toward an adjacent protected wooded area while the buildings are organized around a fully developed terraced garden. *Credit: Zimmer Gunsul Frasca Architects LLP*

ACADEMIC CAMPUS INITIATIVES

When sustainable building initiatives in healthcare buildings were in their infancy, universities around the United States began registering and certifying new academic buildings through the US Green Building Council's LEED program. In 2004, as part of a campuswide initiative for all new construction, the Winship Cancer Institute at Emory University in Atlanta became the third Emory building—and the first American academic clinical medical building—to achieve LEED certification. Other major universities are expanding their sustainable building programs to medical center buildings. Among the next wave are Oregon Health & Science University, the University of Pittsburgh, the University of Florida, the University of Michigan, and Harvard University.

Universities credit increasing student awareness as a driver in both sustainable building and operations. Green transportation initiatives, "garbage-free" athletic events, extensive recycling programs, and organic and/or locally produced food initiatives are among the more visible elements of an increased focus on improved operations. Increasing numbers of LEED-registered projects—as of the end of 2006 the University of Florida boasts a total of ten registered or certified projects, and Harvard has sixteen—signify a sweeping reconsideration of building performance. This is likely to accelerate as universities move forward on carbon-reduction initiatives (see Chapter 12).

As a pioneer, the Winship Cancer Institute team experienced many of the frustrations common among project teams that began this work before a market was in place to service sustainable building initiatives. "During the demolition of the existing building, we found a construction waste recycler. Unfortunately, it went out of business one-third of the way through the process," notes Dan Glotsis of Stanley Beaman & Sears. "But that was 1999—now construction waste recycling is achievable. We also wanted certified wood for the foundation and shoring, but it just wasn't available at the time."

Winship Cancer Institute at Emory University

Atlanta, Georgia

Figure 9-13: Winship Cancer Institute at Emory University. *Credit: Gary Knight & Associates, Inc.*

Owner: Emory University, Woodruff Health Sciences Center
Design team:
ARCHITECT/INTERIOR DESIGN: Stanley Beaman & Sears
ASSOCIATE ARCHITECT: NBBJ
LANDSCAPE ARCHITECT: Hughes Good O'Leary & Ryan
STRUCTURAL ENGINEER: Stanley D. Lindsey and Associates, Ltd.
MECHANICAL, ELECTRICAL, AND PLUMBING ENGINEER: Newcomb & Boyd
LABORATORY PLANNER: GPR Planners Collaborative
GENERAL CONTRACTOR: Turner Construction Co.
Building type: New construction
Size: 260,000 sq ft (24,200 sq m)
Program description: 60 percent outpatient clinical space and 40 percent science and research space; including three floors of research laboratories, radiation oncology and imaging department, four linear accelerators, ambulatory infusion center, bone marrow transplant/hematology and leukemia clinic, and women's center
Completion date: 2003
Recognition: US Green Building Council LEED certified

Emory University's commitment to achieve LEED certification for all its new buildings was the major driver for the project, the first comprehensive cancer center in Atlanta. The on-campus building is nestled among historic structures and an important historic tree, both of which dictated the building's massing and location. The building plan maximizes daylighting in occupied spaces—laboratories and offices—and anchors the laboratory equipment in the central interior building zone. Laboratories are organized in a modular, open plan that allows them to be reconfigured easily as the research staff and casework configuration need changes. An eighty-position ambulatory infusion area is adjacent to a private outdoor garden.

KEY BUILDING PERFORMANCE STRATEGIES

Water

- Condensate-return water recycled, saving 1.9 million gallons (71.9 mil liters) annually
- Nonpotable water used to cool condensing units
- Native landscaping; drip irrigation used only to establish materials, and then abandoned

Energy

- Energy demand reduced 20 percent below baseline through chillers equipped with variable frequency drives (VFDs)
- Building cooling load demand reduced 35 percent below ASHRAE 90.1-1999 through energy-recovery system for the laboratory ventilation system (a "heat wheel" system)
- Expandable energy plant in the building, including additional modulating chiller capacity

One of the building's more innovative water-conservation measures is its use of nonpotable water to cool the condensing units associated with the environmental rooms. While local codes permit the use of domestic water to cool the condensers, the project included a recirculating system using chilled water, which reduced potable water use and sanitary sewer charges. The estimated savings is 1,000,000 gallons (3,785,400 liters) of water per year. In addition, the project uses condensate derived from energy-recovery dehumidification for cooling tower makeup water, yielding an additional savings of 900,000 gallons (3,406,870 liters) annually (see Fig. 9-15).

Source: Stanley Beaman & Sears; Johnson 2005

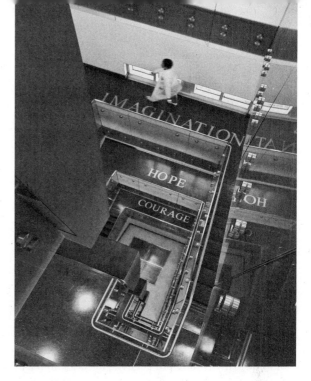

Figure 9-14: A central design feature of the building is an open stair to encourage walking by researchers and ambulatory patients and families. The words inscribed in the floors are components of prominently located quotes meant to inspire building occupants, either in their research or their recovery. *Credit: Gary Knight & Associates, Inc.*

The eight-year payback for heat recovery on the laboratory ventilation system was a tough sell in 1999, but given what's happened with energy pricing, that payback time has been dramatically reduced: the system will pay for itself in just four years.

We challenged the existing campus landscape-planning standards. But we had to design two plant schemes— the xeriscape and the traditional—both to make sure that the cost difference was negligible, and just in case people didn't like the native planting. At the same time, we devised a storage tank for foundation dewatering recovery in order to irrigate the nonnative scheme. In the end, that was more expensive than the xeriscaping.

—DAN GLOTSIS, STANLEY BEAMAN & SEARS

Figure 9-15: Condensate Recovery System
The project also includes a piped gravity system to capture condensate from the laboratory's energy-recovery unit cooling coils for use as cooling tower make-up water. This system will capture approximately 900,000 gallons of water annually and reduce energy demand.
Credit: Newcomb & Boyd

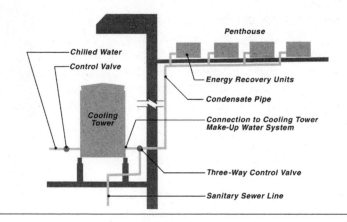

THE ASHE VISTA AWARDS

The 2005 ASHE Vista Awards established the early influence of the ASHE *Green Healthcare Construction Guidance Statement,* the *Green Guide for Health Care,* and LEED. Every award-winning project evidenced the application of sustainable design principles, although none of the Vista Team Award projects formally registered with either LEED or the *Green Guide.* The timing of this group of projects — all were completed by late 2003 — meant that design decisions were made in 2000 and 2001, prior to the release of many of these initiatives. These projects represent early consideration of healthy materials palettes at a time when alternative products were less available. Every project team referenced the use of some form of integrated design process. The D'Amour Center, for example, won the Vista award in the new construction category.

CASE STUDY

The D'Amour Center for Cancer Care

Springfield, Massachusetts

Figure 9-16: D'Amour Center for Cancer Care. *Credit: © Robert Benson*

Owner: Baystate Health
Design team:
   ARCHITECT AND INTERIOR DESIGNER: Steffian Bradley Architects
   CONSTRUCTION MANAGER: George B. H. Macomber Co.
   MECHANICAL, ELECTRICAL, AND PLUMBING ENGINEER: AHA Consulting Engineers
   STRUCTURAL ENGINEER: McNamara/Salvia, Inc.
   CIVIL ENGINEER AND LANDSCAPE ARCHITECT: Vanesse Hangen Brustlin, Inc.
Type: New construction
Size: 64,000 sq ft (5,945 sq m)
Design energy intensity: 50 kWh/sq ft annually
Program description: Adult and pediatric ambulatory cancer services, including comprehensive radiation and systemic oncology programs, and patient and family counseling services
Completion date: 2004

Just outside of downtown Springfield, the D'Amour Center for Cancer Care is located on one of Baystate Health's medical center campuses. Site factors considered in the center's design included maintaining the site's urban edge, the new facility's relationship to the campus as a whole, and maximizing natural light, which influenced the center's orientation. Kurt Rockstroh, AIA, Principal at Steffian Bradley, notes that "throughout the design process, the team was challenged to reject existing cancer treatment metaphors and standard design terminology."

The D'Amour Center creates a patient-focused healing environment that attempts to alleviate patients' anxiety and loneliness, and the overwhelming nature of cancer treatment, by improving their experience of the surrounding environment. Because cancer patients are immunosuppressed and highly sensitive to odors, chemical toxins, mold, and bacteria, "healthy-material" selection criteria informed all decisions relating to the interior furnishings and finishes. The client evaluated choices based on functional use and life cycle costs as well. For example, the woven polyethylene wall covering used in rooms where patient treatment occurs is chlorine and plasticizer free and contains no heavy metals or harmful dyes, and obviates the need for frequent repainting. The accent wall covering is made of recyclable nylon, polyester, and wood pulp.

Figure 9-17: The second floor's gently curved living room traverses the east-west axis below the skylight, while natural light filters through the glass planks. Third-floor conference rooms receive natural light from the atrium. Wood paneling, linoleum flooring, and polyolefin wall covering reflect a concern for creating a healthy indoor environment and a strong association with nature.
Credit: © Robert Benson

KEY BUILDING PERFORMANCE STRATEGIES

Materials
- Material choices that contained recycled content preferred
- Major manufacturers of interior materials and furnishings all ISO 14001 certified
- Linoleum flooring in all patient treatment areas
- Formaldehyde-free building insulation and substrates and low-VOC adhesives throughout
- Low-VOC paint on all painted walls
- Carpet Green Label certified by Carpet and Rug Institute (project completed prior to creation of Green Label Plus standard)
- Fixed casework minimized and freestanding furnishings specified for work areas, team space, and offices
- Custom quick-release brackets allow work surfaces and workstations to be disassembled without tools
- Furnishings 70 percent recyclable and comprised of 40 percent recycled materials
- More than 50 percent of furnishings Greenguard certified

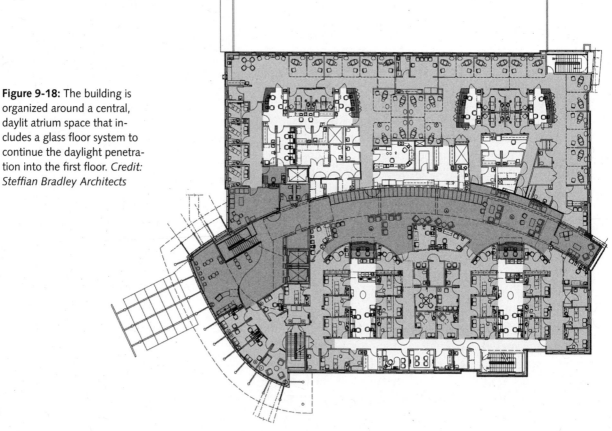

Figure 9-18: The building is organized around a central, daylit atrium space that includes a glass floor system to continue the daylight penetration into the first floor. *Credit: Steffian Bradley Architects*

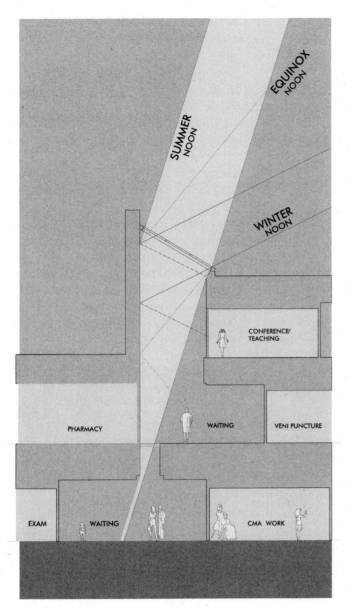

The project's most notable architectural feature is the curved circulation and waiting spine capped by a continuous skylight/roof monitor. This feature, coupled with a glass flooring system, permits the deep penetration of daylight into the building's interior. Challenging the prevailing notion of large atria or circulation as perimeter elements, workspaces line the building's periphery instead. Because of the building's depth and the desire to maximize direct sun penetration, a south-facing skylight (with low-E, high-performance glazing) was selected.

How has this project measured its success? It received more philanthropic support than any project in the Baystate system and achieved its five-year patient projection within six months of opening.

Source: Steffian Bradley Architects

Figure 9-19: Section through Skylight
Extensive daylighting studies resulted in the curved, sloped skylight that traverses the building from east to west and brings year-round daylight deep into the facility's core. *Credit: Steffian Bradley Architects*

HOSPITALS *for a* HEALTHY ENVIRONMENT™

Baystate is going the extra mile to minimize its use of hazardous chemicals. Baystate is recycling xylene and ethanol and has implemented a new technology to reuse methanol. To reduce its use of harmful pesticides, Baystate controls pests through a successful integrated pest management program that employs bait technology and reduces spraying. Additionally, the facility has implemented a new green cleaning program that minimizes chemical use and enhances worker safety. A robust recycling program and a creative surplus equipment donation project round out Baystate's exemplary achievements.

The Fay W. Boozman College of Public Health at the University of Arkansas for Medical Sciences in Little Rock (case study, Chapter 2) received a second VISTA new building award in 2005. Though the project did not proceed with LEED certification, the initial intent to participate in LEED guided the team in establishing and ultimately achieving sustainable design goals and strategies. Because the university identified sustainable design experience as a criterion for architect selection, each team member had LEED-accredited professionals on staff, and environmental stewardship was therefore embedded in the design approach.

Providence St. Peter Hospital in Olympia, Washington, received the ASHE 2005 Vista Award in the renovation category for its expansion and renovation. Providence included a reference to the *Green Guide for Health Care* in its submission, but what really impressed the Vista jurors was the decision to intentionally minimize the building's footprint on a site that they described as an "important natural resource in the local community."

Figure 9-20: The University of Arkansas for Medical Sciences College of Public Health included sustainable design goals from project inception (case study, Chapter 2). *Credit: Tim Hursley*

Owner: Providence St. Peter
Hospital

Design Team:

ARCHITECT: Giffin Bolte
Jurgens

STRUCTURAL ENGINEER:
Putnam Collins Scott
Associates

GENERAL CONTRACTOR:
Sellen Construction Co.

Building type: Expansion and
renovation

Size: Addition: 93,659 sq ft
(8,700 sq m); renova-
tion: 138,478 sq ft
(12,860 sq m)

Design energy intensity:
208 kBTU/sq ft

Program description: 360-
bed existing community
hospital, total building
area 720,000 sq ft
(66,930 sq m); project includes emergency depart-
ment, laboratory, public lobby, and concourse additions; renovation of
surgical suite, diagnostic imaging, cardiac catheterization labs, critical care
and short stay inpatient units, and a new 420-space parking structure

Completion date: phased construction: 2003–2004

Recognition: 2005 ASHE Vista Award; 2003 Energy Star partner

Providence St. Peter Hospital Campus Renewal

Olympia,
Washington

Figure 9-21: Providence
St. Peter Hospital
Campus Renewal.
Credit: Eckert & Eckert

The community cherishes the hospital's beautiful, wooded 173-acre (70 hectare) site. "It is an island of serenity in a sea of suburban development," notes Geoffrey Glass, PE. During the planning and implementation of the project, every effort was made to preserve and repair this setting. This directed renewal project increased the total conditioned area by only 13 percent, but dramatically transformed patients' experience of it, from the time they enter until they depart. The existing building, dating from 1970, never capitalized on the potential of bringing the outside indoors; the renewal project, however, connects the delivery of care to this extraordinary natural setting.

Since 1998, the hospital has cut electricity use by 2 percent, natural gas use by 23 percent, and water use by 26 percent through a variety of creative initiatives. These efficiencies freed capacity for a 13 percent increase in campus built area without added central plant space or equipment. This, in turn, greatly improved the financial feasibility of the campus renewal project. The campus received an EPA Energy Star designation for 2003.

Figure 9-22: Entering the building through the contemplative garden seamlessly transitions visitors from the heavily wooded parking areas to the inpatient elevator core and ambulatory care functions. *Credit: Eckert & Eckert*

Figure 9-23: The addition of a relatively modestly scaled public concourse transforms the public experience within the facility and ties the building to its extraordinary site. *Credit: Giffin Bolte Jurgens*

Figure 9-24: The concourse features simple, natural materials and expansive glazing and daylight.
Credit: Eckert & Eckert

According to the project team, creating a strong, identifiable relationship to the surrounding forest was the overriding consideration in the design of all public spaces. This was accomplished, in part, through the use of coordinated natural materials, organic shapes, warm colors, lighting, and artwork. The design primarily owes its success to the expanses of glass that provide views of trees and sky in all directions. Also noteworthy is the powerful relationship established between the contemplative garden and the architectural elements of the entry canopy and concourse. At a more intimate scale, small gardens have been placed outside each concourse lounge to provide views of native plants and buffer these spaces from the traffic zone.

The palette of colors, materials, and finishes from this project has become the master palette for future renovation and campus construction. Also based on sustainable principles, these materials include polished, tinted concrete; eco-polymeric Stratica and carpet floor coverings; and wood and regional stone. The resulting consistency and harmony are effective in unifying the public spaces throughout the campus renewal project.

Geoffrey Glass describes the journey to the material standards palette as a struggle: "We wanted to support more sustainable materials. It took some experimentation to get to this point, but while we choked a little on the initial cost of the alternatives, we realized that we can service this palette economically."

When the campus was built in 1970, all the parking was tucked between the fir and cedar trees to minimize the impact of the hospital on the one-hundred-year-old forest. Approximately 35 percent of our existing campus is developed—the adjacent Class 1 salmon wetland precludes development of another 40 percent. We regard our site as a valuable community resource—and our community agrees with that.

—GEOFFREY GLASS, PE, DIRECTOR, FACILITY AND TECHNOLOGY SERVICES, PROVIDENCE ST. PETER HOSPITAL

The hospital opted to solve its need for additional parking through construction of a structured employee garage rather than disturb the heavily wooded site. Through negotiation with the city, Providence St. Peter was required to provide only the quantity of parking functionally necessary, which was less than the minimum mandated in city regulations. The 420-car garage satisfies the need for expanded parking with minimal impacts—its curved shape tiers into a hillside to minimize its presence on the site and shares an expanded storm water retention basin.

Source: Giffin Bolte Jurgens

Figure 9-25: The employee parking garage curves to follow the site's natural drainage patterns and shares the storm water retention and filtration basin. *Credit: Eckert & Eckert*

Finally, the Infrastructure Team Award was given to HOK/Flack + Kurtz for the new Energy Center at North Shore University Hospital in Manhassett, New York, an existing 869-bed academic medical center campus. This new 10,000-ton, 156,000-PPH high-pressure steam power plant consists of three dual-fuel 52,000-PPH,150 PSIG steam boilers, three 2,000-ton steam turbine chillers, and two 2,000-ton electric centrifugal chillers. Condenser water plate heat exchangers provide precooling of return chilled water as well as full free cooling when ambient conditions permit. Upgrading the plant equipment reduced cooling costs by an estimated 35 percent. Other benefits include operating simplicity and reduced ongoing maintenance costs.

Figure 9-26: New York State Energy Research and Development Authority recognized the central plant at North Shore University Hospital for innovation in energy efficiency and peak electrical demand reduction, resulting in incentive awards of $2.7 million. *Credit: S. Goferman/Sugodesign © 2003*

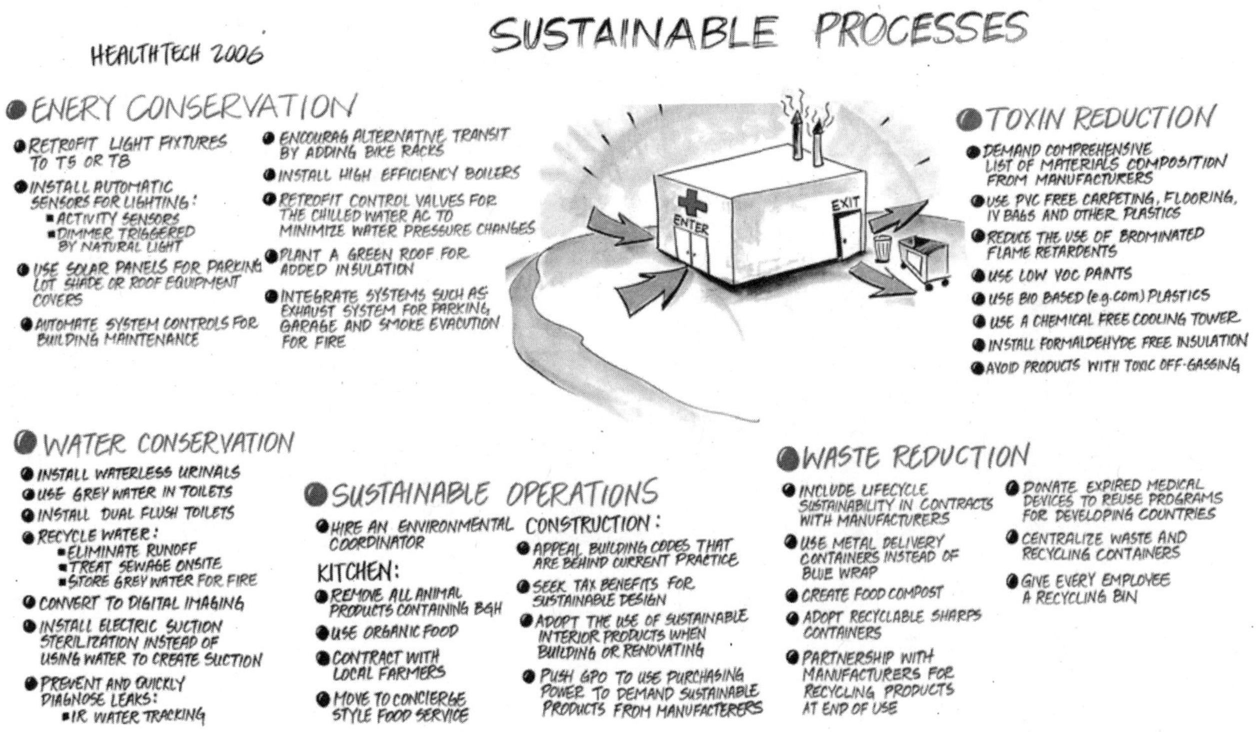

SUSTAINABLE PROCESSES

HEALTHTECH 2006

● ENERY CONSERVATION

- ● RETROFIT LIGHT FIXTURES TO T5 OR T8
- ● INSTALL AUTOMATIC SENSORS FOR LIGHTING:
  - ▪ ACTIVITY SENSORS
  - ▪ DIMMER TRIGGERED BY NATURAL LIGHT
- ● USE SOLAR PANELS FOR PARKING LOT SHADE OR ROOF EQUIPMENT COVERS
- ● AUTOMATE SYSTEM CONTROLS FOR BUILDING MAINTENANCE

- ● ENCOURAG ALTERNATIVE TRANSIT BY ADDING BIKE RACKS
- ● INSTALL HIGH EFFICIENCY BOILERS
- ● RETROFIT CONTROL VALVES FOR THE CHILLED WATER AC TO MINIMIZE WATER PRESSURE CHANGES
- ● PLANT A GREEN ROOF FOR ADDED INSULATION
- ● INTEGRATE SYSTEMS SUCH AS EXHAUST SYSTEM FOR PARKING, GARAGE AND SMOKE EVACUATION FOR FIRE

● TOXIN REDUCTION

- ● DEMAND COMPREHENSIVE LIST OF MATERIALS COMPOSITION FROM MANUFACTURERS
- ● USE PVC FREE CARPETING, FLOORING, IV BAGS AND OTHER PLASTICS
- ● REDUCE THE USE OF BROMINATED FLAME RETARDENTS
- ● USE LOW VOC PAINTS
- ● USE BIO BASED (e.g. corn) PLASTICS
- ● USE A CHEMICAL FREE COOLING TOWER
- ● INSTALL FORMALDEHYDE FREE INSULATION
- ● AVOID PRODUCTS WITH TOXIC OFF-GASSING

● WATER CONSERVATION

- ● INSTALL WATERLESS URINALS
- ● USE GREY WATER IN TOILETS
- ● INSTALL DUAL FLUSH TOILETS
- ● RECYCLE WATER:
  - ▪ ELIMINATE RUNOFF
  - ▪ TREAT SEWAGE ONSITE
  - ▪ STORE GREY WATER FOR FIRE
- ● CONVERT TO DIGITAL IMAGING
- ● INSTALL ELECTRIC SUCTION STERILIZATION INSTEAD OF USING WATER TO CREATE SUCTION
- ● PREVENT AND QUICKLY DIAGNOSE LEAKS:
  - ▪ IR WATER TRACKING

● SUSTAINABLE OPERATIONS

- ● HIRE AN ENVIRONMENTAL COORDINATOR

KITCHEN:
- ● REMOVE ALL ANIMAL PRODUCTS CONTAINING BGH
- ● USE ORGANIC FOOD
- ● CONTRACT WITH LOCAL FARMERS
- ● MOVE TO CONCIERGE STYLE FOOD SERVICE

CONSTRUCTION:
- ● APPEAL BUILDING CODES THAT ARE BEHIND CURRENT PRACTICE
- ● SEEK TAX BENEFITS FOR SUSTAINABLE DESIGN
- ● ADOPT THE USE OF SUSTAINABLE INTERIOR PRODUCTS WHEN BUILDING OR RENOVATING
- ● PUSH GPO TO USE PURCHASING POWER TO DEMAND SUSTAINABLE PRODUCTS FROM MANUFACTERERS

● WASTE REDUCTION

- ● INCLUDE LIFECYCLE SUSTAINABILITY IN CONTRACTS WITH MANUFACTURERS
- ● USE METAL DELIVERY CONTAINERS INSTEAD OF BLUE WRAP
- ● CREATE FOOD COMPOST
- ● ADOPT RECYCLABLE SHARPS CONTAINERS
- ● PARTNERSHIP WITH MANUFACTURERS FOR RECYCLING PRODUCTS AT END OF USE

- ● DONATE EXPIRED MEDICAL DEVICES TO REUSE PROGRAMS FOR DEVELOPING COUNTRIES
- ● CENTRALIZE WASTE AND RECYCLING CONTAINERS
- ● GIVE EVERY EMPLOYEE A RECYCLING BIN

Figure 9-27: The Health Technology Center, San Francisco (healthtech.org), catalogued current sustainable design and operational strategies underway in US healthcare settings in a wall chart graphic, which has been redrawn for this book. The information was derived from interviews conducted in late 2006 with healthcare providers and design teams. *Credit: © 2006 Health Technology Center*

For all the project teams, the Vista Awards validated their innovations and their underlying commitment to sustainable building goals: environmental stewardship in the service of improved occupant experience and community leadership. Given that most of the projects were initiated in the late 1990s, such commitment also reflects leadership: by 2005, these qualities were equated with excellence.

ESTABLISHING A NEW BENCHMARK

Are the cumulative efforts of these innovators and early adopters defining a new benchmark for healthcare design? What is the low-hanging fruit of US sustainable healthcare? To answer these questions, the nonprofit research and education organization HealthTech conducted research in 2006 among healthcare leaders engaged in sustainable building. The results are cataloged in the HealthTech Sustainable Wall Chart, reprinted as Figure 9-27.

By the end of 2006, a total of twelve healthcare projects had achieved LEED certification; three acute care, two long-term care, and seven ambulatory care buildings. Comparing the LEED points achieved by projects collectively provides some insight into the opportunities and challenges facing the current healthcare construction market; Figure 9-28A–B summarizes the achievements of these projects. The graphs that follow (Figure 9-29) compare these achievements, first using the sequence established by LEED, and then ranking by total point achievement.

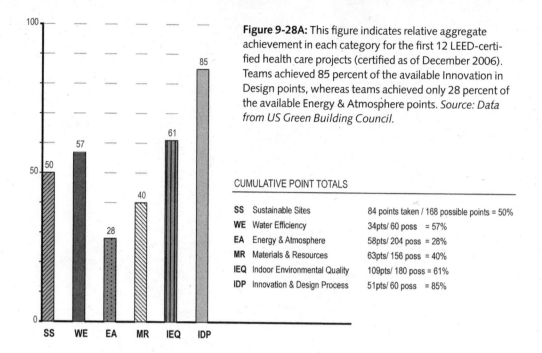

Figure 9-28A: This figure indicates relative aggregate achievement in each category for the first 12 LEED-certified health care projects (certified as of December 2006). Teams achieved 85 percent of the available Innovation in Design points, whereas teams achieved only 28 percent of the available Energy & Atmosphere points. *Source: Data from US Green Building Council.*

CUMULATIVE POINT TOTALS

SS	Sustainable Sites	84 points taken / 168 possible points = 50%
WE	Water Efficiency	34pts/ 60 poss = 57%
EA	Energy & Atmosphere	58pts/ 204 poss = 28%
MR	Materials & Resources	63pts/ 156 poss = 40%
IEQ	Indoor Environmental Quality	109pts/ 180 poss = 61%
IDP	Innovation & Design Process	51pts/ 60 poss = 85%

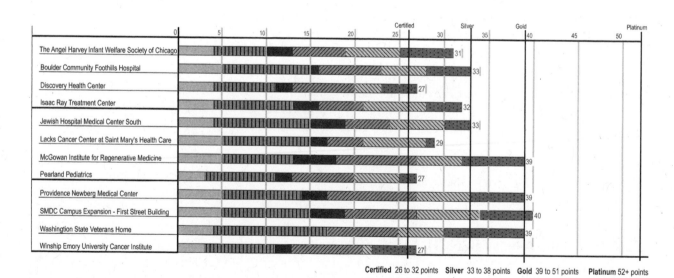

Figure 9-28B: These LEED certified health care projects achieved points across six categories in order to achieve the total score and certification level. See Figure 9-28A for legend. *Source: Data from US Green Building Council.*

Figures 9-29 A–L: These charts compare LEED achievement, first using the point sequence established by LEED for New Construction, followed by rearrangement based upon total points achieved. The database of projects are the twelve LEED-certified health care buildings named in Figure 9-28B. *Source: Data obtained from USGBC checklists; compiled by Guenther 5 Architects.*

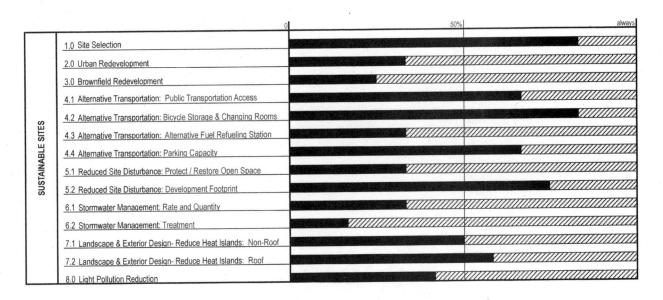

Figure 9-29 A-B: Sustainable Sites

50 percent of certified projects are achieving 50 percent of the points in this section. Credit 1 Site Selection has been achieved by all but one of the 12 projects; Credit 6.2 Stormwater Management: On Site Treatment is the least achieved. With the exception of Credit 4.3, the Credit 4 Alternative Transportation series has been achieved by more than half the certified projects.

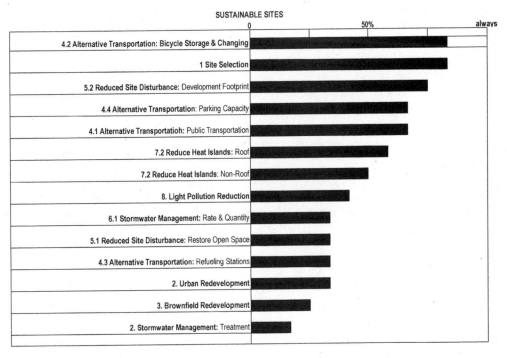

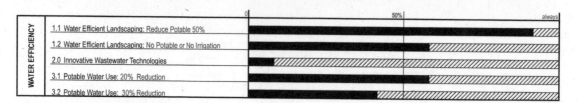

Figure 9-29C-D: Water Efficiency

The vast majority of projects are achieving 50 percent reduction in potable water for landscape irrigation—and more than 50 percent of LEED-certified projects have totally eliminated reliance on potable water for irrigation. Not surprisingly, healthcare projects are challenged to reduce fixture consumption by 30 percent, given the regulatory and infection control challenges around low-flow aerators and waterless urinals. Increased focus on process water uses will yield greater water savings, as evidenced in Winship Cancer Center (case study this chapter).

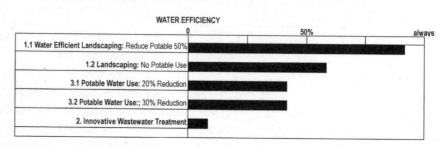

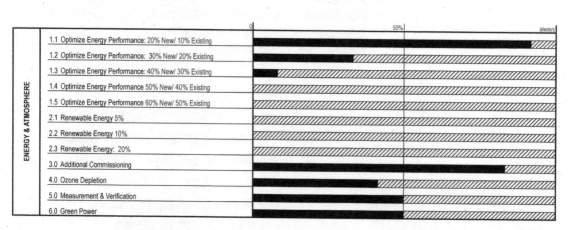

Figure 9-29E-F: Energy & Atmosphere

Sustainable healthcare buildings are achieving energy demand reductions in the range of 20 percent for a total of 2–3 points in this credit; only one of the certified projects has achieved reductions in the range of 40 percent. Projects are increasingly purchasing Green Power to offset 50 percent of their energy demand, and a number have achieved an additional Innovation point for 100 percent offset—including Providence Newberg (case study, Chapter 10). The vast majority of healthcare buildings are engaging in additional commissioning (see Chapter 6).

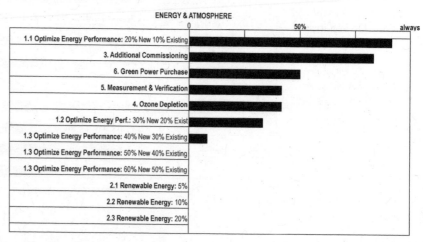

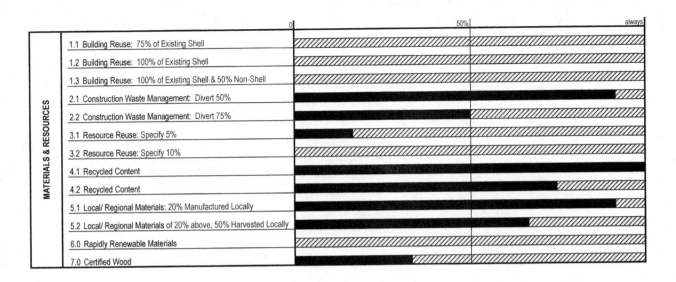

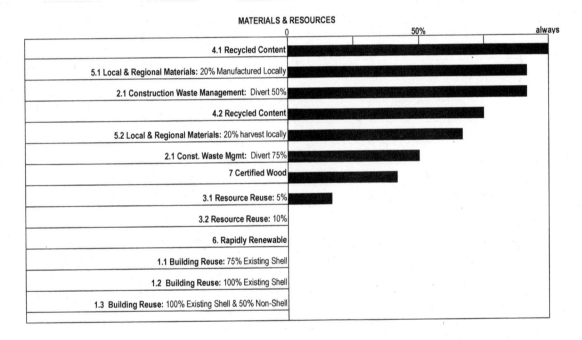

MATERIALS & RESOURCES

Figure 9-29G-H: Materials & Resources
Approximately 50 percent of LEED-certified projects are achieving 75 percent construction waste diversion; the vast majority are able to achieve 50 percent diversion. Recycled content materials as well as Local and Regional materials also appear to be readily achievable across a range of project types, locations, and scales. Resource reuse, that is, salvaging of materials, is proving to be more challenging—as is Building Reuse. The vast majority of initial certified projects are new construction; projects that blend new construction with renovation are challenged to achieve the current LEED points.

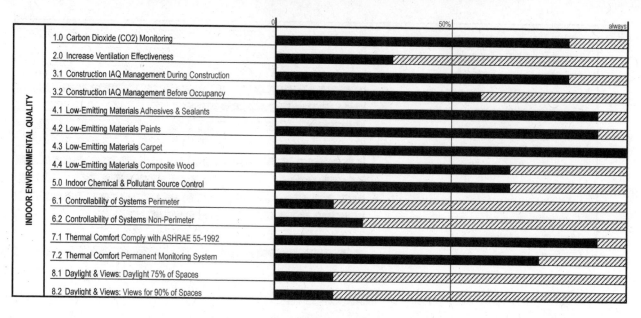

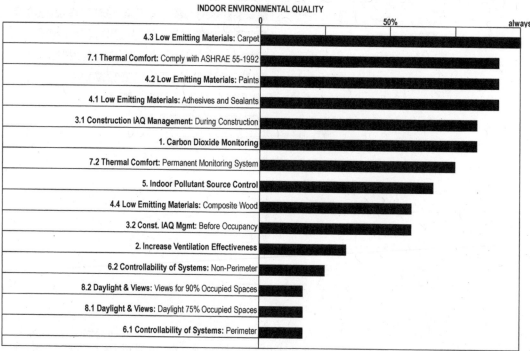

Figure 9-29 I-J: Indoor Environmental Quality
More than 50 percent of the certified projects are achieving more than 50 percent of the available points in this section. Low-emitting materials appear to be readily available through a range of cost-effective market products. Credit 6: Controllability of Systems and Credit 8: Daylight and Views, as drafted for Commercial Office projects, have limited applicability in health care settings; hence the extensive revisions to these credits proposed by the *Green Guide*.

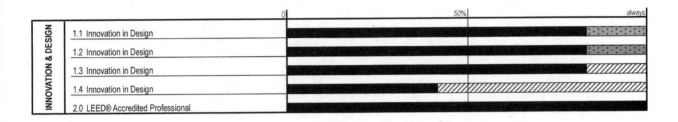

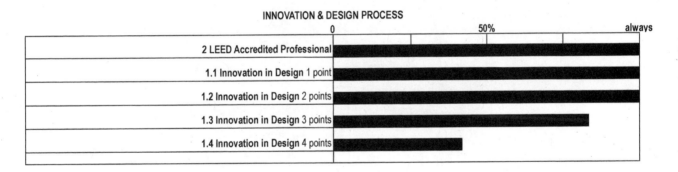

Figure 9-29 K-L: Innovation in Design

Virtually every project receives the point attributed to LEED Accredited Professionals. Most projects achieve at least three Innovation points, though fewer than 50 percent achieved all four. Many projects receive Innovation points for green building educational programs. Two projects received Innovation points for 100 percent purchase of Green Power. Exceeding point thresholds on recycled content is another common Innovation achievement, as has the implementation of green cleaning protocols.

CANADIAN INITIATIVES

In addition to these largely American initiatives, Canadian hospitals also responded early to the challenge of sustainable building. While a number of facilities — including Cambridge Memorial Hospital and Trillium Health Centre — focused on ISO 14001 certification (see Chapter 7), Thunder Bay Regional Health Sciences Centre in Thunder Bay, Ontario; the Carlo Fidani Peel Regional Cancer Centre at Credit Valley Hospital, in Mississauga, Ontario, (both in Chapter 11); and Bloorview Kids Rehab in Toronto (see below), integrated sustainable design considerations into their buildings. While Canada does not yet have a LEED-certified hospital, the BC Cancer Agency Research Center (see Chapter 1) is a Canada Green Building Council gold-certified research building.

CASE STUDY

Bloorview Kids Rehab

Toronto, Ontario

Figure 9-30: Bloorview Kids Rehab. *Credit: Tom Arban Photography*

Owner: Bloorview Kids Rehab
Design team:
   ARCHITECTS: Montgomery Sisam/Stantec, architects in joint venture
   LANDSCAPE ARCHITECT: Vertechs Design Inc.
   STRUCTURAL ENGINEER: Halcrow Yolles
   MECHANICAL, ELECTRICAL, AND PLUMBING ENGINEER: H. H. Angus & Associates Ltd.
   GENERAL CONTRACTOR: EllisDon Corp.
Building type: Replacement pediatric rehabilitation facility
Size: 353,000 sq ft (32,800 sq m)
Program description: Seventy-five-bed pediatric rehabilitation facility and community facility, including pool
Completion date: 2006

Bloorview Kids Rehab brings together multiple functions formerly housed in two separate sites. Part hospital, part community resource, part research and education center, the new facility is between a midtown residential neighborhood and a wooded ravine that slopes downward to a tributary of the Don River. A portion of the site bordering the ravine was transferred to the regional conservation authority as a public trail.

Sustainable design initiatives were explored and developed through an integrated design process. Early integration of all building systems (mechanical, electrical, and structural) with the architectural and site design resulted in a building that is more cost-effective, energy efficient, and environmentally benign.

Figure 9-31: The pool is heated using waste heat generated by the building's cooling systems. *Credit: Tom Arban Photography*

KEY BUILDING PERFORMANCE STRATEGIES

Site
- Native plantings selected for landscaped area
- Green roof; three accessible roof terraces for inpatients

Water
- Occupancy sensors and low-flow fixtures
- Underground storage of roof storm water connected to on-site irrigation systems

Energy
- Effected a 19 percent energy reduction compared with a building of similar program designed to meet the standards of the Model National Energy Code for Buildings
- Improved glazing system: low-E coating, argon-filled airspace with insulating edge spacer, high-performance thermal break, 25 mm (0.9 in) overall thickness
- Occupancy sensors on lighting

- Variable-speed drives on cooling towers
- Pool water heated by waste heat generated by cooling systems
- Chiller heat recovery assists with domestic hot-water heating loads
- Reuse of existing 60 kW photovoltaic array for on-site electricity production

Environmental Quality

- Low-emitting materials, materials requiring simple fabrication processes, and exposed structural finishes
- Maximized daylight and view opportunities afforded by sloping ravine site

Source: Stantec

Figure 9-32: The project focuses on providing daylight and views of the ravine and water. This third-floor deck offers inpatients access to the outdoors. *Credit: Tom Arban Photography*

In its 2006 operations survey, *FacilityCare* magazine received responses from 250 healthcare facility managers and executives. Asked whether they were addressing sustainable design in their design, construction, and operations, 12 percent indicated it was a "top priority"; 48 percent indicated they were "looking for affordable solutions"; and 21 percent reported that it was "under research" (Helmer 2006). Fewer than 20 percent indicated a total lack of knowledge or interest. In *The Tipping Point*, Malcolm Gladwell (2000) identifies three key conditions that must be present to create widespread change:

1. *The wisdom of the few:* More than 40 million square feet of healthcare are engaged in sustainable building strategies.

2. *The "stickiness factor":* Increasing regulatory interest, references in 2006 Guidelines for Construction of Hospitals and Healthcare Facilities, and escalating resource costs ensure that this is not a fad.

3. *The power of context:* As healthcare leaders recognize the connection between environmental stewardship and mission, a powerful context emerges that propels this work forward.

As the next generation of projects is realized — led by both innovators and fast followers — they will collectively demonstrate a commitment to environmental stewardship that creates a rich context for design exploration. Chapter 10 continues the examination of sustainable design strategies in support of the concept of stewardship.

CHAPTER 10

Resource Stewardship

In healthcare, sustainable building represents a bold move toward precaution and prevention. The building stands for health. In creating it, the organization is essentially saying, 'We're investing in keeping people healthier.' And that is different from the way that the US has traditionally approached healthcare. But it's consistent with a physician's value system. It represents a mindset and a culture of health as opposed to sickness treatment. Healing is an intangible concept. Creating the right environment for people mentally, physically, and spiritually is so important. Being attentive to sustainability, wellness, and resource stewardship presents a holistic view of healthcare that has an impact. We may not be able to measure or test it, but I'm convinced it has a tremendous impact on a person's ability to attain health. Not just to be not sick, but to be in health.

—JOHN KOSTER MD, CEO, Providence Health & Services

INTRODUCTION

Chapter 1, "Design and Stewardship," provided the global context for defining *stewardship*. Within the healthcare sector, the concept of stewardship is often embedded in the core mission of healthcare organizations. Since the Setting Healthcare's Environmental Agenda (SHEA) conference in 2000 (see Chapter 8), the notion of environmental leadership as fundamental to healthcare's mission and goals has gained recognition and momentum. Environmental stewardship is becoming a hallmark of leadership, excellence, and quality. Increas-

ingly, healthcare executives are viewing sustainable building as the right thing to do.

In 2006, a series of interviews with healthcare executives engaged in sustainable building formed the basis of a white paper titled *Values-Driven Design and Construction: Enriching Community Benefits through Green Hospitals* (Guenther, Vittori, and Atwood 2006). This chapter reflects on those interviews and features case studies that support a comprehensive demonstration of resource stewardship that furthers the possibilities for sustainable healthcare architecture. Each of the five essays interspersed throughout this chapter focuses on a singular aspect of the built environment—site, water, energy, materials, and environmental quality—and make an explicit connection between stewardship and human health.

Without exception, healthcare executives engaged in sustainable construction and operation view resource stewardship as intrinsic to their mission. For many religion-based healthcare organizations, "stewardship of God's resources" is embedded in their core principles. For Micki Benz, vice president of development for St. Mary's Health Care in Grand Rapids, Michigan, "It's about what you value and how well you know what you value. Are you concerned about the environment? Are you willing to reflect those values in what you're building and show that you'll do something about it? Our values are oriented toward a concern for the environment, a concern for people's welfare, and a concern for excellence and quality delivery." In secular healthcare organizations, executives note that connecting sustainability to mission may require a more expansive view, but the explicit relationship between human health and ecological health provides a compelling case. Roger A. Oxendale, president and CEO of Children's Hospital of Pittsburgh of University of Pittsburgh Medical Center, says, "Our responsibility as a pediatric healthcare organization is not just to care about the kids that come into our organization, but to care for all the kids in the community and what impacts their lives and informs their health—including the quality of the environment. Environmental advocacy is part of our broader view of mission."

> *I always start by talking about our mission and vision. And they both encompass stewardship—I don't even have to use the word. Our mission is to improve the health of those we serve. And our vision is to be where people want to work, where physicians want to practice, and, most importantly, where people turn when they need healthcare services. By building a better building, we are clearly going to improve the health of all those we serve—our patients, our families, our staff, and our physicians.*
>
> —CHERYL HERBERT, RN, PRESIDENT, DUBLIN-METHODIST HOSPITAL, OHIOHEALTH

LAND USE

Healthcare campuses continue to grow. Building area increases to accommodate private rooms and expanding diagnostic and treatment technologies; parking requirements continue to increase in auto-dependent communities. As sprawl has redefined our cities at their edges, US healthcare institutions have increasingly used site-selection criteria similar to those of commercial real estate interests, choosing greenfield campus sites based on their proximity to arterial highways. For the most part, healthcare organizations have not been vocal advocates for smart growth, responsible land planning, or public transportation.

Sustainable building initiatives are beginning to challenge this reality. In their essay "We All Live Downstream," landscape architects Carol Franklin and Teresa Durkin argue that conflicts between land development and the environment have become urgent.

We All Live Downstream

Carol Franklin, ASLA, and Teresa Durkin

> The residents..., according to parable, began noticing increasing numbers of drowning people caught in the river's swift current and so went to work inventing ever more elaborate technologies to resuscitate them. So preoccupied were these heroic villagers with rescue and treatment that they never thought to look upstream to see who was pushing the victims in.
>
> —SANDRA STEINGRABER, *Living Downstream*, 1998

We are living in an age when the conflicts between ongoing development efforts and maintaining a safe and healthy environment are of critical concern. In the United States, urban land use has increased in the last six decades from roughly 15 million acres to 60 million acres as the population has doubled. As the population grows, healthcare planners must keep pace with evolving needs. At the same time, they must also consider the full spectrum of implications for every land-use decision.

The healthcare industry is currently experiencing the largest building boom in history. This represents a significant opportunity to adopt a process that connects public health, quality of life, and a healthy built environment. Planning for a healthy physical environment requires a mode of thinking and making decisions that considers the importance of community design goals, such as alternative transportation, brownfield recovery, and better water and waste management practices. It must also recognize the interdependence of the environment and public health by not contributing to air and water pollution, urban sprawl, habitat destruction, and global warming, and by protecting natural areas and open spaces.

Conventional site development is having a negative impact on our fundamental resources—land and water. A typical 10-acre site will generally have 3 acres of buildings, 5 acres of paved parking, and 1 acre of interior and perimeter landscaping. The infrastructure required to drain the storm water will consume another acre or more to accommodate a detention basin. This type of development is generating greater volumes of polluted storm water runoff—the root cause of many water-quality problems.

Impervious surfaces collect pathogens, metals, sediment, and chemical pollutants that are directly transmitted to receiving waters during rain and snowmelt events. Nonpoint source pollution from storm water runoff is a major threat to public health and is increasingly linked to chronic and acute illnesses from exposure through drinking water, seafood, food production, and contact with pathogen-contaminated water bodies that are used for recreation. Water-quality problems are compounded by the increased rate of urbanization coupled with combined sewer overflow (CSO) systems and the aging infrastructure in many American cities and towns. CSO systems discharge untreated human and industrial waste during periods of heavy rain or snowmelt. The US Environmental Protection Agency (EPA) estimates improvement costs to abate CSO storm events that impact 40 million citizens in 32 states and 772 cities to be $45 billion dollars (EPA 2004). Decades of federal, state, and local storm water regulations have not successfully reversed the degradation of streams, waterways, and coastal areas. Treating only the symptoms of the problem with large and expensive infrastructure investments is proving to be an unsustainable practice.

The overarching question becomes, how can we protect, preserve, and restore key components of the environmental system as development proceeds? The solution requires integrated design strategies that provide beneficial and cost-effective solutions for every aspect of site planning, site design, and architecture.

Integrated design solutions such as green roofs, pervious parking lots, infiltration trenches, and underground recharge beds have proven highly effective. Landscape techniques such as rain gardens, vegetated swales, and wetland meadows work as biofilters to remove pollutants and facilitate storm water infiltration while recharging groundwater that sustains the base flow in area streams. Design strategies that capture rainfall can serve a number of purposes, including irrigation and gray water use. Using these methods, planners and designers can address the root cause of the problem, practice conservation, and protect the public health at the lowest possible cost.

TOWARD A HEALTHY FUTURE

The benefits of providing a healthy indoor healing environment for patients, families, and staff are well documented. Extending the healing concept to the landscape and the site—an environment that reduces stress and increases health benefits—will provide a healthy physical environmental that nurtures the human spirit. To start, the facility itself must not pollute, contaminate, or destroy the site on which it is built. The landscape should reflect good stewardship and can play an important educational and aesthetic role in preserving and celebrating the local and regional character; people should be able to enjoy the natural world in a serene and tranquil atmosphere. Stream corridors and native plant communities should be protected to enhance and reveal inherent beauty and reinforce its sense of place.

Air-quality problems and urban heat islands are another threat to public health, contributing to respiratory disease and heat stress–related illness. Strategically planted trees, shrubs, and vines improve air quality and shade buildings and hard surfaces, reduce the overall solar gain and heat radiation of built structures, and remove pollutants such as nitrogen oxides, sulfur oxides, particulate matter, and ozone from the air.

Planting trees is one of the most cost-effective ways to reduce solar heat gain and ambient temperature. Shading and evapotranspiration from trees can reduce surrounding air temperature by as much as 9°F (5°C). Because cool air settles near the ground, air temperature directly under trees can be as much as 25°F (14°C) cooler than blacktop areas nearby. Summer daytime air temperatures tend to be 3° to 6°F (1.5° to 3°C) cooler in tree-shaded neighborhoods than in treeless areas.

A commitment to better landscape management and site-protection practices can make a quantifiable difference. During construction, careful site protection can limit site disturbance, soil damage, and the removal of natural vegetation. After construction, select plants that are well adapted to the site. A landscape based on native plant species saves water, requires less maintenance, and fosters important ecological interactions with indigenous plants, animals, insects, fungi, and microbes. Native plants have practical value in maintaining healthy ecosystems and increasing resource efficiency. Replacing lawn with native ground covers, grasses, and shrubs saves energy and reduces the use of chemical fertilizers, pesticides, and herbicides.

SUSTAINABLE SITE-DESIGN PRINCIPLES

Establish sustainable goals: Early in the process, evaluate sites under consideration for environmental opportunities and constraints. Develop an environmental management master plan during the first phase of site development to ensure the preservation of the site's ecologically significant areas. An environmental management master plan will inform design decisions so that the footprint of the proposed development does not overwhelm the capacity of the site. Minimize grading by fitting the building to the site, not the site to the building.

Identify partners for collaboration: Environmental issues, such as flood control or water quality, are not confined to property boundaries and are most effectively addressed through collaboration at the watershed or ecosystem scale. Increased impervious areas in a watershed directly contribute to increased runoff and generate greater pollutant loads. Understand how postdevelopment runoff needs to be managed to preserve a good balance within the watershed. Involve public health agencies and advocacy groups in planning for new healthcare facilities, since they may be responsible for coordinating community health and land-use efforts.

Interface with community health concerns: Consult regional watershed, open-space preservation, and smart growth plans before selecting a healthcare site to ensure a project is aligned with local sustainability goals. Coordinate site selection and development with local mass transit plans to reduce the use of automobiles, reduce required on-site parking, promote walking and bicycling, and ensure better access. Do not develop on greenfield sites if previously developed site options exist.

Adopt the precautionary principle: "Where there are threats of serious or irreversible damage, lack of full scientific certainty shall not be used as a reason for postponing cost-effective measures to prevent environmental degradation" (United Nations 1992).

Provide for public education and awareness: The project can become a community outreach vehicle and a teaching tool about integrated site planning and landscape design if the public is included in communications and a well-planned education program. Consider design solutions allowing public access to a site's significant natural areas and engaging the community in preserving and strengthening its ecology.

Practice conservation, restoration, and regeneration: Understand the resource flows on-site to balance resource use and protect, manage, restore, and regenerate the natural ecosystems — such as croplands, forests, grasslands, and river basins — upon which we and future generations depend.

Studies have shown that perceived higher costs and lack of awareness are the real barriers to change. However imperfect our present process, if we work collaboratively toward shared principles, we can raise awareness, measure our success, share information, and explore inclusive new partnerships in order to develop effective mitigation strategies to solve multidimensional problems in a holistic way.

Site-selection criteria for healthcare facilities that consider appropriate development locations — and avoid prime farmland, floodplains, endangered species habitats, and fragile waterfront and wetland sites — are now being discussed, not only as they relate to sustainable design, but also the nation's security. Hurricane Katrina's destruction of virtually all of New Orleans' medical infrastructure, for example, challenges us to reexamine locating critical-access facilities in the midst of floodplains.

In some instances, healthcare organizations are actively selecting urban sites over greenfield suburban locations, preferring connectivity to public transportation infrastructure and participation in urban economic development initiatives. For example, the University of Pittsburgh Medical Center chose to rehabilitate an existing urban hospital campus for its expanded children's hospital rather than relocate to a suburban site, citing concerns about the loss of a connection to the community (see Chapter 5). The decision to participate in the economic revitalization of a surrounding neighborhood provides an extension of such community-based benefits.

Perhaps related to this decision, a number of sustainable healthcare projects are remediating and redeveloping urban brownfield sites. In some instances, the brownfield site catalyzes a broader approach to sustainable design, construction, and operation. The Dell Children's Medical Center of Central Texas in Austin (this chapter) and Spaulding Rehabilitation Hospital in Boston (Chapter 8) exemplify sustainable projects located on sites that required substantial remediation — the former Austin airport and the Charlestown Navy Yard, respec-

tively. Robert Bonar, CEO of Dell Children's Medical Center of Central Texas, viewed the development of the site "as an opportunity to be particularly careful about the development example we set, and the city of Austin encouraged us to set a high bar for the subsequent development of the airport parcel."

Alternative transportation connectivity is increasingly viewed as essential, given the large volume of traffic generated by 24/7 operation and increased employee expenses for transportation. Many of the people in the case studies have become active, vocal advocates for improved public transportation. In urban areas well served by public transportation, organizations are effective in reducing the required on-site parking. Where there is limited public transportation, project teams often find creative alternatives to private auto use. Palomar Pomerado Health in Escondido, California (Chapter 11), for example, is expanding van pools and is in discussions with the county transit authority about an extension to connect with the Sprinter, the local light rail system. Michael Covert, CEO of Palomar Pomerado, believes that "part of solving the transportation dilemma is the creation of a mixed-use site with other commercial businesses in close proximity." Still others, like the Lacks Cancer Center at St. Mary's Health Care in Grand Rapids, Michigan (Chapter 9), point to centralizing related services as a necessary strategy to reduce transportation impacts on both the environment and the patient experience.

Accommodating massive parking requirements is a major challenge in sustainable site planning. Projects seek creative ways to minimize total parking through public transportation connectivity, and also to minimize the development footprint associated with surface parking through the implementation of structured or underground parking solutions. Fletcher Allen Hospital in Burlington, Vermont (below); Providence St. Peter Hospital in Olympia, Washington (Chapter 9); and Ryan Ranch in Monterey, California (Chapter 11) all demonstrate the use of underground or structured parking in a conscious effort to reduce overall site impacts in suburban sites.

Fletcher Allen Health Care Renaissance Project

Burlington,
Vermont

Figure 10-1: Fletcher Allen Health Care Renaissance Project. *Credit: © Robert Benson Photography. All rights reserved.*

Owner: Fletcher Allen Health Care, University of Vermont College of Medicine
Design team:
    ARCHITECT: Tsoi/Kobus & Associates
    ASSOCIATE ARCHITECT: Freeman French Freeman, Inc.
    LANDSCAPE DESIGN: SE Group
    STRUCTURAL ENGINEER: Weidlinger Associates, Inc.
    MECHANICAL, ELECTRICAL, AND PLUMBING ENGINEER: Bard, Rao + Athanas
      Consulting Engineers, LLC
    CIVIL ENGINEER: Dufresne-Henry Inc.
    CONSTRUCTION MANAGERS: Macomber Builders/Barton Malow Co., joint
      venture
Building type: Campus expansion
Size: 550,000 sq ft (51,100 sq m) ambulatory care center; 84,000 sq ft (7,800
    sq m) medical education center; 56,000 sq ft (5,200 sq m) central utilities
    plant
Program description: Consolidation of ambulatory, diagnostic, and inpatient
    services; medical education center; central utilities plant; and underground
    parking structure
Completion date: 2005

Major project objectives included establishing a clear sense of place, creating a unified architectural design, reconnecting the campus with the natural environment, and improving access and wayfinding by providing a single point of entry with separate patient and service traffic. While the site area would have supported at-grade parking, the solution instead incorporates a single level of below-grade parking adjacent to the medical education center. The site, which is high on a hilltop overlooking the city of Burlington, features spectacular views of the Green Mountains, Lake Champlain, and the Adirondacks. The design solution employs the varied topography to bring daylight and views to programs below the entry level, reducing the height and apparent mass of the developed area.

Source: Tsoi/Kobus & Associates

Figure 10-2: The major expansion is nestled into the hillside, with the highly glazed education center (foreground) that links the existing medical school to the acute care hospital oriented to take advantage of the captivating views. *Credit: Tsoi/Kobus & Associates*

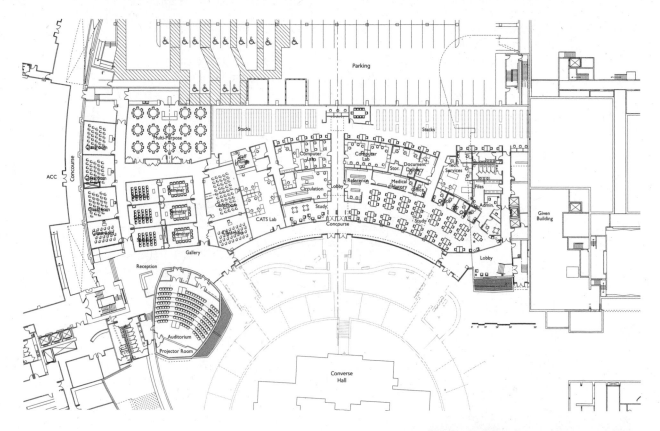

Figure 10-3: Education Center Floor Plan
Despite the availability of land for surface parking, Fletcher Allen elected to construct structured parking adjacent to the education center, reserving the roof of the addition for landscape development. *Credit: Tsoi/Kobus & Associates*

Figure 10-4: The expansive, south-facing lobby is shielded from summer sun by strategically sized, large overhangs while benefiting from passive heating during the cold months. *Credit: © Robert Benson Photography. All rights reserved*

Sustainable healthcare projects located on sites with fragile or degraded ecosystems often protect and restore those ecosystems and use stewardship to frame their approaches. Providence St. Peter Hospital (Chapter 9) is located on a densely wooded second-growth forest site, bordering a Class I salmon wetland. Boulder Community Hospital in Boulder, Colorado (Chapter 9), restored a damaged wetland ecosystem, relocated a prairie dog colony, and returned more than half its site to the city of Boulder as permanent open space.

Creative approaches to storm water management and treatment are emerging in sustainable projects — bioswales with natural vegetation and landscape features are used on projects with sufficient land and proper soil characteristics. Kaiser Permanente Modesto Medical Center in Modesto, California (Chapter 5), pioneered the use of porous paving — the city of Modesto has been so impressed that it now requires its use. At Thunder Bay Regional Health Sciences Centre, in Thunder Bay, Ontario (Chapter 11), a system of bioswales also functions as a water filtration device.

Green roof systems — either as components of therapeutic landscapes, or purely as strategies to retain storm water and cool roofs — are being installed. In some instances, municipalities are mandating green roofs as part of an integrated strategy to mitigate urban heat island impacts and storm water runoff. Advocate Lutheran General Hospital in Park Ridge, Illinois (Chapter 7), for example, is located in a metropolitan area that encourages installation of green roofs. Meyer Children's Hospital (Ospedale Pediatrico Meyer) in Florence, Italy (this chapter), describes its green roof as "an active skin" that mediates solar radiation (Sala, Trombadore, and Alcamo 2006).

As diagnostic and treatment areas slide out from beneath inpatient units, major exposed roof areas (often seen from adjacent inpatient areas) require design reconsideration and provide landscape development opportunities. Metro Health in Wyoming, Michigan (Chapter 7), and Palomar Pomerado in Escondido, California (Chapter 11) are examples of diagnostic and treatment blocks with extensive green roof areas.

Outdoor places of respite are both transformative and increasingly prevalent programmatic features of sustainable healthcare buildings, whether manifested in therapeutic gardens, solaria or terraces on inpatient units, or individual terraces adjacent to patient rooms. Dell Children's Medical Center; Palomar Pomerado; Legacy Salmon Creek Hospital in Vancouver, Washington; REHAB Basel in Switzerland (Chapter 11); and Spaulding Rehabilitation Hospital are only a few examples of the many case study projects that feature extensive integration with the outdoors. In the case of San Juan Regional Medical Center in Farmington, New Mexico (Chapter 6), the outdoor terraces adjacent to each patient room are the direct result of the reintroduction of solar-shading devices in a hot climate.

Finally, sustainable healthcare buildings are converting conventional turf grass landscaping to native planting and xeriscape solutions. While healing and therapeutic gardens may utilize nonnative species in enclosed settings, overall site landscape strategies are increasingly moving toward native planting. The use of native plants for landscaping conserves water, requires less maintenance, and significantly reduces the need to apply chemical fertilizers and herbicides. At the Winship Cancer Institute at Emory University in Atlanta (Chapter 9), the project team designed two alternative landscape solutions — one a traditional scheme with irrigation and the other a native planting solution — because of the university's initial reluctance to embrace the aesthetics of native landscape. Ultimately, the native scheme prevailed. Legacy Salmon Creek (Chapter 9) features a healing garden with native and adapted plantings.

WATER CONSERVATION

Healthcare institutions are consistently within the top ten water users in their communities. A 2002 estimate by H2O Applied Technologies, corroborated by the Hospital Corporation of America, reported that total annual water consumption ranges between 250,000 and 700,000 gallons (946,000 and 2,650,000 liters) per bed in US acute care settings (see Figure 10-5). The Federal Energy Management Program reports usage of 80 to 150 gallons (300 to 550 liters) of water per bed per day, roughly equivalent to European hospitals, though estimates from the Massachusetts Water Resources Authority (1996) put the upper range as high as 350 gallons (1,325 liters). The wide variation in water use may be attributable to the size of the facility or number of beds (it appears that larger hospitals use more water per bed than smaller), types of services on site (e.g., laundry and sterilization), equipment, facility age, and mechanical equipment types (e.g., water-cooled versus air-cooled equipment).

Biologist Peter Warshall, PhD, in the essay titled "Sustainability, Water, and Healthcare," identifies four principles central to the sustainable use of water in healthcare settings. In the case studies that accompany this section, projects have focused on innovative technologies in reducing overall potable water usage. Taken together, the case studies demonstrate regional variations in water conservation strategies. Water conservation strategies are often huge money savers, particularly when facilities are charged for both supply and discharge. The Massachusetts Water Resources Authority (1996) estimates that in Boston, water and sewer charges averaged 22 percent of a hospital's total utility cost.

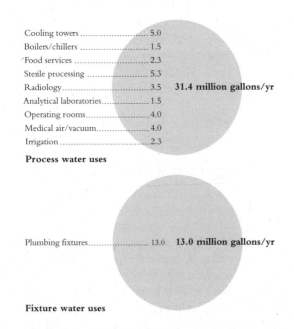

Cooling towers 5.0
Boilers/chillers 1.5
Food services 2.3
Sterile processing 5.3
Radiology..................... 3.5   **31.4 million gallons/yr**
Analytical laboratories..................... 1.5
Operating rooms..................... 4.0
Medical air/vacuum..................... 4.0
Irrigation 2.3

Process water uses

Plumbing fixtures..................... 13.0   **13.0 million gallons/yr**

Fixture water uses

Figure 10-5: Water Use in Hospitals. Seventy percent of potable water in a typical four-hundred-bed hospital is used for process applications. *Source: Loranger 2004*

Sustainability, Water, and Healthcare

Peter Warshall, PhD

Our bodies are but molded water.
—NOVALIS

*W*ater creates an inescapable contract. We cannot choose to be part of or separate from its flows. Without water flowing through our bodies, we die within a few days. We may live upstream or downstream, drink surface or groundwater, eat fish from the ocean, swim in a river, be fed plasma intravenously, inhale water vapor from an air-conditioning system: we can never free our bodies from water's flow or quintessence. We are wedded to the water in the biosphere, and there can be no divorce clause; but to maintain matrimonial hydro-harmonies—both within our bodies and between our bodies and the environment—this hydro-contract must include healthcare clauses.

These hydro-harmonies are not so easy to achieve. First of all, water's qualities are hard to characterize. More than any other substance on the planet, water promiscuously assimilates organic and inorganic chemicals. It may start out clean, then absorb harmful molecules, such as plasticizers from polyvinyl chloride (PVC) pipes, en route. It may come to earth as pure rainwater but wash over farm fields and absorb nitrates that pollute groundwater used for drinking. Humans may even add chemicals to water, such as chlorine, to kill off harmful bacteria, only to discover that, in certain quality waters, the chlorine produces trihalomethanes that have been implicated in cancer: and so the solution to one water problem causes another.

Second, water flow is erratic and can exploit the tiniest imperfections in man-made waterworks. The one-hundred-year storm flow may bring harmful microbes into an otherwise healthful lake. An undetected leak in a pipe may jeopardize the safety of a massive drinking water system. A broken valve in a nuclear power plant's waterworks can lead to overheating and threaten the safety of a neighborhood.

Third, water flows are hard to model or generalize. To the great frustration of sustainability dreamers and their hopes for widely applicable paradigms, water flows are maddeningly site specific, embedded in unique watershed landscapes. The ways a watershed gathers, stores, concentrates, dilutes, and biochemically transforms water quality depends on details — the specific weather, the specific configuration of the aquifer, the specific loading and concentrations of chemical ingredients. If you make an aqueous generalization and ignore the individuality of a watershed's persona and its need for custom design, the water flow will play you for a sucker. Healthcare workers, epidemiologists, and civil engineers know water management is a complex (if not the most complex) aspect of sustainability.

PRINCIPLE ONE: PROTECT THE SOURCE, PROTECT THE DELIVERY SYSTEM, AND CUSTOM DESIGN THE WATERWORKS

Any point in the water cycle can be a source of disease. The big picture of water and health starts with ensuring that the atmosphere does not become contaminated with acids and sulfates, smog, and volatile organic chemicals (VOCs) that can poison wildlife and humans. It continues by protecting watersheds so that they will not leak pesticides, toxic metals, fertilizer residues, and specific harmful organics into the water supply, swimmable rivers, or coastal beaches. Then, at the water treatment plant, humans must ensure that the treatment itself is benign, and that the pipes do not leach toxics into drinking water or crack and allow contaminants to enter. Finally, at the wastewater treatment plant, the equipment must effectively treat and eliminate the contaminants of the local sewage. With poorly designed treatment, harmful viruses and molecules may be sent back into the environment. (This view of the hydrological cycle might be considered a form of preventative medicine — or the precautionary principle in action.)

The diagnosis of water's health-giving or disease potential can be difficult. What is clean water and what causes harm to the human body can be confusing. Consider any beach in Southern California. Does the bacteria Enterococcus cause sickness in saltwater, when most of the studies have been done in freshwater? How much Enterococcus is dangerous? Should we allow one infection for every thousand swimmers, or one in ten thousand? Are swimming restrictions caused by politicians exploiting local fears so they can appear to be white knights who save children? Have they received campaign contributions from an engineering

firm that will profit from "solving" what may not really be a problem? Is the source a wastewater-treatment plant or storm runoff? Is it from humans or pet dogs? Is the health department in need of more federal funds — and is Enterococcus a good way to drum up financing? On the other hand, is the department actually doing its duty to protect the public health? Who really understands the risk assessment models of successive approximation, correlation, and regression, extreme or central values that allegedly prove safety or harm? Given imperfect knowledge, how much should taxpayers shell out — and for which technology — to reduce Enterococcus along the shoreline?

Although the truth is central to preventing water-related human illness, the truth alone rarely ensures success. Only a combo of empirical hydro-truths and a sense of fairness can hold sway. For instance, the environmental justice movement, a movement among minorities whose watersheds became the dumping grounds for waterborne pollutants, gained strength by combining meticulous water-quality data, epidemiology, and ethical arguments for civil rights. Central to all sustainable solutions to health/water entanglements are human fears, belief in experts, citizen actions, the wily ways of water, and how comfortable we are with certain levels of risk.

PRINCIPLE TWO: CUSTOM DESIGN TO PROTECT THE BENEFICIARY (THE HUMAN BODY)

Healthcare facilities have shifted toward service specializations. Because of specialization, water-quality strategies must be custom designed for the medical processing equipment. Medical processes with distinct water needs include laboratory testing, producing medical air, washing X-ray film, steam and vacuum sterilization, washing glassware, and dialysis with reverse osmosis, all of which require the purest water.

Medical air for various medical procedures, for instance, must be clean and oil free. In oxygen supply systems, water, not oil, is used as a lubricant to ensure that the air will be clean and oil free. Water maintains the seal, provides lubrication, and absorbs the heat produced by the process. But perhaps the most exacting requirement in healthcare is for extremely clean water in dialysis and laboratory testing. Poor water quality in these settings can harm the kidneys or lead to false diagnoses.

PRINCIPLE THREE: SAVE WATER, SAVE ENERGY, SAVE MONEY

While water consumption by hospitals and healthcare facilities is minor compared to that of agriculture, power plants, and other industrial uses, healthcare facilities are among the building types that use water most intensively. In general, most water conservation strategies for fixtures such as toilets, cafeteria sinks, and heating, ventilating, and air-conditioning (HVAC) systems are identical with those for commercial buildings. Equipment such as ultra-low-flush toilets and faucet timers need no review. Within the healthcare sector, the majority of water is consumed by process uses—sterilization, kitchen, laundry, irrigation, film processing, and the like. The main purpose of water conservation in the healthcare sector is to save on water and energy bills, especially in hospitals, long-term care centers, and outpatient facilities. Facilities often pay for water use at both ends—for water supply as it enters the building, and for sewerage charges as it is discharged after use. Conservation strategies can target one or both of these points.

X-ray processing, for instance, gulps huge amounts of water for film washing. In labs that operate 24/7 in Southern California, the water used for X-ray washing has typically been used only once. A device that recirculates the wash water lowers film processing water use by 97 percent, a savings that dropped X-ray water use from 3.2 to less than 0.01 acre feet per year in one major lab. Likewise, the shift from film processing to digital imaging is cited as a water conservation strategy at San Juan Regional Medical Center.

A good example of how saving water saves energy and operational costs occurred in the Medical Dental Building in Seattle. Formerly one of the city's largest downtown water users, it discovered that its once-through heating and cooling system was its major water waster (single-pass cooling systems remove heat in buildings to a stream of water and then send the heated water off to the sewer). The building replaced its water-cooled system with an air-cooled one. The project cost $440,000 and was 50 percent subsidized by the city's Water Smart Technology Program. It saved over 57,000 gallons per day and paid for itself in two years. It also saved the water-treatment plant the cost of upgrading the input water to drinking levels (even though it would only be used for cooling) and the municipal sewerage plant both energy and money to treat the cooling discharge.

The larger question for healthcare, water conservation, and sustainability is: what happens with these conservation savings? Do they lower patient care costs? Raise salaries? Get invested in research or equipment purchases? Add more water to rivers? Encourage suburban sprawl? How water, energy, and cash savings are spent and allocated is important. The savings should not be squandered on other activities that weaken the health of citizens or the environment. Otherwise, why conserve?

PRINCIPLE FOUR: TECHNO-FIXES ARE IMPORTANT BUT INSUFFICIENT

This big picture view of water and health would be incomplete without mentioning the importance of water beyond healthcare facilities and waterworks. Water has always been included in the contemplative and spiritual lives of humans. The ability to take time off to fish, swim, boat, ski, hang out on a beach, or simply watch and listen to ripples in a stream connects healthcare to water in a larger context. Sustainable health and water mean both the planet's bodies of water and the human body require stewardship.

Reducing potable water for landscape use is a widely embraced goal, but the strategies for achieving it vary by region and setting. A number of projects, like Boulder Community Hospital (Chapter 9) or Discovery Health Center in Harris, New York (Chapter 11), eliminate irrigation systems entirely through the specification of native, drought-resistant plants. Others, like Dell Children's (this chapter) and Palomar Medical Center West in Escondido, California (Chapter 11), use municipal reclaimed water systems for irrigation. Finally, others use drip or other high-efficiency irrigation systems to reduce the overall potable water consumption. Collectively, these are viewed as low-hanging fruit in sustainable healthcare.

Broader application of municipal or on-site reclaimed water is subject to approval by local regulatory authorities or infection-control professionals—lack of clear regulatory guidance has hindered industry-wide implementation to date. The Oregon Health & Science University (OHSU) Center for Health and Healing (this chapter) was one of the first healthcare projects to implement on-site gray water for broader building applications and on-site wastewater treatment. At OHSU, gray water is filtered and recycled from the on-site wastewater-treatment plant and used to flush staff toilets throughout the building. On-site wastewater treatment is slowly making its way into US sustainable healthcare projects, as most healthcare campuses have access to municipal wastewater-treatment infrastructure. At OHSU, lack of available city sewage capacity led to the innovative on-site solution. Like many urban areas, Portland has an overburdened combined storm water/sewage system.

Potable water use reduction strategies are moving rapidly into healthcare, despite both real and perceived challenges of infection control and asepsis. Dual-flush toilets, waterless urinals, and low-flow and metered devices are increasingly utilized in sustainable hospital projects to achieve reductions of 20 percent or more in total domestic water use. At the BC Cancer Agency Research Centre, in Vancouver, British Columbia (Chapter 1), the dual-flush toilets are one of the features researchers consistently applaud. According to Mary McNeil, CEO of the BC Cancer Foundation, "the building occupants have more than simply a sense of control — they can interact with the building to exercise their values."

DO LOW-FLOW FIXTURES ACTUALLY PERFORM?

Low-flow plumbing fixtures are often perceived to be less effective. A consortium of twenty-two North American water resource organizations and plumbing fixture manufacturers sponsored the development of the maximum performance (MaP) testing protocol for fixtures. The report has become the standard performance measure for both traditional and low-flow devices, with performance data on approximately three hundred specific fixture models. (http://www.cwwa.ca/home_e.asp or www.cuwcc.org/ MapTesting.lasso) (Veritech and Koeller 2006)

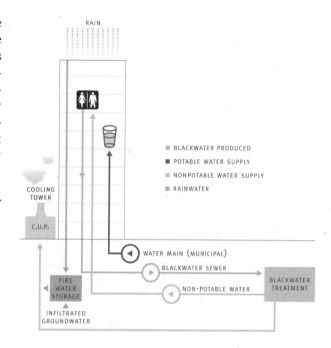

Figure 10-6: When analyzing water flows, it's important to aim for maximum conservation before trying new forms of supply. In the Oregon Health & Sciences University Center for Health and Healing, most of the water conservation came from reducing faucet flow rates (a medical building involves a lot of hand washing). Use of lower-flow toilets and urinals is a secondary source of conservation. *Credit: Interface Engineering and Yudelson 2005*

Projects that focus on process-water reduction report impressive results — in some instances more than 50 percent reductions — through strategies ranging from capturing rainwater for process uses to clever means of recycling process water. As a baseline measure, sustainable healthcare buildings are, in general, eliminating once-through potable water use for cooling towers and other mechanical equipment. The Winship Cancer Institute (Chapter 9) reduced potable water consumption by 19 million gallons annually through recycling the building condensate return and the cooling water for the environmental rooms. The rural Discovery Health Center (Chapter 11) captures rainwater from its 15,000 sq ft (1,394 sq m) roof to provide make-up water for the fire suppression system; when the holding tank is full, the ex-

Water Conservation Strategies

Description	Baseline (mil gal/ yr)	Demand Reduction (%)	Design (mil gal/yr)	Water Source
Fixtures potable	5.0	37	3.3	potable
Cooling towers	1.5	0	1.5	nonpotable
Project irrigation	1.0	0	1.0	nonpotable
Total water use	7.5		5.8	
Total potable	7.5		3.3	
Total potable reduction			56 percent	

Source: Interface Engineering

cess rainwater is diverted for farm irrigation (the site is farmed up to the edge of the building). Finally, the OHSU Center for Health and Healing in Portland, Oregon (this chapter), developed a strategy for rainwater collection and sewage treatment that reduces potable water use by 56 percent (see Figure 10-6 and table above). The business case for this approach reflects the significant fees for both water usage and sewage contribution.

CASE STUDY

Waitakere Hospital

Auckland, New Zealand

Figure 10-7: Waitakere Hospital. *Credit: Nicole Bassett, West Auckland Health Services Foundation*

Owner: Waitemata District Health Board
Design team:
  ARCHITECT: Di Carlo Potts & Associates
  STRUCTURAL ENGINEER: Buller George Turkington
  CIVIL ENGINEER: Harrison Grierson Consultants Ltd.
  SERVICES ENGINEER/ENERGY CONSULTANT: Connell Mott MacDonald

PROJECT MANAGER: Carson Group
SUSTAINABLE DESIGN CONSULTANT: Robert Vale
Building type: Renovation/addition
Size: 158,230 sq ft (14,700 sq m)
Design energy intensity: 34 kWh/sq ft/yr (366 kWh/sq m/yr)
Program description: 120-bed and ambulatory care addition to an existing hospital
Completion date 2005
Recognition: New Zealand Ministry for the Environment Green Ribbon Award for storm water management system

---

Located in urban Waitakere City, which incorporates districts in the west of Auckland, New Zealand, this renovation and extension to an existing 1974 hospital building serves 180,000 inpatients and outpatients per year. The project represents half of what the regional authority — the Waitemata District Health Board — is spending on a redevelopment program begun in 2000. It is characterized by attention to daylighting, natural ventilation, patient preferences, water conservation, and energy savings.

Figure 10-8: Rapid growth has made storm water management a high priority in beachside Auckland. The hospital renovation site became a proving ground for storm water reduction and on-site treatment of runoff to offset increased impervious cover. *Credit: Courtesy of Waitakere Hospital*

Figure 10-9: Rainwater collection is expressed through a visible system of exterior downspouts that provide for 100 percent capture of the rain that falls on the roof. *Credit: Nicole Bassett, West Auckland Health Services Foundation*

Initial interest in incorporating regionally appropriate sustainable design principles, especially storm water management, was backed by an advisory group including Waitakere City Council, the New Zealand Energy Efficiency and Conservation Authority, and consultant Robert Vale representing the University of Auckland. High capital costs for energy and storm water features, which initially seemed insurmountable, were eventually offset by loans and grants from the Energy Efficiency and Conservation Authority for energy strategies and Infrastructure Auckland (a public works funding agency now part of Auckland Regional Holdings) for storm water measures.

KEY BUILDING PERFORMANCE STRATEGIES

Site
- Storm water management system uses 1,475 ft (450 m) of linear swales to collect storm water from surrounding 44 acres (18 ha)

Water
- Dual-flush toilets
- High-capacity gutters collect rainwater, which is stored in six 8,860-ft^3 (250-m^3) cisterns for toilet and sewage conveyance, reducing roof-generated storm water by 70 percent

Energy
- Filtration permits partial air recirculation in lieu of full fresh air in hospital clinical areas, saving heating and cooling energy
- Occupancy-sensor lighting, high-efficiency ballasts, and more localized switches for task-specific lighting
- Use of natural ventilation instead of air-conditioning in assessment, treatment, and rehabilitation areas and public spaces
- Operable windows in patient rooms and on corridors
- Added insulation (R-2.0 in walls, R-3.5 in ceilings)
- Small-scale solar water-heating demonstration installation in the hospital's cultural health area
- High-efficiency HVAC features efficient motors and low-pressure loss ducts; central plant variable air volume (VAV) air-conditioning system

Designers were focused on creating a hospital with a noninstitutional feel. This is accomplished through daylight and natural ventilation, the interior color choices, the artwork, and access to outdoor space through internal courtyards.

Energy performance is compared to conventional New Zealand hospitals. The estimated annual reduction in annual carbon dioxide (CO_2) emissions is 476 tons, while overall energy consumption was reduced by an estimated 772,000 kilowatt hours for electricity, with an estimated 85 kilowatt hours reduction in peak electrical demand. At this rate, cost premiums for energy-saving features have an estimated simple payback time of about four years.

Sources: Waitakere Hospital; New Zealand Ministry for the Environment 2005

Figure 10-10: The storm water management system begins with the bioswales. The water is then passed through an underground sand filtration plant and a 20,000-sq-ft (1900-sq-m) collection pond before it is released into a creek. The pond is landscaped and visible from the hospital grounds. *Credit: Nicole Bassett, West Auckland Health Services Foundation*

Oregon Health & Science University CASE STUDY

Portland, Oregon

OHSU is actively engaged in sustainable building initiatives that demonstrate leadership and creativity in the area of resource stewardship. The three projects profiled in this case study reflect a growing awareness of and comfort with strategies for improved energy and water use. Presented chronologically, they illustrate how sustainable design can develop from humble beginnings to transform an organization's attitude about building.

Located on a hilly site in downtown Portland, OHSU is expanding to the South Waterfront. In order to reduce transportation associated with a dispersed campus, the university is installing a tram to move staff and students between the two campus locations. In addition, the campus is served by bus lines and, despite the hills, encourages bicycle commuting by providing ample parking, showers, and changing facilities.

Peter O. Kohler Pavilion at OHSU

Figure 10-11: This acute care expansion project was under construction when the *Green Guide* pilot process began. Despite the advanced stage of its design, the team was still able to effectively integrate sustainable design features.
Credit: Perkins + Will

Design team:
ARCHITECTS: Perkins + Will/Peterson Kolberg & Associates
MECHANICAL, ELECTRICAL, AND PLUMBING ENGINEER: CBG Engineers (now Mazzetti & Associates)
STRUCTURAL ENGINEER: Degenkolb Engineers
CIVIL ENGINEER: W&H Pacific
LANDSCAPE ARCHITECT: Murase Associates
GENERAL CONTRACTOR: Hoffman-Andersen, a Joint Venture
COST ESTIMATING: Davis Langdon
Building type: New building
Size: 360,000 sq ft (33,400 sq m)
Completion date: 2005
Recognition: *Green Guide for Health Care* pilot

This project was well underway when the *Green Guide* pilot process launched, and is the entry point for OHSU and sustainable building. OHSU and the design team began integrating sustainable building strategies into this project to realize reductions in energy and water demand.

KEY BUILDING PERFORMANCE STRATEGIES

Water
- Storm water retention tank used for landscape irrigation
- Water-consumption monitoring
- Low-flow fixtures
- Initiated conversion of chilled water system from constant to variable flow

Energy

- Perimeter corridors and stairwells harvest daylighting
- Naturally ventilated stairwells
- Long-life, low-power diode lighting integrated in handrail system
- Variable-frequency fans and motors

Source: Perkins + Will

CASE STUDY

Biomedical Research Building at OHSU

Figure 10-12: This research building is the final link between the clinical and research campuses. *Credit: Zimmer Gunsul Frasca Architects LLP*

Design team:

ARCHITECT: Zimmer Gunsul Frasca Architects LLP

STRUCTURAL AND CIVIL ENGINEER: KPFF Consulting Engineers

MECHANICAL AND ELECTRICAL ENGINEERS: Affiliated Engineers N.W., Inc.

GENERAL CONTRACTOR: Hoffman-Andersen, a Joint Venture

SUSTAINABILITY CONSULTANT: Ethos Development Inc.

Building type: New education and research building

Size: 275,000 sq ft (25,500 sq m)

Design energy intensity: 187 kBTUs/sq ft/yr

Program description: Biomedical research building

Completion date: 2006

Figure 10-13: The building configuration provides for deep daylight penetration and extraordinary views. *Credit: Zimmer Gunsul Frasca Architects LLP*

Recognizing the city of Portland's mandate for designing to a minimum standard of LEED silver and drawing on the lessons learned from the *Peter O. Kohler Pavilion*, the biomedical research building expanded the range of sustainable building strategies employed, particularly in the area of site and storm water management. Despite the constrained urban site, the project incorporates landscape strategies that reduce the rate and quantity of storm water runoff and increase on-site infiltration and groundwater recharge.

KEY BUILDING PERFORMANCE STRATEGIES

Environmental Quality

- Daylight in 75 percent of occupied spaces
- Views in 90 percent of occupied spaces
- Low-emitting materials
- Maintain indoor air quality during construction

Open, universal lab space, supplemented by the use of modular laboratory case goods and linear equipment corridors, maximize flexibility as the research staff changes. The implementation of green housekeeping and enhanced chemical management round out the innovation strategies for this LEED registered project.

Source: Zimmer Gunsul Frasca Architects LLP

The Center for Health & Healing at OHSU

Figure 10-14: This developer-sponsored facility is the first building in Portland's South Waterfront area. Oregon Health & Science University is installing a tram (the station is ghosted at right of image) to connect the Center for Health and Healing with the university's existing campus at the top of the hill. *Credit: © GBD Architects*

Design team:
   DEVELOPER: Gerding Edlen Development
   ARCHITECT: GBD Architects
   ASSOCIATE ARCHITECT: Peterson Kolberg Associates
   STRUCTURAL ENGINEER: KPFF
   CIVIL ENGINEER: Otak
   ENERGY AND COMMISSIONING AGENT: Interface Engineering, Inc.
   LANDSCAPE ARCHITECT: Walker Macy
   GENERAL CONTRACTOR: Hoffman Construction
   LEED CONSULTANT: Brightworks Northwest
Building type: New building
Size: 400,000 sq ft (37,160 sq m)
Design energy intensity: 130 kBTUs/sq ft/yr
Program description: Medical office and wellness center, including biomedical research, clinical space, outpatient surgery, educational space, and ground-floor retail space
Completion date: 2006
Recognition: US Green Building Council LEED platinum certification

---

Built on the site of a former shipyard, the project is an expansion of the university's main campus into Portland's developing South Waterfront. From the start, the developer, Gerding Edlen, insisted on a sustainable design that would reduce operating costs, reduce consumption of natural resources, and improve occupant comfort, health, and productivity. Those goals meshed with OHSU's mission to promote health and the building's purpose as a mixed-use facility. "From the very first charrette, we knew we were going to go beyond the LEED criteria," recalls Andy Frichtl, PE, of Interface Engineering. "We wanted to really concentrate on the source energy—where it comes from in the first place, not just how it is used on the site."

The multidisciplinary integrated design process facilitated the development of building components that serve multiple functions. For example, the building's sunshades are architectural features that also serve mechanical and electrical purposes. By designing the sunshades into the south facade, to keep the sun off the windows in the summer and lower the HVAC system requirements for cooling, a free surface became available for solar electricity–generating panels.

Not only did the design team want to demonstrate the capability of this alternative energy source that produces no greenhouse gas emissions; Frichtl explains that there were also "significant incentives for using photovoltaic panels: state and federal tax credits, accelerated depreciation and bonus payments from the Oregon Energy Trust to account for the full value of clean power."

The Center for Health & Healing demonstrates in bricks and mortar OHSU's belief that a healthy built environment is integral to healthy living.
—JOSEPH ROBERTSON, MD, PRESIDENT OF OHSU (2006)

KEY BUILDING PERFORMANCE STRATEGIES

Site

▪ Vegetated roof over more than 50 percent of roof surface

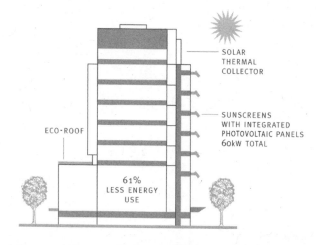

Figure 10-15: Conceptual Design for Energy Efficiency.
With a goal of 60 percent energy demand reduction, dozens of energy-efficiency measures were examined. The design captures and uses as much solar energy as possible. A total of forty-two specific energy efficiency measures are incorporated in the building. *Credit: Interface Engineering and Yudelson 2005*

Water

- On-site sewage treatment, with effluent used for toilet flushing and irrigation
- 100 percent on-site rainwater capture and reuse system

Energy

- 61 percent more efficient than ASHRAE 90.1-1999 requirements
- Natural ventilation
- Displacement ventilation in exam rooms
- Radiant heating and cooling with thermal energy storage
- 60-kW solar photovoltaic panels integrated into south-facing facade as solar shading devices
- 300-kW output from five microturbines
- Integrated daylighting controls and occupancy sensors in perimeter offices

Source: Interface Engineering, Inc.

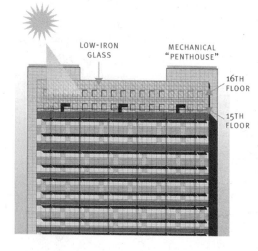

Figure 10-16: Another form of solar energy harnessed is its site-built solar air heater. On the fifteenth and sixteenth floors of the building's south side, the facade was transformed into a giant solar air heater, 190 ft long by 32 ft high (57.9 m by 9.7 m). *Credit: © GBD Architects*

Figure 10-17: The building during construction with the solar air heater facade element. *Credit: Sally Painter Photography*

ENERGY-DEMAND REDUCTION

The healthcare sector is a massive consumer of energy. Figure 10-18 depicts the total usage by energy sources in US healthcare buildings, which in 1999 was just above 500 trillion BTUs. Given that almost half of that energy is site electricity, and the generation and transmission of electricity is relatively inefficient, the source energy equivalent of the total climbs to 701 trillion BTUs in electricity alone, for a total of 984 trillion BTUs, or 9 percent of the commercial building total.

Acute care hospitals represent approximately 60 percent of the total floor area of the healthcare sector, at 1.7 billion sq ft (160 million sq m) of a total of 2.9 billion sq ft (260 million sq m). According to the Commercial Buildings Energy Consumption Survey (CBECS), the average age of an acute care hospital building in the US is 26.5 years—completed about 1980. Since then, energy intensity has continued to increase as hospitals have accommodated improved medical and information technology, with attendant thermal loads and ever-escalating mandatory ventilation standards.

A comparative review of energy consumption in hospitals worldwide was conducted in 1996 by the Centre for Analysis and Dissemination of Demonstrated Energy Technologies (CADDET) (see Figure 10-19) using representative hospitals from each of nine nations (Jakelius 1996). North American healthcare institutions were found to consume energy at levels at least twice those of other industrialized nations, both in electrical and thermal energy values. Electrical consumption varies widely, from a low of 61 kilowatt hours per sq m (Switzerland) to 339 kilowatt hours per sq m (Canada). Thermal consumption varies between 168 kilowatt hours per sq m (Sweden) and 690 kilowatt hours per sq m (US), with an average of 367 kilowatt hours per sq m. CADDET attributes some of Canada's high electrical energy consumption to the fact that the subject Canadian hospital was smaller, on average, than other countries' (1,300 sq ft, or

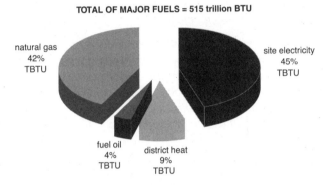

TOTAL OF MAJOR FUELS = 515 trillion BTU

natural gas
42%
TBTU

site electricity
45%
TBTU

fuel oil
4%
TBTU

district heat
9%
TBTU

Figure 10-18: Energy Consumption in Healthcare Buildings.
The US healthcare industry consumed 515 trillion BTUs of source energy in 1999, distributed among a range of fuel sources. *Source:* EIA 1999

Figure 10-19: Comparative Energy Consumption for Hospitals.
This chart shows approximate data for an acute care hospital's average annual thermal and electrical energy consumption per square meter (kWh/sq m). *Source:* CADDET 1999

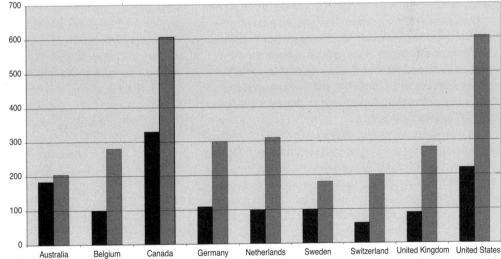

- electrical energy
- thermal energy

Australia | Belgium | Canada | Germany | Netherlands | Sweden | Switzerland | United Kingdom | United States

121 sq m, per bed). Some of the relatively high consumption by the United States was attributed to the relatively large size (3,000 sq ft, or 280 sq m, per bed) and academic teaching component of the subject hospitals. On average, the other hospitals were in the range of 1,800 sq ft (160 sq m) per bed.

In the following essay, "Energy Use, Energy Production, and Health," architect Alexis Karolides from the Rocky Mountain Institute outlines strategies for reducing energy demand and supporting efficient, environmentally responsible energy production in healthcare environments.

Energy Use, Energy Production, and Health

Alexis Karolides, RA

In the service of healing people, healthcare institutions use a tremendous amount of energy, the conventional production of which is associated with public health hazards. Fortunately, solutions exist to reduce and even eliminate this paradox, while also reducing operating costs, enhancing patient outcomes, and boosting staff productivity.

THE MAGNITUDE OF THE PROBLEM
Fifty percent of US power comes from coal-fired power plants, which generate the fine-particle pollutant sulfur dioxide, smog-forming nitrogen oxide, global warming–causing carbon dioxide, and toxic mercury. Pollution from power plants is associated with lung cancer, heart attacks, and asthma. Children, infants, the elderly, and people with compromised immune systems are disproportionately susceptible to power plant pollution (Clear the Air 2003).

According to Worldwatch Institute (1992; 1994), building construction and operation is responsible for 40 percent of total worldwide energy use. (In the United States, construction and material production account for 9 percent of energy use and building operation accounts for 30 percent). In 1999 the operation of US commercial buildings used 5,733 trillion BTUs of energy; of this, the healthcare sector alone used 515

trillion BTUs. Healthcare is consistently the third-most energy-intensive building sector (EIA 2007a). Given this prodigious energy use, healthcare has a major opportunity to dramatically reduce energy use and be a leader in fulfilling its energy needs in ways that promote local and global health.

REDUCE DEMAND
Building Design: For new buildings or major renovations, the most effective and least expensive first step is to reduce energy demand with high-performance, integrated building design, starting with energy-mindful building massing and orientation and superefficient building envelopes—especially glazing and roof design that reduces unwanted heat gain or loss.

Lighting: Improving lighting quality can dramatically reduce energy use. Effective, glare-free daylighting, light-colored surfaces, and high-performance, task-ambient lighting systems controlled by occupancy sensors and daylight-sensitive dimmers and that employ efficient lamps will use far less energy than conventional overhead electric lighting systems.

HVAC: Healthcare design must prioritize indoor environmental quality, infection control, and optimal energy efficiency. All three can be enhanced by using air monitoring controls (such as spore traps and carbon dioxide sensors) to inform airflow rates. If providing 100 percent outside air for infection control, energy efficiency can be enhanced by compartmentalizing the hospital and providing air according to need while employing heat recovery, efficient dehumidification, and ventilation flow controls as appropriate. Energy associated with air distribution can also be radically reduced by using big, short, straight pipes and smaller pumps. (It is helpful to design the pipe layout first, then place the equipment; this requires early coordination between mechanical engineers and architects and can be a focus at integrated design sessions.)

The type of HVAC system installed can have a profound effect on both performance and energy efficiency. A displacement ventilation system can greatly improve air quality (compared with an overhead ventilation supply system) while also reducing energy use, with nominal (if any) additional upfront costs. It works by displacing stale air with fresh air—which can be provided through low-wall or baseboard diffusers— rather than through the conventional process of diluting stale air by mixing it with fresh air from above. In addition to improved air quality (even with fewer air changes per hour), advantages can include: reduction or elimination of ductwork (and the associated reduction in pressure drop, thereby requiring smaller fans and chillers and also potentially permitting an increase in floor-to-floor space); reduced chiller lift and improved chiller efficiency (due to higher supply-air temperatures); and reduced air-handling noise (Rocky Mountain Institute 2005).

Natural or mixed-mode ventilation may be a possibility for some locations or seasons. Radiant heating and cooling (which heats or cools people rather than air) and ground- or water-coupled heat pump systems can also reduce energy use. Finally, nonrefrigerative cooling methods (evaporative, desiccant, absorptive, and hybrids) can also improve efficiency. For any system, utilize waste heat wherever possible, and allow the systems to modulate with varying loads.

Equipment and appliances: *Major diagnostic equipment, such as MRIs and linear accelerators, typically consume large quantities of energy continually, even in standby mode. A large hospital or hospital consortium can demand more energy efficient equipment, sending a signal to manufacturers, for whom energy efficiency has not traditionally been a priority. (At a minimum, a hospital should install the most energy-efficient appliances and equipment available.) Reducing loads from inefficient equipment and/or equipment in standby mode can reduce the energy intensity required from both primary and emergency power sources.*

Water efficiency: *When considering resource efficiency, water should not be overlooked (both for the water savings itself and for the energy savings associated with heating or purifying it). Water-efficiency measures can pay back 40 percent of their installation investment in the first year through reduced water and energy costs. From an energy perspective, wasteful water heating can be avoided by, for example, fixing leaks on hot water fixtures or running full loads in process equipment, and heat exchangers should be installed to capture heat from hot wastewater—especially that from sterilizers, autoclaves, and other process equipment (Loranger 2004).*

Special considerations for surgery suites: *Energy use in operating rooms has increased as standards have evolved that require colder temperatures (partly to counteract more heat-generating equipment and lighting), more floor space, higher ceilings, and supplementary disinfection, such as ultraviolet lights in ducts and mechanical equipment. Despite these hurdles, the following design recommendations can optimize efficacy: use thermodynamic modeling to assess airflow; consider cooling the occupants locally to the standard 55 to 65°F (13 to 18°C) rather than ultrachilling the entire room; design for infection control by providing the most effective locations for exhaust vents; and use a diversity factor in load calculations if all the potential loads will never be in effect simultaneously (Loranger 2004).*

Continuous commissioning: *Providing upfront commissioning followed by periodic recommissioning will optimize equipment and system performance. Studies conducted at Lawrence Berkeley National Laboratory suggest that in typical cases, commissioning and improving building operations could save 20 percent of current energy use in existing buildings (Berkeley Lab 2000).*

PROMOTING HEALTH AND ENERGY EFFICIENCY WITHIN A HEALTHCARE FACILITY

Sometimes the most technically energy-efficient hospital design strategy may not be optimal for patients. A case in point: while reducing square footage per patient with multiple-occupancy patient rooms may seem to be more energy efficient, evidence from multiple studies indicates that infection rates are lower in single-bed rooms (Ulrich and Zimring 2004). Hospitals must first consider the core purpose of their facility and how best to achieve it: whole-system solutions should solve problems without creating new ones. But many design measures are win-win-win, for patient outcomes, staff productivity, and energy efficiency. Providing natural daylight (and simultaneously providing views of nature) is a prime example, as it is linked to energy efficiency as well as improved patient outcomes — faster healing, fewer complaints, the need for less pain medication (Ulrich 1984) and improved staff effectiveness (fewer mistakes and lower stress levels) (Ovitt 1996). Well-designed daylighting allows electric lights to be dimmed or turned off (of note, these should be automatically controlled with manual override), thereby reducing lighting electricity use and the associated heat gain, which in turn re-

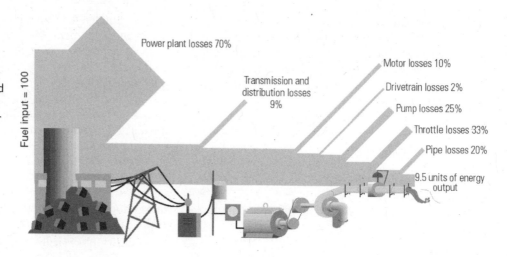

Figure 10-20: "An on-site CCHP [combined cooling, heating, and power] plant is a form of 'distributed' energy production, yielding many benefits. As compared to centralized power plants, smaller power modules provide portability, lower risk, and shorter lead times. Additional benefits include lower grid costs, lower transmission losses, better fault management, better reactive support and better power quality and reliability" (Lovins 2002). *Credit: Courtesy of ESource.*

In figure: Fuel input = 100 · Power plant losses 70% · Transmission and distribution losses 9% · Motor losses 10% · Drivetrain losses 2% · Pump losses 25% · Throttle losses 33% · Pipe losses 20% · 9.5 units of energy output

duces the cooling load, thus even further reducing the building's energy use. As described above, underfloor air distribution in nonclinical areas should represent a win on all fronts, as it can provide better air quality with less energy use (Bauman and Webster 2001).

EFFICIENT, ENVIRONMENTALLY RESPONSIBLE ENERGY PRODUCTION

After reducing energy demand, a plan to procure environmentally responsible energy sources should be developed to fulfill remaining energy needs. Options include purchasing green power from off-site clean and renewable energy sources (The nonprofit Center for Resource Solutions, based in San Francisco, California, offers the leading independent third-party certification system for green power in the US through its Green-e program—look for it at www.green-e.org), on-site renewable energy generation systems, and combined cooling, heating, and power (CCHP) plants.

Hospitals are ideal candidates for CCHP plants because of their high demand for both heat and power and because their 24/7 operations mean the plant can be sized for a relatively flat load profile. The CCHP system can also provide hospitals with the high reliability they require. These plants can increase energy production efficiency by 56 percent (Moroz 2004) because they make use of both the power and the heat produced by the plant; since they are located on-site, they also eliminate the major transmission losses associated with the electricity grid (see Figure 10-20).

Reducing energy demand and an on-site CCHP plant is not the end of the story, however; the fuel choice for energy generation is also important. An on-site CCHP plant powered by coal or diesel will compromise air quality. By contrast, the healthcare sector can promote both energy efficiency and environmental health by relying on clean, renewable energy sources. Fuel cells, even if powered by nonrenewable natural gas, are both clean and quiet. Renewable energy production includes photovoltaics, wind turbines, biofuels, active solar water heating, geothermal power, and environmentally sound hydroelectric (including microhydro) power.

Since the advent of central air conditioning, the healthcare sector has continued to increase its use of fossil fuel–generated thermal and electric energy in the interest of supporting the health of patients. As the global implications of continued reliance on energy produced from fossil fuels becomes better understood, it is those hospitals and healthcare systems that increase energy efficiency and support clean energy technologies that truly support their mission of promoting human health and associated environmental health. They acquire a leadership role in reducing air and water pollution and the associated disease risks by protecting habitats from the risks of mining and drilling and by reducing global warming potential and the associated risks of natural disasters and human health epidemics.

Virtually every case study in this book has achieved some measure of energy-demand reduction. The pioneers appear to have averaged approximately 20 percent reduction below ASHRAE 90.1 baseline energy demand using relatively standard mechanical system designs. These savings have been achieved through measures that include the selection of high-efficiency equipment, variable frequency drives and motors, shorter duct runs, optimized building orientation, and improved thermal envelopes.

As many hospitals move toward 100 percent outside air systems for improved air quality, energy-recovery technologies are increasingly included. The Winship Cancer Institute and the BC Cancer Agency Research Centre both included heat-recovery systems for their laboratories. Dell Children's Medical Center of Central Texas (immediately below) intentionally stacked mechanical equipment rooms in order to optimize energy-recovery technology.

Figure 10-21: Dell Children's Medical Center of Central Texas. *Credit: Karlsberger*

Dell Children's Medical Center of Central Texas

Austin,
Texas

Owner: Seton Healthcare Network
Design team:
ARCHITECT AND INTERIOR DESIGNER: Karlsberger
LANDSCAPE DESIGNER: TBG Partners
MECHANICAL, ELECTRICAL, AND PLUMBING ENGINEER: ccrd partners
STRUCTURAL ENGINEER: Datum Engineers, Inc.
CIVIL ENGINEER: Bury + Partners
PRECONSTRUCTION SERVICES/CONSTRUCTION MANAGER: White Construction Co.
SUSTAINABILITY CONSULTANT: Center for Maximum Potential Building Systems

Building type: New acute-care hospital

Size: 455,000 sq ft (42,300 sq m); site: 32 acres (12.9 ha)

Design energy intensity: Excluding process and plug load, 222 kBTUs/sq ft/yr; with process and plug load, 291 kBTUs/sq ft/yr

Program description: 169-bed acute-care children's hospital

Completion date: 2007

Recognition: *Green Guide for Health Care* pilot

This replacement hospital building is the first development parcel on the former municipal airport and will anchor the subsequent redevelopment of the 700-acre (283-hectare) brownfield site. Seton made an initial decision to integrate ambitious sustainability goals into the project, partially because of the selection of the airport property. Reintegrating the scarred brownfield site into the surrounding residential communities while constructing a large complex of buildings necessitated a creative approach to site planning, energy- and water-demand reduction, and other resource-conscious design considerations.

The goal was to support health for children, native wildlife, and the local economy at a whole new scale—the project is seeking LEED platinum certification. According

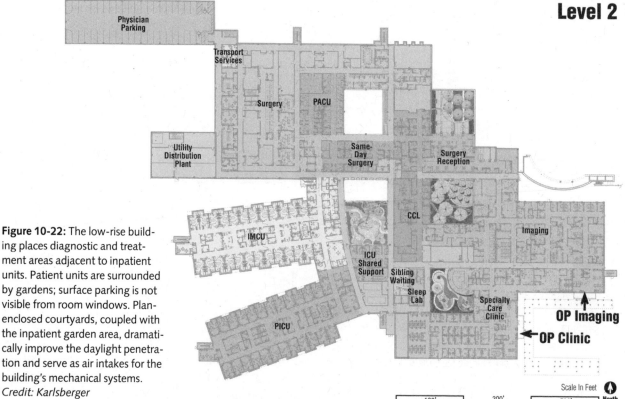

Figure 10-22: The low-rise building places diagnostic and treatment areas adjacent to inpatient units. Patient units are surrounded by gardens; surface parking is not visible from room windows. Plan-enclosed courtyards, coupled with the inpatient garden area, dramatically improve the daylight penetration and serve as air intakes for the building's mechanical systems. *Credit: Karlsberger*

to Tom Snearey, AIA, of Karlsberger: "To achieve this level of performance, the project team had to invent possibilities and then actualize them. It was an aggressive process that engaged a large group of stakeholders—an integrated process that became a way of thinking."

KEY BUILDING PERFORMANCE STRATEGIES

Site
- Brownfield remediation
- Xeriscaping and native planting

Water
- 30 percent potable water reduction in fixtures through use of dual-flush toilets and low-flow devices

Energy
- 35 percent improvement in source energy efficiency through the use of a CCHP-generating facility, accomplished in partnership with Austin Energy
- Additional 15 percent energy-demand reduction attributable to a range of system enhancements, including air intakes through courtyards, distributed air-handling units, heat-recovery technology, and variable frequency motors and drives
- Roof shape and slope accommodates future installation of photovoltaic panels

Materials
- 92 percent of construction and demolition waste recycled through aggressive site source separation program
- 47,000 tons of airport paving material removed and reprocessed
- Local, regional and recycled content materials utilized; exterior features regionally quarried stone
- Coal fly ash as replacement for portland cement

Environmental Quality
- Extensive access to daylight and views for patients and staff
- Low-emitting materials installed throughout building's interior
- Chemical-free termite control: physical barrier method
- Integrated pest management policy

One of the key features of the project is the gas-fired CCHP plant developed in partnership with Austin Energy, dramatically increasing efficiency and reducing emissions as compared to conventional grid-based electricity. The increased efficiency of on-site power generation, coupled with the ability to utilize the waste heat for thermal energy needs, boosted the source energy efficiency equivalent to a 35 percent energy demand reduction. By eliminating approximately $6 million in mechanical infrastructure costs, the project team was able to invest in additional sustainable building strategies. While the installation of photovoltaic panels did not meet the agreed upon payback or investment guidelines, the design includes a roof angled and oriented for future installation of the technology.

The seven plan-enclosed courtyards, referred to as "the lungs of the building," function as air-intake locations, resulting in intake air up to 6°F (3°C) cooler than conventional rooftop intakes. They also increase daylight penetration into the interior. The nursing units feature glass-enclosed staff lounges that offer the best views of the healing garden and, in some instances, the Austin skyline. (The gardens are featured as a case study in Chapter 4.)

Source: Karlsberger

Figure 10-23: Staff lounges, located on the corners of inpatient units, feature large windows with views to the garden areas. *Credit: Karlsberger*

As Karolides points out in her essay—and Dell Children's illustrates—there are major efficiency gains achievable through the implementation of CCHP technologies and systems in healthcare settings. To achieve greater levels of energy demand reduction (with or without CCHP), projects are beginning to innovate system selection and integrate natural ventilation. The OHSU Center for Health & Healing (page 279) demonstrates how a combination of natural and displacement ventilation, radiant heating, and high-efficiency equipment can boost energy demand reduction close to 50 percent. At the Discovery Health Center (Chapter 11), a high-performance envelope coupled with ground-source heat pumps and radiant-slab heating achieves a 42 percent demand reduction and eliminates all on-site combustion.

Renewable energy systems are beginning to appear on hospital buildings, despite the fact that renewable technologies can barely supply more than a fraction of the electrical energy demand of the buildings. Kaiser Permanente Modesto Medical Center (Chapter 5) uses photovoltaic panels as the screening device for its mechanical equipment. The OHSU Center for Health & Healing features photovoltaic panels as solar shading devices on its south-facing facade. Meyer Children's Hospital (page 316) incorporates integral photovoltaics in the glazing system of the south-facing atrium. These installations are often heavily subsidized by grants from utilities or local governments. While installation of photovoltaics may not meet return-on-investment (ROI) thresholds today, many projects are including design provisions for their installation in the future.

Figure 10-24: Salinas Valley Memorial Hospital, Monterey, California, installed an array of photovoltaic panels on the roof of the 100,000-sq-ft (9,290-sq-m) facility, offsetting 2.5 percent of its annual electrical usage. The array produces 225,000 kWh annually. *Credit: Adam Pattantyus*

Another method of supporting clean, renewable energy systems is through the purchase of "green power." Green power purchasers sign contracts with renewable power suppliers for a per kilowatt hour price that both pays for the power and finances further development of renewable sources. Depending on the regional market, the cost of purchasing green power may be greater than the cost of conventional fossil-fuel power, though that is shifting due to the global volatility of fossil fuel prices. The US Green Building Council provides a major impetus for this practice by rewarding green power purchasers through LEED point achievement — Providence Newberg (below) is the first hospital to purchase 100 percent renewable power. And when the Discovery Health Center made the decision to eliminate on-site combustion and rely on electricity to fuel its ground-source heat-pump system, a key element of that decision was the ability to purchase 100 percent of the power through a renewable energy contract.

Figure 10-25: Providence Newberg Medical Center. *Credit: Eckert & Eckert*

CASE STUDY

Providence Newberg Medical Center

Newberg,
Oregon

Owner: Providence Health & Services
Design team:
  ARCHITECT: Mahlum Architects
  MECHANICAL, ELECTRICAL, AND PLUMBING ENGINEER: Glumac International
  CONSTRUCTION MANAGER: Skanska USA Building Inc.
  SUSTAINABILITY CONSULTANT: Green Building Services
Building type: New acute care hospital campus
Size: Hospital: 143,000 sq ft (13,300 sq m); medical office building: 44,000 sq ft (4,100 sq m); site area: 60 acres (24.28 hectares)
Program description: Forty-bed community hospital, medical office building
Completion date: 2006
Recognition: US Green Building Council LEED gold certified

In 2000, Providence Health System began planning for a new hospital campus in Newberg, a town that has evolved to become a suburb of Portland, Oregon. As this was the health system's first such facility in almost three decades, and a relatively modestly scaled campus, the Providence team used the project to test an innovative, integrated

Figure 10-26: Providence Newberg evolved as two separate but interconnected floor plates, requiring a greater building perimeter while improving access to daylight and views. *Credit: Mahlum Architects*

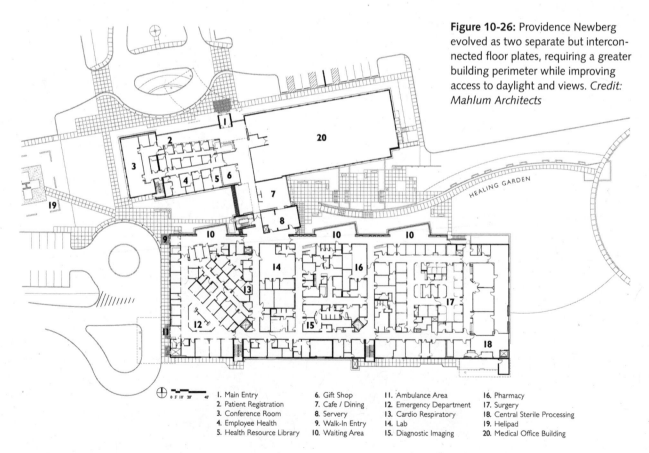

1. Main Entry	6. Gift Shop	11. Ambulance Area	16. Pharmacy
2. Patient Registration	7. Cafe / Dining	12. Emergency Department	17. Surgery
3. Conference Room	8. Servery	13. Cardio Respiratory	18. Central Sterile Processing
4. Employee Health	9. Walk-In Entry	14. Lab	19. Helipad
5. Health Resource Library	10. Waiting Area	15. Diagnostic Imaging	20. Medical Office Building

planning process to achieve sustainable design goals. "Hospitals are huge investments," notes John Koster MD, CEO of Providence Health & Services, the project's owner. "When we have the opportunity to build one, we have to be able to express what we stand for as an organization and ministry."

KEY BUILDING PERFORMANCE STRATEGIES

Site

- Existing on-site structures donated to community for adaptive reuse
- High-reflectance, low-emissivity roofing
- Public transportation access, bicycle parking, and showers
- Healing and wellness gardens positioned to enjoy morning sunlight and views of the mountain
- Network of walking and biking trails in undeveloped portion of the 60-acre site

Energy

- Occupancy sensors, daylight controls, and a centralized lighting-control system turn off lights when spaces are unoccupied or lighting is not needed
- Building refrigerant cooling systems utilize minimal ozone depleting refrigerants
- 28 percent energy cost savings compared to ASHRAE 90.1-1999
- 100 percent Green Power purchased for building

Materials

- 80 percent of construction waste was recycled and/or salvaged
- More than 25 percent of all building material contained recycled content
- Over 30 percent of the building materials were manufactured locally, with over 50 percent of these materials extracted locally

Environmental Quality

- Air quality was improved by maintaining indoor air quality management standards during construction and by performing a pre-occupancy flush out of the HVAC systems
- Tobacco smoking on the campus allowed in one designated outdoor area only, located away from all major entries and air intakes
- All materials specified to ensure a high level of air quality by using low-VOC paints, coatings, adhesives, sealants, and carpets

GREEN POWER PURCHASE

Providence has agreed to purchase 183,294 kilowatt hours of renewable power per month through the Clean Wind Program of PG&E, the local utility. By doing this, Providence will offset the impacts from conventional power generation that would send more than three million pounds of CO_2 emissions into the atmosphere each year. The CO_2 emissions avoided will be equivalent to taking 272 cars off the road.

Source: Providence Health & Services

The design process included the development of an ongoing BOAT, or a business opportunity assessment team, comprised of Providence leaders from diverse functional areas, such as medicine, finance, and engineering. The BOAT developed a financial template for all capital projects—one that integrated capital and operational costs in an initial attempt to instill a life cycle approach into capital and environmental de-

Figure 10-27: The forty-bed community hospital features spacious single-bed inpatient accommodations. *Credit: Eckert & Eckert*

cision making. For the Newberg project, the process was defined to include life cycle costs and benefits related to energy use.

Providence defined the direct cost of additional capital requirements, the monetary value of rebate programs (including direct utility programs and tax credits), and the estimated operational savings related to each energy-saving strategy. Provided the strategies meet the defined return on investment—"hurdle rate"—additional capital is then approved. Even before the opening of Providence Newberg, Richard Beam, director of energy management services, Office of Supply Chain Management, estimated that the process had yielded upward of $600,000 annually in savings and avoided costs through a range of system initiatives. With a twenty-five percent reduction in energy demand for Newberg, that number is now above $1 million.

Within this overall framework, each Providence site develops specific regional and local responses to the challenge. As a system, the values are what resonate consistently throughout: "Respect, compassion, justice, stewardship, and excellence—these are our values," says Beam. "Every single institution lives those values—stewardship and excellence speak to our role in being environmentally conscious."

Sources: Mahlum Architects; Providence Health & Services

MATERIALS AND RESOURCES

The healthcare sector is a prodigious consumer of materials and resources, both during the initial construction of buildings and during the ongoing layout reconfiguration and system modifications that continue throughout their useful life. As discussed in Part I, these resources are not only unsustainable in terms of sheer quantity; many products have negative life cycle health impacts. As part of demonstrating resource stewardship, many healthcare organizations are taking on the challenges of innovating their approach to building material selection, specification, and maintenance. Recognizing that constructing cancer centers without materials containing known or suspected carcinogens should be both possible as well as cost-effective, hospitals are using their purchasing power and sustainable healthcare projects to bring to market a new generation of high-performance, healthy building products.

This market transformation is not without its challenges for owners and design professionals alike, as Greg

You can't create a healing environment with visual amenities alone. We looked holistically at pollutants in the environment from materials, seeking to avoid those that could potentially have negative impacts on the occupants of our building, our community, and beyond.

—SUZEN HEELEY, DIRECTOR OF DESIGN AND CONSTRUCTION, HACKENSACK UNIVERSITY MEDICAL CENTER (ROSSI AND LENT 2006)

Roberts chronicles in "Specifying for Health." Not only does it require new types of evaluation criteria, it asks specifiers and owners to consider and trust new information sources presenting life cycle data. In the absence of a comprehensive, coherent product evaluation system, industry "greenwashing" is rampant. Inevitably, products are better in some aspects of their life cycle impacts than in others, and project teams must choose which attributes govern selection.

Specifying for Health

Greg Roberts, AIA

In today's lexicon of sustainability, the term green material takes on a different meaning than it did in the past. A green material used to be raw, fresh, or new, such as green lumber or green concrete. Today, the greenness of a material means something quite different: green lumber may come from a certified well-managed forest; green concrete may be a material with a high percentage of fly ash, a byproduct from coal-burning power plants. When it comes to healthcare, a material's impact on preserving natural resources and reducing environmental degradation are only a few of the factors designers should consider when "going green." Equally important to healthcare is a material's toxicity and impact on air quality, both of which can pose grave consequences to human and global health.

The designer's and specifier's increased knowledge of what makes a material green and how such materials can improve the healing environment for patients and caregivers without causing harm is very challeng-

ing. For example, urea formaldehyde is an off-gassing substance used extensively for decades in construction materials (70 percent of all use is construction related, historically). Latex paints, glues, lacquers, plywood, particleboard, decorative laminates, fiberglass insulation—all are frequently urea formaldehyde–emitting materials, especially when they are new. Formaldehyde levels are normally much higher indoors than outdoors and can irritate tissue upon direct contact, resulting in nose, throat, and eye irritation and tear inducement. The International Agency for Research on Cancer (2004) recently concluded that formaldehyde is carcinogenic to humans—urea formaldehyde stands out for having a particularly long off-gassing period. Responding to the health concerns raised by consumers, including specifiers and procurers in the healthcare sector, manufacturers now are beginning to offer products free of added urea formaldehyde.

In the past, code compliance, performance, aesthetics, cost, and availability were the key screening attributes for material selection. But today's selection process adds environmentally preferable product criteria. Through such criteria, material selection takes into account many factors, including:

- *Whether the materials were regionally and equitably produced or harvested (i.e., did they replenish on a cycle compatible with their harvesting, as in rapidly renewable or sustainably managed forest products?)*
- *How much energy was consumed in manufacturing and transporting the product, and what fuel type(s) were used (i.e., measuring embodied energy)*
- *Whether the product is recyclable (i.e., a biological or technical nutrient), or whether it can be disassembled and reused somewhere else*

Expanding the selection process to include health impacts, we should ask what chemicals were used in its production and what effect will they have on human and environmental health. This cradle-to-cradle thinking has been advocated by architect William McDonough and chemist Michael Braungart in their McDonough Braungart Design Chemistry Design Protocol (MBDC 2004), as well as elsewhere. This process evaluates a material according to its character-

istics within the desired application and categorizes it based on both human health and environmental relevance criteria.

Whether a material poses a toxicity hazard, and how much it off-gasses into the atmosphere, are two of the primary health issues considered in a materials evaluation. Many chemical hazards currently found in building materials are classified as carcinogens, mutagens, and endocrine disrupters, and pose significant long-term health consequences. As a result, environmentally conscious material selection has gained increased importance and thus drawn much research interest (Lin 2003).

Life cycle assessment can provide a basis for quantifying environmental impacts. Just as the off-gassing of formaldehyde can diminish over time, so, too, can the toxicity impact increase or decrease over a material's useful life. Many life cycle assessment tools and methodologies, however, are ill equipped to account for the health effects of toxic chemicals because of data gaps, uncertainty, and an inability to represent synergistic effects between multiple chemicals. Can we, as designers and specifiers, create a screening process that helps us achieve the goal of selecting only sustainable, healthy, and carcinogen-free materials?

A comprehensive understanding and scientific evaluation of the chemical soup to which we are exposed—and its environmental and human health consequences—may never be within reach. But in the healthcare industry, leading hospitals and health care systems are referencing the precautionary principle in their approach to chemical and construction hazards: "When an activity raises threats of harm to human health or the environment, precautionary measures should be taken even if some cause and effect relationships are not fully established scientifically" (SEHN 1998). As this principle guides more organizations' approaches to chemical evaluation, healthcare moves into a growing number of industries worldwide developing and using high-hazard materials screening methodologies.

Understanding the pros and cons of material life cycle impacts and making informed trade-offs are all a part of the selection and specification process. But finding remedies for a material's negative impact is no easy task. It requires significant time and effort to sift through multiple (and sometimes unclear and inaccurate) infor-

mation sources. Confusing terminology and outright misleading claims of a product's greenness—a process known as greenwashing—further complicates matters. Finding a balance between a product's environmental and health impacts and more conventional selection criteria—a balance that allows us to reduce chemical emissions and health risks while factoring in schedule, cost, and budget considerations—is a daunting task.

Simply specifying a material on the basis of its environmental or health attributes does not in itself lead to the ultimate selection. There are many more questions than answers, often with no right or wrong solution. Variables in fabrication and assembly, packaging, shipping, delivery, installation sequence, cutoff waste, take-back policies, and a material's end-of-use disposition all have bearing on material specification.

Standardization of reporting, evaluating, or measuring a building material's environmental impact has only recently been addressed. Third-party certifiers, such as Green Seal, Scientific Certification Systems, and the Greenguard Environmental Institute, are just a few that have come forward in certain industry segments to test and certify to a product's sustainable attributes. The American Society for Testing and Materials Performance of Buildings' Subcommittee E-6.71, Sustainability, has developed a number of standards focused on evaluating the sustainable merits of materials. Together with standard-setting bodies such as the American Society of Heating, Refrigerating, and Air-Conditioning Engineers (ASHRAE), the International Organization for Standardization (known by its French acronym, ISO), and others, it continues to formulate criteria for evaluating sustainable materials and systems. Commercial resources such as BuildingGreen's Green Spec Directory have developed their own greenness criteria, as have a number of professionals and institutions. However, until more universally accepted standards are written and adopted, specifiers will have to search broadly for answers regarding a material's sustainable properties and its human health impacts.

Many building owners avoid sustainable building practices, fearing added costs; healthcare leaders are no different. However, specifying materials based solely on first cost is shortsighted. There is hope, however, as informed leaders render decisions based on the triple bottom-line concept necessary for businesses to succeed in today's socially responsible and environmentally concerned climate.

For example, careful selection of materials low in VOCs and without persistent bioaccumulative toxic chemicals (PBTs) usually involves no or minimal cost premiums and provides added value by reducing indoor pollution. In many cases, it also reduces maintenance and premature replacement costs while avoiding potential liabilities (Kats 2003). Others have feared premium costs or inferior performance and safety from building materials with recycled content, an integral element of green building strategies. For them, cost difference is becoming a nonissue as more recycled content products come to market at price points equal to or less than those of virgin materials. And a recent study funded by the California Integrated Waste Management Board (2003) found recycled-content materials perform about the same as virgin-content materials. Both recycled and virgin-content products do have the potential to emit chemicals of concern; the study found, however, that low-emitting building materials are readily available in both categories.

In its 2003 Principles for Green Specifications, the Construction Specifications Institute's Environmental Task Team recognized that green and environmentally preferable product attributes address health, safety, and welfare issues (CSI 2003). Such recognition is even more important in the healthcare environment, where a material can compromise indoor air quality, spread infections, and contribute to toxic contamination—to name just a few potential hazards. The statutory responsibility of each licensed architect is to safeguard the health, safety, and welfare of the public through the practice of architecture. Selecting and specifying materials that offer green attributes and do not present harm contribute to fulfilling that responsibility.

Additionally, studies have shown that buildings designed using sustainable strategies and green building materials have many other benefits—including the increased productivity, safety, morale, and general well-being of their occupants and extended building life and value.

CONCLUSIONS
The goal in healthcare facility construction is to provide a safe environment for care; equally important is a fa-

cility's ability to enrich and enhance the lives of the occupants who work and receive care within it. Green building materials free of toxic elements and low in off-gassing can contribute to improved recovery times, diminished medical complications, and reduced staff absenteeism, all while improving productivity.

Designers and specifiers delving deep into the consequences of selected materials and demanding sustainable, healthy, and safe performance will drive manufacturers to meet the challenge with new and improved products. This transformation has occurred very rapidly over the past five years and will continue, becoming the standard of everyday best practices, as more healthcare facilities increase their focus on the connection between environmental factors and human health, and particularly the environmental health performance of the materials making up the healing environment. Hopefully, in the future, when a material is referred to as "green," it will mean it's a safe and healthy material for the environment and for us.

The most effective advocate for materials transformation in healthcare has been the National Facilities Services group at Kaiser Permanente. Since 2001, it has been engaged in transforming the healthcare materials marketplace through its industry purchasing agreements. Its story is summarized in the sidebar "Changing the Course of Production."

One of Kaiser's most compelling material evaluations is its assessment of resilient flooring. In seeking a substitute product for vinyl composition tile because of life cycle health concerns, the National Facilities Services group beta tested a range of alternative products at sites throughout the West Coast for eighteen months in order to develop and test the business case. Key findings from the study supported the use of alternative products. In particular, the study found that eco-polymeric and rubber (Slotterback 2006):

- Do not require waxing and stripping maintenance protocols
- Improve traction, reducing slip-and-fall incidents
- Improve acoustics, and are quieter underfoot
- Offer improved stain resistance

CHANGING THE COURSE OF PRODUCTION

The First Steps

In the mid-1990s, Kaiser Permanente began incorporating environmentally preferable purchasing specifications into its contracts for medical, chemical, and building products. Mercury-free thermometers, PVC-free medical and building products, latex-free examination gloves, greener cleaners, and recyclable solvents are among the many resulting product changes it has implemented over the past ten years. The power of large-scale purchasing to drive changes in the market is demonstrated in the case of how Kaiser Permanente catalyzed innovation in the carpet sector.

Purchasing Specifications and Partnerships

In the summer of 2002, Kaiser set out to find a high-performance, environmentally preferable carpet tile. To evaluate whether a carpet is indeed environmentally preferable, Kaiser Permanente asked leading manufacturers detailed questions about the impacts of their products from cradle to grave. For product content, Kaiser Permanente evaluated the carpets for PVC content, PBTs, carcinogens, and post-consumer recycled content. For sustainable manufacturing practices, Kaiser Permanente assessed the progress carpet manufacturing facilities were making in minimizing waste, water use, nonrenewable energy, and air emissions. For the use stage, it examined whether the carpets posed problems to indoor air quality, including off-gassing VOCs—that "new carpet" smell. And for the end-of-life stage, carpets were evaluated on whether they could be closed-loop recycled (carpet to carpet)

or down-cycled (carpet to other products of lower value). This scale of investment in evaluating the environmental performance of products set Kaiser Permanente apart from its peers.

The Decision: Catalyze Innovation

After evaluating the products and the company responses, no carpet emerged that was both PVC-free and met Kaiser Permanente's demanding performance specifications. The ideal product, it turned out, did not yet exist. Lacking such an ideal product, Kaiser Permanente added an innovation question to evaluate the interest, commitment, and capacity of suppliers to develop a new product that met its needs. "Kaiser Permanente is seeking to develop long-term partnerships with companies that are committed to developing the products we need," emphasized Tom Cooper of Kaiser Permanente's standards, planning, and design team. "We want to collaborate with manufacturers to create products that have the design features Kaiser Permanente wants, at affordable prices. Partnering is about dialogue, finding shared interests, and moving forward with better products."

With the goal of creating a new product, Kaiser Permanente chose two vendors with the understanding, specified in a contract, that they would develop a PVC-free product with the necessary performance characteristics—at the same cost as existing products—within two years. The contract required each firm to submit quarterly reports, including indicators of progress toward PVC-free backing. One firm, Collins & Aikman (C&A), based in Dalton, Georgia, met the challenge. "In direct response to our request, C&A developed a new durable, low-emission, PVC-free carpet, with backing made primarily from postconsumer recycled plastic," said Cooper. The achievement earned C&A a sole-source contract with Kaiser Permanente. In responding to Kaiser's challenge, C&A created a new carpet line for the system—and for other healthcare and institutional uses. The C&A trademarked Ethos carpet is made with a polyvinyl butyral (PVB) backing, a chlorine-free material that is recov-ered from PVB laminate in automobile safety glass. The C&A carpet backing is made from over 75 percent postconsumer recycled product, which can be recycled into more carpet backing at the end of its life. The combination of mission, capacity to evaluate products, willingness to partner with suppliers, commitment to reducing PVC use—and Kaiser Permanente's market size—led C&A to design a new carpet product.

Source: Excerpted with permission from Clean Production Action 2007

CASE STUDY

The Sarkis and Siran Gabrellian Women's and Children's Pavilion at Hackensack University Medical Center

Hackensack, New Jersey

Figure 10-28: The Sarkis and Siran Gabrellian Women's and Children's Pavilion at Hackensack University Medical Center. *Credit: Courtesy of Hackensack University Medical Center*

Owner: Hackensack University Medical Center
Design team:
   ARCHITECT: Architecture for Health Science & Commerce (AHSC)
   INTERIOR DESIGN: Hackensack University Medical Center
   MECHANICAL AND ELECTRICAL ENGINEER: Goldman Copeland Associates
   STRUCTURAL ENGINEER: Severud Associates
   CONSTRUCTION MANAGER: Wm. Blanchard Co.

Building type: New acute care hospital addition

Size: 300,000 sq ft (27,900 sq m)

Program description: 192 private rooms, pediatric inpatient services, maternal-fetal medicine suite, labor and delivery suite, restaurant and kitchen, laundry facility

Completion date: 2005

Recognition: *Green Guide for Health Care* pilot

In 2000, the Hackensack University Medical Center (HUMC) made a commitment to create a high-performance healing environment for its new women's and children's center. An initial discussion about shifting cleaning products to reduce impacts on occupant health campuswide led to a broader investigation of building materials and their health impacts.

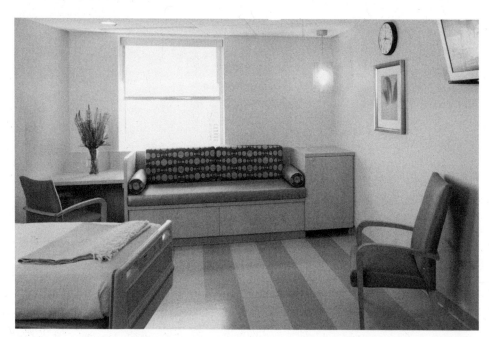

Figure 10-29: The patient rooms focus on healthy materials. Cabinets are made from wheat-based agriboard, which is both rapidly renewable and formaldehyde free. Synthethic rubber flooring is free of phthalate plasticizers and can be maintained without waxing or stripping. *Credit: Courtesy of Hackensack University Medical Center*

A discussion with HUMC's president, John Ferguson, led to an investigation of healthier alternatives to traditional commercial cleaning products, which are loaded with known or suspected human carcinogens, hormone and endocrine disruptors, and neurotoxins. In response, the medical center's Dierdre Imus Environmental Center for Pediatric Oncology developed the Greening the Cleaning program, which has developed into a full-scale cleaning protocol based on environmentally friendly, nontoxic cleaning products that utilize natural or naturally derived ingredients.

KEY BUILDING PERFORMANCE STRATEGIES

Materials

- Millwork contains a wheat/strawboard core that utilizes rapidly renewable resources and eliminates the formaldehyde commonly used in wood product binders and adhesives
- Doors contain recycled-content core materials
- Interior wood veneer is Forest Stewardship Council certified and finished with a low-VOC sealant
- Cotton insulation made from preconsumer recycled denim jeans eliminates formaldehyde sometimes found in conventional insulation; it also protects from fiberglass irritation
- PVC-free, phthalate-free, halogen-free, resilient flooring is maintained without waxing and stripping protocols
- PVC-free, phthalate-free wall protection system
- Construction waste recycling initiative redirected 75 percent of construction waste

Focusing on innovative building materials presented challenges during design and construction. For example, HUMC traded the benefit of local and regionally available formaldehyde-free fiberglass for that of the recycled denim product, which is manufactured in Arizona, becoming the largest installation to date of recycled denim insulation product in the process. As construction progressed through 2004, product availability was continuously shifting—the bidding and contract award process made the shift in material specification complex and demanding. The result, however, is a building that provides both a regional and national model for materials innovation.

Figure 10-30: The gracious Dr. Michael B. Harris Atrium for Tomorrow's Children visually connects the two floors of the birthing center with a skylit space that celebrates the same healthier materials approach. *Credit: Courtesy of Hackensack University Medical Center*

OPERATIONAL INITIATIVES

Toys for pediatric patients and the waiting areas were chosen using environmentally responsible criteria; the result was formaldehyde-free wooden toys and PVC-free plastic toys. Patient gowns, robes, and pajamas are constructed of fabrics made of 25 percent organic and 75 percent green (i.e., processed without chemicals) cotton. The room service menu and on-site restaurant feature organic food choices.

Source: Hackensack University Medical Center

Since the mid-1990s, Guenther 5 Architects has successfully integrated innovative, healthier materials in a range of healthcare interiors projects. Initially motivated by independent research on emissions and asthma triggers, the firm has moved to specification standards that recognize the health and life cycle impacts of commonly used building materials.

At the Continuum Center for Health and Healing, an integrative medicine center in New York City, the medical providers recognized that patients seeking integrative services often believe that their chronic medical issues are linked to environmental stressors. To create a healthy interior, the materials palette included cork, linoleum, sealed concrete floors, formaldehyde-free insulation and cabinet substrate, and low-emitting paints and adhesives. Consult rooms feature wood case goods and area carpets made of natural fibers.

Figure 10-31: The Continuum Center for Health and Healing features cork flooring in circulation areas, linoleum flooring in exam rooms, and a combination of Tectum suspended ceiling tiles and open ceiling areas. *Credit: © Peter Mauss, Esto Photography*

Figure 10-32: Consult rooms feature rapidly renewable cork flooring, freestanding wood case goods, low-emitting paints and sealants, and operable windows. *Credit: © Peter Mauss, Esto Photography*

The Jay Monahan Center for Gastrointestinal Health, on the campus of the Weill Medical College of Cornell University in New York City, features rapidly renewable bamboo flooring, linoleum, recycled glass tiles, and formaldehyde-free, low-emitting casework substrates, paints, and sealants. Together, these materials reinforce a connection to nature on a high-density urban site that affords little opportunity for a direct experience of nature. Daylight penetration is maximized through careful planning and extensive use of translucent and clerestory glazing.

Figure 10-33: Rapidly renewable bamboo flooring provides a strong biophilic natural materials reference point on a high traffic, urban site. Wood veneers are FSC-certified and millwork substrate is formaldehyde-free. *Credit: © Adrian Wilson*

During the construction process, construction-waste recycling of up to 75 percent of the total waste stream is now readily achievable in North America; many project teams are reporting up to 90 percent diversion. In some markets, recycling waste contractors permit mixed materials on-site and convey them to a central, off-site location for separation (Figure 10-34). More construction and demolition waste is diverted from landfill as "tipping fees" for landfill disposal are rising and municipalities are beginning to ban construction and demolition waste from landfills altogether. A goal of zero construction and demolition waste to landfill is ambitious, but regional partnerships between building materials manufacturers and waste handlers can lead to diversion rates of greater than 90 percent.

An increased emphasis on local and regional building materials (an idea developed further in the case studies in Chapter 11) is beginning to suggest a renewed bioregional aesthetic, as it energizes new connections between healthcare construction and local economies. Likewise, considerations of flexibility and durability are influencing building form, scale, and the method of construction procurement. Collectively, the issues surrounding materials and the wise use of resources have the potential both to link to the core mission of healthcare — "first, do no harm" — and to support transformation of the physical footprint of healthcare delivery.

Figure 10-34: At the Dell Children's Medical Center of Central Texas in Austin, construction waste is source separated on-site; the contractor maintains multiple tipping locations for distinct waste stream constituents. *Credit: Karlsberger*

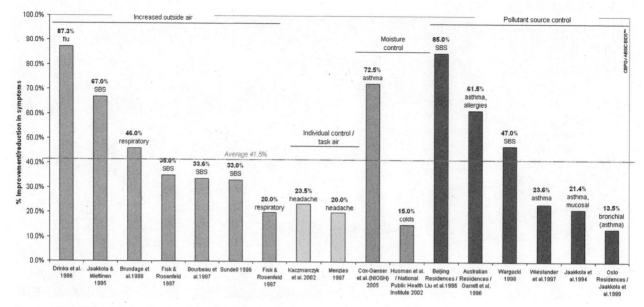

Figure 10-35: Health Gains from Improved Indoor Air Quality
Carnegie Mellon University identified seventeen international studies that document the relationship between improved indoor air quality and positive health impacts on illnesses, including asthma, flu, sick building syndrome, respiratory problems, and headaches; the improvements ranged from 13.5 to 87.3 percent. *Credit: Carnegie Mellon University, Center for Building Performance and Diagnostics*

BREATHING EASIER: ENVIRONMENTAL QUALITY

Environmental quality encompasses those elements of the built environment that influence the direct experience of the building — lighting (both natural and artificial), air quality (ventilation and indoor air pollution sources), the acoustic environment (sound and noise), and occupant control over all of these factors. Insofar as natural light and ventilation can profoundly impact building form, discussion of those features in the healthcare environment is developed in Chapter 11. However, more fundamental consideration of ventilation and air quality are included here, supplemented by case studies of healthcare buildings that demonstrate innovation in the resource stewardship of air quality, light, and sound.

Strategies for improved environmental quality focus on the relationship among air quality, occupant health, and productivity. In 2005, the Center for Building Performance and Diagnostics at Carnegie Mellon University released a graphical compilation of seventeen credible research studies linking health with improved indoor air quality (see Figure 10-35). These studies attribute health improvements to various air quality strategies — increased outside air, improved occupant control, improved moisture control, and pollutant source control. Collectively, these studies provide compelling evidence of the importance of access to outside air for building occupants and underscore the importance of building ventilation, the topic of building ecologist Hal Levin's essay, "Building Ventilation."

Building Ventilation

Hal Levin

*D*esigning ventilation for a specific building depends strongly on the type of occupancy, the quality of outdoor air, the character of indoor pollutant sources, and the level of pollutant exposure considered acceptable. These factors determine the appropriate amount and quality of ventilation with outdoor air, as well as filtration and air cleaning requirements. One size does not fit all: building design is always case specific, and exceptions are the rule in buildings. But source control is by far the most effective means of providing good indoor air quality. Reducing sources of pollutants indoors reduces proportionally the need for outdoor air ventilation. In nearly every case, source control is more cost-effective than ventilation.

WHY VENTILATE?

The fundamental reasons to ventilate are to dilute and remove contaminants generated indoors in order to protect occupants and building contents, and to provide a comfortable indoor environment for occupants. The stronger the indoor contaminant sources, the more dilution air is needed. But ventilation for health and comfort is not as simple as just bringing in more outdoor air. The economic, environmental, and energy-related costs of ventilation require us to design building ventilation carefully. Some of the key determinants and decisions involve the amount of outdoor air, the source of that air, the nature and extent of filtration and cleaning required for that air, the amount of indoor air to be recirculated, the best temperatures and relative humidity for ventilation air, and the means to control and deliver ventilation air most effectively.

There are many sources of indoor contaminants, not the least of which is people. In addition, chemicals are emitted from building materials, especially when new, and from furnishings and other building contents. Processes such as food preparation, and those that involve cleaning products, appliances, and office equipment, can also be serious sources of contaminants. A myriad of other important building-related sources exist, including pesticides, plasticizers, and fire retardants.

Outdoor air is brought into a building to dilute contaminants with indoor sources. In order to improve indoor air, the outdoor air must have lower concentrations of the indoor contaminants than the indoor air. Therefore, it is important to prevent harmful pollutants from entering the indoor environment via outdoor air through filtration and air cleaning. This is done by scheduling ventilation operation to minimize intake of outdoor air during peak pollution periods and through the deliberate location of outdoor air intakes.

Outdoor air may contain a myriad of chemicals and particles, including motor vehicle exhaust, and it may contain urban air pollution (smog) formed by the photochemical transformation of certain VOCs. Ozone and other pollutants in outdoor air may react with common indoor air pollutants to form far more irritating, odorous, or toxic chemicals. Some of the most common "green" chemicals (such as the citrus and pine oils used in cleaning products and interior finishes) actually react with ozone to form formaldehyde, higher molecular-weight aldehydes, acidic aerosols, and fine particles that may be far worse from a health perspective than the chemicals from which they are formed—and, in some cases, the chemicals they are designed to replace. Outdoor air may also contain exhaust from commercial or industrial processes, as well as pollen and mold from natural sources. Finally, outdoor air may be relatively high in humidity that, if not controlled indoors, can ultimately lead to moisture-related problems for building materials and contents (mold and mildew, for example) and to health problems for occupants.

In rare cases, building ventilation has been shown to bring in and spread outdoor air contaminated with the bacteria Legionella, the organisms responsible for Legionnaires' disease. These bacteria are found in soil and sometimes originate in cooling towers that are part of building air-conditioning systems. There is also concern about ventilation systems being vehicles for spreading tuberculosis bacteria and other organisms—especially in healthcare institutions—or spreading viruses and bacteria that cause common respiratory infections in schools, airplanes, and other densely populated indoor environments.

Another reason to ventilate is to create comfortable thermal conditions. In fact, until the mid-1970s, very little emphasis was placed on the role of ventilation in maintaining good indoor air quality in modern buildings; far more was placed on the use of ventilation to provide heating, cooling, humidity control, and air movement for comfort. Building materials changed in the fifties and sixties, with plastics and composite materials replacing solid wood, plaster, and other traditional building products. It was only when significant problems occurred—after energy conservation efforts in the seventies and eighties led to reduced outdoor air ventilation—that the indispensable role of ventilation in maintaining indoor air quality was acknowledged and the impacts from indoor pollutant sources recognized.

Ventilation can also reduce occupant exposure to airborne infectious agents, pollen, and allergens. Even recirculated air can help reduce exposures to such health hazards if appropriate circulation patterns and filtration are employed. In instances such as healthcare facilities and homeless shelters, where highly infectious occupants may be present, upper-room-air ultraviolet radiation is sometimes used to control the risks of infectious agent exposure while minimizing potential ultraviolet exposure. Ventilation must be carefully planned to deliver contaminated air to the sterilizing devices while minimizing the exposure of uninfected occupants to infectious agents.

HOW MUCH VENTILATION IS NEEDED? WHAT WE KNOW—AND WHAT WE DON'T
Numerous studies of the relationship between building ventilation rates and occupant health suggest that, on average, more mechanical ventilation with outdoor air correlates to lower rates of building-related symptoms (also known as sick building syndrome, or SBS). Such general findings are only relevant, however, when setting broad guidelines or standards. In fact, although the data are limited, naturally ventilated buildings usually have lower outdoor air ventilation rates than mechanically ventilated buildings, yet they have lower rates of SBS symptoms. Higher rates of SBS have been found in air-conditioned buildings (Seppänen, Fisk, and Mendell 1999).

For the design of specific buildings, the type of occupancy, the quality of outdoor air, and the character of indoor pollutant sources must be considered in determining the appropriate amount of outdoor air. As a result of these determinants, this amount can vary greatly from season to season, from place to place in a particular building—even from day to day. As noted earlier, one size does not fit all: design is always case specific, and exceptions are the rule.

CHALLENGES TO DELIVERING VENTILATION AT THE DESIGNED RATE
Even when the desired amount of outdoor air is known, it can be difficult to ensure delivery of specific amounts of outdoor air. Airflow measurement problems and system inefficiencies or losses can contribute to large variations between designed ventilation rates and actual delivered rates. Measurement of the actual supply of outdoor air, either at outdoor air intakes or at the delivery points in the building, is difficult at best.

While much attention is paid to regulating the amount of outdoor air delivered to spaces, the actual rates are rarely as intended. Oversimplified assumptions about a building's conformance to design intent are used in practice, and excessive credence is given to their use. System inefficiencies involve the unintended mixing of outdoor and recirculated air, losses through ducts, and poor distribution within spaces. Unbalanced systems are common, and improper pressure relationships between and among spaces often cause pollution penetration or movement.

The most critical ventilation rates are the designed rates and the actual minimum rates, which are often specified by codes and regulations, and the rates under typical building operation. Variations in measured minimum ventilation rates have been documented at less than half to more than twice the designed value, and half the one hundred buildings measured in one study had rates lower than the designed rate—some as low as one-fourth the designed rate. In that random stratified sample of US office buildings, organized by the US Environmental Protection Agency, 17 percent of the buildings' measured outdoor air rates were below the ASHRAE Standard 62.1 minimum of 20 cubic feet per minute per person, although in general these ventilation rates were high relative to the standard's minimum requirements (Persily et al. 2005; Persily and Gorfain 2004). Thus, both underventilation and overventilation are more common than generally assumed.

While commissioning can usually reduce the discrepancies between design and performance, the measurement problems themselves reduce the effectiveness and reliability of commissioning. The simplest means to deliver a minimum ventilation rate is through the use of a dedicated outdoor air injection fan. As we have seen, inadequate ventilation increases the exposure of occupants to contaminants from indoor sources. But excessive ventilation results in a waste of energy for fan power and the conditioning of outdoor air. Researchers and designers are now working on more reliable ways to measure and control outdoor air supply rates.

LIMITS TO VENTILATION'S ABILITY TO PROVIDE GOOD INDOOR AIR QUALITY

Pollution sources (or loads) vary greatly within and among buildings in the same way that thermal loads do. Since the major role of ventilation is pollutant dilution and removal, source control is therefore considered by most authorities the foremost means of controlling occupant exposure to pollutants. In nearly every case, it is more cost-effective than ventilation. Careful selection of building materials and products, proper system sizing and controls, correct system operation and maintenance, and good housekeeping practices are all critical. Yet shortcomings in one or more of these crucial areas are far more common than most designers assume. Careful and thorough commissioning and periodic recommissioning have been found to be important —and cost-effective—means for achieving good indoor air quality and efficient building operation.

THE WAY FORWARD: TOWARD SUSTAINABLE BUILDINGS

The measurement challenges must be overcome in order to enable commissioning and periodic or routine verification of ventilation. While outdoor air ventilation clearly reduces occupant exposure to pollutants from indoor sources, the first line of defense should be the elimination, reduction, encapsulation, or isolation of pollutant sources. New technologies, such as individual- or user-controlled ventilation and delivery, as well as underfloor ventilation supply, hold promise for reducing ventilation while improving indoor air quality. Demand-controlled ventilation is effective in variably high-occupant density situations. More sophisticated approaches to the design of buildings with natural (passive) ventilation and hybrid ventilation systems have produced many (often very large) buildings that do not depend on mechanical ventilation systems. Yet the control of pollutants in outdoor ventilation air for naturally ventilated buildings is a challenge remaining to be addressed.

In an age when preventing climate change has taken center stage as the number one environmental

---

VENTILATION PRINCIPLES

- Deliver what is needed, where it is needed, when it is needed.
- Maximize occupant/user control over air temperature, velocity, and direction; personal (i.e., individual occupant or task) ventilation approaches, when appropriate, are preferable.
- Know what is in the outdoor air brought in for ventilation and what is in the air inside that is being dumped outdoors.
- Keep systems properly adjusted (continuous commissioning).
- Keep ventilation systems very clean.
- Use local and system/building-specific solutions. Avoid standardized solutions for regular inspections, time between filter changes, settings for amount of outdoor air, calibration of sensors and dampers, and so on.

---

challenge, the elimination of unnecessary fossil fuel consumption will increasingly be a driving force behind building design. Reducing cooling and heating loads, along with effective source control, can dramatically reduce the amount of ventilation necessary to maintain indoor air quality and the energy required to deliver outdoor air. In the future, cleaning the outdoor air may become a much more common pursuit, since ventilation with polluted outdoor air can itself produce deteriorated indoor air quality.

Pollutant source control will be the most effective strategy for outdoor air as well. This will require changes in our transportation systems to bring about reductions in greenhouse gas emissions, urban smog, and dependence on fossil fuels. The quality of the indoor environment is inextricably linked to that of the outdoor environment in the immediate community context and on a broader, even global, scale. A stronger commitment to environmental protection and an enhanced understanding of the human behaviors that affect building ecology will be necessary to place ventilation in its proper role in buildings.

One of the major shifts in healthcare ventilation strategies is the move to air systems based exclusively on outside air. Aimed primarily at improving infection control and reducing the risks associated with bioterrorism and the contamination of hospital ventilation systems, these designs are coupled with heat-recovery technology to reduce the energy demand that would otherwise be associated with the solution. In North America, regulations governing pressurization and ventilation air changes limit the ability to consider natural ventilation strategies in acute care settings.

However, North American sustainable healthcare projects are beginning to pilot displacement-ventilation strategies. With displacement ventilation, air is introduced at the floor, at low velocity, at a temperature only slightly lower than the desired room temperature. The cooler air displaces the warmer room air, creating a fresh, cool zone at the occupied level. Heat and contaminants rise to the ceiling level, where they are exhausted. Because displacement-ventilation systems typically use 100 percent outdoor air, air pollutants generated within the building are removed at the source and are not recirculated. In addition, heat generated by ceiling lighting is removed, and thus not included when estimating building cooling loads. Finally, because displacement systems rely on the natural convective movement of air,

they require less fan energy and are quieter. The OHSU Center for Health & Healing (page 279) includes displacement ventilation in its exam rooms. The New Rikshospitalet University Hospital in Oslo (page 323) employs displacement ventilation as the standard system in inpatient units (this system was developed in the 1970s in Scandinavia, where it is seen as a proven technology).

The reliance on natural ventilation in many of the international case studies in this book (e.g., Waitakare and Meyer Children's Hospital) is a striking energy performance differentiator between American hospitals and those abroad. The Washington State Veterans Home in Retsil, Washington (below), features natural cooling and operable windows, with predicted annual energy reduction of close to 50 percent below a standard, mechanically cooled long-term care facility.

DISPLACEMENT VENTILATION IN HEALTHCARE SETTINGS

Two firms—Mazzetti & Associates of San Francisco and Stantec of Vancouver, British Columbia—worked independently, but in concert, to develop displacement ventilation schemes specifically for hospitals. At GreenBuild 2006, Denver, the US Green Building Council's annual conference, the two firms presented their initial findings: Stantec on diagnostic and treatment areas, and Mazzetti on inpatient areas and waiting rooms.

In response to Kaiser Permanente's desire to push sustainable practices on its Hayward, California replacement hospital project, Mazzetti researched displacement ventilation in a low sidewall configuration for an inpatient room and an emergency waiting room. (After an in-house charrette on sustainable practices that included renowned infection-control expert Andrew Streifel and officials from California's Office of Statewide Health and Planning Development, those areas looked to have the highest promise for displacement ventilation.) The research hypothesis was that low-sidewall displacement ventilation—at less than current code air-exchange rates—would perform better than traditional overhead mixing ventilation systems at current code air-exchange rates. If the hypothesis proved to be true, the energy savings potential would be dramatic.

Initial research was conducted using full-scale laboratory mock-ups at the Canadian test labs of E. H. Price and corroborated by computational fluid dynamic modeling. All aspects of ventilation were tested, including environmental comfort (ASHRAE Standard 55), ventilation effectiveness (ASHRAE Standard 62), and particle dispersion—via a test devised and validated by Andrew Streifel. (Particle dispersion is an indicator for infection control, the critical issue that differentiates healthcare ventilation from other commercial building types.)

The hypothesis was proven. In all aspects, low-sidewall displacement ventilation, at lower than code air-exchange rates, performed better than traditional overhead mixing ventilation at code air-exchange rates. Stantec's parallel research on exam rooms corroborated Mazzetti's research on the ventilation's effectiveness, thermal comfort, and particle dispersal characteristics of displacement ventilation, and explored the potential to control airflow in natural ventilation mode using airflow sensors linked to an intelligent facade and the mechanical exhaust system.

Research continues with the following goals: to determine optimal displacement ventilation exchange rate(s) for safety, comfort, and energy use; to determine under what conditions hybrid natural/displacement systems can be implemented in healthcare facilities; to upgrade codes to accept the recommended systems; and to apply the findings to integrated, sustainable design solutions. The research consortium has grown, driven by the momentum to apply sustainability to healthcare. To validate the research, independent oversight committees have been established to advise on infection control and standards and codes.

Sources: Bob Gulick, PE, Mazzetti & Associates; Ray Pradinuk, MBAIC, Stantec Architecture

---

Owner: Washington State Department of Veterans Affairs

Design team:
    ARCHITECT: NBBJ
    MECHANICAL, ELECTRICAL, AND PLUMBING ENGINEER: Stantec Consulting, Inc.
    CONSTRUCTION MANAGER: M.A. Mortenson Company

Building type: New skilled nursing facility

Size: Residential and administration building: 160,000 sq ft (14,860 sq m); kitchen and dining facility: 10,000 sq ft (929 sq m)

Program description: 240-bed residential facility; kitchen and dining facility

Completion date: 2005

Recognition: US Green Building Council LEED gold certification

Washington State Veterans Home

Retsil, Washington

Figure 10-36: Washington State Veterans Home. *Credit: Matt Milios/NBBJ*

Figure 10-38: The curving pedestrian spine links the resident neighborhoods in a celebration of daylight and access to the outdoors through a sequence of "living" spaces. A natural materials focus includes wood flooring and stone accents; light colors allow daylight to adequately light the interior much of the time. *Credit: Michelle Litvin*

Figure 10-37: The kitchen, with its expressed structure, high ceilings, and large windows, invites residents to move between the indoors and outdoors. A design process acknowledging the resident experience led to a concept focused on connecting residents to the immediate exterior surroundings. *Credit: Michelle Litvin*

When the Washington State Department of Veterans Affairs began planning for a new skilled nursing facility, residents and staff were actively engaged to define the qualities of the best skilled nursing care environment for veterans. During an initial work session, a resident read aloud the slogan on his cap: "You work where I live." Emphasizing respect for residents, those words became the project's planning and design mantra. When the project team asked residents to describe their ideal environment, they identified many sustainable design solutions. "We realized that the residents were already asking to choose, to be able to open windows, to have more daylight and access to the outdoors," said Liz Jacks, NBBJ project manager.

Recognizing the Sinclair Inlet, with its mild microclimate and sea breezes, as a unique, manageable natural resource, the design team developed a naturally ventilated cooling solution. The decision to emphasize access to the outdoors supported energy demand reduction. "The site is very hilly," explained Jacks, "and we wanted to be able to get the residents outside. We realized burying the building into the site would give us grade access on multiple levels and help us with insulation. It also avoided large-scale excavation."

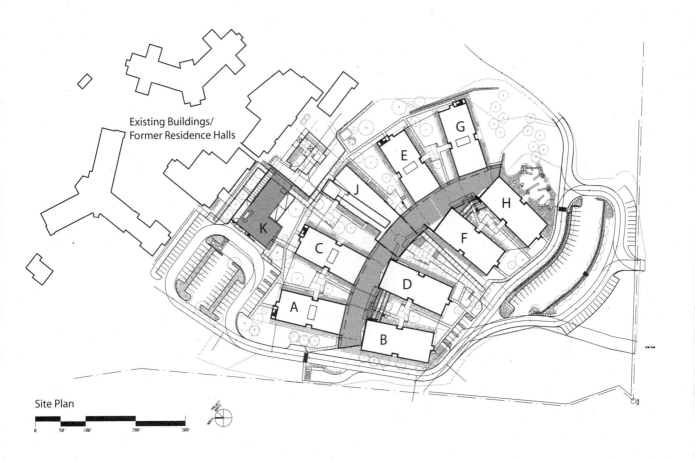

Existing Buildings/
Former Residence Halls

Site Plan

0   50'   100'   200'   300'

Figures 10-39 and 10-40: The building orients resident wings to maximize passive cooling and prevailing winds. There is no mechanical cooling system in the facility. The aerial photo demonstrates the relationship between the site and the tempering influences of the Sinclair Inlet microclimate. *Credits: Figure 10-39: NBBJ Architects; Figure 10-40: © George White Location Photography*

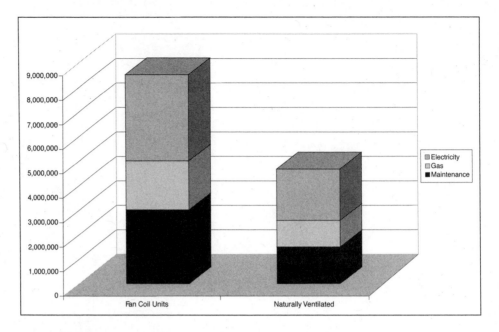

Figure 10-41: Energy Cost Savings
The cost of fan coil units for cooling, including power, chilled water, and maintenance, was conservatively estimated at more than $8 million, while the passive cooling saved not only energy, but maintenance costs—a total estimated savings of $4.5 million over the thirty-year life span of the system. *Credit: Stantec Consulting, Inc.*

THE JOURNEY TO NATURAL VENTILATION AND PASSIVE COOLING

The successful implementation of these strategies begins with the microclimate of the site—an analysis that supported the use of natural systems provided that the thermal mass of the building was increased and that deep floor plates (windowless spaces) were eliminated. The cost analysis indicated a $400,000 premium for additional thermal mass (concrete plank versus steel structure), which was more than offset by the elimination of the mechanical cooling system. Stantec analyzed the energy cost savings over thirty years associated with the shift in systems; its analysis is summarized in Figures 10-41 and 10-42.

Source: Stantec Consulting, Inc.

KEY BUILDING PERFORMANCE STRATEGIES

Energy
- Natural ventilation
- Passive cooling

Environmental Quality
- Fresh air exchanges in resident rooms and common areas
- High and low operable windows
- Resident control over environment
- Daylight and views of Sinclair Inlet
- Outdoor spaces that front the wooded waterfront site

The architects developed their own assessment criteria to meet state requirements while using sustainable methods and the LEED checklist. The team rejected design strategies that did not support the sustainable character of the project, and a strict budget was maintained. The facility is the first in the state of Washington to be approved for natural ventilation and passive cooling, while the system itself is the first sustainable solution to receive an exception to the Washington Administrative Code for comfort.

Source: NBBJ

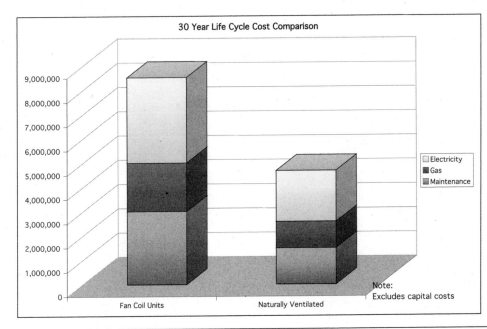

30 Year Life Cycle Cost Comparison

Legend:
- Electricity
- Gas
- Maintenance

Note:
Excludes capital costs

X-axis: Fan Coil Units, Naturally Ventilated

Y-axis: 0 / 1,000,000 / 2,000,000 / 3,000,000 / 4,000,000 / 5,000,000 / 6,000,000 / 7,000,000 / 8,000,000 / 9,000,000

Figure 10-42: Energy Savings by Building System This graph indicates the relative energy demand for services and system components of a "standard" base building (with a fan coil heating and cooling system) compared with the passive systems utilized at the Washington State Veterans Home. The naturally ventilated building yields a major decrease in energy demand for both heating and auxiliary equipment (pumps and fans). *Credit: Stantec Consulting, Inc.*

Minimizing pollutant source control is a central focus of the majority of sustainable healthcare projects. Project teams prioritize the use of materials with reduced VOCs — including paints, adhesives, sealants — and eliminate formaldehyde in insulation and cabinet substrate. Patrick Dollard, CEO of the Discovery Health Center (Chapter 11), summed it up for his medically fragile, developmentally disabled residents: "If I'm caring for the canaries of the planet, I want the healthiest possible environment that I can create." In most instances, low-emitting materials are paired with the implementation of greener, cleaner protocols and integrated pest management; in fact, the majority of LEED-certified healthcare projects have received a "greener cleaner" innovation point.

SIGHT AND SOUND

Consideration of the acoustic environment of healthcare settings, as pioneered by the *Green Guide for Health Care,* is gaining momentum in the industry. A task force working with the Facility Guidelines Institute issued *Interim Sound and Vibration Design Guidelines for Hospital and Healthcare Facilities* (ASA 2006), which form the basis

for the *Green Guide's* acoustics credits. Recognizing the interconnection among community noise sources, mechanical system impacts, and occupant-generated sounds (ranging from alarms to human voices), sustainable building strategies that improve hospitals' acoustic environments as a key component of their environmental quality are emerging.

Finally, access to daylight, the outdoors, and views of nature frame our perception of environmental quality. Ever since Roger Ulrich (1984) linked improved patient recovery and views of nature, the healthcare industry has been stymied by a building typology that celebrates immediate horizontal adjacency of diagnostic and treatment modalities. This has led to massive, deep floor plates and buildings that leave workers daylight deprived and consume more energy (Williams, Knight and Griffiths 1999). Chapter 11, "Toward a New Language of Form," considers how sustainable building is challenging the prevailing notion of hospital design. The final case study in this chapter, Meyer Children's Hospital in Florence, Italy, features what at first glance appears to be a low-rise, deep-plate building. But the building actually utilizes courtyards, light pipes, and a large, daylit atrium to both reduce energy needs and improve the occupants' experience.

Meyer Children's Hospital (Ospedale Pediatrico Meyer di Firenze)

Florence, Italy

Figure 10-43:
Meyer Children's Hospital. *Credit: Courtesy of CSPE Florence*

Owner: Italian National Health System, Tuscan Region

Design team: Anshen + Allen, San Francisco/Centro Studi Progettazione Edilizia (CSPE), Florence

Type: New acute-care construction and renovation

Size: Building: 361,667 sq ft (33,600 sq m); site: 17.83 acres (7.2 ha)

Design energy intensity: Projected from models: 18 kWh/sq ft (188 kWh/sq m)

Program description: 152-bed children's hospital

Completion date: 2007

Recognition: EU Hospitals Project

Adding on to an existing historic villa adjacent to parkland, the competition-winning design team delivered a pediatric hospital that uses sustainable technologies to realize a daylit, child-centered design. The hospital replaces an older facility elsewhere in Florence and is arguably the most ambitious of the five demonstration hospitals built under the European Union (EU) Hospitals Project. It will function as a regional demonstration project for the use of integrated and applied building photovoltaics.

The hospital is an independent health institute of the Italian National Health System managed by Azienda Ospedaliera Meyer. Its overall objectives were the reduction and control of solar radiation and the provision of natural ventilation and natural cooling of the external building surfaces using evaporative principles (Sala, Trombadore, and Alcamo 2006).

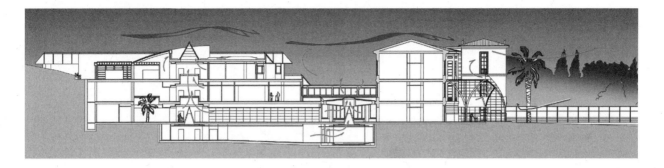

Figure 10-44: A section of the Meyer Children's Hospital is partially bermed into the hill to diminish the building's impact on the site and to reduce energy demand. *Credit: Courtesy of CSPE Florence*

KEY BUILDING PERFORMANCE STRATEGIES

Site

▣ Old-growth trees on-site incorporated into parkland plan
▣ 53,800 sq ft (5,000-sq-m) green roof integrates building with site

Energy

▣ High-performance envelope, including 2.5 inches (6 cm) of external wall insulation
▣ 35 percent energy demand reduction below baseline through heat pump heating and cooling systems
▣ 36 kW photovoltaic embedded glass system in solarium
▣ Daylighting expected to provide 36 percent lighting energy savings below standard practice (about 60 percent reduction from prior hospital use if operated as modeled)

Materials

▣ Low-VOC surface paints
▣ Wood window frames, doors, ceilings, siding, and trim
▣ Pre-patina copper cladding in Tuscan tradition

Environmental Quality

▣ 36.8 sq ft (3.42 sq m) of double-glazed windows in every patient room
▣ Skylights, courtyards, and sun pipes (light ducts) serving up to three floors provide daylight to deeper plan areas
▣ Daylit corridors precluding need for electrical light during morning hours
▣ Motorized blinds control glare

Financial savings are estimated at €92,000 ($119,600) per year based on an annual maintenance cost of €9,000 ($12,000). Hospital administration reports that after an initial investment cost of €1.5 million ($1.9 million), simple payback time for energy-related features, including photovoltaic array, is calculated at 17.7 years—or 11.5 years when EU financial support of €500,000 ($650,000) is considered. Project engineers expect a reduction in emissions of 899 tons of CO_2, 0.77 tons of SOx (sulfur oxide), and 7.91 tons of NOx (nitrogen oxide) per year compared with the emission levels of the old hospital.

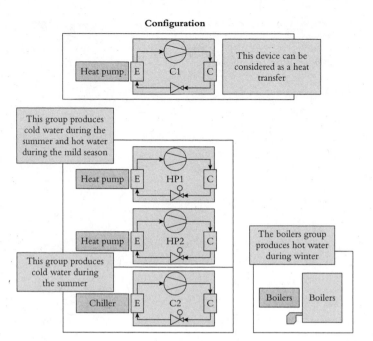

Configuration

This device can be considered as a heat transfer

Heat pump | E | C1 | C

This group produces cold water during the summer and hot water during the mild season

Heat pump | E | HP1 | C

Heat pump | E | HP2 | C

The boilers group produces hot water during winter

This group produces cold water during the summer

Chiller | E | C2 | C

Boilers | Boilers

Figure 10-45: Heating and cooling systems at Meyer are based on air-to-air heat pumps. *Credit: Marco Sala, 2006, European Union Hospitals Project*

"A combination of shading and ventilation systems can keep the [building] temperature to within 10°C above ambient. To save on energy for cooling, passive cooling and ventilation techniques are used as much as possible, with air-conditioning [used] only where necessary. A sun space functions as a buffer area for the building. The heated air is used to create solar drafts providing a natural airflow through the building. Trees will be planted around the hospital, and part of the roof will be covered with grass. The respiration of the vegetation will provide a cool microclimate. A centralized energy-management system selects the operational strategy in each case" (Russ 2006).

Sources: Anshen + Allen; Centro Studi Progettazione Edilizia (CSPE)

CONCLUSION

Most of the healthcare organizations and design teams engaged in green building do not set out to change the industry — they embark on this journey because they no longer view environmental stewardship as optional but rather as an essential component of leadership. They determine, initially, what it is possible to do, seizing the low-hanging fruit of sustainable building. But they also question the status quo, recognizing that the present model was derived in an era of inexpensive, expendable fossil fuel, when there was a seemingly inexhaustible "away" to which to discard the waste from building and operations.

Many describe this journey as transformative — John Kouletsis, AIA, director of planning and design services for Kaiser Permanente, notes, "People are reluctant to embrace change. But at some point in time, the idea becomes so pervasive that it becomes the common wisdom." And John Ferguson, the CEO of Hackensack University Medical Center, sums it up: "This is not that complicated. It's really common sense. All we are doing is challenging things we've been doing for a long time. And why do we do things for a long time? Only because we are used to the status quo."

Figure C-1: Evelina Children's Hospital. This passively conditioned atrium contains both an educational program area and building circulation, transforming the perception of an urban London hospital (Chapter 8). *Credit: © Paul Tyagi/ VIEW*

Figure C-2: Gravesham Community Hospital. Daylighting and natural ventilation are facilitated through the building massing and light-colored courtyard materials (Chapter 8). *Credit: James Brittain Photography*

Figure C-3: Gravesham Community Hospital. This hospital situates a 102-bed acute care geriatric hospital alongside housing for the elderly—this unique garden is shared by both. The entire complex is integrated in a low-rise row house neighborhood in London (Chapter 8). *Credit: James Brittain Photography*

Figure C-4: Kaleidoscope, Lewisham Children and Young People's Centre. This neighborhood primary care and social service center creates a healing oasis in London. The plan facilitates deep penetration of daylight and moves the operable windows away from the heavily trafficked urban streetscape. Note the solar-shading devices on the south-facing facade (Chapter 8).
Credit: © Nick Kane

Figure C-5: Kaleidoscope, Lewisham Children and Young People's Centre. The central garden is visible from all public and waiting areas, fostering a profound connection between nature and healing. Through the garden, the rectilinear plan transforms into organic shapes, which are then echoed in ceilings and lighting (Chapter 8).
Credit: © Nick Kane

Figure C-7: REHAB Basel Centre for Spinal Cord and Brain Injuries. Patient rooms surround the perimeter of the large floor plates, and feature sliding glass doors opening on to a continuous balcony that doubles as a solar-shading device. Above the bed, a 6-ft diameter spherical skylight bathes the patient rooms in daylight. Natural wood floors and ceilings complement the wood exterior (Chapter 11). *Credit: © Margherita Spilluttini*

Figure C-6: REHAB Basel Centre for Spinal Cord and Brain Injuries. This two-story, 240,000-sq-ft (22,000-sq-m) rehabilitation hospital is organized around four distinctive plan-enclosed courtyards that provide places of respite, powerful wayfinding cues, and permit all occupied spaces to have operable windows (Chapter 11). *Credit: © Margherita Spilluttini*

Figure C-8: Meyer Children's Hospital. This replacement hospital, appended to a historic mansion, features vegetated roofs. Skylights and light tubes bring daylight deep into the interior. The building barely disrupts the landscape it appears to emerge from (Chapter 10). *Credit: Alessandro Ciampi*

Figure C-9: Meyer Children's Hospital. The central atrium brings daylight deep into the interior. Integrated photovoltaic panels in the atrium provide on-site electrical generation (Chapter 10). *Credit: Alessandro Ciampi*

Figure C-10: Rikshospitalet-Radiumhospitalet Medical Centre. Widely regarded as a model hospital, the central atrium spine separates the diagnostic and treatment areas from inpatient units. The atrium provides daylight to occupied workspaces, which line the upper floors (Chapter 11). *Credit: Rikshospitalet-Radiumhospitalet Medical Center*

Figure C-11: BC Cancer Agency Research Centre. The building massing separates laboratory and office blocks to achieve daylighting and ventilation objectives (Chapter 1). *Credit: © Nic Lehoux, Nic Lehoux Photography*

Figure C-12: BC Cancer Agency Research Centre. The 16-ft diameter circular "petri dish" windows extend through the labs and associated interstitial space, and integrate operable sections and shading devices (Chapter 1). *Credit: © Nic Lehoux, Nic Lehoux Photography*

Figure C-13: BC Cancer Agency Research Centre. Open, flexible research laboratories are bathed in daylight; researchers can manually open windows (Chapter 1). Credit: © Nic Lehoux, Nic Lehoux Photography

Figure C-14: Thunder Bay Regional Health Sciences Centre. Expressing the bioregional influence of the timber industry, the atrium of this 375-bed regional acute care hospital curves to follow the path of the sun (Chapter 11). *Credit: Peter Sellar, Klik Photography*

Figure C-15: Thunder Bay Regional Health Sciences Centre. The atrium space is 100 percent passively heated and cooled. The cafeteria occupies the ground floor (Chapter 11). *Credit: Peter Sellar, Klik Photography.*

Figure C-16: Carlo Fidani Peel Regional Cancer Centre and Ambulatory Centre at Credit Valley Hospital. The large-scale timber structure supports biophilic design principles. Triangular skylights at the intersection of the roof and structure bathe the large lobby in daylight (Chapter 11). *Credit: Peter Sellar, Klik Photography*

Figure C-18: University of Texas Health Science Center School of Nursing and Student Community Center. This pioneering sustainable building features natural materials, including regional cypress, and includes provisions for the future installation of photovoltaic panels on its roof (Chapter 3). *Credit: © Paul Hester*

Figure C-17: Bloorview Kids Rehab. A sloping ravine site with river views provides the inspiration for a series of sustainable design strategies in this seventy-five-bed rehabilitation facility (Chapter 9). *Credit: Tom Arban Photography*

Figure C-19: University of Texas Health Science Center School of Nursing and Student Community Center. The central atrium allows deep daylight penetration and organizes the plan (Chapter 3). *Credit: © Paul Hester*

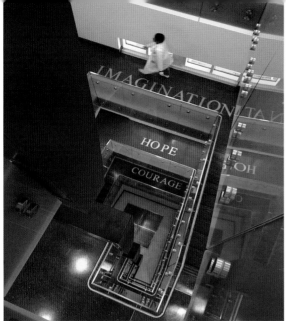

◀ **Figure C-20:** Winship Cancer Institute at Emory University. An open stair in this research and clinical building facilitates communication among patients and researchers while promoting active, walking behaviors (Chapter 9). *Credit: Gary Knight Photography*

▶ **Figure C-21:** University of Wisconsin Cancer Center. This building celebrates its connection to nature through a simple and honest use of natural materials that provide both finish and structure. The sloping roof and clerestory glazing bathe the building in daylight (Chapter 1). *Credit: James Steinkamp*

◀ **Figure C-22:** University of Wisconsin Cancer Center. The "connection to nature" experience extends throughout the treatment spaces, with infusion bays that cluster near windows, providing views of the changing seasons (Chapter 1). *Credit: James Steinkamp*

Figure C-23: Legacy Salmon Creek Hospital. The meditation room is prominently placed, and is a a focus of the rooftop therapeutic garden. Natural materials and strategically placed exterior glazing extend the experience deep into the room (Chapter 9). *Credit: © Eckert & Eckert*

Figure C-24: Legacy Salmon Creek Hospital. Patient units are organized with views of an adjoining nature preserve. The design team completed daylighting studies to determine glazing configurations in patient rooms (Chapter 9). *Credit: © Eckert & Eckert*

Figure C-25: Legacy Salmon Creek Hospital. This expansion campus includes an acute care hospital, ambulatory care buildings, and structured parking organized around a central entrance court and garden (Chapter 9). *Credit: © Eckert & Eckert*

Figure C-26: The Jay Monahan Center for Gastrointestinal Health. This modest renovation demonstrates the intersection between natural materials and daylight in urban settings. In a Pebble Project postoccupancy study of outpatient treatment settings, patients ranked this facility highest and believed their wait times were much shorter than they actually were (Chapter 10). *Credit: © Adrian Wilson*

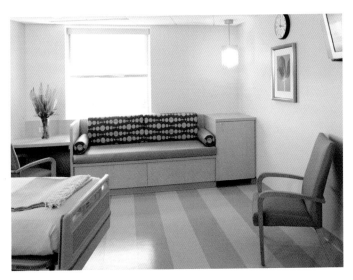

Figure C-27: The Sarkis and Siran Gabrellian Women's and Children's Pavilion at Hackensack University Medical Center. A strong focus on healthier building materials informs the patient room design. Formaldehyde-free substrate, rubber flooring, and low-emitting finishes contribute to improved indoor air quality (Chapter 10). *Credit: Courtesy of Hackensack University Medical Center*

Figure C-28: D'Amour Cancer Center. A central, daylit circulation spine delivers daylight to the building interior. Conference rooms on the third floor overlook the spine, and a glass floor allows daylight penetration to the lowest level (Chapter 9). *Credit: © Robert Benson*

► **Figure C-29:** Providence Newberg Medical Center. This LEED gold-certified, forty-bed acute care hospital is the first hospital to offset 100 percent of its electrical usage with Green-e certified power (Chapter 10). *Credit: © Eckert & Eckert*

► **Figure C-31:** Washington State Veterans Home. Residents engaged in the design process propelled the sustainable building strategies forward. Valuing the unique Sinclair Inlet microclimate, they pursued operable windows and passive cooling throughout the building (Chapter 10). *Credit: Matt Milios/NBBJ*

◄ **Figure C-32:** Washington State Veterans Home. The exterior solar-shading devices are operated by residents. Resident wings radiate to capture prevailing breezes (Chapter 10). *Credit: Michelle Litvin*

▲ **Figure C-30:** Providence Newberg Medical Center. The patient rooms are focused on views of the natural landscape (Chapter 10). *Credit: © Eckert & Eckert*

Figure C-33: Patrick H. Dollard Discovery Health Center. Dubbed a "barn with attitude," this LEED-certified ambulatory care building features bris-soleil, daylighting, and views (Chapter 11). *Credit: David Allee*

Figure C-34: Patrick H. Dollard Discovery Health Center. Improved occupant thermal comfort and substantial energy savings are derived from the radiant heating system linked to ground-source heat pumps. A related key feature is the elimination of exposed heating elements, an important consideration for the largely wheelchair-bound pediatric population (Chapter 11). *Credit: David Allee*

Figure C-35: Ryan Ranch Outpatient Campus. At Ryan Ranch, the 90,000-sq-ft (8,361-sq-m) program is separated into two freestanding buildings nestled into the heavily wooded site. The wood exterior includes integrated solar shading and clerestory glazing. A central utility plant frees the roof from equipment, permitting expressive shed roof forms (Chapter 11). *Credit: Tim Griffith*

Figure C-36: Ryan Ranch Outpatient Campus. The waiting areas celebrate the stunning natural views from the hilltop site (Chapter 11). *Credit: Sharon Risedorph*

Figure C-37: St. Mary's/Duluth Clinic First Street Building. On a site overlooking Lake Superior, this LEED gold certified cancer care building restored an industrial brownfield site to a healing place (Chapter 6). *Credit: Ed LaCasse*

Figure C-38: St. Mary's/Duluth Clinic First Street Building. The urban building emphasizes native landscaping and creative storm water management, ensuring that runoff is filtered before entering the lake (Chapter 7). *Credit: Blake Marvin*

Figure C-39: Legacy Salmon Creek Hospital Garden. The forecourt garden juxtaposes geometric and organic forms as it terraces from the entrance road beyond to the hospital entrance. Paving blocks and porous paving recharge groundwater; the water feature (left) introduces the sound of water in the court (Chapters 4 and 9). *Credit: Walker Macy*

▲ **Figure C-40:** Lacks Cancer Center at St. Mary's Garden. This rooftop garden offers panoramic views of downtown Grand Rapids, Michigan. Adjacent to an interior solarium, the rooftop program includes both interior and outdoor places of respite for staff and families (Chapter 9). *Credit: HKS Architects*

▶ **Figure C-41:** The Howard Ulfelder, Healing Garden at the Yawkey Center for Outpatient Care, Massachusetts General Hospital. This eighth-floor healing garden overlooks the Charles River and an adjacent historic prison cupola, which has been converted to hospital use. The use of a glass rail system expands the boundaries of the urban setting, and its height allows viewers to lose the middle landscape in favor of the distant river view (Chapter 4). *Credit: Ben Watkins, Halvorson Design Partnership, Inc.*

Figure C-42: Thunder Bay Regional Health Sciences Centre. Thunder Bay uses its landscape design to support on-site storm water retention and filtration. The ponds are designed as coldwater fish breeding areas to help repopulate the adjacent river with native species (Chapter 11). *Credit: Peter Sellar, Klik Photography*

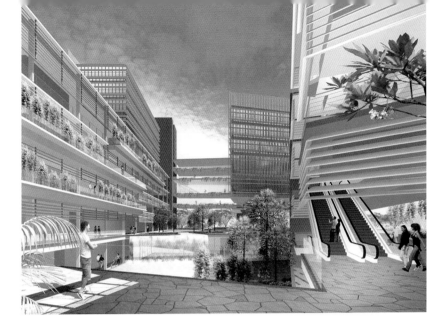

Figure C-43: Alexandra Hospital at Yishun. This 1.1 million-sq-ft (102,245-sq-m) project is being planned with an energy demand 50 percent below the standard for such a building in Singapore. Only 30 percent of the building will be air conditioned, with remaining areas dependent on passive strategies (Chapter 7). *Credit: Courtesy of Hillier Architecture*

Figure C-44: Alexandra Hospital at Yishun. The section demonstrates the courtyard section, deep in the building, achieving daylighting. A key feature of the program is a 100,000-sq-ft (10,000-sq-m) disaster-preparedness facility (Chapter 7). *Credit: Courtesy of Hillier Architecture*

Figure C-45: Spaulding Rehabilitation Hospital. Located on the former Charleston Navy Yard site, this replacement hospital project began with the rehabilitation of that urban brownfield. It maintains public boardwalk access to the waterfront, patient rooms, and physical rehab departments with river views, and integrates interior and outdoor experiences (Chapter 8). *Credit: Perkins + Will*

Figure C-46: Carl and Ruth Shapiro Cardiovascular Center at Brigham and Women's Hospital. This major expansion is part of a master plan that restores a formal axis green (to the left of this bridge) for the medical center. The project, anticipating LEED silver certification, incorporates energy and water reduction, healthier material selection, and a focus on improved indoor air quality (Chapter 8). *Credit: Cannon Design*

Figure C-47: The Centro de Reabilitação Infantil. The newest of the Sarah Network hospitals opened in 2002. Located in Rio de Janeiro, it treats children from infants through sixteen-year-olds. The facility provides generous daylight in its physical therapy areas, using prefabricated metal building elements designed to maximize daylight while minimizing solar heat gain, and allowing for natural ventilation (Chapter 11). *Credit: Photos courtesy of the Sarah Network and João Filgueiras Lima*

Figure C-48: Sarah Lago Norte Support Center for the Seriously Handicapped. This is the second Sarah hospital to be located in Brasília—on an expansive site. It exemplifies the network's core principles of humanistic design, scale, abundant daylight, and vegetation that guide the construction of all its therapeutic treatment areas (Chapter 11). *Credit: Photos courtesy of the Sarah Network and João Filgueiras Lima*

CHAPTER 11

Toward a New Language of Form

> The hospital as a machine for healing has become an anachronism. As a building type, the hospital remains a curious amalgam, with medical technology often pitted against humanist concerns.... There is little doubt that architecture can, and should, play a crucial role in humanizing the hospital. At first glance, this seems rather unlikely. How can architecture contribute to revolutionizing healthcare?
>
> — STEPHEN VERDERBER

INTRODUCTION

If "architecture is the clothing we put on our institutions" (Guenther 2006), what is the shape of the medical delivery system that determines the current fashion of healthcare buildings? What aspects of the medical delivery system have informed current design archetypes? What is emerging in medicine's relationship to ecology that will inform the delivery system and shape the healthcare system — and its buildings — in the future? Architectural historian Stephen Verderber postulated a near-term challenge to create a "sustainable health architecture" based on a new aesthetic — "one in which the dominant and depressing parking garage no longer symbolizes an unquestioning acceptance of the role of the automobile in our lives" (Verderber and Fine 2000). As public health and medical practitioners question the role of the automobile in chronic disease, possibilities for new hospital archetypes emerge.

This chapter explores the typology of architecture for health — both its historic evolution and ideas about its future. The case studies in this book demonstrate key differences between the typologies of international and North American healthcare buildings — differences based on fundamentally different responses to the relationship between the built environment and natural world. North American hospitals have become completely uninhabitable without massive inputs of electric lighting and mechanical ventilation — a permanent "life support" infrastructure — for the sake of efficiency and technological accommodation. Elsewhere in the developed world, building regulations requiring access to daylight and operable windows in occupied buildings have ensured that hospitals remain fundamentally "habitable" without these artificial inputs. Medical technology and processes are accommodated within the definition of a habitable building. The European hospital building becomes, to North Americans, a demonstration of "the road not taken."

The differences in building typology, which have profound implications for resource consumption, must be acknowledged, debated, and resolved. For much of the developing world, the creation of a medical service delivery structure is just beginning. The forms of those systems, and the buildings that partner in care delivery, have yet to be designed. The biggest challenge is also the biggest opportunity: how to evolve an appropriate healthcare building typology that reflects twenty-first-century realities of climate change and ecological stewardship and, by doing so, resists exporting a tried-and-true model reliant on an excessive ecological footprint. The first path encourages innovation and the entrepreneurial creativity to flourish, with the promise to bolster local economies and enhance human and ecosystem health. Continuing to enable the latter will further exacerbate economic and social inequities.

In North America, sustainable building principles are just beginning to influence building form; elsewhere in the world, these deeply grounded, centuries old principles remain clearly evident in contemporary building design. This chapter examines how the inherent qualities of habitability and sustainability influence healthcare building form. Architect Ray Pradinuk argues for a rediscovery of daylight as a determinant of building form through an examination of European precedents. Architects Tye Farrow and Sean Stanwick discuss the importance of bioregional design in developing a meaningful architecture for health. Finally, research architect and educator Stephen Kendall examines how the scale and complexity of twenty-first-century healthcare construction demands a reconsideration of design and construction processes and how reorganizing decision making can lead us to new building forms that respond more effectively to forces of change in the healthcare field. The building case studies demonstrate the emergence of a new "architecture for the body" reflecting the powerful confluence between a health culture, sustainability, and the sophisticated technology of twenty-first-century healthcare delivery. Understanding the precursors to this transformational moment is essential to effectively navigating the course ahead.

THE DEVELOPMENT OF THE MODERN HOSPITAL

The mega-hospital was conceived in strict opposition to nature.... The triumph of minimalism and high technology was everywhere to be found in the modern hospital: the lack of natural ventilation, the shrinkage of the window aperture and a diminution of the total amount of glazed area, adoption of the hermetically sealed building envelope, dependence on artificial lighting over natural daylight, the rise of the block hospital and its rejection of courtyards and other green spaces for use by patients, and a de-emphasis on overall patient amenity were but a few technologically driven modern developments (Verderber and Fine 2000).

The twentieth-century hospital, in its quest to accommodate rapid and chaotic changes in urbanization and suburbanization, medical care delivery, and medical and construction technologies, relegated a vision of healing, wholeness, and connection to nature to the past.

Improved understanding of bacteria eliminated the need to construct elaborate natural ventilation systems for asepsis; the development of artificial ventilation and air conditioning systems further diminished the perceived need for operable windows. In addition, the proliferation of innovative and expensive medical technology, including inventions like the X-ray machine, concentrated medical knowledge in the hospital and gave rise to diagnostic and treatment departments that required the movement of bedridden patients across larger campuses. Nineteenth-century pavilion hospitals necessitated long travel distances. Efficiency of patient movement to and from diagnostic departments demanded adjacency; travel distance analyses optimized deep floor plates and vertical arrangements.

By 1910, it was clear that the increasing specialization of medicine, coupled with real estate pressure, necessitated the development of a skyscraper or block hospital typology. By 1920, flexibility was consistently emphasized to allow for expansion and response to scientific discovery (i.e., medical technology). Educator and cultural critic Neil Postman (1992) once noted, "Technology was to be the weapon with which disease and illness would be vanquished." He also summarized two key revolutionary ideas promoted by the stethoscope, considered the first medical technology invention:

1. Medicine is about the disease, not the patient.
2. What the patient knows is untrustworthy; what the machine knows is reliable.

Coupled with the pervasive twentieth-century notion of progress, the provision and accommodation of ever more complex and challenging medical technology came to define the twentieth-century hospital.

Vertical plans became possible with the advent of improved vertical transportation systems. The 1930s' urban block-plan hospital rejected courtyards and green spaces used by patients as the building height precluded direct connection with the ground plane for large numbers of patients. With this, the hospital ceased once and for all to be concerned with celebrating the connection between nature and healing. In *Medicine and Culture,* journalist Lynn Payer (1988) summed it up: "The once seemingly limitless lands gave rise to a spirit that anything was possible if only the natural environment . . . could be conquered. Disease could also be conquered, but only by aggressively ferreting it out diagnostically and just as aggressively treating it, preferably by taking something out rather than adding something to increase the resistance."

THE END OF NATURE IN HOSPITALS

The beginning of suburban development provided infrastructure and land that facilitated a massive hospital construction boom. Architectural historian Cor Wagenaar (2006) recounts that this era of building "epitomized the promise of science, the victory of technology, and the prospect of a successful battle against old and new diseases. What better way to express the new era than by employing the International Style?" Situated in suburban and rural areas, these hospitals reintroduced a connection to nature through courtyards and solaria.

While this seemed initially positive, the earlier generation of hospitals—many of which included end-of-corridor solaria or terraces, courtyards, and other explicit program areas that brought patients and staff in contact with nature—were losing these humanistic features to the ever-expanding spatial requirements of medical technology. At the same time, larger and deeper horizontal floor plates were made possible as mechanical ventilation systems emerged in the 1950s and 1960s. Postman (1992) continues, "Like some well-known diseases, the problems that have arisen as a result of the reign of medical technology came slowly and were barely perceptible at the start. Through it all, the question of what was being undone had a low priority if it was asked at all."

At the same time, declining air and water quality in urban environments, increasing concerns about respiratory illnesses linked to pollen and dust, and the advent of more sophisticated air filtration systems for medical environments created the perception that outdoor air was, in fact, less healthy than the conditioned indoor air. The response was to separate the natural world, with its particulates, insects, and dirt, from the clean, aseptic hospital environment.

REINTRODUCING LIGHT AND AIR

A *New York Times* feature article on health in September 2004 exclaimed: "If there is one universal truth about hospitals, it is that they are drab, dismal places . . . not at all designed to soothe and heal" (Alvarez 2004). Why? In a talk to the American Institute of Architects (AIA) Academy on Architecture for Health barely one month later, architect Paul Hyett, principal at Ryder HKS in the UK, summarized the problem this way: "new technologies in modern architecture produced new building forms—high rise, deep plan, sealed environments—that are inappropriately low in thermal mass and too heavily dependent on artificial systems" (Hyett 2004).

Bellevue Hospital in New York, one of the first hospitals in the United States, demonstrates this transformation as it evolved on its Manhattan site overlooking the East River. In the late 1800s, McKim, Mead & White developed one of the last pavilion master plans for the site—a plan that was never fully realized. By the 1970s, a twenty-two-story block tower with approximately 1.5 acres per floor replaced all the acute care functions in a one-million-square-foot sealed high rise.

While this example may be extreme, the prevalent typology of North American hospitals, which places deep

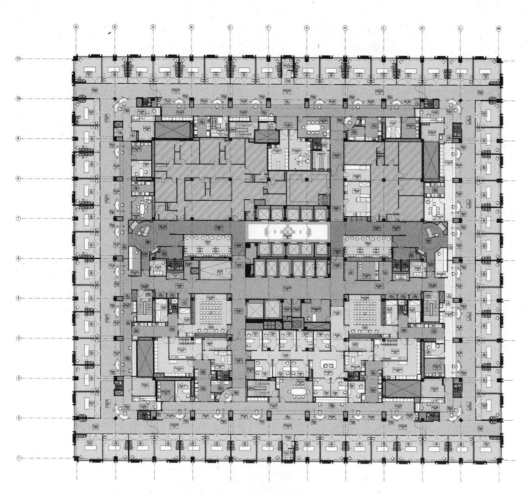

Figure 11-1: Bellevue Hospital in New York City, a high-rise, deep-plan, sealed building, is typical of block-plan buildings. In this plan of a renovated critical care floor, fifty-six patient rooms occupy the entire perimeter, except in four locations where the corridor extends to the exterior. All staff spaces and diagnostic and treatment support are located in the massive core. *Credit: Courtesy of Guenther 5 Architects*

Figure 11-2: The Bellevue Hospital pavilion-plan campus dates from 1916. The master plan and buildings, designed by McKim, Mead & White, were never fully realized; today, only two of the original pavilions remain. *Credit: Dattner Architects*

floor plate diagnostic and treatment (D&T) bases below towering inpatient units, has evolved into completely artificially lit and conditioned spaces. That *New York Times* writer contrasted the "drab, dismal" state of American healthcare with the New Rikshospitalet-Radiumhospitalet Medical Centre (below) in Oslo, of which architect Tony Monk (2004) said, "The philosophy that permeates throughout the scheme is to create an environment for people, like a living beautiful town where the different functional activities fuse together and every opportunity is exploited to stimulate interesting spatial experiences."

Owner: University of Oslo/Norwegian Statsbygg (Directorate of Public Construction and Property)
Design team: Medplan Arkitekter Norway
Building type: New construction
Size: 2,072,000 sq ft (192,500 sq m)
Design energy intensity: 41 kWh/sq ft (441 kWh/sq m)
Program description: 585-bed major trauma hospital specializing in cardiac surgery and transplants that treats about 190,000 patients per year and employs 4,000. Since construction, the hospital organization has merged with Radiumhospitalet.
Completion date: 2001

Rikshospitalet-Radiumhospitalet Medical Centre

Oslo, Norway

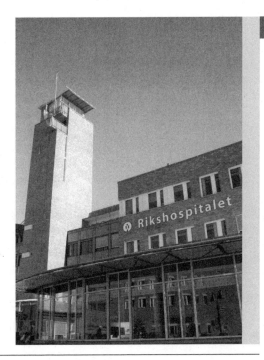

Figure 11-3: Rikshospitalet-Radiumhospitalet Medical Centre. *Credit: Rikshospitalet-Radiumhospitalet Medical Centre*

Located on a landscaped suburban site with views of the city of Oslo and the nearby fjord, the New Rikshospitalet was heralded by the press as a model of new hospital design upon its opening. The hospital appears low rise but contains as many as seven levels in some areas; it is built into the bowl-shaped site to keep the hospital's profile at a more human scale.

Figure 11-4: The four-story interior street bisects the hospital, with diagnostic and treatment blocks to the left and inpatient units to the right. Glass bridges on each floor allow patients to traverse the atrium when moving between program components. The offsets in the axis create framed events along the concourse. *Credit: Rikshospitalet-Radiumhospitalet Medical Centre*

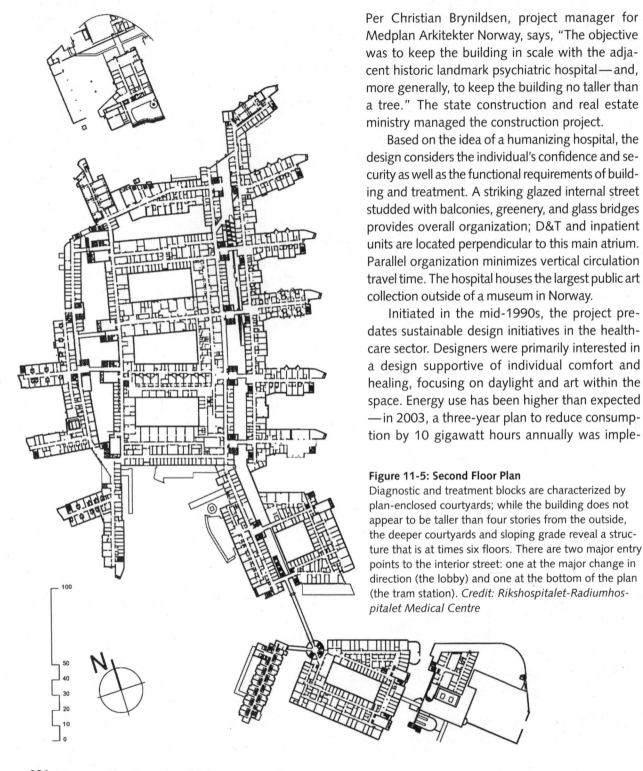

100

50
40
30
20
10
0

N

Per Christian Brynildsen, project manager for Medplan Arkitekter Norway, says, "The objective was to keep the building in scale with the adjacent historic landmark psychiatric hospital — and, more generally, to keep the building no taller than a tree." The state construction and real estate ministry managed the construction project.

Based on the idea of a humanizing hospital, the design considers the individual's confidence and security as well as the functional requirements of building and treatment. A striking glazed internal street studded with balconies, greenery, and glass bridges provides overall organization; D&T and inpatient units are located perpendicular to this main atrium. Parallel organization minimizes vertical circulation travel time. The hospital houses the largest public art collection outside of a museum in Norway.

Initiated in the mid-1990s, the project predates sustainable design initiatives in the healthcare sector. Designers were primarily interested in a design supportive of individual comfort and healing, focusing on daylight and art within the space. Energy use has been higher than expected — in 2003, a three-year plan to reduce consumption by 10 gigawatt hours annually was imple-

Figure 11-5: Second Floor Plan
Diagnostic and treatment blocks are characterized by plan-enclosed courtyards; while the building does not appear to be taller than four stories from the outside, the deeper courtyards and sloping grade reveal a structure that is at times six floors. There are two major entry points to the interior street: one at the major change in direction (the lobby) and one at the bottom of the plan (the tram station). *Credit: Rikshospitalet-Radiumhospitalet Medical Centre*

mented. While the plan has successfully reduced building thermal energy consumption, new energy-intensive surgical equipment keeps actual total energy consumption essentially static. The hospital treats almost twice the number of patients assumed in the hospital's design and those figures are still rising; this also accounts for higher than expected energy use.

KEY BUILDING PERFORMANCE STRATEGIES

Site
- The hospital is designed with narrow "fingers" or wings, which jut out from a core building, improving access to daylight and fresh air
- Structured parking preserves views from all occupied areas
- Dedicated public transportation provides links from downtown

Energy
- Glass areas limited (aside from glazed "main street") to reduce heat loss
- Increased building insulation levels (7.87 in) (20 cm)

Environmental Quality
- Norwegian code requires daylighting in all areas where work is performed for four or more hours per day, so even basement work areas of the facility are daylit
- Operable windows throughout, including clinical laboratories and patient rooms
- Displacement ventilation in patient rooms

Sources: Medplan Architekter Norway; Brynildsen (2006); Rikshospitalet-Radiumhospitalet Medical Centre

---

Monk captures a fundamental shift in healthcare-building design: the reemergence of buildings designed with a focus on people rather than technology. In describing the Rikshospitalet, Knut Bergsland (2005), of SINTEF Health Research, straightforwardly describes "a building designed by human beings for human beings." A new market focus on "the experience," as articulated in *The Experience Economy* (1999), describes an economy where market leaders in all sectors of the economy "stage experience" as they deliver services. But, in describing healthcare, business writers Pine and Gilmore (1999) note that "sick patients want more than pharmaceutical goods, medical services or even a hospital 'experience' — they want to be well." This notion of transforming people from illness to wellness is embedded in the core ideology of healthcare's approach to sustainability and has been articulated throughout the earlier chapters of this book.

As hospitals connect their buildings and operation with a transformation to health-based, ecological thinking, they will enter what Pine and Gilmore describe as the ultimate form of goods and services delivery. It should come as no surprise that these leaders will gain market share, economic success, and community stature.

In his essay "Doubling Daylight," architect Ray Pradinuk proposes a new typology for healthcare that restores the relationship between the built environment and the natural world, transforming the experience of the hospital building for its occupants and surrounding community in the process. Drawing on the extensive research linking daylight and views to improved patient outcomes and productivity, as well as new European hospitals (some of which are featured as case studies throughout this book), Pradinuk forcefully argues for a fundamental change in healthcare culture and architecture.

Doubling Daylight

Ray Pradinuk, MBAIC

CURRENT DAYLIGHTING LEVELS AND THE EVIDENCE FOR MORE

At the Healthcare Design Conference in 2003, Boston surgeon and author Dr. Richard Selzer marveled during his keynote address at the selfless commitment of a nurse who had worked her entire career in a windowless post-op recovery area without ever treating a conscious patient. His single plea to the assembled design professionals was for daylight and views for staff, in the operating room and beyond. Many years ago, in "An Absence of Windows," an essay in Confessions of a Knife, Selzer (1979) wrote, "I have spent too much time in these windowless rooms. Some part of me would avoid them if I could."

Healthcare architects have been talking to each other at conferences about designing healing environments filled with daylight since about the time that Richard Selzer first wrote those words, yet a "window that opens" remains the most asked for, least delivered characteristic of the caregiver work environment in North American hospitals. Returning from the conference, the next project proposal extols the benefits of daylighting as the foundation of a healing environment, but somehow, inevitably, not far into the schematic design process, the successful design team is drawn back into the very same deep floor plates they'll criticize in their next proposal.

North American hospital diagnostic and treatment (D&T) blocks have devolved to accept the lowest percentage of daylit space of any densely and regularly inhabited building type. Massive D&T floor plates with as little as 15 percent of their area within 15 feet of the perimeter are not uncommon. Because windows are code required for inpatient rooms, the percentage of daylit space on the inpatient unit is higher, but it is often only the patient rooms that have windows. Staffers in North American hospitals continue to spend the majority of their workdays in artificially lit spaces, and many do not experience daylight for hours, or in midwinter, even days at a time. While the negative impact on the well-being of patients in the outpatient or diagnostic and treatment areas of a new hospital may not extend beyond their relatively short visit, evidence suggests the effects on the staff working in those many small rooms all day long, day after day, are detrimental.

The effect of daylight on patient outcomes is becoming more widely known, primarily through the evidence-based research compiled by the Center for Health Design. Researchers Ulrich and Zimring (2004) reference several strong studies linking daylight to reductions in depression, agitation, and drug use. They report on an Italian research group's finding that patients with unipolar and bipolar disorder randomly assigned to eastern rooms exposed to direct sunlight in the morning had a mean 3.67-day shorter hospital stay than patients in west-facing rooms (Benedetti et al. 2001). Seemingly, it not only matters that you get your dose of sunlight, it matters when in the day you get it.

Possibly because there are so few daylit hospital staff work environments in North America to study, there is correspondingly less research here linking daylighting to staff well-being and performance. One study concluded that nurses in Alaska had twice the errors in the darker months (Ulrich and Zimring 2004); but just how serious is the medical error problem? One Canadian study, The Canadian Adverse Events Study (2004), reported that 7.5 percent of admitted patients experienced an adverse event (AE), and 1.5 percent of admitted patients died of an adverse event (equal to 24,000 Canadian in-hospital patient deaths annually) (Baker et al. 2004). While almost 50 percent of adverse events are nosocomial infections, most of the rest result from medical error; the study also found that 40 percent of all adverse events were preventable. Time magazine recently quoted a physician, compelled to stand as a sentinel for his wife during her hospitalization, despairing that "no day passed—not one— without a medication error" (Gibbs and Bower 2006).

The absence of natural light in the nursing station, report room, office, treatment room, and operating theater must be considered a likely contributor to medical error. Heschong Mahone Group's famous study of 21,000 students in school districts throughout California, Washington, and Colorado found a 20 percent and 26 percent difference in math and reading test score results, respectively, between students in the worst and best lit classrooms. As more evidence linking daylight deprivation to medical error and productivity loss comes in, it seems likely that the performance of caregivers in windowless workplaces will be found to be not unlike that of students in windowless classrooms: increasing daylight in staff spaces will profoundly benefit patients. "[E]xperts suggest that the greatest gains in improving patient safety will come from modifying the work environment [emphasis added] of health care professionals, creating better defenses for averting [adverse events,] and mitigating their effects" (Baker et al. 2004). Dr. Robert Reid, one of the study's authors, commented on the day of its release: "We need a cultural change in healthcare. It's not individuals; it's underlying systems. It's not bad apples; it's bad barrels." (Reid 2004).

The gathering evidence identifying the impact of daylighting—or its absence—on medical outcomes and patient well-being, combined with general research on daylighting's effect on knowledge-worker productivity, must even now be considered sufficient to warrant a precautionary approach in setting daylighting requirements for new healthcare projects. It's time to significantly increase daylighting in North American healthcare facilities.

WHY ARE HOSPITALS SO LIGHT DEPRIVED?
When and why did daylight lose significance as a hospital form generator? Daylight has been undervalued in North America since the advent of air-conditioning, with the solid, 56,000-square-foot, massive footprint of New York's Bellevue Hospital (Figures 11-1 and 11-2) representing "the triumph of conditioned compact utility over fresh air and daylit habitability in health care facility design" (Verderber and Fine 2000).

With daylight expectations so low for so long, programming and design teams readily succumb to forces compacting the D&T plan. Urban hospitals overprogram confined sites and are compelled to retain existing buildings during the construction of their replacements. On suburban sites, clinicians all want to be on the main floor and planners want the rest of the site for surface parking. In cities and suburbs, and even when site area is virtually unlimited, big, deep-plan D&T blocks predominate. On inpatient units, the ubiquitous racetrack layout continues to deprive caregivers of daylight at their workstation. Regardless of their shape—square, rectangular, or triangular—patient rooms monopolize the daylit perimeter, leaving staff corralled in the middle with the utility and equipment rooms.

CATALYSTS TOWARD DAYLIGHT
Of late, the deep-plan D&T has been exposed to renewed criticism by North American healthcare architects encouraged by mounting evidence from clinicians' research, the sustainable design movement's interest in daylight, and by a growing awareness of the substantially higher quantity of daylighting continually achieved by European hospitals. Of these, it may ultimately be close scrutiny of buildings in Europe—if not forays by European architects into the healthcare design sector here—that will most influence the hospital configuration paradigm in North America.

Among the most compelling of the newest generation of European hospitals are Oslo's New Rikshospitalet University Hospital by Medplan Arkitekter (page 328), and José Rafael Moneo's Hospital Materno Infantil de Madrid (Mother's and Children's Hospital of Madrid) in Spain (page 332). Rikshospitalet combines a three-courtyard D&T block, a village street fully lit by skylight, and L-shaped inpatient units on a beautiful forest-edged site to achieve 45 percent D&T daylighting (defined by the Green Guide for Health Care as the percentage of space within 15 feet of a perimeter wall) and direct daylight for 95 percent of staff- and patient-occupied spaces on inpatient units. On a tight urban site in central Madrid, Moneo composed an elegant rectangular block around four small and four even smaller rectangular courtyards to achieve 55 percent daylighting overall. Each of the eight courtyards illuminates corridors on two sides and patient care and staff workspaces on two sides. Bassinets are wheeled to nursery and birthing room windows and displayed to families gathered along the corridor windows across the courtyards. We are indeed phototropic!

THE COSTS AND BENEFITS OF DAYLIGHTING
Increasing daylighting in any building increases capital costs. Doubling the daylit area in the D&T and providing daylight for virtually all staff workstations on the inpatient unit will add roughly C$16 per square foot, or 4 percent, to the cost of constructing an acute care hos-

Figures 11-6 and 11-7: In the Mother's and Children's Hospital of Madrid, the plan-enclosed courtyards facilitate a sense of community. Newborns are wheeled to the courtyard windows for viewing; families congregating in the daylit circulation zone have both privacy and connection to the larger community. *Credit: Ray Pradinuk*

pital for the increased perimeter wall and window alone. Additional costs might include courtyard landscaping, a glazed roof, and atria-scaled artwork. Since the courtyards within a daylit D&T are typically 20 percent of its gross floor area, the overall floor plate will increase, or on confined sites, the building will expand vertically to include an additional floor's worth of stairs and elevator and service shafts. The energy saved by daylighting and responsive artificial lighting controls will make a significant contribution toward reducing overall energy consumption, but even where energy costs are highest, they can only contribute a fraction to the return required for a ten-year payback on an investment in more perimeter wall and window. The only opportunity to recoup the additional capital investment in daylighting, save a relatively small contribution from the recruitment budget, arises from a combination of cost avoidances and productivity gains in the delivery of medical care — which can be substantial.

On a typical inpatient unit with 600 square feet per bed, the cost of the error portion of those adverse events equates to C$40 per square foot per year, so preventing 40 percent of those errors would avoid C$16 per square foot per year in adverse event treatment costs: about the same as the capital cost of providing every caregiver workstation with a window.

What daylighting's contribution might be to that optimal error reduction is currently anybody's guess.

Error reduction is perhaps the most compelling of the likely care-delivery benefits of daylighting, but a mere 2 percent productivity increase in just the additional daylit area of a healthcare facility would by itself pay for the wall and window in less than three years. Additional daylighting would allow hospital staff to provide better treatment to patients while reducing the costs and patient days associated with treating medical error. It would also enhance caregiver recruitment and retention.

Once a line appears in healthcare construction accounting practice for care-delivery benefits, additional daylight will be viewed as self-financing. Eventually, we, too, may come to design for daylight without having to think much about it, as is the case now in Scan-

MEASURABILITY

While the benefits of daylight on caregiver attentiveness and productivity may be difficult to measure in the field, it is unimaginable that the most desired characteristic of their work environment would not impact positively on caregiver performance.

dinavia. As Knut Bergsland put it when speaking about the extraordinary daylighting of Oslo's Rikshospitalet, "It's just the way we do it—no cost/benefit required" (Bergsland 2004).

CONFIGURING FOR DAYLIGHT

The Rikshospitalet uses three large plan-enclosed courtyards to daylight its D&T areas. The plan-enclosed courtyard has been the strategy of choice in European cities to achieve both density and daylight for centuries. Plan-enclosed courtyards allow a simple overall D&T plan shape to be retained; allow departments to ebb and flow around their corners, front and back; and allow treatment and service spaces to be shared at the back-of-house of departments. A matrix of sixty-foot wings accommodate most caregiver work paths, adding a minimal amount of travel for caregivers (Fig. 11-8. left). But plan-enclosed courtyards provide contained views, the antithesis of the North American longing for vistas and outward projections. Culturally, North Americans are unfamiliar with courtyard typologies and are predisposed to criticize the most effective strategy for increasing D&T daylight as too costly to build and maintain and certain to reduce patient care time because of increased caregiver travel.

A second D&T daylight configuration strategy articulates the D&T footprint (Fig. 11-8, center). However, this strategy is surprisingly ineffective in increasing daylight levels. While contained courtyard views are avoided, the articulated plan can't come close to providing the access to daylight that plan-enclosed courtyards can provide without seriously impacting the functionality of the plan. The articulated plan replicates the highly inflexible pavilion plans of the early twentieth century that trapped departments up dead-end corridors, giving them nowhere to grow but the front-of-house and leaving no possibility of any back-door sharing of support and treatment spaces. Universally employed in Europe for that specific purpose, clearly, the plan-enclosed courtyard is the only viable means of significantly increasing D&T daylighting.

For inpatient units, the only strategy to achieve daylight in all staff workplaces is by revisiting the double-loaded corridor plan that the racetrack unit replaced. As the evidence from clinicians suggests, by distributing caregiver workstations and support rooms within single-room-double-loaded corridor pods, more patients will be in view as they stir to rise from their beds, so fewer will be untended and at risk of falling. With supplies at hand and fewer unnecessary trips, nurse travel times of 30 percent will drop toward 20 percent. More patient

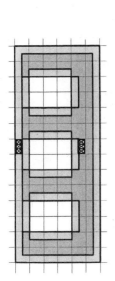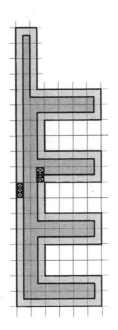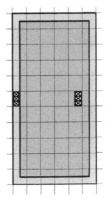

Figure 11-8: All three diagnostic and treatment (D&T) plans are 59,400 sq ft (5,518 sq m). Less than one-quarter (24.2 percent) of the deep-plan D&T's area (right) is within 15 feet of its perimeter. Just over half (51.5 percent) of both narrow-plan D&Ts are daylit spaces, but only the plan-enclosed courtyard (left) retains operational efficiency and flexibility. *Credit: Stantec Architecture*

bed heads will be seen with each nurse step. Families will have more opportunities to meet and support each other. It will be found, coincidently, that these reminted, daylit L- and T-shaped nursing units will join together rather well around courtyards, either off to the side of or above D&Ts.

QUALITIES OF LIGHT
Once hospital construction budgets have been adapted to accommodate increased daylighting, qualitative de-

sign issues will need to be addressed, particularly those dealing with working and convalescing near courtyards. Looking out a courtyard window, the building that is enclosing the viewer is seen, so the architecture—not just the interior of the hospital—is present in the patient experience, putting Heidegger's "critical lack of nearness" (Frampton 1999) in modern architecture back on the healthcare architecture agenda. While some walls, materially, merit close viewing more than others, more than details are at issue. The simultaneity

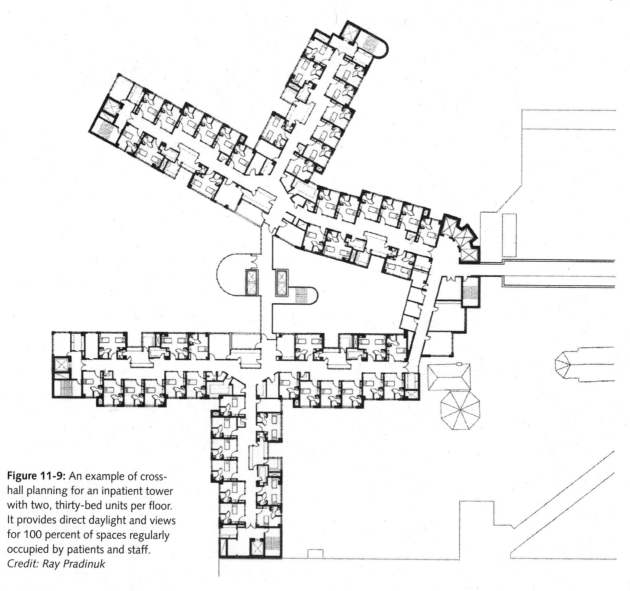

Figure 11-9: An example of crosshall planning for an inpatient tower with two, thirty-bed units per floor. It provides direct daylight and views for 100 percent of spaces regularly occupied by patients and staff.
Credit: Ray Pradinuk

Figure 11-10: At Rikshospitalet-Radiumhospitalet Medical Centre, the quality of the interior street recalls a townscape; the scale, window patterns, and color subtly recall the urban fabric of Oslo, Norway. *Credit: Rikshospitalet-Radiumhospitalet Medical Centre*

of being sheltered while seeing the building providing that shelter magnifies the psychological and social dimensions of dwelling: the room is situated in the building; its occupant is situated in the building community; and the hidden labyrinth of corridors and stairs that choreographs the connection among its members is imagined. The kind of building patients see will inform their perception of the character of its community.

Some walls, in the way that they're windowed, balance the provision of privacy with a connection to world and thereby express sheltering more appreciably than others. The sounds within courtyards are proprietary to the hospital community. For patients, footsteps crossing the courtyard in the morning or a quiet conversation overheard are somehow related, more or less directly, to their care. This reification of the community of care for patients within the hospital building must in itself be comforting, reassuring. (Of course, for patients to hear morning sounds at the courtyard floor, their windows have to be left open overnight.)

In the design of these courtyard hospitals, would use influence character? Could a certain courtyard be perfect for staff offices and lounges, for example—maybe a greenhouse courtyard with meeting balconies? Could tree branches provide just the right filtering of views between examination rooms in another? Will orientation influence material if light will bounce across from walls that see the sun? How will soundless air handling be achieved? How will the landscape be maintained and the wildlife accommodated? A new architecture of the healthcare courtyard with building systems to match awaits: designers might pin a reproduction of van Gogh's famous courtyard landscape painting, the Hospital at Arles, *over the drawing table for inspiration.*

Hospital Materno Infantil de Madrid in Spain and the REHAB Basel in Switzerland (both below) are powerful examples of the design potential of an enclosed courtyard typology. At REHAB Basel, the Swiss architectural firm Herzog & de Meuron achieved a variety of spatial experiences by using five courtyards varying in scale, materiality, and shape throughout the 100,000-square-foot (9,300-square-meter) floor plate. Both buildings fundamentally transform the healthcare experience, creating spatial variety and a sense of private community for people at a moment of vulnerability.

Mother's and Children's Hospital of Madrid (Hospital Materno Infantil de Madrid)

Madrid,
Spain

Figure 11-11: Hospital Materno Infantil de Madrid (Mother's and Children's Hospital of Madrid). *Credit: Ray Pradinuk*

Owner: Comunidad de Madrid (City Government of Madrid)
Design team: ARCHITECTS: José Rafael Moneo and José Maria de la Mata
Type: New construction on existing hospital site
Size: 539,412 sq ft (50,113 sq m)
Program description: 326-bed, nine-story hospital specializing in obstetrics, gynecology, and pediatrics
Completion date: 2003

This replacement for Madrid's well-known maternity hospital combines under one roof the Instituto Provincial de Obstetricia y Ginecología (known as Maternidad de O'Donnell after the street where it was located) and Hospital Infantil. The collocated facilities have separate entrances but share some administrative and functional areas. The metal and glass facade creates a striking street presence while providing ample daylight to waiting areas arranged around the perimeter of the floor plan. Wards, located in deeper plan areas to avoid street noise, are daylit by eight internal courtyards. These courtyards also serve to divide the two hospitals' functions while providing views to the outdoors.

The hospital was designed with the stated aim of reducing patient length of stay through more comfortable accommodations. The design of the maternity wards, in particular, was driven by concern for domestic-style patient privacy. Maternity areas are designed to foster closeness between mother and child; one private room provides birth and recovery accommodations for both mother and child, who remain together during their stay. Patient rooms combat institutional aesthetics with wooden window frames and Mallorcan shutters.

Source: Maternity and Children's Hospital of Madrid

Figure 11-12: A series of plan-enclosed courtyards provide opportunities for daylight and ventilation. Courtyards are open to circulation on two sides and provide windows in program space on two sides. *Credit: Ray Pradinuk*

Figure 11-13: One plan-enclosed courtyard becomes a skylit atrium at the second floor. *Credit: Ray Pradinuk*

Figure 11-14: REHAB Basel Centre for Spinal Cord and Brain Injuries. *Credit: © Margherita Spiluttini*

REHAB Basel Centre for Spinal Cord and Brain Injuries (Zentrum für Querschnitt-gelähmte und Hirnverletzte)

Basel, Switzerland

Owner: REHAB Basel AG (a private nonprofit organization)

Design team:

ARCHITECT: Herzog & de Meuron

CONSTRUCTION MANAGER: Hardegger Planung & Projektmanagement

Type: New rehabilitation hospital

Size: 246,386 sq ft (22,890 sq m)

Program description: 92-bed private inpatient and outpatient spinal cord and brain injury rehabilitation clinic on a 6-acre (2.4-ha) site that includes 450-sq-ft (41.8-sq-m) double and single patient rooms, a day clinic, exam and therapy rooms, a gym and swimming pool, and overnight accommodations for visitors

Completion date: 2002

Located in a suburban Basel neighborhood, the privately run REHAB Basel blends into the style of the neighborhood and puts a premium on patient privacy. The clinic is low rise and organized with all beds on one floor to make it easier for patients in wheelchairs to get around, and elevators connect all three stories. As a place where patients learn how to cope with life changes after a severe injury, the clinic functions as a treatment facility while fulfilling patients' diverse needs as a home.

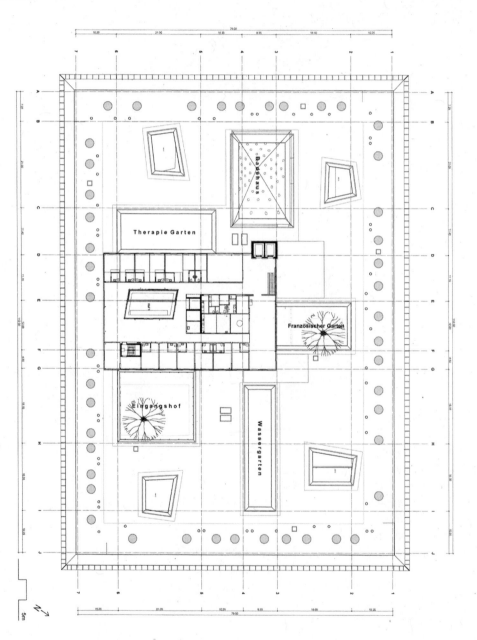

Figure 11-15: Roof Plan.
The 100,000 sq ft (3,048 sq m) vegetated roof is visible from the third-floor penthouse spaces; plan-enclosed courtyards penetrate the large floor plate. The circles on the roof plan are the spherical patient room skylights (see cover photo).
Credit: © Herzog & de Meuron

Because patients may stay for as long as eighteen months, the building was organized like a small town, connecting indoors and outdoors with separations between residential/private and social/public spaces. Daylight permeates the building. Space is ample and flexible, with many nondedicated areas where patients can spend free time, linger between treatment sessions, or meet family and friends. Rather than declare a green agenda, the architects emphasized the noninstitutional ambiance created by materials in an untreated state. To meet the Swiss energy code's high standards, the building capitalizes on energy savings achieved through passive solar techniques and natural ventilation.

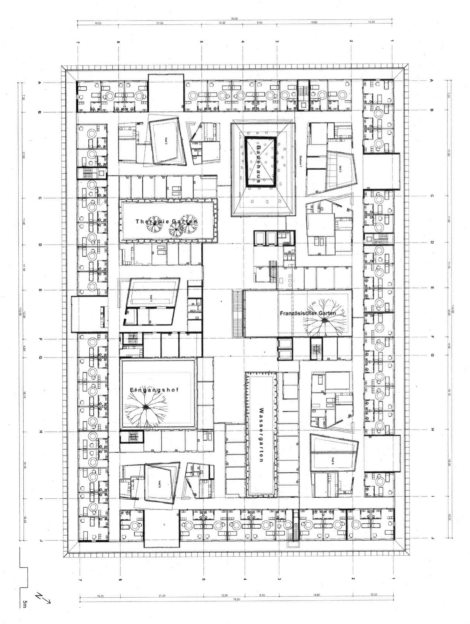

Figure 11-16: Second-Floor Plan
The patient rooms are arranged around the building perimeter, with ancillary and staff functions clustered around the plan-enclosed courtyards. *Credit: © Herzog & de Meuron*

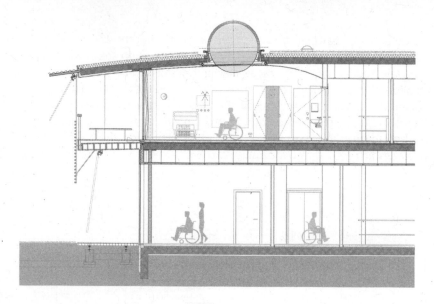

Figure 11-17: The building section illustrates the continuous wood deck that acts as a solar shading device for the building perimeter. Each patient room is outfitted with a transparent plastic sphere, 6.5 feet (2 meters) in diameter, that eliminates the need for artificial lighting during daylight hours. *Credit:* © *Herzog & de Meuron*

KEY BUILDING PERFORMANCE STRATEGIES

Site
- Kitchen and ornamental gardens on-site
- Expansive views of countryside and cityscape from rooftop painting workshop and library
- 262-foot (80-meter) wheelchair training course and playing field
- Intensive green roof, viewable from third-story conversation areas, filters rainwater

Energy
- Ample daylighting makes daytime artificial light in patient rooms unnecessary
- Green roof functions as insulation
- User-controlled passive ventilation through large, operable windows and sliding doors

Materials
- Untreated oak, larch, ironwood, and waxed pine used for exterior cladding, *brise-soleils,* and interior wall and ceiling paneling
- Sealed oak floors

Environmental Quality
- Transparent plastic spherical skylights measuring 6.5 feet (2 meters) in diameter embedded in patient room ceilings minimize the need for artificial light during daylight hours (see this book's cover photo)
- Patient rooms located around the perimeter of the second story open to wood decks via sliding glass doors; decks are wide enough to accommodate rolling beds
- Five courtyards within the orthogonal plan correspond to various therapy areas, bring daylight to all parts of the building, and contribute to wayfinding with identifiable plantings and water features
- Privacy and shade provided by oak *brise-soleils* wrapping building, supplemented by textile window shades

Sources: Herzog & de Meuron; Stephens 2005

Palomar Medical Center West (still in the formative stages of design) has developed a nature-responsive approach by integrating vertically stacked, discrete outdoor places of respite for patients and staff on inpatient units. Placing staff space on the perimeter in inpatients units, separating the D&T base from the inpatient towers, and moving ambulatory care support functions into a standalone structure all demonstrate a fundamental shift in the typology of healthcare buildings. Green roofs temper the view of the large D&T footprint from the patient rooms above, and plan-enclosed courtyards penetrate the two-story block. Other related examples of this shift in typology include Spaulding Rehabilitation Hospital in Boston (page 208) and Metro Health Hospital in Grand Rapids, Michigan (page 162).

Palomar Medical Center West

Escondido, California

Figure 11-18: Palomar Medical Center West. *Credit: Anshen + Allen Architects for Palomar Pomerado Health: An Association of CO Architects and Anshen + Allen*

Owner: Palomar Pomerado Health
Design Team: Anshen + Allen Architects for Palomar Pomerado Health: An Association of CO Architects and Anshen + Allen
Building type: Replacement acute care hospital on greenfield site
Size: 750,000 sq ft (69,700 sq m)
Program description: Located in San Diego County, the 360-bed tertiary-care facility includes emergency department services (56 positions), state-of-the-art cardiac, oncology, 192 acuity adaptable beds, and 186 general medical/surgical beds; a 96-bed Women and Children's Pavilion including inpatient and outpatient women's services, inpatient pediatrics, and a level-two neonatal intensive care unit are planned for a separate building on the same campus
Completion date: 2011
Recognition: *Green Guide for Health Care* pilot

Figure 11-19: Solar shading devices become a prominent architectural design feature in the Southern California climate. This is one of a series of studies for patient-room solar shading. *Credit: Anshen + Allen Architects for Palomar Pomerado Health: An Association of CO Architects and Anshen + Allen*

Underpinning the medical center's design philosophy is the concept of a garden hospital set within a campus framework. Site planning, landscaping, noninstitutional architectural expression, and materials selection have all been strongly influenced by that concept. The project's design narratives reflect a commitment to environmental stewardship: Frances Moore, CO Architects, describes the drivers for energy demand reduction, "Most of the energy used in buildings comes from fossil fuels, the burning of which contributes to acid rain, global warming, and air pollution. Reducing energy use and using clean fuels helps mitigate these effects. Palomar Medical Center West's energy-efficiency measures include a robust energy management system, capturing

Figure 11-20: One key design concept is the integration of nature through planting that extends vertically on a series of inpatient unit terraces. Each inpatient unit includes discrete landscaped exterior lounge and terrace areas for both patients and staff. *Credit: Anshen + Allen Architects for Palomar Pomerado Health: An Association of CO Architects and Anshen + Allen*

waste heat for reuse, efficient lighting strategies, daylight controls, variable air volume air handling, efficient equipment, and building commissioning."

KEY BUILDING PERFORMANCE STRATEGIES

Site
- Green roof systems on D&T block and administrative wings assist in storm water management strategies and reduce heat-gain and heat-island impacts
- Plan-enclosed courtyards provide outdoor places of respite for the emergency department, surgery, and radiology

Water
- Native, drought-tolerant landscaping and connection to municipal reclaimed-water system; no potable water used for landscaping
- Low-flow and waterless plumbing fixtures

Energy
- North–south building orientation minimizes heat gain
- Solar-shading devices reduce energy demand
- Robust energy-management system, heat recovery, efficient lighting strategies, daylight controls, high-efficiency equipment, and building commissioning

Source: CO Architects

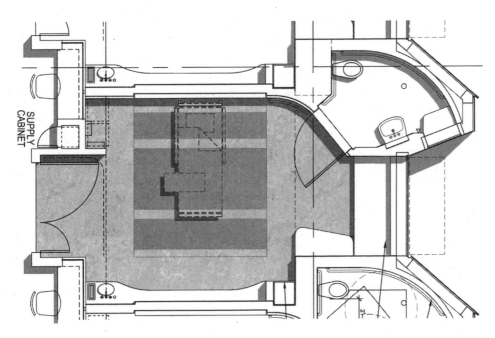

SUPPLY CABINET

Figure 11-21: The same-handed patient room design optimizes the view from the bed and uses the articulation of the facade as a component of the solar shading design. *Credit: Anshen + Allen Architects for Palomar Pomerado Health: An Association of CO Architects and Anshen + Allen*

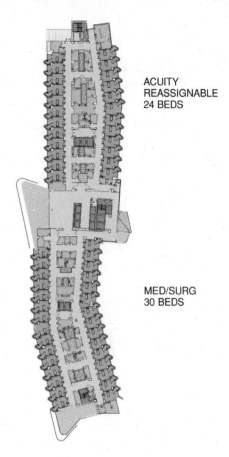

ACUITY
REASSIGNABLE
24 BEDS

MED/SURG
30 BEDS

Figure 11-22: Typical inpatient floors feature central exterior terrace spaces and lounges linking the north and south entry sequences. South-facing spaces (to the left) are for visitors and patients; north-facing spaces (to the right), for staff. *Credit: Anshen + Allen Architects for Palomar Pomerado Health: An Association of CO Architects and Anshen + Allen*

BIOREGIONALISM

Increasingly, global markets for goods and services homogenize hospital design both nationally and internationally. Architectural historian Cor Wagenaar characterized the adoption of the International Style in healthcare design as expressing progress and modernity. Over the last 30 years, healthcare buildings have adopted a range of typological models — the medical mall, hospitality, and the corporate headquarters. Healthcare has not evolved a unique typology in re-

sponse to cultural or philosophical notions of health, community history, or meaning. In contrast, sustainable design challenges the standardization of building typology by recognizing:

- *Bioregional differences in climate:* Temperature, wind, and moisture require unique, climate-responsive architecture.
- *Indigenous materials:* Using locally and regionally sourced materials supports distinctive architectural typologies, strengthens local economies, and safeguards the environment from the burdens of long-distance transport.
- *Buildings connect people to place:* By constructing buildings using local resources, people recognize the familiar and are more keenly aware of place.
- *Biophilic response is universal and operative in times of stress:* The unique function of hospital buildings — occupied in times of impaired health and stress — demands a typology that recognizes the spiritual and psychological dimensions of the encounter.

Architects Tye Farrow and Sean Stanwick, in their essay "Humanism in the Art of Sustainable Healing," argue that healthcare buildings need to be synchronized with their environment and grow from their communities, celebrating the local culture and becoming enmeshed in the local economy. The hospitals in the case studies that follow, Thunder Bay Regional Health Sciences Centre and Credit Valley Hospital, both in Ontario, embody these key principles.

Humanism in the Art of Sustainable Healing

Sean Stanwick, MEDesArch, and
Tye Farrow, MArch

If the delivery of health and the process of sustainable design share the common goal of improving our quality of life, then the role of healthcare architecture has never been more important. To enhance their meaning and relevance to an increasingly diverse popu-

lation, and to minimize their environmental footprint, hospitals can no longer afford to operate as isolated facilities with tenuous connections to the community. Instead, they should be like natural habitats: areas full of energy, life, and diversity, fostering relationships between the land and the water and embracing their role as comprehensive resources for healing at all levels.

While sustainability is generally accepted as the right goal, it has largely been defined through quantitative returns, such as energy performance or payback period. However, a more holistic approach to sustainability suggests that it encompasses many threads woven together, and not just individual pieces as conceived by the architect. In this light, sustainability should be considered part of a larger symbiotic paradigm in which appropriate technological solutions are responsive to the cultural identities intrinsically linked to local geography, environmental attunements, and essential cultural values. This way of thinking—and doing—begins to address the debate between the often-polarized forces of universalizing technology and localizing place identity.

A critical mass of related research supporting the connection principles of a regionally informed, sustainable architecture is beginning to circulate. Historically, early roots can be traced to the writings of German sociologist Ferdinand Tönnies (1957) wherein he identified gemeinschaft, a process by which the character of a place results in functional and meaningful characteristics and associations. In "Towards a Critical Regionalism: Six Points for an Architecture of Resistance," Kenneth Frampton (1983) yearns for a regional architecture that resists the culture of nostalgia in favor of creating an identity and language of vernacular traditions. Canadian architects John McMinn and Marco Polo (2006) extend this when they posit:

> The enduring presence of regionalism in Canadian architecture has been accompanied by, and is often linked to the development of sustainable green strategies. The two phenomena offer potential common ground for the pursuit of an architecture that addresses both local climatic and environmental conditions and cultural and material traditions.

With this in mind, the broader question is no longer whether we should embrace a more intuitive approach to sustainability and health, but rather, by what means.

To achieve meaningful design in healthcare, it is vital that designers consider a parallel paradigm: humanism in the service of sustainable healing. With a desire to heal the body, the mind, and also the spirit, humanism speaks to the symbiotic relationship between contextual aspects, the quality of hospital design, and the overall psychological well-being of patients and staff. Rooted in the belief that concern for human values is of the utmost importance to the care of the sick, humanism bridges the gap between science and nature.

The human connection between nature and healing is an intuitive and deeply emotional one. Harvard biologist E. O. Wilson wrote in The Biophilia Hypothesis of humans' deep attachment to nature—an attachment extending far beyond the narrow demand for physical sustenance to include a broader range of intellectual, emotional, and spiritual needs. Wilson infers that it is impossible to detach from nature without also compromising human spiritual existence (Kellert and Wilson 1993). As a paradigm for healthcare design, humanism agrees.

While humanism as a philosophical precept serves to guide designers and clients in the search for a more relevant architecture, can these ideas move beyond the theoretical to deliver inspiring physical environments? Indeed they can. Humanism in healthcare can manifest itself in several innovative ways: verdant courtyards, natural ventilation, photovoltaic panels, animated water features, and atria with natural light—all of which provide a more positive healing environment. But perhaps the most salient means to foster sustainable design and health from a holistic and biophilic perspective is the adoption of bioregionally specific materials and construction methods. By using local and regional materials and methods of construction, our buildings participate in defining a unique sense of place with both cultural and ecological relevance.

Each time we construct a building we impact the environment in some way. The key is to minimize the environmental footprint and positively contribute to the health of the whole, meaning community and patients alike. Consider, for example, the use of wood in forested regions. As a renewable resource—and, subject to forestry practices, a sustainable building material—wood can lessen the environmental footprint by reducing resource and energy use.

At the community level, the use of sustainably harvested and manufactured local and regional natural materials has great potential to benefit the local economy. McMinn and Polo (2006) further the cause for a broader measure of sustainability when they write, "[T]o be truly sustainable, buildings need to remain relevant and functional to the community they serve. Energy-efficient buildings that fail to address cultural needs and values may suffer premature obsolescence and invite major modifications or outright demolition or replacement." In parts of North America, reflecting the historical economic association with the great forests, wood has the power to drive and sustain local economies, to generate tourism dollars, and even promote the generational succession of woodworking trades by giving new life to an old and reborn methods of construction. A parallel dynamic can play out in other regions with distinct indigenous resource bases.

When adopting green design principles, we must embrace the duty of stewardship bestowed upon us as designers and create a cohesive system of wellness for the environment and the people who inhabit its spaces. And while the advantages of using local and regionally based materials and construction methods are numerous and well evidenced in built works, embracing this principle, particularly in institutional healthcare facilities, is indeed an uphill charge that requires designers, clients, and municipalities alike to dissolve their standard approaches and adopt new methodologies. Yet when placed in the context of Wilson's biophilia hypothesis or Polo and McMinn's analysis of regionalism, the validation of this approach and its benefits to the community, the environment, and to patients becomes self-evident. Returning once again to the notion that concern for human values is of the utmost importance to the care of the sick, a regionally inspired architecture that bridges the gap between science and nature has the capacity to uniquely connect people to place in the service of healing.

CASE STUDY

Thunder Bay Regional Health Sciences Centre

Thunder Bay, Ontario

Figure 11-23: Thunder Bay Regional Health Sciences Centre. *Credit: Farrow Partnership Architects, Inc.*

Owners: Thunder Bay Regional Hospital; Cancer Care Ontario; Northwestern Ontario Regional Cancer Centre

Design team:

ARCHITECT: Salter Farrow Pilon Architects Inc. (successor firms: Farrow Partnership Architects Inc. and Salter Pilon Architects, Inc.)

ASSOCIATE ARCHITECT: Kuch Stephenson Gibson Malo, Architects & Engineers

LANDSCAPE ARCHITECTS: Schollen & Co. Inc. with Kuch Stephenson Gibson Malo

STRUCTURAL ENGINEERS: Mickelson/Cook joint venture

MECHANICAL AND ELECTRICAL ENGINEER: H. H. Angus & Associates Ltd.

CIVIL ENGINEER: Wardrop Engineering

CONSTRUCTION MANAGERS: EllisDon/Tom Jones Corp.

INTERIORS: Salter Farrow Pilon Architects Inc.

Type: New replacement regional acute care hospital

Size: 680,000 sq ft (63,170 sq m); site area: 60 acres (24.2 ha)

Program description: 375-bed hospital, including acute care, maternity, emergency services, mental health, and cancer center

Completion date: 2004

Thunder Bay is a community of approximately 120,000 on Lake Superior in northwestern Ontario, close to the Manitoba border. Replete with the rugged vernacular of the Canadian north, Thunder Bay's history is rooted in local pulp and paper industries and the national railway that helped unify the country.

Conceptually, the building is organized in a T-configuration. Oriented north–south, inpatient units are located on the east side, with clinical departments on the west and north. Architecturally, the project features a dramatic three-story wood-and-glass walkway that serves as the main public corridor. "The fully glazed arcade curves to follow the path of the sun to allow deep penetration of light and enhance the comforting perception of the hospital," observes Sean Stanwick of Farrow Partnership. "Conceived as a path through a forest lined with trees, the corridor symbolizes and fosters a direct connection to nature." The goal was to give occupants of the building, both staff and patients, "the feeling that they had spent the day outdoors"—a real challenge in a northern climate, with its limited winter daylight hours. The concourse has been designed to use passive solar energy; it uses virtually no fossil-fuel generated energy for cooling or heating in the summer or winter.

Figure 11-24: Aerial view of the hospital and adjacent rugged terrain. The building massing and main concourse is oriented to follow the sun's path, allowing natural light penetration. *Credit: Farrow Partnership Architects, Inc.*

Figure 11-25: Natural light illuminates the concourse and cafeteria spaces in the main concourse. *Credit: Peter Sellar, Klik Photography*

Figures 11-26 and 27: This conceptual sketch of the wood-structured main concourse at the main entry illustrates the layering of the facade and structural elements; the photograph captures the actualized building. *Figure 11-26 credit: Farrow Partnership Architects, Inc.; Figure 11-27 credit: Peter Sellar, Klik Photography*

Sustainable site planning is realized through a series of connected ponds and wetlands that divert storm water runoff and filter the water before returning it to the adjacent McIntyre River. The ponds are also designed as cold-water fish habitat breeding areas to help repopulate the river with native species. Of the 60-acre site, 50 percent has been restored as bogs and wetlands for the river ecosystem.

The building's exterior is clad in a mix of native cut tindal stone and an aggregate masonry unit comprised of crushed tindal stone and cement. The material was selected to create a specific connection to the regional geology and history.

Thunder Bay is also the first cancer center in Canada to incorporate direct-light skylights within the radiation treatment rooms, enhancing the patients' therapeutic experience, and accomplished without compromising user safety. The center's main nursing stations are oriented with direct views outside through three-story mini-atria in each of the inpatient areas.

Source: Farrow Partnership Architects, Inc.

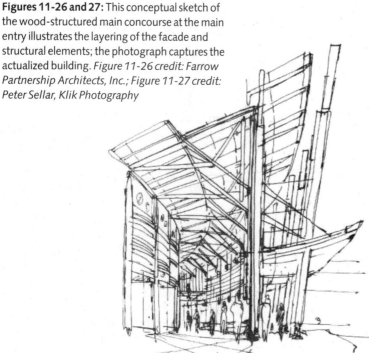

Figure 11-28: Carlo Fidani Peel Regional Cancer Centre & the Vijay Jeet and Neena Kanwar Ambulatory Care Centre at the Credit Valley Hospital. *Credit: Peter Sellar, Klik Photography*

The Carlo Fidani Peel Regional Cancer Centre & the Vijay Jeet and Neena Kanwar Ambulatory Centre at Credit Valley Hospital

Mississauga, Ontario

Owner: Credit Valley Hospital

Design team:

ARCHITECT: Farrow Partnership Architects, Inc.

LANDSCAPE ARCHITECT: EDA Collaborative Inc.

STRUCTURAL ENGINEER: Halsall Associates Ltd.

MECHANICAL AND ELECTRICAL ENGINEER: Rybka Smith and Ginsler Ltd.

GENERAL CONTRACTORS: PCL Constructors Ltd.

Building type: Lobby and clinical space addition with associated renovation

Size: 320,000 sq ft (29,728 sq m)

Program description: Peel Regional Cancer Centre, rehabilitation, complex continuing care, maternal child care, laboratory services, and emergency room renovations, along with extensive renovations to adjacent departments in three phases

Completion date: 2005

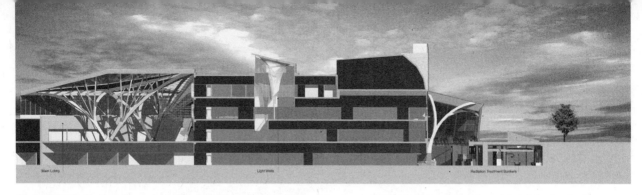

Figure 11-29: Section through atrium (at left) and mini-lanterns of cancer radiation treatment bunkers (at right). *Credit: Farrow Partnership Architects, Inc.*

Beginning with a strong site planning and design framework to accommodate growth, this award-winning addition maximizes usable site area while protecting existing landscaped areas. Conceived as trees in a forest, the vision for the lobby is that of a village gathering place linking the new cancer center and the adjacent existing renovated spaces. Embracing the comforting and warming qualities inherent to wood, the complex yet delicate network of curving wooden members gently bend and intertwine like the branches of a tree to create the appearance of a tree-lined courtyard. (The structure utilizes a water-mist fire-suppression system to meet fire-protection requirements.)

The undulating roof incorporates large, triangular glazed sections at the structure's cleaves. Also, a series of smaller, two-story light wells, constructed, in a similar fashion, of laminated beams and glazing, permit direct natural light to penetrate deep into the main nursing stations in the cancer treatment waiting areas on the lower floors.

Source: Farrow Partnership Architects, Inc.

Figure 11-30: The atrium was conceived as a "village gathering place." Wood materials were selected to humanize, personalize, and demystify the healthcare experience. *Credit: Peter Sellar, Klik Photography*

Figure 11-31: The building has a direct connection to nature and to its occupants' inner social lives. The design of the structural forms mimic nature. *Credit: Farrow Partnership Architects, Inc.*

Shifting scales to community-centered ambulatory care, sustainable projects are responding to bioregional influences. The University of Wisconsin Cancer Center in Johnson Creek, Wisconsin (Chapter 1), not only uses simple local materials in a building that emphasizes connection to nature, it recalls regional prairie school architecture. The Sambhavna Trust Clinic in Bhopal, India (Chapter 3), also exemplifies a bioregional focus. Among the British National Health Service projects, Kaleidoscope, Lewisham Children's and Young People's Centre in London, England (Chapter 8), demonstrates a community-focused and -scaled approach to building that blends medical and social service programs in a nature focused, neighborhood setting. Collectively, these projects and the following case studies illustrate a departure from the medical mall typology that has prevailed in the last generation of ambulatory care design.

The Patrick H. Dollard Discovery Health Center in Harris, New York (below), inhabits a rural landscape among whose residents it has earned the moniker "a barn with attitude." Constructed largely of wood, it transcends institutional definition and lives in a landscape of farm buildings. The Ryan Ranch outpatient campus in Monterey, California (below), reduced the apparent scale of a multispecialty outpatient program by producing a cluster of smaller structures with tuck-under parking. With a modular central plant, the campus preserved mechanical efficiencies of scale, while the decentralized buildings preserve much of the wooded site.

Figure 11-32: Patrick H. Dollard Discovery Health Center. *Credit: David Allee*

Owner: The Center for Discovery
Design team:
ARCHITECT: Guenther 5 Architects PLLC
LANDSCAPE ARCHITECTURE: Billie Cohen; Dirtworks US
MECHANICAL, ELECTRICAL, AND PLUMBING ENGINEER: Lilker Associates
ENERGY MODELING: Joseph R. Loring & Associates, Inc.
COMMISSIONING: EME, LLC
GENERAL CONTRACTOR: Storm King Contracting
Building type: New ambulatory diagnostic and treatment facility
Size: Building: 28,000 sq ft (2,600 sq m); site: 9 acres (3.65 ha)

Program description: Primary adult and pediatric medical, dental, physical, and occupational therapy, and psychiatric and social services for developmentally disabled and medically fragile children and adults

Completion date: 2003

Recognition: 2004 ASHE Vista Sustainability Award; US Green Building Council LEED certified

Figure 11-33: The building features a roof terrace accessible to building occupants with views of the adjacent organic farm and pastures. *Photo Credit: David Allee*

This project, initiated prior to LEED or the *Green Guide*, sought to evolve a noninstitutional ambulatory medical facility nested within a rural, residential campus. The Discovery Health Center houses approximately two hundred developmentally disabled adults and children in a decentralized group home model on a 350-acre site bisected by a major highway.

The center emphasizes a nature-based program that includes community-supported agriculture manifested in its organic farm. Goats and horses pasture in the fields adjacent to the building—the goats actually come up to the buildings and gnaw on the windowsills. The center also has a therapeutic horseback riding facility and a historic dairy farm; it is also now raising beef cattle. The project site, a 9-acre former "industrial" egg farm, created significant pollution runoff to the adjacent organic farm. Although it might have been less expensive to develop on a greenfield parcel, the Center for Discovery realized that the ecological remediation of the project site would improve irrigation water quality on the farm and safeguard against future potential contamination.

KEY BUILDING PERFORMANCE STRATEGIES

Site
- High-reflectance roofing
- On-site organic farming

Water
- Rainwater harvested from roof used for fire suppression system, ground-source heat pump system make-up, and farm irrigation

Energy
- 42 percent energy reduction below ASHRAE 90.1-1999 achieved via high-performance building envelope (approximately 100 percent better than New York State's energy code), ground-source heat pumps for heating and cooling, and variable-frequency drives in pumps and air-handling units
- Radiant (hydronic) heating system
- 100 percent green power purchase

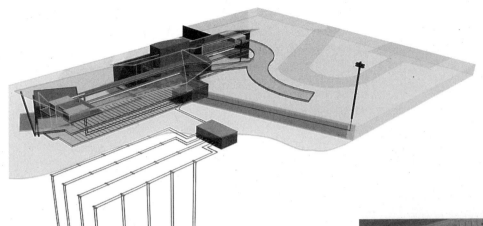

Materials

- Avoidance of polyvinyl chloride (PVC)
- 75 percent construction-waste recycling

Environmental Quality

- Low-emitting materials; formaldehyde-free insulation and agriboard cabinets
- Operable windows throughout exam rooms and offices
- Daylight and views from more than 90 percent of occupied spaces

Operations

- Mercury reduction
- Green housekeeping

The center utilizes radiant heating systems in residential buildings because they provide superior thermal comfort, reduce maintenance, and improve resident safety, leaving no exposed heating equipment in the wheelchair zone. Linking hydronic heating to ground-source heat pumps eliminated all on-site combustion, contributing to reduced airborne emissions. Expressing the Center for Discovery's commitment to renewable energy production, 100 percent of the building's electrical demand is offset through the purchase of green power.

Source: Guenther 5 Architects

Figure 11-35: The soaring interior achieves a high degree of thermal comfort due to the radiant system. Brise-soleils provide shading from solar gain and activate the largely daylit space. *Credit: David Allee*

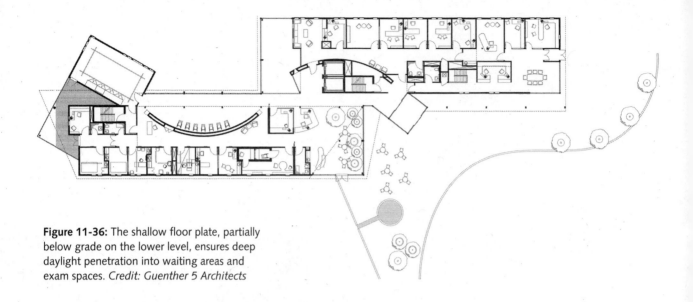

Figure 11-36: The shallow floor plate, partially below grade on the lower level, ensures deep daylight penetration into waiting areas and exam spaces. *Credit: Guenther 5 Architects*

Ryan Ranch Outpatient Campus

Monterey, California

Figure 11-37: Ryan Ranch Outpatient Campus. *Credit: Tim Griffith*

Owner: The Community Hospital of Monterey Peninsula

Design team:

    ARCHITECT: Chong Partners Architecture

    LANDSCAPE ARCHITECT: Bellinger Foster Steinmetz

    MECHANICAL, ELECTRICAL, AND PLUMBING ENGINEER: Guttmann & Blaevoet

    STRUCTURAL ENGINEER: Umerani Associates

    GENERAL CONTRACTOR: Rudolph & Sletten

Building type: New ambulatory care center

Size: Ancillary building: 44,000 sq ft (4,087 sq m); medical office building: 46,000 sq ft (4,273 sq m); parking: 24,000 sq ft (2,230 sq m); site: 21 acres (8.5 ha)

Program description: Imaging center, sleep center, diabetes and nutrition center, medical office building

Completion date: 2004

Awards/recognition: First project to qualify for PG&E's Savings by Design Healthcare Program

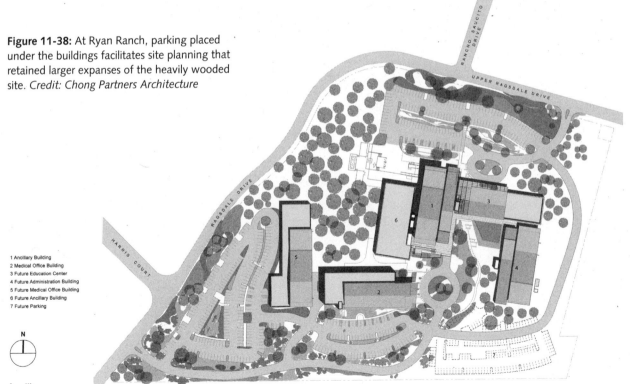

Figure 11-38: At Ryan Ranch, parking placed under the buildings facilitates site planning that retained larger expanses of the heavily wooded site. *Credit: Chong Partners Architecture*

1 Ancillary Building
2 Medical Office Building
3 Future Education Center
4 Future Administration Building
5 Future Medical Office Building
6 Future Ancillary Building
7 Future Parking

N

0   50ft

An owner who understood this magnificent site's inherent natural beauty and unique-ness led to a series of sustainable site preservation strategies. The design for the new outpatient campus, which extends an existing community hospital in Southern Cali-fornia, focused on minimizing development impacts on the previously undeveloped site and mitigating noise from both mechanical equipment and the air traffic overhead. The decision to preserve the heavily wooded landscape led to structured parking below the buildings. Once the impact of this decision on the quality of the site became appar-ent, a series of additional sustainable design initiatives followed, including the central utility plant. The central plant freed each building from rooftop mechanical equipment, which permitted the design team to develop sloping roof shapes. Glass curtain walls maximizing natural light and serene views of hillsides dotted with live oaks provide a less stressful environment and improve the occupants' experience.

Cathy Barrett, associate partner of Chong Partners Archi-tecture, commented, "Our role was to help the client see the site for what it is—not just for our purposes today, but for the future. And a physician with a keen interest in design headed the Community Hospital of Monterey team. We prepared a se-ries of alternative scenarios demonstrating the impact of paving and parking on the natural site features. When you have a great view and want to take advantage of it, who wants to look at a sea of cars?" she asked.

KEY BUILDING PERFORMANCE STRATEGIES

Energy
- Design of separate on-site central plant minimized noise, re-duced unsightly equipment (allowing for greater design op-tions), extended equipment life in a seaside climate, and guaranteed future building efficiencies
- Employs design elements that help facility qualify for PG&E's Savings by Design Healthcare Program
- Exceeds 2001 California energy code by 22 percent

Materials
- Carpet and Rug Institute Green Label carpet with renewable resource backing system

Environmental Quality
- Extensive daylight and views
- High-performance glazing and additional acoustical treat-ment on the roofs protect facilities (including its in-house sleep studies laboratory) from noise caused by local airport's flight patterns
- Low-emitting materials

Source: Chong Partners Architecture

Figure 11-39: Clerestory windows and brise-soleil shading devices provide daylighting and animate the waiting spaces. *Credit: Sharon Risedorph*

Figure 11-40: The promontory site offers stunning views, a key component of the occupant experience. *Credit: Sharon Risedorph*

CONSIDERATIONS OF FORM, SCALE, AND TIME

The sharp contrast between the scale of Thunder Bay Regional Medical Centre (page 342) and the ambulatory care projects featured above leads to at least two provocative questions about the formal typology of healthcare buildings:

1. Are building form and scale driven by the need to compress the design and construction process (i.e., the cost of money)?
2. Are building form and scale driven by the complexity of technology (i.e., the need for universal bay sizing and medical planning expertise)?

The centralization of services in mega-hospitals increases transportation impacts, limits the project delivery approaches, and has led to the perception of hospitals as dehumanizing institutions. In urban areas, the mega-hospital creates the mega-campus, often disrupting the pedestrian and retail fabric. In suburban sites, the greenfield mega-hospital floats in a sea of surface parking, isolating the building from public transportation access and nature. Further, as scale increases, the time required to design and construct these buildings impacts their ability to respond to innovation in technology and service delivery.

In his essay "Open Building: Healthcare Architecture on the Time Axis," research architect and educator Stephen Kendall examines a paradigm shift in project delivery methods to address the massive scale issues of the contemporary healthcare building boom. Arguing that owners increasingly look to disaggregating building components in order to improve scheduling, generate more timely solutions, or have multiple skilled professionals working on specific aspects of complex projects simultaneously, Kendall proposes "open building" across the time axis.

Open Building: Healthcare Architecture on the Time Axis A New Approach

Stephen Kendall, PhD

Hospitals are, in an important sense, no longer being designed, built, and operated as they were during the time of Florence Nightingale, when the modern hospital was born. Hospitals today are much more complex and quickly evolving. Conceiving of today's hospitals as "whole buildings" — as might have made sense in simpler times — makes as little sense as saying that cities are designed, delivered, and managed as "wholes." Their "wholeness" is understood as being in a perpetual in-between state.

In the context of the main theme of this book— sustainability—comparing hospitals to cities is important. Hospitals, like cities, are artifacts. They grow or decay largely through organized human care and cultivation—or the lack thereof. As such, cities and hospitals are sustainable only to the extent that they exhibit both durability and adaptability—durability at a higher level (e.g., the network of streets in a city), and adaptability at a lower level (e.g., the buildings that come and go in the street network). And like sustainable cities, no single firm designs today's complex hospital campus. Design is distributed and is almost continuous.

Pioneering healthcare systems, coming to grips with the need for sustainable facilities, are asking that their hospitals be designed much in the way office buildings and shopping centers are designed, and as a surprising amount of multifamily housing around the world is now being delivered. They are more consciously organizing themselves on the time axis, taking into account the differential obsolescence of the physical parts and spaces making up their facilities. Pioneering clients in the United States and Europe are adopting new mandates because they understand that hospitals are never finished and that design and procurement methods must be reorganized. Consequently, architecture and engineering (A/E) teams, construction managers, suppliers, and financing organizations are being asked (albeit not often enough) to organize their work in fundamentally new ways. Here is what some of these pioneers are doing.

A/E teams are hired to design a base building that has the principal building circulation paths, building structure, and envelope, and the primary mechanical, electrical, and plumbing pathways and equipment. In some important cases in Europe, the design is shown, in drawings, to have accommodation capacity for a variety of functional scenarios. In these projects, A/E teams are being asked to go beyond the rhetoric of flexibility and instructed to demonstrate in unequivocal ways that the building they are designing can adapt over time. Designed for a specific place, in a specific climatic and regulatory context, the base building is then constructed by a firm specializing in this work.

Independently, and using the base building as its site, another A/E company designs the fit-out, providing the functional layout and associated installations. Since function is a moving target, the design methods and technology must permit layouts to be decided at the last minute and allow for reconfiguration later on; close attention must be paid to facility users and to critical interfaces with the base building. The fit-out is installed by specialized contractors. Finally, another provider is hired to supply the fixtures, equipment, and other medical items needed to make the facility run smoothly.

OPEN BUILDING IS NOT NEW

This is open building. It is not new. It recognizes change and distributed design as normal facts of facility life and offers formalized approaches to deal with these realities. What may be new—or at least reawakened by considering how cities exist and transform—is that open building distinguishes levels of intervention, each level operating on its own time scale and under the control of a party that has executive decision-making authority over it (Habraken 1998).

Further, open building recognizes that a successful facility does not depend on the same design firm having top-down control of all levels. For example, some of the mechanical, electrical, and plumbing systems will be in the base building (designed by one firm), but the rest of these systems are in the fit-out and even the furnishings (e.g., cabling and piping is found in some medical equipment)—designed perhaps by another firm. In an open building perspective, facility change is understood to be both territorial and technical—a change of a pediatric wing under the control of a doctor, for example, involves spatial redistribution that implicates parts of many technical systems. Distinguishing "levels of intervention" and organizing design accordingly enables an efficient response to demands for change over time. Doing so is entirely congruent with the distribution of design and building responsibilities over clearly partitioned work domains. Open building, therefore, provides methods to help resolve the question, who controls what, when?

The open building approach recognizes and formalizes what is already happening in the real world, although there is not yet any commonly used term for the practice. In addition, efforts to manage facilities change are not without precedent. We have seen related but different experiments in the School Construction Systems Development initiative (Boice 1968), in the Veterans Administration interstitial hospitals (BSD 1977), and in the US General Services Administration/Public Building Service Peach Book experiments (Hattis and Ware 1971). In any case, open building is not wishful thinking.

But, while some pioneers push practice in these new directions, there is resistance. Why? There are basically two reasons—one ideological, the other practical.

The ideological reason to resist delivering hospitals as open buildings springs from functionalism and the idea of whole-building integration. The belief seems to be that with sufficient scientific research on human behavior, we can design buildings by first defining function in great detail. But as many point out (Denise Scott Brown, John Habraken, Stewart Brand, Frank Duffy, and many others), form must now accommodate (changing) function (Venturi and Scott Brown 2004; Brand 1994). This goes against the grain of decades of traditions that tell us to start with function and make architecture to fit. Turning this around is troublesome.

The other reason to resist is more pragmatic. The delineation of levels of intervention and the natural distribution of design that follows require new ways of working and coordination and ask us to reconsider ingrained habits and conventions. This is always painful and demands an extra effort before it pays off. We fear losing control, and our instinctive reaction is to avoid such change as long as possible.

From the days of the modern movement we have tried to come to grips with change, and the complexity it brings, by adhering to forecasting and claims of predicting human behavior. Now, to paraphrase John Habraken, the reason we need to study what is actually happening is to learn to make provisions for what cannot be foreseen, instead of trying to forecast what will (Habraken 1998). The uncertainty of the future itself must be the basis on which present decisions are made. Unfortunately, much in our current methods in building design and construction cannot do that. If we don't have a stable program of functions, how can we design? The open building approach points to an answer, but also raises many questions about architectural knowledge and methods.

One of the clearest examples of how an open building approach can be implemented in the design of a large medical facility is the Office of Properties and Building of the canton of Bern in Switzerland. This is a public organization responsible for the canton's large portfolio of buildings, including universities, hospitals, and prisons. A decade ago, it decided to implement a major hospital facilities expansion program following what it calls "systems separation." The story of its effort is recounted elsewhere in detail (Kendall 2004) but can be summarized here (see Figures 11-41 through 11-48) (Hochbauamt des Kantons Bern 1997; 1998).

THE SYSTEMS SEPARATION MODEL
The Systems Separation Model is a design strategy conceived by Giorgio Macchi, the chief architect of Bern's Office of Properties and Building. His idea was to provide hospital facilities with the capacity for change—during the planning and implementation stages, but also along the time axis into the future. The defining characteristic of his idea is a definition, in performance-specification language, of autonomous systems levels encompassing both spatial and technical elements, defined by their period of usefulness and by separated design contracts. Separate A/E teams, selected in separate invited competitions, designed each level. In fact, based on the successes achieved so far, future projects under the office's jurisdiction will be required to maintain a strict systems separation in terms of technical definition and contract scope, defining key interfaces but leaving maximum decision flexibility to the next level, even if one design firm is responsible for designing all levels (Macchi 1997; 1999; 2000).

Figure 11-41: The site of the INO addition (in the foreground) to the Insel-spital on the campus of the University of Bern. *Credit: Courtesy of the Canton of Bern Office of Properties and Buildings*

SPATIAL ORGANIZATION

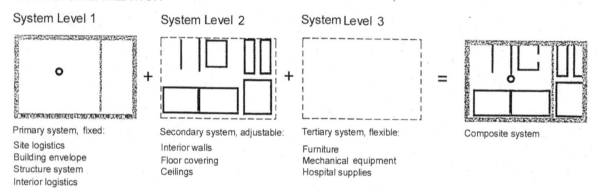

System Level 1

System Level 2

System Level 3

Primary system, fixed:

Site logistics
Building envelope
Structure system
Interior logistics

Secondary system, adjustable:

Interior walls
Floor covering
Ceilings

Tertiary system, flexible:

Furniture
Mechanical equipment
Hospital supplies

Composite system

TECHNICAL SYSTEM ORGANIZATION

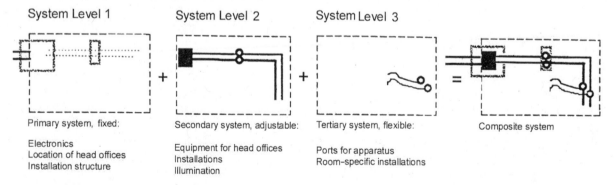

System Level 1

System Level 2

System Level 3

Primary system, fixed:

Electronics
Location of head offices
Installation structure

Secondary system, adjustable:

Equipment for head offices
Installations
Illumination

Tertiary system, flexible:

Ports for apparatus
Room-specific installations

Composite system

Figure 11-42: The basic organizational diagram shows the system separation on levels. *Credit: Courtesy of the Canton Bern Office of Properties and Buildings*

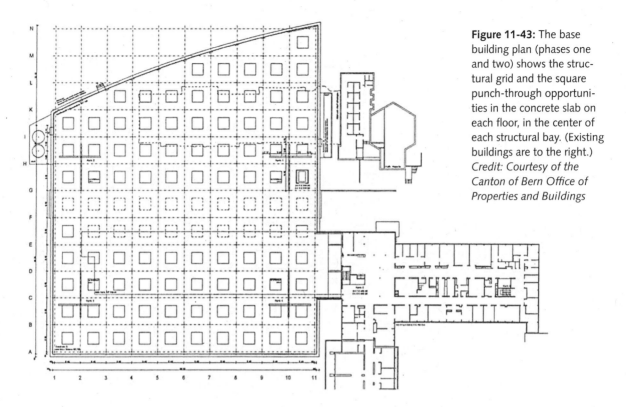

Figure 11-43: The base building plan (phases one and two) shows the structural grid and the square punch-through opportunities in the concrete slab on each floor, in the center of each structural bay. (Existing buildings are to the right.) *Credit: Courtesy of the Canton of Bern Office of Properties and Buildings*

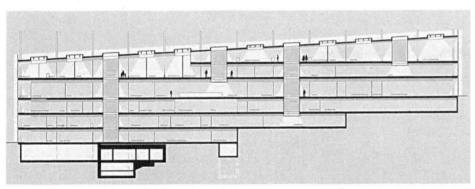

Figure 11-44: The north-south cross-section through the primary system shows possible penetrations for light shafts, stairs, installation risers, and so on in phases one and two. *Credit: Courtesy of the Canton of Bern Office of Properties and Buildings*

Figure 11-45: This is phase one's primary system green roof, with skylights. The foreground building is to be demolished; its functions will be moved into phase one, followed by construction of phase two in its place. *Credit: Courtesy of Stephen Kendall*

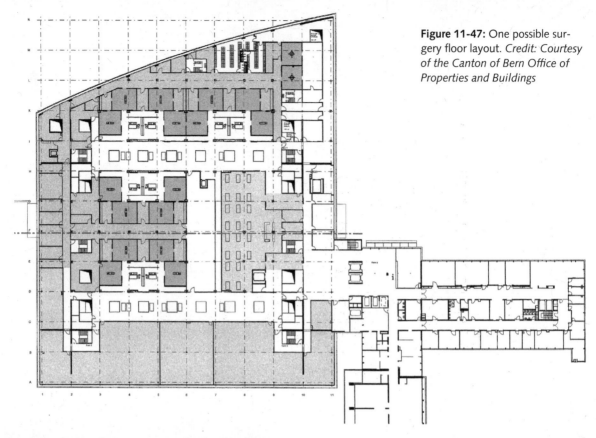

Figure 11-47: One possible surgery floor layout. *Credit: Courtesy of the Canton of Bern Office of Properties and Buildings*

Figure 11-46: The phase one primary system interior ready for fit-out installation. *Credit: Courtesy of Stephen Kendall*

QUESTIONS WE NEED TO ASK

Returning to the analogy of the sustainable city and a complex facility like a hospital, what Giorgio Macchi and his staff are doing in Bern seems quite natural. The whole is partitioned into sensible, hierarchically organized parts, with each part designed by a different architect's office (something that is becoming increasingly commonplace in the US). But it is also a struggle against ingrained habits, attitudes, and methods. If we consider this pioneering process and the projects that it is spawning, we cannot avoid asking uncomfortable questions that cut to the core of what architects and clients have come to believe and to practice.

How can clients organize themselves to get the new generation of change-ready buildings they need and also avoid large future expenditures or an unsustainable scrap-and-build cycle? What are the new client mandates, and how are they formulated? If clients try to procure buildings in an open building way, can A/E teams deliver? And can architecture ac-

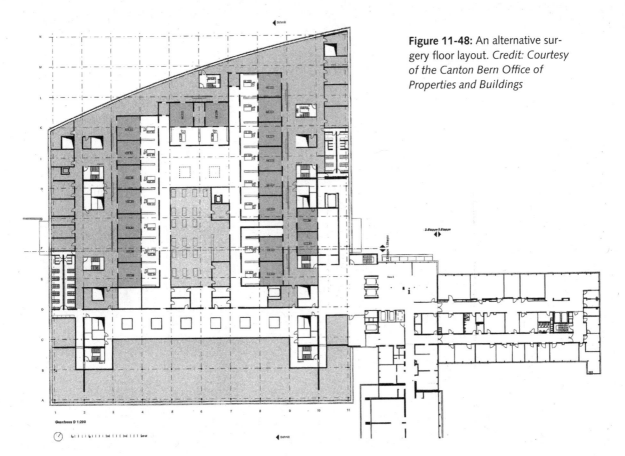

Figure 11-48: An alternative surgery floor layout. *Credit: Courtesy of the Canton Bern Office of Properties and Buildings*

commodate change and yet endure as part of a local culture, contributing to our collective sense of place, offering stability and composure in an otherwise churning environment? We do not want anonymous buildings that we cannot have affection for and have to demolish after they are exhausted in twenty years. We can no longer make tight-fit buildings based on immutable programs of use. So what is the basis for a new open architecture, and what are the new methods needed to design it?

The open building concept is akin to a "long life, loose fit" strategy, which views buildings as less specifically "purpose built" and more inherently adaptable, and looks at adaptability through a broad lens — a lens beyond the current iteration of medical uses. Prior to the advent of deep floor plate buildings, hospitals built in the nineteenth and early twentieth centuries — with their high ceilings and large windows — could be adaptively reused by other markets. Jersey City Medical Center, for example, a 1920s-era high-rise hospital building, has been converted to luxury condominiums. (Conversely, in the early 1970s, Lutheran Medical Center made news by converting a 1920s New York City industrial building into an acute care hospital.) However, since the advent of mechanical ventilation, the vast majority of schools, industrial buildings, and hospitals have developed into inherently nonadaptable structures — the exact opposite of "long life, loose fit."

NEW URBANISM AND HEALTHCARE

The twentieth-century urban megahospital, when it abandons its urban site and moves to greenfield suburbia, must often be completely demolished to reclaim the land. As medical responses to disease shift, what does it mean for our special-purpose healthcare buildings? If tomorrow, cancer could be treated with oral pharmaceuticals, for what purposes might the cancer center infrastructure be recycled?

St. Olav's Hospital in Trondheim, Norway, a one-thousand-bed tertiary-care replacement hospital with only the first of six phases completed, provides a provocative example of a strikingly different urban hospital typology. Located on an existing urban site, St. Olav's is replacing its entire campus—both its acute care infrastructure and medical school—on its current site. In the

process, the master plan is reintroducing the underlying urban street grid (which was interrupted by the prior megahospital) and constructing a system of discrete, narrow floor plate pavilions, each of which is a unique center of excellence. Below the street, a massive concourse connects the buildings, while above the street, the structures are interconnected by bridges. Each of the buildings responds to the surrounding urban scale and context. Although COWI Denmark completed the overall master plan, multiple teams are individually designing and constructing plan components.

St. Olav's Hospital

Trondheim, Norway

Figure 11-49: St. Olav's Hospital. *Credit: Team St. Olav*

Owner: Helse-Midt-Norge RHF (Central Norway Regional Health Authority)
Design team:
    ARCHITECT: Frisk Architects
    CONTRACTOR: Reinertsen Anlegg AS
    MASTER PLANNING AND CONSULTING: COWI Denmar
Building type: Replacement hospital on existing campus
Size: 2,152,782 sq ft (200,000 sq m)
Design energy intensity: Less than 300 kWh/sq m/yr per Norwegian code
Program description: 1,187-bed acute care teaching hospital, including mental health facilities
Completion date: Phase one: 2006; final completion: 2015

Figure 11-50: The scale of the St. Olav's structures are six-story or less, with a below grade level and two-story bridges that interconnect the buildings above the street grid. Each building is a distinct clinical service. *Credit: Team St. Olav*

Figure 11-51: An aerial view illustrating the overall plan for a series of court-yard buildings that comprise the more than 2-million-square-foot replacement campus and urban grid. Individual buildings are designed and executed by individual design and construction teams. *Credit: Team St. Olav*

Replacing a century-old facility on the same site on the Øya Peninsula near downtown Trond-heim, the new St. Olav's Hospital will serve a regional population of 650,000. Comprising treatment as well as research and teaching functions, the 5 billion NOK ($810.5 million) facil-ity will employ 7,500, admitting 60,000 patients and serving another 300,000 outpatients per year. The complex includes a 150-room hotel, opened in 2004, responding to the needs of rural patients for whom area fjords and mountains make commuting to the hospital difficult.

The hospital's design is based on the Planetree Model, which centralizes services around each patient: rather than move patients around the hospital for treatment, a team of spe-cialists (remaining as consistent as possible in composition) brings medical processes to each patient's room. The hospital affirms that this is a democratic shift from the institution's for-mer hierarchy, which was based on medical specialty (i.e., surgeons set apart from day-to-day care), and aims to facilitate cross-specialty collaboration.

Research and teaching functions are integrated into the hospital fabric rather than being isolated in a separate center. Related medical services are organized within six clinic blocks shaped like fingers along a landscaped boulevard. (As Norwegian code requires employee workstations used for four or more hours at a time to have access to daylight, the finger-like building wings, along with the narrow floor plates, also serve to allow natural light to permeate.) Tunnels and glazed pedestrian overpasses connect the distinct, human-scale buildings.

St. Olav's consulted patient representatives during all stages of the hospital planning process and promises to continue to consult them during the operation of the hospital. This has led to a focus on patient rights, privacy, and closeness to family. Nursing stations are de-signed as the nucleus of care wards and surrounded by six to eight single-patient rooms; the hospital's only multibed rooms are in special open wards used for procedures such as dialysis. The hospital's goal is to reduce patient length of stay by 24 percent. Meanwhile, the hospital's physical design and newfound reliance on information and communications technology aims to promote staff comfort, satisfaction, and job efficiency.

KEY BUILDING PERFORMANCE STRATEGIES

Energy
- Facility will not exceed 300 kWh/sq m/yr, per Norwegian code

Materials
- Goal to divert 90 percent of demolition debris from landfills; maximize on-site reuse
- Generate less than 27 kg of waste per sq m (5.5 lbs per sq ft) built during construction
- Consider life cycle costs in materials selection, including performance, maintainability, durability, and final disposal
- Select wood and other natural materials for finishing

Environmental Quality
- Patient courtyards provide access to fresh air and daylight
- Narrow floor plates ensure daylighting to all occupied spaces
- Vertical planted screens provide shade, privacy, and greenery to upper floors, while landscaped areas function as park space

Due to efficiency improvements, the hospital estimates that it will require 10 percent fewer staffers than the former hospital to treat the same number of patients, reducing necessary labor by 430 worker-years. The design strategies meant to achieve the reduction in patient length of stay include larger outpatient clinics with more examination rooms, more day hospital beds, the addition of observation rooms (which were not a part of the previous facility), and hotel rooms that allow patients to have minor surgery or receive continuous treatment such as chemotherapy without occupying a hospital bed.

Source: Helsebygg Midt-Norge (Hospital Development Project for Central Norway)

CONCLUSION

Sustainable design considerations are influencing hospital building typologies. As buildings become more climate responsive, bioregional influences will create distinctive, signature design elements — imagine "the hospital as a machine" replaced by "the hospital as a flower." Connecting healthcare buildings to the communities they grow from within can provide a powerful pattern language.

European and global south hospital buildings, with their continued reliance on natural ventilation, daylight, and passive heating and cooling, can inform this new language of form. The Norwegian examples (Rikshospitalet and St. Olav's) are provocative glimpses into two different approaches; many others are throughout this book.

This chapter cannot close, however, without celebrating the Sarah Network of Hospitals for Rehabilitation, a total of one thousand beds distributed throughout eight hospitals in six Brazilian cities. They are, collectively, the work of João da Gama Filgueiras Lima (affectionately known throughout Brazil as Lelé). Executed over a span of more than twenty years, the projects embody sustainable design features, industrialized construction methods, exquisite connections to their physical and social contexts — and offer a celebration of the power of healing architecture.

The Sarah Network of Hospitals for Rehabilitation

Brasília, Salvador,
São Luís,
Belo Horizonte,
Fortaleza, and
Rio de Janeiro,
Brazil

Figure 11-52: Sarah–Brasília, a 294-bed hospital designed by João Filgueiras Lima, opened in 1980; it provides daylight and natural ventilation. It features large-scale use of prefabricated concrete building elements, which allow for efficient construction while establishing a humanistic aesthetic. *Credit: Courtesy of the Sarah Network and João Filgueiras Lima*

Owner: Brazilian government funded; managed by NGO Associação das Pioneiras Sociais (Social Pioneers Association), a nongovernmental organization

Design team:

 ARCHITECT: João Filgueiras Lima (Lelé)

Building types: Some new construction, some renovation of existing hospital facilities

Size: 1,000 beds distributed through eight hospitals in six cities

Program description: Rehabilitation and treatment of malformations, traumas, locomotor system diseases, and neurodevelopmental problems

Completion dates: From 1980 (Brasília) to 2002 (Rio de Janeiro)

The Sarah Network, named for Sarah Kubitschek, wife of former president of Brazil Juscelino Kubitschek, is comprised of daylit and naturally ventilated orthopedic rehabilitation hospitals in six cities in eastern Brazil. Developed incrementally over a twenty-two-year period beginning in 1980, many of the hospitals use custom-prefabricated structural elements of metal, concrete, plastic, and wood, all produced at the network's own 21,500-square-foot (2,000-square-meter) industrial production facility, the Centro de Tecnologia da Rede Sarah, near the Sarah Network hospital in Salvador, Brazil.

The hospitals are renowned for the progressive nature of the rehabilitative care they offer, exceeding the standards established by the World Health Organization (WHO). In line with its medical philosophy, the design of the Sarah Network of Hospitals is focused on humanizing treatment and on reintegrating patients with their communities. Daylighting, natural ventilation, and passive cooling are motivated primarily by the mental and physical health and comfort of patients and staffers, rather than by energy savings. Climate and site conditions were central to architect João Filgueiras Lima's design for each facility. The designs are striking, often playfully highlighting the aesthetics of functional spaces such as hydrotherapy pools and gymnasiums, and feature prefabricated structural elements that contribute to the public facilities' material and cost-efficiency without betraying their mass-produced nature.

Each successive hospital has benefited from the experience gained through the previous designs in the network, with thematic repetition, as well as prefabrication, helping to control costs. Despite some standardization, however, the most important element of the hospitals' respective designs is arguably the responsiveness of each to its site and microclimate. The Fortaleza clinic, for example, is located farther from the water than some of its sister facilities, presenting different wind patterns to aid ventilation; preservation of a large wooded area on the site demanded a less horizontal plan than that employed in Salvador and São Luís.

Sarah–Brasília, the original Sarah hospital and the network's headquarters, embodies many of the ideas echoed throughout the later hospitals. The site is landscaped to catch breezes off of Lake Paranoá and to filter the air and moderate humid conditions. Gardens are generously landscaped to soften interconnections among spaces, with indoor spaces connecting directly with the outdoors. The building is solar oriented; all spaces are designed for natural ventilation and daylight. The passive ventilation system is augmented with mechanical exhausters used to achieve thermal comfort when necessary. Additional passive strategies, such as shade structures and abundant vegetation, cool areas in direct sunlight, while thermoacoustic roof tiles and an insulative air gap between roof layers mitigates heat buildup. The building's specific programmatic functions are located to benefit from solar gain based on use patterns; for example, less frequently used reception areas are located in the building's north end (subequatorial sun is strongest from the north), while frequently used gymnasiums and treatment rooms are located in the cooler south end. "Stimulation rooms" are positioned to take advantage of the comforting morning sun.

Everything we do and practice rigorously follows these principles.

—Sarah Network 2006

Create a specialized healthcare center that treats the patient as a human being who is not merely the object upon which techniques are applied, but rather, is the agent of that action.

Live the reality of locomotor system medicine as a conglomeration of unified knowledge and techniques aimed at the restitution of the universal right to come and go among the physically challenged.

Participate actively in society and work at the prevention of disability and deformity while at the same time combating prejudice against the physically disabled; after all, life is characterized by infinitely varied forms that change with time.

Defend the principle that no human being should be discriminated against for being different in his or her physical form or way of performing an activity.

Freedom from technological dependency by rejecting a passive attitude in the face of consumerism and imitation and by utilizing our culture's creative potential.

Develop a critical attitude toward imported standards, be they techniques or conduct.

Simplify technique and procedures in order to adapt them to the genuine necessities born of Brazil's contrasting economies and regions. Simplification is the critical synthesis of the most complex systems and processes: one cannot simplify that which one does not understand.

Appreciate innovative initiative and the exchange of experience, in education and research, stimulating the creativity of persons and groups; "the individual is the institution," and each person represents it, answers on its behalf, and dedicates his or her life to it.

Live for health instead of merely to survive illness.

Transform each individual into an active agent responsible for his or her own health.

Work so that the utopia of this hospital is educating for health until each individual, protected from illness, no longer needs it.

The community bears the primary responsibility for this work, whose purpose is the fulfillment of the community's will. It is everyone's duty, then, to demand of this institution the commitment consolidated here today.

Source: Sarah Network 2006

Figure 11-53: Invented by Lima, the *cama-maca* (literally "bed stretcher") or mobile bed facilitates movement of patients, enabling them to be comfortably transported to outside spaces during their rehabilitation. *Credit: Courtesy of the Sarah Network and João Filgueiras Lima*

Figure 11-54: Sarah–Fortaleza, opened in 1991, is a sixty-one-bed inpatient and outpatient rehabilitation hospital for children and adults. It includes an open-air physical therapy area that provides patients with a lush, vegetated setting and offers easy access to a therapeutic swimming pool for strengthening exercises. *Credit: Courtesy of the Sarah Network and João Filgueiras Lima*

CHAPTER 12

Ecological Footprint and Beyond

> If you can't measure it, you can't manage it.
> — PETER DRUCKER

> We have at most ten years — not ten years to decide upon action, but ten years to alter fundamentally the trajectory of global greenhouse emissions.
> — JAMES HANSEN, DIRECTOR,
> NASA Goddard Institute for Space Studies

INTRODUCTION

Charting the course toward sustainable healthcare design and construction requires perspective and tools: a conceptual framework, metrics (i.e., what we measure), and the basis for measurement — or how we measure it. As with the tools described in Chapter 8, these efforts imply a definition of the *measures of success.* Just what defines a high-performance healing environment? Is it a carbon neutral, zero-waste hospital, free of persistent bioaccumulative toxic chemicals? If so, how is that performance defined and measured? The concept of "ecological footprint" is both a framework for measuring environmental impacts and a platform from which to track continuous improvement and catalyze policies. Since its inception in 2003, the nonprofit Global Footprint Network has been developing a range of tools and

policy frameworks to advance the application of the ecological footprint to quantify humanity's demand on nature — as carried out by governments, communities, and businesses.

This chapter proposes an expanded view of the ecological footprint responding to the layered ecological urgencies of our time: climate change, global toxification, and zero waste, echoing the themes in Michael Lerner's essay in Chapter 3. The parallels between these seemingly disparate ecological markers are striking: they each have global reach independent of political boundaries, geography, and generation.

Healthcare has deep roots and successes in both the policy and implementation arenas associated with toxics and waste reduction. On the other hand, reducing climate change impacts, while grabbing headlines in the first decade of the twenty-first century, is just beginning to emerge among healthcare's priorities. A health-based ecological footprint framework — with carbon neutrality, persistent bioaccumulative toxic chemical (PBT) elimination, and zero waste as the measures of success — builds on healthcare's pioneering leadership and provides sharp focus to global ecological stewardship efforts.

ECOLOGICAL FOOTPRINT: AN INTRODUCTION

In 1994, Mathis Wackernagel, a PhD student at the University of British Columbia's School of Community and Regional Planning, submitted his dissertation, "The Ecological Footprint and Appropriate Carrying Capacity: A Tool for Planning toward Sustainability" (Wackernagel 1994). The following year, Wackernagel and his professor, Dr. William Rees, coauthored *Our Ecological Footprint: Reducing Human Impact on the Earth*. Defined as "a resource management tool that measures how much land and water area a human population requires to produce the resources it consumes and to absorb waste under prevailing technology" (GFN 2006), ecological footprinting is increasingly being employed as a conceptual framework, and as a planning, management, and policy tool — including as a sustainability indicator for the European Union, and integrated into the Canadian Index of Well-Being (GFN 2006).

Wackernagel and Rees postulate that from a global perspective, current development patterns exceed the earth's carrying capacity by about 23 percent (GFN 2006), with a broad range of footprint ratios worldwide (Figure 12-1). The average available global footprint — based on available biocapacity — is about 4.95 acres (2 ha) per person. As a basis of comparison, per capita footprint in the US is estimated at 23.72 acres (9.6 ha), while India's is 1.97 acres (0.8 ha) (WWF 2005).

Ecological footprint analysis relies on two primary inputs: energy use, and goods and services required for ongoing operations. Over more than a decade of application, these datasets have been augmented with other considerations. Two of them — materials used in the orig-

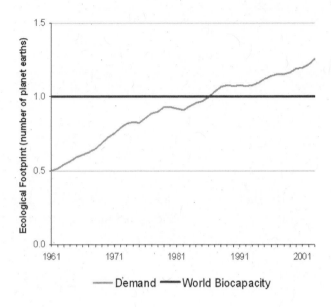

Figure 12-1: Global Ecological Footprint illustrates the ratio between the global demand and biocapacity, beginning in 1961, and its increase through 2003. The horizontal line represents the Earth's biocapacity. Beginning in 1997, demand exceeded biocapacity, resulting in a condition termed ecological overshoot. *Credit:* Global Footprint Network *2006*

inal construction of buildings and medical waste incineration — have particular relevance to healthcare (Germain 2001/2002). To credibly measure actual operations requires access to reliable data and accounting practices aligned with the footprint criteria. Ecological footprint analysis can be conducted at any scale — nationally, for an individual organization, or a single household.

HEALTHCARE'S ECOLOGICAL FOOTPRINT

With just over a decade of ecological footprint analysis development, there are few examples of specific applications in the healthcare sector. The handful of studies undertaken to date, notably in Canada and the UK, provide both a window into healthcare's intensive demands on productive biocapacity and opportunities to measurably reduce those impacts through coordinated policy and action. In 2001, Dr. Susan Germain, a general practitioner, conducted what is acknowledged as the first ecological footprint analysis of a hospital for her masters thesis in environmental science. The Lions Gate Hospital, British Columbia, served as the subject facility. Germain's study, summarized here, reveals the formidable ecological responsibility resting on healthcare's shoulders.

> *The US health care system has a disproportionately large ecological footprint. Although there is no exact measure of the footprint, financial measures offer a rough surrogate: The US health care system is the most expensive in the world.... [I]f the US is to reduce its environmental impact to a sustainable level, it must also substantially reduce the scale of its health care system.*
>
> SOURCE: THE GREEN HEALTH CENTER 2004

THE ECOLOGICAL FOOTPRINT OF LIONS GATE HOSPITAL

Located in North Vancouver, British Columbia, Lions Gate Hospital is a 335-bed midsize hospital. Upon examining energy use, consumption of goods, construction, and incinerated waste, Lions Gate's ecological footprint was calculated to be 7,020 acres (2,841 ha), corresponding to an area 719 times larger than its physical footprint of 9.76 acres (3.95 ha). As a basis of comparison, the entire city of Vancouver's ecological footprint (Rees 2000) was estimated to be about 180 times its physical footprint. This dramatic contrast between the two footprints provides a window into the magnitude of healthcare's ecological impacts. As Germain notes, "These figures give us an idea of the scale at which hospitals consume—however, they do not give us a complete picture."

The Lions Gate's operational ecological footprint (EF) cites the following four examples:

1. Energy footprint—the single largest contributor to Lions Gate's EF (Germain 2001/2002)—is equivalent to 5,913 acres (2,393 ha), representing 85 percent of the hospital's total footprint (By comparison, energy accounts for about 50 percent of the total footprint in other analyses [Rees 2001].)
2. Over 1.7 million pairs of gloves used in year of study, yielding 35 tons of waste.
3. Plastic bags for IV solutions weighing over 17 tons, with packaging weighing 7 tons.
4. About 426,000 diapers used, mostly for adults, in addition to incontinence pads, resulting in 58 tons of waste annually.

In her article "The Ecological Footprint of Lions Gate Hospital," Germain acknowledges that toxic emissions are unaccounted for in standard ecological footprint methodology. "The EF technique does not address the issue of toxics. The only waste product considered in the EF technique is carbon dioxide (CO_2). Thus, the environmental impacts of potentially toxic materials in the waste flow are not considered. This includes medications, both discarded and excreted, cleaning materials and other wastes. There is currently no technique used to quantify environmental impacts that includes this evaluation" (Germain 2001/2002). Recognizing the significance of medical waste incineration in the context of a hospital's ecological footprint, Germain's analysis accounted for the health effects associated with incineration—releases of dioxins, methyl mercury, and other toxic chemicals. This, too, extended the boundaries of standard ecological footprint analysis while being fully consistent with healthcare's interest in these issues.

Because most of the buildings on the Lions Gate campus were more than thirty years old, Germain calculated the ecological footprint associated with construction materials based on conversion factors from the Green Building Challenge (Cole 2001) combined with the hospital's floor area. This yielded a basis from which to calculate carbon dioxide linked to the manufacture of construction materials. The footprint was amortized for a thirty-year time frame, considered the

(continued)

estimated life expectancy of similar buildings. Overall, the ecological footprint for Lions Gate Hospital's construction materials was 355.82 acres (144 ha).

Complexities of the analysis included the particulars of Lions Gate's energy generation. Its electricity is generated by hydropower and natural gas. Ecological footprint measures the amount of productive land required to offset emissions impacts of fossil-fuel based power generation—cleaner and renewable technologies require less land area to sequester carbon dioxide impacts. According to Germain, "If the same amount of energy were consumed in an area that produced electricity solely from natural gas, the energy footprint would have been 9,995 acres (4,045 hectares), while the use of coal would have increased the

energy footprint to 12,098 acres (4,896 ha) (Germain 2001/2002)." Germain further notes that at 85 percent, Lions Gate's energy-related ecological footprint is substantially higher than the 50 percent energy-related share calculated in other ecological footprint analyses (Germain 2001/2002)—yet another indicator of healthcare facilities' significant energy intensity.

The comparison footprint for Vancouver also included many EF inputs not included in the Lions Gate Hospital study; including them would likely have yielded an even larger differential. In summary and perhaps not surprisingly, hospitals appear to have more intensive ecological footprints than the communities in which they are situated.

Source: Germain 2001/2002

TABLE 1: Numbers and Weights of Some Items Purchased by LGH from April 2000 to March 2001

Item	Number of Items	Paper	Synthetics	Latex	Metal	Total Weight
Gloves	3,535,800 (1,767,900 prs)	6,650.4 kg	21,080.4 kg	7,851.9 kg		35,583 kg
Injection and Irrigation Solutions (not incl. H₂O)	35,794.2 L (Inj) + 12,487.2 L (Irrig)	6,662.1 kg	17,632.3 kg			24,294 kg
Diapers, Incontinence Products	Children: 20,880 Adult: 405,276 Incont. Pads: 94,320	31,799.9 kg	25,920.7 kg			57,721 kg
Disposable Surgical Drapes		2,002.3 kg	13,504.1 kg			15,506 kg
Sterilization Wrap		860.5 kg	6,462.7 kg			7,323 kg
Paper, Books, Brochures		95,977.5 kg				95,977 kg
Paper Cups and Plates		5,205.0 kg				5,205 kg
Plastic Cups, Lids, Cutlery, Dishes		1,926.3 kg	8,898.9 kg			10,825 kg
Toilet Paper, Tissues, Paper Towels		42,945.6 kg				42,946 kg
Paper X-Ray Pouches		5,832.0 kg				5,832 kg
Plastic Bags		927.6 kg	14,181.8 kg			15,109 kg
Sharps Containers		63.7 kg	3,224.5 kg			3,288 kg
Skin Staplers 35mm	2,094	90.0 kg	420.9 kg			511 kg
Needles, Syringes		1,460.1 kg	4,753.3 kg		86.5 kg	6,300 kg
Tongue Depressors		1,366.5 kg				1,367 kg
Preassembled Trays	51,072 trays (49,572 included in weights)	2,057.1 kg	4,262.9 kg			6,320 kg
Sutures	27,640.5 metres					
Alcohols	3,705 L					
Peri-Care Cleanser	5,178 L					
Phenokil	13,296 L					

Figure 12-2: The Lions Gate Hospital's ecological footprint analysis accounted for the quantity and material composition and associated weights of purchased items over the one-year study period (Germain 2001/2002). *Source:* Reprinted from *Healthcare Quarterly* with permission.

Soon after the release of Germain's study, the UK's nonprofit Best Foot Forward (BFF) released *Material Health: An Assessment of the Environmental Sustainability of the NHS in England and Wales* (BFF 2004), which provided a comprehensive ecological footprint analysis of the national healthcare system; as noted in Chapter 8, the National Health Service (NHS) is Europe's largest organization. The report's executive summary provides a snapshot of the NHS's operations in England and Wales: its ecological footprint is 4,964,825 global hectares, or 0.09 hectares per capita.

In addition to architectural designer Malcolm Stroud's analysis depicted in Figure 12-3, the *Material Health* report also estimated 3.19 million tons of emissions to air, 99.6 percent of which was CO_2. As with the Germain study, above, the NHS analysis did not measure other chemical emissions to air and water.

Figures 12-3: Malcolm Stroud's (2006) graphic analysis of contributions to the National Health Service's ecological footprint, with energy (source + use) about 60 percent, while transport (humans + food) represents 29 percent. These data highlight areas with the best opportunities for making significant reductions in the ecological footprint. *Source: © Malcolm Stroud*

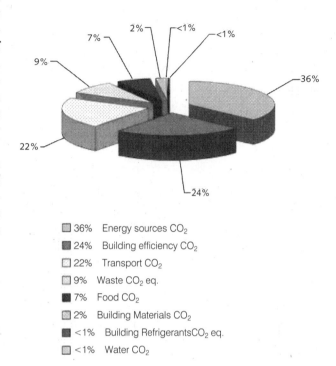

EXISTING SUBURBAN BRITISH HOSPITAL OVER 60-YEAR LIFETIME

- 36% Energy sources CO_2
- 24% Building efficiency CO_2
- 22% Transport CO_2
- 9% Waste CO_2 eq.
- 7% Food CO_2
- 2% Building Materials CO_2
- <1% Building Refrigerants CO_2 eq.
- <1% Water CO_2

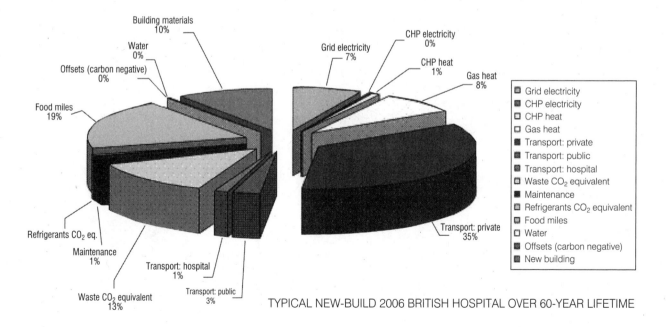

TYPICAL NEW-BUILD 2006 BRITISH HOSPITAL OVER 60-YEAR LIFETIME

Based on the *Material Health* analysis, the report outlined three specific policy and implementation potentials for the NHS:

1. *Solar water heating:* identified three options with potential to reduce ecological footprint, ranging from a 2 to 63 percent reduction and yielding associated CO_2 emissions reductions
2. *Waste:* determined that waste minimization, coupled with accelerated recycling, needed to be a core part of the waste reduction strategy
3. *Staff, patient, and visitor travel:* recommended switching modes of transportation and promoting car sharing.

Following the report's release, the NHS advanced policies relating to improved energy performance, waste reduction, and the location of healthcare facilities, favoring a decentralized network of smaller-scale buildings to reduce automobile dependence for patients, staff and visitors (see Chapter 8 for a more detailed discussion of NHS's tools and initiatives).

The Lions Gate and NHS footprint analyses point to energy use as a major contributor—particularly at Lions Gate, where energy use represented 85 percent of the total footprint. This finding corroborates the significance of the carbon footprint as a widely acknowledged metric of ecological stewardship.

CLIMATE CHANGE

The 1997 signing of the Kyoto Protocol amendment to the United Nations Framework Convention on Climate Change positioned global climate change as a political, social, and ecological reality. Signed and ratified by 169 nations and other governmental organizations as of 2006, representing 55 percent of global atmospheric greenhouse emissions, the Protocol's objective is the "stabilization of greenhouse gas concentrations in the atmosphere at a level that would prevent dangerous anthropogenic interference with the climate system" (UNFCC 1992). Kyoto Protocol goals include reducing CO_2 emissions to 5 percent below 1990 levels in an effort to reverse climate change—given increased emissions worldwide, this goal could result in global reductions of 29 percent below anticipated 2010 levels without the Protocol (UNEP 1998).

Global climate change, also termed global warming, has the potential to fundamentally alter life on this

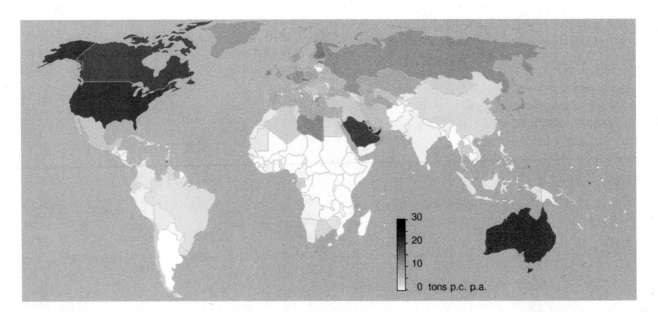

Figure 12-4: This map displays the per capita carbon dioxide emissions of countries around the world. *Source: Wikimedia Commons 2006*

planet and specifically, to redefine the conditions and context for human health. The numbing consequences of global climate change have become synonymous with the human experience: from the relentless heat wave that overcame much of central Europe in August 2003 to the devastating 2004 southeast Asian tsunami and the calamitous Gulf Coast hurricanes in 2005, the nature of natural disasters — their intensity, scale, and the magnitude of their human and ecological toll — is unprecedented in modern times. Climate change is directly linked to CO_2 emissions worldwide.

CARBON NEUTRALITY

Along with healthy building materials, resource efficiency, and enhanced indoor air quality, carbon neutrality is emerging as a litmus test of twenty-first-century green buildings. Indeed, on November 13, 2006, Oxford University Press proclaimed *carbon neutral* as its 2006 word of the year. Its definition: ". . . calculating your total climate-damaging carbon emissions (your "carbon footprint"), reducing them where possible, and then balancing your remaining emissions, often by purchasing a carbon offset." According to *New Oxford American Dictionary* editor Erin McKean, lexicographers select a word that "is both reflective of the events and concerns of the past year and also forward looking: a word that we think will only become more used and more useful as time goes on" (OUP 2006).

Calculating carbon footprint is fundamental to assessing climate change impacts. Carbon footprint is defined as "a measure of the impact human activities have on the environment in terms of the amount of greenhouse gases produced, measured in units of carbon dioxide" (Carbon Footprint Ltd. 2006). The carbon footprint (measured in tons of CO_2) is a vital component of a broader ecological footprint (measured in acres or hectares) associated with human development impacts on planetary ecosystems. Generic tools to measure both carbon footprint and ecological footprint are rapidly evolving.

Because buildings represent 48 percent of US energy use and a corresponding percentage of CO_2 releases (*Architecture 2030* 2006), buildings must be a central focus in the global dialogue and strategy to achieve meaning-

ful CO_2 emission reductions. In January 2006, architect Edward Mazria, AIA, launched the 2030 ° Challenge: to achieve zero emissions and carbon neutrality for all building operations by 2030, beginning with an initial 60 percent reduction of fossil fuel consumption by 2010, and continuing with an additional 10 percent incremental reduction in every subsequent five-year period (Architecture 2030 2006). Many US organizations are adopting this bold initiative, including the American Institute of Architects (AIA); the US Green Building Council (USGBC); the American Society of Heating, Refrigerating, and Air-Conditioning Engineers (ASHRAE); and the US Conference of Mayors (see Chapter 2 for a discussion of the origins of this initiative) (Ulam 2006).

Globally, the World Business Council on Sustainable Development's goals for its building energy efficiency project are energy self-sufficiency and carbon neutrality at reasonable costs by 2050. As these initiatives take hold, reducing carbon emissions is proving to deliver economic value. In "Carbon Down, Profits Up," the Climate Group (2005) illustrates how, over a four-year period, many companies and governments have realized financial and economic benefits through reducing their greenhouse gas emissions. In the international banking sector, HSBC made a commitment at the end of 2004 to be the first major carbon neutral bank. This aspiration was the third part of HSBC's carbon management plan. The first two, being as energy efficient as possible and buying renewable energy, have already been implemented.

At Greenbuild 2006, the US Green Building Council unveiled specific actions to address climate change, including a commitment to become a carbon neutral organization by 2007. As it has done at prior Greenbuild conferences, the USGBC offset carbon emissions associated with travel for all twelve thousand participants at the 2006 Denver conference. LEED projects will reflect this organizational commitment: Beginning June 26, 2007, all new LEED-registered projects will be required to achieve at least two energy optimization points, representing a 50 percent reduction in CO_2 emissions, compared with current levels. Further, USGBC will launch a new educational program to aid industry professionals in implementing energy-efficient design and construction practices with immediate and measurable impact on CO_2 emissions (USGBC 2006).

HEALTHCARE'S CARBON FOOTPRINT

Aligning the healthcare industry with carbon neutral principles and practices represents much more than a token gesture in the race to reverse global climate change. Indeed, the healthcare sector has a direct stake in the consequences of global warming: its alarming health consequences have been articulated by medical and public health professionals. Healthcare is also a key actor given its opportunity to radically curb its contribution to CO_2 emissions by strategically and comprehensively reducing its carbon footprint.

But the industry also faces formidable challenges. Unlike the commercial office sector, whose energy intensity (measured in kilowatt hours per square foot) has peaked according to US Department of Energy estimates, healthcare continues to increase energy intensity and overall consumption as it replaces an earlier generation of building infrastructure. According to Department of Energy data, healthcare is now the second most energy-intensive building sector per square foot in the US, behind food service (EIA 2003). Contributing factors are 24/7 operations and reliance on an ever-increasing array of energy-consuming technologies with correspondingly rigorous ventilation requirements (see below).

In 2005, the US Environmental Protection Agency (EPA) issued the Energy Star Challenge, calling on businesses and organizations across the nation to reduce energy use in existing buildings. By challenging building owners to reduce energy consumption by ten percent, the EPA estimates "by 2015 Americans would reduce greenhouse gas emissions by more than 20 MMTCE [see sidebar above], equivalent to the emissions of 15 million vehicles, while saving about $10 billion" (EPA 2007a). In response, the American Society for Healthcare Engineering (ASHE) launched the Energy Efficiency Commitment (E2C) in order to both educate hospital staffers on the environmental and economic value of improving energy efficiency within their organizations and recognize members who achieve at least 10 percent savings in energy consumption. The EPA's Energy Star Challenge program goal to reduce energy use in commercial buildings with consequent CO_2 emission reductions supports the 2030 °Challenge. Hospitals can use the range of existing EPA Energy Star tools, such as Target Finder, to establish energy performance targets that meet the 2030 °Challenge goal. EPA's Target Finder calculates energy consumption for a new facility, and compares estimated energy use with an established relative regional baseline target and to the top 10 percent of facilities of similar type and location.

Similar emphasis on reducing healthcare's carbon footprint is being seen internationally. For example, the UK's Carbon Trust's NHS Carbon Management Programme issued a challenge to the NHS in late 2006: reduce the NHS's annual carbon footprint by 15 percent, representing approximately 40,000 tons of carbon emissions. Within two months of the declaration, the British government committed £100 million ($197.25 million) toward the NHS's carbon reduction action. As UK Health Minister Andy Burnham noted, "The reduction of carbon emissions and greenhouse gases is important for the environment and helps people lead a healthy life" (Department of Health 2007).

In a groundbreaking study for Royal Liverpool University Hospital, London-based architectural designer Malcolm Stroud (2006) illustrates how a carbon neutral hospital development could be created using current technology. Based on British policies and metrics, Stroud's study categorizes estimated CO_2 sources and relative percentages for a typical existing acute care hospital (see Figure 12-5). Stroud contends that changing energy sources has a greater potential to lower a healthcare facility's carbon footprint than building design, assigning a 60:40 ratio to these two categories.

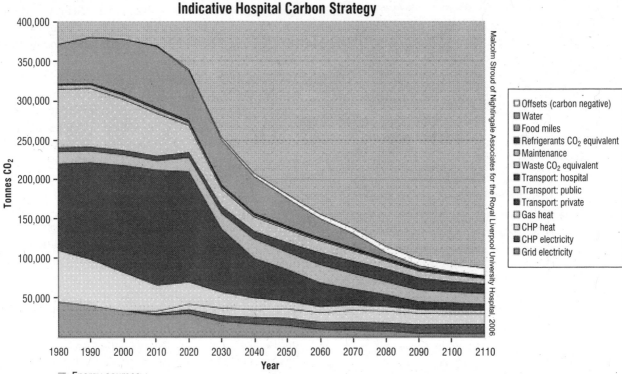

Indicative Hospital Carbon Strategy

Malcolm Stroud of Nightingale Associates for the Royal Liverpool University Hospital, 2006

Legend:
- Offsets (carbon negative)
- Water
- Food miles
- Refrigerants CO_2 equivalent
- Maintenance
- Waste CO_2 equivalent
- Transport: hospital
- Transport: public
- Transport: private
- Gas heat
- CHP heat
- CHP electricity
- Grid electricity

Y-axis: Tonnes CO_2 (50,000 to 400,000)
X-axis: Year (1980 to 2110)

■ Energy sources
36 percent: carbon emissions associated with different energy sources and technologies (e.g., grid-connected coal-, natural gas-, nuclear-, or hydro-generated electricity; on-site combined heat and power; on-site renewables

■ Energy efficiency
24 percent: building performance reflecting design, mechanical, and operational measures

■ Transport
22 percent: reliance on cars, ambulances, public transportation, and associated fuels as a function of building location

■ Waste
9 percent: methane emissions from landfilling and emissions avoidance from recycling

■ Food miles
7 percent: transporting food from source to facility

■ Materials
2 percent: embodied energy associated with material sourcing, processing, transporting, and manufacture prior to use

■ Refrigerants
<1 percent: global warming potential associated with refrigerants

■ Water
<0.1 percent: embodied energy associated with water conveyance and treatment

Figure 12-5: The graph illustrates the potential to radically alter a hospital's carbon footprint over a 130-year time span by implementing a full spectrum of carbon reduction efforts. *Credit: Royal Liverpool University Hospital*

In line with Stroud's model, a number of activities in the healthcare sector demonstrate both individual facility and systemic initiatives aimed at reducing carbon footprint. The Maine Green Power Connection, for example, recommends the actions highlighted above for Maine's hospitals. Many of these are relevant to hospitals on a broader scale. Additional initiatives include:

- Providence Health System's Newberg Medical Center, in Newberg, Oregon (page 293), is the first US hospital building to meet all its energy needs with 100 percent renewable wind-generated electricity (PHS 2007). This shift to renewables will offset more than 3 million pounds of carbon dioxide emissions each year. To support this commitment, Providence has agreed to purchase 183,294 kilowatt hours per month through Pacific Gas and Electric's Clean Winds Program.
- At Boulder Community Hospital in Boulder, Colorado (page 234), the central plant and mechanical equipment were specified to reduce airborne emissions. High-efficiency, partial load, low-nitrogen oxide (NOx) boilers reduce annual NOx emissions by 70 percent, carbon monoxide (CO) by 50 percent, and energy fuel consumption by 20 percent over standard boilers. Variable supply and return fan controls reduce carbon dioxide (CO_2) emissions by 5.5 million pounds per year (2.49 million kilograms), sulfur dioxide (SO_2) by 18,298 pounds per year (8299 kilograms, and NOx by 17,857 pounds per year (8100 kilograms). The payback period is less than one year.
- Whitchurch Community Hospital in Shropshire, UK, is the first NHS hospital to fulfill its energy needs with a biomass boiler, using wood chips derived from sawmill residues and forestry by-products as its fuel source; it is considered a possible path to achieving both financial and carbon savings. The wood-fueled boiler is offsetting an estimated 115 tons of CO_2 per year while also shifting reliance to a renewable, local fuel resource; this is already resulting in an estimated 20 percent cost savings over gas (Jones 2006).

TOWARD A CARBON NEUTRAL, PBT-FREE, ZERO WASTE HOSPITAL

The hospital of the future is emerging today, with its defining characteristics shaped by the global realities of climate change, toxic pollution, and natural resource depletion, among others. Case studies throughout this book illustrate how these considerations are influencing design and operations. For some issues, like waste reduction, healthcare has had more than a decade of successes to build upon; for others, such as carbon neutrality, the work is just beginning. But what brings these issues together are parallel trends: carbon dioxide emissions are increasing at an alarming rate as PBT levels in humans rise and the global stock of resources decreases. These indicators—each with significant health consequences—warrant attention and action. Architect Simon Shaw's essay, "Toward a Carbon Neutral Hospital," explores a range of strategies aimed at reducing carbon footprint.

Toward a Carbon Neutral Hospital

Simon Shaw, RIBA

*W*hat does it mean for a healthcare organization or hospital campus to become carbon neutral? What would Kyoto Protocol compliance require? How does the carbon footprint today compare with the 1990 baseline—how is it calculated?

The carbon footprint will be reduced greatly if the building itself is considered as part of the process of healthcare. While Malcolm Stroud's prioritizing of energy sources (Figure 12-5) is statistically correct—that is, that the choice of fuel source may have a larger overall impact on the carbon footprint than overall energy consumption—the investment in renewable energy sources before the adoption of load-reduction measures is wasteful. An understanding of energy use patterns is critical to identifying potential efficiencies. Utilizing the climate change impact categories presented by Stroud, the following is a blueprint for carbon neutral hospitals.

1. BUILDING/ENERGY EFFICIENCY

Minimizing energy demand is the highest priority toward a carbon neutral hospital. Factors that contribute to building energy efficiency can be divided into three areas: siting and planning, external envelope, and internal environment. The following descriptions are not exhaustive, but provide a framework for reducing the effects of climatic impact.

Siting and Planning: *Site and building orientation significantly impact the carbon footprint. The density of site development has a direct impact, affecting the scale, massing, and planning of the new facility. Solar and wind orientation, favorable geothermal conditions, and optimum site development are fundamental. Correct solar orientation will allow sunlight to be managed for seasonal demands, while rightsizing the building will minimize material consumption and reduce demand on necessary systems.*

Responsible land use can benefit the carbon footprint. In giving a low priority to water consumption, conveyance, and treatment, Stroud excludes the off-site impacts of storm water handling. However, if intro-

duced on-site, bioswales and rainwater retention ponds will eliminate the negative impact of the development on surrounding infrastructure. Additionally, this retained water may be reused for irrigation, cooling tower makeup, sewage conveyance, or even drinking.

External Envelope: *A building's skin can play a significant role in minimizing the energy needed for its operation. A high-performance, thermally resistant, airtight building will significantly reduce heat losses during the winter and also reduce heat gains during the summer months.*

Buildings are now wearing more sophisticated skins. Architects are integrating ventilation, shading, and other technologies into double-wall facades that serve as primary space conditioners. Careful control of sunlight will eliminate unwanted summer heat gains and reduce the cooling load, but could also reduce the winter heating load by controlling admission of the solar heat. To achieve carbon neutrality, future hospitals could gain considerable advantage by employing their building envelope to maximize natural daylight and generate heat—and potentially, even power—by integrating solar thermal collectors and solar photovoltaics.

Internal Environment: *Analyzing the many environmental needs of a hospital could potentially lead to more efficient control over the heating, cooling, and ventilating systems. For example, the demands of an operating room are different from those of a patient room and different still from those of an administration space. Using a single system design to serve them all may not be energy efficient. Decoupling the heating and cooling systems from ventilation, as with displacement ventilation, could easily improve efficiency. The separation of cooling and ventilating tasks not only improves comfort conditions, it also improves indoor air quality and the control and zoning of the system.*

Night purging is a very simple process that involves letting the cool air during evening and early morning into a building to replace the warm air that has built up during the day. It can be as simple as opening a window or carefully controlled by a monitoring computer. In hospitals, the incidental heat gains from equipment and people are considerable; when combined with twenty-four-hour use, the frequent lack of operable windows, and well-insulated, well-sealed envelopes, there is little chance of night purging. Other systems, such as geothermal, ground-source, or bore-hole heating and cooling, can reduce the building's energy requirement.

2. ENERGY SOURCES

After reducing energy demand, the next consideration is the way energy is generated—either on- or off-site.

Healthcare facilities are not only affected by the cost, reliability, and availability of utilities, but also by regulation in the form of environmental directives, taxes, and liabilities. An element of future-proofing must therefore be considered. As this book goes to press, policy initiatives aimed at taxation of carbon emissions are under discussion in the United States. Future buildings will need the capacity to survive, adapt, and grow in the face of unforeseen changes. There are many operational advantages to having on-site sources of energy.

Using current technology, the huge power demands of a hospital could preclude energy being provided by on-site renewable measures alone. However, there are a number of other opportunities for source energy improvements. The choice of fuel used to operate buildings greatly impacts emissions. All fuels contain impurities that become pollutants, so the choice of fuel has a huge impact on the carbon footprint. For example, burning coal emits about 1.7 times as much carbon per unit of energy as natural gas, and 1.25 times as much as oil. For the same amount of energy produced, natural gas emits 50 percent less CO_2 than coal, and 25 percent less than oil. Cogeneration, also known as combined heat and power (CHP),simultaneously generates both on-site thermal energy for heating and electric power, and is considered about 56 percent more efficient than grid-connected power due to the dramatic reduction of transmission losses and capture of waste heat. A further development of this technology is trigeneration, which expands capability to include the generation of chilled water for evaporative cooling.

Conventional combined heat and power facilities have predominantly used oil or gas. However, wood-chips and other sustainably managed biofuels, including wood by-products, have the potential to provide carbon neutral energy sources (Stroud 2006). The low caloric value of agricultural products such as straw bales and cereal crops, and forestry waste such as branches and tree-tops from thinning and timber harvesting, prevents them from becoming a viable economic alternative unless they are available locally. But even without burning, biomass can be used as fuel. Anaerobic digestion, a process similar to composting, will produce low-grade heat, nutrient rich products, and biogas. This gas—mainly methane—can be used as a clean fuel.

3. MATERIAL EFFICIENCY

A life cycle perspective is a valuable standpoint from which to grasp the full range of consequences associated with specific materials and products, including embodied energy—the energy associated with the extraction, process, manufacture, and transport of a building's materials, and for its construction (see Figure 1-6). The analysis enables a comparison based on identified environmental and health-evaluative criteria. Choosing nontoxic materials with high postconsumer recycled and industrial by-product content, such as steel and fly ash–based cement, respectively, coupled with low-energy manufacturing processes, can lower a building's carbon footprint.

The UK's Building Research Establishment's Green Guide to Specification provides, for every building material or assembly, a rating from A (least environmental impact) to C (most environmental impact). In simplifying the presentation of material assessments, the Green Guide to Specification provides an easy desktop reference that is widely used in the UK (Anderson, Shiers, and Sinclair 2005). As embodied energy calculation methodologies unfold, it is possible that building materials will include their embodied energy values as a component of their product data, with calculations for transportation energy from point of assembly to the project site.

4. TRANSPORT STRATEGY

Stroud's analysis shows that transport is a hospital-related activity for which carbon emissions are already high and consistently rising. Stroud begins with the assumption that technological improvements will lead to a 50 percent improvement in emissions for individual vehicles. Carbon neutrality, however, cannot be achieved by improved fuel-efficiency standards alone, as long as fossil fuels remain a component of automobile design—the rate of individual vehicle use needs to be reduced from 83 to 25 percent of total vehicle use in order to achieve a total emissions reduction of 70 percent. (One fortunate repercussion: the number of parking spaces could then be reduced by 75 percent, making more of a site available for other development or productive landscaping.)

With regard to managing transportation carbon impacts, a new hospital's location and proximity to public transportation will become very important. Hospital staff will be encouraged to use public transportation, car share, or bicycle. The resultant site planning will provide for bus drop-offs, priority parking for car sharers, bicycle facilities, and potentially, the provision of electric or fuel-cell vehicles powered by on-site renewable energy.

Some existing hospitals' locations may prove to be a real obstacle to achieving carbon neutrality. In the context of achieving an "excellent" rating in the UK Building Research Establishment Environmental Assessment Method (BREEAM), Stroud highlights a study suggesting that a less than ideally located hospital should consider converting to a more local facility—or even abandonment (Stroud 2006).

5. FOOD STRATEGY

Unlike housing, for which surrounding land can be allocated for growing produce, it is unlikely that the land owned by healthcare facilities would be sufficient to provide the food quantities required by its occupants. Therefore, the production and transport of food will always be a contributing factor to a hospital's carbon footprint. A low-impact food program, based on minimizing food miles—or the distance that food travels from "farm to fork"—is recommended.

A carbon neutral hospital must recognize its purchasing power. The sheer quantity of meals consumed gives the hospital commercial leverage over the procurement of its food or food service. Room-service meal distribution both reduces waste and improves patient satisfaction. Local and seasonal foods should be used wherever possible, giving the meals a distinctive, local flavor and a connection to the land, the climate, and the time of year.

As described in Gary Cohen's essay in Chapter 3, Kaiser Permanente and Catholic Healthcare West in California are joining a growing number of hospitals piloting new programs for purchasing produce from small, local farms instead of from the large-scale industrial farms that typically supply hospitals and other big institutions. The results of these programs will answer a question vital to the future of sustainable agriculture and to the livelihood of small farmers in California and across America (Ness 2005). The reduction of food miles is only one of the measurable outcomes being tracked as these programs unfold.

6. WASTE STRATEGY

In a review of the CleanMed 2006 conference, healthcare environmental management expert and essayist Janet Brown (2006) writes: "The back door of a health care facility can teach you a lot. The sheer volume of waste is astounding—from construction waste to food, packaging, corrugated boxes, medication, electronics, surplus equipment, mercury-contaminated material, and plastic medical apparatus, to name just a few."

According to unpublished research by Hospitals for a Healthy Environment (H2E), most hospitals generate roughly 25 pounds of waste per occupied bed per day. Because health care space is always at a premium, any missed or late pickups can quickly result in a mountain of material.

Increased environmental health awareness, combined with a shortage of landfill space and incineration facilities, has resulted in waste disposal regulations that make disposal ever-more controversial and expensive. Stroud estimates that the methane and CO_2 released from hospital waste in landfill sites could, in theory, make up about 15 percent of the carbon footprint. Therefore, in order of priority, a waste strategy should consider:

- Avoidance: *Avoid material consumption by modifying a process or procedure to design out redundancy or disposability.*
- Re-use: *To eliminate cross-contamination, articles being reused must be cleaned, disinfected, and, if necessary, sterilized. This may have a financial impact and would need to be reviewed on a case-by-case basis.*
- Recycling: *Recyclable materials need to be collected, sorted, and delivered to central storage areas to be prepared for transportation. This will require extra areas designated for these activities. These need to be sensibly located.*

- Proper disposal: *Due to the nature of some procedures, hospitals produce many wastes—from nonhazardous domestic waste to infectious, chemical, mercury, hazardous and radioactive waste. With current technology, many of these waste products are unavoidable. However, sorting and pretreating these waste materials on site considerably reduces the environmental and health impacts of disposal.*

Finally, if we accept that a certain level of waste is inevitable, the potential to reduce the carbon footprint ultimately lies in an ability to recapture landfill gases.

7. CARBON OFFSETS
Even after a strategic implementation of the six steps described above, a facility's carbon footprint may require offsets to achieve carbon neutrality. A carbon offset is achieved by either reducing emissions or increasing carbon absorption, such as is thought to occur through tree planting. While outstanding questions about the ability of carbon offsets to achieve the desired result of balancing carbon emissions exist, several strategies, ranging from purchasing renewable energy credits (RECs) and carbon trading, are marketed.

As the bar for the design, construction, and operation of healthcare buildings rises, the green standards of today become the standard practice of tomorrow. As this occurs, achieving carbon neutrality in all aspects of a hospital's operation will become the new objective. While achieving carbon neutrality is an unrealized aspiration for the healthcare sector, it has the potential to transform current design methodologies and inform the sustainable future of healthcare.

THE ZERO WASTE HOSPITAL

Both Shaw's essay and Chapter 7 consider the topic of waste reduction. What is a zero waste hospital? In 2005, the University of Florida announced a target goal of "zero waste by 2012," after achieving "garbage-free games" in its athletic program. A commitment to a zero waste future, as espoused by the GrassRoots Recycling Network's Zero Waste Business Principles and described here, is gathering momentum in the US and internationally, as businesses explore ways to reduce their carbon and broader ecological footprint. These principles can be applied to healthcare organizations, too. As H2E demonstrates, leading healthcare organizations are already approaching 50 percent diversion rates in their operational waste streams; at the same time, many hospital environmental managers engaged in the work acknowledge they are just getting started (see Chapter 7).

ZERO WASTE BUSINESS PRINCIPLES

The GrassRoots Recycling Network adopted the following principles on January 13, 2004, to guide and evaluate current and future zero waste policies and programs established by businesses. These Zero Waste Business Principles establish the commitment of companies to achieve zero waste and further establish criteria by which workers, investors, customers, suppliers, policymakers and the public in general can assess the resource efficiency of companies.

1. *Commitment to the triple bottom line:* We ensure that social, environmental and economic performance standards are met together. We maintain clear accounting and reporting systems and operate with the highest ethical standards for our investors and our customers. We produce annual environmental or sustainability reports that document how we implement these policies. We inform workers, customers and the community about environmental impacts of our production, products or services.

2. *Use the precautionary principle:* We apply the precautionary principle before introducing new products and processes to avoid products and practices that are wasteful or toxic.

(continued)

3. *Zero waste to landfill or incineration:* We divert more than 90 percent of the solid wastes we generate from landfill and incineration from all of our facilities. No more than 10 percent of our discards are landfilled. No mixed wastes are incinerated or processed in facilities that operate above ambient biological temperatures (more than 200° F (93.3° C)) to recover energy or materials.

4. *Responsibility—takeback products packaging:* We take financial and/or physical responsibility for all the products and packaging we produce and/or market under our brand(s), and require our suppliers to do so as well. We support and work with existing reuse, recycling and composting operators to productively use our products and packaging, or arrange for new systems to bring those back to our manufacturing facilities. We include the reuse, recycling or composting of our products as a design criteria for all new products.

5. *Buy reused, recycled and composted:* We use recycled content and compost products in all aspects of our operations, including production facilities, offices and in the construction of new facilities. We use LEED [accredited] architects to design new and remodeled facilities as green buildings. We buy reused products where they are available and make our excess inventory of equipment and products available for reuse by others. We label our products and packaging with the amount of postconsumer recycled content and for papers, we label if chlorine-free and forest-friendly materials are used.

6. *Prevent pollution and reduce waste:* We redesign our supply, production and distribution systems to reduce the use of natural resources and eliminate waste. We prevent pollution and the waste of materials by continual assessment of our systems and revising procedures, policies and payment policies. To the extent our products contain materials with known or suspected adverse human health impacts, we notify consumers of their content and how to safely manage the products at the end of their useful life.

7. *Highest and best use:* We continuously evaluate our markets and direct our discarded products and packaging to recover the highest value of their embodied energy and materials according to the following hierarchy: reuse of the product for its original purpose; reuse of the product for an alternate purpose; reuse of its parts; reuse of the materials; recycling of inorganic materials in closed loop systems; recycling of inorganic materials in single-use applications; composting of organic materials to sustain soils and avoid use of chemical fertilizers; and composting or mulching of organic materials to reduce erosion and litter and retain moisture.

8. *Use economic incentives for customers, workers and suppliers:* We encourage our customers, workers and suppliers to eliminate waste and maximize the reuse, recycling and composting of discarded materials through economic incentives and a holistic systems analysis. We lease our products to customers and provide bonuses or other rewards to workers, suppliers and other stakeholders that eliminate waste. We use financial incentives to encourage our suppliers to adhere to zero waste principles. We evaluate our discards to determine how to develop other productive business opportunities from these assets.

9. *Products or services sold are not wasteful or toxic:* We evaluate our products and services regularly to determine if they are wasteful or toxic and develop alternatives to eliminate those products that we find are wasteful or toxic. We evaluate all our products and offer them as services whenever possible. We design products to be easily disassembled to encourage reuse and repair. We design our products to be durable—to last as long as the technology is in practice.

10. *Use nontoxic production, reuse and recycling processes:* We eliminate the use of hazardous materials in our production, reuse and recycling processes, particularly persistent bioaccumulative toxics. We eliminate the environmental, health and safety risks to our employees and the communities in which we operate. Any materials exported to other countries with lower environmental standards are managed according to the current standards in the United States.

Source: GrassRoots Recycling Network 2004
Reprinted with permission

THE PBT-FREE HOSPITAL

An essential element of an ecological footprint strategy is reducing toxic chemicals. At the 2004 United Nations' Johannesburg +2 Sustainable Development Conference, the commitment to "achieve, by 2020, that chemicals are used and produced in ways that lead to the minimization of significant adverse effects on human health and the environment, using transparent science-based risk assessment procedures and science-based risk management procedures, taking into account the precautionary approach" was renewed (WSSD 2004). As materials expert Tom Lent and attorney Julie Silas describe in their essay "The PBT-Free Challenge," momentum is well underway in the healthcare industry to achieve what may seem to some an elusive goal.

The PBT-Free Challenge

Tom Lent and Julie Silas

1989: *Researchers working with indigenous Inuit women in the Arctic find record-breaking levels of polychlorinated biphenyls (PCBs)—probable carcinogens and developmental toxicants—and other toxic industrial chemicals thousands of miles from the nearest manufacturing plant that releases these chemicals (Dewailly, Nantel, Weber, et al. 1989).*

1999: *Scientists discover that polybrominated diphenyl ethers (PBDEs)—halogenated flame-retardant chemicals linked in animal studies to disruptions in thyroid function and immune suppression—are concentrating in Swedish mothers' milk, with a fiftyfold increase in levels between the early 1970s and the late 1990s (Meironyte, Noren, and Bergman 1999).*

2001: *A study of the US food supply shows that contamination with dioxins—the most potent synthetic carcinogens known to science and strong endocrine disruptors—is universal across the nation at levels of concern, despite government efforts to reduce dioxin releases into the environment (Schecter et al. 2001).*

2004–2006: *Record levels of perfluorinated chemicals (PFCs) — known to cause liver damage and reproduc-*

tive problems—are found in studies of human blood and mothers' milk around the world; an EPA advisory panel determines that perfluorooctanoic acid, a primary PFC, is a likely human carcinogen. Nearly every man, woman, and child now has some type of PFC in his or her blood (Kannan, Corsolini, Falandysz, et al. 2004; Calafat, Kuklenyik, Reich, et al. 2003; Yeung, So, Jiang, et al. 2006; Inoue, Okada, Ito, et al. 2004; Chase 2006).

These disparate stories have a common thread. In each case, a toxic chemical is accumulating in our blood and flesh, rapidly increasing in quantity, hitting—and surpassing—levels of concern, with no end in sight. Each of the cited chemicals is from a class of chemicals known as persistent bioaccumulative toxicants (PBTs).

These toxic chemicals are often dangerous in very small quantities, doing harm to humans and other living organisms at concentrations of mere parts per billion or trillion. Efforts to manage these chemicals have been ineffective: landfills do not diminish the hazardous properties of these chemicals, and waste incineration and landfill fires can generate new, hazardous PBT compounds. Spread by winds, water, and animals, these worst-in-class chemicals now contaminate the most pristine environments; ironically the highest con-

THE ABCs OF PBTs

Persistent bioaccumulative toxicants (PBTs) are "persistent" because they do not break down rapidly via natural processes once they are emitted into the environment. Many persist for months or years, allowing them to travel long distances on wind and water currents from where they were manufactured—for example, from chemical plants in Louisiana to Inuit women in the Arctic. PBTs "bioaccumulate"—they love to build up in living beings, often in fatty tissues, increasing their concentrations by orders of magnitude as they move up the food chain to humans at the top and becoming most concentrated in mothers' milk. And PBTs are "toxic"—and include some of the most potent carcinogens, mutagens, and reproductive toxicants known to humankind.

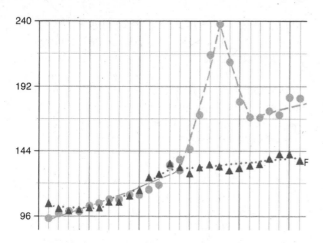

Figure 12-6: The graphs illustrate the increasing incidence rates of the two most common cancers—breast cancer and prostate cancer—based on National Cancer Institute data from 1975 through 2002. *Source: National Cancer Institute*

centrations are now found in the peoples and animals of the Arctic regions. PBTs are a global problem that require concerted efforts to solve. In response, scientists and medical professionals from around the world—concerned by the rising incidence of breast cancer and other chronic diseases linked to PBT exposure (see Figure 12-6)—are voicing concerns that the same chemicals that have provided such a boon to industry are creating new health crises.

PRIORITY PBTS
Products that contain or create PBTs of concern can be found throughout a modern medical facility—in building materials and in the products and devices used on a daily basis. Fortunately, in most situations, high-performance, cost-effective, PBT-free alternatives exist.

Dioxins: *Dioxins are an unavoidable by-product of the manufacture, combustion, and disposal of materials containing chlorine—most notably polyvinyl chloride (PVC)—and of cement kilns fired by hazardous waste fuel. Dioxins are the most potent human carcinogens; they cause developmental damage, are associated with endometriosis, and can alter the reproductive, immune, and endocrine systems even at infinitesimally low doses. Building materials such as flooring, pipes, wall*

coverings, roofing membranes, furniture, carpet backings, and curtains account for three-quarters of all PVC; however, its use in medical devices is also widespread—it is found in IV tubing and bags, blood bags, and a host of other devices. As customer demand for PVC-free products increases, manufacturers are responding by investing in research, development, and product innovation, as evidenced by the steady stream of chlorine-free alternatives now coming to market (HCWH 2007a; 2007c; HBN 2007).*

Halogenated flame retardants (HFRs): *These chemicals are used to reduce the flammability of fabrics, foams, and other plastics. They get their name from the halogens attached to the carbon in the molecule—usually bromine (called brominated flame retardants, or BFRs) or chlorine. Polybrominated diphenyl ethers (PBDEs) and other HFRs are linked to thyroid disruption, reproductive and neurodevelopmental problems, and immune suppression. HFRs are widely used in curtains, drapery, and other textiles; mattress and furniture foam padding; a host of electronics, including computers, fax and copy machines, and monitors; and ventilators, pulse oximeters, IV pumps, and other plastic products needing fire protection. As states begin to institute bans on PBDEs and other HFRs, manufacturers are actively substituting alternative chemicals, using inherently flame-resistant plastics, and redesigning products to avoid needing flame retardants altogether.*

Perfluorochemicals (PFCs): *These are a family of compounds used to create nonstick and stain-repellant treatments and materials for carpets, medical components, and household products, including Teflon, Scotchguard, Stainmaster, Gore-Tex, and Zonyl. Linked to thyroid and developmental problems, the EPA is scrutinizing this family of compounds, and several manufacturers are beginning to phase out fluoropolymers, including perfluorooctanoic acid (PFOAs) (EPA 2007b).*

Heavy metals: *Lead is often used as a stabilizer in other materials, most notably wiring and PVC products, and can be found in roofing, solder, and radiation shielding. Mercury is found in fluorescent lamps; thermostats and other control equipment; thermometers, sphygmo-*

manometers, and other medical devices; laboratory equipment; and is still used in the manufacture of PVC at some chlor-alkali plants. Lead and mercury are both potent neurotoxicants, particularly damaging to the brains of fetuses and growing children. Cadmium, used as a dye in paint and as a stabilizer in PVC, is carcinogenic and can damage the kidneys and lungs (GBPSR 2000). The healthcare industry has made major strides in procuring mercury-free medical equipment and controls and reducing mercury levels in fluorescent lamps (see Chapter 7).

ORGANIZATIONAL COMMITMENTS TO CHANGE
Responding to the weight of evidence linking PBT releases and threats to living systems, governments and institutions worldwide are initiating efforts to reduce or eliminate the use of products that contain or contribute to the release of PBTs into the environment. Dioxins, furans, and PCBs are among twelve top PBTs already targeted for elimination by international treaty—the 2001 Stockholm Convention on Persistent Organic Pollutants. It is expected that halogenated flame retardants and some perfluorochemicals will be added to the treaty soon (WWF 2005). The EPA has prioritized thirty-one chemicals for elimination and targeted healthcare-related activities as an important source of two of the twelve most hazardous PBTs: mercury and dioxin (EPA 1998). Some of these efforts are bearing fruit: Swedish PBDE levels plummeted in the early twenty-first century after a national ban was instituted. During the same period in the United States, where production continued, PBDE concentrations soared even higher (Lunder 2003; Hites 2004).

Specific to healthcare, the American Hospital Association and the EPA entered into a landmark memorandum of understanding in 1998 to advance pollution prevention efforts in US healthcare facilities and prioritized PBTs for elimination (EPA and AHA 1998). The state of Washington's Department of Ecology and the Washington State Hospital Association initiated their own memorandum of understanding in 2005 that committed to minimize PBTs in healthcare, focusing particularly on mercury elimination (WSDE 2005). Kaiser Permanente's national environmental purchasing policy incorporates specific environmental criteria

for all purchasing decisions, including criteria to "avoid products containing persistent bioaccumulative toxic compounds" (Kaiser Permanente 2006). And group purchasing organizations for healthcare have incorporated efforts to avoid products that contain PBTs —or contribute to their release into the environment —into their environmentally preferable purchasing goals (Premier 2004; Consorta 2007).

Driven by buyer demands, manufacturers are responding. Some are reducing the use of specific PBTs in their products, such as Shaw Carpets (PVC-free and flame-retardant-free carpet) and Herman Miller (PVC-free, heavy-metal-free furniture). Some are establishing goals to comprehensively remove all PBTs from their products. In 2001, SC Johnson established its "greenlist" to help its chemists avoid harmful chemicals and "remove PBT chemicals from our product line" (Weeks 2006), leading to many successful product reformulations to eliminate PBTs and PVC, a primary source of dioxin. Market demand for PBT alternatives is growing, particularly from the healthcare sector: more than one hundred healthcare organizations have undertaken efforts to reduce PVC and di(2-ethylhexyl) phthalate (DEHP) use in their facilities (HCWH 2007).

PATHWAY TO A PBT-FREE HOSPITAL
As major consumers of PBT-related building and operations products—and as influential community specialists on health—healthcare leaders have a critical role to play in impelling not only the healthcare industry, but also society at-large, to eliminate PBTs from the environment. A PBT-free hospital policy can become the cornerstone of a bigger effort to eliminate all high-hazard toxics from construction and operations. By incorporating PBT-free specifications in construction and implementing environmentally preferable purchasing policies for operations, hospitals can undertake healthy practices that simultaneously consider their own patients, staff, and local communities, and their global responsibility.

The path to the PBT-free hospital ideally starts with the establishment of clear policy directives at the healthcare system level. Policies such as Kaiser Permanente's national environmental purchasing policy, which articulates the goal of avoiding products and materials that contain or create PBTs, provide important guidance to construction project designers and purchasing departments alike. Such policies send a compelling message to suppliers and help build momentum to move the marketplace to expand the availability of high-performance, PBT-free options — keys to reversing the growing crisis.

Construction and renovation projects provide the ideal opportunity to establish a PBT-free environment. Ideally the PBT-free goal should be established early in the project's goal-setting process and become a priority throughout the building program. Explicitly addressing the goal and rationale early on and carrying it through to specifications and criteria for product substitution will help ensure that all parties understand the priority of the goal and reduce the likelihood of its being disregarded in the inevitable process of value engineering and contractor material substitution.

Operations are equally important to creating and maintaining the PBT-free hospital. Establishing environmentally preferable purchasing policies that prioritize PBT elimination should be complemented by supporting purchasing staff in efforts to find alternative products that meet the goals while fulfilling other perfomance requirements. Similarly, maintenance and renovation policies that establish the PBT-free goal will help ensure that PBT-free building designs are kept PBT-free as hospitals replace materials through the course of building operations, repair, and maintenance.

A clearly articulated PBT elimination goal in construction and operations is a solid foundation to establishing a toxic-free environment. Further, a hospital can work to eliminate the whole range of carcinogens, mutagens, reproductive toxicants, teratogens, neurotoxicants, and endocrine disruptors from the products they use. Clearly signaling to the marketplace a commitment to eliminate PBTs and other toxics is critical and should be carried consistently through conversations with vendors, requests for proposals, screening questionnaires, and contract and specification language.

By demanding disclosure of ingredients and making clear preferences for PBT-free alternatives, hospitals can influence the changing marketplace for the better. In the long run, signaling a preference for PBT-free products to the market spurs innovation, even though in some cases, a hospital may find that vendors are unable to supply a satisfactory alternative immediately. Even then, hospitals can add to the market push that is creating rapid change in the industry.

CONCLUSION
The growing threat to human health posed by PBTs is urgent, but it can be reversed, bolstered by clear signals from the healthcare industry. Creating model PBT-free hospitals protects staff, patients, and the community while signaling larger change. Leveraging manufacturers to replace their PBT products with safer high-performance, PBT-free options ensures that the changes undertaken by hospitals quickly cascade through society. To arrive at a day when all product choices will be PBT- and toxic-free, the assertive leadership of healthcare is critical.

CONCLUSION

The roadmap to a sustainable healthcare facility begins to unfold when specific goals within the context of the ecological footprint are identified. The ones outlined in this chapter — carbon neutrality, zero waste, and PBT elimination — can be achieved in this new generation of buildings; indeed, some hospitals are already well along that path. What is clear is that the work does not reside just within the walls of the healthcare facility — success requires coordination at the community, regional, and global scales, and among manufacturers and educators as much as policy makers. Carbon neutral schemes rely on effective technologies and a trained cadre of professionals who understand how to employ energy-efficiency measures and renewable resources in a cost-effective manner. Zero waste requires commodities that are manufactured for reuse, recycling, and composting and a waste management infrastructure that recognizes discards as resources rather than merely looking at them as garbage. Finally, fulfilling the PBT-free challenge requires a materials manufacturing sector that eliminates the use of these worst-in-class chemicals from their feedstocks while maintaining or enhancing fundamental performance attributes. The healthcare sector can be the clarion call that sees these as both opportunities and imperatives.

CHAPTER 13

Creating the Twenty-First Century Hospital

> The fatal metaphor of progress, which means leaving things behind us, has utterly obscured the real idea of growth, which means leaving things inside us.
> —G. K. CHESTERTON

> Of course, there is no such thing as the twenty-first century either. It is only a name, and we have no reason to suppose that how we have thought or behaved in the twentieth century need be, or will be, different because the Earth made another turn around the sun. But it is a name we use to foster hope, to inspire renewal, to get another chance to do it right.
> —NEIL POSTMAN, *Building a Bridge to the 18th Century*

INTRODUCTION

Educator Neil Postman begins with the idea that imagined futures are always more about where we have been than where we are going (Postman 1999). In a sense, buildings are also always manifestations of the past: what we were thinking about when they were designed —whether that was five or fifty years ago. The challenge for all of us is to look back at history but envision the path ahead. There seems to be no question that our future depends on this vision.

The challenges ahead are daunting: Kyoto Protocol compliance by 2012; carbon neutrality, PBT elimination and zero waste by 2030 (see Chapter 12). While this may seem a daunting undertaking for an industry with so many fundamental economic, occupational, regulatory,

and safety challenges, healthcare leaders are nonetheless embarking on this journey.

This final chapter postulates that the healthcare industry is in a pivotal position to lead the twenty-first-century reintegration of environment, health, and economic prosperity. By critically reinventing the hospital as a regenerative place of healing, marshaling purchasing power, and modeling health and wellness within a society in critical need of alternatives to fast food and retail culture, the healthcare industry can signal a new relationship to healing and health.

If the healthcare industry put its own house in order, what a model of optimism it would be to the broader building world! If people experience hospitals that promote health, they will demand schools and homes and office environments that do the same. In his essay "Design and Stewardship," environmental advocate Bill Walsh postulates how healthcare can support sustainable building to further this mission. The final essay, "Towers of Illness to Cathedrals of Health" by Charlotte Brody, RN (page 392), celebrates the healthcare leaders who are actualizing this transformation.

In the coming years, there is likely to be a flurry of renewed policy initiatives linked to the growing awareness of climate change, and the need for carbon, waste, and toxics reduction. Unlike policy initiatives of the 1960s, which were focused primarily on the agricultural and manufacturing sectors (e.g., the effort to eliminate DDT and the Clean Air Act, first passed in 1963), this generation of policy initiatives must include the ever-expanding services sector. Can the healthcare industry shed its culture of compliance in favor of informed environmental leadership and begin to shape environmental health policy direction? What leadership position might healthcare hold on behalf of the broader ecological sustainability agenda? How can a culture predicated on prevention and precaution elevate the public discourse on climate change, toxification, and zero waste?

REDUCING HEALTHCARE'S ECOLOGICAL FOOTPRINT

Today, manufacturing, mining, and agriculture — activities often associated with environmental damage — account for less than 25 percent of the US gross domestic product (GDP). The US services sector — from real estate to retail, fast food to healthcare — accounts for more than 75 percent of the country's economic activity and 80 percent of employment nationwide (Chertow and Powers 1997). Healthcare alone accounts for just over 16 percent of total US GDP — more than 20 percent of the services sector's economic activity (CMMS 2007).

Environmental impacts associated with the services sector are as varied as the components that comprise it. Think about the retail sector: a handful of enormous retailers — Wal-Mart, Target, Home Depot — define the environmental choices of US consumers through the choices they make about stocking their shelves. Their purchasing decisions determine the success or failure of environmentally responsible products.

Environmental law and policy advocates Marian Chertow and Daniel Esty (Chertow and Powers 1997) note three important services sector areas from which to leverage environmental improvements:

> In sum, the environmental consequences of service activities in the US are great, varied, often technologically sophisticated, and largely determined by a set of private, for-profit business decision-makers. Additionally, the environmental footprint of services extends into manufacturing, agriculture, and other natural resource industries since all are connected by the value chain which begins with extraction and manufacturing and ends with reuse or disposal. The tremendous impact of service companies on the environment can be divided into three basic categories: *upstream leverage,* where the service company influences its suppliers and others up the value chain; *downstream influence,* where the service company influences its customers toward the end of the value chain; and *environmentally responsible production,* which requires us to consider how the "production" of services can be done more efficiently [emphasis added].

As the purchasing agents for millions of healthcare consumers, healthcare organizations and their group-purchasing organizations have tremendous leverage over their suppliers. This book contains multiple examples of healthcare organizations employing upstream leverage — note Kaiser Permanente's focus on moving markets (Chapter 10), as well as the myriad innovators and leaders who have purchased emerging products and technologies in support of more environmentally responsible solutions. Whether in search of better building products or organic food, the healthcare industry is beginning to exert upstream leverage on manufacturers and suppliers. By joining with education, healthcare has forced milk producers nationwide to eliminate the growth hormone rBST (recombinant bovine somatotropin) from dairy production for a negligible difference in product cost (*New York Times* 2006). In the building industry, manufacturers are transforming the design, packaging, shipment, and end-of-life management of products based on healthcare-system advocacy.

Downstream influence is subtler. Chertow and Esty maintain that service industries play a key role in both satisfying and creating consumer preferences for goods and services, including their environmental dimensions. When a hospital serves patients local and organic food as part of their treatment, patients and families gain a new awareness of the importance of healthy eating. Likewise, patients experiencing a green building leave with an increased understanding of the importance of sustainable architecture on occupant, community, and global health. Higher education institutions, philanthropic foundations, and organizations such as the US Green Building Council recognize the intrinsic pedagogical value of sustainable buildings. This can also be linked to business strategist B. Joseph Pine II and James H. Gilmore's *The Experience Economy* (1999), which contends that "health care customers want more than goods and services, or even a positive 'experience'—they want to be well." Insofar as hospitals can charge for the benefit customers (i.e., patients) receive as a result of spending time within their walls, they are in the transformation business—the final stage in the evolution of goods and services industries. They argue that the value of the *transformation* is the final value added in the healthcare transaction, over and above basic medical care delivery.

Equally as important is the healthcare industry's clout in educating its peers in other services sectors. Just as bankers often draw real estate investors' attention to environmental liabilities associated with a building, the healthcare industry is poised to take a leadership position in informing other services sectors about an explicit, health-based approach to sustainable building technologies and operation. For example, the healthcare sector, through development of infection control risk assessment protocols, has evolved a strong set of guidelines for conducting construction activities adjacent to occupied buildings. These guidelines, ultimately, have wide applicability in other construction market sectors—wherever construction activities may impact building occupants. Who better than the healthcare sector to lead a health-based approach to sustainable building?

Finally, the concept of environmentally responsible production recognizes that services must also be "produced," often through complex operations requiring prodigious energy use and generating voluminous waste streams. According to US Department of Energy data, the two most energy-intensive building sectors are food service and healthcare, both services sectors (DOE 2006). The largest paper users are all in the services sector. Chapter 3, "Environment and Medicine," introduces the complex issue of the expanding scale of the healthcare system. Chapter 7, "Integrating Operations," describes many components associated with the environmental impacts of healthcare services delivery. Facilities are units of production in the healthcare industry, supporting the delivery of a broad range of services. Throughout this book, case studies demonstrate healthcare's leadership in environmentally responsible production.

Design and Stewardship: How the Design of Facilities Helps Create Better Neighborhoods and Communities

Bill Walsh

Imagine: hospitals designed to help people get better, and to not make anyone sick. The notion seems unremarkable at first. In practice, it is not as easy as you might think. In principle, it is a notion that is profoundly subversive to the dominant design paradigm of our day.

If we can imagine hospitals that heal, then we will soon come to expect them. This book has introduced you to studies that link improved patient outcomes—and, not incidentally, improved performance by professional staff—to improvements in building design and materials selection. Long before these findings are parsed, challenged, and replicated (or not), the market is going to speak loud and clear. Given the choice, would you rather send an ailing loved one, birth a premature infant, or sustain a chronically ill elder in an institution that is committed to healthy building, or not?

If we come to expect healthy hospitals, then we might soon come to expect school buildings that help students learn better, offices that stimulate creativity, and factories designed to increase workers' productivity, as well as their job satisfaction and even their personal health. We might expect that when we undertake a do-it-yourself improvement at home, we don't need to special-order green materials from distant locales like Berkeley, California. The plastic, paint, or caulk we buy from the big-box hardware store will be healthy, or it won't be for sale. We might even have reason to expect that the factory, forest, or field from which our purchase was extracted or manufactured was a healthy place, too.

If that is what we expect from the buildings we occupy, will we expect less from the buildings that populate the landscape around us? After all, if the facilities in medical meccas such as Boston, Houston, or midtown Manhattan can maintain their medical standards of quality, service, and cleanliness without feeding their solid waste into incinerators that belch dioxin into the surrounding neighborhood, why can't the rest? If one hospital, dormitory, or high-rise building can be built to benefit, rather than denigrate, the community, why accept less? If we are unwilling to tolerate toxic off-gassing in our home or office, will we continue to simply regulate the high-volume pollution of those same harmful chemicals into the skies and waters of the towns that make the products we use?

Indeed, how long will it be before we expect our buildings to be living buildings[1] that are net contributors to the communities they populate, generating their own energy with renewable resources, capturing and treating all of water used on-site, and using all materials efficaciously to maximize the health and beauty of our world (CRGBC 2007)?

Not long. This is the nature of the tectonic shift in public policy toward health and the environment that is foreshadowed by the trailblazers, strategies, and case studies that you have encountered in this book.

Our society owes a great debt to the leaders in the field of healthcare facilities design and administration.

For a decade now, they have worked in harmony with their professional mantra — "first, do no harm" — but against conventional wisdom, seeking and finding solutions for the environmental health challenges embedded in the aspects of their mission as seemingly unrelated as solid-waste disposal and neonatal intensive care. Their efforts have braided three common threads — holistic thinking, thoughtful design, and the recognition that materials matter — into a lifeline for our civilization.

Holistic thinking: Leaders in healthcare design and administration have done a remarkable job of implementing holistic thinking, in particular through consensus-driven organizations such as Hospitals for a Healthy Environment, Health Care Without Harm, and related efforts like the Green Guide for Health Care. These forums have fashioned solutions to challenges involving multiple interests of patients, staff, and society at large, making particularly impressive strides in bridging the gulf between construction and operations. These should be studied and replicated in other fields.

Thoughtful design: Leaders in healthcare design and administration have applied holistic thinking to the design of their facilities as well, and courageously blazed a trail in evidence-based design. At a minimum, this approach places the health of people, society, and the planet where they belong: in the forefront of facilities planning, design, and operations. No less importantly, the approaches recounted in this volume break through the ceiling of expectations rooted in conventional green building wisdom and point toward a future as yet to be designed. Without such inspirational leadership, we cannot meet the environmental health challenges of our generation.

Materials matter: Perhaps the most consistent theme woven through the various challenges confronted by the leaders you have met in this book is the recognition that materials selection and management matter. The premature infant in the neonatal intensive care unit benefits from careful materials selection, which eliminates the uncontrolled ingestion of chemicals from a vinyl IV tube replaced with a safer plastic, as does the health-compromised toddler from the Gulf Coast of the US, where most vinyl originates and communities live

---

[1]The author relies upon the definition of a "living building" by Jason McLennan, CEO, Cascadia Region Green Building Council, and Bob Berkebile, FAIA, principal, BNIM Architects.

with appallingly high dioxin contamination. The thriving adolescent who lives a block away from the hospital benefits too, when that baby's IV is autoclaved rather than burned in a dioxin-belching incinerator on-site. The maintenance crew benefits from reduced exposure to stripping and waxing chemicals that are not needed to maintain a carefully chosen floor covering, as do the night-shift nurses and the immunocompromised patients who are confined to the unit during its cleaning. From medical devices to building materials, leaders in the healthcare field are at the forefront of defining the green building materials market—and influencing millions of dollars of product sales in the process.

The penultimate lesson of the work that is recounted in this book is this: healthy building practices do not compromise the essential missions of our most important institutions; they further those missions. There is no downside to a hospital that heals, a school building that increases adolescent attention spans, a factory that reduces fatigue and illness on the shop floor, or a building that does not just stand, but rather "lives" in its community.

THE NEXT GENERATION OF ENVIRONMENTAL POLICY

In the first generation of environmental law, policy focused on the manufacturing sectors. There is less certainty in approaching the services sector, where the pollution is less obvious than in smokestack industries. "When we think of making steel, we imagine pollution. When we think of hospitals delivering health services, we do not immediately focus on the difficulty of disposing of hypodermic needles or radioactive waste" (Chertow and Powers 1997).

The next generation of public policy may emerge as systems oriented, with pollution prevention initiatives giving way to more comprehensive, life cycle approaches to environmental issues. Green building tools in the healthcare sector, such as the *Green Guide for Health Care* and *LEED for Health Care*, are important early indicators of this evolution.

> A central thrust of next-generation environmental policy must be to move beyond the regulatory and organizational barriers that single-media, single-species, single-substance and single-life-stage approaches create to a more holistic and longer term consideration of environmental threats. It must resist fragmentation, overcome cultural barriers, and deal with questions of complex interactions between the economic and natural worlds. It must also resourcefully avoid the problems created by categories that are too narrow, tools that are too blunt, and thinking that is too narrow.
> —CHERTOW AND POWERS (1997)

Healthcare faces the challenges of a system of regulation based on technology mandates rather than performance standards. Many regulatory obstacles to innovation reside in this place. The healthcare industry will need to conceive, propose, and test new practices through expanded investment in building-related research—examples such as the ventilation study profiled in Chapter 10, the collaborative effort of Kaiser Permanente in California, Providence Health Services in Oregon, and Partners HealthCare in Massachusetts are the cornerstone of regulatory policy innovation. Key to such research is the explicit understanding that its intent is to modify core regulation—not to be a case-by-case "waiver recipient."

The industry must rigorously examine innovative ideas and overcome regulatory challenges to improved energy performance and begin to embrace sustainable ideology as an essential component of "passive survivability" of healthcare infrastructure. On-site renewable energy, daylighting, and passive ventilation are examples of strategies that contribute to extending the critical services of a healthcare facility in the event of major ongoing utility disruptions. Likewise, careful management of potable water will require the healthcare industry to develop clear, research-based infection-control guidance on the safe uses of reclaimed water (gray water) and captured rainwater, including standards for its on-site treatment. Support for the continued development of life cycle assessment methodologies for materials will become more important in an industry that must commit to building cancer centers without materials containing known or suspected carcinogens and pediatric facilities that avoid materials that trigger asthma.

WHO WILL GUIDE THIS TRANSFORMATION?

Businesses, government, and nonprofits are the three major sectors of the US economy. With few exceptions, business has proven to be self-interested in matters of the environment. As the public exerts more pressure on private business to take an active role in environmental stewardship, the business sector is challenged to integrate the public good into its core decision making — it is simply not designed to manage it. Government has proven effective at macroscale matters (such as chlorofluorocarbon [CFC] elimination), but increasing globalization has reduced its influence, and bureaucracy has slowed its pace. Nonprofits, historically dependent on contributions from foundations and private donors, are viewed as a sector characterized by a dearth of entrepreneurial capacity — these days, nonprofits are expected to include an objective, entrepreneurial skill set. Healthcare, which straddles all three sectors, is oddly unlike any of its sector counterparts, given its overarching mission for the public good.

Whether nonprofit or for-profit, healthcare largely functions and is perceived as providing community benefit — a term rooted in an 1891 definition as "charitable activities that benefit the community as a whole" (Everson 2005). The Internal Revenue Service's "community benefit standard," revised in IRS Ruling 83-157, notes "[T]he promotion of health . . . is deemed beneficial to the community as a whole" (IRS 1983). With twenty-first-century businesses' increasing emphasis on triple bottom-line imperatives — not only for competitive advantage but also for planetary survival — healthcare's singular blend of environmental, economic, and social agendas is a model worthy of replication by other sectors.

According to writer and sustainable development strategist Carl Frankel (2004), "This adds up to an emerging demand for a fundamentally new sort of institution that is sustained by profits yet committed to serving humanity — that is, that reconciles the traditional tension between private enterprise and the public good." This emerging for-benefit "fourth sector" is gaining ground (Fourth Sector 2007). In some regards, the nonprofit healthcare industry is a keystone of fourth-sector thinking.

Along with companion fourth-sector organizations, the healthcare industry is beginning to transform itself in the service of ecological health. Visionary healthcare leaders, like those profiled in this book, are beginning this journey. Collectively, they represent Tier 3 organizations that, according to physician and public health advocate Ted Schettler, MD, MPH, "are informed by the inextricable link between environment and human health and are moving beyond both compliance and monetary savings with a long-term plan to reduce environmental footprint" (2001). In the following essay, Charlotte Brody, RN, describes those leaders, and the journey they are taking.

From Towers of Illness to Cathedrals of Health

Charlotte Brody, RN

*W*hen the Health Care Without Harm campaign formed in 1996, a reasonable person might have concluded that the healthcare industry had far too much to worry about to add dioxin in the air and mercury in fish to the list of problems it was supposed to solve. Now, ten years later, every major group purchasing organization in the United States, and thousands of hospitals around the world, have replaced their mercury-containing thermometers and blood pressure devices, reduced their waste stream, replaced incineration with safer alternatives for the destruction of medical waste, demonstrated their preference for other materials over the use of polyvinyl chloride (PVC) plastic, and constructed buildings that are healthier for the environment and for people, too.

All of these improvements have been made in an industry that is under severe stress. Increasing costs and decreasing reimbursements, more patients with less insurance, competition for the fully insured patients, nursing shortages, occupational injuries, and medical errors are just a few of the many daily problems that can elevate the blood pressure of any healthcare provider.

We learn in school that a rise in blood pressure is designed to help us survive under stress. The heart and lungs and big muscles gear up as the body shuts down all the systems that are unnecessary for fight or flight. Digestion and peripheral circulation turn off to increase the capacity for the heart pumping and breathing, stress responses that our animal bodies still believe are the most useful. The human brain can create a version of the stress response, too. It shuts stuff out, focusing on the few problems it deems most important to our survival. It limits input, hoping that by focusing on a prioritized set of issues we can actually get something accomplished.

We isolate so we can manage. We ignore what we don't have the capacity to address. So how did the thirty-one people from twenty-eight nonprofit environmental and health organizations who started Health Care Without Harm garner the engagement of enough of the healthcare sector to encourage the closure of more than 5,000 medical waste incinerators in the United States, the engagement of more than 70 percent of the purchasing power of the healthcare industry, and the commitment of more than 1,206 healthcare partners representing 6,700 healthcare facilities to phase out the use of mercury and cut their waste stream in half? At the same time, how did Health Care Without Harm convince all of the major pharmacy chains in the country to eliminate the sale of mercury-based thermometers and move major medical-device manufacturers away from using phthalates and PVC in their products?

The answer can help us reach the vision of this book: the transformation of hospitals from towers of disease into cathedrals of health. The answer is courage. Not the Cowardly Lion kind, and not the racing-into-battle kind, either. Rather, an uplifting kind of courage that leads to the hope and sustenance needed for problem solving; a quiet kind of courage not intimidated by change and grounded in the recognition of the high cost of inaction.

Early in its history, Health Care Without Harm recognized that the standard model of activist campaigns wouldn't work for the healthcare industry. That recognition was built from the courage of the nurses, waste specialists, and healthcare administrators who first engaged with the campaign. Those brave representatives from Catholic Healthcare West, the American Nurses Association, Beth Israel Medical Center in New York City, Dartmouth-Hitchcock Medical Center in New Hampshire, and Fletcher Allen Health Care in Vermont, among others, challenged the social change activists and organizers to understand that we could not and should not make the argument that environmental responsibility was the most important issue facing the healthcare industry. And in an equal act of courage, an experienced group of social change activists set their standard ways of working aside and created a campaign that did not ignore patient care and employee safety — or any other health issue — when addressing the environmental issues of waste disposal or product selection.

Instead of proposing that Health Care Without Harm issues be prioritized by the healthcare industry because they were the most important, the campaign adopted a solution-based framework — a "let's make this improvement because we can" orientation. Solving the solvable and applying the lessons we learned along the way to address more intractable problems became Health Care Without Harm's approach to making social change.

It worked. First on incineration and mercury-containing devices. Then on PVC, phthalates, and pesticides. Most recently on green healthcare building design and on sourcing sustainable, organic, and healthier food choices. Incremental accomplishments achieved by courageous people who were interested in Health Care Without Harm's approach and found a way out of whatever stress-induced silos they were in to move their institutions to do something positive.

Some of the change makers say they have been motivated by their love for the outdoors. Some explain their actions as an expression of concern for their children and other people's children. Very few of them

> *Every building is a unique blend of site, program, people, budget, with a unique set of challenges and opportunities. Innovative, integrative design practices recognize that new solutions emerge from a process that engenders creative problem solving and 'thinking out of the box.' We encourage you to delve into an exploratory process to discover new benchmarks for 21st century health care facilities.*
>
> *Source:* THE AMERICAN SOCIETY OF HEALTHCARE ENGINEERING *Green Healthcare Construction Guidance Statement* (ASHE 2004)

were sure that making change would be good for their careers. Yet very few of them stopped with one victory. Most of them have been surprised by what they've been able to accomplish and by how proud they and others are of what they've done. Each of their incremental steps has added up. Because of them, there is less dioxin in breast milk and cottage cheese and less mercury in tuna and the nervous systems of developing children.

A mere increase in blood pressure may not be a healthy response to modern day stressors; it may be that the best way to solve problems is to face the fact that still more problems exist. Perhaps it is healthier to recognize that everything is interconnected, that it is all important, and that rather than creating hierarchies of importance we should look for opportunities to fix the fixable. Perhaps the Cathedral of Health will be built by quietly courageous master builders who learned their craft through years of constructing solutions to increasingly difficult problems. I look forward to sitting with all of you in its pews.

CONCLUSION

People and place, consciousness and commitment, vision and value. This journey links to moments that eloquently define the full range of human experience — sickness and healing, from birth to death — all in a continuum that is known as life. Healthcare buildings — as the artifact of a culture of healing — may finally emerge as an architectural typology distinct from corporate, residential, or hospitality spaces, one in a regenerative partnership with nature and health that models a paradigm of wellness. We will sit with Charlotte Brody in those pews — and share her invitation to all our readers to do the same.

Bibliography and References

CHAPTER 1

American Institute of Architects [AIA]. (2005). *High-Performance Building Position Statements.* AIA: Washington, DC. http://www.aia.org/SiteObjects/files/HPB_position_statements.pdf

Benyus, J. (1997). *Biomimicry: Innovations Inspired by Nature.* New York: William Morrow.

Berkebile, R. J., and J. McLennan. (1999). The Living Building. *The World & I* (October): 160–8.

Brundtland, G., ed. (1987). *Our Common Future: The World Commission on Environment and Development.* Oxford: Oxford University Press.

Cascadia Region Green Building Council [CRGBC]. (2006). *The Living Building Challenge v1.0: In Pursuit of True Sustainability in the Built Environment.* Portland, Ore.: Cascadia Region Green Building Council.

Costanza, R., R. D'Arge, R. DeGroot, et al. (1997). The value of the world's ecosystem services and natural capital. *Nature* 387 (May): 253.

Earth Charter Initiative. (2000). *The Earth Charter.* http://www.earthcharter.org/files/charter/charter.pdf

Eberhard, J. (2005). *Final Report of Latrobe Fellowship.* http://www.latrobefellow.org/exsummary.pdf

Frumkin, H., ed. (2005). *Environmental Health: From Global to Local.* New York: John Wiley & Sons.

Hawken, P. (1993). *The Ecology of Commerce: A Declaration of Sustainability.* New York: HarperBusiness.

Hawken, P., A. Lovins, and L. H. Lovins. (2000). *Natural Capitalism: Creating the Next Industrial Revolution.* Back Bay Books.

International Union of Architects [UIA] and American Institute of Architects [AIA]. (1993). *Declaration of Interdependence for a Sustainable Future.* Authored at the World Congress of Architects, Chicago, June 18–21. http://www.uia-architectes.org/texte/england/2aaf1.html

McDonough, W., and M. Braungart. (2002). *Cradle to Cradle: Remaking the Way We Make Things.* New York: North Point Press/Farrar Strauss and Giroux.

McKibben, B. (1989). *The End of Nature.* New York: Anchor Books.

Millennium Ecosystem Assessment. (2005). *Ecosystems and Human Well-Being: Current State and Trends: Findings of the Condition and Trends Working Group.* New York: Island Press.

Orr, D. W. (2004). *The Nature of Design: Ecology, Culture, and Human Intention.* Oxford: Oxford University Press.

Szenasy, S. (2004). Ethics and sustainability: Graphic designers' role. Speech given at the annual American Institute of Graphic Arts National Design Conference, Vancouver, BC, October 23–26. http://powerofdesign.aiga.org/content.cfm/szenasy

Union of Concerned Scientists. (1992). World Scientists' Warning to Humanity. http://www.ucsusa.org/ucs/about/1992-world-scientists-warning-to-humanity.html

United Nations Department of Economic and Social Affairs. Division for Sustainable Development. (2004). Documents. http://www.un.org/esa/sustdev/documents/agenda21/index.htm

United Nations Environment Programme [UNEP]. (1989). Cleaner Production—Key Elements. http://www.uneptie.org/pc/cp/understanding_cp/home.htm

Vitousek, P. M., H. Mooney, J. Lubchenco, and J. Melillo. (1985). Human domination of Earth's ecosystems. *Science* 227: 494–9.

Wackernagel, M., L. Onisto, A. C. Linares, et al. (1997). *Ecological Footprints of Nations: How Much Nature Do They Use? How Much Nature Do They Have?* Xalapa, Mexico: Center for Sustainability Studies.

World Wildlife Fund International, Zoology Society of London, and Global Footprint Network (2006). *Living Planet Report 2006.* http://www.panda.org/news_facts/publications/living_planet_report/lp_2006/index.cfm

Less is Better ▥ Bill Valentine

Gladwell, M. (2000). *The Tipping Point: How Little Things Can Make a Big Difference.* New York: Little, Brown.

Life Cycle Design: Toward an Ecology of Mind
▥ Pliny Fisk III

Bateson, G. (1972). *Steps to an Ecology of Mind.* Chicago: University of Chicago Press.

Biederman, I., and E. A. Vessel. (2006). Perceptual pleasure and the brain. *American Scientist* 94 (3): 247–53.

Brickey, J. (1994). The effects of pattern scale in the near environment on preschool play behavior. Masters thesis, University of Tennessee–Knoxville.

De Long, A. J., and J. F. Lubar. (1979). Effect of environmental scale of subjects on spectral EEG output. *Society for Neuroscience Abstracts* 5:203.

De Long, A. J., D. W. Tegano, J. D. Moran III, J. Brickey, D. Morrow, and T. L. Hunter. (1994). Effects of spatial scale on cognitive play in preschool children. *Early Education and Development* 5 (3): 237–46.

Durham, D. F. (1992). Cultural carrying capacity. *Focus* 2: 5–8.

Durning, A. B. (1989). *Poverty and the Environment: Reversing the Downward Spiral.* Worldwatch Institute: Washington, DC.

Gould, E., A. J. Reeves, S. Michael, A. Graziano, and C. G. Gross. (1998). Neurogenesis in the neocortex of adult primates. *Science* 286 (5439): 548–52.

Kursweil, R. (2005). *The Singularity Is Near: When Humans Transcend Biology.* New York: Viking/Penguin.

Rheingold, H. (2003). *Smart Mobs: The Next Social Revolution.* New York: Basic Books.

Teilhard de Chardin, P. (1955). *The Phenomenon of Man.* New York: Harper & Row.

Von Foerster, H. (2003). *Understanding Understanding: Essays on Cybernetics and Cognition.* New York: Springer.

Wright, K. (2002). Times of our lives. *Scientific American,* September.

Restoring Our Buildings, Restoring Our Health, Restoring the Earth ■ Bob Berkebile

Burns, C. M., and H. Eubank. (2002). Green schools: enlightenment in Brazil. *RMI Solutions,* Summer.

David and Lucille Packard Foundation [Packard]. (2002). *Building for Sustainability.* Los Altos, Calif: David and Lucille Packard Foundation, Los Altos Project.

Green Guide for Health Care [GGHC]. (2007). *Best Practices for Creating High Performance Healing Environments.* Version 2.2. http://www.gghc.org/about.cfm

Kats, G. (2005). *National Review of Green Schools: Costs, Benefits, and Implications for Massachusetts: A Report for the Massachusetts Technology Collaborative.* Washington, DC: Capital E. http://www.cap-e.com/ewebeditpro/items/O59F7707.pdf

Marks, R. W. (1963). The Comprehensive Man: Directions for the Student. In *Ideas and Integrities: A Spontaneous Autobiographical Disclosure,* ed. R. B. Fuller. Englewood Cliffs, NJ: Prentice-Hall.

CHAPTER 2

Centers for Disease Control and Prevention [CDC]. Division of Nutrition and Physical Activity. National Center for Chronic Disease Prevention and Health Promotion. (2005). U.S. Obesity Trends 1985 to 2004. http://www.cdc.gov/nccdphp/dnpa/obesity/trend/maps/index.htm.

Chivian, E., M. McCally, H. Hu, and A. Haines, eds. (1993). *Critical Condition: Human Health and the Environment.* Cambridge: MIT Press.

Christiani, D. (1993). Urban and transboundary air pollution: Human health consequences. In Chivian, McCally, Hu, et al.

Congress for the New Urbanism. (2007). www.cnu.org

Crisci, M. (1990). Public health in New York City in the late nineteenth century. In *Services UDoHaH,* ed. National Library of Medicine, History of Medicine Division. New York: National Library of Medicine.

Davis, D. (2002). *When Smoke Ran Like Water: Tales of Environmental Deception and the Battle Against Pollution.* New York: Basic Books.

Environmental Protection Agency [EPA]. (2006). *Indoor Air Quality.* http://www.epa.gov/docs/iedweb00/index.html

———. (2000). *National Water Quality Inventory,* Ch. 6: "Ground Water." http://www.epa.gov/305b/2000report/

———. (1998). *Characterization of Building-Related Construction and Demolition Debris in the United States.* Report No. EPA530-R-98-010. Prairie Village, Kan.: Franklin Associates. www.epa.gov/epaoswer/hazwaste/sqg/c&d-rpt.pdf

Field, A. E., E. H. Coakley, A. Must, et al. (2001). Impact of overweight on the risk of developing common chronic diseases during a 10-year period. *Archive of Internal Medicine* 161:1581–6.

Friedman, M. S., K. E. Powell, L. Hutwagner, L. M. Graham, and W. G. Teague. (2001). Impact of changes in transportation and commuting behaviors during the 1996 summer Olympic Games in Atlanta. *Journal of the American Medical Association* 285 (7): 897–905. Quoted in Frumkin, Frank, and Jackson (2004).

Friends of Gaviotas. (2007). www.friendsofgaviotas.org

Frumkin, H., L. Frank, and R. Jackson. (2004). *Urban Sprawl and Public Health.* Washington, DC: Island Press.

Geiser, K. (2001). *Materials Matter.* Boston: MIT Press.

Hu, H., and N. Kim. (1993). Drinking-Water Pollution and Human Health. In Chivian, McCally, Hu, et al.

Kay, D., A. Prüss, and C. Corvalan. (1999). Methodology for assessment of environmental burden of disease: Report on the ISEE session on environmental burden of disease, Buffalo, New York, August 22, 2000. (WHO/SDE/WSH/00.7). Geneva: World Health Organization. http://www.who.int/docstore/peh/burden/wsh00-7/Methodan1.htm

Kyoto Protocol. (1997). United Nations Framework Convention on Climate Change. http://unfccc.int/resource/docs/convkp/kpeng.html

Lawton, T. K. (2001). The Urban Structure and Personal Travel: An Analysis of Portland, or Data and Some National and International Data. Rand Infrastructure, Safety and Environment. http://www.rand.org/scitech/stpi/Evision/Supplement/lawton.pdf

Little, A. G. (2005). City city bang bang: An interview with Seattle Mayor Greg Nickels on his pro-Kyoto cities initiative. *Grist*, June 15. http://www.grist.org/news/maindish/2005/06/15/little-nickels

Mazria, E. (2003). Turning down the global thermostat. *Metropolis*, October.

National Institute for Occupational Safety and Health [NIOSH]. (1988). *Proposed National Strategies for the Prevention of Leading Work-Related Diseases and Injuries, Part 1*. Washington, DC: Association of Schools of Public Health.

Newman, P., and J. Kenworthy. (1993). *Automobile Dependence: "The Irresistible Force."* Murdoch, Australia: Institute for Sustainability and Technology Policy.

Newman, P., J. Kenworthy, F. Laube, and P. Barter. (1998). *Indicators of Transport Efficiency in 37 Global Cities: A Report to the World Bank*. Murdoch, Australia: Institute for Sustainability and Technology Policy.

Preston, S. (1996). American longevity: past, present, and future. Syracuse University Policy Brief No. 7.

Redefining Progress. (2007). http://www.redefiningprogress.org

Riis, J. A. (1890). *How the Other Half Lives: Studies Among the Tenements of New York*. New York: Charles Scriber's Sons.

Roodman, D. M., and N. Lenssen (1995). *A Building Revolution: How Ecology and Health Concerns are Transforming Construction*. (Worldwatch Institute Paper #124). Washington, DC: Worldwatch Institute.

Rosenberg, C. E. (1987). *The Care of Strangers: The Rise of America's Hospital System*. New York: Basic Books.

Rosenman, K. D., M. J. Reilly, D. P. Schill, et al. (2003). Cleaning products and work related asthma. *Journal of Occupational and Environmental Medicine* 45 (5): 557–63.

Smart Growth Network. (2006). *Getting to Smart Growth: 100 Policies for Implementation*. Washington, DC: International City/County Management Association. http://www.smartgrowth.org/pdf/gettosg.pdf

Starr, P. (1949). *The Social Transformation of American Medicine*. New York: Basic Books.

Stein, C. J., and G. A. Colditz. (2004). The epidemic of obesity. *The Journal of Clinical Endocrinology and Metabolism*, June 89 (6): 2522–5.

Thornton, J. (2003). *The Environmental Impacts of Polyvinyl Chloride (PVC) Building Materials*. Washington DC: Healthy Building Network. http://www.healthybuilding.net/pvc/ThorntonPVCSummary.html

Turner, B. (1995). *Medical Power and Social Knowledge*. 2nd ed. London: Sage. Quoted in C. Samson, ed. *Health Studies: A Critical and Cross-Cultural Reader*. Oxford: Blackwell Publishers.

US Conference of Mayors. (2005). US Mayors Climate Protection Agreement. http://www.usmayors.org/uscm/resolutions/73rd_conference/env_04.asp

US Global Change Research Program [USGCRP] National Assessment Synthesis Team. (2001). *Climate Change Impacts on the United States: The Potential Consequences of Climate Variability and Change*. Washington, DC: USGCRP.

Vermont Forum on Sprawl (1998–2006). www.vtsprawl.org

Weisman, A. (1995). Colombia's model city. *Context* 42 (Fall).

———. (1999). *Gaviotas: A Village to Reinvent the World*. White River Junction, Vermont: Chelsea Green.

World Bank Group. (2001). Chart 1. World Population and Access to Safe Water, 1990–96. http://www.worldbank.org/depweb/english/modules/environm/water/chart1.html

World Health Organization [WHO], UNICEF, and UN Environment Programme [UNEP]. (2002). *Pollution-Related Diseases Kill Millions of Children a Year*. http://www.nyo.unep.org/pdfs/cbpr.pdf

Good Places — Good Health ▪ Richard Jackson and Marlon Maus

Allen, K. G. (2006). A Look At Our Future: When Baby Boomers Retire. PowerPoint slides. http://aspe.hhs.gov/medicaid/mar/KathrynAllen.pdf

California Department of Finance. (2004). *Population Projections by Race/Ethnicity for California and Its Counties 2000–2050*. http://www.dof.ca.gov/html/demograp/ReportsPapers/Projections/P1/P1.asp

Centers for Disease Control and Prevention and National Center for Chronic Disease Prevention and Health Promotion [CDC]. (2006). *Health-Related Quality of Life*. http://apps.nccd.cdc.gov/HRQOL/

Cervero, R., and R. Gorham. (1995). Commuting in transit versus automobile neighborhoods. *Journal of the American Planning Association* 61 (2): 210–25.

Colditz, G. A. (1999). Economic costs of obesity and inactivity. *Medicine & Science in Sports & Exercise* 31 (11 Supplement): S663–7.

Cooper, A. R., L. B. Andersen, N. Wedderkopp, A. S. Page, and K. Froberg. (2005). Physical activity levels of children who walk, cycle, or are driven to school. *American Journal of Preventive Medicine* 29 (3): 179–84.

Corburn, J. (2004). Confronting the challenged in reconnecting urban planning and public health. *American Journal of Public Health* 94 (4): 541–6.

Dannenberg, A. L., R. J. Jackson, H. Frumkin, et al. (2003). The impact of community design and land-use choices on public health: A scientific research agenda. *American Journal of Public Health* 93 (9): 1500–8.

Davis, M. M., K. Slish, C. Chao, and M. D. Cabana. (2006). National trends in bariatric surgery, 1996–2002. *Archives of Surgery* 141 (1): 71–4.

Day, J. C. (2001). National Population Projections. Washington, DC: U.S. Census Bureau. http://www.census.gov/population/www/pop-profile/natproj.html

Duhl, L., and A. Sanchez. (1999). *WHO: Healthy Cities and the City Planning Process: A Background Document on Links Between Health and Urban Planning.* Copenhagen: World Health Organization Regional Office for Europe.

Flegal, K. M., D. F. Williamson, E. R. Pamuk, and H. M. Rosenberg. (2004). Estimating deaths attributable to obesity in the United States. *American Journal of Public Health* 94 (9): 1486–9.

French, S. A., M. Story, and R. W. Jeffrey. (2001). Environmental influences on eating and physical activity. *Annual Review of Public Health* 22: 309–35.

Frumkin, H. (2005). Health, equity, and the built environment. *Environmental Health Perspectives* 113 (5): A290–1.

Frumkin, H., L. Frank, and R. Jackson. (2004). *Urban Sprawl and Public Health.* Washington, DC: Island Press.

Gregg, E. W., R. B. Gerzoff, C. J. Caspersen, D. F. Williamson, and K. M. Venkat Narayan. (2003). Relationship of walking to mortality among U.S. adults with diabetes. *Archives of Internal Medicine* 163 (12): 1440–7.

Hanna, K., and C. Coussens. (2001). *Rebuilding the Unity of Health and the Environment: A New Vision of Environmental Health for the 21st Century.* Washington, DC: National Academy Press.

Hetzel, L., and A. Smith. (2001). *The 65 Years and Over Population: 2000.* Washington, DC: U.S. Census Bureau. http://www.census.gov/prod/2001pubs/c2kbr01-10.pdf

Koplan, J. P., C. T. Liverman, and V. A. Kraak, eds. (2005). *Preventing Childhood Obesity: Health in the Balance.* Washington: National Academies Press.

Kouzis, A. C., and W. W. Eaton. (1994). Emotional disability days: Prevalence and predictors. *American Journal of Public Health* 84 (8): 1304–7.

Lee, R., and J. Skinner. (1999). Will aging baby boomers bust the federal budget? *Journal of Economic Perspectives* 13 (1): 117–40.

Martin, S., and S. Carlson. (2005). Barriers to children walking to or from school—United States, 2004. *Journal of the American Medical Association* 294 (17): 2160. (Reprinted from *Morbidity and Mortality Weekly Report, 2005* (54): 949–52.)

Miller, N. L., K. E. Bashford, and E. Strem. (2003). Potential impacts of climate change on California hydrology. *Journal of the American Water Resources Association* 39 (4): 771–84.

Mutangadura, G. B. (2004). World health report 2002: Reducing risks, promoting healthy life. *Agricultural Economics* 30 (2): 170–2.

Myers, D. G., and E. Diener. (1995). Who is happy. *Psychological Science* 6 (1): 10–19.

National Center for Health Statistics [NCHS]. (2003). Table 119: Gross domestic product, federal and state and local government expenditures, national health expenditures, and average annual percent change: United States, selected years. In *Health, United States, 2003.* Washington, DC: Department of Health and Human Services. ftp://ftp.cdc.gov/pub/Health_Statistics/NCHS/Publications/Health_US/hus03/

Northridge, M. E., and E. Sclar. (2003). A joint urban planning and public health framework: contributions to health impact assessment. *American Journal of Public Health* 93 (1): 118–21.

Olfson, M., S. C. Marcus, B. Druss, L. Elinson, T. Tanielian, and H. A. Pincus. (2002). National trends in the outpatient treatment of depression. *Journal of the American Medical Association* 287 (2): 203–9.

Pucher, J., and L. Dijkstra. (2003). Promoting safe walking and cycling to improve public health: Lessons from the Netherlands and Germany. *American Journal of Public Health* 93 (9): 1509–16.

Sallis, J. F., R. B. Cervero, W. Ascher, K. A. Henderson, M. K. Kraft, and J. Kerr. (2006). An ecological approach to creating active living communities. *Annual Review of Public Health* 27 (1): 297–322.

Santry, H. P., D. L. Gillen, and D. S. Lauderdale. (2005). Trends in bariatric surgical procedures. *Journal of the American Medical Association* 294 (15): 1909–17.

Simpson, G. A., B. Bloom, R. A. Cohen, S. Blumberg, and K. H. Bourdon. (2005). U.S. children with emotional and behavioral difficulties: Data from the 2001, 2002, and 2003 National Health Interview surveys. *Adv Data* (360): 1–13.

Stein, C. J., and G. A. Colditz. (2004). The epidemic of obesity. *The Journal Of Clinical Endocrinology and Metabolism* 89 (6): 2522–5.

US Census Bureau. (2004). Census bureau projects tripling of Hispanic and Asian populations in 50 years. Press release, March 18. http://www.census.gov/Press-Release/www/releases/archives/ population/ 001720.html

Zito, J. M., D. J. Safer, S. dosReis, J. F. Gardner, M. Boles, and F. Lynch. (2000). Trends in the prescribing of psychotropic medications to preschoolers. *Journal of the American Medical Association* 283 (8): 1025–30.

Zuvekas, S. H., B. Vitiello, and G. S. Norquist. (2006). Recent trends in stimulant medication use among U.S. children. *American Journal of Psychiatry* 163 (4): 579–85.

Good Air, Good Health   Anthony Bernheim

Agency for Toxic Substances and Disease Registry [ATSDR]. (2005). Minimal Risk Level (MRLs) for Hazard Substances. http://www.atsdr.cdc.gov/mrls./index.html

Alevantis, L., K. Frevert, R. Muller, H. Levin, and A. Sowell. (2002). Sustainable building practices in California state buildings. In *Proceedings of Indoor Air 2002: 9th International Conference on Indoor Air Quality and Climate*, vol. 3. Monterey, California.

Bernheim, A., H. Levin, and L. Alevantis. (2002). Special environmental requirements for a California state office building. In *Proceedings of Indoor Air 2002: 9th International Conference on Indoor Air Quality and Climate*, vol. 4. Monterey, California.

Bornehag, C., J. Sundell, C. J. Weschler, et al. (2004). The association between asthma and allergenic symptoms in children and phthalates in house dust: A nested case-control study. *Environmental Health Perspectives* 112 (14): 1393–7.

California. Office of Environmental Health Hazard Assessment [OEHHA]. (2000). Air-Hot Spots-Acute RELs. http://www.oehha.org/air/acute_rels/allAcRELs.html

———. (2005). Air-Chronic RELs. http://www.oehha.org/air/chronic_rels/allchrels.html

Carpet and Rug Institute [CRI]. (2007). http://www.carpet-rug.org/

Green Guide for Health Care [GGHC]. (2007). Best Practices for Creating High Performance Healing Environments, Version 2.2. http://www.gghc.org/about.cfm

GreenGuard. (2007). GreenGuard Environmental Institute. http://www.greenguard.org/Default.aspx?tabid=110

Levin, H. (1998). Toxicology-based air quality guidelines for substances. In *Indoor Air: International Journal of Indoor Air Quality and Climate*, Supplement 5: 5–7.

McCarthy, J. F., and J. D. Spengler. (2001). Indoor Environmental Quality in Hospitals. In *Indoor Air Quality Handbook*, eds. J. D. Spengler, J. M. Samet, and J. F. McCarthy, Chapter 65.3–16. New York: McGraw-Hill.

McLennan, J. F. (2004). *The Philosophy of Sustainable Design*. Kansas City, MO: Ecotone.

Scientific Certification Systems [SCS]. (2007). www.scscertified.com/

State of California Integrated Waste Management Board. (2007). Sustainable (Green) Building Section 01350: Special Environmental Requirements. http://www.ciwmb.ca.gov/greenbuilding/Specs/Section01350/

US Green Building Council [USGBC]. (2007). www.usgbc.org/

CHAPTER 3

Ausubel, K., ed. (2004). *Ecological Medicine: Healing the Earth, Healing Ourselves.* San Francisco: Sierra Club Books.

Battisto, D., D. Allison, and L. Crew. (2006). A green community wellness center: Expanding the scope of design for health. *Academy Journal,* October 18.

Clemson University. (2004). A Collaborative Initiative to Improve Health and Well-Being for Residents of Clemson and Surrounding Communities. PowerPoint slides. http://virtual.clemson.edu/groups/wellness/A%20collaborative%20initiative%20to%20improve%20the%20health-green.ppt

Corvalan, C., S. Hales, and A. McMichael. (2005). *Health Synthesis Report of the Millennium Ecosystem Assessment.* Geneva: World Health Organization.

Elliott, H. (1997). A General Statement of Hardin's Tragedy of the Commons. *Population & Environment* 18 (6): 515–31.

Elliott, H., and R. Lam. (2002). A moral code for a finite world. *Chronicle of Higher Education,* November 15. http://www.cairco.org/ethics/elliott_lamm_ethics.html

Environmental Science Center with Bristol-Myers Squibb Company. (n.d.). *Greener Hospitals: Improving Environmental Performance.* Augsberg, Germany: Wissenschaftszentrum Umwelt. http://www.bms.com/static/ehs/sideba/data/greenh.pdf

Gaydos, L. M., and J. E. Veney. (2002). The nature and etiology of disease. In *World Health Systems: Challenges and Perspectives*, eds. B. J. Fried and L. M. Gaydos. Chicago: Health Administration Press.

Jameton, A. (2005). Environmental health ethics. In *Environmental Health: From Global to Local*, ed. H. Frumkin. San Francisco: Jossey-Bass.

Kaiser Permanente. (2006). Medical Center and Grocery Store? Find a Farmer's Market near You. http://members.kaiser-permanente.org/redirects/farmersmarkets

Mannino, D. M., D. M. Homa, L. J. Akinbami, J. E. Moorman, C. Gwynn, and S. C. Redd. (2002). Surveillance for asthma—U.S. 1980–1999. In *Surveillance Summaries, Morbidity and Mortality Weekly Report*. Atlanta: Centers for Disease Control and Prevention.

Myers, N., A. Jameton, C. Raffensperger, et al. (2002). *What is Ecological Medicine?* Bolinas, California: Commonweal Foundation.

The Paris Appeal. (2004). http://www.artac.info/static/telechargement/PARISAPPEAL_SIGNATR.pdf

Pierce, J., and A. Jameton. (2004). *The Ethics of Environmentally Responsible Health Care*. Oxford: Oxford University Press.

Potter, V. R. (1971). *Bioethics: Bridge to the Future*. Englewood Cliffs, NJ: Prentice-Hall.

Schettler, T. (2001). Environmental challenges and visions of sustainable health care. Presented at CleanMed Conference, Boston, May 4. http://www.cleanmed.org/2002/documents/schettler.pdf

Tickner, J. A., and C. Raffensperger. (1999). *Protecting Public Health and the Environment: Implementing the Precautionary Principle*. Washington, DC: Island Press.

Toxic Substances Control Act, U.S. Code 15 (1976) Ch. 53 §§ 2601–92.

Trasande L., and P. J. Landrigan. (2004). The National Children's Study: A critical national investment. *Environmental Health Perspectives* (October) 112 (14): A789–90.

United Nations Development Programme [UNDP]. (1997). *Human Development Report 1997*. New York: United Nations Development Programme.

Wilson, S. (2004). Design for Health: Summit for Massachusetts Health Care Decision Makers, September 28. PowerPoint slides.

World Bank. (1993). *World Development Report, 1993: Investing in Health*. Washington, DC: World Bank.

Transforming Healthcare ■ Gary Cohen

American Cancer Society [ACS]. (2005a). *Detailed Guide: Breast Cancer. What are the Key Statistics for Breast Cancer?* http://www.cancer.org/docroot/STT/content/STT_1x_Breast_Cancer_Facts__Figures_2003-2004.asp

———. (2005b). Probability of Developing Invasive Cancers over Selected Age Intervals, by Sex, U.S. 1999–2001. http://www.cancer.org/docroot/MED/content/downloads/MED_1_1x_CFF2005_Probability_of_Developing_Invasive_Cancers_Selected_Age_Intervals_by_Sex_1999-2001.asp

American Obesity Association [AOA]. (2006). AOA Fact Sheets: Obesity in the U.S. http://www.obesity.org/subs/fastfacts/obesity_US.shtml

Catholic Healthcare West [CHW]. (2006). *CHW Food & Nutrition Services Vision Statement.* http://www.noharm.org/details.cfm?ID=1298&type=document

Centers for Disease Control and Prevention [CDC]. (2005a). Chronic Disease Overview. http://www.cdc.gov/nccdphp/overview.htm

———. (2005b). *National Health Interview Survey. Incidence of Diagnosed Diabetes per 1,000 Population Aged 18–79 Years, by Sex and Age, United States, 1997–2004.* Atlanta: National Center for Health Statistics, Division of Health Interview Statistics.

———. (2005c). *Third National Report on Human Exposure to Environmental Chemicals.* Atlanta: National Center for Environmental Health, Division of Laboratory Sciences. (NCEH No. 05-0570: 111).

Collaborative on Health and the Environment [CHE]. (2006). CHE Toxicant and Disease Database. http://database.healthandenvironment.org/

Electronic Industries Alliance Regularly Tracking Tool [EIA]. (2005). Matrix of Enacted Mercury-Containing Product State Laws in the USA. http://www.eiatrack.org/p/219

Environmental Protection Agency [EPA]. (2001). Information Sheet 1 / Dioxin: Summary of the Dioxin Reassessment Science. www.epa.gov/ncea/pdfs/dioxin/factsheets/dioxin_short2.pdf

Food and Drug Administration [FDA]. (2002). Public Health Notification: FDA Public Health Notification: PVC Devices Containing the Plasticizer DEHP. http://www.fda.gov/cdrh/safety/dehp.html

———. (2006). Questions and Answers about Dioxins. http://www.cfsan.fda.gov/~lrd/dioxinqa.html

Fox, J. E. (2005). Non-traditional targets of endocrine disrupting chemicals: The roots of hormone signaling. *Integrative and Comparative Biology* 45 (1): 179–88. http://icb. oxfordjournals.org/cgi/content/abstract/45/1/179

Goldman, L. (2001). Environmental contamination and chronic diseases/disease clusters. Testimony before the Senate Committee on Environment and Public Works. 107th Congress. 1st sess. June 11.

Green Guide for Health Care [GGHC].(2007). Best Practices for Creating High Performance Healing Environments, Version 2.2. http://www.gghc.org/about.cfm

Health Care Without Harm [HCWH]. (2005). The Luminary Project. www.theluminaryproject.org

Heberer, T., U. Duennbier, C. Reilich, and H. J. Stan. (1997). Detection of drugs and drug metabolites in ground water samples of a drinking water treatment plant. *Fresenius Environmental Bulletin* 6 (7-8): 438–43.

Heindel, J. J. (2003). Endocrine disruptors and the obesity epidemic. *Toxicological Sciences* 76:247–9.

Heinzmann, B. (2005). Occurrence and behavior of trace substances in the partly closed water cycles of Berlin and its relevance to drinking water. Paper presented at the International Workshop on Rainwater and Reclaimed Water for Urban Sustainable Water Use, Tokyo, June 9–10. http://env.t.u-tokyo.ac.jp/furumailab/j/crest/workshop05/june10pm_1.pdf

Hemminger, P. (2005). Damming the flow of drugs into drinking water. *Environmental Health Perspectives* 113 (10): A678–A681.

Holloway M. (1994). An epidemic ignored: Endometriosis linked to dioxin and immunologic dysfunction. *Scientific American* 270 (4): 24–6.

Hospitals for a Healthy Environment [H2E]. (2005). Making Medicine Mercury Free: A 2005 Report on the Status of Virtual Mercury Elimination in the Health Care Sector. http://www.h2e-online.org/pubs/mercuryreport.pdf

Huffling, K. (2006). Effects of environmental contaminants in food on women's health. *Journal of Midwifery & Women's Health* 51 (1): 19–25.

Jahnke, G. D., A. R. Iannucci, A. R. Scialli, and M. D. Shelby. (2005). Center for the evaluation of risks to human reproduction—the first five years. *Birth Defects Research Part B: Developmental and Reproductive Toxicology* 74 (1): 1–8.

Kaiser Permanente. (2005). Kaiser Permanente Comprehensive Chemicals Policy. http://www.sehn.org/rtfdocs/Chemicals_Policy_3.23.05.doc

———. (2006). Medical Center and... Grocery Store? Find a Farmer's Market near You. http://members.kaiserpermanente.org/redirects/farmersmarkets/

Keitt, S. K, T. F. Fagan, and S. A. Marts. (2004). Understanding sex differences in environmental health: A thought leaders' roundtable. *Environmental Health Perspectives* 112 (5): 5.

KnowledgeSource. (2006). Group Purchasing Organizations Market Overview. http://knowsource.ecnext.com/coms2/summary_0233-3641_ITM

Koc, M., and K. A. Dahlberg. (2004). The restructuring of food systems: Trends, research, and policy issues. *Agriculture and Human Values* 16 (2): 109–16.

Mahaffey, K. (2000). Recent advances in recognition of low-level methylmercury poisoning. *Current Opinion in Neurology* 13 (6): 699–707.

Mannino, D. M., D. M. Homa, L. J. Akinbami, J. E. Moorman, C. Gwynn, and S. C. Redd. (2002). Surveillance for asthma—U.S. 1980–1999. In *Surveillance Summaries, Morbidity and Mortality Weekly Report.* Atlanta: Centers for Disease Control and Prevention.

National Toxicology Program [NTP]. Center for the Evaluation of Risk to Human Reproduction [CERHR]. (2000). *NTP-CERHR Expert Panel Report on Di(2-Ethylhexyl) Phthalate.* Washington, DC: Department of Health and Human Services. http://cerhr.niehs.nih.gov/chemicals/dehp/DEHP-final.pdf

Roswell Park Cancer Institute [RPCI]. (2005). RPCI Investigators Present Promising Research for Non-Hodgkin's Lymphoma at Hematology Meeting. Press release. http://www.roswellpark.org/Site/Home/MMNR/Press/Clinical_News/2005_Releases/RPCIInvestigatorsPresentPromisingResearchfor

Shea, K. M. (2004). Nontherapeutic use of antimicrobial agents in animal agriculture: Implications for pediatrics. *Pediatrics* 114 (3): 862–8.

Suchy, T., and J. Stepan. (2004). Extragenital endometriosis as a subject of interest for the surgeon. *Rozhl Chir.* 83 (5): 239–41.

Wilson, M. P. (2006). *Green Chemistry in California: A Framework for Leadership in Chemicals Policy and Innovation.* Berkeley: Northern California Center for Occupational and Environmental Health, School of Public Health, University of California.

From Medicine to Ecological Health ▪ Ted Schettler

Berry, W. (1983). Solving for Pattern. In *The Gift of the Good Land.* New York: North Point Press.

———. (1995). Health is Membership. In *Another Turn of the Crank.* Washington, DC: Counterpoint.

Jameton, A. (2005). Environmental Health Ethics. In *Environmental Health: From Global to Local*, ed. H. Frumkin. San Francisco, CA: Jossey-Bass.

Jonas, H. (1984). *The Imperative of Responsibility: In Search of an Ethics for the Technological Age.* Chicago: University of Chicago Press.

Leopold, A. (1949). *A Sand County Almanac.* New York: Oxford University Press.

Millennium Ecosystem Assessment [MEA]. (2005). Ecosystems and Human Well-Being: Current State and Trends: Findings of the Condition and Trends Working Group. New York: Island Press.

Pierce, J., and A. Jameton. (2003). *The Ethics of Environmentally Responsible Health Care.* New York: Oxford University Press.

Potter, V. R. (1971). *Bioethics: Bridge to the Future.* Englewood Cliffs, NJ: Prentice-Hall.

———. (1988). *Global Bioethics: Building on the Leopold Legacy.* East Lansing: Michigan State University Press.

CHAPTER 4

Berry, L., D. Parker, R. C. Coile Jr., et al. (2004). The business case for better buildings. *Frontiers of Health Service Management* 21 (1): 3–24.

Carson, Rachel. (1962). *Silent Spring.* Houghton Mifflin.

Gould, S. J. (1991). Enchanted evening. *Natural History*, September 14.

Kellert, S. (2005). *Building for Life: Designing and Understanding the Human–Nature Connection.* Washington, DC: Island Press.

Leopold, A. (1966). *A Sand County Almanac, with Other Essays on Conservation from Round River.* New York: Oxford University Press.

Mann, Thomas. (1996). *The Magic Mountain.* New York: 1st Vintage int'l. ed.

Marcus, C. C. (1999). *Healing Gardens: Therapeutic Benefits and Design Recommendations.* Hoboken, NJ: John Wiley & Sons.

McHarg, I. (1969). *Design with Nature.* Garden City, NY: Natural History Press.

McLennan, J. F. (2000). Living buildings. In *Sustainable Architecture White Papers.* New York: Earth Pledge Foundation.

National Cancer Institute. (2002). Taxanes in Cancer Treatment. http://cancerweb.ncl.ac.uk/cancernet/600715.html.

Nightingale, F. (1859). *Notes on Hospitals.* London: John W. Parker.

Orians, G., and J. Heerwagen (1992). Evolved responses to landscapes. In *The Adapted Mind: Evolutionary Pyschology and the Generation of Culture*, eds. J. H. Barkow, L. Cosmides, and J. Tooby. New York: Oxford University Press, p. 558.

Porteous, J. D. (1996). *Environmental Aesthetics: Ideas, Politics and Planning.* London: Routledge.

Ravanesi, B. (2006). Personal communication with Robin Guenther.

Simpson, D. (2004). Designed healing: Healthcare architecture changing with the times. *Northwest Construction*, July. http://northwest.construction.com/features/archive/0407_Feature4.asp

Sorvig, K. (2006). Building on—or haunted by—McHarg's legacy. Letters. *Landscape Architecture* (May): 13–14.

Stephenson, F. (2002). A tale of taxol. *Research in Review* (Florida State University), Fall. http://www.rinr.fsu.edu/fall2002/taxol.html

Ulrich, R. S. (1984). View through a window may influence recovery from surgery. *Science* 224:420–1.

Wilson, E. O. (1984). *Biophilia: The Human Bond with Other Species.* Cambridge: Harvard University Press.

Wines, J. (1998). The art of architecture in the age of ecology. New York: Taschen. Quoted in *Sustainable Architecture White Papers*, eds. D. Brown, M. Fox, and M. R. Pelletier. New York: Earth Pledge Foundation.

Nature and Healing: The Science, Theory, and Promise of Biophilic Design ▪ Stephen R. Kellert and Judith H. Heerwagen

Beauchemin, K. M., and P. Hays. (1996). Sunny hospital rooms expedite recovery from severe and refractory depression. *Journal of Affective Disorders* 40:49–51.

———. (1998). Dying in the dark: Sunshine, gender and outcomes in myocardial infarction. *Journal of the Royal Society of Medicine* 91:352–4.

De Vries, S. (2001). Nature and health: The importance of green space in urban living environment. Paper presented at the Open Space Functions Under Urban Pressure Conference, Ghent, Belgium, September 19–21.

Frumkin, H. (2001). Beyond toxicity: Human health and the natural environment. *American Journal of Preventative Medicine* 20 (3): 234–40.H.

Heerwagen, J. H., and G. H. Orians. (1986). Adaptations to windowless: The use of visual décor in windowed and windowless offices. *Environment and Behavior* 18 (5): 623–9.

———. (1993). Humans, Habitats and Aesthetics. In Kellert and Wilson.

Heschong Mahone Group. (2003). *Windows and Offices: A Study of Worker Performance and the Indoor Environment.* Report prepared for the California Energy Commission.

Kaplan, R. (1992). Urban forestry and the workplace. In *Managing Urban and High-Use Recreation Settings* (USDA Forest Service, General Technical Report NC-163), ed. P. H. Gobster. Chicago: North Central Forest Experiment Station.

Kellert, S. (Forthcoming). Elements of biophilic design. In *Bringing Buildings to Life: The Science, Theory, and Practice of Biophilic Building Design*, eds. S. Kellert, J. Heerwagen, and M. Mador.

———. (1997). *Kinship to Mastery: Biophilia in Human Evolution and Development*. Washington, DC: Island Press.

———. (2005). *Building for Life: Designing and Understanding the Human-Nature Connection*. Washington, DC: Island Press.

Kellert, S., and E. O. Wilson, eds. (1993). *The Biophilia Hypothesis*. Washington, DC: Island Press.

Kiraly, S. J., M. A. Kiraly, R. D. Hawe, and N. Makhani. (2006). Vitamin D as a neuroactive substance: Review. *The Scientific World Journal* 6:125–39.

Kweon, B.S., W.C. Sullivan, and A. Wiley. (1998). Green common spaces and the social integration of inner-city older adults. *Environment and Behavior* 30 (6): 832-858.

Lechtzin, N., and G. Diette, et al. (2001). Effect of nature sights and sounds during fiberoptic bronchoscopy on pain and anxiety. Abstract presented at the American Thoracic Society International Conference, Lubeck, Germany.

Marcus, C. C., and M. Barnes. (1995). *Healing Gardens: Therapeutic Benefits and Design Recommendations*. New York: John Wiley & Sons.

Mendler, S., W. Odell, M. Lazarus, and Hellmuth, Obata + Kassabaum [HOK]. (2006). *The HOK Guidebook to Sustainable Design*. 2nd ed. Hoboken, NJ: John Wiley & Sons.

Morris, N. (2003). *Health, Well-Being and Open Space*. Edinburgh: Edinburgh College of Art and Heriot–Watt University.

Pretty, J., M. Griffin, M. Sellens, and C. Pretty. (2003). *Green Exercise: Complementary Roles of Nature, Exercise, and Diet in Physical and Emotional Well-Being and Implications for Public Health Policy*. (CES Occasional Paper 2003-1). Essex: Center for Environment and Society, University of Essex.

Pretty, J., J. Peacock, M. Sellens, and M. Griffin. (2005). The mental and physical health outcomes of green exercise. *Journal of Environmental Health Research* 15 (5): 319–37.

Sullivan, W. C., E. F. Kuo, and S. F. Depooter. (2004). The fruit of urban nature: Vital neighborhood spaces. *Environment and Behavior* 36 (5): 678–700.

Tennessen, C. M., and B. Cimprich. (1995). Views to nature: Effects on attention. *Journal of Environmental Psychology* 15: 77–85.

Ulrich, R. S. (1984). View through a window may influence recovery from surgery. *Science* 224:420–1.

———. (1993). Biophilia and Biophobia. In Kellert and Wilson.

———. (2002). Health benefits of gardens in hospitals. Paper presented at the Plants for People Conference, International Exhibition Floriade.

Ulrich, R. S., O. Lumden, and J. L. Eltinge. (1993). Effects of exposure to nature and abstract pictures on patients recovery from heart surgery. Paper presented at the 33rd meeting of the Society for Psychophysiological Research, Rottach-Egern, Germany. Abstract published in *Psychophysiology* 30 (Supplement 1): 7.

Ulrich, R. S., R. F. Simons, B. D. Losito, E. Fiorito, M. A. Miles, and M. Zelson. (1991). Stress Recovery during Exposure to Natural and Urban Environments. *Journal of Environmental Psychology* 11 (3): 201–30.

Walch, J. M., B. S. Rabin, R. Day, J. N. Williams, K. Choi, and J. D. Kang. (2005). The effect of sunlight on post-operative analgesic medication usage: A prospective study of spinal surgery patients. *Psychosomatic Medicine* 67 (1): 156–63.

Wilson, E. O. (1984). *Biophilia: The Human Bond with Other Species*. Cambridge: Harvard University Press.

Design with Rhythm ■ Jody Rosenblatt-Naderi and Jerry Smith

Abram, D. (1996). *Spell of the Sensuous: Perception and Language in a More-Than Human World*. New York: Vintage.

Alexander, C., S. Ishikawa, M. Silverstein, et al. (1977). *A Pattern Language: Towns, Buildings, Construction*. New York: Oxford University Press.

American Society of Landscape Architecture. (2000). *Therapeutic Landscapes Data Base*. www.healinglandscapes.org.

Barrie, T. (1996). *Spiritual Path, Sacred Place: Myth, Ritual and Meaning in Architecture*. Boston and London: Shambhala.

Berlyne, D. E. (1971). *Aesthetics and Psychobiology*. New York: Appleton-Century-Crofts.

Downing, Frances. (2000). *Remembrance and the Design of Place*. College Station: Texas A&M University Press.

Francis, C. and C. C. Marcus. (1991). Places People Take Their Problems. In *Proceedings of the 22nd Annual Conference of Environmental Design Research Association, Oklahoma City*, eds. J. Urbina-Sotia, P. Ortega-Andeane, and R. Bechtel.

Gehls, J. (1987). *Life Between Buildings: Using Public Space*. New York: Van Nostrand Reinhold.

Geva, A. (2002). Unpublished conversations on the sacred. Texas A&M University.

Hall, E. T. (1969). *The Hidden Dimension.* Reprint, New York: Anchor Books, 1990.

Horsburgh, C. R. (1995). Healing by design. *The New England Journal of Medicine* 11 (333): 735–40.

Jay, R. (1998). *Gardens of the Spirit.* New York: Sterling.

Kaplan, R., and M. E. Austin. (2004). Sprawl and the quest for nearby nature. *Landscape and Urban Planning* 69:235–43.

Kaplan, R., and S. Kaplan (1990). Restorative experience: The healing power of nearby nature. In *The Meaning of Gardens,* eds. M. Francis and R. T. Hester Jr. Cambridge: MIT Press, 238–43.

Kaplan, R., S. Kaplan, and T. Brown. (1989). Environmental preference: A comparison of four domains of predictors. *Environment and Behavior* 21: 509–30.

Koestler, A. (1964). *Act of Creation.* Middlesex, England: Penguin.

Krishna, H. J. (2005). *Texas Manual on Rainwater Harvesting.* Austin: Texas Water Development Board.

Lane, B. C. (1988). *Landscapes of the Sacred: Geography and Narrative in American Spirituality.* New York: Paulist Press.

Malkin, J. (1992). *Hospital Interior Architecture.* New York: Van Nostrand Reinhold.

Marcus, C. C. (1997). *House as a Mirror of Self: Exploring the Deeper Meaning of Home.* Berkeley: Canari Press.

Marcus, C. C., and M. Barnes. (1995). *Gardens in Health Care Facilities: Uses, Therapeutic Benefits, and Design Considerations.* Martinez, Calif.: The Center for Health Design.

Marcus, C. C., and C. Francis, eds. (1997). *People Places: Design Guidelines for Urban Open Space.* 2nd ed. Hoboken, NJ: John Wiley & Sons.

McAvoy, G. (2006). *Bamboo: Symbol of Strength and Longevity.* LaBelle: University of Florida Cooperative Extension Service. http://hendry.ifas.ufl.edu/HCHortNews_Bamboo.htm

Messervy, J., and S. Abell. (1995). *The Inward Garden: Creating a Place of Beauty and Meaning.* Boston: Little, Brown.

Myss, C. (2005). *The Language of Archetypes.* Compact disc. Louisville, Colo.: Sounds True Publishers.

Naderi, J. R. (2001). Placemaking and mother tongue. Proceedings of the Council of Educators in Landscape Architecture Conference.

———. (2003). Landscape design in the clear zone: Effect of landscape variables on pedestrian health and driver safety. *Transportation Research Record* 1851:119–230.

———. (2004). Design of walking environments for spiritual renewal. *China Magazine.*

Ndubisi, F. (2002). *Ecological Planning: A Historic and Comparative Synthesis.* Baltimore: Johns Hopkins University.

Robinson, P. (1913). St. Francis of Assisi. *New Advent Catholic Encyclopedia* vol. 6. http://www.newadvent.org/cathen/06221a.htm

Stigsdotter, U. A., and P. Grahn. (2003). Landscape planning and stress. *Urban Forestry & Urban Greening* 2 (1): 1–18.

Tabb, P. (2003). Personal communication with Jody Rosenblatt-Naderi.

Tuan, Y. F. (1977). *Space and Place: The Perspective of Experience.* Minneapolis: University of Minneapolis Press.

Ulrich, R. S. (1999). Effects of Gardens on Health Outcomes: Theory and Research. In Marcus and Barnes, 27–86.

Wilhelm, R. and C. Baynes, trans. (1987). *The I Ching.* 22nd printing. New York: Princeton University Press.

Wilkin, P. (2006). Places of spirit: The Iona community. *Spirituality and Health International* 7 (4): 181–6. http://doi.wiley.com/10.1002/shi.300

Wright, M. S. (1997). *Co-creative Science: A Revolution in Science Providing Real Solutions for Today's Health and Environment.* Jeffersonton, Va: Perelandra Center for Nature Research.

Yancey, W. C. (1972). Architecture, interaction and social control: The case of large-scale housing project. In *Environment and the Social Science: Perspectives and Applications,* eds. J. F. Wohlwill and D. H. Carson. Washington, DC: American Psychological Association.

Zeisel, J., and J. Eberhard. (1981). *Inquiry by Design: Environment/Behavior/Neuroscience in Architecture, Interiors, Landscape, and Planning.* Monterey, Calif.: Brooks/Cole.

CHAPTER 5

Berry, L., D. Parker, R. C. Coile Jr., D. K. Hamilton, D. D. O'Neill, and B. L. Sadler. (2004). The business case for better buildings. *Frontiers of Health Service Management* 21 (1): 3–24.

Building Design and Construction [BDC]. (2006). White Paper on Sustainability. http://www.bdcnetwork.com/article/ca6390371.html

Building Design Partnership [BDP]. (2004). *Learning from French Hospital Design.* http://www.bdp.co.uk/healthcare/frenchlessons.asp

Cassidy, R. (2003). White Paper on Sustainability. *Building Design & Construction* (November): 1.

David and Lucille Packard Foundation [Packard]. (2002). *Building for Sustainability.* Los Altos, Calif.: David and Lucille Packard Foundation Los Altos Project. http://www.hpsarch.com/careers/2002-Matrix.pdf

Dean, L. (2000). Remarks, *Setting Healthcare's Environmental Agenda Conference,* San Francisco, October 16. In *Papers and proceedings from the conference.* http://www.noharm.org/details.cfm?type=document&ID=477

Elkington, J. (1998). *Cannibals with Forks: The Triple Bottom Line of 21st Century Business.* Oxford: Capstone.

Fisk, W. (2000). Review of health and productivity gains from better IEQ. In *Proceedings of Healthy Buildings 2000 Conference,* vol. 4., Espoo, Finland, August 6–10.

Frankel, C. (2004). *Out of the Labyrinth: Who We Are, How We Go Wrong and What We Can Do About It.* Rheinbeck, NY: Monkfish.

Gladwell, M. (2000). *The Tipping Point: How Little Things Can Make a Big Difference.* New York: Little, Brown.

Green Guide for Health Care [GGHC]. (2007). Best Practices for Creating High Performance Healing Environments, Version 2.2. http://www.gghc.org/about.cfm

Hawken, P., A. Lovins, and L. H. Lovins. (1999). *Natural Capitalism: Creating the Next Industrial Revolution.* Boston: Little, Brown.

Kats, G. (2003). *Green Building Costs and Financial Benefits.* Washington, DC: Capital E. http:www.cap-e.com/eweb editpro/items/O59F3481.pdf

Kresge Foundation. (2007). www.kresge.org

Lawrence, D. (2000). Remarks, *Setting Healthcare's Environmental Agenda Conference,* San Francisco, October 16. In *Papers and proceedings from the conference.* http://www.noharm.org/details.cfm?type=document&ID=477www.noharm.org/details.cfm?type=document&ID=477

Lovins, A. B. (2004). Energy efficiency, taxonomic overview. *Encyclopedia of Energy* 2: 383–401.

Matthiessen, L. F., and P. Morris. (2004). *Costing Green: A Comprehensive Cost Database and Budgeting Methodology.* Davis Langdon. www.usgbc.org/Docs/Resources/Cost_of_Green_Full.pdf

Mills, E., and E. Lecomte. (2006). *From Risk to Opportunity: How Insurers Can Proactively and Profitably Manage Climate Change.* Boston: Ceres.

Porter, M., and E. O. Teisberg. (2006). *Redefining Health Care: Creating Value-Based Competition on Results.* Chicago: American College of Healthcare Executives.

Powers, T. (2006). Environmental sensitivity in children's healthcare. *Environmental Design & Construction,* April 1.

Pradinuk, R. (2005). Arguing for a better hospital with the skeptic, the angst-ridden, and the zealous. Presentation to AIA Academy on Architecture for Health, Los Angeles, October 21.

PricewaterhouseCoopers. (2002). *Sustainability Survey Report.* August. http://www.pwc.com/fas/pdfs/sustainability%20survey%20report.pdf

Reed, C. (2000). U.S. Environmental Protection Agency research on Energy Star hospital partners. Unpublished data.

Roberts, G., and R. Guenther. (2006). Environmentally Responsible Hospitals. In *Improving Healthcare With Better Building Design,* ed. S. Marberry. Chicago: Health Administration Press.

Schlessinger, M., and B. Gray. (1998). A broader vision for managed care, part I: Measuring the benefit to communities. *Health Affairs* 17 (3): 152–68.

Secretan, L. (2005). Reclaiming higher ground. Keynote address, EnvironDesign 9, New York, April 19.

SustainAbility and United Nations Environment Programme [UNEP]. (2002). *Trust Us: The Global Reporters 2002 Survey of Corporate Sustainability Reporting.* London: SustainAbility. http://www.sustainability.com/trust-us

Yudelson, J., ed. (2005). *Engineering a Sustainable World: Design Process and Engineering Innovations for the Center for Health and Healing at Oregon Health and Science University, River Campus.* Portland, OR: Interface Engineering.

CHAPTER 6

Alexander, C., S. Ishikawa, M. Silverstein, et al. (1977). *A Pattern Language: Towns, Buildings, Construction.* New York: Oxford University Press.

Batshalom, B., and B. Reed. (2005). Mental model diagram. In The mindset thing: Exploring the deeper potential of integrated design. *Environmental Building News* 14 (12).

Day, C. (1990). *Places of the Soul: Architecture and Environmental Design As a Healing Art.* New York: HarperCollins.

Einstein, A. (1935). *The World As I See It.* New York: Citadel.

Facilities Guidelines Institute [FGI] and American Institute of Architects [AIA]. (2006). *Guidelines for Construction of Hospitals and Health Care Facilities.* Washington, DC: Facility Guidelines Institute.

Hamilton, D. K., and R. D. Orr. (2005). In *Improving Healthcare with Better Building Design,* ed. S. Marberry. Chicago: Health Administration Press, p.145.

Kats, G. (2003). *Green Building Costs and Financial Benefits.* Washington, DC: Capital E. http://www.cap-e.com/eweb editpro/items/O59F3481.pdf

Malin, N. (2005). The mindset thing: Exploring the deeper potential of integrated design. *Environmental Building News* 14 (12).

Matthiessen, L. F. (2006). *Costing Green Revisited.* Los Angeles: Davis Langdon.

Matthiessen, L. F., and P. Morris. (2004). *Costing Green: A Comprehensive Cost Database and Budgeting Methodology.* Los Angeles: Davis Langdon.

Meadows, D. H. (1999). *Leverage Points: Places to Intervene in a System.* Harland, Vt.: Sustainability Institute: Vermont. http://www.sustainabilityinstitute.org/pubs/Leverage_ Points.pdf

Orr, D. W. (2004). *The Nature of Design: Ecology, Culture, and Human Intention.* Oxford: Oxford University Press.

Salvatore, A. (2002). The built environment as a component of idealized design. Presentation at the Institute for Healthcare Improvement: 3rd Annual International Summit, May 13.

Senge, P. (1990). *The Fifth Discipline: The Art and Practice of the Learning Organization.* New York: Currency.

Shaw, A. (1989). *Energy Design for Architects.* Englewood Cliffs, NJ: Prentice Hall.

Shein, E. H. (1992). *Organizational Culture and Leadership.* San Francisco: Jossey-Bass.

Ulrich, R., and C. Zimring. (2004). *The Role of the Physical Environment in the Hospital of the 21st Century: A Once-in-a-Lifetime Opportunity.* Concord, Calif.: Center for Health Design. http://www.healthdesign.org/research/reports/ physical_environ.php

Wilson, J. Q. (1989). *Bureaucracy: What Government Agencies Do and Why They Do It.* New York: Basic Books.

Womack, J. P., and D. T. Jones. (1996). *Lean Thinking: Banish Waste and Create Wealth in Your Corporation.* New York: Simon & Schuster.

Yudelson, J., ed. (2005). *Engineering a Sustainable World: Design Process and Engineering Innovations for the Center for Health & Healing at Oregon Health & Science University, River Campus.* Portland, OR: Interface Engineering.

The Integrative Design Process: Changing our Mental Model ■ Bill Reed

Peat, D. (1995). *Blackfoot Physics: A Journey into the Native American Universe.* Weisner Books. Quoted in S. Sterling. (2003). Whole systems thinking as a basis for paradigm change in education: Explorations in the context of sustainability. PhD diss., University of Bath.

Senge, P. (1990). *The Fifth Discipline: The Art and Practice of the Learning Organization.* New York: Currency.

Commissioning ■ Tia Heneghan and Rebecca T. Ellis

Lewis, J. (2003). Presentation at the Federal Energy Management Advanced Metering Workshop, Golden, Colo., September 25.

CHAPTER 7

Bisson, C. L., G. McRae, and H. Shaner. (1993). *An Ounce of Prevention: Waste Reduction Strategies for Health Care Facilities.* Chicago: American Hospital Association.

Brannen, L. (2006). Preventative Medicine for the Environment: Developing and Implementing Environmental Programs that Work. In *Designing the 21st Century Hospital: Environmental Leadership for Healthier Patients and Facilities.* Concord, Calif.: Center for Health Design. http://www.health design.org/research/reports/documents/CHD_Brannen.pdf

Environmental Protection Agency [EPA]. (1997). *Mercury Study Report to Congress, Volume II: An Inventory of Anthropogenic Mercury Emissions in the United States.* (EPA-452/R-97-004). Washington, DC: EPA.

———. (2006). *An Inventory of Sources and Environmental Releases of Dioxin-Like Compounds in the United States for the Years 1987, 1995, and 2000.* (EPA/600/P-03/002f, Final Report, November 2006). Washington, DC: EPA.

Environmental Protection Agency and American Hospital Association [EPA and AHA]. (1998). Memorandum of Understanding between the American Hospital Association and the U.S. Environmental Protection Agency. http://www.noharm.org/library/docs/going_green_memorandum_of_understanding_betwee.pdf

Facility Guidelines Institute [FGI]. (2001). www.fgiguidelines .org/

Facilities Guidelines Institute [FGI] and American Institute of Architects [AIA]. (2001). *Guidelines for Construction of Hospitals and Health Care Facilities.* Washington, DC: Facilities Guidelines Institute.

———. (2006). *Guidelines for Construction of Hospitals and Health Care Facilities.* Washington, DC: Facility Guidelines Institute.

Green, M., S. Gifford, and H. McCarter. (2006). Lessons from Singapore. *Healthcare Design* (December).

Health Care Without Harm [HCWH]. (2001). Making Medicine Mercury Free: A Resource Guide for Mercury-Free Medi-

cine. http://www.noharm.org/details.cfm?type=document
&id=1274

Guenther, R. (2001). Sustainable Healthcare. *Healthcare Design* (October).

————. (2005). Stericycle Burns Waste and Endangers Shareholder Investments, Communities' Health. Press release, April 28. http://www.noharm.org/details.cfm?type=document&id=1067

Hospitals for a Healthy Environment [H2E]. (2005). *A 2005 Report on the Status of Virtual Mercury Elimination in the Health Care Sector.* www.h2e-online.org/pubs/mercuryreport.pdf

International Standards Organization [ISO]. (2006). www.iso.org

Schettler, T. (2001). Environmental challenges and visions of sustainable health care. Paper presented at CleanMed Conference, Boston, May 4.

University of Michigan Health System [UMHS]. (2001). U-M Health System Named Tops in Recycling among State's Public Institutions. Press release, May 23. http://www.med.umich.edu/opm/newspage/2001/recycling.htm

Wright, H. A. I., M. J. Hanley, and T. Quigley. (2001). Healthy Hospitals: A Journey to ISO 14001 Certification. *Healthcare Quarterly* 4 (4): 32–4.

CHAPTER 8

American Institute of Architects [AIA], J. A. Demkin, eds. (1996). *Environmental Resource Guide.* New York: John Wiley & Sons.

American Society of Healthcare Engineering [ASHE]. (2002). Green Healthcare Construction Guidance Statement. www.healthybuilding.net/healthcare/ASHE_Green_Healthcare_2002.pdf

Anderson, J., D. Shiers, M. Sinclair. (2002). *The Green Guide to Specification.* 3rd ed. Oxford: Blackwell Science.

Austin Energy. (2007). City of Austin Green Building Program. http://www.austinenergy.com/Energy%20Efficiency/Programs/Green%20Building/index.htm

Building Research Establishment [BRE]. (1990). The Building Research Establishment's Environmental Assessment Method. http://www.breeam.org

Cannon Design. (2007). Brigham & Women's Hospital. http://cannondesign.com/start_frameset.htm

Cascadia Region Green Building Council [CRGBC]. (2006). *The Living Building Challenge v1.0: In Pursuit of True Sustainability in the Built Environment.* Portland, Ore.: Cascadia Region Green Building Council.

Cassidy, R. (2004). Progress Report on Sustainability. *Building Design & Construction* (November): Supplement.

Clinton, W. J., President. (1998) Greening the Government through Waste Prevention, Recycling, and Federal Acquisition. Executive Order no. 13101, *Code of Federal Regulations*, title 3, 63 (179) 49643–51, September 14. http://www.epa.gov/oppt/epp/pubs/13101.pdf

Dean, L. (2000). Remarks, *Setting Healthcare's Environmental Agenda Conference*, San Francisco, October 16. In *Papers and proceedings from the conference.* http://www.noharm.org/details.cfm?type=document&ID=477

Environmental Building News [EBN]. (1992). ASTM Green Building Committee (September/October) 1 (2).

Fowler, K. M., and E. M. Rauch. (2006). *Sustainable Building Rating Systems Summary.* Pacific Northwest National Laboratory, General Services Administration (DE-AC05-76RL061830).

Glaser, D. (2006). Personal communication with Gail Vittori, December 20.

Green Building Council of Australia [GBCA]. (2007). Rating Tool Fact Sheet: Green Star—Healthcare PILOT. http://www.gbcaus.org/gbc.asp?sectionid=89&docid=953

Green Guide for Health Care [GGHC]. (2004). Best Practices for Creating High Performance Healing Environments, Version 2.0 Pilot. http://www.gghc.org

————. (2007). Best Practices for Creating High Performance Healing Environments, Version 2.2. http://www.gghc.org

Helmer, S. (2006). *FacilityCare's 2006 Operations Survey. FacilityCare* (November).

Lawrence, D. (2000). Remarks, *Setting Healthcare's Environmental Agenda Conference*, San Francisco, October 16. In *Papers and proceedings from the conference*, p. 54. http://www.noharm.org/details.cfm?type=document&ID=477

LEED for Health Care Core Committee. (Forthcoming). LEED for Health Care. Washington, DC: U.S. Green Building Council.

Lerner, M. (2000). Remarks, *Setting Healthcare's Environmental Agenda Conference*, San Francisco, October 16. In *Papers and proceedings from the conference*, p. 66. http://www.noharm.org/details.cfm?type=document&ID=477

Norman, D. A. (1998). *The Invisible Computer.* Cambridge: MIT Press.

Solomon, N. B. (2004). Environmentally-friendly building strategies slowly make their way into medical facilities. *Architectural Record* (August): 179–88.

US Green Building Council [USGBC]. (2003). www.usgbc.org

———. (2007). LEED Initiatives in Governments and Schools. https://www.usgbc.org/ShowFile.aspx?DocumentID=691

Vittori, G. (2000). Green and Healthy Buildings for the Healthcare Sector. Paper presented at *Setting Healthcare's Environmental Agenda*, San Francisco, October 16. In *Papers and proceedings from the conference*, pp. 1–10. http://www.noharm.org/details.cfm?type=document&ID=477

Whole Building Design Guide. (2007). www.wbdg.org

Great Britain's National Health Service

Borger, C., S. Smith, C. Truffer, et al. (2006). Health spending projections through 2015: Changes on the horizon. *Health Affairs* 25:w61–w73. http://content.healthaffairs.org/cgi/content/full/25/2/w61

Commission for Architecture and the Built Environment [CABE]. (2006a). *Corporate Strategy 2006/7–2008/9*, p. 5. London: Commission for Architecture and the Built Environment.

———. (2006b). *The Cost of Bad Design*. London: Commission for Architecture and the Built Environment. http://www.cabe.org.uk/default.aspx?contentitemid=1342

———. (2006c). *Designed with Care: Creating a Good Healthcare Building*. London: Commission for Architecture and the Built Environment. http://www.cabe.org.uk/default.aspx?contentitemid=1154

———. (2006d). *Designed with Care: Design and Neighbourhood Healthcare Buildings*. London: Commission for Architecture and the Built Environment. http://www.cabe.org.uk/default.aspx?contentitemid=1158

Coote, A. (2006). *Health and Sustainable Development*. London: Commission for Architecture and the Built Environment. http://www.cabe.org.uk/default.aspx?refid=182&sl=4.2&contentitemid=1299

Hockridge, E., and J. Longfield. (2005). *Getting more sustainable food into London's hospitals: Can it be done? And is it worth it?* London: Sustain.

Jenkin, N., ed. (2004). Material Health: A Mass Balance and Ecological Footprint Analysis for the NHS. Executive summary. Oxford: Best Foot Forward. http://www.material-health.com/download.htm

Macgregor, L. (2007). Hospitals get cash to fight global warming. Reuters, January 4.

National Health Service [NHS]. (2000). Health Facilities Scotland. http://www.hfs.scot.nhs.uk

———. (2006). www.nhs.uk

———. (2007a). NHS Careers. http://www.nhscareers.nhs.uk/

———. (2007b). *Achieving Excellence Design Evaluation Toolkit Evolution*. http://design.dh.gov.uk/downloads/aedet_evolution/AEDET_Evolution_promotional_booklet.pdf

National Health Service Department of Health. (2004). *Choosing Health: Making Healthy Choices Easier*. London: HMSO, p. 5.

———. (2006a). IDEAs. http://design.dh.gov.uk/ideas/

———. (2006b). NHS Environment Assessment Tool Guidance. http://www.dh.gov.uk/PublicationsAndStatistics/Publications/PublicationsPolicyAndGuidance/PublicationsPolicyAndGuidanceArticle/fs/en?CONTENT_ID=4119943&chk=/zNIF4

———. (2006c). Sustainable Development in the NHS. http://www.dh.gov.uk/PolicyAndGuidance/Organisation Policy/EstatesAndFacilitiesManagement/Sustainable Development/SustainableDevelopmentArticle/fs/en?CONTENT_ID=4119123&chk=sS5n8V

National Health Service Estates. (2005). *ASPECT: Staff and Patient Environment Calibration Toolkit*. Norwich, UK: TSO. http://design.dh.gov.uk/downloads/aspect/ASPECT_documentation_v010705.pdf

National Health Service Purchasing and Supply Agency [NHS PASA]. (2005). Draft Sustainable Purchasing Action Plan.

———. (2006a). Food Procurement Action Plan. http://www.pasa.doh.gov.uk/sustainabledevelopment/food/action plan.stm

———. (2006b). Public Sector Food Procurement Initiative Action Plan, p. 7.

———. (2006c). Sustainable Procurement Action Plan. http://www.pasa.nhs.uk/pasa/Doc.aspx?Path=[MN][SP]/About%20procurement%20in%20the%20NHS/Sustainable%20procurement/Action%20Plan%20sustainable%20procurement%204%2010%2006.pdf

———. (2006d). Sustainable Procurement Strategy 2006. http://www.pasa.doh.gov.uk/sustainabledevelopment/Strategy%20sustainable%20procurement%20draft%20DW3%2010%2006.pdf

Nightingale, M. (2006). University Hospital in Coventry: Light and space. *Hospital Development* (November).

Norman, D. A. (1998). *The Invisible Computer*. Cambridge: MIT Press.

Sustainable Development Commission [SDC]. (2004). *Healthy Futures: Food and Sustainable Development*. London: SDC.

———. (2006). *Healthy Futures: Are You a Good Corporate Citizen?* London: SDC.

United Kingdom. Parliament. (2005). *Securing the Future: Delivering UK Sustainable Development Strategy.* Cm 6467. http://www.sustainable-development.gov.uk/publications/pdf/strategy/SecFut_complete.pdf

US Green Building Council. (2007). LEED Initiatives in Governments and Schools. https://www.usgbc.org/ShowFile.aspx?DocumentID=691

World Health Organization Regional Office for Europe [WHO]. (2004). Highlights on Health, United Kingdom 2004. http://www.euro.who.int/eprise/main/who/progs/chhunk/system/20050315_1

CHAPTER 9

American Society for Healthcare Engineering [ASHE]. (2002). ASHE Green Healthcare Construction Guidance Statement. http://www.healthybuilding.net/healthcare/ASHE_Green_Healthcare_2002.pdf

Gladwell, M. (2000). *The Tipping Point: How Little Things Can Make a Big Difference.* New York: Little, Brown.

Green Guide for Health Care [GGHC]. (2007). Best Practices for Creating High Performance Healing Environments, Version 2.2. http://www.gghc.org/about.cfm

Guenther, R., G. Vittori, and C. Atwood. (2006). Values Driven Design and Construction: Enriching Community Benefits through Green Hospitals. In *Designing the 21st Century Hospital: Creating Safe and Healthy Environments for Patients and Staff.* Concord, Calif.: Center for Health Design. http://www.healthdesign.org/research/reports/documents/CHD_GuentherVittoriAtwood_edit_v2.pdf

Hassel, J., J. Walleck, and R. Ramachandran. (2006). Interview with Maya Sheppard, December 1.

Helmer, S. (2006). *FacilityCare's* 2006 Operations Survey. *FacilityCare* (November).

Johnson, G. (2005). Caring for patients and the environment. *Healthcare Design* 5 (3): 421.

Meadows, D. (2001). Dancing with Systems. *Whole Earth,* Winter.

CHAPTER 10

Acoustical Society of America [ASA], Institute of Noise Control Engineering, and National Council of Acoustical Consultants: Joint Subcommittee on Speech Privacy. (2006). *Interim Sound and Vibration Design Guidelines for Hospital and Healthcare Facilities.* Draft.

American Chemistry Society Green Chemistry Institute. (2007). www.greenchemistryinstitute.org

American Institute of Architects [AIA]. (2001). *Guidelines for Construction of Hospitals and Health Care Facilities.* Washington, DC: Facility Guidelines Institute.

Anastas, P. T., and J. C. Warner. (1998). *Green Chemistry: Theory and Practice.* New York: Oxford University Press.

BuildingGreen. (2007). *GreenSpec Directory,* 7th ed. Brattleboro, Vt.: BuildingGreen.

California Urban Water Conservation Council. (2006). Maximum Performance (MaP(tm)) Testing: A New and Better Measurement of Toilet Performance! http://www.cuwcc.org/MapTesting.lasso

Chen, Q., and L. Glicksman. (2003). *System Performance Evaluation and Design Guidelines for Displacement Ventilation.* Atlanta: American Society of Heating, Refrigerating, and Air Conditioning Engineering.

Clean Production Action. (2007). Healthy Business Strategies for Transforming the Toxic Chemical Economy. http://www.cleanproduction.org/Green.Healthy.php

Consulting Specifying Engineer. (2006). Displaced Ventilation in Hospitals? http://www.csemag.com/article/CA6401710.html

Energy Information Administration [EIA]. (1999). Commercial Buildings Energy Consumption Survey. http://www.eia.doe.gov/emeu/cbecs/pba99/intro.html

Guenther, R., G. Vittori, and C. Atwood. (2006). Values Driven Design and Construction: Enriching Community Benefits through Green Hospitals. In *Designing the 21st Century Hospital: Creating Safe and Healthy Environments for Patients and Staff.* Concord, Calif.: Center for Health Design. http://www.healthdesign.org/research/reports/documents/CHD_GuentherVittoriAtwood_edit_v2.pdf

Herbert, C. (2006). Quoted in Guenther, Vittori and Atwood.

Jakelius, S. (1996). *Learning from Experiences with Energy Savings in Hospitals.* Centre for the Analysis and Dissemination of Demonstrated Energy Technologies (CADDET). http://www.caddet.org/public/uploads/pdfs/Report/ar_20.pdf

Koster, J. (2006). Quoted in Guenther, Vittori, and Atwood.

Massachusetts Water Resources Authority [MWRA]. (1996). Water Use Case Study: Norwood Hospital. http://www.mwra.state.ma.us/04water/html/bullet1.htm

New Zealand Ministry of the Environment. (2005). Value Case for Sustainable Building in New Zealand: Three Case Studies. http://www.mfe.govt.nz/publications/sus-dev/value-case-sustainable-building-feb06/html/page6d.html

Robertson, J. (2007). OHSU Center First Medical Facility in Nation to Win LEED Platinum Award. Press release, February 22. http://www.ohsu.edu/ohsuedu/newspub /releases /022207_leedaward.cfm

Rossi, M., and T. Lent. (2006). Creating Safe and Healthy Spaces: Selecting Materials that Support Healing. In *Designing the 21st Century Hospital: Creating Safe and Healthy Environments for Patients and Staff.* Concord, Calif: Center for Health Design. http://www.healthdesign.org/research/ reports/documents/CHD_RossiLent.pdf

Russ, C. (2006). *Hospitals: Exemplary Energy Conscious European Hospitals and Health Care Buildings.* Freiburg, Germany: Fraunhofer Institute for Solar Energy Systems. http://www .eu-hospitals.net/results/pdf/future/evaluation-compari son-recommendations_for_future_applications.pdf

Sala, M., A. Trombadore, and G. Alcamo. (2006). Energy-Saving Strategies for the New Design Meyer Children Hospital in Florence. In *Design & Health IV: Future Trends in Healthcare Design,* ed. A. Dilani. Huddinge, Sweden: International Academy for Design and Health.

Slotterback, S. (2006). Kaiser Permanente's Sustainable Building Program. PowerPoint slides. Institute of Medicine.

Ulrich, R. S. (1984). View through a window may influence recovery from surgery. *Science* 224:420–1.

Veritec Consulting Inc. and Koeller & Co. (2006). Maximum Performance (MaP) Testing of Popular Toilet Models, 8th ed. Mississauga, Ont., and Yorba Linda, Calif: Veritec Consulting and Koeller & Co.

Williams, J. M., I. P. Knight, and A. J. Griffiths. (1999). Hospital energy performance: New indicators for UK National Health Service estate. *Building Services Engineering Research & Technology* 20 (1): 9–12.

Yudelson, J., ed. (2005). *Engineering a Sustainable World: Design Process and Engineering Innovations for the Center for Health & Healing at Oregon Health & Science University, River Campus.* Portland, OR: Interface Engineering.

We All Live Downstream ▪ Carol Franklin and Teresa Durkin

Energy Information Administration [EIA] and Department of Energy. (2004). *Emission of Greenhouse Gases in the U.S. 2004.* Washington, DC: Energy Information Administration.

Environmental Protection Agency [EPA]. (2004). *Report to Congress on Impacts and Control of Combined Sewer Overflows and Sanitary Sewer Overflows.* Washington, DC: EPA.

Gaffield, S. J., R. L. Goo, L. A. Richards, and R. J. Jackson. (2003). Public health effects of inadequately managed stormwater runoff. *American Journal of Public Health* 93 (9): 1527–33.

Jackson, R. J., and C. Kotchtitsky. (2000). *Creating a Healthy Environment: The Impact of the Built Environment on Public Health.* Atlanta: Centers for Disease Control and Prevention.

Steingraber, S. (1998). *Living Downstream: An Ecologist Looks at Cancer and the Environment.* New York: Vintage.

United Nations Conference on Environment and Development [UNCED]. (1992). Report from the UN Conference on Environment and Development, Rio de Janeiro, June 13–14 (The Earth Summit).

Energy Use, Energy Production and Health
▪ Alexis Karolides

Bauman, F., and T. Webster. (2001). Outlook for Underfloor Air Distribution. *ASHRAE Journal,* June.

Berkeley Lab. (2000). New Commercial Building Energy Efficiency Program Launched. Press release. http://www.lbl .gov/Science-Articles/Archive/combldg-energy.html

Energy Information Administration. [EIA]. (2007a). Commercial Building Sector Energy Intensities: 1992–1999. http://www.eia.doe.gov/emeu/efficiency/cbecstrends/cbecs _tables_list.htm#Commercial%20Buildings%20Pri mary%20Energy

———. (2007b). Health Care Buildings: How Do They Use Electricity? http://www.eia.doe.gov/emeu/consumptionbriefs/ cbecs/pbawebsite/health/health_howuseelec.htm

Flavin, C., and N. Lenssen. (1994). Powering the Future: Blueprint for a Sustainable Electricity Industry. (Worldwatch Paper #119). Washington, DC: Worldwatch Institute.

Lenssen, N. (1992). Empowering Development: The New Energy Equation. (Worldwatch Paper #111). Washington, DC: Worldwatch Institute.

Loranger, R. (2004). Presentation, Design for Health: Summit for Massachusetts Health Care Decision Makers, September 28.

Lovins, A., E. K. Datta, T. Feiler, et al. (2002). *Small Is Profitable: The Hidden Economic Benefits of Making Electrical Resources the Right Size.* Snowmass, Colo.: Rocky Mountain Institute.

Moroz, R. (2004). Presentation, Design for Health: Summit for Massachusetts Health Care Decision Makers, September 28–29.

Ovitt, M. A. (1996). The effect of a view of nature on performance and stress reduction of ICU nurses. Master's thesis,

Department of Landscape Architecture, University of Illinois–Urbana-Champaign.

Rocky Mountain Institute. (2005). Report given at Design for Health: A Summit for Massachusetts Health Care Decision Makers, September 28–29.

Ulrich, R. (1984). View through a window may influence recovery from surgery. *Science* 224:420–1.

Ulrich, R., and C. Zimring. (2004). *The Role of the Physical Environment in the Hospital of the 21st Century: A Once in a Lifetime Opportunity.* Concord, Calif.: Center for Health Design. http://www.healthdesign.org/research/reports/physical_environ.php

Wu, B. (2003). *Lethal Legacy: A Comprehensive Look at America's Dirtiest Power Plants.* Washington, DC: U.S. Public Interest Research Group Education Fund. http://www.cleartheair.org/reports/lethal_legacy_report.pdf

Specifying for Health ▮ Greg Roberts

California Integrated Waste Management Board. (2003). Building Materials Emissions Study. http://www.ciwmb.ca.gov/greenbuilding/specs/section01350

Construction Specifications Institute Environmental Task Team. (2003). 2003 Principles for Green Specifications.

International Agency for Research on Cancer. [IARC] (2004). IARC Classifies Formaldehyde as Carcinogenic to Humans. Press release, June.

Kats, G. (2003). *Green Building Costs and Financial Benefits.* Washington, DC: Capital E. http://www.cap-e.com/ewebeditpro/items/O59F3481.pdf

Lin, F., and L. Lin. (2003). A discussion of the state-of-art research on environmentally conscious material selection methodologies for the reduction of products' toxic impact. *The Journal of Sustainable Product Design* 3 (3-4): 119–34.

McDonough Braungart Design Chemistry. (2004). The Cradle-to-Cradle Design Protocol. http://www.mbdc.com/ref_protocol.htm

Science & Environmental Health Network. (1998). Precautionary Principle: Wingspread Consensus Statement on the Precautionary Principle. http://www.sehn.org/wing.html

Scorecard: The Pollution Information Site. (2005). Chemical Profiles/High Production Volume (HPV) Chemicals. http://www.scorecard.org/chemical-profiles/def/hpv.html

Building Ventilation ▮ Hal Levin

Persily, A. K., and J. Gorfain. (2004). Analysis of Ventilation Data from the U.S. Environmental Protection Agency Building Assessment Survey and Evaluation [BASE] Study. (NISTIR 7145). Gaithersburg, MD: National Institute of Standards and Technology. http://www.eere.energy.gov/buildings/highperformance/pdfs/nist-oa_study_2005.pdf

Persily, A. K., J. Gorfain, and G. Brunner. (2005). Ventilation design and performance in U.S. office buildings. *ASHRAE Journal* (April): 6.

———. (2005). Ventilation Rates in U.S. Office Buildings from the EPA BASE Study. National Institute of Standards and Technology. Proceedings: Indoor Air. Washington, DC: Environmental Protection Agency.

Seppanen, O. A., W. J. Fisk, and M. J. Mendell. (1999). Association of ventilation rates and CO_2 concentrations with health and other responses in commercial and institutional buildings. *Indoor Air* 9:226–52.

CHAPTER 11

Alvarez, L. (2004). Where the healing touch starts with the hospital design. *New York Times,* September 7.

Gibbs, N., and A. Bower. (2006). Q: What scares doctors? A: Being the patient. *Time,* April 23. http://www.time.com/time/magazine/article/0,9171,1186553-1,00.html

Guenther, R. (2006). How should healthcare lead? Panel discussion at CleanMed Conference, Seattle, April 20.

Hyett, P. (2004). New developments in the healthcare estate in England. Presentation at the AIA Academy of Architecture for Health Conference, Washington, DC.

Lima, João Filgueiras. (2000). *João Filgueiras Lima: Lelé.* Lisbon and São Paulo: Blau and Instituto Lina Bo e P. M. Bardi.

Monk, T. (2004). *Hospital Builders.* London: Academy Press.

Payer, L. (1988). *Medicine & Culture: Varieties of Treatment in the U.S., England, West Germany and France.* New York: Penguin.

Pine, B. J., II, and J. H. Gilmore. (1999). *The Experience Economy: Work Is Theater and Every Business a Stage.* Boston: Harvard Business School Press.

Postman, N. (1992). *Technopoly: The Surrender of Culture to Technology.* New York: Knopf.

Sant'Ana, D. (2006). Case Study: Sarah Network of Hospitals for Reabilitation [sic]. (2006). These Are the Principles of the Sarah Network. http://www.sarah.br/paginas/institucao/en/e-03-principios.htm

———. (2007). The Sarah Network. www.sarah.br [English version].

Stephens, S. (2005). REHAB Center for Spinal Cord and Brain Injuries. *Architectural Record* (June).

Verderber, S. (2006). Hospital Futures: Humanism Versus the Machine. In *The Architecture of Hospitals,* ed. C. Wagenaar. Rotterdam: NAi.

Verderber, S., and D. Fine. (2000). *Healthcare Architecture in an Era of Radical Transformation.* New Haven: Yale University Press.

Wagenaar, C. (2006). Five Revolutions: A Short History of Hospital Architecture. In *The Architecture of Hospitals,* ed. C. Wagenaar. Rotterdam: NAi, p. 35.

Doubling Daylight ■ Ray Pradinuk

Alexander, C., S. Ishikawa, M. Silverstein, et al. (1977). *A Pattern Language: Towns, Buildings, Construction.* New York: Oxford University Press.

Baker, G. R., P. G. Norton, V. Flintoft, et al. (2004). The Canadian Adverse Events Study: The incidence of adverse events among hospital patients in Canada. *Canadian Medical Association Journal* 170 (11).

Benedetti, F., C. Colombo, B. Barbini, E. Campori, and E. Smeraldi. (2001). Morning sunlight reduces length of hospitalization in bipolar depression. *Journal of Affective Disorders* 62 (3): 221–3.

Bergsland, K. (2005). Keynote address, annual HealthCare Design Conference, Scottsdale, Ariz., November 6–9.

Berry, L., D. Parker, R. C. Coile Jr., D. K. Hamilton, D. D. O'Neill, and B. L. Sadler. (2004). Can better buildings improve care and increase your financial returns? *Frontiers of Health Services Management,* Fall.

Blomkvist, V., C. A. Eriksen, T. Theorell, R. S. Ulrich, and G. Rasmanis. (2004). Acoustics and psychosocial environment in intensive coronary care. *Occupational and Environmental Medicine* 62 (3).

Commission for Architecture and the Built Environment [CABE]. (2004). *The Role of Hospital Design in the Recruitment, Retention and Performance of NHS Nurses in England.* London: CABE.

Fisk, W. (2000). Review of health and productivity gains from better IEQ. In *Proceedings of Healthy Buildings 2000 Conference,* vol. 4. Espoo, Finland, August 6–10.

Fisk, W., and A. Rosenfeld. (1997). Estimates of improved productivity and health from better indoor environments. *Indoor Air* 7 (3): 158–72.

Frampton, K., T. Grajewski, and A. Eggleton. (1999). Counting the cost of people and materials movement within hospital buildings. Unpublished research report, Cardiff University, Wales.

Green Guide for Health Care [GGHC]. (2004). Best Practices for Creating High Performance Healing Environments, Version 2.0 Pilot. http://www.gghc.org

Kats, G. (2003). *Green Building Costs and Financial Benefits.* Washington, DC: Capital E. http://www.cap-e.com/eweb editpro/items/O59F3481.pdf

Kroner, W., and J. Stark-Martin. (1992). Environmentally responsive workstations and office worker productivity. In *Proceedings of Indoor Environment and Productivity, June 23–26, Baltimore,* ed. H. Levin. (2000). Atlanta: ASHRAE.

Lowe, G., G. Shellenberg, and H. Shannon. (2003). Correlates of employees' perceptions of a healthy work environment. *American Journal of Health Promotion* 17 (6): 390–9.

Reid, R. (2004). Interview by CBC Radio. *The Early Edition,* May 25.

Selzer, R. (1979). An Absence of Windows. In *Confessions of a Knife.* East Lansing: Michigan State University Press.

Shepley, M. M., and K. Davies. (2003). Nursing unit configuration and its relationship to noise and nurse walking behavior: An AIDS/HIV unit case study. *Academy Journal* (American Institute of Architects), 6th ed. http://www.aia.org/aah_a_jrnl_0401_article4

Ulrich, R. (1984). View through a window may influence recovery from surgery. *Science* 224: 420–1.

———. (2001). Effects of interior design on wellness: Theory and recent scientific research. *Journal of Healthcare Design* (November): 97–100.

Ulrich, R., and C. Zimring. (2004). *The Role of the Physical Environment in the Hospital of the 21st Century: A Once in a Lifetime Opportunity. Report to the Center for Health Design.* http://www.healthdesign.org/research/reports/physical_environ.php

VanderKaay, S. (2004). Calculating the value of intangibles. *Canadian Architect,* July.

Verderber, S., and D. Fine. (2000). *Healthcare Architecture in an Era of Radical Transformation.* New Haven: Yale University Press.

Walch, J. M., B. S. Rabin, R. Day, J. N. Williams, K. Choi, and J. D. Kang. (2005). The effect of sunlight on post-operative analgesic medication usage: A prospective study of spinal surgery patients. *Psychosomatic Medicine* 67 (1): 156–63.

Wyon, D. P. (1996). Individual microclimate control: Required range, probable benefits, and current feasibility. *Proceedings of Indoor Air* 96 1:1067–72.

Zoutman, R. (2002). Video presentation to the Romanow Commission on the Future of Health Care at the annual Community and Hospital Infection Control Association of Canada Conference, April 2.

Humanism in the Art of Sustainable Healing
▓ Sean Stanwick and Tye Farrow

Frampton, K. (1983). Towards a Critical Regionalism: Six Points for an Architecture of Resistance. In *The Anti Aesthetic: Essays on Postmodern Culture*, ed. H. Foster. Port Townsend, Wash.: Bay Press.

Kellert, S., and E. O. Wilson, eds. (1993). *The Biophilia Hypothesis*. Washington, DC: Island Press.

McMinn J., and M. Polo. (2006). 41° to 66°, Regional Responses to Sustainable Architecture in Canada. Museum exhibit. Cambridge, Ont.: Cambridge Galleries.

Tönnies, F. (1957). *Community and Society: Gemeinschaft und Gesellschaft*. East Lansing: Michigan State University Press.

Open Building: Health Care on the Time Axis
▓ Stephen Kendall

Boice, J. R. (1968). *A History and Evaluation of the School Construction Systems Development Project 1961–1967*. Menlo Park, Calif.: Building Systems Information Clearinghouse, Educational Facilities Laboratories.

Brand, S. (1994). *How Buildings Learn: What Happens After They're Built*. New York: Viking.

Building Systems Development and Stone, Marraccini & Patterson [BSD]. (1977). *Development Study—VA Hospital Building System*. Washington, DC: U.S. Government Printing Office.

Hattis, D. B., and T. E. Ware. (1971). *The PBS Performance Specification for Office Buildings*. (NBS Report 10 527). Washington, DC: Department of Commerce, National Bureau of Standards, Institute for Applied Technology, Building Research Division.

Hochbauamt des Kantons Bern, ed. (1997). Jurybericht: INO Inselspital Bern, Wettbewerb 1997, Primärsystem. Bern.

———. (1998). Jurybericht: INO Inselspital Bern, Wettbewerb 1998, Sekundärsystem. Bern.

Habraken, J. N. (1998). *The Structure of the Ordinary: Form and Control in the Built Environment*. Cambridge: MIT Press.

Kendall, S. (2004). Open building: A new paradigm in health care architecture. *AIA Academy of Health*, October 27. http://www.aia.org/aah_journal 20041027

Macchi, G. (1997). Prävention beim Bauen: Projektorganisatorische Vorkehrungen im Hinblick auf einen langfristig hohen Gebrauchswert. In *Bauwerkserhaltung und Wirtschaftlichkeit: Perspektiven einer modernen Aufgabe, Referate der FEB-Studientagung vom Donnerstag*. (Dokumentation SIA D 0141). Zürich: Schweizer Ingenieur und Architekten-Verein.

———. (1999). Eine neue Werterhaltungspolitik für Bauverwaltungen. In *Umbau? Über die Zukunft des Baubestandes*. Berlin: Wasmuth Verlag Tübingen.

———. (2000). Reflexiones y cambios. In *Hospitales, La arquitectura del insalud, 1986–2000*. Instituto nacional de la salud.

Venturi, R., and D. S. Brown. (2004). *Architecture as Signs and Systems: For a Mannerist Time, The William E. Massey Sr. Lectures in the History of American Civilization*. London: Belknap Press.

CHAPTER 12

Architecture 2030. (2006). www.architecture2030.org

Barrett, J., N. Cherrett, R. Birch, and C. Simmons. (2004). An analysis of the policy and educational application of the ecological footprint. Oxford: Best Foot Forward.

Best Foot Forward [BFF] (2004). *Material Health: A Mass Balance and Ecological Footprint Analysis of the NHS in England and Wales*. Oxford: BFF.

Brown, J. (2006). Reduce, reuse, recycle—and save. *Healthcare Design* (June). http://www.healthcaredesignmagazine.com /CleanDesign.htm

Carbon Footprint Ltd. (2006). What Is a Carbon Footprint? www.carbonfootprint.com/carbon_footprint.html

Climate Group. (2005). *Carbon Down, Profits Up*. 3rd ed. http://theclimategroup.org/index.php/resources/

Cole, R. (2001). Numbers used to estimate embodied energy and CO_2 for the Green Building Challenge. Personal communication with professor at School of Community and Regional Planning, University of British Columbia–Vancouver.

EcoBridge. (2006). Causes of Global Warming. http://www .ecobridge.org/content/g_cse.htm

Energy Information Agency [EIA] and U.S. Department of Energy. (2003). Commercial Building Energy Consumption Survey, Table C3: Consumption and Gross Energy Intensity for Sum of Major Fuels for Non-Mall Buildings, 2003. www.eia.doe.gov/emeu/cbecs/cbecs2003/detailed_ tables_2003/2003set9/2003pdf/c3.pdf

Environmental Protection Agency [EPA]. (2007a). The Energy Star Challenge: Build a Better World 10% at a Time. http:// www.energystar.gov/index.cfm?c=leaders.bus_challenge

———. (2007b). Perfluorooctanoic Acid (PFOA) and Fluorinated Telomars. http://www.epa.gov/oppt/pfoa/

GrassRoots Recycling Network [GRRN]. (2004). GRRN Zero Waste Business Principles. http://www.grrn.org/zerowaste/business/index.php

Green Guide for Health Care [GGHC]. (2007). Best Practices for Creating High Performance Healing Environments, Version 2.2. http://www.gghc.org/about.cfm

Germain, S. (Winter 2001/2002). The ecological footprint of Lions Gate Hospital. *Healthcare Quarterly* 5 (2): 61–6.

———. (2007). Determination of the Ecological Footprint of a Hospital. http://www.c2p2online.com/documents/Lionsgate.pdf

Global Footprint Network [GFN]. (2006).www.footprintnetwork.org

Green Building Council Australia. (2007). Green Star – Health care PILOT. http://www.gbcaus.org

Green Health Center. (2004). Exploring Bioethics Upstream. http://www.unmc.edu/green/main_conclusions.htm

Hancock, T. (2001). *Doing Less Harm: Assessing and Reducing the Environmental and Health Impact of Canada's Health Care System.* Canadian Coalition for Green Health Care.

Hancock, T., and K. Davies. (1997). The health implications of global change: A Canadian perspective. A paper for the Rio +5 Forum prepared for Environment Canada under the auspices of the Royal Society of Canada's Canadian Global Change Program. Ottawa: The Royal Society of Canada.

Health Care Without Harm [HCWH]. (2002). Making Medicine Mercury Free. http://www.noharm.org/library/docs/Going_Green_Making_Medicine_Mercury_Free.pdf

———. (2007). Healthy Building: The Issue. http://www.noharm.org/us/healthyBuilding/issue

Jones, C. (2006). Energy management: Saving carbon, saving cash. *Hospital Development* (August). www.hdmagazine.co.uk/story.asp?storyCode=2037734

Maine Green Power Connection [MeGPC]. (2007). www.mainegreenpower.org

Meironyte, D., K. Noren, and A. Bergman. (1999). Analysis of polybrominated diphenyl ethers in swedish human milk: A time-related trend study, 1972–1997. *Journal of Toxicology and Environmental Health Part A*, 58 (6) 329–41.

Oxford University Press [OUP]. (2006). Carbon Neutral: Oxford Word of the Year. http://blog.oup.com/oupblog/2006/11/what_do_al_gore.html

Providence Health System [PHS]. (2007). The West Coast's First Green Hospital. http://www.providence.org/yamhill/new_medical_center/green.htm

Reed, C. (2006). Personal communication, September 14.

Rees, W. (2000). Ecological Footprints and the Pathology of Consumption. In *Fatal Consumption: Rethinking Sustainable Development*, eds. R. Woollard and A. Ostry. Vancouver: University of British Columbia Press.

———. (2001). Personal communication with professor at the School of Community and Regional Planning.

Schecter, A., P. Cramer, O Päpke, et al. (2001). Intake of dioxins and related compounds from food in the U.S. population. *Journal of Toxicology and Environmental Health* 63 (1): 1–18.

Stein, J., T. Schettler, D. Wallinga, and M. Valenti. (2002). In harm's way: Toxic threats to child development. *Journal of Developmental and Behavioral Pediatrics* 23 (0): Supplement, S13–S22.

Stroud, M. (2006). Health care buildings and climate change. PhD diss., University of Huddersfield. http://stroud14.net

United Kingdom. Department of Health. (2007). Burnham Announces £100m Funding to Help NHS Increase Energy Efficiency. Press release, January 4. http://www.gnn.gov.uk/environment/fullDetail.asp?ReleaseID=254163&NewsAreaID=2&NavigatedFromDepartment=True

Ulam, A. (2006). U.S. Mayor's Conference president says 2030 Challenge is realizable. *Architectural Record*, July 25. http://archrecord.construction.com/news/daily/archives/060725challenge.asp

United Nations Environment Programme [UNEP]. (1998). Kyoto Protocol on Climate Change Opens for Signature. Press release: Bonn, March 16. http://www.iisd.ca/climate/ba/opening.html

United Nations Framework Convention on Climate Change [UNFCC]. (1992). Article 2. http://unfcc.int/resource/docs/convkp/conveng.pdf

US Green Building Council [USGBC]. www.usgbc.org

Wackernagel, M. (1994). The ecological footprint and appropriate carrying capacity: A tool for planning sustainability. PhD diss., School of Community and Regional Planning, University of British Columbia. http://en.scientificcommons.org/6213480

Wackernagel, M., and W. Rees. (1996). *Our Ecological Footprint: Reducing Human Impact on the Earth.* Gabriola Island, BC and Philadelphia: New Society Publishers.

Wikipedia Commons. (2006). CO_2 Emissions Per Capita Per Country. Map. http://en.wikipedia.org/wiki/Image:CO2_per_capita_per_country.png

World Business Council for Sustainable Development [WBCSD]. (2000). *Eco-Efficiency: Creating More Value with Less Impact.* Geneva: WBCSD.

World Summit on Sustainable Development. (2004). *Plan of Implementation of the World Summit on Sustainable Development.* United Nations Treaty Series 1954 (33480): 13.

World Wildlife Fund [WWF]. (2005). *Stockholm Convention "New" POPs: Screening Additional POPs Candidates.* Washington, DC: WWF.

Toward a Carbon Neutral Hospital ▪ Simon Shaw

Anderson, J., D. Shiers, and M. Sinclair. (2005). *The Green Guide to Specification.* Oxford: Blackwell Science.

Brown, J. (2006). Reduce, reuse, recycle—and save. *Healthcare Design* (June). http://www.healthcaredesignmagazine.com/CleanDesign.htm

Green Guide for Health Care [GGHC]. (2007). Best Practices for Creating High Performance Healing Environments, Version 2.2. http://www.gghc.org/about.cfm

Ness, C. (2005). Hospital experiment putting locally grown produce on patients' plates. *San Francisco Chronicle*, August 6.

Stroud, M. (2006). Health care buildings and climate change. PhD diss., University of Huddersfield. http://stroud14.net

The PBT-Free Challenge ▪ Tom Lent and Julie Silas

Calafat, A. M., Z. Kuklenyik, J. A. Reich, J. L. Butenhoff, and L. L. Needham. (2003). Quantitative analysis of serum and breast milk for perfluorochemical surfactants. *Organohalogen Compounds* 62: 319–22.

Chase, R. (2006). Board: Teflon chemical a likely carcinogen. Associated Press, February 16.

Clean Production Action. (2007). http://www.cleanproduction.org/

Consorta. (2007). Consorta's EPP Program: Green Building and The Green Guide for Healthcare Construction. http://www.consorta.com/wings/resource_mgmt/epp/greenbuilding.asp

Dewailly, E. A. Nantel, J.-P. Weber, and F. Meyer. (1989). High levels of PCBs in breast milk of Inuit women from Arctic Quebec. *Bulletin of Environmental Contaminations and Toxicology* 43 (5), November.

Environmental Protection Agency [EPA]. (1998). A Multimedia Strategy for Priority Persistent, Bioaccumulative, and Toxic [PBT] Pollutants. http://www.epa.gov/pbt/pubs/pbtstrat.htm

———. (2007a). National Partnership for Environmental Priorities. http://www.epa.gov/epaoswer/hazwaste/minimize/chemlist.htm

———. (2007b). Perfluorooctanoic Acid (PFOA) and Fluorinated Telomars. http://www.epa.gov/oppt/pfoa/

Environmental Protection Agency and American Hospital Association. [EPA and AHA] (1998). Memorandum of Understanding between the American Hospital Association and the U.S. Environmental Protection Agency. http://www.noharm.org/library/docs/going_green_memorandum_of_understanding_betwee.pdf

Health Care Without Harm [HCWH]. (2002). Making Medicine Mercury Free. http://www.noharm.org/library/docs/Going_Green_Making_Medicine_Mercury_Free.pdf

———. (2007). Health Care Institutions Undertaking Efforts to Reduce Polyvinyl Chloride [PVC] and / or Di(2-Ethylhexyl) Phthalate (DEHP). http://www.noharm.org/us/pvcDehp/hospitalsreducingpvc

Hites, R. (2004). Polybrominated diphenyl ethers in the environment and people: A meta analysis of concentrations. *Environmental Science Technology* 38: 945–56.

Inoue, K., F. Okada, R. Ito, et al. (2004). Perfluorooctane sulfonate (PFOS) and related perfluorinated compounds in human maternal and cord blood samples: Assessment of PFOS exposure in a susceptible population pregnancy. *Environmental Health Perspectives* 112 (11): 1204–7.

Kaiser Permanente. (2006). National Environmental Purchasing Policy. http://www.sehn.org/rtfdocs/KP_EPP_Policy_rev._04.12.06.doc

Kannan, K., S. Corsolini, J. Falandysz, et al. (2004). Perfluorooctanesulfonate and related fluorochemicals in human blood from several countries. *Environmental Science and Technology* 38 (17): 4489–95.

Lunder, S., and R. Sharp. (2003). *Mother's Milk: Record Levels of Toxic Fire Retardants Found in American Mothers' Breast Milk.* Washington, DC: Environmental Working Group.

Meironyte, D., K. Noren, and A. Bergman. (1999). Analysis of polybrominated diphenyl ethers in Swedish human milk: A time-related trend study, 1972–1997. *Journal of Toxicology and Environmental Health Part A*, 58 (6) 329–41.

Premier. (2004). Premier's Position Statement: Environmentally preferable purchasing. http://www.premierinc.com/safety/topics/epp/#Premier's position on EPP

Schecter, A., P. Cramer, O Päpke, et al. (2001). Intake of dioxins and related compounds from food in the U.S. population. *Journal of Toxicology and Environmental Health* 63 (1): 1–18.

Stein, J., T. Schettler, D. Wallinga, and M. Valenti. (2002). In harm's way: Toxic threats to child development. *Journal of Developmental and Behavioral Pediatrics* 23(0): Supplement, S13–S22.

Stockholm Convention on Persistent Organic Pollutants (POPs). (2001). www.pops.int

Washington State Department of Ecology [WSDE]. (2005). Memorandum of Understanding: Washington State Department of Ecology and Washington State Hospital Association.http://www.ecy.wa.gov/mercury/hospitals/hospital_mou.html

Weeks, J. (2006). PBT Profiler Use in Industry to Screen HPV Chemicals: SC Johnson Case Study. PowerPoint presentation at First U.S. Conference on Characterizing Chemicals in Commerce: Using Data on High Production Volume (HPV) Chemicals, Austin, Tex., December.

World Wildlife Fund [WWF]. (2005). "New" POPs: Screening additional POPs candidates. World Wildlife Fund Report.

Yeung, L.W.Y., M. K. So, G. Jiang, et al. (2006). Perfluorooctanesulfate and related fluorochemicals in human blood samples from China. *Environmental Science Technology* 40 (3): 715–20.

CHAPTER 13

American Society of Healthcare Engineering [ASHE]. (2004). *Green Healthcare Construction Guidance Statement.* http://www.ashe.org/ashe/products/pdfs/ashe_guidance_sustainconst_rev2_0410.pdf

Cascadia Region Green Building Council [CRGBC]. (2007). Living Building Challenge, v. 1.2. www.cascadiagbc.org/lbc

Centers for Medicare and Medicaid Services (CMMS), Office of the Actuary, National Health Statistics Group. (2007). www.cms.hhs.gov/NationalHealthExpendData.

Chertow, M., and C. Powers. (1997). Industrial Ecology: Overwhelming Policy Fragmentation. In *Thinking Ecologically: The Next Generation of Environmental Policy,* eds., M. Chertow and D. Etsy. New Haven, CT: Yale University Press, 19-36.

Chertow, M., and D. Etsyr, eds. (1997). *Thinking Ecologically: The Next Generation of Environmental Policy,* New Haven: Yale Univ. Press,

Department of Health & Human Services. [DHHS] Centers for Medicare and Medicaid Services. (2007). National Health Expenditure Data. http://www.cms.hhs.gov/NationalHealthExpendData/

Department of Energy [DOE]. (2006). Commercial Buildings Energy Consumption Survey (CBECS). http://www.eia.doe.gov/emeu/cbecs/contents.html

Everson, M. (2005). Testimony before the House Committee on Ways and Means. May 26. 109th Congress. 1st sess. May 26. http://www.nacua.org/documents/Hearing_TaxExemptHospitals.asp

Fourth Sector. (2007). www.fourthsector.net

Frankel, C. (2004). *Out of the Labyrinth: Who We Are, How We Go Wrong and What We Can Do About It.* Rheinbeck, NY: Monkfish.

Green Guide for Health Care [GGHC]. (2007). Best Practices for Creating High Performance Healing Environments, Version 2.2. http://www.gghc.org/about.cfm

Internal Revenue Service. Department of the Treasury. (2007). Rev. Rul. 83-157, 1983-2 C.B. 94. http://www.irs.gov/pub/irs-tege/rr83-157.pdf

Pine, B. J. II, and J. H. Gilmore (1999). *The Experience Economy: Work Is Theater and Every Business a Stage.* Boston: Harvard Business School Press.

Postman, N. (2000). *Building a Bridge to the 18th Century: How the Past Can Improve Our Future.* New York: Vintage.

Schettler, T. (2001). Environmental challenges and visions of sustainable health care. Paper presented at CleanMed Conference, Boston, May 4. http://www.sehn.org/Sustainable_Health_Care.html

Public Policy and Quality of Life ■ Bill Walsh

Cascadia Region Green Building Council. (2007). www.cascadiagbc.org

Contributors

Bob Berkebile, FAIA; principal, BNIM Architects

Bob Berkebile is a founding principal of BNIM. For the past thirty years, and through sustainable design, he has helped restore social, economic, and environmental vitality to our communities. He thinks like people used to: he is mindful of the generations that will follow. Bob was founding chairman of the American Institute of Architects' Committee on the Environment and has served on the board of the US Green Building Council. Highly regarded by fellow professionals and the recipient of numerous awards, Bob focuses on improving the quality of life in our society through the integrity and spirit of his firm's work.

Anthony Bernheim, FAIA, LEED-AP; principal and western regional director, Sustainable Design Solutions, HDR Architecture, Inc.

Anthony Bernheim is a nationally known pioneer in green building with specific expertise in collaborative integrated green building design and building occupant health. Anthony is a member of the International Society of Indoor Air Quality and Climate. In 2004, he was awarded the Nathaniel A. Owings Award by the American Institute of Architects, California Council "in recognition of a lifetime of service, commitment, and advocacy for the principles of sustainable design and preserving the earth's natural resources." In 2002, he received the California Governor's Environmental and Economic Leadership Award.

Laura Brannen, Sarah O'Brien, and Janet Brown, Hospitals for a Healthy Environment (H2E)

Laura Brannen, Sarah O'Brien, and Janet Brown make up the core staff of H2E— a nonprofit organization whose goal is to transform the environmental performance of the healthcare sector. With dozens of years of combined experience in facility waste management, toxics reduction efforts, environmental health advocacy, and environmentally preferable purchasing, H2E's staffers provide practical solutions, educational tools, and awards programs to support facilities as they embrace a long-term commitment to environmental health.

Charlotte Brody, RN; executive director, Commonweal

Charlotte Brody is a registered nurse and a founder of Health Care Without Harm. She currently acts as executive director for Commonweal, a thirty-year-old health and environmental organization in Bolinas, California. She also serves on the boards of Smith Farm Center for Healing and the Arts and the Environmental Working Group, the advisory boards of the Environmental Health Strategy Center and Kaiser Permanente's Environmental Stewardship Council, and the steering committee of the Safe Cosmetics Campaign. She has worked with civil rights, women's rights, and labor union groups, and before helping to form Health Care Without Harm, was the organizing director for the Center for Health, Environment and Justice (CHEJ).

Gary Cohen, executive director, Environmental Health Fund; coexecutive director, Health Care Without Harm

Gary Cohen is a founder of Health Care Without Harm, the international campaign for environmentally responsible healthcare. As the executive director of the Environmental Health Fund, he works on issues of domestic and global chemical safety. He is the coauthor of *Fighting Toxics* (Island Press, 1990) and the groundbreaking report, *The US Military's Toxics Legacy*. He is also a program consultant on environmental health issues to the Marisla Foundation and the John Merck Fund. In 2006, he received the Skoll Global Award for Social Entrepreneurship.

Teresa Durkin, RLA, AICP; vice president, The HOK Planning Group

Teresa Durkin is a landscape architect and a planner who specializes in directing planning and design projects for communities, educational institutions, public parks, arboretums, and urban landscapes. Teresa merges her strong interest in community collaboration with her passion for creating viable and meaningful places rooted in context.

Rebecca T. Ellis, PE, LEED-AP, CCP

Rebecca Ellis is a mechanical engineer with degrees from the University of Minnesota and the Massachusetts Institute of Technology. Rebecca is also a nationally recognized leader in the commissioning industry. She has helped define mainstream commissioning services and is a much sought after speaker, author, and trainer. Prior to founding Questions & Solutions Engineering, she developed and led the largest commissioning service group in the US.

Tye Farrow, BArch, MArchUD, OAA, MRAIC; partner in charge of design, Farrow Partnership Architects, Inc.

Tye Farrow is recognized as a leader in collaborating with clients to expand their thinking and see new possibilities through design. His approach to the creative process engages participants in an eye-opening journey of learning and discovery. In 2003, Tye was awarded Canada's Top 40 Under 40 Award, which recognizes leaders shaping the country's future; in 2002, his firm was awarded the prestigious Ontario Association of Architects Innovative Practice Award.

Rick Fedrizzi, president and CEO, US Green Building Council

Rick Fedrizzi, founding chairman of the US Green Building Council, was appointed its president and CEO in April 2004. Prior to that, Rick was president of Green-Think, Inc., a consulting firm he founded after a twenty-five-year career at United Technologies Corporation.

Pliny Fisk III, MArch, MLArch; cofounder and codirector, Center for Maximum Potential Building Systems

Pliny Fisk III co-founded and is co-director of the Center for Maximum Potential Building Systems in 1975, and holds the signature faculty position in sustainable urbanism at Texas A&M University, with a joint position as Associate Professor in Architecture, Landscape Architecture and Planning. Pliny is the recipient of numerous awards, including the U.S. Green Building Council's first Sacred Tree Award in the public sector category and the American Solar Energy Society's Passive Solar Pioneer Award. Pliny received B.Arch., M.Arch., and M.L.Arch. degrees from the University of Pennsylvania, where he focused on ecological land planning under the guidance of Ian McHarg.

Carol Franklin, FASLA, Andropogon Associates, Ltd.

Carol Franklin is a founding principal for Andropogon with more than thirty years experience in master planning and site design. She is nationally recognized in the field of sustainable design, particularly for her expertise in the design and management of native plant communities and habitats. Carol specializes in developing strategies for the reestablishment of natural systems in a wide range of sensitive, degraded, and developed environments.

Judith Heerwagen, PhD, J. H. Heerwagen & Associates, Inc.

Judith Heerwagen is an environmental psychologist whose research and writing have focused on workplace ecology, the psychosocial value of space, and the human factors of sustainable design. She was on the research faculty at the University of Washington in the College of Architecture and Urban Planning and has been a staff scientist at the Pacific Northwest National Laboratory since 1994. Currently, she operates her own consulting and research business in Seattle.

Tia Heneghan, PE, LEED AP CTG Energetics

Tia Heneghan has over twenty-five years' experience in the built environment and has held positions at virtually every level of facilities management. Tia brings a pragmatic perspective and a broad facilities background to greening existing facilities, having worked on both public and private sector projects. She serves on the Federal Energy Management Advisory Council, the LEED Energy & Atmosphere Technical Advisory Group, and the LEED for Existing Buildings core committee. Director of CTG Energetics' Colorado office, she heads the firm's LEED for Existing Buildings team nationwide.

Richard Jackson, MD, MPH, University of California School of Public Health

Dr. Richard Jackson headed the National Center for Environmental Health at the Centers for Disease Control for close to ten years. While there he instigated much interest in the built environment for the public health community. He first worked as a pediatrician and then an epidemiologist before earning a masters degree in public health from the University of California–Berkeley in 1979. In 2004, he was appointed state public health officer and chief deputy director of the California Department of Health Services. That same year, Dick received a presidential citation from the American Institute of Architects for his work on the built environment and health.

Alexis Karolides, principal, breakthrough design team, Rocky Mountain Institute

Alexis Karolides is a registered architect with experience in commercial, institutional, and industrial architecture. Her primary research area at the Rocky Mountain Institute is healthy building and biologically inspired design, energy efficiency, and environmental sensitivity for commercial and residential building projects.

Stephen Kendall, PhD; director, Building Futures Institute, College of Architecture and Planning, Ball State University

Stephen Kendall is a registered architect and a professor of architecture at Ball State University, where he also directs the Building Futures Institute. His research focuses on both architectural pedagogy and open building practices. He addresses the issues of distributed design control, intervention on a range of environmental issues, and change.

Stephen Kellert, PhD; Tweedy Ordway Professor of Social Ecology, Yale University School of Forestry and Environmental Studies

Stephen Kellert studies methods of design that harmonize the natural and built environments and has a particular interest in the value and conservation of nature. Kellert has received several awards in the field of environmental conservation, and was one of three hundred individuals listed in American Environmental Leaders: From Colonial Times to the Present. He has authored more than one hundred publications, including several books; Building for Life: Designing and Understanding the Human–Nature Connection (Island Press, 2005) is his most recent.

Tom Lent, policy director, Healthy Building Network

Tom Lent has over twenty-five years of experience with energy and environmental issues, primarily focused on healthy and resource-efficient building technologies. Tom is a founding co-coordinator of the Green Guide for Health Care and developer of the Healthy Building Network's Pharos system, a comprehensive assessment tool to compare building materials based on health, environment and social justice criteria. He works closely with product manufacturers and healthcare systems, such as Kaiser Permanente, working to spur the development of new, environmentally sound products.

Michael Lerner, PhD; founder, Commonweal

Michael Lerner is president and cofounder of Commonweal, a health and environmental research institute in Bolinas, California. He is also a cofounder of the Commonweal Cancer Help Program, Health Care Without Harm, and the Collaborative on Health and the Environment. He is the president and cofounder of the Smith Farm Center for Healing and the Arts in Washington, DC, and a cofounder of the Health and Environmental Funders Network.

Hal Levin, Building Ecology Research Group

Hal Levin received degrees in English and architecture during the tumultuous 1960s from the University of California–Berkeley. From 1978 to 1989 he was a research specialist at the College of Environmental Design and from 1978 to 1983, a lecturer in the architecture departments at the University of California in Berkeley and Santa Cruz. Most recently he was scientist of the indoor environment department at the Lawrence Berkeley National Laboratory, where he worked from 2000 until he retired in 2005. He is founder and editor of www.BuildingEcology.com

Marlon Maus, MD, MPH; PhD candidate, University of California School of Public Health

Dr. Marlon Maus is a board certified ophthalmologist who served as director of medical education at Wills Eye Hospital in Philadelphia before resuming postgraduate education. He has been involved in numerous professional organizations, including the American Council of Graduate Medical Education, the American Academy of Ophthalmology, and the American Medical Association, at which he has held various positions related to medical education. His dissertation focuses on the relationship between public health and the built environment.

Ray Pradinuk, MAIBC, LEED-AP; senior associate, Stantec

Ray Pradinuk was born and raised in Saskatchewan. He received a BArch from the University of British Columbia and an MS in Architecture from the Bartlett School of Architecture, University College, London. The focus of Ray's work has been on the social and psychological implications of complex urban and architectural spatial arrangements and on sustainable design in healthcare. Ray studied space syntax theory with Professor Bill Hillier and has since applied the theory and analytical methods of space syntax to urban and architectural planning and design problems.

Bill Reed, AIA; president, Integrative Design Collaborative

Bill Reed has been a practicing architect for the past twenty-five years and is an internationally recognized specialist on issues related to green design. He emphasizes process and systems thinking in order to fully integrate the practice of green building design into real-world living systems. He consults to and is a former board member of the US Green Building Council and the national executive committee of the American Institute of Architecture's Committee on the Environment. He is always on the lookout for beneficial alternatives to conventional design.

Greg Roberts, AIA, FCSI, CCS, CCCA, LEED-AP, ACHA; principal, WHR Architects

Roberts is a principal and specifications manager with WHR Architects, a firm specializing in healthcare architecture in Houston and Dallas. He serves on the steering committee of the Green Guide For Health Care and the core committee of LEED for Health Care, two national initiatives focused on green healthcare facilities. Greg has also served on the national environmental task team of the Construction Specifications Institute. He lectures on sustainability and has published articles in a number of national magazines.

Jody Rosenblatt-Naderi, MArch, ASLA

Jody Rosenblatt-Naderi is a registered landscape architect and has practiced and conducted research in pedestrian transportation, community design, and health since graduating from Harvard in 1980. She is currently a member of the graduate faculty at Texas A&M University and operates a private consultancy focused on landscapes of recovery in the Florida Keys.

Mark Rossi, PhD; research director, Clean Production Action

Mark Rossi's recent research includes coauthoring: "Healthy Business Strategies for Transforming the Toxic Chemical Economy" (Clean Production Action), "Alternatives Assessment Framework" (Lowell Center for Sustainable Production), and "Creating Safe and Healthy Spaces" (Health Care Without Harm). Mark also serves on the steering committee of Health Care Without Harm and is a research fellow at the Lowell Center for Sustainable Production. His doctorate, from MIT, is in environmental policy.

Ted Schettler, MD, MPH; science director, Science and Environmental Health Network

Dr. Ted Schettler coauthored Generations at Risk (MIT Press, 1999), which examines the reproductive health effects of exposure to a variety of environmental toxicants, and "In Harm's Way: Toxic Threats to Child Development" (Journal of Developmental and Behavioral Pediatrics, February 2002). He has served on the advisory committees of the Environmental Protection Agency and the National Academy of Sciences. Ted has a medical degree from Case Western Reserve University and a masters degree in Public Health from Harvard University.

Simon Shaw, RIBA, LEED-AP; project architect, Architerra

Simon is an RIBA-registered architect trained in both the UK and Italy. He worked for seven years in London for Feilden Clegg Bradley, a practice with an international reputation for design quality and environmental expertise. He has experience in the sustainable design of education facilities and heritage-led regeneration projects. More recently, Simon has been assisting Steffian Bradley Architects with their Sustainable Architecture in Healthcare Program and is currently working with Architerra, a new architecture and development advisory firm dedicated to sustainable design and smart growth.

Julie Silas; program coordinator, Healthy Building Network

Julie Silas is based in Oakland, California. Before joining the Healthy Building Network, Julie was the program director for the San Francisco Bay Area Physicians for Social Responsibility and on the steering committee of Health Care Without Harm, partnering with healthcare organizations to promote more environmentally responsible practices within the healthcare system.

Jerry Smith, ASLA, LEED-AP; senior associate, HOK Planning Group

Jerry Smith serves on the steering committee of the Green Guide for Health Care, is the landscape architecture representative on the Environmental Standards Council of the Center for Health Design, and is on the faculty of the healthcare garden design certificate program at the School of the Chicago Botanic Garden.

Sean Stanwick, BArch, ME DesArch, OAA intern architect; associate, Farrow Partnership Architects

With a particular interest in contemporary urban design, Sean is a frequent contributor of project features and book reviews to architectural journals and conferences worldwide. He is a coauthor of Design City: Toronto (March 2007) and Wine By Design (October 2005), both for John Wiley & Sons UK. Sean received research funding through the Ontario Hospital Association Change Foundation in 2004.

Bill Valentine, FAIA; chairman, HOK Groups Inc.

Bill Valentine is chairman and design principal of HOK, a global architectural design and services firm. Valentine joined HOK shortly after earning his MArch from Harvard forty-four years ago and became president in 2000; he was named chairman in 2005. Bill is considered one of the pioneers of the green building movement—and one of its staunchest advocates. He actively promotes his definition of good design as a simple idea, elegantly executed and inspiring, with social significance, and in harmony with the environment.

J. A. Vanegas, PhD; director, Center for Housing and Urban Development, College of Architecture, Texas A&M University

Jorge Vanegas is responsible for establishing and maintaining an institutional infrastructure that delivers innovative solutions to enhance quality of life and the built environment within disadvantaged populations in urban and semiurban settings. Jorge has twenty years of experience and accomplishments in education, research, and service.

Bill Walsh, founder and national coordinator, Healthy Building Network

Bill is a lawyer with over twenty years' experience working with public interest organizations, including Greenpeace and the Public Interest Research Groups. In 2000 he founded the Healthy Building Network in an effort to build coalitions of nontraditional allies dedicated to accelerating the transformation of the multibillion dollar building and materials market toward healthier materials.

Peter Warshall, PhD, founder and principal, Peter Warshall and Associates

Peter Warshall has worked with water problems on Native American reservations, in Africa, in Latin America, and North America for thirty-five years. He was an elected official to a public utilities district in California and wrote Septic Tank Practices, a book on home-site sewage treatment and water conservation. He also served on the California Drought Emergency Task Force, wrote the first gray water ordinance for a US municipality, oversaw the first total recycling sewage plant in northern California, and helped Commonweal with its biomonitoring program.

Index

WILEY BOOKS ON
Sustainable Design

For these and other Wiley Books on Sustainable Design, visit www.wiley.com/go/sustainabledesign

Alternative Construction: Contemporary Natural Building Methods
by Lynne Elizabeth and Cassandra Adams

Cities People Planet: Liveable Cities for a Sustainable World
by Herbert Girardet

Design with Nature
by Ian L. McHarg

Ecodesign: A Manual for Ecological Design
by Ken Yeang

Green Building Materials: A Guide to Product Selection and Specification, Second Edition
by Ross Spiegel and Dru Meadows

Green Development: Integrating Ecology and Real Estate
by Rocky Mountain Institute

The HOK Guidebook to Sustainable Design, Second Edition
by Sandra Mendler, William O'Dell, and Mary Ann Lazarus

Land and Natural Development (Land) Code
by Diana Balmori and Gaboury Benoit

Sustainable Construction: Green Building Design and Delivery
by Charles J. Kibert

Sustainable Commercial Interiors
by Penny Bonda and Katie Sosnowchik

Sustainable Design: Ecology, Architecture, and Planning
by Daniel Williams

Sustainable Healthcare Architecture
by Robin Guenther and Gail Vittori

Sustainable Residential Interiors
by Associates III

Environmental Benefits Statement

This book is printed with soy-based inks on presses with VOC levels that are lower than the standard for the printing industry. The paper, Rolland Enviro 100, is manufactured by Cascades Fine Paper Group and is made from 100 percent post-consumer, de-inked fiber, without chlorine. According to the manufacturer, the following resources were saved by using Rolland Enviro 100 for this book:

Mature trees	Waterborne waste not created	Water flow saved (in gallons)	Atmospheric emissions eliminated	Energy not consumed	Natural gas saved by using biogas
225	103,500 lbs.	153,000	21,470 lbs.	259 million BTU	37,170 cubic feet